Social psychology
an introduction

Michael Hogg received his BSc in 1977 from the University of Birmingham and his PhD in 1983 from the University of Bristol. After lecturing for three years at Bristol University, he took up a postdoctoral research fellowship at Macquarie University in Sydney in 1985, and then in 1986 moved to a lectureship at the University of Melbourne. In 1989 he became a senior lecturer, and in 1991 moved to the University of Queensland in Brisbane where, since 1992, he has been reader in social psychology. He has also held honorary visiting appointments at the University of California, Los Angeles, for six months in 1990 and at the University of California, Santa Cruz, for the whole of 1994. Michael Hogg is a social psychologist whose research interests are intergroup relations and group processes. He has been involved for fifteen years in the development of social identity theory and self-categorisation theory. In addition to publishing more than seventy books, chapters and articles, he is an editorial consultant for the *British Journal of Social Psychology*, the *European Review of Social Psychology*, and the *Blackwell Encyclopaedia of Social Psychology*. His other books include *The Social Psychology of Group Cohesiveness: From Attraction to Social Identity* (1992), *Rediscovering the Social Group: A Self-categorization Theory* (1987) in collaboration with John Turner and others, and a number of books in collaboration with Dominic Abrams; *Social Identification: A Social Psychology of Intergroup Relations and Group Processes* (1988), *Social Identity Theory: Constructive and Critical Advances* (1990), and *Group Motivation: Social Psychological Perspectives* (1993).

Graham Vaughan is professor of psychology at the University of Auckland. He was a student at three New Zealand universities, completing a BA at Auckland, an MA at Canterbury and a PhD at Victoria. He was a Fulbright Fellow and visiting assistant professor at the University of Illinois at Champaign-Urbana in 1966; a visiting lecturer in 1973 and a Ford Foundation Fellow in 1975 at the University of Bristol; a visiting associate professor at Princeton University in 1981; a visiting directeur d'études at the Maison des Science de l'Homme in Paris in 1981; and a visiting senior fellow at the National University of Singapore in 1988. He is a former editor of the *New Zealand Journal of Psychology*, an occasional reviewer for a number of journals including the *British Journal of Social Psychology*, the *Journal of Personality and Social Psychology* and the *Psychological Bulletin*, and is currently on the board of editors of the *Journal of Intercultural Studies*. His primary areas of interest in social psychology include attitudes, group processes, ethnic relations and identity, and the history of social psychology. A fellow and former president of the New Zealand Psychological Society, he is the author of sixty papers and current editor of *Racial Issues in New Zealand*.

Social psychology
an introduction

MICHAEL A. HOGG
University of Queensland

GRAHAM M. VAUGHAN
University of Auckland

Prentice Hall
Harvester Wheatsheaf

LONDON   NEW YORK   TORONTO   SYDNEY   TOKYO   SINGAPORE
MADRID   MEXICO CITY   MUNICH

First published 1995 by
Prentice Hall/Harvester Wheatsheaf
Campus 400, Maylands Avenue
Hemel Hempstead
Hertfordshire, HP2 7EZ
A division of
Simon & Schuster International Group

Typeset in 10/12 pt Ehrhardt
by Mathematical Composition Setters Ltd, Salisbury, UK

Printed and bound in Great Britain
by Hartnolls Limited, Bodmin, Cornwall

Library of Congress Cataloging in Publication Data

Hogg, Michael A., 1954–
    Social psychology : an introduction / Michael A. Hogg, Graham M.
Vaughan.
        p.   cm.
    Includes bibliographical references and index.
    ISBN 0-13-433129-X (pbk.)
    1. Social psychology.   I. Vaughan. Graham M.   II. Title.
HM251.H623   1995
302–dc20   94-38461
                                                               CIP

British Library Cataloguing in Publication Data

A catalogue record for this book is available from
the British Library
ISBN 0-13-433129-X

---

1 2 3 4 5   99 98 97 96 95

Contents
....

7 Group processes *214*

Foreword
·················

Ideas should pass borders without much difficulty. But the migration of ideas, as Levi-Strauss has shown for mythologies, is often accompanied by systematic transformations. Scientific ideas should be more immune to the consequences of transplantation and borders should have less effect on them. To some extent this may be the case for natural sciences, but it certainly is not the case for all social sciences. Borders do exist at least in social psychology. This certainly was the case when Mussolini (see Doise 1986) utilised social psychological ideas developed in the writings of Le Bon (1985) and Orano (1902), just as the Nazis returned to versions of *Völkerpsychologie* in order to rationalise their calamitous undertakings. At the same time, migrants, such as Asch, Lewin and Sherif, developed in the United States another social psychology aimed at understanding, unmasking and demystifying authoritarian and ethnocentric theories currently fashionable at that time. Their experimental approach moved back again to western Europe where it became successful, probably as an alternative to the dogmatism characterising much of the official social psychological thinking in eastern Europe during the Cold War.

Borders of another kind are apparent in the different 'scientific' cultures that exist in European and North American social psychological journals. Articles by Fisch and Daniel (1982) and Jaspars (1986) pointed out systematic differences in frequencies of themes treated in journals on both sides of the Atlantic. Some years ago I expressed the opinion that there is as much variety in the work of North American social psychologists as in the work of their West-European colleagues but that the dominant traditions in the United States and in Europe are not the same (Doise 1986). Briefly stated, I would now say that societal concerns, in the sense used by Himmelweit (see Himmelweit and Gaskell 1990) are more often encountered in Europe than in the United States.

However, nowadays it is no longer possible to speak only about European and North American social psychology. In Africa, Australia, Asia, eastern Europe, South America – and I should not forget Canada and New Zealand – social psychologists are developing approaches with concerns that are not necessarily those characterising mainstream research in western Europe or in the United States. What are the characteristics of this 'international social psychology'? They are still to be defined, but this book already shows how ideas are often transformed when they migrate across cultures. Such transformations are not as radical as when mythological deities of one culture become demons of other cultures. Ideas developed in one scientific culture at a specific level of analysis are applied in another culture for analyses at other levels. One example was the accentuation of contrasts model in perception when Tajfel applied it to intergroup relations, and another was attribution theory when it was revisited in Europe by Deschamps, Jaspars and Hewstone. But I leave to the readers of this book the task of finding other instances of the same trend.

The problem of migration of ideas cannot be fully comprehended without dealing with migration of persons. In the foregoing I have mentioned the names of Asch, Himmelweit, Lewin and Sherif. The names of many other social psychologists who emigrated from their home countries, often in dramatic circumstances, could be added to this list. Serge Moscovici and Henri Tajfel, who both shaped typical 'European approaches' are examples. People who migrate have to think about social relationships and about societal dynamics. A lot of people travel today but few really make their living in other countries. The authors of this book are both migrants in the real sense. Moreover, they have worked in close connection with Henri Tajfel at some period of their life. There are important personal reasons that made me feel immediately sympathetic with the idea of this book when Graham Vaughan told me about it in August of 1992. I really enjoyed the prospect of reading a text by two colleagues, greatly respected for their professional competences, and at the same time far away from, but closely connected with, the social psychological centres in Europe and North America. In reading their manuscript my expectations have been completely realised.

One last word about migration. Not only persons and ideas migrate, but also vine stocks. To some extent social psychology was salvaged by the Americans during the plague of the Second World War – in a similar way they also salvaged vines during the phylloxera plague in Europe. For a long time, however, good wine was considered to be produced only in Europe. This has now changed. Australia, New Zealand and California are prize winners for fine wines adapted from European stocks. It was Graham Vaughan who introduced me to the art of winetasting in the area of Auckland in 1978, and he convinced me that quality of wine could be regenerated during the migration of plants. I sincerely hope that my Australian and New Zealand colleagues will convince students in social psychology that what can happen with viniculture can also happen with social psychology.

Willem Doise
University of Geneva

REFERENCES

Doise, W. (1986). *Levels of Explanation in Social Psychology*. Cambridge: Cambridge University Press.

Doise, W. (1986). 'Mass psychology, social psychology and the politics of Mussolini' in C. F. Graumann and S. Moscovici (eds), *Changing Conceptions of Crowd Mind and Behaviour*, (pp. 69–82). New York: Springer-Verlag.

Fisch, R., Daniel, H. D. (1982). 'Research and publication trends in experimental social psychology; 1971–1980'. *European Journal of Social Psychology*, **12**, 395–413.

Himmelweit, H. and Gaskell, G. (1990). *Societal Psychology*. London: Sage.

Jaspars, J. (1986). 'Forum and focus: A personal view of European social psychology'. *European Journal of Social Psychology*, **16**, 3–15.

LeBon, G. (1985). *The Crowd: A Study of the Popular Mind*. London: Ernest Benn (1952).

Orano, P. (1902). *Psicologia Sociale*. Bari: Laterza.

Preface and acknowledgements

·····································

We decided to write this book because we felt there is a great need for a comprehensive social psychology text written specifically for university students in Britain and continental Europe. Such a text, we felt, must approach social psychology from a European rather than American perspective not only in terms of the topics, orientations and research of interest but also in terms of the style and level of presentation of social psychology, and the cultural context of the readership. However, a European text can no longer ignore or gloss over American social psychology – so, unlike other European texts, we have located mainstream American social psychology within the framework of the book, covered it in detail and integrated it fully with European work. We intend this to be a self-contained coverage of social psychology, so that you do not need to switch between American and European texts in order to make sure you have a proper understanding of social psychology as a truly international scientific enterprise – an enterprise in which European research now has a very high profile.

We are both very closely associated with European social psychology and to varying degrees consider ourselves to be European social psychologists in terms of our research and teaching interests and our intellectual roots. During the late 1960s and early 1970s Michael Hogg attended the same school in Bristol from which the subjects for the original minimal group studies were being drawn, though he cannot quite recall if he ever took part. In the mid-1970s he was an undergraduate at the University of Birmingham where his initial interest in social psychology was fired by Ray Cochrane and Mick Billig, and then in 1978 he went to Bristol University to begin his PhD studies with John Turner – in the same year Stephen Reicher, Margaret Wetherell and Penny Oakes also started. Bristol was an exciting place which felt like a crucible for European social psychology: Henri Tajfel, John Turner and Howard Giles were still there, and, in addition to a constant stream of international visitors, postgraduate numbers were swelled by the arrival of Susan Condor, Karen Henwood and Nick Pidgeon. In 1981 Michael Hogg attended the European summer school (that year it was in the incomparable setting of a Jesuit retreat in Aix-en-Provence) where he established continuing links with, for example, Carmen Huici, José Marques, Fabio Lorenzi-Cioldi and Jacques-Philippe Leyens. Also in 1981, he began lecturing at Bristol – joined at the end of 1983 by his now long-time colleague and collaborator

Dominic Abrams. Despite leaving Britain in 1985, Michael Hogg remains a European social psychologist in terms of his intellectual orientation, his research interests, and his editorial and professional commitments. He is probably best known for his continuing work on social identity theory and self-categorisation theory. Subsequent research and teaching experiences in Australia and the United States have, perhaps paradoxically, given added perspective to the increasingly important role that contemporary European social psychology occupies internationally.

Graham Vaughan has considerable experience as a social psychology teacher and researcher in the United States, Britain and western Europe. He was a Fulbright Fellow at the University of Illinois in 1966–67, a visit which provided him with an early acquaintance with the work of Martin Fishbein. As a visiting professor at Princeton University in 1981 he had the opportunity to interact closely with Joel Cooper, John Darley and the late Ned Jones. Between these trips he was a visiting lecturer at the University of Bristol in 1973–74, and returned there as a research associate in 1975. This period coincided with major developments in the study of intergroup relations and the development of social identity theory spearheaded by Henri Tajfel. Fruitful interchanges took place at Bristol with John Turner, Glynis Breakwell, Howard Giles, Rupert Brown, Susan Skevington and Colin Fraser, and early contacts were made with Willem Doise at Geneva, Ad van Knippenburg at Leiden and Gerard Lemain in Paris. A later period as a visiting directeur d'études at the Maison des Science de l'Homme in Paris in 1981 provided the context for discussions with Serge Moscovici, Rom Harré and Miles Hewstone. Graham Vaughan's excitement with European social psychology also rubbed off on his erstwhile University of Auckland undergraduates, Margaret Wetherell and Diane Mackie.

From these backgrounds we bring substantial experience in teaching European social psychology or social psychology from a European perspective – either to students in Britain and Europe or to students in Australia, New Zealand and the United States. Our conviction that an introductory social psychology textbook such as this is needed has arisen from these experiences. It has, however, taken us a long time to write the book, and along the way we have been helped and supported in a great variety of ways by different people in different places. The writing spans three continents: the initial writing was done in Auckland in New Zealand and Brisbane in Australia, and the later stages in Bristol in the UK and at Santa Cruz in the United States. Michael Hogg would like to thank the University of California, Santa Cruz, for hosting his sabbatical in 1994 which enabled him to dedicate time to completing the text. We would like to thank Mark Haxell, Kathryn McPhillips, Pam Oliver and Josta van Rij-Heyligers at the University of Auckland for their contribution to some chapters in an earlier inhouse text. Debbie Terry and Cindy Gallois at the University of Queensland, and Ron Borland, Val Clarke and Mike Innes from Melbourne and Townsville all commented and advised on an earlier draft of the text. Willem Doise at the University of Geneva, Dominic Abrams at the University of Kent and Ad van Knippenberg at the University of Nijmegen all provided enormously helpful advice on the content and structuring of the text. We would like to thank all these people for the invaluable advice they have given us – we only hope we have done it justice. Special thanks must go to Farrell Burnett, formerly of Harvester Wheatsheaf, for inspiring us to produce the book in the first place and for keeping us going in the early days. Also a special thanks to the current team at Harvester Wheatsheaf, especially Clare Grist and Nicola Horton, for their enthusiasm and encouragement. Writing a book involves a great deal of time-consuming and meticulous indexing, referencing and searching out of details: we would like to thank Cate Hey, Sarah Hains, Sarah Nicoll and Bridget Hogg for relieving us of these responsibilities – they did a magnificent job. Book writing is also a great strain on one's friends and families. We hope they will forgive us. A very special thanks to them all, but especially Jan Vaughan and Bridget Hogg, and little Jessica Hogg who was born into the middle of it all.

Although the book has a logical structure, with earlier chapters flowing into later ones, it is not essential to read from beginning to end. The chapters are cross-referenced so that, with a few exceptions, chapters or groups of chapters can be read independently in almost any order. It is better to read Chapter 4 before tackling Chapter 5, and Chapter 7 before Chapter 8. Chapter 1 describes the structure of the book, why we decided to write it, and how it should be read: it is worthwhile reading the last section of Chapter 1 before starting later chapters. Chapter 1 also defines social psychology, its aims, its methods and its history. Some of this material might benefit from being reread after you have studied some of the other chapters and have become familiar with some of the theories, topics and issues of social psychology. It is not always possible to write in a gender-neutral way without being either pedantic or clumsy. We have opted occasionally to refer to 'she' and 'he' to help smooth the style – when we do, we alternate these pronouns.

The primary target of our book is the student, though we hope it will be of some help to the teacher, and to the researcher, as well. We will be grateful to any among you who might take the time to share your reactions with us.

Michael Hogg and Graham Vaughan
Santa Cruz and Auckland
December 1994

INSTRUCTOR'S MANUAL

Social Psychology: An Introduction is accompanied by an Instructor's Manual, which provides further guidance on how to make the most of the textbook, including ideas for classroom exercises and student assessments.

The Instructor's Manual is available free of charge to anyone who adopts *Social Psychology* for use on their courses; please apply to the publisher for further details.

1 Introduction

FOCUS QUESTIONS

A man enters a café, greets with a kiss on each cheek a young woman waiting for him at a table, and sits opposite her. He orders them both a cappuccino and subsequently rather dominates the conversation of a recent film.

♦ How would a social psychologist go about explaining this rather ordinary social event?

♦ How would we assess whether the explanation was correct?

WHAT IS SOCIAL PSYCHOLOGY?

▶ Social psychology
▶ Behaviour

Social psychology has been defined as *the scientific investigation of how the thoughts, feelings and behaviours of individuals are influenced by the actual, imagined or implied presence of others* (for example, Allport 1935). But what does this mean? What do social psychologists actually do, how do they do it, and what do they study?

Social psychologists are concerned to explain human behaviour, and generally do not study animals. Certain principles of social psychology may be applicable to animals, and animal research may provide evidence for some processes that are generalised to people (for example, social facilitation – see Chapter 7). Furthermore, certain principles of social behaviour may be general enough to apply to both humans and, for instance, to other primates (for example, Hinde 1982), but as a rule, social psychologists believe that the study of animals does not take one very far in explaining human social behaviour.

Social psychologists study behaviour because it is behaviour that can be observed. *Behaviour* refers not only to gross motor activities (such as running, punching, jumping), but also to more subtle actions such as a raised eyebrow or a smile, and, of course, to what we say and write. In this sense, behaviour is publicly verifiable. However, the meaning to be attached to behaviour is a matter of theoretical perspective, cultural background or personal interpretation.

Social psychologists are interested not only in behaviour but also in feelings, thoughts, beliefs, attitudes, intentions, goals and so forth. These are not

Social psychology and everyday life. Social psychology impinges on almost all aspects of our day to day life – at home, at work, even moving about in a city.
Source: Nicola Horton

directly observable but can, with varying degrees of certainty, be inferred from behaviour. These unobservable processes are also very important because they may, quite directly, govern overt behaviour. This point is crucial in understanding the relationship between attitudes and behaviour (see Chapter 4). They are also the psychological dimension of social behaviour as they occur within the human brain. Social psychologists usually wish to go one step further. They attempt to relate psychological aspects of social behaviour to even more fundamental cognitive processes and structures (see Chapter 2).

What makes social psychology *social* is that it deals with how people are affected by other people who are physically present (for example, an audience – see Chapter 7), or who are imagined to be present (for example, anticipating performing in front of an audience), or even whose presence is implied. This last influence is more complex and addresses the fundamentally social nature of our experiences as humans. For instance, we tend to think in terms of words, and words derive from language and communication which would not exist without social interaction. As such, thought, which is an internalised and private activity that can occur when we are alone, is clearly based on implied presence (see Chapter 14). As another example of implied presence, consider that most of us do not drop litter, even if no-one is watching and even if there is no possibility of being caught. This is because people, through the agency of society, have constructed a powerful social convention or norm that proscribes such behaviour. Such a norm implies the presence of other people and 'determines' behaviour even in their absence (see Chapters 6 and 7).

▶ Science
▶ Data
▶ Theory

Social psychology is a *science* because it uses the scientific method to construct and test theories. Just as physics has concepts such as electrons, quarks and spin to explain physical phenomena, social psychology has concepts such as dissonance, attitude, categorisation and identity to explain social psychological phenomena. The scientific method dictates that no theory is 'true' simply because it is logical and makes internal sense. On the contrary, a *theory* is valid on the basis of its correspondence with fact. Social psychologists construct theories from *data* and/or previous theories and then conduct empirical research in which data are collected to test the theory (see below).

Social psychology and related disciplines

Social psychology is poised at the crossroads of a number of related disciplines and subdisciplines (see Figure 1.1). It is a subdiscipline of general psychology, and as such is concerned with explaining human behaviour in terms of processes which occur in the human mind. It differs, however, from individual psychology in that it seeks to explain *social* behaviour, as defined in the previous section. For example, a general psychologist might be interested in perceptual processes that are responsible for people overestimating the size of coins, but a social psychologist might focus on the fact that coins have value (a case of implied presence) and that perceived value might influence the judgement of size. A great deal of social psychology is concerned with face-to-face interaction between individuals or among members of groups, while general psychology focuses on people's reactions to stimuli which do not have to be social (for example, shapes, colours, sounds).

The boundary between individual and social psychology is often approached from both sides. For instance, having developed a comprehensive and highly

FIGURE 1.1 *Social psychology and related disciplines.*

influential theory of the individual human mind, Sigmund Freud set out to develop a social psychology in his 1921 book *Group Psychology and the Analysis of the Ego*. Freudian, or psychoanalytic, notions have left a significant mark on social psychology (Billig 1976), in particular in the explanation of prejudice (see Chapter 9). Since the late 1970s, social psychology has been influenced by cognitive psychology in a concerted attempt to employ its methods (for example, reaction time) and its concepts (for example, memory) to explain a wide range of social behaviours. In fact, what is now called social cognition is in many ways the dominant force in contemporary social psychology (Fiske 1993; Fiske and Taylor 1991), and it surfaces in almost all areas of the discipline.

In dealing with, for example, groups, social and cultural norms, language and intergroup behaviour, social psychology has links with sociology and social anthropology. In general, sociology focuses on how groups, organisations, social categories and societies are organised, how they function and how they change. The unit of analysis (that is, the focus of research and theory) is the group as a whole rather than the individuals who constitute it. Social anthropology does much the same but, historically, has focused on 'exotic' societies (that is, non-industrial, tribal societies that exist or have existed largely in developing countries). Social psychology deals with many of the same phenomena but seeks to explain how individual human interaction and human cognition influences 'culture' and, in turn, is influenced by culture (Smith and Bond 1993). The unit of analysis is the individual within the group. In reality, some forms of sociology (for example, microsociology, psychological sociology, sociological psychology) are closely related to social psychology.

Just as the boundary between social and individual psychology has been approached from both sides, so has the boundary between social psychology and sociology. From the sociological side, for example, Karl Marx's theory of cultural history and social change has been extended to incorporate a consideration of the role of individual psychology (Billig 1976). From the social psychological side, intergroup perspectives on group and individual behaviour draw on sociological variables and concepts (Hogg and Abrams 1988 – see Chapter 10). Contemporary social psychology also abuts sociolinguistics and the study of language and communication (Giles and Coupland 1991 – see Chapter 14), and even literary criticism (Potter *et al.* 1984). It also feeds a variety of applied areas of psychology, such as sports psychology and organisational psychology.

Social psychology's location at the intersection of different disciplines is part of its intellectual and practical appeal. However, it is also a cause of much debate about what precisely constitutes social psychology as a distinct scientific discipline. If one leans too far towards individual cognitive processes then perhaps one is pursuing individual psychology or cognitive psychology. If one leans too far towards the role of language, then perhaps one is being a scholar of language and communication. If one emphasises the role of social structure in intergroup relations too much then perhaps one is being a sociologist. The issue of exactly what constitutes social psychology provides an important ongoing metatheoretical debate (that is, a debate about what sorts of theories are appropriate for social psychology) that forms the background to social psychology (see below).

Topics of social psychology

One way to define social psychology is by identifying what social psychologists study. This book is intended to be a comprehensive coverage of the principal phenomena that social psychologists study now and have studied in the past. As such, social psychology can be defined by the contents of this and other books that present themselves as social psychology texts. A brief look at the contents of this book will give a flavour of the scope of social psychology. Social psychologists study an enormous range of topics which includes conformity, persuasion, power, influence, obedience, prejudice, prejudice reduction, discrimination, stereotyping, bargaining, sexism and racism, small groups, social categories, intergroup relations, crowd behaviour, social conflict and harmony, social change, overcrowding, stress, the physical environment, decision-making, the jury, leadership, communication, language, speech, attitudes, impression formation, impression management, self-presentation, identity, emotion, attraction, friendship, the family, love, romance, sex, violence, aggression, altruism and prosocial behaviour (acts that are positively valued by society).

One problem with defining social psychology solely in terms of its topics is that it does not properly differentiate it from other disciplines. For example, intergroup relations is a focus not only of social psychology but also of political scientists and sociologists. The family is studied not only by social

Social psychology and interpersonal relationships. Race and sex and their social significance can influence intimate relationships. Relating to another involves considerable 'give and take' or social exchange. (Source: Andrew Lukey.)

psychologists but also clinical psychologists. What makes social psychology distinct is a combination of *what* it studies, *how* it studies it and what *level of explanation* is sought.

METHODOLOGICAL ISSUES

Scientific method

Social psychology employs the scientific method to study social behaviour (Figure 1.2). Science is a *method* for studying nature, and it is the method, not the people who use it, the things they study, the facts they discover or the explanations they propose, that distinguishes science from other approaches to knowledge. In this respect the main difference between social psychology and, say, physics, chemistry or biology is that the former studies human social behaviour while the others study non-organic phenomena and chemical and biological processes.

▶ Hypotheses
Science involves the formulation of *hypotheses* (predictions) on the basis of prior knowledge, assumption and casual or systematic observation. Hypotheses are formally stated speculations about what factor or factors may cause something to occur, and are stated in such a way that they can be empirically tested to see if they are true. For example, one might hypothesise that ballet dancers perform better in front of an audience than when alone. This hypothesis can be empirically tested by assessing performance alone and in front of an audience. Strictly speaking, empirical tests can falsify hypotheses

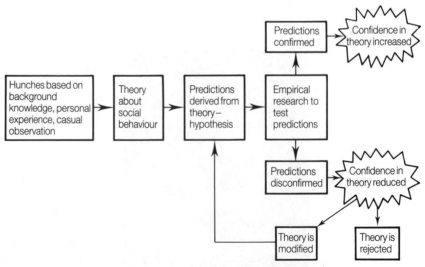

FIGURE 1.2 *A model of the scientific method.*

(causing the investigator to reject the hypothesis, revise it or test it in some other way) but not *prove* them (Popper 1969). If a hypothesis is supported, then confidence in its accuracy increases and one may generate more finely-tuned hypotheses. For example, if we find that ballet dancers do indeed perform better in front of an audience, we might then go on to hypothesise that this effect only occurs when the dancers are already very well rehearsed. An important feature of the scientific method is replication – it guards against the possibility that a finding is tied to the circumstances of the way in which a test was conducted, and also, of course, guards against fraud.

The alternative to science is dogma, or rationalism where understanding is based on authority: something is true ultimately because authorities (for example, the ancient philosophers, the religious scriptures, charismatic leaders) say it is so. Valid knowledge is acquired by pure reason: that is by learning well, and uncritically accepting, the pronouncements of authorities. Even though the scientific revolution, which was championed by people such as Copernicus, Galileo and Newton, occurred in the sixteenth and seventeenth centuries, dogma and rationalism still exist as influential alternative paths to knowledge.

As a science, social psychology has at its disposal an array of different methods for conducting empirical tests of hypotheses. There are two broad types of method: *experimental* and *non-experimental*; each has advantages and limitations. The choice of an appropriate method is determined by a range of factors to do with the nature of the hypothesis under investigation, the resources available for doing the research (for example, time, money, participants) and the ethics of the method. Confidence in the validity of a hypothesis is greatly increased if it has been supported a number of times by different research teams using different methods. Methodological pluralism helps minimise the possibility that the finding is an artifact of a particular method, and replication by different research teams helps avoid confirmation bias – a tendency for researchers to become personally involved in their own theories to such an extent that they lose a degree of objectivity in interpreting data (Greenwald and Pratkanis 1988; Johnson and Eagly 1989).

Experiments

An experiment is a hypothesis test in which one does something to see its effect on something else. For example, if I hypothesise that my car consumes excessive petrol because the tyres are under-inflated, then I can conduct an experiment. I can note petrol consumption over an average week, then I can increase the tyre pressure and again note petrol consumption over an average week. If consumption is reduced then my hypothesis is supported. Casual experimentation is one of the most important and common ways in which people learn about their world: it is an extremely powerful method because it allows one to identify the causes of events and thus gain control over one's destiny.

▶ Independent
variable
▶ Dependent variable

Not surprisingly, systematic experimentation is the most important research method in science. Experimentation involves *intervention* in the form of *manipulation* of one or more *independent variables*, and then the measurement of the effect of the treatment (manipulation) on one or more focal *dependent variables*. In the example above, the independent variable is tyre inflation which was manipulated to create two experimental conditions (lower versus higher pressure), and the dependent variable is petrol consumption which was measured on refilling the tank at the end of the week. More generally, independent variables are dimensions that the researcher hypothesises will have an effect, and that can be varied – for example, tyre pressure in the present example, and the presence or absence of an audience in the ballet dancing example. Dependent variables are dimensions that the researcher hypothesises will vary as a consequence of varying the independent variable – for example, petrol consumption or quality of the ballet dancer's performance. Variation in the dependent variable is *dependent* on variation in the independent variable.

Social psychology is largely experimental in that most social psychologists would prefer to test hypotheses experimentally if at all possible, and much of what we know about social behaviour is based on experiments. Indeed, two of the most prestigious scholarly societies for the scientific study of social psychology are, in America, the *Society for Experimental Social Psychology* and, in Europe, the *European Association of Experimental Social Psychology*.

▶ Confounding

A typical social psychology experiment might be designed to test the hypothesis that violent television programmes increase aggression in young children. One way to do this would be randomly to assign twenty children to each of two conditions in which they individually watch a violent or a non-violent programme, and then monitor the degree of aggression expressed immediately afterwards by the children while they are at play. Random assignment of subjects (here, children) ensures that there are no systematic differences between the subjects in the two conditions. If there were any systematic differences in, say, age, sex or parental background, then any significant effects on aggression might be due to age, sex or background rather than the violence of the television programme. That is, age, sex or parental background are *confounded* with the independent variable. Likewise, the television programme viewed in each condition should be identical in all respects except the degree of violence. For instance, if the violent programme also contained more action, then we would not know if subsequent differences in aggression were due to the violence, the action or both. The circumstances surrounding the viewing of the two programmes should also be identical: if the violent programmes were viewed in a bright red room and the non-violent programmes in a blue room, then any effects might be due to room colour, the violence or both. It is vitally important in experiments to avoid confounding – the conditions must be identical in all respects except for those represented by manipulation of the independent variable.

One must also be careful about how one measures *effects*, that is the dependent measures that assess the dependent variable. In our example, it would probably be inappropriate, because of the children's age, to administer a questionnaire measuring aggression. A better technique would be unobtrusive observation of behaviour: but then what would one code as 'aggression'? The criterion would have to be sensitive to changes: in other words, loud talk or violent assault with a weapon might be insensitive since all children talk loudly when playing (there is a *ceiling effect*) and virtually no children violently assault one another with a weapon while playing (there is a *floor effect*). In addition, it would be a mistake for whoever records or codes the behaviour to know which experimental condition the child was in: such knowledge would undermine objectivity. The coder(s) should know as little as possible about the experimental conditions and hypotheses.

The example used here is of a simple experiment which has only two levels of only one independent variable – called a *one-factor design*. Most social psychology experiments are more complicated than this. For instance, we might formulate a more detailed hypothesis that aggression in young children is increased by television programmes that contain *realistic* violence. To test this hypothesis a two-factor design would be appropriate. The two factors (independent variables) would be (1) the violence of the programme (low versus high), and (2) the realism of the programme (realistic versus fantasy). The subjects would be randomly assigned to each of four experimental conditions in which they watched a non-violent fantasy programme, a non-violent realistic programme, a violent fantasy programme or a violent realistic programme. Finally, independent variables are not restricted to two levels. For instance, in our example we might predict that aggression is increased by moderately violent programmes while extremely violent programmes are so distasteful that aggression is actually suppressed – our independent variable of programme violence could now have three levels (low versus moderate versus extreme).

The laboratory experiment

▶ Laboratory

The classic social psychology experiment is conducted in a *laboratory* in order to be able to control as many potentially confounding variables as possible. The aim is to isolate and manipulate a single aspect of a variable, an aspect which may not normally occur in isolation outside the laboratory. Laboratory experiments are intended to create artificial conditions. Although a social psychology laboratory may contain machines, wires, flashing lights and so forth, usually it is simply a room containing tables and chairs. For example, our ballet hypothesis could be tested in the laboratory by formalising the hypothesis to one in which we predict that someone performing a well-learned task performs the task more quickly in front of an audience. We could unobtrusively time individuals taking off their clothes and then putting them back on again (a well-learned task) either alone in a room or while being watched by two other people (that is, an audience). We could compare these speeds with someone dressing up in unusual and difficult clothing (a poorly learned task). Indeed, this method was actually used by Markus (1978) when she investigated the effect of an audience on task performance – see Chapter 7 for details.

▶ External validity/
mundane realism
▶ Internal validity/
experimental
realism

Laboratory experiments allow one to establish cause and effect relationships among variables. However, laboratory experiments have a number of drawbacks. Because experimental conditions are artificial and highly controlled, laboratory findings cannot be generalised directly to conditions outside the laboratory. However, laboratory findings address theories about human social behaviour, and on the basis of laboratory experimentation we can generalise these theories to apply to conditions other than those in the laboratory. Laboratory experiments are intentionally low on *mundane realism* or *external validity* (that is, how similar the circumstances are to those usually encountered by subjects in the real world) but should always be high on *experimental realism* or *internal validity* (that is, the manipulations must be full of psychological impact and meaning for the subjects; Aronson *et al.* 1990).

▶ Subject effects
▶ Demand
characteristics
▶ Experimenter effect
▶ Double-blind

Laboratory experiments can be prone to a range of biases. There are *subject effects* that can cause subjects' behaviour to be an artifact of the experiment rather than a spontaneous and natural response to a manipulation. Artifacts can be minimised by carefully avoiding *demand characteristics* (Orne 1962) and *evaluation apprehension* and *social desirability* (Rosenberg 1969). Demand characteristics are features of the experiment that seem to 'demand' a particular response – they give information about the hypothesis and thus inform helpful and compliant subjects about how to react to confirm the hypothesis. Subjects are thus no longer naive or *blind* regarding the experimental hypotheses. Subjects in experiments are real people, and experiments are real social situations. Not surprisingly, subjects may wish to project the best possible image of themselves to the experimenter and other subjects present. This can influence spontaneous reactions to manipulations in unpredictable ways. There are also *experimenter effects*. The experimenter is often aware of the hypotheses and may inadvertently give cues that cause subjects to behave in a way that confirms the hypothesis. This can be minimised by a *double-blind* procedure in which experimenters are unaware of which experimental condition they are running.

Since the 1960s, laboratory experiments have tended to be reliant on psychology undergraduates as subjects (Sears 1986). The reason is a pragmatic one – psychology undergraduates are readily available in large numbers. In most major universities there is a 'subject pool' scheme whereby psychology students act as experimental subjects in exchange for course credits or as a course requirement. Critics have often suggested that this over-reliance on a particular type of subject may provide us with a somewhat distorted view of social behaviour – one that is not easily generalised to other sectors of the population. In their defence, experimental social psychologists point out that theories, not experimental findings, are generalised, and that replication and methodological pluralism will ensure that social psychology is about people – not just psychology students.

The field experiment

Social psychology experiments can be conducted in more naturalistic settings outside the laboratory. For example, we could investigate the hypothesis that prolonged eye contact is uncomfortable and causes flight by having an experimenter stand at traffic lights and either gaze intensely at the driver of a car stopped at the lights or gaze in the opposite direction. The dependent measure would be the speed with which the car sped away once the lights changed (Ellsworth *et al.* 1972 – see Chapter 14). Field experiments have high external validity and, since subjects are usually completely unaware that an experiment is taking place, are not reactive (that is, no demand characteristics are present). However, there is less control over extraneous variables, random assignment can sometimes be difficult, and it can be difficult to obtain accurate measurements or measurements of subjective feelings (generally, overt behaviour is all that can be measured).

Non-experimental methods

Systematic experimentation tends to be the preferred method of science, and indeed it is often equated with science. However, there are all sorts of circumstances where it is simply impossible to conduct an experiment to test a hypothesis. For instance, theories about planetary systems and galaxies can pose a real problem – we cannot move planets around to see what happens. Likewise, social psychological theories about the relationship between biological sex and decision-making are not amenable to experimentation because we cannot experimentally manipulate biological sex and see what effects emerge. Social psychology also confronts ethical issues that can proscribe experimentation. For instance, hypotheses about the effects on self-esteem of being a victim of violent crime are not at all easily tested experimentally – we would not be able randomly to assign subjects to two conditions and then subject one group to a violent crime and see what happened.

▶ Correlation

Where experimentation is not possible or not appropriate, social psychologists have a range of non-experimental methods to choose from. Because these methods do not involve the manipulation of independent variables against a background of random assignment to condition, it is almost impossible to draw causal conclusions. For instance, we could compare the self-esteem of a group of people who have been victims of violent crime with those who have not. Any differences could be attributed to violent crime, but could also be due to other uncontrolled differences between the two groups. One can only conclude that there is a *correlation* between self-esteem and being the victim of violent crime. There is no evidence that one causes the other (that is, that being a victim lowers self-esteem, or that having lower self-esteem increases one's likelihood of becoming a victim). Both could be *correlated* or co-occurring effects of some third variable, for instance chronic unemployment, which independently lowers self-esteem *and* increases the probability that one might become a victim. In general, non-experimental methods involve the examination of correlation among naturally occurring variables, and as such do not permit one to draw causal conclusions.

Archival research

▶ Archival research

Archival research is a non-experimental method that is very useful for investigating large-scale, widely occurring phenomena that may be remote in time. The researcher assembles data collected by others, often for reasons unconnected with those of the researcher. For instance, Janis (1972) used an archival method to show that overly cohesive governmental decision-making groups may make poor decisions with disastrous consequences because they adopt poor decision-making procedures (called 'groupthink' – see Chapter 8). Janis constructed his theory on the basis of examination of biographical, autobiographical and media accounts of the decision-making procedures associated with, for example, the 1961 Bay of Pigs fiasco. Archival methods are often used to make comparisons between different cultures or nations regarding issues such as suicide, mental health or child-rearing strategies. The archival method is, of course, not reactive, but can be unreliable because the researcher usually has no control over the primary data collection, which might be biased or unreliable in other ways (for example, missing vital data). The researcher has to make do with whatever is there.

Case study

▶ Case study

The case study allows an in-depth analysis of a single case (either a person or a group) or a single event. Case studies often employ an array of data-collection and analysis techniques involving structured and open-ended interviews and questionnaires, and the observation of behaviour. Case studies are well suited to the examination of unusual or rare phenomena that could not be created in the laboratory, for instance bizarre cults, mass murderers or disasters. Case studies are very useful as a source of hypotheses, but findings may suffer from researcher or subject bias (the researcher is not blind to the hypothesis, there are demand characteristics, and subjects suffer evaluation apprehension), and findings may not easily be generalised to other cases or events.

Survey research

Another non-experimental method is data collection by survey. Surveys can involve structured interviews, in which the experimenter asks the subjects a number of carefully chosen questions and notes down the responses, or a questionnaire, in which subjects write their own responses to written questions. In either case the questions can be open-ended (that is, respondents can give as much or as little detail in their answers as they wish) or closed-ended (that is, there is a limited number of predetermined responses, for example circling a number on a nine-point scale). For instance, if one wished to investigate immigrant workers' experiences of prejudice in Germany, one could ask respondents a set of predetermined questions and summarise the gist of their responses or simply assign a numerical value. Alternatively, respondents could record their own responses by writing a paragraph or by circling numbers on scales in a questionnaire.

Surveys can be used to obtain a large amount of data from a large sample of subjects, hence generalisation is often not a problem. However, it is a method that, like the case study, can be subject to experimenter bias, subject bias and evaluation apprehension. Anonymous and confidential questionnaires may minimise experimenter bias, evaluation apprehension and some subject biases, but demand characteristics may remain and poorly constructed questionnaires may obtain biased data due to 'response set' (that is, the tendency for some respondents unthinkingly to agree with statements, or to choose mid-range responses or extreme responses).

Field studies

The final non-experimental method is the field study. We have already described the field experiment; the field study is essentially the same, but without any interventions or manipulations. Field studies involve the observation, recording and coding of behaviour as it occurs. Most often, the observer is non-intrusive by not participating in the behaviour, and 'invisible' by not having an effect on the ongoing behaviour. For instance, one could research the behaviour of students in the student cafeteria by concealing oneself in a corner and observing what goes on. Sometimes 'invisibility' is impossible, and so the opposite strategy can be used – the researcher becomes a full participant in the behaviour. For instance, it would be difficult to be an invisible observer of gang behaviour. Instead one could study the behaviour of a street gang by becoming a full member of the gang and surreptitiously taking notes (for example, Whyte 1943 – see Chapter 7). Field studies are excellent for investigating spontaneously occurring behaviour in its natural context but are particularly prone to experimenter bias, lack of objectivity, poor generalisability and distortions due to the impact of the researcher on the behaviour under investigation.

Data and analysis

Research provides data that are analysed to draw conclusions about whether hypotheses are supported. The type of analysis undertaken depends on at least the following:

1. The type of *data* obtained – for example, binary responses such as yes versus no, continuous variables such as temperature or response-latency, defined positions on nine-point scales, rank ordering of choices, open-ended written responses (text).

2. The *method* used to obtain data – for example, controlled experiment, open-ended interview, participant observation, archival search.
3. The *purposes* of the research – for example, to describe in depth a specific case, to establish differences between two groups of subjects exposed to different treatments, to investigate the correlation between two or more naturally occurring variables.

▶ Statistics
▶ *t*-test
▶ Statistical significance

Overwhelmingly, social psychological knowledge is based on statistical analysis of quantitative data. Data are obtained as, or are transformed into, numbers (that is, quantities), and then these numbers are compared in various formalised ways (that is, by *statistics*). For example, to ascertain whether females are more friendly as interviewees than are males, we could compare transcripts of interviews of both males and females. We could then code the transcripts to count how often subjects made positive remarks to the interviewer, and then compare the mean count for say twenty females with the mean for twenty males. In this case we would be interested in knowing whether the difference between males and females was 'on the whole' greater than the difference among males and among females. To do this, we could use a very simple statistic called the *t-test* to compute a single number called the *t*-statistic that is based on a consideration of the difference between the females' and males' mean friendliness scores, and the amount of variability of scores within each sex. The larger the value of *t*, the larger the between-sex difference relative to within-sex differences. The decision about whether the difference between groups is psychologically significant depends on whether it is *statistically significant*. Social psychologists accept the arbitrary convention that if the obtained value of *t* has less than a one in twenty probability of occurring simply by chance (for example, if we randomly selected two lots of twenty people and compared their friendliness, only 5 in 100 times or less would we obtain a value of *t* as great as or greater than that obtained in the study) then the obtained difference is statistically significant and there really is a difference in friendliness between male and female interviewees (see Figure 1.3).

The *t*-test is very simple. However, the principle underlying the *t*-test is the same as underlies more sophisticated and complex statistical techniques used by social psychologists to test whether two or more groups differ significantly. The other major method of data analysis used by social psychologists is correlation, which assesses whether the co-occurrence of two or more variables is significant. Again, although the example below is simple, the underlying principle is the same for an array of correlational techniques.

To investigate the idea that rigid thinkers tend to hold more conservative attitudes (Rokeach 1960 – see Chapter 9), we could have twenty subjects answer a questionnaire measuring cognitive rigidity (dogmatism: a rigid and inflexible set of attitudes) and attitudinal conservatism (for example, endorsement and espousal of right-wing political and social policies). If we rank the twenty subjects in order of increasing dogmatism and find that conservatism also increases, with the least dogmatic subject being the least conservative and the most dogmatic the most conservative, then we can say that the two variables are *positively correlated* (see Figure 1.4, in which dots represent individual subjects positioned with respect to their scores on both the dogmatism and conservatism scales). If we find that conservatism systematically decreases with increasing dogmatism, then we say the two variables are *negatively correlated*. If there seems to be no systematic relationship between the two variables then they are uncorrelated, or there is *zero correlation*. A statistic can be calculated to represent correlation numerically, for instance Pearson's *r* statistic varies from −1 for a perfect negative, to +1 for a perfect positive correlation. Depending on, among other things, the number of subjects, we can also know whether the correlation is statistically significant at the conventional 5 per cent level.

Although statistical analysis of quantitative data is the bread and butter of social psychology, some social psychologists find that this method is unsuited

CASE 1. *A significant difference.* The *t*-statistic is relatively large because the difference between means is large and the variation within sex groups is small.

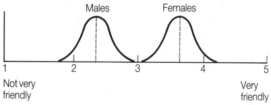

CASE 2. *Not a significant difference.* The *t*-statistic is relatively small because, although the difference between means is still large, the variation within sex groups is much larger.

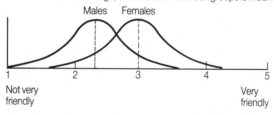

CASE 3 *A significant difference.* The *t*-statistic is large because, although the difference between means is smaller, the variation within sex groups is small.

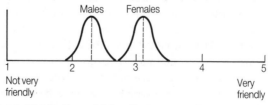

FIGURE 1.3 *Distribution of friendliness scores for twenty male and twenty female interviewees.*

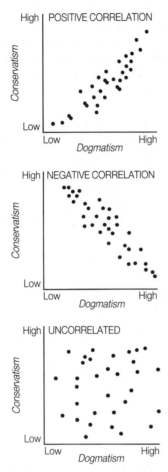

FIGURE 1.4 *The correlation between dogmatism and conservatism for twenty subjects.*

to their purposes and prefer a more *qualitative* analysis. For example, analysis of people's explanations for unemployment or prejudice may sometimes benefit from a more discursive, non-quantitative analysis in which the researcher tries to unravel what is said in order to go beyond superficial explanations and get to the underlying beliefs and reasons. One form of qualitative analysis is *discourse analysis* (for example, Potter and Wetherell 1987; Wetherell and Potter 1992). Discourse analysis treats all 'data' as text: that is, as a communicative event that is replete with multiple layers of meaning, but which can only be interpreted by considering the text in its wider social context. For example, discourse analysts believe that we should not take subjects' responses to attitude statements in questionnaires at face value and subject them to statistical analysis. They believe, instead, that we should interpret what is being communicated. This is made possible only by considering the response as a complex conjunction of social-communicative factors deriving from the immediate context and the wider socio–historical context. Discourse analysis is, however, more than a research method, it is also a systematic critique of 'conventional' social psychology methods and theories (see below).

RESEARCH ETHICS

As researchers, social psychologists confront important ethical issues. For instance, is it ethical to expose experimental subjects to a treatment that is embarrassing or has potential effects on their concept of the self? If such research is important, what are the rights of the subject, what are the ethical obligations of the researcher, and what guidelines are there for deciding? Although ethical considerations surface most often in experiments (for example, Milgram's (1974) obedience studies – see Chapter 6), they can also confront non-experimental researchers. For example, is it ethical for a non-participant observer investigating crowd behaviour to refrain from interceding in a violent assault? To guide researchers, the American Psychological Association (1982) has drawn up a set of principles for ethical conduct in research involving human subjects – these principles are reflected in ethics codes of national societies of psychology in Europe. Researchers design their studies with these guidelines in mind and then obtain official approval from a university or departmental research ethics committee. There are five ethical principles that have received much attention: protection from harm, right to privacy, deception, informed consent and debriefing.

Physical welfare of subjects

Clearly it is unethical to expose subjects to physical harm. For example, the use of electric shocks that cause visible burning would be difficult to justify. However, in most cases it is difficult to establish whether non-trivial harm is involved, and if so, what its magnitude is and whether debriefing (see below) deals with it. For instance, having experimental subjects do badly on a word-association task may have long-term effects on self-esteem, and could therefore be considered harmful. On the other hand, the effects may be so transitory and minor as to be insignificant.

Respect for privacy

Social psychological research often involves invasion of privacy. Subjects can be asked intimate questions, can be observed without their knowledge, and can have their moods, perceptions and behaviours manipulated. It can sometimes be difficult to decide whether the research topic justifies invasion of privacy. At other times it is more straightforward: for example, intimate questions about sexual practices are essential for research into behaviour that may put people at risk of contracting HIV and developing AIDS. Concern about privacy is usually satisfied by ensuring that data obtained from individual subjects are entirely confidential: only the researcher knows who said or did what. Personal identification is removed from data (rendering them anonymous) and research findings are reported as means for large groups of subjects.

Use of deception

Laboratory experiments involve the manipulation of people's cognitions, feelings or behaviours in order to investigate the spontaneous, natural and non-reactive effect of independent variables. Because subjects need to be naive regarding hypotheses, experimenters often conceal the true purpose of the experiment: a degree of deception is often necessary. Between 50 and 75 per cent of published experiments involve some degree of deception (Adair *et al.* 1985; Gross and Fleming 1982). Because the use of deception seems to imply trickery, deceit and lying, it has attracted a great deal of criticism: for example, Baumrind's (1964) attack on Milgram's (1974) obedience studies (see Chapter 6), and social psychologists have been challenged to abandon controlled experimental research (in favour of role-playing or simulations: for example, Kelman 1967) if they cannot do it without deception. This is probably too extreme a request – social psychological knowledge has been enriched enormously by classic experiments that have used deception (many are described in this book). Although some experiments have used a degree of deception that really does seem unacceptable, in practice the deception used in most social psychology experiments is trivial – for example, an experiment may be introduced as a study of group decision-making when in fact it is part of a programme of research into prejudice and stereotyping. In addition, no-one has yet shown any long-term negative consequences of the use of deception in social psychology experiments (Elms 1982), and experimental subjects themselves tend to be impressed rather than upset or angered by cleverly executed deceptions and view deception as a necessary withholding of information or a necessary ruse (Christensen 1988; Smith 1983).

Informed consent

One way to safeguard subjects' rights in experiments is to obtain their informed consent to participate. In principle, subjects should freely give their consent (preferably in writing) to participate on the basis of full information about what they are consenting to take part in, and must be entirely free to withdraw from the research whenever they wish. Researchers cannot lie or withhold information in order to induce subjects to participate, nor can they make it difficult to say no or to withdraw (that is, by social pressure or by exercise of personal or institutionalised power). In practice, however, terms such as 'full information' are difficult to define, and, as we have just seen, experiments often require some deception in order that subjects remain naive.

Debriefing

Subjects should be fully debriefed after taking part in an experiment. Debriefing is designed to make sure that subjects leave the laboratory with an increased respect for and understanding of social psychology. More specifically, debriefing involves a detailed explanation of the experiment and its broader theoretical and applied context. Any deceptions are explained and justified to the satisfaction of all subjects, and care is taken to make sure that the effects of manipulations have been undone.

Social psychologists often conduct and report research into socially sensitive phenomena or research that has implications for socially sensitive issues, for example prejudice, discrimination, racism, sexism, ageism (see Chapters 9, 10 and 14). In these sorts of area the researcher has to be especially careful that both the conducting and reporting of research is done in such a way that it is not biased by personal prejudices and is not open to public misinterpretation, distortion or misuse. For example, early research into sex differences in conformity found that women conformed more than men. This finding is, of course, fuel to the chauvinistic view that women are more dependent than, and intellectually inferior to, men. Later research discovered that men and women conform equally, and that whether one conforms or not depends to a great extent on how much familiarity and confidence one has with the conformity task. Early research used tasks that were more familiar to males than females, and many researchers looked no further because the findings confirmed their assumptions (Chapters 6 and 9).

THEORETICAL ISSUES

Social psychologists construct and test theories of human social behaviour. A social psychological theory is an integrated set of propositions that explains the causes of social behaviour, generally in terms of one or more social psychological processes. Theories rest on explicit assumptions about social behaviour and contain a number of defined concepts and formal statements about the relationship among concepts. Ideally, these relationships are causal ones that are attributed to the operation of social and/or psychological processes. Theories are framed in such a way that they generate hypotheses that can be tested empirically. Social psychological theories vary a great deal in terms of their rigour, testability and generality (Shaw and Costanzo 1982). Some theories are short-range, mini-theories that are tied to specific phenomena, while others are much broader, general theories that explain whole classes of behaviour – some even approach the status of 'grand theory' (such as evolutionary theory, Marxism, general relativity theory, psychodynamic theory) in that they furnish a general perspective on social psychology.

Social identity theory (for example, Hogg and Abrams 1988; Tajfel and Turner 1979; Turner 1982 – see Chapter 10) is an example of a fairly general mid-range social psychological theory. It rests on four assumptions:

1. Interpersonal and group behaviour are separate phenomena.
2. Human cognition is designed to streamline perception of the social world in socially adaptive and meaningful ways.
3. Society is structured into distinct social categories that stand in power and status relations to one another.
4. People have a need for relatively positive self-esteem.

There is a range of precisely defined concepts which include social group, intergroup behaviour, stereotyping, conformity, discrimination, categorisation, social comparison and social belief structures. These are woven together theoretically in terms of three causal processes:

1. *Categorisation* is associated with perceptual 'simplification'.
2. *Social comparison* is associated with people's need for self-esteem.
3. *Social beliefs* are associated with people's choices of different behavioural strategies.

These processes operate together to produce group behaviour, as distinct from interpersonal behaviour. This theory generates testable predictions about a range of group phenomena, including stereotyping, intergroup discrimination, social influence in groups, group cohesiveness, social change, and even language and ethnicity.

Theories in social psychology

▶ Metatheory

Theories in social psychology can generally be clustered into types of theory, with different types of theory reflecting different *metatheories*. Just as a theory is a set of interrelated concepts and principles that explain a phenomenon, a *metatheory* is a set of interrelated concepts and principles concerning which theories, types of theory or perspectives are appropriate.

▶ Radical behaviourism

▶ Neo-behaviourism

Behaviourist or learning perspectives originally derive from Ivan Pavlov's work on conditioned reflexes, and B.F. Skinner's work on operant conditioning. *Radical behaviourists* believe that behaviour can be explained and predicted in terms of reinforcement schedules – behaviours associated with positive outcomes or circumstances increase in strength and frequency. More popular with social psychologists, however, are *neo-behaviourists* who believe that one needs to invoke unobservable intervening constructs (for example, beliefs, feelings, motives) to make sense of behaviour. The behaviourist perspective in social psychology produces theories that emphasise the role of situational factors and reinforcement/learning in social behaviour. One example is the *reinforcement-affect model* of interpersonal attraction (for example, Lott 1961 – Chapter 12): people grow to like those people whom they associate with positive experiences (for example, we like people who praise us). Another more general example is *social exchange theory* (for example, Kelley and Thibaut 1978 – Chapter 12): the course of social interactions depends on subjective evaluation of the rewards and costs involved. Social modelling is another broadly behaviourist perspective: we imitate behaviour that is reinforced in others, and thus our behaviour is shaped by vicarious learning (for example, Bandura 1977 – Chapter 11). Finally, *drive theory* (Zajonc 1965 – Chapter 7) explains decrements and improvements in performance in front of an audience in terms of the strength of a learned response.

▶ Cognitive theories   Critics have argued that behaviourist theories exaggerate the degree to which people are passive recipients of external influences. *Cognitive theories* redress the balance by focusing on the way in which people actively interpret and change their environment, through the agency of cognitive processes and cognitive representations. Cognitive theories have their origins in Kurt Koffka and Wolfgang Köhler's Gestalt psychology of the 1930s, and in many ways social psychology has always been very cognitive in its perspective (Landman and Manis 1983; Markus and Zajonc 1985). One of the earliest cognitive theories in social psychology was Kurt Lewin's (1951) field theory which dealt with the way in which people's cognitive representations of features of the social environment produced motivational forces to behave in various ways. Lewin is generally considered the father of experimental social psychology. In the 1950s and 1960s cognitive consistency theories dominated social psychology (Abelson *et al.* 1968). These theories assumed that cognitions about oneself, one's behaviour, and the world, which were contradictory or incompatible in other ways produced an uncomfortable state of cognitive arousal that motivated people to resolve the cognitive conflict. This perspective has been used to explain attitude change (for example, Aronson 1984 – Chapter 5). In the 1970s, attribution theories dominated social psychology. Attribution theories focus on the way in which people explain the causes of their own and other people's behaviours, and on the consequences of causal explanations (for example, Hewstone 1989 – Chapter 3). Finally, since the late 1970s social cognition has been the dominant perspective in social psychology. This is a perspective which contains a number of theories dealing with the way in which cognitive processes (for example, categorisation) and cognitive representations (for example, schemata) are constructed and influence behaviour (for example, Fiske and Taylor 1991 – Chapter 2).

Social psychologists have often tried to explain social behaviour in terms of enduring (sometimes innate) personality attributes. For instance, good leaders have charismatic personalities (Chapter 8), prejudice is expressed by people with prejudiced personalities (Chapter 9), and people who conform more have conformist personalities (Chapter 6). In general, social psychologists now consider personality to be at best a partial explanation, at worst an inadequate explanation, of social phenomena. There are at least two reasons for this:

1. There is actually very little evidence for stable personality traits. People

behave in different ways at different times and in different contexts – they are influenced by situation and context.

2. Rather than being an explanation for behaviour, personality, as behavioural consistency across contexts, is something to be explained. Why do some people resist social and contextual influences on behaviour? What is it about their interpretation of the context that causes them to behave in this way?

Personality theories can be contrasted with collectivist theories. Collectivist theories focus on the way in which people are socially constituted by their unique location in society: people behave as they do, not because of personality or individual predispositions, but because they internally represent socially constructed group norms that influence behaviour in specific contexts. An early collectivist viewpoint was McDougall's (1920) theory of the 'group mind' (Chapter 10). In groups, people change the way they think, process information and act, so that group behaviour is quite different from interpersonal behaviour – a group mind appears to emerge. More recently this early idea has been elaborated greatly by European social psychologists seeking an intergroup perspective on social behaviour (for example, Tajfel 1984). Of these, social identity theory is perhaps the most developed (for example, Tajfel and Turner 1979 – Chapter 10). Its explanation of the behaviour of people in groups is importantly dependent on an analysis of the social relations between groups. Collectivist theories adopt a 'top down' approach in which individual social behaviour can only be explained with reference to groups, intergroup relations and social forces. Individualistic theories, in contrast, are 'bottom up' – individual social behaviour is constructed from individual cognition or personality.

It is important to note that many social psychological theories have elements of two or more perspectives, and also that these, and other, perspectives often merely lend emphasis to different theories. Metatheory does not usually intentionally reveal itself.

The 'crisis' in social psychology

Social psychology occurs against a background of, often latent, metatheoretical differences. In many respects this is an intellectually appealing feature of the discipline. From time to time these differences come to the fore and become the focus of intense public debate. The most recent occurrence was in the late 1960s and early 1970s when social psychology appeared to many to have reached a crisis of confidence (for example, Elms 1975; Israel and Tajfel 1972; Rosnow 1981; Strickland *et al.* 1976). There were two principal worries about social psychology:

1. It was overly *reductionist* (that is, by explaining social behaviour mainly in terms of individual psychology, it failed to address the essentially social nature of the human experience).

2. It was overly *positivistic* (that is, it adhered to a model of science that was distorted, inappropriate, and misleading).

Reductionism and levels of explanation

▶ Reductionism
▶ Levels of
  explanation

Reductionism is the practice of explaining a phenomenon in terms of the language and concepts of a lower level of analysis. Society is explained in terms of groups, groups in terms of interpersonal processes, interpersonal processes in terms of intrapersonal cognitive mechanisms, cognition in terms of neuropsychology, neuropsychology in terms of biology, and so forth. A problem of reductionist theorising is that it can leave unanswered the original question. For example, the act of putting one's arm out of the car window to indicate an intention to turn can be explained in terms of muscle contraction or nerve impulses, or understanding of and adherence to social conventions, and so on. If the *level of explanation* does not match the level of the question, then the question remains, in effect, unanswered. In researching interpersonal relations, to what extent does an explanation in terms of cognition really address interpersonal relations?

Although a degree of reductionism is possibly necessary for theorising, too great a degree is undesirable. Social psychology has been criticised for being inherently reductionist because it tries to explain social behaviour in terms of asocial intrapsychic cognitive and motivational processes (for example, Moscovici 1972; Pepitone 1981; Sampson 1977; Taylor and Brown 1979). The problem is most acute when social psychologists try to explain group processes and intergroup relations. By tackling these phenomena exclusively in terms of personality, interpersonal relations or intrapsychic processes, social psychology essentially leaves less than adequately explained some of its most important phenomena, for example prejudice, discrimination, stereotyping, conformity, group solidarity (Billig 1976; Hogg and Abrams 1988; Turner and Oakes 1986).

Doise (1986; Lorenzi-Cioldi and Doise 1990) has recently suggested that one way around this problem is to accept the existence of different levels of explanation but make a special effort to construct theories that formally integrate (Doise uses the term 'articulate') concepts from different levels (see Box 1.1). This idea has been adopted to varying degrees by many social psychologists (see Tajfel 1984). One of the most successful attempts is social identity theory (for example, Tajfel and Turner 1979), as we have noted (see Chapter 10), in which individual cognitive processes are articulated with large-scale social forces to explain group behaviour. Doise's ideas have also been employed to reinterpret group cohesiveness (Hogg 1992), attribution theories (Hewstone 1989), and social representations (for example Doise *et al.* 1993).

Positivism

▶ Positivism

Positivism is the non-critical acceptance of scientific method as the only way to arrive at true knowledge. Positivism was introduced in the early nineteenth

---

BOX 1.1 Levels of explanation in social psychology

I Intrapersonal
Analysis of psychological processes to do with individuals' organisation of their experience of the social environment (for example, research on cognitive balance).

II Interpersonal and situational
Analysis of inter-individual interaction within circumscribed situations. Social positional factors emanating from outside the situation are not considered. The object of study is the dynamics of relations established at a given moment by given individuals in a given situation (for example, some attribution research, research using game matrices).

III Positional
Analysis of inter-individual interaction in specific situations, but with the role of social position (for example, status, identity) outside the situation taken into consideration (for example, some research into power and social identity).

IV Ideological
Analysis of inter-individual interaction that considers the roles of general social beliefs and of social relations between groups (for example, some research into social identity, social representations and minority influence, studies considering the role of cultural norms and values).

(Source: taken from Hogg (1992, p. 62) and based on Lorenzi-Cioldi and Doise (1990, p. 73) and Doise (1986, pp. 10–16).)

---

century by the French mathematician and philosopher Auguste Compte, and was extremely popular until the end of that century. The character Mr Gradgrind in Charles Dickens' 1854 novel *Hard Times* epitomises positivism: science almost as a religion.

Social psychology has been criticised for being positivistic (for example, Gergen 1973; Henriques *et al.* 1984; Potter *et al.* 1984; Shotter 1984). It is argued that because social psychologists essentially study themselves they cannot achieve the level of objectivity of, say, a chemist studying a compound or a geographer studying a landform. Since complete objectivity is unattainable, scientific methods, particularly experimental ones, are simply not appropriate for social psychology. Social psychology can only masquerade as a science: it cannot be a true science. Critics argue that what social psychologists propose as fundamental causal mechanisms (for example, categorisation, attribution, cognitive balance, self-concept), are only 'best guess' concepts that explain some historically and culturally restricted data – data which are subject to unavoidable and intrinsic bias. Critics also feel that by treating human subjects as objects or clusters of variables which can be experimentally manipulated we are not only cutting ourselves off from a rich reservoir of subjective or introspective data, but we are also dehumanising people.

These criticisms have produced some quite radical alternatives to traditional social psychology. Examples include: social constructionism (Gergen 1973), humanistic psychology (Shotter 1984), ethogenics (Harré 1979), discourse analysis (Potter and Wetherell 1987), and post-structuralist perspectives (Henriques *et al.* 1984). There are marked differences among these alternatives, but they share a broad emphasis on understanding people as whole human beings who are constructed historically and who try to make sense of themselves and their world. Research methods tend to emphasise in-depth subjective analysis (often called *deconstruction*) of the relatively spontaneous accounts people give of their thoughts, feelings and actions. Subjectivity is considered a virtue of, rather than an impediment to, good research.

▶ Operational definition

Most social psychologists, however, respond to the problem of positivism in a less extreme manner that does not involve abandoning the scientific method. Instead, they deal with the pitfalls of positivism by being rigorous in the use of appropriate scientific methods of research and theorising (for example, Campbell 1957; Kruglanski 1975; Turner 1981a). Included in this is awareness of the need for *operational definitions* of social processes, such as aggression, altruism or leadership. Operationalism is a product of positivism, and refers to a demand that theoretical terms in science be defined in a manner that renders them susceptible to measurement. As scientists, we should be mindful of our own subjectivity and should acknowledge and make explicit our biases. Our theories should be sensitive to the pitfalls of reductionism and, where appropriate, articulate different levels of analysis. We should also recognise that experimental subjects do not throw off their past history and become unidimensional 'variables' when they enter the laboratory. On the contrary, culture, history, socialisation and personal motives are all present in the laboratory – experiments are social situations (Tajfel 1972a). Finally, attention should be paid to language, as that is perhaps the most important way in which people represent the world, think, plan action and manipulate the world around them (Chapter 14). Language is also the epitome of a social variable: it is socially constructed and internalised to govern individual social cognition and behaviour.

HISTORICAL CONTEXT

Social psychology, as we have described it, is not a static science. It has a history, and it is almost always invaluable to consider a science in its proper historical context in order to understand its true nature. In this section, we give an overview of the history of social psychology. Although ancient forms of social and political philosophy addressed such questions as the nature/nurture controversy, the origins of society and the function of the state, it was mostly a speculative exercise and devoid of fact-gathering (Hollander 1967). An empirical approach to the study of social life did not appear until the latter part of the nineteenth century.

Social psychology in the nineteenth century

Anglo-European influences

▶ Völkerpsychologie An important precursor to the development of an independent discipline of social psychology was the work of a number of people in Germany know as the *folk psychologists*. In 1860, a journal devoted to *Völkerpsychologie* was founded by Steinthal and Lazarus, and contained articles of both a theoretical and factual nature. Whereas general psychology (to be elaborated later by Wundt) dealt with the study of the mind, folk psychology was to deal with the study of the collective mind, following the stimulus of the philosopher Hegel. This concept was interpreted in conflicting ways by Steinthal and Lazarus, at once to mean a societal way of thinking within the individual and also a form of super-mentality which could enfold a whole group of people (Haines 1980). This concept of a group mind became a dominant way of accounting for social behaviour in the 1890s and early 1900s. An extreme example of it was found in the work of the French writer Gustav LeBon (1908), in his account of why crowds often behave badly, namely, because the behaviour of the individual becomes subject to the control of the *group mind*. Likewise, the English psychologist William McDougall (1920) subscribed to the group mind explanation when dealing with collective behaviour, devoting a whole book to the topic. The famous American Solomon Asch (1951) observed much later that the issue that such writers wished to deal with has not gone away: that to understand the complexities of an individual's behaviour requires us to address the person in the context of group relations.

Early texts

At the turn of the century there were two texts dealing with social psychology, by Bunge (1903) and by Orano (1901), but because they were not in English, they received no attention in either Britain or the United States. Even earlier, the American Baldwin (1897) touched on the field of social psychology in a work mainly given to the social and moral development of the child. A book by the French sociologist Gabriel Tarde (1898) had definite implications for the kinds of data and the level of analysis that social psychology should adopt. His view was a bottom-up approach and was offered in debate with Emile Durkheim. Whereas Durkheim argued that the way people behave is determined by social laws that are set by society, Tarde proposed that a science of social behaviour must derive laws that deal with the individual case. The way he conceived of social psychology is closer in flavour to most current American thinking than any of the other early texts (Clark 1969).

The two early texts which actually caught the attention of the English-speaking world were written by McDougall (1908) and the American sociologist E.A. Ross (1908). Neither looks much like a modern social psychology text, but we need to remember that living scientific disciplines continue to be redefined. The central topics of McDougall's book, for example were the principal instincts, primary emotions, the nature of sentiments, moral conduct, volition, religious conceptions and the structure of character. Compare these with the chapter topics of the present textbook.

The rise of experimentation

An influential textbook by Floyd Allport (1924) moulded a shape for social psychology which was followed by many teachers in psychology departments for years to come. Following the manifesto for psychology as a whole laid out by the behaviourist John Watson (1913), Allport argued cogently that social psychology would only flourish if it became an experimental science. A little later, Murphy and Murphy (1931) felt justified in producing a book entitled *Experimental Social Psychology*. Not all of the studies reviewed were actually experiments, but the intention of what the discipline should be was clear.

▶ Experimental
method

Although the earlier texts had not shown it, the closing decade of the nineteenth century had set a scene in which social psychology would be inextricably entwined with the broader discipline of general psychology. As such, its subsequent development reflects the way in which psychology was defined and taught in university departments of psychology, particularly in the United States, which rapidly replaced Germany as the leading country for psychological research. Just as the psychological laboratory at Leipzig founded by Wilhelm Wundt in 1879 had provided an experimental basis for psychology in Germany, the laboratories set up at American universities did likewise in the United States. In the period 1890–1910, the growth of laboratories devoted to psychological research was rapid (Ruckmick 1912). Thirty-one American universities established experimental facilities in those twenty years. The subject taught in these departments was clearly defined as an experimental science. In the United States, therefore, it is not surprising that social psychology should quite early on look towards the *experimental method* as a touchstone. By the time Allport published his 1924 text, this trend was well established.

When was social psychology's first experiment?

This is a natural question to ask, but the answer is clouded. One of the oldest psychological laboratories was at Indiana University. It was here that Norman Triplett (1898) conducted a study which some modern textbooks have listed as the first experiment in social psychology (for example, Lippa 1990; Penrod 1983; Sears *et al.* 1991) and quote it as an experiment on social facilitation (for example, Baron and Byrne 1991; Brigham 1991; Deaux and Wrightsman 1988 – see Chapter 7). Gordon Allport (1954) implied that what Wundt did in 1879 for experimental psychology, Triplett did in 1898 for a scientific social psychology. Check Box 1.2 and judge for yourself if you think this was a study in social psychology.

The search for a founding figure, or a first idea, is not a new phenomenon in the history of science or, indeed, in the history of civilisation. Sometimes it

---

BOX 1.2 Triplett's study of pacemaking and competition: psychophysiology, sports psychology or social psychology?

The first experiment in what?

Norman Triplett was a 37-year-old teacher when he returned to graduate studies at Indiana University to work on his masters thesis, published in 1898 as 'The dynamogenic factors in pacemaking and competition'. His supervisors were two experimental psychologists, Bryan and Bergström, and the laboratory (along with that at Clark University) was one of the best-established settings in the country. His experiment is often referred to as a study in social facilitation (a topic discussed later in Chapter 7), and classified by some textbook writers as the first social-psychological experiment ever conducted. Is this claim justified?

Triplett's interest had been stimulated by the popular knowledge that racing cyclists go faster when racing or when being paced than when riding alone. Cycling as an activity had increased enormously in popularity in the closing decade of the nineteenth century and was participated in both as a pastime and as a sport, with spectacular press coverage. Triplett listed a variety of possible explanations for the superior performance of cyclists who are racing or being paced:

1. The pacer in front provided a suction to pull the rider behind along, which helped to conserve energy or else provided shelter from the wind.
2. A 'brain-worry' theory, popular at the time, predicted that solitary cyclists did poorly because they worried about whether they were going fast enough. This exhausted their brain and muscles, possibly because phosphoric acid was released which benumbed the brain and inhibited motor performance.
3. Friends usually rode as pacers and no doubt encouraged the cyclists to keep up their spirits.
4. In a race, a follower might be hypnotised by the wheels in front, and so rode automatically, leaving more energy for a later controlled burst.
5. A dynamogenic theory, favoured by Triplett, proposed that the presence of another person racing aroused a 'competitive instinct'.

▶

The competitive instinct released 'nervous energy' (a concept fairly close to the modern idea of arousal). The sight of movement in another suggested a higher speed and inspired greater effort. Other racers released a level of nervous energy which an isolated rider cannot achieve alone. The energy of a movement was in proportion to the idea of that movement.

In the psychology of Triplett's day it was thought that to perform a movement there had to be an 'idea' of that movement present. This idea 'suggested' the action to be performed, and the stronger the idea, the stronger the movement.

In the most famous of his experiments, he recorded the perform-ance of forty boys and girls aged from 8 to 17 years. They worked in two conditions: in pairs and alone. The apparatus consisted of two fishing reels which turned silk bands around a drum. Each reel was connected by a loop or cord to a pulley two metres away, and a small flag was attached to each cord. To complete one trial, a flag sewn to the silk band had to travel four times around the wheel.

The result showed that some children were slower in competition some were faster in competition, and others were little affected. He interpreted the faster ones as showing the effects of both 'the arousal of their competitive instincts and the idea of a faster movement' (Triplett 1898, p. 526). For those who were slower, he thought that they were overstimulated and 'going to pieces' (a nice modern turn of phrase).

In expanding on the dynamogenic theory, his main interest was on the ideo-motor responses, that is, the effects of one competitor's bodily movements acting as a cue to the other competitor. It is interesting that essentially *non-social* cues are highlighted by Triplett to illustrate the idea of movement being used as a cue by his subjects.

The leading American psychological journals in the decade following Triplett's study made scarcely a reference to it. It was catalogued in general sources but not under any headings with a 'social' connotation. In Baldwin's 1901 dictionary it was located under 'will' but not under 'individual and social'. Likewise, in the 1899 volume of *L'Année Psychologique* it was excluded from the section called 'Sociology', which in turn subsumed social psychology. Instead, it was listed under 'Movement and volition' in a section with other papers which were mostly physiological or psychophysiological in nature.

What is clear is that Triplett himself cannot be considered a social psychologist. By adopting a revisionist view of history, the spirit of his experiment emerges as a precursor to the theme of social facilitation research.

has the trappings of an origin myth. In the present case, there were studies earlier than 1898 which might just as easily be called the first in social psychology (Burnham 1910; Haines and Vaughan 1979). Vaughan and Guerin (1994) have pointed out that Triplett has also been claimed by sports psychologists as one of their own. Certainly, his work dealt with competition rather than social facilitation.

Later influences

▶ Behaviourism

Social psychology's development after the early impact of *behaviourism* was redirected by a number of other important developments, some of which came from beyond mainstream psychology.

Attitude scaling

One of these developments was the arrival of several methods for scaling attitudes (Bogardus 1925; Likert 1932; Thurstone 1928), two of which were published in sociological journals, and are further discussed in Chapter 4. The discipline of sociology has often thrown up approaches to social psychology which have been critical of an individual-behaviour level of analysis. Thomas and Znaniecki (1918), for example, defined social psychology as the scientific study of attitudes rather than of social behaviour.

Studies of the social group

A central part of social psychology is an abiding interest in the structure and function of the social group (see Chapters 7, 8 and 10). A major figure in psychology who gave special impetus to the long-term development of social psychology was Lewin. One of his imaginative studies was an experiment dealing with the effect of leadership style on small group behaviour (Lewin *et al.* 1939 – see Chapter 8). By 1945 Lewin had founded a research centre devoted to the study of group dynamics. Another important thread in research on the nature of the social group came from the field of industrial psychology. A famous study carried out in a factory setting showed that work productivity can be more heavily influenced by psychological properties of the workgroup and also by the degree of interest which managers show in their workers (Roethlisberger and Dickson 1939) than by mere physical working conditions. A major outcome of research of this kind was to reinforce an approach to social psychology in which theory and application can develop together.

Famous textbooks

The 1930s marked several quite different themes which had a striking impact on the continuing development of the discipline. Murchison (1935) produced the first handbook for the subject: a weighty tome which suggested that here was a field to be taken seriously. A later, expanded edition of the Murphy and Murphy text (1931) appeared which summarised the findings of more than one thousand studies, though it was used mainly as a reference work. Perhaps the most widely used textbook of this period was that by LaPiere and Farnsworth (1936). Another by Klineberg (1940) was also popular. It featured contributions from cultural anthropology and the crucial role that culture plays in the way that an individual's personality develops. Just after the Second World War, a mainstream work by Krech and Crutchfield (1948) appeared which emphasised a *phenomenological approach* to social psychology: that is, an approach which focuses on the way in which people actually experience the world and account for their experiences.

In the 1950s and thereafter, the number of textbooks appearing on the bookshelves increased exponentially. Most have been published in the United States, and their reliance on both American data and theory has been heavy.

Famous experiments

For different reasons, several experiments stand out over the years which have fascinated teachers and students alike. The following have had an impact beyond the immediate discipline to the wider perspective of general psychology, and some out further to other disciplines. We will not go into detail about these studies here, since they are treated in later chapters.

Muzafer Sherif (1935) carried out an experiment on *norm formation* which caught the attention of psychologists eager to pinpoint what could be 'social' about social psychology (Chapter 6). Solomon Asch (1951) demonstrated the stunning effect that *group pressure* can have in persuading an individual to conform (Chapter 6). Muzafer and Carolyn Sherif (1953) looked at the role that competition for resources can have on intergroup conflict (Chapter 10). Leon Festinger used his theory of *cognitive dissonance* to show that a smaller reward can induce more attitude change than a larger reward (Festinger and Carlsmith, 1959), a finding which annoyed orthodox reinforcement theory at that time (Chapters 4 and 5). Stanley Milgram's (1963) study of *destructive obedience* picked up the dilemma faced by a person ordered by an authority figure to perform an immoral act, a study which unwittingly took a central place in a crisis period of questioning of the future of the experimental method in social psychology (Chapter 6). Henri Tajfel (1970; Tajfel *et al.* 1971) conducted an experiment to show that the mere fact of being categorised into groups was sufficient to generate *intergroup discrimination* (Chapter 10).

Famous programmes

One way of viewing the network within which a discipline develops is to ask the question 'who's who?', and then 'who influenced whom?' Looked at in this way, the group-centred research of the charismatic Lewin (Marrow 1969) had a remarkable impact on other social psychologists in the United States. One of his students was Leon Festinger, and one of Festinger's students was Stanley Schachter. The latter's work on the cognitive labelling of emotion is a derivative of Festinger's notion of social comparison (that is, the way that individuals use other people as a basis for assessing their own thoughts, feelings and behaviours).

There have been other groups of researchers whose impact is more obvious by the nature of the concepts that derived from their programmes. There were two influential groups whose research concerned questions posed during the Second World War. One was the study of the *authoritarian personality* by Adorno and his colleagues (1950). Stimulated by the possibility that an explanation for the rise of German autocracy resided in the personality and child-rearing practices of a nation, they embarked on an ambitious cross-cultural check in the United States (Chapter 9). Another product of the war was the Yale *attitude change* programme, led by Carl Hovland and designed to uncover the theory and techniques of propaganda (Hovland *et al.* 1953 – see Chapter 5).

Later developments

What is later, or 'modern', is a relative concept and is continuously updated and reinterpreted. From our perspective, one such example is the work of Thibaut and Kelley (1959). They developed an approach to the study of interpersonal relationships based on an economic model of *social exchange* (see Chapter 12) which continued to stimulate theory-building into the 1980s. Likewise, Deutsch (Deutsch and Krauss 1960) applied exchange theory to open up the field of interpersonal bargaining to the psychologist. The remarkable contribution made by Lewin to the manner in which social psychology was to develop is indicated by the fact that all of these innovators (Thibaut, Kelley, Deutsch) were his students.

The modern period, however, has been dominated by cognitive approaches. *Attribution theory* was set on its path by Jones (Jones and Davis 1965) who focused attention on the ordinary person's ideas about causality (Chapter 3). Darley and Latané (1968) used an innovative cognitive model to open up research on *prosocial behaviour* by throwing light on the way in which people interpret an emergency, and sometimes fail to help a victim (Chapter 13).

Following earlier work by Heider (1946) and Asch (1946) in a field loosely described as social perception, a major restructuring led this avenue towards the topic area of *social cognition* (see Chapter 2). Several researchers made major contributions to this development, including Mischel (Cantor and Mischel 1977), who dealt with the way that perceived traits of behaviour can function as prototypes, and Nisbett and Ross (1980), who opened up the domain of cognitive heuristics (mental short cuts in social thinking).

The journals

Traditional journals which were important up to the 1950s were the *Journal of Abnormal and Social Psychology* and the *Journal of Personality*. A sociological journal, *Sociometry*, also catered for social psychological work.

From the 1960s there was an increased demand for further outlets. This reflected not only the increase in the number of actively researching social psychologists around the world, but also the demand for some regional representation. The patriarchal *Journal of Abnormal and Social Psychology* divided into two: one part devoted to abnormal psychology and the other titled *Journal of Personality and Social Psychology* (founded in 1965). *Sociometry* was retitled *Social Psychology Quarterly* (1979) to reflect better its heavy social psychological content. Anglo–European interests were represented by the *British Journal of Social and Clinical Psychology* (1963) (which split in about 1980 to produce the *British Journal of Social Psychology*) and the *European Journal of Social Psychology* (1971). Room for a second, American journal dedicated to experimental research was found for the *Journal of Experimental Social Psychology* (1965), and then in 1975 a third major American social psychology journal was launched, called *Personality and Social Psychology Bulletin*. Other journals devoted to the area are *Journal of Applied Social Psychology* (1971) and *Social Cognition* (1982).

From the point of view of articles published, therefore, there was an explosion of interest in the subject during the decade bridging the 1960s and 1970s.

SOCIAL PSYCHOLOGY IN EUROPE

Although, as our historical overview has shown, the beginnings of social psychology, and indeed psychology as a whole, were in Europe, America quickly took over leadership in terms not only of concepts but also of journals, books and organisations. One important reason for this shift in hegemony was the rise of fascism in Europe in the late 1930s. For instance, in Germany in 1933 Jewish professors were dismissed from the universities, and from then until the end of the Second World War the names of Jewish authors were expunged from university textbooks in the service of National Socialism and to promulgate Aryan doctrine (Baumgarten-Tramer 1948). This led, during the immediate pre-war period, to a massive exodus of European social psychologists and other scholars to the United States. By 1945 social psychology in Europe had been significantly weakened, particularly when compared with the rapid development of the field in the United States. By 1945 there remained very little European social psychology.

From 1945 into the 1950s the United States provided resources (for example, money and academic links) to (re-)establish centres of European social psychology. Although partly a scientific gesture this was also part of a general Cold War strategy to provide an intellectual environment in western Europe to combat the potential encroachment of communism. These centres were linked to America rather than to one another – in fact there were very few links among European social psychologists who were often unaware of one another and who tended to have lines of communication with American universities. Europe, including Britain, was largely an outpost of American social psychology. In the period from 1950 to the end of the 1960s, social psychology in Britain was largely based on American ideas. Likewise in the

Netherlands, Germany, France and Belgium most work was influenced by American thinking (Argyle 1980).

Gradually, however, European social psychologists became more conscious of the hegemony of American ideas and of the intellectual, cultural and historical differences between Europe and America. For instance, the recent European experience was one of war and conflict while America's last major conflict within its own borders was the Civil War in the 1860s. Not surprisingly, Europeans considered themselves to be more concerned with intergroup relations and groups while Americans were perhaps more interested in interpersonal relations and individuals. Europeans pushed for a more *social* social psychology. There was a clear need for some degree of intellectual and organisational independence.

This came to a head in the 1960s, when European social psychologists started to meet to establish a *European Association of Experimental Social Psychology*. The main figures behind the development of an indigenous European social psychology were Henri Tajfel in Britain and Serge Moscovici in France, although many other prominent European social psychologists were involved (for example, Codol, Doise, Jaspars, Leyens, Rabbie, Stroebe, von Cranach). The *European Journal of Social Psychology* was launched in 1971 and is now generally considered one of the five most prestigious social psychology journals in the world. In 1990 another European periodical was launched: the *European Review of Social Psychology*. Although largely relying on American social psychology texts, there have been some European texts, probably beginning with Moscovici's *Introduction à la psychologie sociale* (1973), followed by Tajfel and Fraser's *Introducing Social Psychology* (1978), and then Moscovici's *Psychologie sociale* (1984). The most recent text, excluding this one of course, is Hewstone *et al.*'s *Introduction to Social Psychology* (1988).

Since the early 1970s, then, European social psychology has undergone a powerful and continuing renaissance (Doise 1982; Jaspars 1980, 1986). Initially it self-consciously set itself up in opposition to American social psychology and adopted an explicitly critical stance. However, since the late 1980s European social psychology, although not discarding its critical orientation, has attained a degree of self-confidence and international recognition. Its impact on American social psychology, and thus on international perspectives, is significant and acknowledged – Moreland *et al.* (1994) document how a recent upsurge in research into group processes (as evidenced from publication trends over the past twenty years in the three major American social psychology journals) was almost exclusively due to European research and perspectives. It is, perhaps, through work on social representations (Chapter 3), social identity and intergroup behaviour (Chapter 10), and minority influence (Chapter 6), that Europe has, to date, had its most most visible international impact.

Europe is a continent of many languages and a historical diversity of national emphases on different aspects of social psychology: for example, social representations in France, political psychology and small group processes in

Germany, social justice research and social cognition in the Netherlands, social development of cognition in French-speaking Switzerland, goal-oriented action in German-speaking Switzerland, and discourse analysis and intergroup relations in Britain. A great deal of research is published in national social psychology journals. However, in recognition of the fact that English is now the international language of scientific discourse, European social psychologists publish in English so that their ideas might have the greatest impact both internationally and within Europe – most major European journals, series and texts publish in English.

ABOUT THIS BOOK

We have written this introductory text to reflect the more mature European social psychology discussed above: a social psychology that incorporates American and European research with an emphasis which is framed by European, not American, intellectual and socio-historical priorities. Traditionally, students of social psychology in Britain and Europe have had to use a mixture of American and European texts. American texts are comprehensive and detailed but pitched at too low a level for British and European universities, do not cover European topics well or at all, and quite naturally are grounded in the day-to-day cultural experiences of Americans. European texts, which are generally edited collections of chapters by different authors, address European priorities but tend to be idiosyncratic and uneven, and very incomplete in their coverage of social psychology. We feel there is a clear need for a single comprehensive introduction to social psychology for British and European students of social psychology.

Our aim has been to write an introduction to social psychology for first, second and, possibly, third year university students of psychology. Its language addresses intelligent adults. However, since it is an *introduction* we pay careful attention to sensitive use of specialist language (that is, scientific or social psychological jargon). It is intended to be a comprehensive introduction to mainstream social psychology, with no intentional omissions. We cover classic and contemporary theories and research, generally adopting a historical perspective as that most accurately reflects the unfolding of scientific inquiry. The degree of detail and scope of coverage are determined by the scope and intensity of undergraduate social psychology courses in Britain and Europe. We have tried to write a text that combines the most important and enduring features of European and American social psychology. As such, this can be considered an international text, but one that specifically caters for the British and European intellectual, cultural and educational context.

This book is structured so that Chapters 2 to 5 deal with what goes on in one's head: cognitive activities and cognitive representations. This includes discussion of attitudes and how they may change. Chapter 6 deals with the pivotal notion of social influence: how people influence one another. Because an important class of influence relies on being a member of a group, this chapter flows logically into Chapters 7 and 8 which deal with group processes. Chapters 9 and 10 broaden the discussion of groups to consider what happens between groups: prejudice, discrimination, conflict and intergroup behaviour. That the nature of intergroup behaviour involves so many instances of conflict invites a discussion of human aggression, which is dealt with in Chapter 11. Lest we become disillusioned with our species, Chapter 12 deals with interpersonal relations, including attraction, friendship and love, but also the topic of breakdowns in relationships. Continuing the emphasis on more positive aspects of human behaviour, Chapter 13 discusses how people can be altruistic and can engage in selfless, prosocial acts of kindness and support. At the core of interpersonal interaction lies communication, of which spoken language is the richest form – Chapter 14 deals with language and communication. Chapter 15 covers an important applied area of social psychology: the effect of the physical environment on social behaviour.

Each chapter is self-contained, though integrated in the general logic of the entire text. There are plentiful cross-references to other chapters, and at the end of each chapter are some references to further, more detailed coverage of topics. Many of the studies referred to in this book can be found in the social psychology journals which we have already noted in the historical section. You are encouraged to check new issues of these publications to learn about up-to-date research. Other articles, which offer state-of-the-art summaries and reviews of topics in social psychology, appear in the *Annual Review of Psychology*, *Psychological Bulletin*, *Psychological Review*, *Advances in Experimental Social Psychology*, *European Review of Social Psychology* and *Review of Personality and Social Psychology*. Another useful source of reviews is Lindzey and Aronson's (1985) *Handbook of Social Psychology* (currently in its third edition).

SUMMARY

- ◆ Social psychology can be defined as the scientific investigation of how the thoughts, feelings and behaviours of individuals are influenced by the actual, imagined or implied presence of others. Although social psychology can also be described in terms of what it studies, it is probably more useful to describe it as a way of looking at human behaviour.
- ◆ Social psychology is a science. It employs the scientific method to study social behaviour. Although this involves a range of empirical methods to collect data to test hypotheses and construct theories, experimentation is usually the preferred method as it is the best way to reveal causal processes. Nevertheless, methods are obviously matched to research questions, and methodological pluralism is highly valued.
- ◆ Social psychological data are usually transformed into numbers which are analysed by a range of formal numerical procedures, that is, statistics.

Statistics allow conclusions to be drawn about whether a research observation is a true effect or some chance event.

♦ Social psychology is enlivened by fierce and invigorating debates over the ethics of research methods, the appropriate research methods for an understanding of social behaviour, the validity and power of social psychology theories, and the types of theory that are properly *social* psychological.

♦ Although having roots in nineteenth-century German folk psychology and French crowd psychology, modern social psychology really began in America in the 1920s with an adoption of experimental method. An enormous impetus was given to social psychology by Kurt Lewin in the 1940s, and the discipline has grown exponentially ever since.

♦ Despite its European origins, social psychology quickly became dominated by America – a process greatly accelerated by the rise of fascism in Europe during the 1930s. However, since the late 1960s there has been a rapid and sustained renaissance of European social psychology, driven by distinctively European intellectual and socio-historical priorities to develop a more social social psychology with a greater emphasis on collective phenomena and group levels of analysis. In the 1990s European social psychology is a dynamic and rapidly growing discipline which is now an equal but complementary partner to America in social psychological research.

FURTHER READING

Aronson, E., Ellsworth, P. C., Carlsmith, J. M. and Gonzales, M. H. (1990). *Methods of Research in Social Psychology* (2nd edn). New York: McGraw-Hill.
Howell, D. C. (1987). *Statistical Methods for Psychology* (2nd edn). Boston, MA: PWS/Kent.
Shaw, M. E. and Costanzo, P. R. (1982). *Theories of Social Psychology* (2nd edn). New York: McGraw-Hill.

▶ KEY TERMS

archival research	double-blind
behaviour	experimental method
behaviourism	experimental realism
case study	experimenter effect
cognitive theories	external validity
confounding	hypotheses
correlation	independent variable
data	internal validity
demand characteristics	laboratory
dependent variable	levels of explanation

metatheory
mundane realism
neo-behaviourism
operational definition
positivism
radical behaviourism
reductionism
science

social psychology
statistical significance
statistics
subject effects
theory
t-test
Völkerpsychologie

2 *Social cognition and social thinking*

··

FOCUS QUESTIONS

♦ If you wanted to make the best possible impression on someone, should you present only your one best feature or all your positive features, no matter how marginal the latter?

♦ Do first impressions really matter that much or can they actually be changed rather easily by subsequent information?

♦ Do we think of social groups in terms of a checklist of defining features, a more nebulous set of characteristics or a specific concrete exemplar?

♦ How well do we remember other people, and what factors might influence the way we remember them?

♦ When do we actually pay attention to information about people in making inferences about them, and when do we simply rely on our assumptions?

♦ How accurate are people at making inferences about others, what are our shortcomings, and can we learn to be more accurate?

SOCIAL PSYCHOLOGY AND COGNITION

Social psychology is the science of human thought, feelings and behaviour as they are influenced by and have influence on other people. Within this broad definition (see Chapter 1), *thought* has always had a pivotal role: people think about their social world and on the basis of such thought act in certain ways. Thought is very much the internal language and symbols we use. It is often conscious, or at least something we are or could be aware of. In contrast, cognition is largely automatic. We are unaware of it, and would be hard put to notice it, let alone characterise it in language or shared symbols. Perhaps a useful way to think about cognition is that it is like a computer program: it operates in the background to run all the functions of the computer that we are aware of.

▶ Social cognition

Cognition and thought are considered in important ways to be the mental activities that mediate between the world out there and what people subsequently do. Cognition and thinking occur within the human mind: they are mental events. That they occur can be inferred from what people say and do – from people's expressions, actions, writings, sayings and so forth. If we can understand cognition we may gain some understanding of how people behave in the ways they do, that is, of psychology. Social cognition is a major approach in social psychology, which focuses on the way in which cognition is affected by wider and more immediate social contexts, and how such cognition affects our social behaviour.

A history of cognition in social psychology

▶ Behaviourism

Wundt (1897) was one of the founders of modern empirical psychology. He used self-observation and introspection to gain an understanding of cognition (people's subjective experience) which he considered to be the main purpose of psychology. This methodology became unpopular because it was not very scientific. Data and theories were idiosyncratic and almost impossible to refute because one could not use one's own cognition as data to challenge another's theory of their own cognition.

Because psychologists felt that theories should be based on publicly observable and replicable data, there was a shift away from studying internal (cognitive) events toward external, publicly observable events. The ultimate expression of this change in emphasis was American behaviourism of the early twentieth century (for example, Skinner 1963; Thorndike 1940; Watson 1930) – cognition became a dirty word in psychology for almost half a century. Behaviourists focused on overt behaviour (for example, a hand wave) as a response to observable stimuli in the environment (for example, an approaching bus), based on past punishments and rewards for the behaviour (for example, being picked up by the bus).

By the 1960s, psychologists began to take a fresh interest in cognition. This was partly because behaviourism seemed terribly cumbersome and inadequate as an explanation of human language and communication (see Chomsky 1959) – some consideration of how people represent the world symbolically and how they manipulate such symbols was needed. Another reason was that the world was becoming more and more dominated by the manipulation and transfer of information – information processing became an increasingly important focus for psychology (Broadbent 1985). This development has continued with the computer revolution which has encouraged and enabled psychologists to model or simulate highly complex human cognitive processes. The computer has also become a metaphor for the human mind, with computer software/programs standing in for cognition. Cognitive psychology has re-emerged as a legitimate scientific pursuit (for example, Anderson 1990; Neisser 1967).

▶ Gestalt psychology

In contrast to general psychology, social psychology has almost always been strongly cognitive (Manis 1977; Zajonc 1980). This emphasis can be traced at least as far back as Kurt Lewin, who is often referred to as the father of experimental social psychology. Drawing on Gestalt psychology, Lewin (1951) believed that social behaviour is most usefully understood as a function of people's perceptions of their world, and their manipulations of such perceptions. As such, cognition and thought are placed centre stage in social psychology. The cognitive emphasis in social psychology has had at least four guises (Fiske and Taylor 1991): cognitive consistency, naive scientist, cognitive miser and motivated tactician.

▶ Cognitive consistency

After the Second World War, in the 1940s and 1950s, an enormous amount of research was done on attitude change. This produced a number of theories sharing an assumption that people strive for *cognitive consistency*: that is, they are motivated to reduce perceived discrepancies among their various cognitions because such discrepancies are aversive (for example, Abelson *et al.* 1968; Festinger 1957; Heider 1958 – see Chapters 4 and 5). Consistency theories gradually lost popularity in the 1960s as evidence accumulated that people are in fact very tolerant of cognitive inconsistency.

▶ Naive scientist
▶ Attribution

In its place there arose in the early 1970s a *naive scientist* model that characterised people as having a need to attribute causes to behaviours and events in order to render the world a meaningful place in which to act. This model underpins *attribution* theories of human behaviour which dominated social psychology in the 1970s (Chapter 3). The naive scientist model assumes that people are basically rational in making scientific-like cause/effect analyses. They are, however, compromised by limited information and by various motivational factors (for example, self-interest), and so all sorts of error and bias creep in.

▶ Cognitive miser
▶ Motivated tactician

In the late 1970s, however, it became clear that even in ideal circumstances people are simply not very careful scientists. Instead it seems that they are limited in their capacity to process information, and they take all sorts of cognitive short-cuts: they are *cognitive misers* (Nisbett and Ross 1980; Taylor 1981). The various errors and biases associated with social thinking are not motivated departures from some ideal form of information processing, but are intrinsic to social thinking. Motivation has almost disappeared from the cognitive miser perspective. However, as this cognitive miser perspective has matured, the importance of motivation has again become evident (Showers and Cantor 1985) – the social thinker has become characterised as a *motivated tactician*: 'a fully engaged thinker who has multiple cognitive strategies available and chooses among them based on goals, motives and needs. Sometimes the motivated tactician chooses wisely, in the interests of adaptability and accuracy, and sometimes ... defensively, in the interests of speed or self-esteem' (Fiske and Taylor 1991, p. 13).

FORMING IMPRESSIONS OF OTHER PEOPLE

People spend a great deal of time thinking about other people. We form impressions of people we meet, have described to us or encounter in the media. We communicate these impressions to others, and we use them as bases for deciding how we will feel and act. Impression formation and person perception are important aspects of social cognition (Schneider *et al*. 1979).

Asch's configural model

▶ Configural model
▶ Central traits
▶ Peripheral traits

According to Asch's (1946) *configural model*, in forming first impressions we latch onto certain pieces of information, called *central traits*, that have a disproportionate influence over the final impression. Other pieces of information, called *peripheral traits*, have much less influence on the impression formation process. Central and peripheral traits are ones that are more or less intrinsically correlated with other traits, and therefore more or less useful in constructing an integrated impression of a person. Central traits influence the meanings of other traits and the perceived relationship among traits: they are responsible for the integrated configuration of the impression.

To investigate this idea, Asch had students read one of two lists of seven adjectives describing a hypothetical person – the lists differed only in so far as one contained the word 'warm' and the other the word 'cold' (see Figure 2.1). Subjects then evaluated the target person on a number of other bipolar evaluative dimensions, such as generous/ungenerous, happy/unhappy, reliable/unreliable. Asch found that subjects exposed to the list containing 'warm' generated a much more favourable impression of the target than did those exposed to the list containing the trait 'cold'. When the words 'warm' and 'cold' were replaced by 'polite' and 'blunt', the difference in impression was far less marked. Asch argued that warm/cold is a central trait dimension which has more influence on impression formation than polite/blunt which is a peripheral trait dimension.

Asch's experiment was replicated in a naturalistic setting by Kelley (1950), whose introduction of a guest lecturer to students ended with: 'People who know him consider him to be a rather *cold* (or very *warm*) person, *industrious*, *critical*, *practical* and *determined*'. The lecturer gave identical lectures to a number of classes, half of which received the *cold* and half the *warm* description. After the lecture, the students rated the lecturer on a number of dimensions. Those who received the *cold* trait rated the lecturer as more *unsociable*, *self-centred*, *unpopular*, *formal*, *irritable*, *humourless* and *ruthless*. They were also less likely to ask questions and interact with the lecturer. This seems to support the Gestalt view that impressions are formed as integrated wholes based on central cues.

Critics, however, have wondered how we can decide what is a central trait. Gestalt theorists believe that the centrality of a trait rests on its intrinsic degree of correlation with other traits. Others have argued that centrality is a

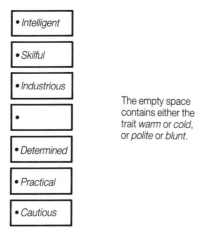

| • Intelligent |
| • Skilful |
| • Industrious |
| • |
| • Determined |
| • Practical |
| • Cautious |

The empty space contains either the trait *warm* or *cold*, or *polite* or *blunt*.

Percentages of subjects assigning additional traits as a function of which focal trait was inserted in the list

Additional traits	Focal traits inserted in the list			
	Warm	Cold	Polite	Blunt
Generous	91	8	56	58
Wise	65	25	30	50
Happy	90	34	75	65
Good-natured	94	17	87	56
Reliable	94	99	95	100

FIGURE 2.1 *Impressions of a hypothetical person, based on central and peripheral traits. (Source: based on Asch 1946.)*

function of context (for example, Wishner 1960; Zanna and Hamilton 1972) – in Asch's experiment warm/cold was central because it was distinct from the other cue dimensions and was semantically linked to the response dimensions. People tend to employ two main dimensions for evaluating other people: good/bad social and good/bad intellectual (Rosenberg *et al.* 1968). Warm/cold is clearly good/bad social, and so are the traits used to evaluate the impression (generous, wise, happy, good-natured, reliable). However, the other cue traits (intelligent, skilful, industrious, determined, practical, cautious) are clearly good/bad intellectual.

Biases in forming impressions

Primacy and recency

▶ Primacy

The order in which information about a person is presented can have profound effects on the subsequent impression. Asch (1946), in another experiment, used six traits to describe a hypothetical person to subjects. For half the subjects the person was described as intelligent, industrious, impulsive, critical, stubborn, envious (that is, positive traits first and negative traits last). The order of presentation was reversed for the other group of subjects. Asch found evidence for a *primacy* effect – the traits presented first disproportionately influenced the final impression so that the person was evaluated more favourably when positive information was presented first than when negative information was presented first. Perhaps early information acts in much the same way as central cues, or perhaps people simply pay more attention to earlier information.

▶ Recency

A *recency* effect can emerge where later information has more impact than earlier information. This might happen, for example, when one is distracted (for example, overworked, bombarded with stimuli, tired) or when one has little motivation to attend to someone. Later, when you learn, for example, that you may have to work with this person, you may attend more carefully to cues. All things being equal, however, primacy effects are more usual (Jones and Goethals 1972), with the clear implication that first impressions are indeed very important.

Positivity and negativity

Research indicates that in the absence of information to the contrary, people tend to assume the best of others and form a positive impression (Sears 1983). However, if there is any negative information this tends to attract our attention and assume a disproportionate importance in the subsequent impression: we are biased towards negativity (Fiske 1980). Furthermore, once formed, a negative impression is much more difficult to change in the light of subsequent positive information than is a positive impression likely to change in the light of subsequent negative information (for example, Hamilton and Zanna 1972). We may be sensitive in this way to negative information for two reasons:

1. The information is unusual and distinctive (unusual, distinctive or extreme information attracts attention – Skowronski and Carlston 1989).
2. The information indirectly signifies potential danger, and so its detection has survival value for the individual and ultimately the species.

Personal constructs and implicit personality theories

▶ Personal constructs
▶ Implicit personality theories

Kelly (1955) has suggested that even within shared cultures individuals tend to develop their own idiosyncratic ways of characterising people. These *personal constructs* can, for simplicity, be treated as sets of bipolar dimensions. So, for example, I might consider *humour* as the single most important organising principle for forming impressions of people, while you might consider *intelligence* as more important. We have different personal construct systems and would be likely to form very different impressions of the same person. Personal constructs develop over time as adaptive forms of person perception, and so are very resistant to change. We also tend to develop our own *implicit personality theories* (Bruner and Tagiuri 1954; Leyens 1983) or *philosophies of human nature* (Wrightsman 1964). These are general principles about what sorts of characteristic go together to form certain types of personality. For instance, Rosenberg and Sedlak (1972) found that people assumed that intelligent people are also friendly but not self-centred. Like personal constructs, implicit personality theories and philosophies of human nature are relatively idiosyncratic and are resistant to change.

Stereotypes

▶ Stereotype

Impressions of people are also strongly influenced by widely shared assumptions about the personalities, attitudes and behaviours of people based on group membership, for example ethnicity, nationality, sex, race and class. These are *stereotypes*, which are discussed below, and in detail in Chapters 3, 9 and 10. One of the most salient characteristics of people we first meet is their category membership (for example, sex), and this tends to engage a stereotype-consistent impression. For instance, Haire and Grune (1950) found that subjects had little difficulty composing a paragraph describing a 'working man' from stereotype-consistent information, but enormous difficulty incorporating one piece of stereotype-inconsistent information – that the man was intelligent. Subjects either ignored the information, distorted it, took a very long time, or even promoted the man from worker to supervisor.

Social judgeability

▶ Social judgeability

People form impressions largely to make judgements about other people – whether they are mean, friendly, intelligent, helpful, and so forth. Recent research suggests that people are unlikely to form impressions and make judgements if the target is deemed not to be socially judgeable in the specific context, that is if social rules (norms, conventions, laws and so forth) prevail that proscribe making judgements (Leyens *et al.* 1992; Yzerbyt *et al.* 1994). If, however, the target is deemed *socially judgeable*, then judgements are more polarised and are made with greater confidence the more socially judgeable the target is considered to be. One implication is that people will not make stereotype-based judgements if conventions or legislation proscribe such behaviour, but will readily do so if conventions encourage such behaviour.

Cognitive algebra

▶ Cognitive algebra

Impression formation involves the integration of sequential pieces of information about a person (that is, traits presented over time) into a complete image. The image is generally evaluative and so are the pieces of information themselves. Imagine being asked your impression of a person you met at a party. You might answer: 'He seemed very friendly and entertaining – all in all a nice person.' The main thing we learn from this is that you formed a positive/favourable impression. Impression formation is very much a matter of evaluation, not description. *Cognitive algebra* refers to an approach to the study of impression formation which focuses on how we assign positive and negative valence to attributes, and how we then combine these pluses and minuses into a general evaluation (Anderson 1965, 1978, 1981). There are three principal models of cognitive algebra: summation, averaging and weighted averaging (see Table 2.1).

Summation

▶ Summation

Summation refers to a process where the overall impression is simply the cumulative sum of each piece of information. For instance, say that we have a mental rating scale that goes from −3 (very negative) to +3 (very positive), and that we can assign values to specific traits such as intelligent (+2), sincere (+3) and boring (−1). If we met someone who had these characteristics, our overall impression would be the sum of the constituents: (+2 + 3 − 1)= + 4 (see Table 2.1). If we now learned that the person was humorous (+1), our impression would improve to +5. It would improve to +6 if we then learned that the person was also generous (+1). Every bit of information counts, and in order to project a favourable impression you would be advised to present every facet of yourself that was positive, even marginally positive. In this example, you would be wise to conceal the fact that you were boring – your impression on others would then be (2 + 3 + 1 + 1)= +7.

TABLE 2.1 Forming an impression by summation, averaging and weighted averaging

	Summation	Averaging	Weighted averaging	
			Potential 'friend'	Potential 'politician'
	All traits weighted 1	All traits weighted 1	weighting	weighting
Initial traits:				
intelligent (+2)			2	3
sincere (+3)			3	2
boring (−1)			3	0
Initial impression	+4.0	+1.33	+3.33	+4.00
			(weight = 1)	(weight = 0)
Revised impression on learning that the person is also humorous (+1)	+5.0	+1.25	+2.75	+3.00
			(weight = 2)	(weight = 1)
Final impression on learning that the person is also generous (+1)	+6.0	+1.20	+2.60	+2.60

Projecting a good impression. At an interview it is crucial to project the best impression possible. Should you highlight *all* your positive qualities or just your very best? (Source: Andrew Lukey.)

Averaging

▶ Averaging

Averaging refers to a process where the overall impression is the cumulative average of each piece of information. So, from our example above, our initial impression would be: $(2 + 3 - 1)/3 = +1.33$ (see Table 2.1). The additional information that the person was humorous $(+1)$ would actually worsen the impression to $+1.25$: $(2 + 3 - 1 + 1)/4 = +1.25$ It would worsen still further to $+1.20$ with the information that the person was generous $(+1)$: $(2 + 3 - 1 + 1)/5 = +1.20$. The implication is that in order to project a favourable impression you would be advised to present only your very best facet. In this example, you would be wise to present yourself as sincere, and nothing else – your impression on others would then be $+3$.

Weighted averaging

▶ Weighted averaging

Although research tends to favour the averaging model, the model has some limitations. The valence of separate pieces of information may not be fixed, but may depend on the context of the impression formation task. Context may also influence the relative importance of pieces of information, and thus weight them in different ways in the impression. These considerations led to the development of a weighted averaging model. For example (see Table 2.1), say the target person was being assessed as a potential friend. We might assign relative weights to intelligent, sincere and boring of 2, 3 and 3. The weighted average would be $+3.33$: $((+2 \times 2) + (+3 \times 3) + (-1 \times 3))/3 = 3.33$. If the person was being assessed as a potential politician we might assign weights of 3, 2 and 0, to arrive at a weighted average of $+4$: $((+2 \times 3) + (+3 \times 2) + (-1 \times 0))/ = 4.00$. Table 2.1 shows how additional information with different weighting might affect the overall impression.

Weights reflect the context-dependent, subjective importance of information in forming an impression. They may be determined in a number of different ways. For instance, we have already seen that negative information may be weighted more heavily (for example, Kanouse and Hanson 1972). Earlier information may also be weighted more heavily – the primacy effect we discussed above. Paradoxically, we may now have come full circle to Asch's central traits – the weighted averaging model seems to allow for something like central traits which are weighted more heavily in impression-formation than are other traits. With respect to central traits, the difference between Asch and the weighted averaging perspective is that for the latter they are simply more heavily weighted and salient information, while for Asch they actually influence the meaning of surrounding traits and reorganise the entire way we view the person. Asch's perspective retains the descriptive or qualitative aspect of traits and impressions, whereas cognitive algebra focuses only on quantitative aspects and suffers accordingly. Recent developments in social cognition have tended to supplant central traits with the more general concept of cognitive schema (Fiske and Taylor 1991).

SOCIAL SCHEMATA AND CATEGORIES

▶ Schema

A schema is a 'cognitive structure that represents knowledge about a concept or type of stimulus, including its attributes and the relations among those attributes' (Fiske and Taylor 1991, p. 98). It is a set of interrelated cognitions (for example, thoughts, beliefs, attitudes) that allows us quickly to make sense of a person, situation, event, place and so forth on the basis of limited information. Certain cues activate a schema, which then 'fills in' missing details.

▶ Script

For example, imagine you are visiting Paris. Most of us have a place schema about Paris, a rich repertoire of prior knowledge about what one does when in Paris – sauntering along boulevards, sitting in parks, sipping coffee at pavement cafés, browsing in bookshops, eating at restaurants, and so forth. The reality of life in Paris is, of course, much more diverse, yet this schema helps to interpret events and guide one's choices about how to behave. While in Paris you might visit a restaurant. Arrival at a restaurant might invoke a 'restaurant schema' which is a set of assumptions about what ought to occur (for example, someone seats you, you study the menu, someone comes to take your order, you eat, talk and drink, you pay the bill, you leave). An event schema such as this is called a *script* (see below). While at the restaurant, your waiter may have a rather unusual French accent that identifies him as English, and engages a whole set of assumptions about his attitudes and behaviours – a schema about a social group is a stereotype (Chapters 9, 10 and 14).

Once invoked, schemata (or schemas) facilitate top-down, conceptually driven or theory-driven processing, as opposed to bottom-up or data-driven processing (Rumelhart and Ortony 1977) – we tend to fill in gaps with prior knowledge and preconceptions, rather than seek information gleaned directly from the immediate context. The concept of cognitive schemata first emerged in Bartlett's (1932) early non-social memory research, which focused on the way memories are actively constructed and organised to facilitate understanding and behaviour. It also has a precedence in Asch's (1946) *configural model* of impression formation (discussed above), Heider's (1958) *balance theory* of person perception (see Chapter 4), and ultimately in Gestalt psychology (Brunswik 1956; Koffka 1935). These are all approaches in which simplified and holistic cognitive representations of the social world act as relatively enduring templates for interpretation of stimuli and the planning of action. The alternative to a schema approach is one in which perception is treated as an unfiltered, veridical representation of reality (for example, John Stewart Mill 1869), impression formation is, as discussed above, the cognitive algebra of trait combination (for example, Anderson 1981), and memory is passively laid down through the repetitive association of stimuli (for example, Ebbinghaus 1885).

Types of schema

There are many types of schema; however, they all influence the encoding (taking in and interpretation) of new information memory of old information and inferences about missing information. The most common schemata, some of which have been used as examples above, are person schemata, role schemata, event schemata or scripts, content-free schemata and self-schemata.

Person schemata

Person schemata are individualised knowledge structures about specific people. For example, you may have a person schema about your best friend (for example, that she is kind and intelligent but tends to clam up in company and would rather frequent cafés than go mountain-climbing), or about a specific politician, a well-known author or a next-door neighbour.

Role schemata

▶ Roles

Role schemata are knowledge structures about role occupants, for example airline pilots (they fly the plane and should not be seen swigging whisky in the cabin) and doctors (although often complete strangers, they are allowed to ask personal questions and get you to undress). Although role schemata can quite properly apply to roles (that is, types of function or behaviour in a group – see Chapter 7 for a discussion of roles), they can sometimes be better understood as schemata about social groups, in which case if such schemata are shared they are essentially social stereotypes (Chapters 9 and 10).

Scripts

Schemata about events are generally called scripts (Abelson 1981; Schank and Abelson 1977). We have scripts for attending a lecture, going to the movies, having a party, giving a presentation, eating out at a restaurant, and so forth. For example, people who often go to soccer matches might have a very clear script for what goes on both on and off the pitch. This makes the entire event meaningful. Imagine how you would fare if you had never been to a soccer match and had never heard of soccer (see Box 3.2 in Chapter 3 which describes one such scenario). The lack of relevant scripts can often be a major contributor to feelings of disorientation, frustration and lack of efficacy encountered by sojourners in foreign cultures (for example, new immigrants).

Content-free schemata

Content-free schemata do not contain rich information about a specific category but rather a very limited number of rules for processing information. Content-free schemata might specify that if you like John, and John likes Tom, then in order to maintain balance you should also like Tom (see balance theory – Heider 1958, chapter 5), or they might specify how to attribute a cause to someone's behaviour (for example, Kelley's (1972a) idea of causal schemata which we discuss in Chapter 3).

Self-schemata

Finally, people represent and store information about themselves in a very similar but more complex and varied way than information about others. Information about self constitutes the self-concept. It is stored as separate context-specific nodes such that different contexts activate different nodes and thus, in effect, different aspects of self (Breckler *et al.* 1991; Higgins *et al.* 1988). People tend to have clear conceptions of themselves (that is, self-schemata) on some dimensions but not others: they are schematic on some but aschematic on others. People are self-schematic on dimensions that are important to them, on which they think they are extreme, and on which they are certain the opposite does not hold (Markus 1977). For example, if you think you are athletic, definitely not unathletic, and being athletic is important to you, then you are self-schematic on that dimension – it is part of your self-concept. If you do not consider yourself athletic and you do not really care much about being athletic or about the attribute 'athletic', then you are aschematic on that dimension. Most people have a complex self-concept with a relatively large number of self-schemata. Linville (1987) has suggested that this variety helps buffer people from the negative impact of life events by making sure that there are always self-schemata from which one can derive a sense of satisfaction. Self-schemata influence information processing and behaviour in much the same way as do schemata about other people (Markus and Sentis 1982): self-schematic information is more readily noticed, is over-represented in cognition and is associated with longer processing time.

Self-schemata do not only describe how we are. Markus and Nurius (1986) have suggested that we have an array of possible selves – future-oriented schemata of what we would like to become. For example, a postgraduate student may have future selves as a university lecturer or a singer in a rock-and-roll band. Another perspective is offered by Higgins (1987) who suggests that we have three types of self-schema:

1. *Actual self* – how we currently are.
2. *Ideal self* – how we would like to be.
3. *'Ought' self* – how we think we should be.

Discrepancies between actual on the one hand, and ideal or 'ought' on the other, can motivate change to reduce the discrepancy. Failure to resolve the actual/ideal discrepancy produces dejection-related emotions (for example, disappointment, dissatisfaction, sadness), while failure to resolve the actual/ought discrepancy produces agitation-related emotions (for example, anxiety, threat, fear).

Categories and prototypes

▶ Prototype
▶ Family resemblance
▶ Fuzzy set

To apply schematic knowledge, you first need to be able to categorise a person, event or situation as fitting a particular schema. Based on principles first noted by the philosopher Wittgenstein (1953), cognitive psychologists now believe that categories are best described as collections of instances that have a *family resemblance* (for example, Cantor and Mischel 1977, 1979; Mervis and Rosch 1981; Rosch 1978). What is meant by this is that there is rarely a set of attributes that are necessary criteria for category membership; instead instances are more or less typical in terms of a range of attributes, with a most

How accurate are prototypes? A typical university student? People tend to have fuzzy prototypes of social categories and use these prototypes as the basis of more general impressions. (Source: Andrew Lukey.)

typical or *prototypical* instance representing the category.. In general, however, since prototypes are abstracted or constructed from instances, no instances may actually fit the prototype: they vary in prototypicality. Prototypes are cognitive representations of the category – standards against which family resemblance is assessed, and category membership decided. Since instances within a category are not identical, but differ from one another to varying degrees, categories can be considered *fuzzy sets* centring around a prototype (see Box 2.1).

Although prototypes are generally considered to represent the average category member, this may not have to be the case (Chaplin *et al.* 1988). Under certain circumstances the prototype may be the ideal member (for example, the ideal environmentalist) or an extreme member (the most anti-logging

---

BOX 2.1 Categories are fuzzy sets organised around prototypes

Here is a short exercise to illustrate the nature of categories as fuzzy sets.

1. Consider the category *university lecturer*. Whatever comes immediately to mind is your prototype of a university lecturer – most likely it will be a set of characteristics and images.
2. Keep this in mind, or write it down. You may find this rather more difficult than you imagined – prototypes can become frustratingly nebulous and imprecise when you try to document them.
3. Now, picture all the university lecturers you can think of. These will be lecturers who have taught you in large lecture halls or small classes, in their offices, or lecturers just seen lurking around your psychology department. Also include lecturers whom you have read about in books and the media, or seen in films or on television. These are all instances of the category university lecturer. Which of these instances is most prototypical? Do any fit the prototype perfectly, or are they all more or less prototypical? Which of these instances is least prototypical? Are any so non-prototypical that they have hardly any family resemblance to the rest? You should discover that there is an enormous range of prototypicality (the category is relatively diverse – a fuzzy set containing instances which have family resemblance) and that no instance fits the prototype exactly (the prototype is a cognitive construction).
5. Finally, compare your prototype with those of your classmates. You may find a great deal of similarity, your prototype is shared among students. Prototypes of social groups (for example, lecturers) that are shared by members of a social group (for example, students) can be considered social stereotypes.

member of the category). These sorts of prototype may prevail when social categories are in competition (for example, environmentalists versus developers) – this analysis is used in Chapter 6 to explain how people may conform to more extreme or polarised group norms (for example, Wetherell 1987).

The relationship between categories is thought to be hierarchical, with less inclusive categories nested beneath more inclusive categories (that is, categories that include fewer members and fewer attributes are nested under categories that include more members and more attributes) – see Figure 2.2. In general, people are more likely to rely on intermediate-level categories than ones which are very inclusive or very exclusive – these basic-level categories are neither too broad nor too narrow. For instance, we are more likely to identify something as a car than a vehicle (too inclusive) or an early model Volvo estate (too exclusive). Basic-level categories are the default option, but they may not be at all common in social perception where contextual and motivational factors may dominate the choice of level of categorisation (Cantor and Kihlstrom 1987; Hampson *et al.* 1986; Turner 1985).

▶ Exemplars

In addition to representing categories in terms of prototypes (that is, abstractions from many instances), people may represent them in terms of *exemplars* (specific instances one has encountered). To categorise new instances, people may sometimes use exemplars rather than prototypes as the standard. For instance, Brewer (1988) suggests that as people become more familiar with a category they shift from prototypical to exemplar representation, and Judd and Park (1988) suggest that people use both prototypes and exemplars to represent groups to which they belong, but only exemplars to represent outgroups. Social psychologists are still not certain about the conditions of use of prototypes versus exemplars (Fiske and Neuberg 1990; Linville *et al.* 1989; Park and Hastie 1987).

Once a person, event or situation is categorised, a schema is invoked.

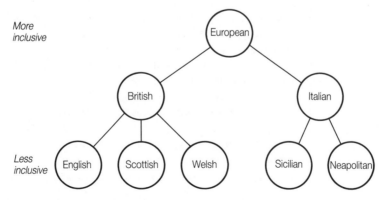

FIGURE 2.2 *Categories organised hierarchically by level of inclusiveness.*

Schemata and prototypes are very similar, and indeed are often used interchangeably. One way to distinguish them is in terms of their organisation. Prototypes, as just described, are relatively nebulous, unorganised, fuzzy representations of a category; however, schemata are highly organised specifications of features and their interrelationships (Wyer and Gordon 1984).

Categorisation and stereotyping

Stereotypes are widely shared generalisations about members of a social group (for example, Tajfel 1978, 1981a). They are usually highly simplified images, and they are often derogatory when applied to outgroups. Box 2.2 describes a study of Europeans' stereotypes of northern and southern European nations (Linssen and Hagendoorn 1994). Stereotypes and stereotyping are central aspects of prejudice and discrimination (see Chapter 9) and of intergroup behaviour as a whole (see Chapter 10).

First described scientifically by Lippman (1922), stereotypes were treated as simplified mental images that act as templates to help interpret the huge diversity of the social world. Decades of research aimed at describing the content and form of stereotypes have produced a number of clear findings (Brigham 1971; Hogg and Abrams 1988; Katz and Braly 1933; Oakes *et al.* 1994; Tajfel 1978):

1. People show an easy readiness to characterise vast human groups in terms of a few fairly crude common attributes.

BOX 2.2 European students' stereotypes of northern and southern European nations

During December 1989 and January 1990 Linssen and Hagendoorn (1994) administered a questionnaire to 277 16- and 18-year-old school pupils in Denmark, England, the Netherlands, Belgium, Germany, France and Italy. The respondents indicated the percentage of each national group who they thought had each of twenty-two characteristics. The twenty-two characteristics tended to cluster into four general dimensions: dominant (e.g. proud, assertive, aggressive), efficient (e.g. industrious, scientific, rich), empathic (e.g. helpful, friendly) and emotional (e.g. enjoying life, religious). In general, there was a clear north/south polarisation with southern European nations being seen as distinctly more emotional and less efficient than northern European nations. These stereotypes were independent of other differences between northern and southern European nations (e.g. size, political power, social organisation).

2. Stereotypes are very slow to change.
3. Stereotype change is generally in response to wider social, political or economic changes.
4. Stereotypes are acquired at a very young age, often before the child has any knowledge about the groups that are being stereotyped.
5. Stereotypes become more pronounced and hostile when social tensions and conflict arise between groups, and then they are extremely difficult to modify.
6. Stereotypes are not inaccurate or wrong; rather they serve to make sense of particular intergroup relations.

Although stereotypes have usually been thought to be associated in some way with social categories (for example, Allport 1954; Ehrlich 1973), it was Tajfel (1957, 1959) who specified exactly how the process of categorisation might be responsible for stereotyping. Tajfel reasoned that in making judgements on some focal dimension, people recruit any other peripheral dimension that might be of some assistance (see also Bruner and Goodman 1947). So, for example, if you had to judge the length of lines (focal dimension), and you knew that all lines labelled *A* are bigger than all lines labelled *B* (peripheral dimension), then you might use these labels to help your judgement. Tajfel and Wilkes (1963) tested this idea. They had subjects judge the length of a series of lines presented one at a time, a number times and in varying order. There were three conditions: (1) the lines were randomly labelled *A* or *B*; (2) all the shorter lines were labelled *A*, and all the longer ones *B*; and (3) there were no labels. Subjects appeared to use the information in the second condition to aid judgement, and tended to underestimate the average length of *A*-type lines and overestimate the average length of *B*-type lines. The relevance of this experiment to social stereotyping becomes clear if, for example, you substitute, singing ability for line length and Welsh/non-Welsh for the *A/B* labels. Because people might believe that singing ability and 'Welshness' are correlated (that is, a social stereotype exists) the categorisation of people as Welsh or non-Welsh produces a perceptual distortion on the focal dimension of singing ability – that is, categorisation produces stereotyping.

▶ Accentuation principle

This, and a number of other experiments with physical and social stimuli (see Doise 1978; Eiser 1986; Eiser and Stroebe 1972; McGarty and Penny 1988; Taylor *et al.* 1978; Tajfel 1981a) uphold Tajfel's (1957, 1959) *accentuation principle*:

1. The categorisation of stimuli produces a perceptual accentuation of intracategory similarities and intercategory differences on dimensions believed to be correlated with the categorisation.
2. The accentuation effect is enhanced where the categorisation has importance, relevance or value to the subject.

▶ Social identity
theory
▶ Self-categorisation
theory

The accentuation principle lies at the core of Tajfel's work on intergroup relations and group membership, which has fed into the subsequent development by Turner and his associates of *social identity theory* and *self-categorisation theory* (for example, Hogg and Abrams 1988; Tajfel and Turner 1979; Turner, 1982; Turner *et al.* 1987) – these theories are described in Chapter 10. Tajfel (1981a) felt, however, that while categorisation might explain the process of stereotyping as a context-dependent perceptual distortion of varying strength, it could not explain, for example, the origins of specific stereotypes about specific groups. He believed that a full explanation of social stereotyping needed some wider analysis of intergroup relations and the social functions of stereotypes (Tajfel 1981a; see also Hogg and Abrams 1988; Oakes *et al.* 1994) – this idea is pursued in Chapters 3 and 10.

SCHEMA USE AND DEVELOPMENT

Schema use

People, situations and events possess so many features that it may not be immediately obvious which features will be used as a basis of categorisation, and consequently which schemata will apply (see Figure 2.3). For instance, a specific person may be a British, female Catholic from Aberdeen, who is witty, well read, not very sporty and works as an engineer. What determines which cues will be used as a basis of categorisation and schema use?

Because people tend to use basic-level categories that are neither too

A script gives meaning to an entire event. Street café behaviour. People have event schemata or scripts which guide them in what to expect and how to behave. (Source: Andrew Lukey.)

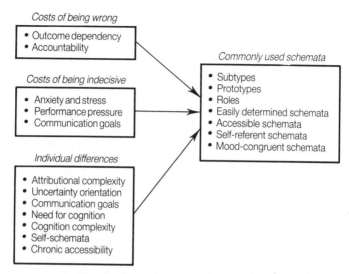

FIGURE 2.3 *Some major influences on commonly used schemata.*

inclusive nor too exclusive (Mervis and Rosch 1981; Rosch 1978 – see above), they initially access subtypes rather than superordinate or subordinate categories (for example, career woman, not woman or female lawyer – Ashmore 1981; Pettigrew 1981), and they access social stereotypes and role schemata rather than trait schemata (for example, politician, not intelligent). People are also more likely to use schemata that are cued by easily detected features, such as skin colour, dress or physical appearance (Brewer and Lui 1989), or features that are contextually distinctive (for example, a single male in a group of women). Accessible schemata, ones that are habitually used or are salient in memory (Bargh *et al.* 1988; Bargh and Pratto 1986; Wyer and Srull 1981) and schemata that have bearing on features that are important to oneself in that context have a high probability of being invoked. So, for example, a racist (someone for whom race is important, salient in memory and habitually used to process person information) would tend to use racial schemata more than would someone who was not racist. Finally, people tend to cue mood-congruent schemata (Erber 1991) and schemata that are based on earlier rather than later information (a primacy effect – see above).

These fairly automatic schema–cueing processes access schemata that are typically functional and accurate enough for immediate interactive purposes. They have *circumscribed accuracy* (Swann 1984). Sometimes, however, people need to use more accurate schemata that correspond more closely to the data at hand, in which case there is a shift from theory-driven towards data-driven cognition (Fiske 1993) – see Figure 2.3. If the costs of being wrong are increased, people are more attentive to data and may use more accurate schemata. The costs of being wrong can become important where people's outcomes (that is, rewards and punishments) are dependent on the actions or attitudes of others (Erber and Fiske 1984; Neuberg and Fiske 1987). Under these circumstances people probe for more information, attend more closely to data, particularly to schema-inconsistent information, and generally attend more carefully to other people. The costs of being wrong can also be important where people need to be more accountable, that is to explain or justify their decisions or actions. Under these circumstances, there is greater vigilance and attention to data, and generally more complex cognition that may improve accuracy (Tetlock and Kim 1987; Tetlock and Boettger 1989).

If the costs of being indecisive are high then people tend to make a quick decision or form a quick impression – indeed any decision or impression, however inaccurate, may be preferable to no decision or impression, and so people rely heavily on schemata. Performance pressure (that is, making a judgement or performing a task with insufficient time) can increase schema use. For example, in one study, time pressure caused males and females with conservative sex-role attitudes to discriminate against female job applicants, and females with more radical sex-role attitudes to discriminate against male applicants (Jamieson and Zanna 1989). Distraction and anxiety can also increase the subjective cost of indecisiveness, and cause people to become more reliant on schematic processing (Wilder and Shapiro 1989). When one has the task of communicating information to others (for example, formal presentations), it often becomes more important to be well organised, decisive and clear, and thus more important to rely on schemata (Higgins 1981). This may particularly be the case when the communication is in a scientific mode rather than a narrative mode, that is when one is communicating about something technical, rather than telling a story which requires rich description and characterisation (Zukier 1986).

People can be aware that schematic processing is inaccurate and, in the case of schemata of social groups, undesirable because it involves stereotyping and prejudice. Consequently, people can actively try not to be over-reliant on schemata. Although this can have some success, it is often rather insignificant against the background of processes described above (Ellis *et al.* 1993). There are, however, some general *individual differences* that may influence the degree and type of schema use:

1. Attributional complexity – people vary in the complexity and number of their explanations of other people (Fletcher *et al.* 1986).
2. Uncertainty orientation – people vary in their interest in gaining information versus remaining uninformed but certain (King and Sorrentino 1988).
3. Need for cognition – people differ in how much they like to think deeply about things (Cacioppo and Petty 1982).
4. Cognitive complexity – people differ in the complexity of their cognitive processes and representations (Crockett 1965).

▶ Accessibility

People also differ in the sorts of schema they have about themselves (Markus 1977 – see above). In general, components which are important in one's self-schema are also important in the schematic perception of others (Markus *et al.* 1985). Individual differences in the chronic *accessibility* (that is, frequent use, memorableness) of schemata can also quite obviously impact on schema use for perceiving others. For instance, Battisch *et al.* (1985) have conducted a programme of research showing that people differ in terms of their habitual orientations to others in social interaction (some being more dominant and controlling and some more dependent and reliant), and that this influences schematic processing. Two types of schema that have been extensively researched and on which people differ are gender and political schemata. People tend to differ in terms of the traditional or conservative nature of their gender or sex-role schemata (Bem 1981) and this influences, among other things, the extent to which they perceive others as being more or less masculine or feminine (see Chapter 9 for more on gender). Political schemata appear to rest on political expertise and knowledge, and their use predicts rapid encoding, focused thought, relevant recall and so forth (Fiske *et al.* 1990; Krosnick 1990).

Acquisition, development and change

We can acquire schemata secondhand. For example, you might have a lecturer schema based only on what you have been told about lecturers. In general, however, schemata are constructed, or at least modified, from encounters with category instances (for example, exposure to individual lecturers in literature, the media, or face to face). *Schema acquisition* and *development* involve a number of processes:

1. Schemata become more *abstract*, less tied to concrete instances, as more instances are encountered (Park 1986).
2. Schemata become richer and more *complex* as more instances are encountered – greater experience with a particular person or event produces a more complex schema of that person or event (Linville 1982).
3. With increasing complexity, schemata also become more tightly *organised* – there are more and more complex links between schematic elements (McKiethen *et al.* 1981).
4. Increased organisation produces a more *compact* schema – one that more resembles a single mental construct that can be activated in an all-or-nothing manner (Schul 1983).
5. Schemata become more *resilient* in so far as they are more able to incorporate exceptions, rather than disregard exceptions because they might threaten the validity of the schema (Fiske and Neuberg 1990).
6. All things being equal, this entire process should make schemata generally more *accurate*.

Schemata lend a sense of order, structure and coherence to a social world that would otherwise be highly complex and unpredictable. For this reason, there are strong pressures to maintain schemata (Crocker *et al.* 1984). People are enormously resistant to schema-disconfirming information, which they generally disregard or reinterpret. For example, Ross *et al.* (1975) informed subjects that they were especially socially sensitive. Although the information was false, subjects rapidly constructed a 'socially sensitive' self-schema that was unaffected by subsequently being told that the feedback was not in fact genuine. Schemata are also maintained by thought – people think a great deal about schemata, which in effect involves a process of cognitively mustering schema-consistent evidence (Millar and Tesser 1986). People also protect their schemata by uncritically relying on their own earlier judgements – they construct justifications and rationalisations based on prior judgements that are in turn based on even earlier judgements, and so forth. The original basis of the schema is lost in the mists of time and is rarely unearthed let alone critically re-examined (Schul and Burnstein 1985).

The possession of relatively stable and unchanging schemata, even slightly inaccurate ones, provides us with significant information-processing advantages. Gross inaccuracy, however, will lead to schema change. For example, a schema that characterised wild lions as cuddly, good-natured and playful pets might, if you encountered one on foot in the wild, change rather dramatically – assuming that you survived the encounter.

▶ Bookkeeping

▶ Conversion

▶ Subtyping

Rothbart (1981) has suggested three processes of schema change:

1. Bookkeeping – a slow process of gradual change in response to new evidence.
2. Conversion – disconfirming information gradually accrues until something like a critical mass has been attained, at which point there is a sudden and massive change.
3. Subtyping – schemata change their configuration, in response to disconfirming instances, by the formation of subcategories.

Research tends to favour the subtyping model (Weber and Crocker 1983 – see Chapter 10 for a discussion of stereotype change). For example, a woman who believes that all men are instinctively violent might, through encountering many who are not, form a subtype of non-violent men to contrast with violent men.

Schema change may also depend on the extent to which schemata are *logically disconfirmable* or *practically disconfirmable* (Reeder and Brewer 1979). Logically disconfirmable schemata are more easily changed by disconfirming evidence – if my schema of Paul is that he is *honest*, then evidence that he has cheated is very likely to change my schema (honest people do not cheat). Practically disconfirmable schemata are also more easily changed: they are ones for which the likelihood of encountering discrepant instances is relatively high, for example friendliness, because it is frequently displayed in daily life (Rothbart and Park 1986). There is less opportunity to display, for example, cowardice, and so a cowardly schema is less practically disconfirmable.

SOCIAL ENCODING

Social encoding refers to the process whereby external social stimuli are represented in the mind of the individual. There are several stages to this process (Bargh 1984):

1. Preattentive analysis – a general automatic and non-conscious scanning of the environment.
2. Focal attention – once noticed, stimuli are consciously identified and categorised.
3. Comprehension – stimuli are given semantic meaning.
4. Elaborative reasoning – the semantically represented stimulus is linked to other knowledge to allow for complex inferences. Clearly, the process of social encoding is heavily dependent on what captures our attention.

Salience

▶ Salience

Attention-capturing stimuli are salient stimuli. In social cognition, *salience* refers to the property of a stimulus that makes it stand out relative to other stimuli in that context. For example, a single male is salient in an all-female group, but not salient in a sex-balanced group, a woman in the late stages of pregnancy is salient in most contexts except at the obstetrician's clinic, and someone wearing a bright T-shirt is salient at a funeral but not on the beach. Salience is 'out there' – a property of the stimulus domain. People can be salient for the following reasons:

1. They are novel (single male, pregnant woman) or figural (bright T-shirt) in the immediate context (McArthur and Post 1977).
2. They are behaving in ways that do not fit prior expectations of them as individuals, as members of a particular social category or as people in general (Jones and McGillis 1976).

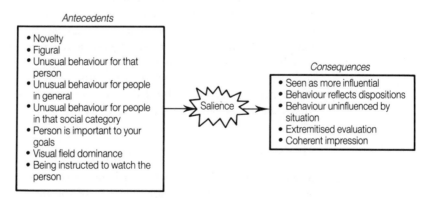

FIGURE 2.4 *Some antecedents and consequences of social salience.*

3. They are important to your specific or more general goals, they dominate our visual field, or they are foci of instructed attention (Erber and Fiske 1984; Taylor and Fiske 1975 – see Figure 2.4)

Salient people attract attention and, relative to non-salient people, tend to be considered more influential in a group, more personally responsible for their behaviour and less influenced by the situation. They are generally evaluated more extremely (McArthur 1981; Taylor and Fiske 1978 – see Figure 2.4). Because we attend more to salient people, they dominate our thoughts and, consequently, increase the coherence (that is, organisation and consistency) of our impressions. People do not necessarily recall more about salient people, but rather find it easier to access a coherent impression of the person. For example, imagine you generally do not like very tall men. If you now go to a party where one particularly tall man stands out, you may feel very negative about him and feel that he took the lead and was relatively uninfluenced by others. Although you will not necessarily recall much accurate information about his behaviour, you will have formed a fairly coherent impression of him as a person.

Vividness

▶ Vividness

While salience is a property of the stimulus in relation to other stimuli in a particular context, *vividness* is an intrinsic property of the stimulus itself. Vivid stimuli are ones that are:

1. Emotionally interesting (for example, a violent crime).
2. Concrete and imagery-provoking (for example, a gory and detailed description of a violent crime).
3. Close to you in time and place (for example, a violent crime committed yesterday in your street) (Nisbett and Ross 1980).

Vivid stimuli ought to attract attention just like salient stimuli, and therefore ought to have very similar social cognitive effects. However, research has not confirmed this (Taylor and Thompson 1982). Vividly presented information (for example, through direct experience or colourful language accompanied by pictures or videos) may be more entertaining than pallidly presented information, but it is not more persuasive or cognitively impactful than pallidly presented information. Apparent effects of vividness can often be attributed to other factors which occur with vividness. For example, vivid stimuli may convey more information, and thus it may be the information not the vividness that influences social cognition.

Accessibility

▶ Priming

Attention can often be directed not so much by stimulus properties 'out there', but by the accessibility, or ease of recall, of categories or schemata that we already have in our heads. Accessible categories are readily and automatically *primed* by features of the stimulus domain to make sense of the intrinsically ambiguous nature of social information. They are ones that we often use, have recently used, and are consistent with current goals, needs and expectations (Bruner 1957, 1958). For example, people who are very concerned about sex discrimination (that is, it is an accessible category) may find that they see sexism almost everywhere – it is readily primed and used to interpret the social world. Some categories are chronically accessible in so far as they are habitually primed in very many contexts (Bargh *et al.* 1988), and this can have pervasive effects. Bargh and Tota (1988) suggest that depression may in part be attributed to chronic accessibility of negative self-schemata.

Research on accessibility exposes people to cues that prime particular categories. This is done in such a way that subjects do not consciously detect the cue/category link. Subjects then interpret ambiguous behaviours (Higgins 1989; Higgins *et al.* 1985). Subjects could be exposed to words such as adventurous or reckless, and then asked to interpret behaviour such as shooting rapids in a canoe. The interpretation of the behaviour would be different depending on the category primed by the cue word. For example, studies in America have shown that racial categories can be primed by words relating to Afro-Americans – white subjects so primed interpreted ambiguous behaviour as being more hostile and aggressive, which is consistent with racial stereotypes (Devine 1989).

Once primed, a category tends to encode stimuli by assimilating them to the primed category: that is, interpreting them in a *category-consistent* manner. This is particularly true of ambiguous stimuli. However, when people become aware that a category has been primed, they often contrast stimuli to the category, that is interpret them in a *category-incongruent* manner (Herr *et al.* 1983; Martin 1986). For example, gender is often an accessible category that is readily primed and used to interpret behaviour (Stangor 1988). However, if one becomes aware that gender has been primed, then one might make a special effort to interpret behaviour in a non-sex-stereotypic manner.

PERSON MEMORY

▶ Associative network

Social behaviour depends very much on how we store information about other people, that is what we remember about other people (Fiske and Taylor 1991; Martin and Clark 1990; Ostrom 1989a). Social psychological approaches to person memory draw on cognitive psychological theories of memory, and mainly adopt what is called an *associative network* or *propositional* model of memory (for example, Anderson 1990). The general idea is that we store *propositions* (for example, 'the student reads the book', 'the book is a social psychology text' 'the student wears a ponytail') that consist of nodes or ideas (for example, book, ponytail, student, reads) which are linked by relationships between ideas. The links are *associative* in so far as nodes are associated with other nodes (for example, student and ponytail), but some associative links are stronger than others. Links become strengthened the more they are activated by cognitive rehearsal (for example, recalling or thinking about the propositions), and the more different links there are to a specific idea (that is, alternative retrieval routes) the more likely it is to be recalled. Recall is a process in which nodes become activated and the activation spreads to other nodes along established associative links, for example the node 'student' activates the node 'ponytail' because there is a strong associative link. Finally, a distinction is made between *long-term memory* which is the vast store of information that can potentially be brought to mind, and *short-term memory* (or working memory) which is the much smaller amount of information that you actually have in consciousness, and is the focus of your attention, at a specific time.

This sort of memory model has been applied to person memory (Hastie 1988; Srull and Wyer 1989), with the important feature that information which is inconsistent with one's general impression of someone is generally better recalled than impression-consistent information. This is because impression-inconsistent information attracts attention and generates more cognition and thought, and thus strengthens linkages and retrieval routes. However, inconsistent information is not better recalled in the following circumstances:

1. If one already has a very well-established impression (Fiske and Neuberg 1990).
2. If the inconsistency is purely descriptive and not evaluative (Wyer and Gordon 1982).
3. If one is making a complex judgement (Bodenhausen and Lichtenstein 1987).
4. If one has time afterwards to think about one's impression (Wyer and Martin 1986).

Contents of person memory

Consider your best friend for a moment. No doubt an enormous amount of detail comes to mind – her likes and dislikes, her attitudes, beliefs and values, her personality traits, the things she does, what she looks like, what she wears, where she usually goes, and so forth. This information varies in terms of how concrete and directly observable it is: it ranges from appearance which is concrete and directly observable, through behaviour, to traits which are not directly observable but are based on inference (Park 1986). Cutting across this continuum is a general tendency for people to cluster together features that are positive and desirable, and, separately, those that are negative and undesirable.

Most person memory research concerns *traits*. Traits are stored in the usual propositional form ('Mary is mean and nasty'), but are based on elaborate inferences from behaviours and situations. The inference process rests heavily on making causal attributions for people's behaviour (the subject matter of

Chapter 3). The storage of trait information appears to be organised with respect to two continua: social desirability (for example, warm, pleasant, friendly) and competence (for example, intelligent, industrious, efficient – see Schneider *et al*. 1979). Trait memories can be quite abstract and they can colour more concrete memories of behaviour and appearance.

Behaviour is usually perceived as purposeful action, and so memory for behaviour may be organised with respect to people's goals: the behaviour 'Angelo runs to catch the bus' is stored in terms of Angelo's goal to catch the bus. In this respect, behaviour, although more concrete and observable than traits, also involves some inference – inference of purpose (Hoffman *et al*. 1981).

Memory for *appearance* is usually based on directly observable concrete information ('Winston has long blonde hair and an aquiline nose'), and is stored as an analogue rather than a proposition. In other words, appearance is stored directly like a picture in the mind, which retains all the original spatial information, rather than as a deconstructed set of propositions that have symbolic meaning. Laboratory studies reveal that we are phenomenally accurate at remembering faces – we can often recall faces with total accuracy over very long periods of time (Freides 1974). However, we tend to be less accurate at recognising the faces of people who are of a different race from our own (Malpass and Kravitz 1969). One explanation of this effect is that we simply pay less attention to, or process more superficially, outgroup faces (Devine and Malpass 1985). Indeed, superficial encoding undermines memory for faces in general, and one remedy for poor memory for faces is simply to pay greater attention (Wells and Turtle 1988). We are also remarkably inaccurate at remembering appearances in natural contexts where eyewitness testimony is required, for example identifying or describing a stranger we saw commit a crime (Kassin *et al*. 1989; Loftus 1979). This is probably because witnesses or victims often do not get a clear look at the offender – the offence may be frightening, unexpected, confusing and quickly over, and the offender may only be glimpsed through a dirty car window or may even wear a mask or some other disguise. Eyewitness testimony, even if confidently given, should be treated with caution. However, its accuracy is more assured if certain conditions are met (Shapiro and Penrod 1986 – see Box 2.3).

Organisation of person memory

In general we remember people as a cluster of information about their traits, behaviours and appearances. However, we can also store information about people in a very different way: we can cluster people under attributes or groups. Social memory, therefore, can be organised by *person* or by *group* (Pryor and Ostrom 1981) – see Figure 2.5. In most settings the preferred mode of organisation is by person, probably because it produces richer and more accurate person memories that are more easily recalled (Sedikides and Ostrom 1988). Organisation by person is particularly likely when people are significant

---

BOX 2.3 Factors that improve the accuracy of eyewitness testimony

- The witness goes back over the scene or the crime to reinstate additional cues.
- The witness has already associated the person's face with other symbolic information.
- The witness was exposed to the person's face for a long time.
- The witness gave testimony a very short time after the crime.
- The witness is habitually attentive to the external environment.
- The witness generally forms vivid mental images.
- The person's face was not altered by disguise.
- The person looked dishonest.

(Source: based on Shapiro and Penrod 1986.)

---

to us because they are familiar, real people with whom we expect to interact across many specific situations (Srull 1983).

Organisation by group membership is likely in first encounters with strangers – the person is pigeon-holed, described and stored in terms of stereotypic attributes of a salient social category (for example, sex, age, ethnicity – see Chapter 9). Over time, the organisation may change to one based on the person (for example, Duck 1977). For example, your memory of a lecturer you have encountered only a few times lecturing on a topic in which you are not very interested will most likely be organised in terms of the

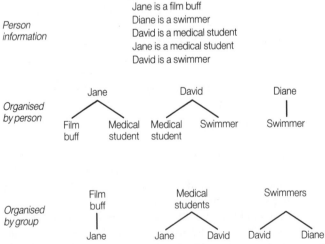

FIGURE 2.5 *Person memory organised by person or by group.(Source: based on Fiske and Taylor 1991.)*

stereotypic properties of the social group 'lecturers'. If you should happen to get to know this person a little better, you might find that your memory would gradually or suddenly become reorganised in terms of the lecturer as a distinct, individual person. There is, however, an alternative perspective on the relationship between person-based and group-based person memory, and that is that they can co-exist as essentially distinct forms of representation (Srull and Wyer 1989; Wyer and Martin 1986). These distinct forms of representation may be associated with different sorts of identities that people may have, based either on interpersonal relationships or on group memberships. This idea is consistent with *social identity theory* which is a theory of group behaviour as something quite distinct from interpersonal behaviour (for example, Hogg and Abrams 1988; Tajfel and Turner 1979; Turner 1982) – see Chapter 10.

Using person memory

Presumably, in making social judgements we draw upon person memory. In fact, it appears that sometimes we do, but sometimes we do not. Hastie and Park (1986) have integrated the findings from a large number of studies to conclude that, by default, people tend to form impressions of people *on-line* – that is, they rely disproportionately on incoming data which are assimilated by schemata in order to produce an impression. There is little correlation between memory and judgement. It is more unusual for people to draw on memory and make *memory-based* judgements, but when they do, there is a stronger correlation between memory and judgement. Whether people make on-line or memory-based judgements or impressions is influenced by the sorts of goal and purpose they bring to the interaction or to the judgement task.

BOX 2.4 Goals and their effects on person memory

Goal	Effect
• Comprehension	Limited memory
• Memorising	Variable memory, organised in an *ad hoc* manner often by psychologically irrelevant categories
• Forming impressions	Good memory, organised by traits
• Empathising	Good memory, organised by goals
• Comparing to oneself	Excellent memory, organised by psychological categories (traits or goals)
• Anticipated interaction	Excellent, well-organised memory, type of organisation not yet clear
• Actual interaction	Variable memory depending on concurrent goals

(Source: after Fiske and Taylor 1991.)

The general principle is that recall of information about other people improves as the purpose of the interaction becomes more psychologically engaging and less superficial (Srull and Wyer 1986, 1989; Wyer and Srull 1986). Psychologically engaging interactions entail information processing at a deeper level that involves the elaboration of more complex and more varied links among elements, and consequently a more integrated memory (Greenwald and Pratkanis 1984). Paradoxically, then, instructing someone to memorise someone (psychologically not very engaging) will be less effective than asking someone to form an impression, which in turn will be less effective than asking someone to empathise. Box 2.4 shows a number of goals and how they affect person memory.

SOCIAL INFERENCE

▶ Normative models
▶ Behavioural
   decision theory

Social inference is, in many respects, the core of social cognition. It addresses the inferential strategies (they can be quite formal and abstract or they can be intuitive and concrete) by which we identify, sample and combine information to form impressions, make judgements, and so forth. Researchers usually study these inferential processes in comparison with ideal processes, called *normative models*, that produce the best possible inferences. Collectively these normative models are known as *behavioural decision theory* (Einhorn and Hogarth 1981). In general, the intuitive strategies of social inference involve a range of biases and errors that produce suboptimal inferences – inferences that fall short of those dictated by the principles of behavioural decision theory (for example, Fiske and Taylor 1991; Nisbett and Ross 1980).

Departures from normality

Gathering and sampling social information

The first stage in making an inference involves the gathering of data and the sampling of information from those data. In doing this, people tend to be over-reliant on schemata, which can cause them to overlook information that is potentially useful or to exaggerate the importance of information that is misleading. For example, members of selection committees believe they are objectively assessing candidates on the basis of information provided by the candidate. However, what frequently seems to happen is that person schemata are quickly, and often unconsciously, activated and used as the basis for candidate assessment. This reliance on person schemata is referred to as 'clinical judgement', and although by no means all bad, it can produce suboptimal inferences and judgements (Dawes *et al.* 1989).

People can also be over-influenced by extreme examples, and small samples (small samples are rarely representative of larger populations, called the *law of large numbers*), and be inattentive to typicality information about a sample and to biases in samples. For example, in Europe there is a great deal of media coverage of dangerous and criminal driving by male youths, leading to injury and death of innocent bystanders. From this, people tend to infer that male youths generally behave like this. However, this is based on a possibly biased source (most mass media present extreme, not ordinary, cases) which presents a small sample of atypical youths behaving in an extreme manner.

Regression

▶ Regression

Individual cases or instances are often more extreme than the average of the population from which they are drawn – over a number of cases or instances there is a *regression* to the population mean. For example, a restaurant you have just visited for the first time may have been truly excellent, causing you to extol its virtues to all your friends. However, the next time you go it turns out to be rather mediocre. On the next visit, moderately good, on the next fairly average. This is an example of regression. The restaurant is probably actually moderately good, but this would not become apparent from one visit – a number of visits would have to be made. The way to control for regression effects in forming impressions is to be conservative and cautious in making inferences from limited information (one or a few cases or instances). People tend, however, not to do this: they are generally ignorant of regression, and do not control for regression in forming impressions and making judgements (Kahneman and Tversky 1973). People can, however, be induced to make more conservative inferences if the initial information is made to seem less diagnostic by the presence of other information. For example, knowing that Hans shoots cats may generate a very extreme and negative impression of him – shooting cats is relatively diagnostic of being a nasty person. However, if this piece of information is *diluted* (Nisbett *et al.* 1981) by other information that he is a committed conservationist who writes poetry, collects antiques, drives an old Citroën 2CV and cares for his infirm mother, the impression is likely to become less extreme, because the tendency to use the diagnosis 'he shoots cats' is weakened.

Base-rate information

▶ Base-rate information

Base-rate information is general information, usually factual and statistical, about an entire class of events. For instance, if we knew that only 5 per cent of university lecturers gave truly awful lectures, or that only 7 per cent of social security recipients preferred being on the dole to working, this would be base-rate information. Research shows that people chronically under-use this information in making inferences, particularly when more concrete anecdotal case studies exist (Bar-Hillel 1980; Taylor and Thompson 1982). So, on the basis of vivid and colourful media exposés of dull lecturers or of social security cheats, people would tend to infer that these are stereotypic properties of the parent categories, even if they have to hand the relevant base-rate information. The main reason that base-rate information is ignored is not so much that it is pallid and uninteresting in comparison with vivid individual instances, but rather that people often fail to see the relevance of base-rate information, relative to other information, to the inference task (Bar-Hillel 1980). People increase their use of base-rate information when it is made clear that it is more relevant than other information (for example, case studies) to the inferential task.

Covariation and illusory correlation

Judgements of covariation are judgements of how strongly two things are related. They are essential to social inference and form the very basis of schemata – schemata, as we have seen above, are beliefs about the covariation of behaviours, attitudes, traits and so forth. To judge covariation accurately, for example the relationship between hair colour and how much fun one has, we should consider the number of blondes having fun and not having fun, and the number of brunettes having fun and not having fun. The scientific method provides formal statistical procedures that we could use to assess covariation (see Chapter 1). However, in making covariation judgements, people fall far short of normative expectations (Alloy and Tabachnik 1984; Crocker 1981). In general this is because they are influenced by prior assumptions (that is, schemata) and tend only to search for or recognise schema-consistent information – people are generally not interested in disconfirming their cherished schemata. So, in assessing the relationship between hair colour and fun, people may have available the social schema that blondes have more fun, and instances of blondes who have more fun will come to mind much more readily than blondes who are having a miserable time, or brunettes who are having a ball.

▶ Illusory correlation
▶ Associative meaning
▶ Paired distinctiveness

When people assume that a relationship exists between two variables, they tend to overestimate the degree of correlation or see a correlation where none actually exists. This phenomenon, called *illusory correlation*, was demonstrated by Chapman (1967). Chapman presented student subjects with lists of paired words such as lion/tiger, lion/eggs, bacon/eggs, blossoms/notebook, and notebook/tiger. Subjects then had to recall how often each word was paired with each other word. Although every word was paired an equal number of times with every other word, subjects overestimated meaningful pairings (for example, bacon/eggs) and distinctive pairings (for example, blossoms/notebook – these words were much longer than all the other words in the list). Chapman reasoned that there are two bases for illusory correlation: *associative meaning* (items are seen as belonging together because they 'ought' to, on the basis of prior expectations), and *paired distinctiveness* (items are thought to go together because they share some unusual feature).

Distinctiveness-based illusory correlation may help explain stereotyping, in particular negative stereotypes of minority groups (Hamilton 1979). Hamilton and Gifford (1976) had subjects recall statements describing two groups, A and B. There were twice as many statements about group A than there were about group B, and there were twice as many positive than negative statements about each group. Subjects mis-recalled that more negative statements (the less common statements) were paired with group B (the less common group). The

experiment was replicated but with more positive than negative statements –
subjects now overestimated the number of positive statements paired with
group B. In real life, negative events are distinctive, they are perceived to be
more rare than positive events (Parducci 1968), and minority groups are
distinctive, people have relatively few contacts with them. Thus, the conditions for distinctiveness-based illusory correlation are met. There is also
evidence for an associative meaning basis to negative stereotyping of minority
groups – people have preconceptions that negative attributes go with minority
groups (McArthur and Friedman 1980).

Heuristics

▶ Heuristics

We have now seen how bad we are, in comparison to standards from
behavioural decision theory, at making inferences. Perhaps the reason for this
is that we have limited short-term memory available for on-line processing but
enormous capacity for long-term memory. It pays, then, to store information
schematically in long-term memory and to call up schemata to aid inference.
Social inference is thus likely to be heavily theory/schema-driven with the
consequence that it is biased towards conservative, schema-supportive
inferential practices. Despite doing this, and being so poor at social inference,
humans seem to muddle through. Perhaps the process is quite adequate for
most of our inferential needs most of the time, and we should study these
'adequate' rather than optimal processes in their own right. Addressing just
this idea, Tversky and Kahneman (1974; Kahneman and Tversky 1973) detail
the sorts of cognitive short-cut, called *heuristics*, that people use to reduce
complex problem-solving to simpler judgemental operations. There are three
main heuristics that have been researched: representativeness, availability, and
anchoring and adjustment.

Representativeness heuristic

▶ Representativeness

In deciding how likely it is that a person or an event is an instance of one
category or another, people often simply estimate the extent to which the
instance represents or is similar to a typical or average member of the category.
The *representativeness heuristic* is basically a relevancy judgement that
disregards base-rate information, sample size, quality of information and
other normative principles. Nevertheless, it is fast and efficient and produces
inferences which are accurate enough for our purposes most of the time. For
example, consider the following information. 'Steve is very shy and withdrawn, invariably helpful, but with little interest in people, or in the world of
reality. A meek and tidy soul, he has a need for order and structure, and a
passion for detail' (Tversky and Kahneman 1974). The representativeness
heuristic would very quickly lead to the inference that Steve is a librarian
rather than say a farmer, surgeon or trapeze artist, and in general one would
probably be correct.

Availability heuristic

▶ Availability

The *availability heuristic* is used to infer the frequency or likelihood of an event on the basis of how quickly instances or associations come to mind. Where instances are readily available we tend to inflate frequencies. For example, exposure to lots of media reports of violent crime will make that information available and will tend to inflate one's estimates of the overall frequency of violent crime. Similarly, in forming an impression of Paul, who has very short hair and tattoos, you might over-estimate the likelihood that he will also be violent, because you have just seen the film *Romper Stomper*. Under many circumstances availability is quite adequate as a basis for making inferences – after all, things that come to mind easily are probably fairly plentiful. Availability is, however, subject to bias as it does not control for factors such as idiosyncratic exposure to unusual samples or instances.

Anchoring and adjustment

▶ Anchoring and adjustment

In making inferences we often need a starting point, an anchor from which, and with which, we can adjust subsequent inferences (for example, Wyer 1976). *Anchoring and adjustment* is a heuristic that ties inferences to initial standards. So, for example, inferences about other people are often anchored by beliefs about ourselves – we decide how intelligent, artistic, kind and so forth someone else is, with reference to our own self-schema. Anchors can also come from the immediate context. For example, Greenberg *et al.* (1986) found that subjects in a mock jury study who were instructed to contemplate the harshest verdict first used this as an anchor from which only small adjustments were made. A relatively harsh verdict was rendered. Subjects instructed to consider the most lenient verdict first likewise used this as an anchor and subsequently rendered a relatively lenient verdict.

Improving social inference

Social inference is not optimal. We are biased, we misrepresent people and events, and we make mistakes. Many of these shortcomings, however, may be more apparent than real (Funder 1987). Social cognition experiments may provide rather unnatural contexts for which our inference processes are not adapted. Intuitive inference processes may actually be very well adapted to everyday life. For example, on encountering a pit bull terrier in the street, it might be very adaptive to rely on availability (media coverage of attacks by pit bull terriers) and to flee automatically rather than adopt more time-consuming normative procedures – what is an error in the laboratory may not be in the field.

Nevertheless, inferential errors can sometimes have serious consequences. For example, both negative stereotyping of minority groups and suboptimal group decisions may be partly caused by inferential errors. In which case, there may be something to be gained by considering ways in which we can improve social inference. The basic principle is that social inference will improve to the extent that we become less reliant on intuitive inferential strategies. This may be achieved through formal education in scientific and rational thinking, as well as statistical techniques (Fong *et al.* 1986; Nisbett *et al.* 1982).

COMMENTS ON SOCIAL COGNITION

▶ Reductionism

Social psychology has always been concerned to describe the cognitive processes and structures that influence and are influenced by social behaviour, and there is no doubt that modern social cognition, which only properly emerged in the late 1970s, has made enormous advances in this direction. However, critics have wondered if social cognition may not have been too successful, and that it may have taken social psychology too far in the direction of cognitive psychology while at the same time diverting attention from many of social psychology's traditional topics. There is a worry that there may not really be any 'social' in social cognition (Forgas 1981; Kraut and Higgins 1984; Markus and Zajonc 1985; Moscovici 1982; Zajonc 1989). Many of the postulated processes and structures seem to be unaffected by social context and seem more accurately to represent *asocial* cognition operating on social stimuli (that is, people). Specifically, Moscovici (1982) suggests that the main problem with social cognition is that it focuses too much on the link between an isolated person and a social object. Instead, he suggests, we should focus on the link among people and the social object. The former perspective is asocial; it is the latter that is truly social because it addresses the social construction and maintenance of cognition. In this respect, social cognition has been considered to be *reductionist* (Chapter 1). Three particular problems are:

1. Social cognition generally fails to deal with language and communication, which are two fundamentally social variables (Kraut and Higgins 1984; Markus and Zajonc 1985).
2. It fails to articulate cognitive processes with wider interpersonal, group and societal processes.
3. It overlooks affect, that is people's feelings. Recently, however, social cognition has begun to turn its attention to affect (Fiske and Taylor 1991).

SUMMARY

♦ Social cognition refers to cognitive processes and structures that affect and are affected by social context. It is assumed that people have a limited capacity to process information and are cognitive misers who take all sorts of cognitive short-cuts, or are motivated tacticians who choose, on the basis of their goals, motives and needs, among an array of cognitive strategies.

- The overall impressions we form of other people are dominated by stereotypes, unfavourable information, first impressions and idiosyncratic personal constructs. Research suggests that in forming impressions of other people we weight components and then average them in complex ways, or that certain components influence the interpretation and meaning of all other components and dominate the resulting impression.
- Schemata are cognitive structures that represent knowledge about people, events, roles, the self and general information processing. Once invoked, schemata bias all aspects of information processing and inference in such a way that the schema remains unassailed.
- Categories are fuzzy sets of features organised around a prototype, and are hierarchically structured in terms of inclusiveness such that less inclusive categories are subsets of broader more inclusive categories. The process of categorisation accentuates perceived intracategory similarities and intercategory differences on dimensions believed to be correlated with the categorisation. This accentuation effect is the basis for stereotyping, but requires articulation with a consideration of intergroup relations to provide a full explanation.
- In processing information about other people we tend to rely on schemata relating to subtypes, stereotypes, current moods, easily detected features, accessible categories and self-relevant information. However, people are less dependent on schemata when the cost of making a wrong inference is increased, when the cost of being indecisive is low and when people are aware that schematic processing may be inaccurate.
- Schemata become more abstract, complex, organised, compact, resilient and accurate over time. They are hard to change but can be modified by schema-inconsistent information, mainly through the formation of subtypes.
- The encoding of information is heavily influenced by the salience of stimuli and by the cognitive accessibility of existing schemata.
- We tend to remember people mainly in terms of their traits but also in terms of their behaviour and appearance. They can be stored as individual persons or as category members.
- The processes we use to make inferences fall far short of ideal. We are dominated by schemata, we disregard regression effects and base-rate information, and we perceive illusory correlations. We rely on cognitive short-cuts (heuristics) such as representativeness, availability, and anchoring and adjustment, rather than more optimal information processing techniques.
- Social cognition has been criticised for being too cognitive and for failing to properly relate cognitive processes and structures to higher-level social processes, and consequently failing to address many topics that are of central concern to social psychology.

FURTHER READING

Fiske, S. T. (1993). 'Social cognition and social perception'. *Annual Review of Psychology*, **44**, 155–194.

Fiske, S. T. and Taylor, S. E. (1991). *Social Cognition* (2nd edn). New York: McGraw-Hill.

Markus, H. and Zajonc, R. B. (1985). 'The cognitive perspective in social psychology' in G. Lindzey and E. Aronson (eds), *Handbook of Social Psychology* (3rd edn, vol. 1, pp. 137–229). Reading, MA: Addison-Wesley.

▶ KEY TERMS

accentuation principle
accessibility
anchoring and adjustment
associative meaning
associative network
attribution
availability
averaging
base-rate information
behavioural decision theory
behaviourism
bookkeeping
central traits
cognitive algebra
cognitive consistency
cognitive miser
configural model
conversion
exemplars
family resemblance
fuzzy set
Gestalt psychology
heuristics
illusory correlation
implicit personality theories
motivated tactician

naive scientist
normative models
paired distinctiveness
peripheral traits
personal constructs
primacy
priming
prototype
recency
reductionism
regression
representativeness
roles
salience
schema
script
self-categorisation theory
social cognition
social identity theory
social judgeability
stereotype
subtyping
summation
vividness
weighted averaging

3 *Causal attribution and social knowledge*
....

FOCUS QUESTIONS
You have just arrived in a foreign country and find yourself becoming very irritated at the seemingly aloof and offhand manner in which people respond to your requests for directions to a hotel.
♦ Is their unfriendliness deliberate or unintentional – perhaps it is a cultural practice?
♦ Are you an intolerant person to have taken offence so readily, or perhaps their behaviour simply confirms your expectations about people from that country?
♦ Do you really care, and if so, what factors would you take into account to explain their behaviour and your reactions?
♦ What might the consequences be of the explanation you arrive at?

SOCIAL EXPLANATION

Human thought is greatly occupied with seeking, constructing and testing explanations of our experiences. We seek to understand our world in order to render it sufficiently orderly and meaningful for adaptive action, and we tend to feel uncomfortable if we do not have such an understanding. So, for example, through life most of us gradually construct quite adequate explanations (that is, theories) of why people behave in certain ways: in this respect we are all naive or lay psychologists. This is, of course, enormously useful because it allows us (with more or less accuracy) to predict when someone will behave in a certain way, and it also allows us actually to influence whether someone *will* behave in that way or not. Thus, we gain some control over our destiny.

People construct explanations for both physical phenomena (for example, earthquakes, the seasons) and human behaviour (for example, anger, a particular attitude), and in general such explanations are *causal* explanations in which specific conditions are attributed a causal role. Causal explanations are particularly powerful bases for prediction and control (Forsterling and Rudolph 1988).

▶ Attribution

In this chapter we discuss how people make inferences about the causes of their own and other people's behaviours, and the antecedents and consequences of such inferences. Social psychological theories of causal inference are called *attribution theories* (Harvey and Weary 1981; Hewstone 1989; Kelley and Michela 1980; Ross and Fletcher 1985). There are seven major theoretical emphases which make up the general body of attribution theory:

1. Heider's (1958) theory of naive psychology.
2. Jones and Davis' (1965) theory of correspondent inference.
3. Kelley's (1967) covariation model.
4. Schachter's (1964) theory of emotional lability.
5. Bem's (1967, 1972) theory of self-perception.
6. Weiner's (1979, 1985) attribution theory.
7. Deschamps' (1983), Hewstone's (1989) and Jaspars' (Hewstone and Jaspars 1982, 1984) intergroup perspective.

We discuss the first six of these below and then deal with intergroup attribution by itself in greater detail later on in the chapter.

BASIC ATTRIBUTION PROCESSES

Heider's theory of naive psychology

▶ Naive scientist/ psychologist

Fritz Heider (1958) drew the attention of social psychologists to the importance of studying people's naive, or common-sense, psychological theories. He believed that these theories are important in their own right because they influence behaviour: for example, people who believe in astrology are likely to have rather different expectations and are likely to act in rather different ways from those who do not. Heider believed that people are intuitive psychologists who construct causal theories of human behaviour, and that because such theories have the same form as systematic scientific social psychological theories, people are actually intuitive or *naive scientists*. Heider based his ideas on three main principles:

1. Because we feel that much of our own behaviour is motivated, we tend to look for the causes and reasons for other people's behaviour in order to discover their motives. The search for causes certainly does seem to pervade human thought, and indeed it is extremely difficult to explain or comment upon something without using causal language. Heider and Simmel (1944) demonstrated this in an ingenious experiment in which subjects who were asked to describe the movement of abstract geometric figures described them as if they were humans with intentions to act in certain ways. Nowadays, one can witness the same phenomenon in people's often highly emotional ascription of human motives to inanimate figures in video games. The pervasive need that people have for causal explanation reveals itself perhaps most powerfully in the way that almost all societies construct an

elaborate causal explanation for the origin and meaning of life – for example, religions.

2. Because we construct causal theories in order to be able to predict and control the environment, we tend to look for stable and enduring properties of the world about us. We try to discover personality traits and enduring abilities in people, or stable properties of situations, that cause behaviour.

▶ Internal or dispositional attribution

▶ External or situational attribution

3. In attributing causality for behaviour we distinguish between personal factors (for example, personality, ability) and environmental factors (for example, situations, social pressure). The former are examples of an *internal* (or *dispositional*) *attribution* and the latter of an *external* (or *situational*) *attribution*. So, for example, it might be useful to know whether someone you meet at a party who seems aloof and distant is an aloof and distant person or is acting in that way because she is not enjoying that particular party. Heider believed that because internal causes, or intentions, are hidden from us we can only infer their presence if there are no clear external causes (however, as we will see below, people tend to be biased in preferring internal to external attributions even in the face of evidence for external causality). It seems that we tend very readily to attribute behaviour to stable properties of people – for example, Scherer (1978) found that people made assumptions about the personality traits of complete strangers simply on the basis of hearing their voices on the telephone.

Heider identified the major themes and provided the insights that act as the blueprint for all subsequent, more formalised theories of attribution.

Jones and Davis' theory of correspondent inference

▶ Correspondent inference

Jones and Davis' (1965; Jones and McGillis 1976) theory of *correspondent inference* explains how people infer that a person's behaviour corresponds to an underlying disposition – how we infer, for example, that a friendly action is due to an underlying disposition to be friendly. People are concerned to make correspondent inferences (attribute behaviours to underlying dispositions) because a dispositional cause is a stable one that renders people's behaviour predictable and thus increases our own sense of control over our world.

In order to make a correspondent inference we draw on five sources of information, or cues (see Figure 3.1):

1. *Freely chosen* behaviour is more indicative of a disposition than is behaviour which is clearly under the control of external threats, inducements or constraints.

▶ Non-common effects

2. Behaviour which has effects that are relatively exclusive to that behaviour rather than to other behaviours (that is, behaviour with *non-common effects*) tells us more about dispositions. People assume that others are aware of non-

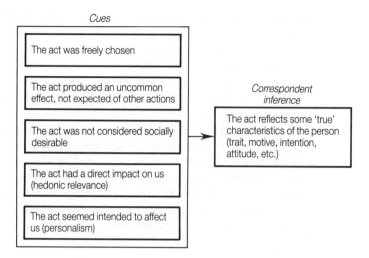

Cues

The act was freely chosen

The act produced an uncommon effect, not expected of other actions

The act was not considered socially desirable

The act had a direct impact on us (hedonic relevance)

The act seemed intended to affect us (personalism)

Correspondent inference

The act reflects some 'true' characteristics of the person (trait, motive, intention, attitude, etc.)

FIGURE 3.1 *How we make a correspondent inference.*

common effects and that the specific behaviour was intentional in order to produce the effect. So, for example, if a person has to choose between behaviours A and B and both behaviours produce roughly the same effects or a very large number of different effects (that is, no, or a large number of non-common effects) then the choice tells us little about the person's dispositions. However, if the behaviours produce a small number of different effects (that is, few non-common effects), then the choice tells us something about that person's disposition.

3. *Socially desirable* behaviour tells us little about a person's disposition because it is considered to be controlled by social roles. However, socially undesirable behaviour is 'out-of-role' and is thus a better basis for making a correspondent inference.

4. We make more confident correspondent inferences about behaviour which has important consequences for ourselves, that is, behaviour which has *hedonic relevance*.

▶ Hedonic relevance

5. We make more confident correspondent inferences about behaviour which appears to be directly intended to benefit or harm us, that is, behaviour which is high in *personalism*.

▶ Personalism

Experiments designed to test correspondent inference theory provide some support. For example, American students making attributions for speeches made by other students tended to make more correspondent inferences for freely chosen socially unpopular positions (for example, freely choosing to make a speech in support of Fidel Castro) (Jones and Harris 1967). In another experiment, Jones *et al.* (1961) found that subjects made more correspondent inferences for out-of-role behaviours (for example, friendly, outer-directed behaviour by someone who was applying for an astronaut job in which the attributes required favour a quiet, reserved, inner-directed person).

Correspondent inference theory does have some limitations and has declined in importance as an attribution theory (Hewstone 1989; Howard 1985). For instance, the theory holds that correspondent inferences depend to a great extent on the attribution of intentionality, yet unintentional behaviours (for example, careless behaviour) can be a strong basis for a correspondent inference (for example, that the person is a careless person). There is also a problem with the notion of non-common effects. While correspondent inference theory maintains that people assess the commonality of effects by comparing chosen and non-chosen actions, other research indicates that people simply do not attend to non-occurring behaviours and so would not be able accurately to compute the commonality of effects (Nisbett and Ross 1980; Ross 1977).

Kelley's covariation model

▶ Covariation model   Perhaps the best known attribution theory is Kelley's *covariation model* (1967, 1973). Kelley believed that in trying to discover the causes of behaviour people act much like scientists. They try to identify what factors covary with the behaviour and then assign that factor a causal role. The procedure is very similar to that embodied by the statistical technique of analysis of variance (ANOVA), and for this reason, Kelley's model is often referred to as an ANOVA model. People use this covariation principle to decide whether to attribute a behaviour to internal dispositions (for example, personality) or to external environmental factors (for example, social pressure).

In order to make this decision people assess three classes of information associated with the co-occurrence of a certain action (for example, laughter) by a specific person (for example, Tom) with a potential cause (for example, a comedian):

▶ Consistency information   1. Consistency information – whether Tom always laughs at this comedian (high consistency) or only sometimes laughs at this comedian (low consistency).

▶ Distinctiveness information   2. Distinctiveness information – whether Tom laughs at everything (low distinctiveness) or only at the comedian (high distinctiveness).

▶ Consensus information   3. Consensus information – whether everyone laughs at the comedian (high consensus) or only Tom laughs (low consensus).

▶ Discounting   Where consistency is low, people *discount* the potential cause and search for an alternative (see Figure 3.2). If Tom sometimes laughs and sometimes does not laugh at the comedian then presumably the cause of the laughter is neither the comedian, nor Tom but some other covarying factor (for example, whether or not Tom inhaled laughing gas before listening to the comedian). Where consistency is high, and distinctiveness and consensus are also high, one can make an external attribution to the comedian (the cause of Tom's laughter was the comedian), but where distinctiveness and consensus are low, one can make an internal attribution to Tom's personality (Tom laughed at the comedian because Tom is the sort of person who tends to laugh a lot).

McArthur (1972) conducted a systematic test of Kelley's theory by having subjects make internal or external attributions for a range of behaviours (for example, 'Tom laughs at the comedian'), each accompanied by one of the eight possible configurations of high or low consistency, distinctiveness and consensus information. Although the theory was generally supported (see review by Kassin 1979), there was a tendency for people to under-use consensus information. There are also some general issues worth considering:

1. Just because people can use prepackaged consistency, distinctiveness and consensus information to attribute causality (the case in experimental tests of Kelley's model), this does not mean that in the normal course of events they do.
2. There is evidence that people are actually rather poor at assessing covariation between events (Alloy and Tabachnik 1984).
3. There is no guarantee that people are actually using the covariation principle – they may attribute causality to the most salient feature or to whatever causal agent appears to be similar to the effect (Nisbett and Ross 1980).
4. If people do attribute causality on the basis of covariance or correlation, then they are indeed being *naive* scientists (Hilton 1988) – covariation is not causation (Chapter 1).

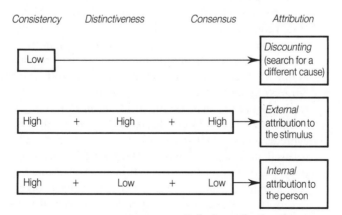

FIGURE 3.2 *Kelley's attribution theory.*

Another drawback of the covariation model is that consistency, distinctiveness and consensus information require multiple observations. Sometimes we may have this information – we may know that Tom does indeed laugh often at almost anything (low distinctiveness), and that others do not find the comedian particularly amusing (low consensus). However, at other times we may have, at best, incomplete information or even no information from multiple observations. How do we attribute causality under these circumstances? To deal with this, Kelley (1972a) introduced the notion of *causal schemata* – beliefs or preconceptions, built up from experience, about how certain kinds of cause interact to produce a specific effect. One such schema is that a particular effect requires at least two causes (called the *multiple necessary cause schema*), for example someone with a drink-driving record must have consumed a certain amount of alcohol and have been in control of a vehicle. Although the notion of causal schemata does have some empirical support (Kun and Weiner 1973) and does help resolve attributional problems raised by the case of a single observation, it is by no means uncritically accepted (Fiedler 1982).

EXTENSIONS OF ATTRIBUTION THEORY

Emotional lability

Schachter (1964, 1971; Schachter and Singer 1962) has suggested the intriguing idea that emotions have two distinct components: a state of physiological *arousal* that does not differentiate between emotions, and *cognitions* that label the arousal and determine which emotion is experienced. Sometimes cognitions may precede arousal (for example, identifying a dog as a Rottweiler may produce arousal that is experienced as fear), but at other times a state of arousal may occur that prompts a search of the immediate environment for possible causes.

To test this idea that emotions may indeed be labile, Schachter and Singer (1962) conducted a now-classic experiment. Student subjects were either given an injection of the drug epinephrine (adrenalin) or else a placebo (salt water), which provided a control condition. Subjects with the drug were then allocated to one of three conditions: (1) they were correctly informed that this would cause symptoms of arousal (for example, rapid breathing, increased heart rate); (2) given no explanation; or (3) misinformed that they might experience a slight headache and some dizziness. All subjects then waited in a room with a confederate to fill out some paperwork. For half the subjects, the confederate behaved in a euphoric manner (engaging in silly antics and making paper aeroplanes), and for the other half in an angry manner (ripping up the papers and stomping around). Schachter and Singer predicted that the 'drug misinformed' subjects would experience unexpected arousal, and would search for a cause in their immediate environment. The behaviour of the confederate would act as a salient cue encouraging subjects in the 'euphoric' condition to feel euphoric, and those in the 'angry' condition to feel angry. The emotions of the other two drug groups and the control group of subjects would be unaffected by the behaviour of the confederate: the control subjects had experienced no arousal from the drug, and the 'informed subjects' already had an explanation for their arousal. The results of the experiment largely supported these predictions.

Perhaps the most significant implication of Schachter's work is its therapeutic application (Valins and Nisbett 1972). If emotions depend on what cognitive label is assigned, through causal attribution, to undifferentiated arousal, then it might, for example, be possible to transform depression into contentment simply by reattributing arousal. A paradigm has been devised to test this idea – the *misattribution paradigm* (Valins 1966). People who feel anxious and bad about themselves because they attribute arousal to internal factors are encouraged to attribute arousal to external factors. For example, someone who is shy can be encouraged to attribute the arousal associated with meeting new people to very ordinary environmental causes rather than to personality deficiencies, and thus no longer feel shy. A number of experiments have employed this type of intervention with some success (for example, Olson 1988; Storms and Nisbett 1970).

Initial enthusiasm for emotional lability, and the therapeutic application of misattribution has, however, gradually waned in the light of subsequent criticisms (Reisenzein 1983):

1. Emotions may be significantly less labile than was originally thought (Maslach 1979). Environmental cues are not very readily accepted as bases for inferring emotions from unexplained arousal, and unexplained arousal is intrinsically unpleasant and so people have a propensity to assign it a negative label.
2. The misattribution effect seems to be very limited (Parkinson 1985). It is largely restricted to laboratory investigations, and is unreliable and short-lived. It is not clear that the effect is mediated by an attribution process, and in any case it is restricted to a limited range of emotion-inducing stimuli.

Self-perception theory

▶ Self-perception theory

One far-reaching implication of treating emotion as cognitively labelled arousal is that people may make attributions for their *own* behaviour. This idea has been explored more fully by Bem (1967, 1972) in his *self-perception theory*. Bem argues that we make attributions not only for others' behaviour but also for our own, and that there is no essential difference between self-attributions and other-attributions. Furthermore, just as we construct an impression of someone else's personality on the basis of being able to make internal dispositional attributions for their behaviour, we construct a concept of who we are not by introspection, but by being able to attribute our own behaviour internally. So, for example, I know that I enjoy eating seafood because I often eat seafood of my own freewill and in preference to other foods, and not everyone likes seafood – I am able to make an internal attribution for my behaviour.

▶ Overjustification
effect

Self-attributions have important implications for motivation. The theory predicts that if someone is induced to perform a task either by enormous rewards or by heavy penalties, task performance is attributed externally and thus motivation to perform is reduced. If there are minimal or no external factors to which performance can be attributed, one cannot easily avoid attributing performance internally to enjoyment, commitment and so forth, and so motivation increases. This has been called the *overjustification effect* (see Figure 3.3), for which there is now a great deal of evidence (Deci and Ryan 1985).

For example, Lepper *et al.* (1973) had nursery school children draw pictures with felt-tip pens. Half the children simply drew of their own freewill while the rest were induced to draw with the promise of a reward that they were subsequently given. A few days later the children were unobtrusively observed playing – the children who had previously been rewarded for drawing spent half as much time drawing as did the other group. The children who had received no extrinsic reward seemed to have greater intrinsic interest in drawing.

In fact, there is evidence that the provision of external rewards for a previously intrinsically motivated task can actually reduce motivation and enjoyment, and worsen performance of that task (for example, Condry 1977). An interesting implication of this is that antisocial behaviour might, paradoxically, be controlled by *rewarding* people for being antisocial rather than punishing them.

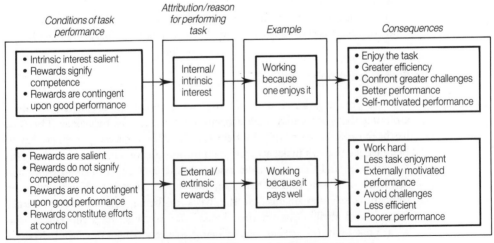

FIGURE 3.3 *The overjustification effect.*

Weiner's attributional theory

Attributional dimensions of task achievement are the focus of another extension of attribution theory by Weiner (1979, 1985, 1986). Weiner was interested in the causes and consequences of the sorts of attribution made for people's success or failure on a task – for example success or failure in a social psychology examination. He believed that in making an achievement attribution we consider three performance dimensions:

1. Locus – was the performance caused by the actor (internal) or the situation (external)?
2. Stability – was the internal or external cause a stable or unstable one?
3. Controllability – to what extent is future task performance under the actor's control?

These produce eight different types of explanation for task performance (see Figure 3.4). For example, failure in a social psychology examination might be attributed to unusual hindrance from others (the top, right-hand box in Figure 3.4) if the student was bright (therefore failure is external) and the student was disturbed by a nearby student sneezing from hayfever (unstable and controllable because in future examinations the sneezing student might not be present, and/or one could choose to sit in a different place away from the sneezing student).

Weiner's model is dynamic in that people first assess whether someone has succeeded or failed, and accordingly experience positive or negative emotion. They then make a causal attribution for the performance, which produces more specific emotions (for example, pride for doing well due to ability) and expectations that influence future performance.

Weiner's model is relatively well supported by research which generally provides subjects with performance outcomes and locus, stability and controllability information, often under role-playing conditions (for example, de Jong *et al.* 1988; Frieze and Weiner 1971). However, critics have suggested that the controllability dimension may be less important than first thought.

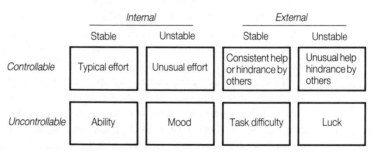

FIGURE 3.4 *Achievement attributions as a function of locus, stability and controllability. (Source: based on Weiner 1979.)*

They have also wondered to what extent people outside controlled laboratory conditions really analyse achievement in this way.

APPLICATIONS OF ATTRIBUTION THEORY

The idea that people need to locate the cause of their own and others' behaviour in order to plan their own action has, in some senses, revolutionised social psychology. We have already seen some ways in which this idea has been applied – for example, achievement attributions, and the reattribution of arousal as a therapeutic technique. In this section we look at two further areas in which attribution ideas have been used: attributional styles and interpersonal relationships.

Individual differences and attributional styles

▶ Attributional style

The investigation of enduring individual differences in the sorts of attributions people make, or their *attributional style*, has been championed by Rotter (1966) who believes that people differ regarding the amount of control they feel they have over the reinforcements and punishments they receive. *Internals* believe they have an enormous amount of personal control over their destiny – things happen because they make them happen. *Externals* are more fatalistic: they believe they have little control over what happens to them – things simply occur by chance, luck or the actions of powerful external agents.

Rotter devised a twenty-nine-item locus of control scale which has been used to relate locus of control to a range of behaviours, including political beliefs, achievement behaviour, reactions to illness and so forth. One problem with the scale is that it may not actually measure a single construct (that is, a single personality dimension) but rather a number of relatively independent beliefs to do with control (Collins 1974).

A number of other questionnaires have been devised to measure attributional styles – a tendency for individuals to make particular kinds of causal inference, rather than others, across different situations and across time (Feather and Tiggerman 1984; Metalsky and Abramson 1981; Sweeney *et al.* 1986). Of these, the attributional style questionnaire or ASQ (Peterson *et al.* 1982; Seligman *et al.* 1979) is perhaps the most widely known. It measures the sorts of explanation people give for aversive events on three dimensions: internal/external, stable/unstable, global/specific. People who tend to view aversive events as being caused by internal, stable, global factors have a 'depressive attributional style' that may promote helplessness and depression, and may have adverse health consequences (Abramson *et al.* 1978; Crocker *et al.* 1988). A more recent attributional complexity scale or ACS has been devised by Fletcher and co-workers (1986). The ACS measures individual differences in the complexity of the attributions that people make for events. Together, however, the ASQ and the ACS provide only limited evidence of cross-situational individual differences in causal attribution (for example, Cutrona *et al.* 1985).

Interpersonal relationships

Attributions assume great importance in interpersonal relationships, particularly close relationships (for example, marriage and friendship), where attributions are *communicated* to fulfil a variety of functions – for instance to explain, justify or excuse behaviour, as well as to attribute blame and instil guilt (Hilton, in press). Harvey (1987) suggests that interpersonal relationships go through three basic phases: formation, maintenance and dissolution (see also Moreland and Levine's (1982, 1984) model of group socialisation in Chapter 7). Fincham (1985) explains that during the formation stage, attributions reduce ambiguity and facilitate communication and an understanding of the relationship. In the maintenance phase the need to make attributions decreases because stable personalities and relationships have been constructed. The dissolution phase is characterised by an increase in attributions in order to regain an understanding of the relationship.

A notable feature of many interpersonal relationships is attributional conflict (Horai 1977), where partners proffer divergent causal interpretations of behaviours and disagree over what attributions to adopt. Often partners cannot even agree on a cause/effect sequence, one exclaiming 'I withdraw because you nag', and the other 'I nag because you withdraw'. Attributional conflict has been shown, from research mainly on heterosexual couples, to be strongly correlated with relationship satisfaction (Kelley 1979; Orvis *et al.* 1976; Sillars 1981).

Attributing blame in a relationship. Couples sometimes cannot agree on what is cause and what is effect. For example, does nagging cause withdrawal or vice versa? (Source: Andrew Lukey.)

The main thrust of research has, however, focused on the role of attributions in marital satisfaction (for example, Fincham 1985; Noller and Ruzzene 1991). An important aim has been to distinguish between distressed and non-distressed spouses in order to provide therapy for dysfuntional marital relationships. Correlational studies (for example, Fincham and O'Leary 1983; Holtzworth-Munroe and Jacobson 1985) reveal that happily married (or non-distressed) spouses tend to credit their partners for positive behaviours by citing internal, stable, global and controllable factors to explain them. Negative behaviours are explained away by ascribing them to causes viewed as external, unstable, specific and uncontrollable. Distressed couples behave in exactly the opposite way. In addition, it appears that while women tend fairly continually to engage in attributional thought about the relationship, men only do so when the relationship becomes dysfunctional. In this respect, and contrary to popular opinion, men rather than women may be the more diagnostic barometers of marital dysfunction.

Do attributional dynamics produce dysfunctional marital relationships, or do dysfunctional relationships distort the attributional dynamic? This important causal question has been addressed by Fincham and Bradbury (1987; see overview by Hewstone 1989) who obtained responsibility attributions, causal attributions and marital satisfaction measures from thirty-nine married couples on two occasions ten to twelve months apart. Attributions made on the first occasion were found reliably to predict marital satisfaction ten to twelve months later, but only for wives. Another longitudinal study (though only over a two-month period) confirmed that attributions do have a causal impact on subsequent relationship satisfaction (Fletcher *et al.* 1987).

BIASES IN ATTRIBUTION

▶ Cognitive miser

The attribution process, then, is clearly subject to bias: it can be biased by personality, by interpersonal dynamics, biased in order to meet communication needs, and so forth. We do not approach the task of attributing causes for behaviour in an entirely dispassionate, disinterested and objective manner, and the cognitive mechanisms that are responsible for attribution may themselves be subject to imperfections that render them suboptimal. Accumulating evidence for attributional biases and 'errors' has occasioned a shift of perspective. Instead of viewing people as naive scientists or even statisticians (in which case biases were considered largely a theoretical nuisance), we now think of people as *cognitive misers* (Taylor 1981). People use cognitive short-cuts (called heuristics) to make attributions that, although not objectively correct all the time, are perfectly satisfactory and adaptive (biases are entirely adaptive characteristics of ordinary, everyday social perception) – Fiske and Taylor (1991); Nisbett and Ross (1980); Ross (1977). In this section we discuss some of the most important attributional biases.

The fundamental attribution error

▶ Fundamental
attribution error

The *fundamental attribution error*, identified by Ross (1977), refers to a tendency for people to make dispositional attributions for others' behaviour even when there are clear external/environmental causal contenders. For example, in Jones and Harris' (1967) study, subjects read speeches about Fidel Castro ostensibly written by fellow students, in order to infer the speech-writers' attitudes concerning Castro. The speeches were either pro-Castro or anti-Castro, and the writers had ostensibly either freely chosen to write the speech or had been instructed to do so. Where there was a choice, subjects not surprisingly reasoned that those who had written a pro-Castro speech were in favour of Castro, and those who had written an anti-Castro speech were against him – an internal, dispositional attribution was made (see Figure 3.5). However, a dispositional attribution was also made even when the speech-writers had been instructed to write the speech. Although there was overwhelming evidence for an exclusively external cause, subjects seemed largely to overlook this information and prefer a dispositional explanation – the fundamental attribution error.

Other studies furnish additional empirical evidence for the fundamental attribution error (Jones 1979; Nisbett and Ross 1980). The fundamental attribution error may also be responsible for a number of more general explanatory tendencies, for example the tendency to over-attribute road accidents to the driver rather than to the vehicle or the road conditions (Barjonet 1980), and the tendency among some people to attribute poverty and unemployment to the person rather than social conditions (see below). Pettigrew (1979) has suggested that the fundamental attribution error may emerge in a slightly different form in intergroup contexts where groups are

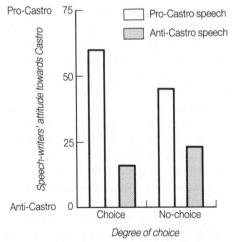

FIGURE 3.5 *Attitude attributions as a function of freedom of choice in writing a speech. (Source: based on data from Jones and Harris, 1967.)*

making attributions about ingroup and outgroup behaviour – this he calls the *ultimate attribution error* (see below).

A number of explanations of the fundamental attribution error have been proposed:

1. *Focus of attention*. The actor's behaviour attracts relatively more attention than the background: it is disproportionately salient in cognition, is, in effect, the figure against the situational background, and thus is over-represented causally (Taylor and Fiske 1978). Thus, the actor and the actor's behaviour form what Heider (1958) called a causal unit. This explanation makes quite a lot of sense: procedures designed to focus attention away from the actor and onto the situation have been shown to increase the tendency to make a situational rather than dispositional attribution (for example, Rholes and Pryor 1982).

2. *Differential forgetting*. Attribution requires the representation of causal information in memory. There is some evidence that people tend to forget situational causes more readily than dispositional causes, thus producing a dispositional shift over time (for example, Moore *et al.* 1979; Peterson 1980). However, other studies show the opposite effect (for example, Miller and Porter 1980), and Funder (1982) has argued that the direction of shift depends on the focus of information processing and occurs immediately after the behaviour being attributed.

3. *Cultural and developmental factors*. Attempts have been made to characterise the fundamental attribution error as an automatic and universal outcome of perceptual experience and cognitive activity (for example, McArthur and Baron 1983). This sort of approach, however, fails to take into account important cultural and developmental factors (Higgins and Bargh 1987; see also below). For example, in western cultures, young children explain action in concrete situational terms, and only learn to make dispositional attributions in late childhood (Kassin and Pryor 1985; White 1988). This process itself may not be universal: Miller (1984, further details below) reports that Indian Hindu children do not drift towards dispositional explanations but rather towards increasingly situational explanations. Perhaps these processes reflect different cultural norms for social explanation. The fundamental attribution error is a relatively ubiquitous, and socially valued feature of western cultures (Beauvois and Dubois 1988; Jellison and Green 1981), but it is distinctly less dominant in non-western cultures (Fletcher and Ward 1988). This all suggests that the fundamental attribution error may not be quite as fundamental as first thought: instead it may be, at least to some extent, a normative way to think (see discussion of norms in Chapters 6 and 7).

4. *Linguistic factors*. One final, interesting observation by Nisbett and Ross (1980) is that the English language is so constructed that it is usually relatively easy to describe an action and the actor in the same terms, but much more difficult to describe the situation in the same way. For example,

we can talk about a kind or honest person, and a kind or honest action, but not a kind or honest situation. The English language seems to facilitate dispositional explanations (Brown and Fish 1983).

The actor/observer effect

▶ Actor/observer effect Imagine the last time a shop assistant was rude to you. You may very likely have thought 'what a rude person' – in other words, you may have made an internal attribution to the shop assistant's enduring personality. In contrast, how did you explain the last time *you* snapped at someone? Probably not in terms of your personality, but more likely in terms of external factors such as time pressures, stress and so forth. The *actor/observer effect* (or the self/other effect) is really an extension of the fundamental attribution error: it refers to the tendency for people to attribute others' behaviour internally to dispositional factors, and their own behaviour externally to environmental factors (Jones and Nisbett 1972). Twenty years of research has provided a great deal of support for this effect (Watson 1982), and has produced some extensions and qualifications. For example, not only do we tend to attribute others' behaviour more dispositionally than our own, but we also tend to consider their behaviour to be more stable and predictable than our own (Baxter and Goldberg 1988).

The actor/observer effect can be influenced by a number of factors. People tend to make more dispositional attributions for socially desirable than socially undesirable behaviours, irrespective of who the actor is (for example, Taylor and Koivumaki 1976), and there is a tendency for actors to be more dispositional in attributing positive behaviours and more situational in attributing negative behaviours than are observers (for example, Chen *et al.* 1988). The actor/observer effect can be overturned if the actor actually knows that actor's behaviour is dispositionally caused: for example, you may 'adopt' an injured hedgehog in the full knowledge that you are a sucker for injured animals and you have often done this sort of thing in the past (Monson and Hesley 1982). Finally, the actor/observer effect can be abolished or reversed if the actor is encouraged to take the role of the observer regarding the behaviour to be attributed, and the observer the role of the actor. Under these circumstances the actor becomes more dispositional and the observer more situational (for example, Frank and Gilovich 1989).

There are two main explanations for the actor/observer effect:

1. *Perceptual focus.* This explanation is almost identical to the 'focus of attention' explanation for the fundamental attribution error (see above). For the observer, the actor and the actor's behaviour are figural against the background of the situation. An actor, however, cannot 'see' himself behaving, and so the background situation assumes the role of figure against the background of self. The actor and the observer quite literally have different perspectives on the behaviour, and thus explain it in different ways (Storms 1973). Perceptual salience does indeed seem to have an important

role in causal explanation. For example, McArthur and Post (1977) found that observers tended to make more dispositional attributions for an actor's behaviour when the actor was strongly illuminated than dimly illuminated.

2. *Informational differences*. Another reason that actors tend to make external attributions and observers internal ones is that actors have a wealth of information to draw upon about how they have behaved in other circumstances. They may actually know that they behave in very different ways in different contexts, and thus they quite accurately tend to see their behaviour as being under situational control. In contrast, observers are not privy to this autobiographical information. They tend simply to see the actor behaving in a certain way in one context, or a limited range of contexts, and have no information about how the actor behaves in other contexts. It is therefore a not unreasonable assumption to make a dispositional attribution. This explanation, first suggested by Jones and Nisbett (1972), does have some empirical support (Eisen 1979; White and Younger 1988).

The false consensus effect

▶ False consensus effect

Kelley (1972b) identified consensus information as one of the three types of information that people used to make attributions about others' behaviour (see above). One of the very first cracks in the naive scientist model of attribution was McArthur's (1972) discovery that attributors in fact tended to under-use or even ignore consensus information (Kassin 1979). Recently it has become apparent that people do not so much ignore consensus information as provide their own – they tend to see their own behaviour as typical and assume that under similar circumstances others would behave in the same way. Ross *et al.* (1977) first demonstrated this *false consensus effect*. They asked students if they would agree to walk around campus for thirty minutes wearing a sandwich board carrying the slogan 'Eat at Joe's'. Those who agreed estimated that 62 per cent of their peers would also have agreed, while those who refused estimated that 67 per cent of their peers would also have refused. There are now over a hundred studies that bear testimony to the robust nature of the false consensus effect (Marks and Miller 1987; Mullen *et al.* 1985).

The false consensus effect may be caused by a number of factors (Marks and Miller 1987; Wetzel and Walton 1985). Since people tend to seek out the company of similar others, they may simply encounter more people who are similar to than different from self – thus experiencing inflated consensus. Another possibility is that our own opinions tend to be so salient that they displace consideration of alternatives, and thus of any comparison that might provide a more accurate estimate of consensus. A third possibility is that we subjectively justify the correctness of our opinions and actions by grounding them in an exaggerated consensus. This suggests the important possibility that false consensus is a mechanism for maintaining a stable perception of reality – reality grounded in consensus.

The false consensus effect. This bungy jumper suddenly discovers the false consensus effect. Bungy jumpers may generally over-estimate the percentage of other people who would indulge in this activity. (Source: *New Zealand Herald.*)

Research into factors influencing the false consensus effect suggests that it is stronger for important beliefs that one cares a great deal about (for example, Granberg 1987), and for beliefs about which one is very certain (for example, Marks and Miller 1985). External threat, positive qualities, perceived similarity of others, and minority group status all also appear to inflate perceptions of consensus (for example, Sanders and Mullen 1983; Sherman *et al.* 1984; van der Pligt 1984).

Self-serving biases

▶ Self-serving bias

There is a range of biases that are quite clearly self-serving in that they seem to protect or enhance self-esteem or self-image. People tend to attribute internally and take credit for their successes (a self-enhancing bias), and attribute externally and deny responsibility for their failures (a self-protecting bias). This is a robust effect that has been found in many different cultures (Fletcher and Ward 1988). Although initial explanations for success and failure may be relatively modest, dispositional attributions for success and situational attributions for failure become more pronounced with time (Burger 1986). In general, self-enhancing biases are more common than self-protecting biases (Miller and Ross 1975) but this may partly be because people with low self-esteem tend not to protect themselves by attributing their failures externally – rather they attribute them internally (Campbell and Fairey 1985).

Self-serving biases are clearly ego-serving (Snyder *et al.* 1978). However, Miller and Ross (1975) suggest that there may also be a cognitive component, particularly for the self-enhancing aspect. People generally expect to succeed, and therefore accept responsibility for success; they try hard to succeed and thus correlate success with own effort, and they generally exaggerate the amount of control they have over successful performances. Together these cognitive factors might encourage internal attribution of success. In general, however, it seems likely that both cognitive and motivational factors have a role (Anderson and Slusher 1986; Tetlock and Levi 1982).

▶ Self-handicapping

Self-serving biases have a number of other ramifications. Self-presentational considerations may influence the degree to which people publicly take credit for success (modesty can often preclude self-enhancement), or deny responsibility for failure (the facts may make attempts at self-protection embarrassingly transparent; for example, Schlenker *et al.* 1990). Riess and colleagues (1981) investigated this idea and found that self-presentational considerations weakened but did not abolish self-serving biases.

There is also evidence for an anticipatory self-serving bias in which people who anticipate failure, intentionally and publicly make external attributions before the event. Berglas (1987) has called this *self-handicapping* (see Box 3.1 and Figure 3.6).

▶ Illusion of control
▶ Belief in a just world

Another self-serving attributional phenomenon is the attribution of responsibility. People tend to attribute greater responsibility to someone who is involved in an accident with larger than smaller consequences (Burger 1981;

BOX 3.1 The self-handicapping phenomenon

Explaining away your failure

Imagine you are waiting to take an examination in a subject you find difficult and in which you fully anticipate failing. You might well make sure that as many people as possible know that you have done no revision, are not really interested in the subject and have a dreadful hangover to boot. Your subsequent failure is thus externally attributed without it seeming that you are making excuses to explain away your failure. Berglas (1987) has called this *self-handicapping*.

To investigate this phenomenon, Berglas and Jones (1978) had subjects perform a problem-solving task where the problems were either solvable or not solvable. They were told they had done very well, and before continuing with a second problem-solving task were given the choice of taking either a drug called 'actavil', which would ostensibly improve intellectual functioning and performance, or 'pandocrin', which would have the opposite effect. As predicted, those subjects who had succeeded on the solvable puzzles felt confident about their ability and so chose actavil in order to further improve (see Figure 3.6). Those who had succeeded on the 'not solvable' puzzles attributed their performance externally to luck and chose pandocrin, in order to be able more easily to explain away the anticipated failure on the second task.

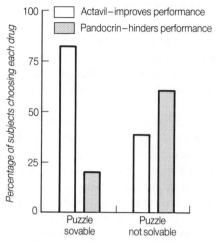

FIGURE 3.6 *Self-handicapping: drug choice as a function of solvability. (Source: based on data from Berglas and Jones 1978.)*

Walster 1966). So, for example, we would attribute greater responsibility to the captain of a tanker that spills millions of litres of oil than the captain of a small boat that spills only a few litres – of course, the degree of responsibility may actually be the same. This effect may be part of a general tendency to cling to an *illusion of control* (Langer 1975) by believing in a *just world* (Lerner 1977). People like to believe that bad things happen to bad people and good things to good people (that is, people get what they deserve), and that people have control over their outcomes. This pattern of attributions makes the world seem a controllable and secure place in which we can determine our destiny.

The belief in a just world can result in a general pattern of attribution in which victims are deemed responsible for their misfortune: poverty, oppression, tragedy and injustice all happen because they are deserved by the victims. A common example of the just world hypothesis in action is the view that the unemployed are responsible for being unemployed. Another example is the view that rape victims are somehow responsible for the violence against them. A final example is the belief held by some people that the six million Jewish victims of the Holocaust were responsible for their fate – that they deserved it (Davidowicz 1975). The belief in a just world may also be responsible for self-blame. Victims of traumatic and violent events such as incest, debilitating illness, rape and other forms of violence can experience a strong and debilitating sense that the world is no longer stable, meaningful, controllable and just. One way to reinstate an illusion of control is by taking some responsibility for the event (Miller and Porter 1983).

INTERGROUP ATTRIBUTION

▶ Intergroup
attribution

Attribution theories are mainly concerned with the way in which people make dispositional or situational attributions for their own and others' behaviour, and the sorts of bias that can occur in this process. The perspective is very much tied to interpersonal relations: people as unique individuals make attributions for their own behaviour or the behaviour of other unique individuals. There is, however, another attributional context, intergroup relations, where individuals as group members make attributions for the behaviours of themselves as group members and others as either ingroup or outgroup members (Deschamps 1983; Hewstone 1989; Hewstone and Jaspars 1982, 1984). Examples of such *intergroup attributions* abound, such as the tendency to attribute economic ills to minority outgroups (for example, West Indian immigrants in Britain, immigrant workers in Germany), or the explanation of behaviours in terms of stereotypic properties of group membership (for example, sex-stereotype consistent attributions for performance – Deaux 1984).

▶ Ethnocentrism

The first point that can be made about intergroup attributions is an extension of the self-serving bias described above. Intergroup attributions are characterised by an *ethnocentric* or ingroup-serving bias in which socially desirable or positive behaviours by ingroup members and socially undesirable or negative behaviours by outgroup members are internally attributed to dispositions, and negative ingroup and positive outgroup behaviours are externally attributed to situational factors (Hewstone and Jaspars 1982; Hewstone 1989; Taylor and Jaggi 1974). This effect is more prevalent in western than non-western cultures (Fletcher and Ward 1988). It is, however, common in team sport contexts, where success of one's own team is attributed to internal stable abilities rather than effort, luck or task difficulty; this group-enhancing bias is stronger and more consistent than the corresponding group-protective bias (Mullen and Riordan 1988; Miller and Ross 1975).

▶ Ultimate
attribution error

Pettigrew (1979) has described a related bias, called the *ultimate attribution error* – an extension of Ross's (1977) fundamental attribution error into the domain of attributions for outgroup behaviours. Pettigrew argued that negative outgroup behaviours are dispositionally attributed, and positive outgroup behaviours are externally attributed or explained away in other ways that preserve one's unfavourable outgroup image. The ultimate attribution error refers to attributions made for outgroup behaviours only, whereas broader intergroup perspectives focus on ingroup attributions as well.

One of the first studies of intergroup attributions was conducted by Taylor and Jaggi (1974) in southern India, against a background of intergroup conflict between Hindus and Muslims. Hindu subjects read vignettes describing Hindus or Muslims acting in a socially desirable (for example, offering shelter from the rain) or socially undesirable (for example, refusing shelter) way towards them, and then chose one of a number of explanations for the behaviour. As predicted, the Hindu subjects made more internal attributions for socially desirable than socially undesirable acts by the ingroup Hindus than by the outgroup Muslims.

Hewstone and Ward (1985) conducted a more complete and systematic follow-up using as subjects Malays and Chinese in Malaysia and Singapore. The subjects made internal or external attributions for desirable or undesirable behaviours described in vignettes as being performed by Malays or by Chinese. In Malaysia, Malay subjects showed a clear ethnocentric attribution bias – they attributed a positive act by a Malay more to internal factors than a similar act by a Chinese, and a negative act by a Malay less to internal factors than a similar act by a Chinese (Figure 3.7). The ingroup enhancement effect was much stronger than the outgroup derogation effect. The Chinese subjects showed no ethnocentric bias – in fact they showed a tendency to make similar attributions to those made by Malays. In Singapore, the only significant effect was that Malays made internal attributions for positive acts by Malays.

▶ Stereotype

Hewstone and Ward explain these findings in terms of the nature of intergroup relations in Malaysia and Singapore. In Malaysia, Malays are the clear majority group and Chinese an ethnic minority. Furthermore, relations between the two groups were tense at that time, with Malaysia pursuing a policy of ethnic assimilation. Both Malays and Chinese generally shared an

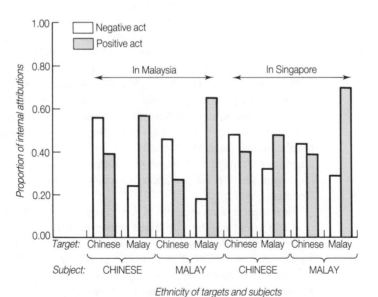

FIGURE 3.7 *Internal attribution of positive and negative acts by Malays and Chinese as a function of attributor ethnicity. (Source: based on data from Hewstone and Ward 1985.)*

unfavourable *stereotype* of Chinese and a favourable stereotype of Malays. In contrast, Singapore is ethnically more tolerant. The Chinese are in the majority, and ethnic stereotypes are markedly less pronounced. The important implication of this analysis is that ethnocentric attribution is not a universal tendency that reflects asocial cognition, but rather it depends on intergroup dynamics in socio-historical context. The sorts of attribution that group members make about ingroup and outgroup behaviour is influenced by the nature of the relations between the groups.

▶ Levels of analysis/ explanation

This is consistent with Hewstone's (1989) argument that a proper analysis of attribution, more accurately described as social explanation, requires a careful articulation (that is, theoretical integration or connection) of different *levels of analysis* (see Doise 1986; also Chapter 1). In other words, we need to know how individual cognitive processes, interpersonal interactions, group membership dynamics and intergroup relations all affect, are affected by and are interrelated with one another.

Further evidence for ethnocentric intergroup attributions has been obtained from studies of interracial attitudes in educational settings in the United States (Duncan 1976; Stephan 1977), from studies of interethnic relations between Israelis and Arabs (Rosenberg and Wolfsfeld 1977), and from studies of race, sex and social class based attributions for success and failure (Deaux and Emswiller 1974; Feather and Simon 1975; Greenberg and Rosenfield 1979; Hewstone *et al.* 1982) – these and other studies are overviewed by Hewstone (1989).

There are at least two processes that may be responsible for ethnocentric intergroup attributions. The first is a cognitive one. Social categorisation generates category-congruent expectations in the form of expectancies (Deaux 1976), schemata (for example, Fiske and Taylor 1991), or group prototypes or stereotypes (for example, Hogg and Abrams 1988; Turner 1985; Turner *et al.* 1987 – see Chapter 10). Research indicates that stereotype- or expectancy-consistent behaviour is attributed to stable internal factors, whereas expectancy-inconsistent behaviour is attributed to unstable or situational factors (for example, Bell *et al.* 1976; Rosenfield and Stephan 1977). When people explain expectancy-confirming behaviour they may simply rely on dispositions implied by a stereotype, without bothering to put cognitive effort into consideration of additional factors (Kulik 1983; Pyszczynski and Greenberg 1981).

▶ Social identity theory

The second process involved in intergroup attributions is the individual need to obtain group membership based self-esteem from intergroup comparisons. This process is described by *social identity theory* (Hogg and Abrams 1988; Tajfel and Turner 1979; Turner 1982 – see Chapter 10). Because people derive their social identity from the groups to which they belong (a description and evaluation of themselves in terms of the defining features of the group), they have a vested interest in maintaining or obtaining an ingroup profile that is more positive than that of comparable outgroups. The ethnocentric attributional bias quite clearly fulfils this aim – it attributes internally good things about the ingroup and bad things about the outgroup, and attributes externally bad things about the ingroup and good things about the outgroup.

Attribution and stereotyping

Attribution processes operating at the societal level in an intergroup context may well have an important role in shaping the profile and dominance of specific stereotypes. Tajfel (1981a) has argued that stereotyping serves a number of adaptive functions not only for individuals but also for social groups (see also Chapter 2). Social groups may activate or accentuate existing stereotypes in order to attribute large-scale distressing events to the actions of specific outgroups, that is scapegoats. For instance, during the 1930s in Germany the Jews were blamed for the economic crisis. It was convenient to activate the 'miserly Jew' stereotype to explain in simplistic terms the lack of money: there is no money because the Jews are hoarding it. Stereotypes may also be elaborated to justify actions committed or planned against an outgroup. For instance, a group might develop a stereotype of an outgroup as dull-witted, simple, lazy and incompetent, in order to explain or justify the economic and social exploitation of that group.

SOCIAL KNOWLEDGE AND SOCIETAL ATTRIBUTIONS

▶ Causal schemata

People do not wake up in the morning and causally reconstruct their world anew every day. In general we rely upon well-learned causal scripts (Abelson 1981) and general *causal schemata* attached to situational, personality and group membership labels. It would appear that we may, so to speak, stop, think and make causal attributions only when events are unexpected or inconsistent with expectations (for example, Hastie 1984; Langer 1978; Pyszczynski and Greenberg 1981), when we are in a bad mood (Bohner *et al.* 1988), when we feel a lack of control (Liu and Steele 1986), or when attributions are occasioned by conversational goals (for example, Hewstone and Antaki 1988; Lalljee 1981; Tetlock 1983). Usually we rely on a wealth of acquired and highly textured cultural knowledge that automatically explains what is going on about us. This knowledge resides in cultural beliefs, social stereotypes, collective ideologies and social representations (see Box 3.2.)

Social representations

▶ Social
representations

One way in which cultural knowledge about the causes of things may be constructed and transmitted is described by Moscovici's theory of *social representations* (for example, Farr and Moscovici 1984; Moscovici 1961, 1981, 1988; see also Chapter 4). Social representations are consensual understandings

BOX 3.2 The cultural context of causal attribution

A very strange custom

Gün Semin (1980) tells a fictitious story about a Brazilian aborigine who visits Rio de Janeiro and then returns to his tribe deep in the Amazonian forest to give an account of the visit:

> 'On particular days more people than all those you have seen in your whole lifetime roam to this huge place of worship, an open hut the size of which you will never imagine. They come, chanting, singing, with symbols of their gods and once everybody is gathered the chanting drives away all alien spirits. Then, at the appointed time the priests arrive wearing colourful garments, and the chanting rises to war cries until three high priests, wearing black, arrive. All priests who were running around with sacred round objects leave them and at the order of the high priests begin the religious ceremony. Then, when the chief high priest gives a shrill sound from himself they all run after the single sacred round object that is left, only to kick it away when they get hold of it. Whenever the sacred object goes through one of the two doors and hits the sacred net the religious followers start to chant, piercing the heavens, and most of the priests embark on a most ecstatic orgy until the chief priest blows the whistle on them.' (Semin 1980, p.292)

This is, or course, a description of a soccer match by someone who does not know the purpose or rules of the game. It illustrates an important point. For causal explanations to be meaningful they need to be part of a highly complex, general interpretive framework that constitutes our socially acquired cultural knowledge.

shared among group members. They emerge through everyday informal communication in order to transform the unfamiliar and complex into the familiar and straightforward, and thus provide a common-sense framework for interpreting our experiences. An individual or a specialist interest group derives a sophisticated, non-obvious, technical explanation of a commonplace phenomenon. This attracts public attention and becomes widely shared and popularised (that is, simplified, distorted and ritualised) through informal discussion among non-specialists. It is now a social representation – an accepted, unquestioned common-sense explanation that tends to oust alternatives and become an orthodoxy.

Moscovici's original formulation focused on the development of the theory of psychoanalysis, but it is just as applicable to other formal theories and phenomena that have been transformed to become part of popular consciousness, for example evolutionary theory, relativity theory, dietary and health

Social representations. Everyday conversations help people to represent the unfamiliar as familiar, the complex as straightforward. (Source: Andrew Lukey.)

theories, Marxist economics and AIDS. Although the theory of social representations has been the subject of some criticism – often for the rather imprecise way in which it is formulated (for example, Augoustinos and Innes 1990) – it does, nonetheless, suggest a way in which ordinary social interaction in society may construct common-sense or 'naive' causal theories that are widely used to explain events (Heider 1958). One source of criticism has been that it has always been rather difficult to analyse social representations quantitatively. Recently, however, some steps have been taken towards the development of appropriate quantitative techniques (Doise *et al.* 1993). In addition, Breakwell and Canter (1993) have assembled a collection of chapters describing in concrete terms the variety of ways that different researchers have approached the measurement of social representations. These methods include qualitative and quantitative analyses of interviews, questionnaires, observational data and archival material.

Rumour

The process through which social representations are constructed has more than a passing resemblance to the way in which rumours develop and are communicated. One of the earliest studies of rumour was conducted by Allport and Postman (1945), who found that if experimental subjects describe a slide to someone else who had not seen the slide, and then this person described it to another person, and so forth, then only 30 per cent of the original detail remained after five retellings. Allport and Postman identified three processes associated with rumour transmission:

1. Levelling – the rumour very quickly becomes shorter, less detailed and less complex.
2. Sharpening – certain features of the rumour are selectively emphasised and exaggerated.
3. Assimilation – the rumour is distorted in line with people's pre-existing prejudices, partialities, interests and agendas.

More naturalistic studies have found rather less distortion as a consequence of rumour transmission (for example, Caplow 1947; Schachter and Burdeck 1955).

Whether rumours are distorted or not, and even whether rumours are transmitted at all, seems to depend on the anxiety level of those who hear the rumour (Buckner 1965; Rosnow 1980). Uncertainty and ambiguity increase anxiety and stress, which in turn leads people to seek out information with which to rationalise anxiety, which in turn enhances rumour transmission. Whether the ensuing rumour is distorted or becomes more precise depends on whether people approach the rumour with a critical or uncritical orientation (Buckner 1965). In the former case the rumour becomes refined, while in the latter (which often accompanies a crisis) the rumour becomes distorted.

Rumours always have a source, and often this source purposely elaborates the rumour for a specific reason – often to discredit individuals or groups. An organisation can spread a rumour about a competitor in order to undermine the competitor's market share (Shibutani 1966), or a social group can spread a rumour to blame another group for widespread crises. A good example of this is the fabrication and promulgation of conspiracy theories (Graumann and Moscovici, 1987).

Conspiracy theories

▶ Conspiracy theory

Conspiracy theories are elementary and exhaustive causal theories that attribute widespread natural and social calamities to the intentional and organised activities of certain social groups which are seen to form conspiratorial bodies set on ruining and then dominating the rest of humanity. The best known conspiracy theory is, of course, the myth of the Jewish world conspiracy (Cohn 1966) that periodically surfaces and often results in massive systematic persecution. Other conspiracy theories include the belief that immigrants are intentionally plotting to undermine the economy, that homosexuals are intentionally spreading the HIV virus, and that witches (in the Middle Ages) and the CIA (nowadays) are behind virtually every world event you care to mention (for example, Cohn 1975).

Conspiracy theories wax and wane in their popularity. They were particularly popular from the mid-seventeenth to the mid-eighteenth century:

> Everywhere people sensed designs within designs, cabals within cabals; there were court conspiracies, backstairs conspiracies, ministerial conspiracies, factional conspiracies, aristocratic conspiracies, and by the last half of the eighteenth century even conspiracies of gigantic secret societies that cut across national boundaries and spanned the Atlantic. (Wood 1982, p. 407)

The accomplished conspiracy theorist can, with consummate skill and breathtaking versatility, explain even the most arcane and puzzling events in terms of the devious schemes and inscrutable machinations of hidden conspirators. Billig (1978) believes it is precisely this that can make conspiracy theories so attractive. They provide a causal explanation in terms of enduring dispositions that can explain a very wide range of events, rather than complex situational factors that are less widely applicable. Furthermore, worrying events become controllable and easily remedied because they are caused by small groups of highly visible people rather than complex socio-historical circumstances (Bains 1983).

Societal attributions

The emphasis on attributions as social knowledge finds an expression in research on the sorts of explanation people give for large-scale social phenomena. In general, this research furnishes evidence for the view that causal attributions for specific phenomena are located within, and moulded by, wider, socially constructed belief systems.

For example, research on explanations for poverty reveals that both rich and poor tend to explain poverty in terms of the behaviour of poor people rather than situationally (for example, Feagin 1972; Feather 1974). This individualistic tendency is not so strong for people with a more left wing or socialist ideology, or for people living in developing countries where poverty is widespread (Pandey et al. 1982). Explanations for wealth tend to depend on political affiliation. In Britain, Conservatives ascribe it to positive individual qualities of thrift and hard work, while Labour supporters attribute it to the negative individual quality of ruthless determination (Furnham 1983). Not surprisingly, there are also cross-cultural differences, for example individualistic explanations are common in Hong Kong (Forgas et al. 1982; Furnham and Bond 1986).

Similarly the sorts of explanation given for unemployment are influenced by people's wider belief and value systems (Chapter 4). Feather (1985) had Australian students give their explanations of unemployment on a number of derived dimensions, and found that they preferred societal over individualistic explanations: for example, defective government, social change and economic recession were seen as more valid causes of unemployment than lack of motivation and personal handicap (see also Feather and Barber 1983; Feather and Davenport 1981). However, students who were politically more conservative tended to place less emphasis on societal explanations. Studies conducted in Britain also reveal that societal explanations are more prominent than individualistic explanations, and that there is a fair degree of agreement between employed and unemployed subjects (Furnham 1982; Gaskell and Smith 1985; Lewis *et al.* 1987).

Other research has focused on the sorts of explanation that people give for riots (social unrest, collective behaviour and riots are discussed in detail in Chapter 10). Riots are enormously complicated social phenomena in that there are both proximal and distal causes: a specific event or action might trigger the riot, but only because of the complex conjunction of wider conditions. For instance, the proximal cause of the 1992 Los Angeles riot may have been the acquittal of the police officers charged with the beating of Rodney King (see Box 10.1 in Chapter 10), however, this alone would have been unlikely to promote a riot without the background of racial unrest and socio-economic distress in the United States. As with explanations of poverty, wealth and unemployment, the sorts of explanation people give for a specific riot seem to be influenced by the person's socio-political perspective (for example, Litton and Potter 1985; Reicher 1984; Reicher and Potter 1985; Schmidt 1972) – more conservative members of the establishment tend to identify deviance or personal or social pathology, while people with more liberal social attitudes tend to identify social circumstances.

For example, Schmidt (1972) analysed printed media explanations of the spate of riots that occurred in American cities during 1967. The explanations could be classified with respect to the three dimensions of: legitimate/ illegitimate, internal/external cause and institutional/environmental cause. The first two dimensions were strongly correlated, with legitimate external causes (for example, urban renewal mistakes, slum conditions) going together and illegitimate internal causes (for example, criminal intent, belief that violence works) going together. Media sources on the political right tended to identify illegitimate internal causes whereas those classified as 'left-centre' (that is, liberal) stressed legitimate external causes.

Finally, Sniderman *et al.* (1986) have investigated the way in which people give explanations for racial inequality and have preferences for different government policies. They used a national sample of whites in the United States (in 1972), and were interested to investigate the influence of level of education. They found that less educated whites employed an 'affect driven' reasoning process. They started with their (mainly negative) feelings about blacks and then proceeded directly to advocate minimal government assistance. Having, done this they 'doubled back' to fill in the intervening link to justify their advocacy, namely that blacks were personally responsible for their own disadvantage. In contrast, more educated whites adopted a 'cognition driven' reasoning process, in which they reasoned both forwards and backwards. Their policy recommendations were based on causal attributions for inequality, and in turn their causal attributions were influenced by their policy preference.

Culture's contribution

It is increasingly clear that specific attributions or causal explanations can only be properly understood by taking into account the wider belief and value systems of individuals. We have already seen, for example, the influence of socio-political values, educational status, group membership and ethnicity, and cultural factors have cropped up throughout.

People from different cultures often make very different attributions, make attributions in different ways, or approach the entire task of social explanation in different ways (Smith and Bond 1993; Triandis 1976; Triandis *et al.* 1972). Consequently, the potential for cross-cultural interpersonal misunderstanding is enormous. For example, the Zande people of West Africa have a dual theory of causality, where common-sense proximal causes operate within the context of witchcraft as the distal cause (Evans-Pritchard 1937; see Jahoda 1979). For the Zande, an internal/external distinction would make little sense. Another example: Lévy-Bruhl (1925) reported that the natives of Motumotu in New Guinea attributed a pleurisy epidemic to the presence of a specific missionary, his sheep, two goats and finally a portrait of Queen Victoria. Although initially quite bizarre, these sorts of attribution are easily explained as social representations – how much more bizarre are they than, for example, the 'string theories' that became popular in physics in the mid 1980s to construct a unified theory of the universe (see Hawking 1988)?

One area in which cross-cultural research on attribution has been done is the fundamental attribution error (see above). We have seen that in western cultures people have a tendency to make dispositional attributions for others' behaviours (Ross 1977). There is also evidence that such dispositional

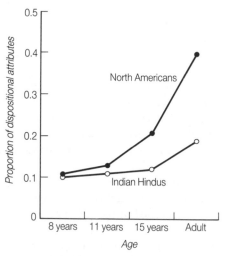

FIGURE 3.8 *Dispositional attributions as a function of age and cultural background. (Source: based on data from Miller 1984.)*

attributions become more evident over ontogeny (for example, Pevers and Secord 1973). In non-western cultures, however, people are less inclined to make dispositional attributions (Carrithers *et al.* 1986; Shweder and Bourne 1982). This is probably partly a reflection of the more pervasive and all-enveloping influence of social roles in more collectivist non-western cultures (Fletcher and Ward 1988; Jahoda 1982).

To investigate further the role of culture in dispositional attributions, Miller (1984) compared middle-class North Americans and Indian Hindus in each of four age groups (adults, 15, 11 and 8 year olds). The subjects narrated prosocial and antisocial behaviours and gave their own spontaneous explanations of the causes of these behaviours. Miller was able to code responses in such a way as to identify the proportion of dispositional and contextual attributions that subjects made. Among the youngest children there was little cross-cultural difference (Figure 3.8). As age increased, however, the two groups diverged, mainly because the Americans came increasingly to adopt dispositional attributions. For context attributions the results were reversed. The important lesson that this study teaches us is that cultural factors have a significant impact on attribution and social explanation.

SUMMARY

♦ People are naive psychologists seeking to understand the causes of their own and other people's behaviour.
♦ Much like scientists, people take account of consensus, consistency and distinctiveness information in deciding whether to attribute behaviour internally to personality traits and dispositions, or externally to situational factors.
♦ The sorts of attribution made can have profound impact on one's emotions, one's self-concept and one's relationships with others. There may be individual differences in propensities to make internal or external attributions.
♦ People are actually very poor scientists when it comes to making attributions. They are biased in many different ways, of which the most significant are a tendency to over-attribute others' behaviour dispositionally and one's own behaviour externally, and a tendency to protect the self-concept by externally attributing our failures and internally attributing our successes.
♦ Attributions for the behaviours of people as ingroup or outgroup members are ethnocentric and in terms of stereotypic group properties. This 'bias' is, however, affected by the real or perceived nature of intergroup relations.
♦ Stereotypes may originate in a need for groups to attribute the cause of large-scale distressing events to outgroups which have (stereotypic) properties that are causally linked to the events.

♦ People may resort to causal attributions only when there is no readily available social knowledge (for example, scripts, causal schemata, social representations, cultural beliefs) to explain things automatically.

FURTHER READING

Fiske, S. T. and Taylor, S. E. (1991). *Social Cognition* (2nd edn). New York: McGraw-Hill.

Hewstone, M. (1989). *Causal Attribution: From Cognitive Processes to Collective Beliefs*. Oxford: Blackwell.

McClure, J. (1991). *Explanations, Accounts, and Illusions: A Critical Analysis*. Cambridge: Cambridge University Press.

▶ KEY TERMS

actor/observer effect
attribution
attributional style
belief in a just world
causal schemata
cognitive miser
consistency information
consensus information
conspiracy theory
correspondent inference
covariation model
discounting
distinctiveness information
ethnocentrism
external/situational attribution
false consensus effect
fundamental attribution error

hedonic relevance
illusion of control
intergroup attribution
internal/dispositional attribution
levels of analysis/explanation
naive psychologist/scientist
non-common effects
overjustification effect
personalism
self-handicapping
self-perception theory
self-serving bias
social identity theory
social representations
stereotype
ultimate attribution error

4 *Nature and measurement of attitudes*

....

FOCUS QUESTIONS
- ◆ Just how meaningful is the term attitude? An animal lover says an attitude is the body posture that a hunting dog takes up when indicating the presence of a prey. A sports coach says that a certain team player has an 'attitude problem', which presumably is something to do with the player's state of mind. Is the term worth keeping in our psychological dictionary if it has several common-place meanings?
- ◆ Citizens often say that polling people's attitudes (or opinions) is a waste of pubic money, and that polls do not predict elections very well. Is there any useful link between attitudes and behaviour?
- ◆ If the concept of attitude turns out to have some use, how might a given attitude be measured? Can it be quantified?

STRUCTURE AND FUNCTION OF ATTITUDES

Background

The term *attitude* is part of our everyday language. Many years ago Gordon Allport referred to it as social psychology's most indispensable concept. In the 1935 *Handbook of Social Psychology*, which was an influential treatise on the discipline at that time, he wrote that:

> The concept of attitudes is probably the most distinctive and indispensable concept in contemporary American social psychology. No other term appears more frequently in the experimental and theoretical literature. (p. 798)

▶ Attitude

In the context within which Allport was writing, his view was not surprising. Others, such as Thomas and Znaniecki (1918) and Watson (1930) had actually defined the whole of social psychology as the scientific study of attitudes. The early 1930s also brought the tangible results of questionnaire-based scales which could be used to measure attitudes. According to Allport, an attitude is:

> a mental and neural state of readiness, organised through experience, exerting a directive or dynamic influence upon the individual's response to all objects and situations with which it is related. (1935, p. 810)

Allport was not to know that so fashionable a concept would become a centre of controversy in the decades ahead, to the point that a radical behavioural view would emerge to argue that an attitude is a figment which one might construct after, but which does not exist before, a particular behaviour has occurred. In looking at broad historical trends in the ways in which attitudes have been treated by social psychologists, McGuire (1986) distinguished three phases of burgeoning attention, punctuated by a waning interest between each:

1. In the 1920s and 1930s, concentration on fairly static issues of attitude measurement and how this related to behaviour.
2. In the 1950s and 1960s, focus on the dynamics of change in an individual's attitudes.
3. In the 1980s and 1990s, swing towards unravelling the structure and function of systems of attitudes.

The word *attitude* is derived from the Latin word *aptus*, which means 'fit and ready for action'. This ancient meaning refers to something that is directly observable, such as a boxer in a boxing ring. Today, however, supporters of the concept see it as a construct which, though not directly observable, precedes behaviour and guides our options for action.

Attitude research in psychology and the social sciences has generated enormous interest and many hundreds of studies covering almost every conceivable topic about which attitudes might be expressed. During the 1960s and 1970s research and theorising into attitudes went into a period of pessimism and decline, to some extent as a reaction to concerns about the apparent lack of relationship between attitudes as measured and behaviour as recorded. During the 1980s, however, attitudes again became a focus of interest for social psychologists, stimulated considerably by modern cognitive psychology (see reviews by Tesser and Shaffer 1990, and Olson and Zanna 1993). This includes applications from experimental research which have focused on how information is processed and the way memory works.

In Chapters 4 and 5, we take the view that attitudes are basic and pervasive in human life. In doing this, we will not take McGuire's evolutionary sequence too literally, since the three foci he refers to have always been, and continue to be, of interest to social psychologists. Without the concept of attitude, we would have difficulty construing and reacting to events, trying to make decisions, and making sense of our relationships with people in everyday life. Attitudes continue to fascinate research workers and remain a key, if controversial, part of social psychology.

How many components?

Constructing models of the parts thought to make up an attitude has long been a source of fascination to social psychologists. Over the years this has led to major differences among theorists, even with respect to such an apparently simple question as how many crucial components are required.

One component

▶ One-component attitude model

Thurstone preferred a one–component model, defining an attitude as 'the affect for or against a psychological object' (1931, p. 261). A later influential text dealing with techniques for constructing attitude scales reiterated this view: an attitude is 'the degree of positive or negative affect associated with some psychological object' (Edwards 1957, p. 2). Such a straightforward view becomes more complex when we examine below how Thurstone went about measuring a 'psychological object' using an early form of attitude scale. Thurstone believed that the concept of attitude was holistic, and that an attitude object had many possible attributes and elements (Ostrom 1989b). The centrality of affect (whether one likes the object or not), however, was the dominant feature of Thurstone's approach, and is also the basis of a more sophisticated socio–cognitive model put forward by Pratkanis and Greenwald (1989), to which we return later.

Two components

▶ Two-component attitude model

Another view, with its roots in Allport's approach, favoured a two–component model. Such an approach stresses that an attitude is, firstly, a state of mental readiness, or an implicit predisposition; and secondly, that it has a generalising and consistent influence on evaluative (judgemental) responses. It is something inside us that influences our decisions about what is good or bad, desirable or undesirable, and so on. An attitude is, therefore, a private event whose existence we can only infer. We might do this by examining our own mental processes, or by introspecting. As we see later, we might also make an inference by examining the way we behave or the way we speak or act. You cannot see, touch or physically examine an attitude: it is a hypothetical construct. According to Petty and Cacioppo (1986), this points to a definition of attitudes as 'lasting, general evaluations of people (including oneself), objects, or issues'.

Three components

▶ Three-component attitude model

Yet a third view is the three-component model, which is an approach to the definition of attitude with ancient philosophical roots:

> The trichotomy of human experience into thought, feeling, and action, although not logically compelling, is so pervasive in Indo-European thought (being found in Hellenic, Zoroastrian, and Hindu philosophy) as to suggest that it corresponds to something basic in our way of conceptualisation,

perhaps ... reflecting the three evolutionary layers of the brain, cerebral cortex, limbic system, and old brain. (McGuire 1989, p. 40)

The three-component model of attitude was particularly popular in the 1960s, following the leads of Rosenberg and Hovland (1960) and Krech *et al.* (1962). It was also sustained in the later work of Himmelfarb and Eagly (1974), who described an attitude as a relatively enduring organisation of beliefs, feelings and behavioural tendencies towards socially significant objects, groups, events or symbols. Note that this definition not only included the three components, but also stressed that:

1. Attitudes are relatively permanent, that is, they persist across time and situations. A momentary feeling in one place is not an attitude.
2. Attitudes are limited to socially significant events or objects.
3. Attitudes are general, involving at least some degree of abstraction. If you drop a book on your toe and find that it hurts, that is not an attitude because it applies to only one event, in one place, at one time. However, if the experience makes you dislike books or libraries or clumsiness in general, that dislike is an attitude.

Each attitude, then, is made up of a cluster of feelings, likes and dislikes, behavioural intentions, thoughts and ideas. Other recent theorists who have favoured the three-component model include Breckler (1984) and Ostrom (1968).

Despite the appeal of the 'trinity', this model presents a problem by presuming a link with behaviour (Zanna and Rempel 1988), itself a thorny issue and of sufficient complexity to be dealt with in Chapter 5. Suffice to say for now that most modern definitions of attitude involve both belief and feeling structures, and worry quite a lot about how, even if each can somehow be measured, the resulting data help to predict the future acts of an individual.

Function of attitudes

If attitudes have a structure they must have a function as well, and the approaches we have considered so far have at least an implicit assumption of purpose. Some writers have been more explicit in this respect. Katz (1960), for example, proposed that there are various kinds of attitude, each serving different functions, such as:

1. Knowledge.
2. Instrumentality (means to a goal).
3. Ego-defence (protecting one's self-esteem).
4. Value-expressiveness (allowing people to display those values which uniquely identify and define them).

According to Smith *et al.* (1956), an attitude saves energy, since we do not have to figure out from scratch how we should relate to the object in question.

We can note a parallel here between the utility of stereotypes and schemata (Chapter 2) and the function of attitudes. Smith *et al.*'s idea is that an attitude enables the person to maximise the probability of having positive experiences and minimise the aversive ones. Fazio (1989) later argued that the main function of any kind of attitude is a utilitarian one: that of object appraisal. This should hold regardless of whether the attitude has a positive or negative valence, that is, whether our feelings about the object are good or bad. Merely possessing an attitude is useful because of the orientation towards the object which it provides for the person. For an attitude truly to fulfil this function, however, it must be accessible. We develop this aspect of Fazio's thinking about attitude function below when we deal with the link between attitude and behaviour.

Cognitive consistency

▶ Cognitive consistency theories

In the late 1950s and 1960s, several theories of attitude structure were developed which emphasised the role of cognition above all else. These became known as the *cognitive consistency theories*. An early dominant example was balance theory, which is dealt with below. Another major contribution was cognitive dissonance theory which, because of its importance in dealing with the connection between attitude and behaviour, we return to in the next chapter.

As well as specifying that beliefs are the building blocks upon which an attitude is structured, such theories also focused on inconsistencies that can arise among some beliefs that an individual might hold. These theories may differ in the terminology used to define consistency and inconsistency in cognitive structures, but they all share the important concept that an attitude structure that is built upon beliefs that are in disagreement (inconsistent) is unpleasant to the holder. Two thoughts are said to be inconsistent if one seems to contradict the other, and this state of mind is a bother. Such an approach to attitude structure goes on to argue that the person will be motivated to change one or more contradictory beliefs so that the set as a whole will be in harmony. The outcome of this is to restore consistency.

Balance theory

▶ Balance theory

The cognitive consistency theory with the clearest implications for attitude structure is *balance theory*, derived from the work of Heider (1946) and extended by Cartwright and Harary (1956). Heider's ideas were rooted in the Gestalt school, a psychological approach to perception popular in Germany in the early twentieth century, and extended further again by Heider to the field of interpersonal relations. The general approach is field-theoretical: aspects of an individual's cognitive field are percepts of people and also of objects and events.

Balance theory focuses on the P–O–X unit of the individual's cognitive field. Imagine a triad consisting of three elements: a person (P), another person (O), and an attitude object or topic (X). Such a triad is said to be consistent if it is balanced, and balance is assessed by counting the number and types of relationships among the elements. P likes X, for instance, is a positive (+) relationship; O dislikes X is negative (−); and P dislikes O is negative (−).

Altogether, there are eight possible combinations of relationships between two people and an attitude object, four of which are balanced and four unbalanced. These are shown in Figure 4.1.

A triad is *balanced* if there is an odd number of positive relationships, which may occur in a variety of ways. If P likes O, O likes X and P likes X, then the triad is balanced. From P's point of view, balance theory acts as a divining rod in predicting interpersonal relationships: if P likes the object X, then any compatible other, O, should feel the same way. Likewise, if P already likes O, then O will be expected to evaluate object X in a fashion similar to P. By contrast, if P likes O, O likes X and P dislikes X, then the relationship is *unbalanced*. As we have noted, the principle of consistency which underlies balance theory means that unbalanced triads make people feel tense and motivated to restore balance (Jordan 1953). Heider proposed that balance would be restored in whatever manner required the least effort. So in the last example, P could decide not to like O or change his opinion about X, depending on which required the least effort.

On the whole, research has shown that unbalanced structures are more unstable and more unpleasant than balanced structures. There are several additional factors that influence how stable and pleasant a structure is. Everything else being equal, people prefer to agree with each other. Furthermore, the theory predicts that we assume that others will like what we like, in

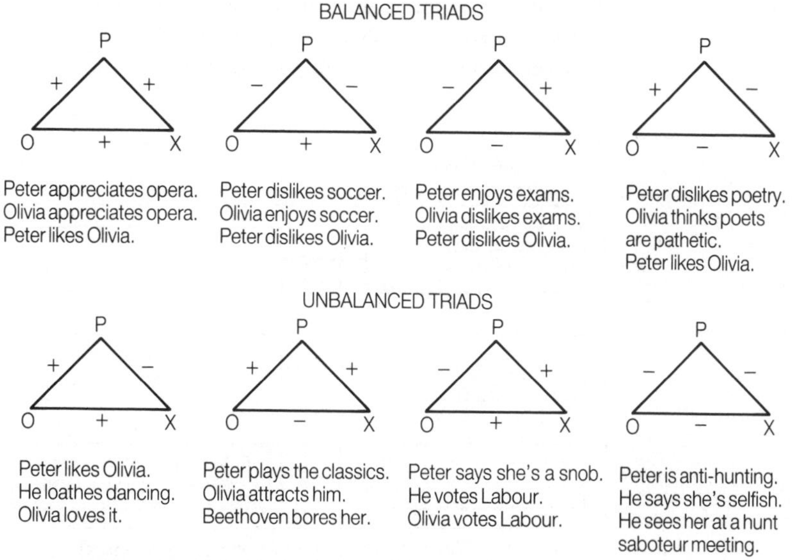

BALANCED TRIADS

Peter appreciates opera. Olivia appreciates opera. Peter likes Olivia.	Peter dislikes soccer. Olivia enjoys soccer. Peter dislikes Olivia.	Peter enjoys exams. Olivia dislikes exams. Peter dislikes Olivia.	Peter dislikes poetry. Olivia thinks poets are pathetic. Peter likes Olivia.

UNBALANCED TRIADS

Peter likes Olivia. He loathes dancing. Olivia loves it.	Peter plays the classics. Olivia attracts him. Beethoven bores her.	Peter says she's a snob. He votes Labour. Olivia votes Labour.	Peter is anti-hunting. He says she's selfish. He sees her at a hunt saboteur meeting.

FIGURE 4.1 *Heider's theory of balanced and unbalanced triads.*

the absence of contradictory information. As well as preferring balanced structures, most people seek out structures in which P and O agree rather than disagree in their evaluations of the third element in the structure (Zajonc 1968).

Despite this, people do not always seek to resolve inconsistency. They sometimes organise their attitudes and beliefs so that elements are isolated from each other and are quite resistant to change (Abelson 1968). Overall, research on balance theory and related issues has been extensive, and mostly supportive of the theory. At about the same time, other researchers developed cognitive dissonance theory (Festinger 1957), which is now more widely known than balance theory. Since this is highly relevant to our treatment of attitude change, it is discussed in Chapter 5.

Cognition and evaluation

▶ Cognition

We have already noted the view that a single component is the essence of an attitude. Thurstone, in the 1930s, saw affect as the cornerstone of an attitude. By the 1950s, Osgood (discussed again later) stressed a central process of evaluation as the essence of an attitude.

▶ Socio-cognitive model

Pratkanis and Greenwald have given recent impetus to this emphasis in their *socio-cognitive model*, defining an attitude as 'a person's evaluation of an object of thought' (1989, p. 247). However, they elaborate this simple picture by drawing on theoretical developments (such as Wyer and Srull 1984) in the field of social cognition, an area we have dealt with an Chapter 2. The attitude object (see Figure 4.2) is represented in memory by:

1. An object label and the rules for applying that label.
2. An evaluative summary of that object.
3. A knowledge structure supporting that evaluation.

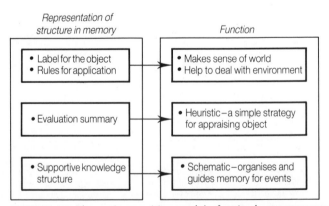

FIGURE 4.2 *The socio-cognitive model of attitude structure and function. (Source: based on suggestions by Pratkanis and Greenwald 1989.)*

Despite the use of the term cognitive, however, Pratkanis and Greenwald actually highlight an evaluative component. In the wider literature, various terms have been used almost interchangeably in denoting this component, such as affect, evaluation, emotion and feeling. More recently, Breckler and Wiggins (1989a,b) have argued that the terminology used in this context needs to be tidied up. They distinguish between affect and evaluation. The former refers to emotional reaction to an attitude object, whereas the latter refers to particular kinds of thought, belief and judgement about the object.

Information processing and attitudes

▶ Information processing
▶ Information integration theory

As a general approach, the ideas behind *information processing* stress the complexity of how people acquire knowledge, and how they form and change their attitudes. According to Anderson's (1971, 1980) *information integration theory*, most of our attitudes are constructed in response to information we receive about attitude objects. Anderson's theoretical position is that people function as sophisticated problem-solvers and as evaluators of new information. How we receive and combine this information provides the basis for attitude structure. For example, the salience of some items and the order in which they are received by the individual become important ingredients for the way in which they are processed. As new information arrives, the person both evaluates it and combines it with information already stored in memory.

Anderson's argument becomes a little more complex with the proposition that an attitude is formed when the individual has assembled a number of discrete items of information into an overall impression by averaging the values attached to them. Such mathematics are performed by ordinary people, who use a form of cognitive algebra to average out the multiple bits of information to which they have been exposed. For example, if you considered a friend to be shy, energetic and compassionate, your overall attitude towards the friend would be an average of the evaluative meanings you attach to those traits. See Chapter 2 for more details and examples about how this averaging might take place.

ARE ATTITUDES PREDICTIVE OF BEHAVIOUR?

Even though the assumption that behaviours might correspond to attitudes seems reasonable, a number of social scientists have questioned this view. In New Zealand, for instance, Stacey found only a small positive correlation between attitudes and self-reported alcohol consumption (Gregson and Stacey 1981). Furthermore, there was no evidence of any benefits in focusing on attitude change rather than on economic incentives to control alcohol use. This sort of finding has caused critics to question the utility of the concept of attitude: if attitude measures bear no relation to what people do, then what is the use of the concept?

A classic study relevant to the attitude/behaviour issue was carried out by LaPiere (1934; see also Chapter 9), who was interested in the difference between prejudiced attitudes towards Chinese in general and discriminatory behaviours towards a Chinese couple in particular. He travelled extensively throughout America with two Chinese friends. They visited 66 hotels, auto-camps and tourist homes and were served in 184 restaurants. They were refused service only once. Six months after these visits, LaPiere sent a questionnaire to all the places visited, asking 'Will you accept members of the Chinese race as guests in your establishment?' Of the 81 restaurants and 47 hotels that replied, 92 per cent replied that they would not accept Chinese customers, 1 per cent said they would accept them and the remainder checked 'Uncertain, depends upon circumstances'. It is clear that these written replies did not correspond to the actual behaviour of the respondents.

After LaPiere's provocative study, dozens of researchers used more sophisticated methods to study the attitude/behaviour relationship. Many obtained relatively low correspondence between questionnaire measures of attitudes and measures of overt behaviour. After reviewing this research, Wicker (1969) concluded that the correlation between attitudes and behaviours is seldom as high as 0.30 (which, when squared, indicates that only 9 per cent of the variability in a behaviour is accounted for by an attitude). Wicker, in fact, found that the average correlation between attitudes and behaviour was only 0.15 (approximately 2 per cent of variance in behaviour is accounted for by attitudes). This startling finding was seized upon during the 1970s as prime evidence that the attitude concept is not worth a great deal since it has little predictive power. Some researchers despaired (Abelson 1972), but presumably not too much – there are two whole chapters of this book dedicated to research into attitudes.

The counter-idea that has formed over the past two decades is that attitudes and overt behaviour are not related in a simple one-to-one fashion. This view has been expressed with increasing frequency. Not all classes of social behaviour can be accurately predicted from verbally expressed atti-tudes. We look now at some recent theoretical developments that cast new light on the difficulty of getting a direct correspondence between attitudes and behaviour.

Beliefs, intentions and behaviour

According to Martin Fishbein (1967a,b, 1971), the basic ingredient of an attitude is affect – a position which follows Thurstone's (1931) early definition. However, a score based entirely on a unidimensional, bipolar evaluative scale (such as good/bad) does not predict reliably how a person will later behave. To do so depends on being able to account for the interaction among attitudes, beliefs and behavioural intentions, and the connections of all of these with later action. In this equation we need to establish both how strong and how valuable an individual's beliefs are: some beliefs will carry more weight than others in relation to the final act. Without this information, trying to predict an outcome for a given individual must be a hit-or-miss affair.

Consider the example in Table 4.1. A young, heterosexually active male might believe, strongly or not, that certain things are true about two forms of contraception, the pill and the condom. *Belief strength* (or expectancy) is a probability estimate, ranging from 0 to 1, about the truth; for example, he may hold a very strong belief (0.90) that the pill is a most reliable method of birth control. Reliability of a contraceptive is a 'good' thing, so his *evaluation* (or value) of the pill is +2, say, on a 5-point scale ranging from +2 to −2. These components interact, producing a product of +1.80. (We can note here that Fishbein's view incorporates the idea that people can perform cognitive algebra – see also Chapter 2). Next, the young man might be fairly sure (0.70) that the condom is less reliable (−1), a product of −0.70. Likewise he thinks that using a condom is potentially embarrassing in a sexual encounter. His further belief that using a condom has no known side-effects is not sufficient to offset the effects of the other two beliefs. Consequently, the young man's intention to use a condom may be quite low – perhaps he hopes that the women who cross his path use the pill. Only by having all of this information could we be fairly confident about predicting his future behaviour.

This approach to prediction also offers a method of measurement, the *expectancy–value technique*, to which we return in a later section. In subsequent work with his colleague Icek Ajzen, Fishbein developed the *theory of reasoned action* to link beliefs to intentions to behaviour. We shall return to this model later. Fishbein and Ajzen's work was a major step forward in understanding issues which had previously complicated the overall relationship between attitudes and behaviour. Predictions can be clarified when the inherent links are brought to the surface. Furthermore, behavioural predictions can be much improved if the measure of attitude is specific rather than general.

Specific attitudes

Ajzen and Fishbein's view is that the success of any attempt to predict the way

TABLE 4.1 A young male's hypothetical attitude towards contraceptive use: the role of the strength and the value of his beliefs

Attribute	Male's belief about female using pill			Male's belief about male using condom		
	Strength of belief[a]	Value of belief[b]	Result	Strength of belief	Value of belief	Result
Reliability	0.90	× +2	= +1.80	0.70	× −1	= −0.70
Embarrassment	1.00	× +2	= +2.00	0.80	× −2	= −1.60
Side-effects	0.10	× −1	= −0.20	1.00	× +2	= +2.00
Outcome			= +3.60			= −0.30

[a] The strength of a belief in this example is the probability (from 0 to 1) that a person thinks that the proposal is true.
[b] The value of a belief is an evaluation on a bipolar scale (in this case, ranging from +2 to −2).

we behave is determined by asking us whether we would perform a given act or series of acts. The key lies in using questions which are specific rather than ones which deal in generalities.

Ajzen and Fishbein argued that much previous attitude research had suffered from either trying to predict specific behaviours from general attitudes, or vice versa, so that low correlations were to be expected. This is, in essence, what LaPiere did. An example of a specific attitude predicting a specific behaviour would be that attitudes towards a particular psychology exam should predict the extent to which students study for that exam. In contrast, an example of a general attitude predicting a general class of behaviours would be attitudes towards psychology as a whole predicting fairly well the tendency to engage in behaviours generally relevant to learning more about psychology, such as reading magazine articles. How interested you are in psychology generally is not likely to be predictive of how well you prepare for a specific psychology exam.

In a longitudinal study over two years by Davidson and Jacard (1979), women's attitudes towards birth control were measured at different levels of specificity and were used as predictors of their actual use of the pill. The measures, ranging from very general to very specific, were correlated with pill use (correlations in parentheses): 'attitude towards birth control' (0.08), 'attitude towards birth control pills' (0.32), 'attitude towards using birth control pills' (0.53) and 'attitude towards using birth control pills during the next two years' (0.57). Quite clearly, the closer the question was to the actual behaviour the more accurately the behaviour was predicted.

General attitudes

▶ Multiple-act criterion Fishbein and Ajzen (1975) also argued that predictions from attitudes to behaviour can be made at a more general level. To do so, however, required that a *multiple-act criterion* be established. This was a general behavioural index based on an average, or combination of, various specific behaviours. General attitudes usually predict multiple-act criteria much better than they predict single acts because single acts are usually affected by many factors. For example, the specific behaviour of participating in a paper-recycling programme on a given day is a function of any number of factors, even the weather. Yet such a person may claim to be environmentally conscious, a general attitude. While environmental attitudes are no doubt one determinant of this behaviour, they are certainly not the only determinant and perhaps not even the major determinant.

Reasoned action

▶ Theory of reasoned action The ideas outlined so far were brought together in a general model dealing with the links between attitude and behaviour: the *theory of reasoned action* (Fishbein and Ajzen 1974; Ajzen and Fishbein 1980). The model comprised three broad processes of beliefs, intention and action, and included the following components:

1. *Subjective norm* – this is a product of what the individual perceives to be others' beliefs. Significant others provide a guide to 'what is the proper thing to do'.
2. *Attitude towards the behaviour* – this is a product of the individual's beliefs about the target behaviour, and also of how these beliefs are evaluated (see the cognitive algebra in Table 4.1). Note that this is an attitude towards behaviour (such as taking a birth control pill in Davidson and Jacard's study) not towards the object (such as the pill itself).
3. *Behavioural intention* – an internal declaration to act.
4. *Behaviour* – the action performed.

Usually, a particular action will be performed if: (1) the person's attitude is favourable; (2) the social norm is also favourable, and (3) the level of perceived behavioural control is high. In early tests of the theory, Fishbein and Coombs (1974) and Fishbein and Feldman (1963) gave subjects a series of statements about the attributes of various attitude objects, for example political candidates. The subjects estimated *expectancies*, that is, how likely it was that the object possessed the various attributes, as well as giving the attributes a *value*. These expectancies and values were then used to predict the subjects' feeling towards the attitude object, assessed by asking the subjects how much they liked or disliked that object. The correlation between the scores and the subjects' feelings was high, pointing to some promise for the model.

Other research reported that voting intentions:

1. correlated 0.80 with how people voted in the 1976 American presidential election (Fishbein *et al.* 1980a);
2. correlated 0.89 with how they voted in a referendum on nuclear power (Fishbein *et al.* 1980b).

Role of volition

▶ Theory of planned behaviour

The theory of reasoned action emphasises not only the rationality of human behaviour but also that the target action is under the person's conscious control – for example, 'I know I can stop smoking if I really want to'. However, some behaviours are less under people's control than others. Consequently, the basic model was extended by Ajzen (1989) to give some prominence to the concept of volition. Perceived behavioural control is the extent to which the person believes it is easy or difficult to perform the act. This can include past experience, as well as present obstacles which the person may envisage. Ajzen and Madden (1986), for example, found that students not surprisingly want to achieve A-grades in their courses: A-grades are highly valued by themselves (attitude) and they are the grades that their family and friends want them to score (subjective norm). However, prediction of actually scoring an A will be faulty unless the students' perceptions of their own ability is taken into account. Ajzen has argued that perceived behavioural control can act on either the behavioural intention or directly on the behaviour itself. He referred to this modified model as the *theory of planned behaviour*. The concepts and their links in both theories are shown in Figure 4.3. The two theories are very closely linked and are not in conflict.

In one study, Beck and Ajzen (1991) started with students' self-reports of the extent to which they had been dishonest in the past. The behaviours sampled included exam cheating, shoplifting and telling lies to avoid completing written assignments – actions which were quite frequently reported. They found that measuring the perception of control which students thought they had over these actions tended to improve the prediction of future action and, to some extent, the actual carrying out of the act. This worked best in the case of cheating, which may well be planned in a more deliberate way than shoplifting or lying. In another study, Madden *et al.* (1992) measured students' perception of control in relation to nine behaviours. These ranged from 'getting a good night's sleep' (quite hard to control) to 'taking vitamin supplements' (quite easy to control). The results were calculated to compare predictive power by squaring the correlation coefficient R between each of the two predictors, sleep and vitamins, and each of the outcomes, intentions and actions. Perceived control improved the predictions for both intentions and actions. This improvement was substantial in predicting the action itself. These effects show up in the steepness of the two lower lines in Figure 4.4.

Features of both models have been used by Terry *et al.* (1993) to show how Fishbein and Ajzen's concepts can be applied to the study of safe sex behaviour as a response to the threat of HIV infection. Specifically, the target behaviours include monogamous relationships, non-penetrative sex and the use of condoms. All of the variables shown in Figure 4.3 can be applied in this

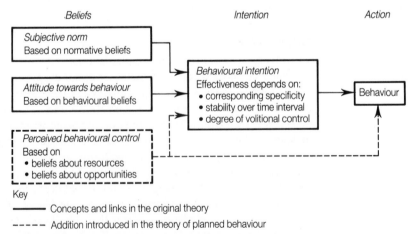

FIGURE 4.3 *A comparison of the theories of reasoned action and planned behaviour. (Source: based on Ajzen and Fishbein 1980, and Madden* et al. *1992.)*

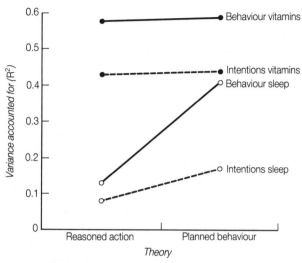

Note: Subjects rated taking vitamins as easy to control but getting a good night's sleep as hard to control.

FIGURE 4.4 *The effect of including perceived behavioural control as a variable in comparing the theories of reasoned action and planned behaviour. (Source: based on Madden* et al. *1992.)*

setting. The particular variable of perceived behavioural control probably needs to be accounted for – the scenario envisages a sex partner, and neither individual may be fully confident of controlling the wishes of the other person. A practical question that may need to be addressed, for example, is the degree of control that a woman might perceive over whether a condom will be used on her next sexual encounter.

In contrast to these models, some researchers have suggested other variables that may play some role in determining action, such as people's moral values (Gorsuch and Ortbergh 1983; Pagel and Davidson 1984; Schwartz 1977). For example, if someone wanted to find out if we would donate money to charity, they would do well to find out whether acting charitably is a priority in our lives. Despite these suggestions, Madden *et al.* (1992) have argued that there is little evidence to show that additional variables improve prediction any further.

A reservation which can be applied to both theories of reasoned action and of planned behaviour is that they assume that attitudes are rational, and that socially significant behaviours are intentional, reasoned and planned. This may not always be true.

Attitude accessibility

We have noted that many models of attitude feature a cognitive component: beliefs are seen as the building blocks of the more general concept of attitude. Even other modern approaches which prefer to stress an evaluative component agree on one matter: attitudes are represented in memory (Olson and Zanna 1993).

Attitude accessibility, or the ease with which an attitude can be recalled from memory, is a factor that can exert a strong influence on behaviour (Fazio 1986).

Attitude strength

▶ Automatic activation Strong attitudes come to mind more readily and exert more influence over behaviour than do weak attitudes. Fazio argued that attitudes are evaluative associations with objects, which makes his approach a one-component model. Associations can vary in strength from (1) not existing (that is, a non-attitude), to (2) a weak association, to (3) a strong association. Only a strong association allows the *automatic activation* of an attitude (Fazio *et al.* 1986). Direct experience of an object and having vested interests in it (that is, something with a strong effect on your life) make the attitude more accessible and increase its effect on behaviour. The more often you have a thought about a particular attitude, the more likely it is to come up again and influence your behaviour. Powell and Fazio (1984) were able to increase attitude accessibility by simply asking subjects six different times what their attitude was, as opposed to only asking them once. A three-step theoretical model was proposed to account for this (Fazio *et al.* 1983; see Figure 4.5). When general attitudes are accessed they can affect behaviour in specific situations. If the general attitude is never accessed, it cannot affect behaviour.

Direct experience

In addition to its strength, the accessibility of an attitude is also a function of direct experience with the attitude object. Attitudes formed through actually experiencing the attitude object show more consistent relationships to behaviour than do those formed less directly (Regan and Fazio 1977). For example, Fazio and Zanna (1978) found that measures of students' attitudes towards psychology experiments better predicted future participation in experiments if students had already taken part in several experiments than if they had only read about experiments. Take another example: your attitude

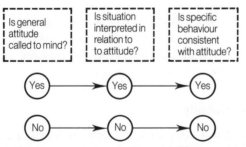

FIGURE 4.5 *Fazio's attitude accessibility model. (Source: based on Fazio* et al. *1983.)*

towards UFOs is far less likely to predict your actual behaviour, should you ever encounter one, than your attitude towards lecturers is likely to predict your lecture-room behaviour. We consider again the role of direct experience in the context of attitude formation.

Moderator variables

▶ Moderator variable

Despite the difficulties of predicting single acts from general attitudes, many researchers remain interested in the task. These researchers typically add moderator variables into the attitude/behaviour equation. A *moderator variable* qualifies an otherwise simple research hypothesis, with the aim of improving prediction. Such variables include the situation, personality, habit, sense of control and direct experience. Ironically, moderator variables may turn out to be more powerful predictors of a behaviour than the more general, underlying attitude. We consider two cases: situational variables and personality variables.

Situational variables

Aspects of the immediate situation, or wider social context, can cause people to act in a manner inconsistent with their attitudes (Calder and Ross 1973). For example, a motorist whose attitude is that a particular speed limit is unnecessary would probably not express this to a police officer who has just stopped her for speeding. Similarly, a student who would actually like to attend classes in formal business dress may nevertheless comply with student dress-code norms and appear instead in casual clothing.

Personality variables

There is a fundamental conflict between explanations which favour situational variables and those that emphasise personality variables – a conflict which extends well beyond the field of attitude research (Ross and Nisbett 1991). Mischel (1968), for example, argued that situational characteristics were more reliable predictors of behaviour than were personality traits (see also the low correlations reported between personality measures and leadership in Chapter 8). Yet Bem and Allen (1974) showed that individuals who identified themselves as consistent on a particular *personality trait*, such as conscientiousness, were more likely to behave in a way that was consistent with that trait, across a variety of situations, than those who identified themselves as variable on that trait.

It has also been proposed that people's *habits* and their *degree of control* over the behaviour of interest, must be considered (Langer 1975; Petty and Cacioppo 1981; Triandis 1980). Triandis (1977) proposed a model similar to Fishbein and Ajzen's, including a habit factor, reflecting the number of times a particular action has been performed by the person in the past. Habits are behaviours that are automatic in certain situations and occur without thinking. Smoking, for instance, is habitual for many people, and is often partly due to a physiological dependency. Thus, the behaviour of smokers may bear little relationship to their attitudes towards cigarettes. In an American national survey, 72 per cent of smokers agreed that smoking was one of the causes of lung cancer, and 71 per cent agreed that 'cigarette smoking causes disease and death' (Oskamp 1984).

ATTITUDE FORMATION

▶ Attitude formation

We have noted that attitudes are learned rather than innate. The learning of attitudes is an integral part of the socialisation process (Fishbein and Ajzen 1975; McGuire 1969; Oskamp 1977), and may occur through direct experiences, or through interactions with others, or be a product of cognitive processes. Social psychologists have generally confined their work to understanding the basic psychological processes that underlie *attitude formation* rather than exploring how particular classes of attitudes develop. The study of these processes most often involves laboratory experiments rather than survey research or public opinion findings.

Behavioural approaches

Effects of direct experience
Many of the attitudes people hold are the products of direct experience with attitude objects. People encounter an attitude object and have a positive or

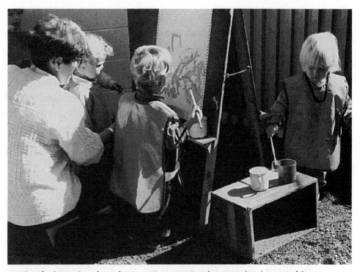

Attitude learning by observation. Attitudes can be learned by modelling other people's behaviours and beliefs. Here, a child carries on painting a scene started by an adult. (Source: Andrew Lukey.)

negative experience, which, at least partially, shapes their attitudes towards that object. A number of researchers have stressed the importance of traumatic or frightening experiences in the formation of attitudes (Oskamp 1977; Sargant 1957), while others have focused on changes in national attitudes as a result of direct exposure while sojourning in a foreign country (Stroebe *et al.* 1988). Several processes have been proposed to explain the effects of personal experiences on attitude formation. Among these are: mere exposure, classical conditioning, operant conditioning, social learning theory and self-perception theory.

Fazio and Zanna (1981) found that the attitudes of students forced to live in makeshift quarters during a campus housing shortage were more predictive of their subsequent behaviour concerning the housing shortage than were the attitudes of students who lacked such direct experience.

Fishbein and Ajzen (1975) have proposed that direct experience can affect attitudes towards an object by providing people with information about the attributes of a particular attitude object. According to the expectancy/value model of attitude structure (see below), this information leads to beliefs that will influence how much people like or dislike the attitude object. Direct experiences that are especially negative or traumatic make certain beliefs more salient than others. For example, if your first visit to the dentist is painful, you may conclude that dentists hurt people.

▶ Mere exposure effect   If you attend rallies or meetings to ban mineral exploration in forest reserves, you might conclude that you are anti-mining, but one component of your attitude might have changed since the first rally: you might feel even more strongly opposed to mining. This is what Zajonc (1968) termed the *mere exposure effect*. He proposed that mere exposure to an object (the number of times one has encountered it) affects one's evaluation of that object. Most people are probably aware of this effect. The first time you hear a new song on the radio, for instance, you may find you neither strongly like nor dislike it. Repetition is likely to strengthen your response in one direction or the other. Mere exposure has most impact when we lack information about an issue. This is a reason why a standing MP, for example, usually has an advantage over other candidates in an election, since her name is more likely to be familiar.

Classical conditioning

Through repeated association a formerly neutral stimulus can elicit a reaction that was previously elicited only by another stimulus. For example, children may be initially indifferent to politics, but later vote as young adults for a party following years of exposure to a parent who has been an enthusiastic supporter – a classically conditioned response has become the basis of a subsequent political attitude. Some have suggested that classical conditioning underlies the formation of a wide variety of attitudes (Staats and Staats 1957; Zanna *et al.* 1970).

Classical conditioning can be a particularly powerful and insidious form of

Classical conditioning. Classical conditioning: pleasant surroundings generate a good mood. This may become associated with other people present and increase liking for them. (Source: Andrew Lukey.)

attitude learning. Janis *et al.* (1965) demonstrated the power of contextual stimuli by reinforcing some subjects with soft drinks at the time that they were reading a persuasive message. Those given soft drinks were more persuaded by what they read than those who were not. Galizio and Hendrick (1972) arranged for their subjects to listen to pleasant guitar music as an accompaniment to persuasive messages presented in the form of folk songs. The songs proved more persuasive when accompanied by guitar music than without. The reasonable interpretation from these experiments is that the positive feelings associated with the soft drinks or with guitar music became associated, via classical conditioning, with the persuasive messages.

Instrumental conditioning

In this form of learning, responses which yield positive outcomes or eliminate negative ones are strengthened. Behaviours that are followed by positive consequences are reinforced and are more likely to be repeated than are behaviours that are followed by negative consequences. Parents use verbal reinforcers constantly in an attempt to encourage acceptable behaviour in their children. Playing quietly and co-operatively with others, for example, is a social behaviour that can win praise. On the other hand, fighting would lead to the withholding of a reinforcer or even to the introduction of a negative one, such as scolding. Instrumental learning can be accelerated or slowed by the frequency, temporal spacing, and magnitude of the reinforcement (Kimble

1961). By rewarding and punishing their children, parents can shape their attitudes on many issues, such as their religious or political beliefs and practices. Even in adulthood, it is possible that attitudes may continue to be shaped by verbal reinforcers. Insko (1965) showed that students' responses to an attitude survey had been influenced by an apparently unrelated telephone conversation which took place a week earlier and in which particular opinions were 'rewarded' by the interviewer responding with the reinforcer 'good'.

Both forms of conditioning (classical and instrumental) emphasise the role of direct reinforcers in the acquisition and maintenance of behaviour in general. The relevance to the topic of attitudes depends on defining an attitude as a class of behaviour. This becomes a relatively straightforward matter if an attitude is operationalised as an *evaluative response*. Such a view has been argued by Osgood *et al.* (1957) and by Fishbein (1967a).

Observational learning

▶ Modelling

Other social psychologists view attitude formation as a social learning process, one which does not depend on direct reinforcers. Bandura (1973) and others have studied social learning and concentrated on a process of *modelling* (see also Chapters 11 and 13) whereby one person's behaviour is modelled on another's. Modelling is learning by observation: individuals learn new responses not only by directly experiencing positive or negative outcomes but also by observing the outcomes of others' responses. Having a successful working mother, for instance, is likely to influence the future career and lifestyle choices of a daughter.

Cognitive development

Other social psychologists prefer to think of attitude formation in terms of cognitive development. The cognitive consistency theories (such as balance, cognitive dissonance) dealt with earlier allow us to view attitude acquisition as an elaborative exercise of building connections (balanced or consonant) between more and more elements, such as beliefs. As the number of related elements increases, the more likely it is that a generalised concept – an attitude – is being formed. Similarly, information integration theory can handle attitude learning as a case in which more and more items of information about an attitude object have been processed (say by averaging their weights).

A difference between cognitive and behavioural approaches is the relative weight that each gives to internal events versus principles of reinforcement. Contemporary social psychology, across many fronts, favours a cognitive interpretation, as we have noted with respect to theory and data treated in Chapters 2 and 3. Despite this trend, we should not ignore certain advantages of behavioural approaches: traditionally, they have been closely linked to the study of learning, and they often deal directly with developmental data (whether generated from studies of animals or children). For this reason, learning theories will continue to be of considerable interest to social psychologists studying attitude acquisition.

▶ Self-perception theory

One interesting approach with both a behavioural and a perceptual flavour is Bem's (1972) *self-perception theory* (also discussed in Chapter 3). Bem proposed that people acquire knowledge about what kind of person they are by attending to their own behaviour and asking 'why did I do that?' All sorts of attitudes could be acquired in this way, with people attributing their behaviour to underlying attitudes which may not actually be the true cause or reason for their behaviour. For example, if you frequently go for long walks, you may conclude that 'I must like them, since I'm always doing that'. Bem's theory suggests that people act, and form attitudes, without thinking.

Sources of learning

Parents

An important source of your attitudes is the actions of other people around you. For the child, parents are a powerful influence, and all of the processes of learning mentioned above (classical conditioning, instrumental conditioning and observational learning) are involved. However, Connell (1972) reported that, although the correlation between the *specific* attitudes of parents and their children towards a given issue is generally positive, it is also weak. On the other hand, when measuring attitudes towards *broad* issues, the relationship is stronger. Jennings and Niemi (1968) found a 0.60 correlation between high-school children's preferences for a particular political party and their parents' choices. The correlation between parents' and children's choices of religious denomination was high at 0.88.

Mass media

The media, particularly television, are also major influences on the learning of attitudes. Although the impact of television on adults is not clear-cut (Barney 1973; Oskamp 1984), there is little question that it plays an important part in attitude formation in children. Young children do not initially have strongly held attitudes, and so are particularly susceptible (Goldberg and Gorn 1974). It is not surprising then to discover that American children under 7 years old get most of their political information from television (Chaffee *et al.* 1977), and that this moulds their political attitudes (Atkin 1977; Rubin 1978). The impact of commercials on children's attitudes has also been investigated. Atkin (1980) found that children who were heavy watchers of television were twice as likely as light watchers to believe that sugar-coated sweets and cereals were good for them. In the same study, it was also found that two-thirds of a group of children who saw a circus strong man eat a cereal believed it would make them strong too.

CONCEPTS RELATED TO ATTITUDES

Values

We have concentrated on attitudes as a relatively high-level concept involving affect as a central dimension. We have also noted that some theorists argue that beliefs constitute an additional dimension. If we accept this view, an attitude could be conceptualised as a set of integrated beliefs with an affective loading. From such an approach springs a further level of analysis, and another term, *value*. An early emphasis on the global concept of values was made in the publication of a psychological test (Allport and Vernon 1931) designed to measure the relative importance of six broad classes of value orientation within the person: *theoretical* – an interest in problem-solving, and the basis of how things work; *economic* – an interest in economic matters, finance, and money affairs generally; *aesthetic* – an interest in the arts, theatre, music, etc.; *social* – a general concern for one's fellows: a social welfare orientation; *political* – an interest in political structures and in power arrangements; and *religious* – a general concern with theology, the afterlife and with morals.

▶ Value
More recently, Rokeach (1973) suggested that values should be conceived less in terms of interests or activities and more as desirable end states of existence and modes of behaviour (goals). He distinguished between *terminal values* – end states such as equality and freedom – and *instrumental values* – modes of behaviour such as honesty and ambition. A terminal value, such as equality, could significantly influence the way someone might feel about racial issues, which is just what Rokeach has found. From this viewpoint, a value is a higher-order concept having broad control over the individual's more specific attitudes. Research dealing with values as a higher-order concept has suggested that they can have strong links with more specific attitudes. For example, measuring values can help predict people's attitudes to the unemployed (Heaven 1990) and to beliefs in a just world (Feather 1991).

Himmelweit *et al.* (1985) conducted a longitudinal study, spanning almost a quarter of a century, of social psychological influences on voting in Britain. They found that specific attitudes were usually poor predictors, while broader socio-political values and party identifications were much better predictors. In another large scale study by Hewstone (1986), this time of attitudes of French, Italian, German and British students towards European integration, general value orientation changes were seen to have had some influence on changed attitudes towards integration.

Feather's extensive research (Feather 1993a,b, 1994) has suggested that values have the following properties:

1. They are general beliefs about desirable behaviour and goals.
2. Unlike wants and needs, they involve goodness and badness and have an 'oughtness' quality about them.

3. They both transcend attitudes and influence the form these attitudes may take.
4. They provide standards for evaluating actions, justifying opinions and conduct, planning behaviour, for deciding between different alternatives, engaging in social influence, and presenting self to others.
5. They are organised into hierarchies for any given person, and their relative importance may alter over the life span.
6. Value systems vary across individuals, groups and cultures.

Ideology

▶ Ideology

The term ideology cuts across that of value. It connotes an integrated system of beliefs, usually with a social or political reference. Tetlock (1989) has proposed that terminal values, such as those described by Rokeach, underlie all kinds of *political ideology*. Ideologies can vary as a function of two characteristics:

1. They may assign different priorities to particular values: traditionally, we might expect liberals and conservatives to rank 'individual freedom' and 'national security' in opposite ways.
2. Some ideologies are pluralistic and others are monistic. A pluralistic ideology can tolerate a conflict of values, for example, 'I want to protect the environment, but I don't want to slow economic growth'. A monistic ideology will be quite intolerant of conflict, seeing issues in black or white terms (see the discussion of authoritarianism in Chapter 9).

Billig (1991) has suggested that a good deal of our everyday thinking comes about as a result of what he calls ideological dilemmas. Teachers, for example, face a dilemma of being an authority figure and yet trying to encourage equality between teacher and student. When conflict between values takes place it can cause a clash of attitudes between groups. For example, Katz and Haas (1988) reported that racial attitudes in a community can become polarised when values such as communalism and individualism clash.

Social representations

▶ Social
representations

A somewhat different emphasis in the study of attitudes has been favoured by European social psychologists. Moscovici (1983; Farr and Moscovici 1984), with the concept of *social representations* (see Chapter 3), describes how people's beliefs are socially constructed – that is, how our ideas and opinions are moulded, through social interaction, by what other people say and believe. Individuals' attitudes are shared with other members of the community, so that the pattern of individual thought is a microcosm of the attitudes of society at large:

> Our reactions to events, our responses to stimuli, are related to a given definition, common to all the members of the community to which we belong. (Moscovici 1983, p. 5)

This view of items of knowledge as data which are socially shared can be traced back to the nineteenth-century notion of 'collective representations' put forward by the French sociologist Emile Durkheim. The emphasis on society, rather than the isolated individual, as the proper basis for and unit of analysis in the understanding of social behaviour, is of course the hallmark of European social psychology in contrast to American social psychology (see Chapter 1). Regarding the study of attitudes, William McGuire (1986) observed that 'the two movements serve mutually supplementary uses' in that the European concept of collective representations highlights how *alike* group members are, while the American individualist tradition shows how *different* they are.

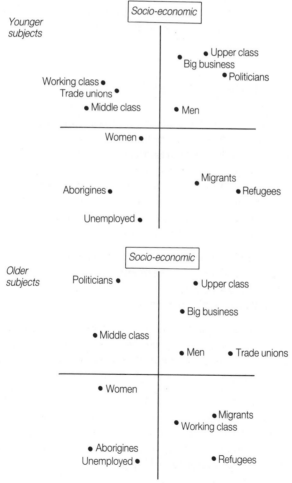

FIGURE 4.6 *Social representations of some groups on two dimensions in Australian society. (Source: adapted from Augoustinos 1991.)*

If social representations are cognitive structures shared on a group basis, we might expect agreement between members to increase with age. This idea was tested by Augoustinos (1991) in a developmental study which compared the images held by high school and university students of twelve groups in Australian society. The groups could be classified with respect to four dimensions reflecting socio-economic, ethnic, political and gender differences. A *multi-dimensional scaling* procedure (discussed later) identified dimensions which allowed the twelve groups to be compared. Figure 4.6 shows two sets of results: one for younger students (13–14 years old) and one for older students (third year at university). For the younger group, the vertical dimension was identified as 'wealth, power and success', but the horizontal dimension was more difficult to describe. For the older group, Augoustinos identified the vertical dimension as socio-economic, whereas the horizontal dimension is possibly male/female. This study illustrates the use of the concept of social representations and indicates that the images held by a community of its own constituent groups can become clearer as a function of age.

MEASURING ATTITUDES

Measuring an attitude is not an easy task since attitudes cannot be observed directly: how can we measure something that is in a person's mind? The usual solution is to ask people. Researchers rely heavily on this approach and often use attitude questionnaires or scales.

Because the study of attitudes has been an active part of social psychology for a long time, a well developed technology exists for measuring attitudes. Several different paper-and-pencil tests have been developed, and four techniques have been refined and used extensively:

1. Thurstone's method of equal-appearing intervals.
2. Likert's method of summated ratings.
3. Guttman's scalogram.
4. Osgood's semantic differential.

We shall see that techniques of attitude measurement assume different things about the nature of the test items that are used or the data that are collected, and about the kind of information these provide about a person's attitudes. They also have assumptions in common:

1. Subjective attitudes can be measured by a quantitative technique, so that each person's opinion can be represented by a numerical score.
2. A particular test item, or other behaviour indicating an attitude, has the same meaning for all respondents, so that a given response is scored identically for everyone making it.

Such assumptions may not always be justified and implicit assumptions should always be treated warily.

▶ Self-rating scale   In a typical attitude questionnaire respondents are asked to indicate whether they agree or disagree with each of a series of belief statements about an attitude object. In view of the important place that the study of attitudes has occupied within social psychology, we need to ask how these belief statements are selected, a topic which is dealt with in detail in relation to each of the techniques outlined below. Occasionally, attitudes are measured by a single question which asks people to make a positive or negative evaluation about a specific topic. Consider the example of a seven-point *self-rating scale* in Figure 4.7.

The respondent checks one of the points on the scale. The scales do not always have seven points; five, six, even one hundred points have been used. Sometimes only the end-points are labelled and the rest are blank. The advantage of such a scale is simplicity. The disadvantage is possible over-simplification of complex issues. Although such a question directly assesses evaluation of an attitude object, the use of a single question to measure an attitude is typically not favoured by psychologists. The reason for employing a larger set of items is that responses to any one question are often affected by irrelevant factors (such as the wording of the question) which create errors. If responses are averaged or summed across a number of questions, a more valid measure is obtained because the error inevitably associated with the individual items tends to cancel out across a number of items. The final statements included in an attitude questionnaire are thus carefully selected. Ideally, each represents a different and independent view about the object and covers both favourable and unfavourable attitudes, so that the nature of the response to one item should not affect the response to another item. There are several systems for choosing appropriate statements and each is known as an attitude scaling method.

Thurstone's method of equal-appearing intervals

The first major technique of attitude measurement was developed by Thurstone (1928) in his study of attitudes towards religion. The scale, derived from psychophysics, introduced precise measurement into an area of research where it had never been used before. Like other attitude theorists, Thurstone viewed attitudes as lying along an evaluative continuum ranging from favourable to unfavourable. Furthermore, the ordering of these statements could be such that there appeared to be an equal distance between adjacent statements on the continuum. Because of the latter assumption, one can make

What is your attitude towards having nuclear power plants in Europe?

1	2	3	4	5	6	7
Strongly approve			*Neutral*			*Strongly disapprove*

FIGURE 4.7 *A seven-point self-rating scale.*

judgements about the degree of discrepancy among different people's attitudes. Thurstone also assumed that the statements are uncorrelated and that each statement has a position that is independent of the others, that is, acceptance of one statement does not necessarily imply acceptance of any others.

▶ Thurstone scale

As originally designed, a *Thurstone scale* is made up of twenty-two independent statements about a particular issue. Each statement has a numerical scale value determined by its average judged position on the continuum, and people's attitudes on the issue are measured by asking them to check those statements with which they agree. Each person's score is the mean scale value of those items which they check. The example in Figure 4.8 is a shortened version of this type of scale. (In practice, the scale values would not be shown. The subject could choose any number of the statements with which to agree.)

The hallmark of a Thurstone scale is that the intervals between the statements are approximately equal, a property which derives from the method of construction. The features involved in constructing this kind of scale are:

1. A large number of statements of opinion about an issue are formulated. Any whose meanings are confusing or ambiguous are discarded.
2. The remaining statements are sorted into eleven categories by a group of judges, who are in practice a group of up to one hundred subjects drawn from the same population as the ultimate subjects whose attitudes are later to be measured.
3. The eleven categories are steps on an equal–intervals scale ranging from favourable through neutral to unfavourable with respect to the attitude object.
4. The task for the judges is to determine to what degree agreement with each item would reflect a favourable, neutral or unfavourable (from 1 through 11) attitude towards the issue.
5. This judgement should be made without regard to the judge's own attitude.
6. By tabulating the ratings of the judges, it is possible to calculate both the

THURSTONE SCALE
Attitude towards contraception

How favourable	Value on 11-point scale	Item
Least	1.3	*Practising contraception should be punishable by law.*
	3.6	*Contraception is morally wrong in spite of possible benefits.*
Neutral	5.4	*Contraception has both advantages and disadvantages.*
	7.6	*Contraception is a legitimate health measure.*
	9.6	*Contraception is the only solution to many of our social problems.*
Most	10.3	*We should not only allow but enforce limitation on family size.*

FIGURE 4.8 *Items on an eleven-point Thurstone equal-intervals scale.*

numerical scale position (the average) of each statement, as well as the extent to which the judges agreed on its placement (its range).

7. The statements selected for use on the final scale are those that have high interjudge agreement and fall at relatively equally-spaced intervals along the continuum. There are twenty-two items, two per scale position, in the final-scale.

8. Other people's attitudes towards the issue are finally derived from their responses to this final set of items. If the scale is statistically reliable, one would expect a person to agree with only two or three items out of twenty-two. The average of the scale values for these endorsed items would reflect that person's position on the eleven-point scale.

9. If there were a sufficient number of reliable items available, it would be possible to make up two twenty-two–item questionnaires as forms A and B, which might for example be used as before and after measures in a study of attitude change.

Likert's method of summated ratings

One of the practical drawbacks of the Thurstone scale is that its construction is very tedious and time-consuming. To cope with this problem, Likert (1932) developed a different technique which produces reasonably reliable attitude scale with relative ease. A series of attitude statements are presented, and respondents check their extent of agreement or disagreement with the statement using a five-point scale with the points usually labelled strongly

Using a rating scale. Questionnaires are widely used to measure people's attitudes. These students are completing a set of Likert-type ratings on items designed to provide a performance assessment of their lecturer. One might worry here about the independence of their responses. (Source: Andrew Lukey.)

agree, agree, undecided, disagree, strongly disagree. Look at the example in Figure 4.9.

▶ Likert scale

In contrast to the Thurstone scale, a person's attitude is measured by asking him to indicate the extent of agreement or disagreement with each item. When a number of these statements are used, a person's score on the various items can be summed and the resulting total used as an index of the person's attitude. When developing a *Likert scale*, researchers find that not all questions will correlate equally with the total – some will be more effective measures of the attitude than others. Those that do not correlate highly with the total are dropped, and the ones that are left are used as the summed index of a person's attitude. Any ambiguous items, or items that do not differentiate between people with differing attitudes, are dropped.

▶ Acquiescent
response set

If possible, items are selected so that for 50 per cent of the items 'agree' represents a positive attitude, and for 50 per cent of the items 'agree' represents a negative attitude. The scoring of the latter set of items is adjusted (5 = 1, 4 = 2, 3 = 3, 2 = 4, 1 = 5) before the item scores are summed. This procedure controls for *acquiescent response set*, that is, a confounding of a highly positive attitude score with a tendency simply to agree with a series of statements.

Likert assumed that each statement that is used in the scale is a linear function of the same attitude dimension. This assumption is the basis for the operations of adding up a person's individual scores (or summating the ratings) to obtain a final score. A further implication is that the items in a scale must be highly correlated with a common attribute and thus with each other, as opposed to Thurstone's distinct and independent items. Likert did not assume equal intervals between scale values. For example, it is quite possible that the difference between 'agree' and 'strongly agree' is much larger than the difference between 'agree' and 'undecided'. This means a Likert scale can

LIKERT SCALE
What are your opinions of the following statements? Your answer is correct if it expresses your real opinion. This is not a test and you are not to be graded. DO NOT OMIT ANY ITEM. In each case place a tick in any *one* of the five places which represent your own ideas about each statement.

Item	Strongly agree	Agree	Undecided	Disagree	Strongly disagree
Farming is a great occupation.	—	—	—	—	—
Farm work is drudgery.	—	—	—	—	—
To be a farmer for the rest of one's life would be terrible.	—	—	—	—	—
The farm is a wonderful place to live.	—	—	—	—	—
The independence of farm life appeals to me.	—	—	—	—	—
Living on a farm sounds too much like hard work.	—	—	—	—	—

FIGURE 4.9 *Items on a five-point Likert summated ratings scale.*

provide information on the ordering of people's attitudes on a continuum but is unable to indicate how close or far apart different attitudes might be.

Likert's method of scale construction is similar to Thurstone's in the initial collecting and editing of a variety of opinion statements. The remaining statements are then rated by a sample group of subjects on the five-point response scale in terms of their own opinions about the statements. This is in contrast to the Thurstone scale approach, where the ratings are made by trained judges, and based not on personal opinions but on some relatively objective evaluation of where the statements fall on a continuum. The Likert scale is composed of those items that best differentiate between sample subjects with the highest and lowest total scores.

In contrast to a Thurstone scale, a Likert scale is usually more statistically reliable (see Table 4.2) and is also less time-consuming to construct. Unlike the Thurstone scale, it is not intended to tap an absolute range of attitude scores (determined by judges); rather, the range reflects directly the attitudes of the subjects who constitute the sample.

Guttman's scalogram method

▶ Guttman scale

A *Guttman scale* (or scalogram) is based on the assumption that a single, uni-dimensional trait can be measured by a set of statements that are ordered along a continuum of difficulty of acceptance. The statements range from those that are easy for most people to accept to those that few people could endorse. Such scale items are cumulative, since the acceptance of one item implies that the person accepts all those of lesser magnitude. To the extent that all this is true, one can predict a person's attitude towards other statements on the basis of knowing the most difficult item they will accept (see the example in Figure 4.10).

To obtain a scale that represents a single dimension, Guttman presents sample subjects with an initial set of items and records the extent to which they respond to the items with specified answer patterns. These patterns, which are referred to as *scale types*, follow a certain step-like order. The subject

GUTTMAN SCALE

Attitude towards mixed-ethnic housing

How acceptable	Statement
Least	*Generally speaking, people should be able to live anywhere they want.*
	Real estate agencies should not discriminate against minority groups.
	The local council should actively support the idea of open housing.
	There should be a local review board that would pass on cases of extreme discrimination in housing.
Most	*There should be laws to enforce mixed-ethnic housing.*

FIGURE 4.10 *Items on a Guttman cumulative scale.*

may accept none of the items in the set (score $= 0$), accept item A only (score $= 1$), accept items A and B only (score $= 2$), accept items A, B and C only (score $= 3$), and so on. If the subject gives a non-scale response pattern (for example, accepts item C only and not those of lesser magnitude), then either the subject has made an error or the items used do not scale in a cumulative fashion.

▶ Unidimensionality   By analysing the numbers of response errors made, Guttman determined *scalability*, that is, the degree to which the initial set of items reflects a uni-dimensional attribute. *Unidimensionality*, then, refers to the extent to which the items being used are scalable, or cumulative. The final scale is obtained by eliminating poor items and retesting sample subjects until a scalable set of items has been developed. People's attitudes are then measured by having them check all of the statements that they find acceptable. To provide an estimate of how scalable a set of items is Guttman developed the coefficient of *reproducibility*. If there are N items to which a person could respond 'yes' or 'no' then there are 2^N possible response patterns, and of these only $N + 1$ should occur if the set is perfectly scalable. Response patterns which are of the non-scale type should, in practice, be low. Such errors detract from the perfection of the scale, that is they reduce reproducibility: $Rep = 1 - (total errors/total responses)$.

It is almost impossible to develop a perfect unidimensional scale. This usually indicates that people respond on multiple dimensions rather than on a single one.

Which is the best scale of the traditional forms that we have considered? There is no simple answer. In metric terms they focus on different properties of the dimension on which the items are located. They also differ somewhat in statistical reliability, which is the property of a measuring instrument to reproduce the same score for a person on different occasions; and, importantly for the researcher, ease of construction. According to Shaw (1966), none of these scales actually achieves equality of intervals, not even the Thurstone scale which was designed to achieve this very purpose. Nor do any of them have a zero point. A comparison of their various qualities is shown in Table 4.2. There is some evidence that judges' own attitudes can influence the way they rate the extremity of items (Edwards 1957; Eiser and Stroebe 1972).

Osgood's semantic differential

▶ Semantic differential   In contrast to approaches where respondents indicate agreement with opinion statements, Osgood studied attitudes by focusing on the meaning that people give to a word or concept. Underlying this technique is the assumption of a hypothetical semantic space of an unknown number of dimensions, in which the meaning of any word or concept can be represented as a particular point.

TABLE 4.2 Thurstone, Likert and Guttman scales compared

Characteristics	Thurstone	Likert	Guttman
Ease of construction	Moderately easy	Easy	Difficult
Item content	Must refer directly to attitude object	Need not refer directly to attitude object	Usually must refer directly to attitude object
Ease of scoring	Moderately easy	Moderately easy	Very easy
Score interpretation	Independent of total distribution of scores	Dependent on total distribution of scores	Relatively independent of total distribution of scores
Respondent's reaction	Neutral to moderately negative	Neutral to moderately negative	Negative
Reliability			
Two-forms	0.60–0.85	0.72–0.94	
Split-half	0.52–0.89	0.78–0.92	
Reproducibility	0.82–0.88	0.79–0.90	0.85–0.95
Validity	Not clearly established	Not clearly established	Not clearly established
Unidimensionality	No	Approximate	Yes
Equality of units	No	No	No
Neutral point	Yes	No	No

Source: Shaw 1966.

The *semantic differential* method of attitude measurement was developed from research on the connotative meanings of words.

The connotative meaning is the meaning a word suggests apart from the thing it explicitly denotes or names. For example, studies of the connotative meanings of words consistently show that one of the major dimensions involves evaluation, the goodness or badness implied by the word (Osgood *et al*. 1957). The word 'friend' tends to be thought of as good, and the word 'enemy' as bad. According to Osgood, this evaluative dimension corresponds to our definition of an attitude. The procedure is to have people judge a particular concept on a set of semantic scales. The idea or topic to be rated is listed at the top of a page, and underneath are several seven-point scales that have words at each end. These scales are defined by verbal opposites with a midpoint of neutrality. In the example in Figure 4.11, the meanings that people attach to the concept of 'nuclear power' are measured by the subjects' ratings of the concept on a set of semantic scales.

SEMANTIC DIFFERENTIAL SCALE
Nuclear power

GOOD	—	—	—	—	—	—	—	BAD
STRONG	—	—	—	—	—	—	—	WEAK
FAST	—	—	—	—	—	—	—	SLOW

FIGURE 4.11 *Measuring a concept on a semantic differential scale.*

Respondents check the space on the scale which indicates their feeling about the topic. Several pairs of words dealing with evaluations are used, some common ones include: good/bad, nice/awful, pleasant/unpleasant, fair/unfair, valuable/worthless. An analysis of the ratings collected by this method may reveal the particular dimensions that people use to qualify their experience, the types of concept that are regarded as similar or different in meaning, and the intensity of the meaning given to a particular concept. Osgood's own research pointed to three major dimensions that people use in judging concepts: evaluative (such as good/bad), potency (such as strong/weak) and activity (such as active/passive).

The major advantage of this approach is that a researcher does not have to make up questions for each attitude being studied. When several pairs of words are used, the resulting attitude score is generally reliable. A disadvantage is that the measure can be too simple. Furthermore, although this method can provide a lot of information about a concept, it is not exactly clear how the concept's meaning for a person is related to opinion statements they make about it. Some research uses variations on the original scales developed by Osgood. The study by Augoustinos (1991) discussed earlier in this chapter compared a variety of groups in Australian society on scales such as: active/passive, wise/foolish, independent/dependent. rich/poor, work hard/ lazy. She used a multi-dimensional scaling procedure (see below) to delineate dimensions, based on data generated from these scales, on which the twelve groups could be plotted (see Figure 4.6).

Fishbein's expectancy-value technique

▶ Expectancy-value
model

We have noted earlier that Fishbein and Ajzen (1974) argued that a better fit with behaviour can follow if an evaluative component is incorporated with a belief component. Fishbein went on to offer a technique of measurement involving a weighting of each contributing belief, underlying an attitude domain, by the strength of its relationship to the attitude object. We noted the main elements of this technique in an earlier section (see Table 4.1). Another example is shown in Figure 4.12.

Despite some criticisms (see Eagly and Chaiken 1992), Fishbein's technique has had considerable impact in a variety of behavioural settings, such as marketing and consumer research (Assael 1981), politics (Bowman and Fishbein 1978), family planning (Vinokur-Kaplan 1978), classroom attendance (Fredericks and Dossett 1983), seat-belt wearing (Budd *et al.* 1984), and even in prediction of how mothers will feed their infants (Manstead *et al.* 1983).

Use of attitude scales today

Combinations of the Likert scale and the semantic differential have been used successfully to deal with quite complex evaluations. For example, voters can be asked to evaluate various issues using a semantic differential scale. Then using a

FISHBEIN SCALE
Attitude towards politicians

Instruction: Rate your degree of <u>belief</u> in each of the following statements by indicating the probability that it is true, on a scale for which:
 	
  0 = not at all true
  10 = certainly true
	Instruction: Rate your <u>evaluation</u> of each of the following attributes on a scale for which:
	
	−10 = Extremely undesirable
	   0 = Neutral
	+10 = Extremely desirable

Politicians are: — Untrustworthy — Honest — Devious — Intelligent	 — Untrustworthy — Honest — Devious — Intelligent

FIGURE 4.12 *Items on a Fishbein expectancy-value scale.*

Likert scale, they can be asked how they think each candidate stands on particular issues. Combining the two measures enables us to predict for whom they will vote (Ajzen and Fishbein 1980).

The Likert scale has also contributed significantly to many modern questionnaires which start from the premise that there will be more than one underlying dimension in the attitude domain being researched. The availability of computer analysis has greatly increased the likelihood that researchers will choose from a variety of multivariate statistical methods, such as *factor analysis*, to analyse psychological data. Whereas Likert tested for uni-dimensionality in a fairly simple way by calculating item/total score correlations, factor analysis starts from a correlation matrix based on correlations between all items making up the questionnaire scale. It is then possible to estimate whether a single general factor (or dimension), or more than one factor, is required to explain the variance in the respondents' pattern of responses to the questionnaire. An example of this could occur if attitudes towards your country's possession of nuclear weapons in turn involved your reactions to war, to nuclear contamination, to relationships with other countries, and so on. Each of these might be measured on a different dimension, so that the questionnaire could well consist of several subscales (see Oppenheim 1992). In the process of extracting factors, decreasing amounts of variance are accounted for: that is, successive factors (dimensions) have weaker explanatory power.

Another multivariate procedure is *multi-dimensional scaling* analysis. In the study by Augoustinos (1991), twelve groups were compared two at a time on seventeen bipolar scales. These data were then analysed using a computer program to yield several orthogonal dimensions, which successively account for decreasing amounts of variance in the data. Augoustinos found that the vertical and horizontal dimensions for her younger subjects accounted for

59 per cent and 23 per cent of variance, and for her older subjects 72 per cent and 28 per cent respectively (see Figure 4.6).

Physiological measures

A variety of physiological measures have been used to assess attitudes. These include skin resistances (Rankin and Campbell 1955), heartbeat, heart cycle (Westie and DeFleur 1959) and pupil dilation (Hess 1965). A subject's attitude is usually inferred by comparing a physiological reading (such as heartbeat) taken in the presence of a neutral object with one taken in the presence of the attitude object. The larger the difference between the responses to the two, the more intense the subject's attitude is assumed to be. Such physiological measures have one major advantage over self-report measures: subjects may not realise that their attitudes are being assessed, and even if they do, may not be able to alter their responses.

However, there are drawbacks. Most physiological measures are sensitive to variables other than attitudes (Cacioppo and Petty 1981). Skin resistance can change in the presence of novel or incongruous stimuli that may have nothing to do with the attitude being assessed. Similarly, heart rate is sensitive to task requirements. Problem-solving tasks increase heart rate, while vigilance tasks (such as watching a VDU screen) lower it. Another problem is that physiological measures provide only limited information about attitudes. They can indicate intensity of feeling but not direction, so that two people who feel equally strongly about an issue, but are totally opposed, cannot be distinguished.

However, one physiological measure is regarded as very useful in distinguishing what kind of attitude people have. It is based on Charles Darwin's suggestion that different *facial expressions* are used to convey different emotions (see Chapter 14). Cacioppo and his colleagues (Cacioppo and Petty 1979; Cacioppo and Tassinary 1990) have linked measures of facial muscle movements to underlying attitudes. Cacioppo and Petty reasoned that people who agreed with a speech that they were listening to would display facial movements different from those of people who disagreed with the speech. To test this, they recorded the movements of specific facial muscles before and during a speech that advocated a conservative or a liberal view: for example, either stricter or more lenient university regulations regarding alcohol. Before the speech, movements of the muscles showed one pattern if students agreed with the topic and a different pattern if they disagreed. The differences in the patterns became more pronounced when the students actually listened to the speeches. Thus, facial muscle movements provide a useful way of distinguishing people with favourable attitudes on a topic from those with unfavourable attitudes. This approach does not indicate the intensity of an attitude present: no single physiological measure assesses both attitude position and strength together, something which is possible with self-report measures.

Measures of overt behaviour

▶ Unobtrusive
measures

Yet another way to measure attitudes is to watch what people do, since their behaviours can be an indication of their attitudes. This technique is only reliable when people do not realise their behaviour is being observed. Several such *unobtrusive measures* for assessing positive attitudes have been developed. Webb *et al.* (1969) suggested that attitudes can be inferred from observing physical traces, archival records and non-verbal behaviours. In a museum, for example, the noseprints on a display case could be counted to determine how popular a particular display is, and the height of the noseprints could indicate the ages of the most interested viewers. Similarly, public records can also provide information about attitudes, and archival information can be used to examine whether significant historical events influence relevant attitudes. Changes in attitudes about sex roles over time could be investigated by examining the roles played by male and female characters in children's books. If attitudes have changed, male and female characters may be more equally represented in recently published books than books of twenty years ago. Library withdrawals also provide archival data: are people reading more fiction or more non-fiction than in the past? Webb *et al.* (1969) described one interesting investigation which found that withdrawals of fiction, but not non-fiction, books dropped after the introduction of television. Library withdrawals can also be used to gauge the effect of the mass media. If a book or play receives a favourable radio review, is it likely to be more popular than if it received an unfavourable review?

Non-verbal behaviour can also serve as an attitude measure. For example, people who like each other tend to sit closer together, allowing a degree of prejudice to be inferred by seating patterns of members of different groups selecting seats in a room. *Interpersonal distance* can also measure fear. Webb and his colleagues described a study where adults told ghost stories to young children seated in a circle. The size of the circle of children grew smaller with each successive scary story. (The *social distance scale* developed by Bogardus (1925) was an earlier attempt to assess attitudes towards different social and ethnic groups based on the distance that people felt was comfortable between themselves and others, as measured by a graduated scale on the floor: a willingness to be more socially intimate with members of a given group would be indicated by the respondent moving further along the scale.)

However, Webb *et al.* (1969) concluded that these unobtrusive measures were not as good as self-report. The value of unobtrusive measures lies in the fact that their limitations are different from those of standard measures, so that when both types are used together, and correlate, a researcher can be more confident of the validity of the results. The major problem with unobtrusive measures is deciding which behaviour reflects an underlying attitude. The ideal behaviour would be one that is affected only by the person's evaluation of an issue and not by any irrelevant variables, which is of course unlikely in real life. Behaviour may not even be a good measure of attitude, and it has been suggested that a person's attitude may determine behaviour the first time a particular action is performed, but with repetition the behaviour becomes a habit and is less likely to be dependent on the relevant attitude (Triandis 1980). These problems can be overcome, however, when the overt behaviour is measured under conditions that enhance the salience, or obviousness of an attitude.

Problems and solutions in measuring attitudes

▶ Bogus pipeline technique

Whenever attitude researchers ask subjects questions, there is the possibility that subjects will be reluctant to reveal their true feelings. Researchers have devised several techniques to overcome such problems. However, these techniques have often raised questions about ethics in the research process, especially if subjects do not know their attitudes are being measured. A good example of this is the so-called *bogus pipeline technique* (Jones and Sigall 1971), which involves convincing subjects that they cannot hide their true attitudes. Subjects are connected to a machine resembling a lie detector and are told that the machine can measure both the strength and direction of a person's emotional responses, thus revealing a person's true attitudes and implying that there is no point in lying. Several studies have shown that subjects are indeed convinced by the bogus pipeline and are less likely to conceal socially undesirable attitudes such as racial prejudice when this technique is used (Allen 1975; Quigley-Fernandez and Tedeschi 1978). This procedure is considered by some researchers to be unethical: it deceives subjects and invades the privacy of those who are fooled by it. Social psychologists using it usually have to demonstrate that the scientific benefits of using it outweigh the ethical costs. (See Chapter 1 for a discussion of research ethics.)

In making comparisons across attitude studies, there are two further problems:

1. A fundamental lack of agreement about the definition of attitudes.
2. The lack of common methods for measurement.

Even when there is agreement about how an attitude might be defined and then measured, the ways in which data are then treated can vary markedly from one investigation to another. To illustrate, consider some of the ways that studies of attitude change (a field treated in detail in Chapter 5) have operationalised 'change.' Suppose that we have measured people's attitudes before and after an intervention and then wish to know how much change has occurred. The following change indexes have been employed:

1. Percentage of subjects showing any positive change at all.
2. Percentage of subjects showing large, moderate, small or no change (categories arbitrarily defined).
3. Net percentage change (positive minus negative changes).
4. Any of the above for an arbitrarily determined combination of opinion items.

5. Absolute mean scale distance changed.
6. Distance changed relative to amount of change possible.
7. Scale distance change weighted (corrected) for the subjective distance between scale points (that is, two units movement across neutral is 'worth more' than two units within one side of the scale).

If you are dubious about how valid it is to compare findings across a group of studies, you are not alone.

Rating scales have varied in the number of scale points (from four to one hundred); in the presence or absence and in the number of verbal labels at various points; and in their arrangement horizontally (across the page) or vertically (up and down the page). Attitudes have been measured by scale ratings of verbal statements (agree/disagree, true/false, like/dislike, and so on), of objects (good/bad, desirable/undesirable), of other people (like/dislike), and of self (degree of esteem, confidence). They have been measured by ratings of acceptance and rejection of individual opinion statements (latitudes of acceptance or of rejection) and by choices, rankings of alternatives, perceived instrumental value of items or actions, ratings of mood, ratings of intention, willingness to endorse an action or product, and likelihood of future behaviour.

Behavioural (non-questionnaire) measures of attitude have similarly spanned a huge variety. Verbal reports (about smoking, serving certain foods, dental hygiene practices) have been used, as well as observations of actual compliance with recommendations (taking an X-ray, getting tetanus shots, agreeing with group norms, and so on). Time measures (decision time, time spent listening to supportive information, and so on), physiological measures (galvanic skin response to indicate reactions of an ethnically prejudiced person to stimuli associated with a certain ethnic group), and learning measures (recall of stimuli) have all been conceived of as attitude indicators. There are many others that rely on unobtrusive observational methods – for example, a count of empty beer and whisky bottles in dustbins as indicators of attitudes towards alcohol in a given neighbourhood, chemists' records of which doctors prescribe new drugs). You can now begin to see some of the problems.

Attitudes have been treated as comprising three components: cognitive, affective and behavioural. However, what is traditionally done in attitude research is to present a set of belief or cognitive statements in a communication, and then to measure only changes in affect. Even more curious and alarming is that the areas of psychological scaling (psychometrics and attitude change) have largely ignored each other. Few of the hundreds of studies performed on attitude change make use of the scaling techniques developed by Thurstone, Likert, Guttman, Osgood and others. On the other hand, it is equally rare for those interested in measurement and scaling procedures to be interested in applied, empirical research on attitude change (Osgood's use of the semantic differential is a notable exception).

Having seen the great variety of measures (and operational definitions) employed for attitudes, we should not be surprised that results in this area often conflict. Some investigators using attitude scales do so on the basis of ease of measurement, or intuition. The area of attitude measurement needs to be treated with caution, and it is easy to see why some researchers wanted to abandon the attempt during the 1960s and early 1970s.

SUMMARY

- ◆ Attitudes have been a major interest of social psychologists since the early days of the field. They have also been described as the most important concept in social psychology.
- ◆ Theories dealing with structure generally agree that attitudes are lasting, general evaluations of socially significant objects (including people and issues). Some theories also stress that attitudes are relatively enduring organisations of beliefs, and behavioural tendencies towards social objects.
- ◆ Attitude structure has been studied mostly from a cognitive viewpoint. Heider's balance theory stimulated interest in the phenomenon that people strive to be internally consistent in their beliefs.
- ◆ The link between attitudes and behaviour has been controversial. The apparently poor predictive power of attitude measures led to a loss of confidence in the concept itself. Fishbein argued that attitudes can indeed predict behaviour. However, if the prediction concerns a specific act the measure of attitude must also be specific.
- ◆ Fishbein and Ajzen's theory of reasoned action included the need for relating a specific act to a measure of the intention to perform that act. Other variables which can affect the predicted behaviour are norms provided by other people and the extent to which the individual has control over the act.
- ◆ A strong attitude, according to Fazio, has a powerful evaluative association with the attitude object. This makes it more accessible in memory and more likely to be activated and the related behaviour performed.
- ◆ Attitudes are learned. They can be formed by means of: direct experience, conditioning, observational learning; and by drawing inferences from one's own behaviour (self-perception).
- ◆ A value is a higher-order concept which can play a guiding and organising role in relation to attitudes. Ideology and social representations are other related concepts.
- ◆ Measuring attitudes is both important and difficult. Traditional techniques include: Thurstone's method of equal-appearing intervals, Likert's method of summated ratings, Guttman's scalogram and Osgood's semantic differential. A more recent method is Fishbein's expectancy-value scale.
- ◆ Physiological and overt behavioural measures are further, indirect attitude measurement techniques.

FURTHER READING

Dawes, R. M. and Smith, T. L. (1985). 'Attitude and opinion measurement' in G.
 Lindzey and E. Aronson (eds), *The Handbook of Social Psychology* (3rd edn).
 New York: Random House.
Eagly, A. H. and Chaiken, S. (1992). *The Psychology of Attitudes*. San Diego, CA:
 Harcourt Brace Jovanovich.
Oppenheim, A. N. (1992). *Questionnaire Design, Interviewing and Attitude
 Measurement*. London: Pinter.
Oskamp, S. (1991). *Attitudes and Opinions* (2nd edn). Sydney: Prentice Hall.

▶ KEY TERMS

acquiescent response set
attitude
attitude formation
automatic activation
balance theory
bogus pipeline technique
cognition
cognitive consistency theories
expectancy-value model
Guttman scale
ideology
information integration theory
information processing
Likert scale
mere exposure effect
modelling

moderator variable
multiple-act criterion
one-component attitude model
self-perception theory
self-rating scale
semantic differential
social representations
socio-cognitive model
theory of planned behaviour
theory of reasoned action
three component attitude model
Thurstone scale
two-component attitude model
unidimensionality
unobtrusive measures
value

5 Changing attitudes

....

FOCUS QUESTIONS

♦ Someone offers you £500 for your prized racing bike, which you think is a fair price. After checking their bank balance, the offer is reduced to £450, saying that's all they can afford. Could such a tactic work?

♦ You have just joined the army. Along with the other cadets you listen to an amazing talk by an officer skilled in the use of survival techniques in difficult combat conditions. Among other things, he asks you to eat some fried grasshoppers. 'Try to imagine this is the real thing! You know, you might have to do this to save your life one day,' he says. Despite your first reaction, you go ahead and eat them. Would you end up liking the delicacy more if the officer's style of presentation was warm and friendly or cold and distant?

ATTITUDES, ARGUMENTS AND BEHAVIOUR

▶ Attitude change

We noted in the previous chapter that a good deal of concern has been expressed by many researchers about the link between attitudes and behaviour, a relationship which at times seems so tenuous that some have even suggested that the concept of attitude should be abandoned. In this chapter, we attend to the way in which attitudes can change over time, concentrating our attention in particular on what kinds of intervention might bring about such change and the nature of the processes involved. By the time we have finished, we trust you might conclude that much of this criticism is misdirected. In particular, it will be argued that discrepancies between attitudes and behaviour, rather than being an embarrassment for attitude theory, provide a crucial way for *attitude change* to occur. Given the many hundreds of studies which have dealt with the topic of changing attitudes and the variety of perspectives that have been used in interpreting the findings, this chapter concentrates on two general approaches which have guided the development of explanation.

The first is an orientation which concentrates on using arguments to convince the recipient that a change of mind, and hopefully of behaviour, is in order. Research in this area has concentrated on the nature of the message, that is, the persuasive communication which will be effective. It picks up on a large number of variables that can determine what will do the trick in trying to change another person's mind. Obvious areas of application relate to political propaganda and advertising. Not surprisingly, these contexts have provided compelling needs for both basic and applied research to be done and have stimulated many studies over several decades.

▶ Cognitive dissonance

The second orientation focuses on the active participation of the person. By engaging people in carrying out certain activities we may have in mind to change underlying attitudes. A special field of research which has concentrated heavily on this issue is *cognitive dissonance*, one of the consistency theories of attitude referred to in Chapter 4. Whereas the first orientation starts from the premise that you reason with someone else to change how they think and act, the second orientation goes straight for the jugular. Find a way to persuade someone to act differently, even if you have to trick them; later they may come to think differently, and then should continue to act in the way that you want.

PERSUASIVE COMMUNICATIONS

▶ Persuasive
communication

Research dealing with the relationship between a *persuasive communication* and attitude change is most closely associated with advertising. According to Schwerin and Newell (1981, p. 7), behavioural change 'obviously cannot occur without [attitude change] having taken place.' For a long time, social psychologists have been interested in the nature of successful versus unsuccessful persuasion. Yet, despite the large role that persuasive messages play in determining human social behaviour, only in the last thirty or so years have social scientists studied what makes a persuasive message effective.

Systematic investigation began towards the end of the Second World War. Carl Hovland was employed by the United States War Department to investigate problems in the extensive use of wartime propaganda. After the war, he continued this work at Yale University in what was the first co-ordinated research programme dealing with the social psychology of persuasion. Research funding was again politically motivated. This time it was the United States' concern at the perceived threat posed by the Soviet Union during the Cold War and the 'wish to justify its ways to the classes and win the hearts and minds of the masses' (McGuire 1986, p. 99). The main features of this pioneering work were outlined in the research team's book *Communication and Persuasion* (Hovland et al. 1953). They suggested that the key to understanding why people would attend to, understand, remember and accept a persuasive message was to study the characteristics of the person presenting the message, the contents of the message and the characteristics of the receiver of the message. The general model of the Yale approach is shown in Figure 5.1.

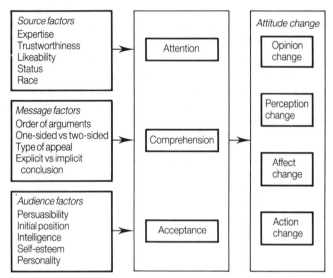

FIGURE 5.1 *The Yale approach to communication and persuasion. (Source: Fishbein and Ajzen 1975, after Janis and Hovland 1959.)*

They asked, 'who says what to whom with what effect?', and studied four variables:

▶ Source
▶ Message
▶ Audience

1. The communicator, or the *source* (who).
2. The communication, or *message* (what).
3. The *audience* (to whom).
4. The *context* within which persuasion takes place.

Hovland and his colleagues identified four distinct steps in the persuasion process: attention, comprehension, acceptance and retention. This research programme spanned nearly three decades and produced an enormous amount of data. Box 5.1 is a summary of the main findings:

Not all the findings based on the early Yale research programme have lasted. Baumeister and Covington (1985) found that people with high self-esteem are just as easily persuaded as those with low self-esteem, but they do not want to admit it. When persuasion does occur, people may even deny it. Bem and McConnell (1970) found that when people do succumb to persuasion, they conveniently fail to recall their original opinion.

Most contemporary social psychologists see the persuasion process as a series of steps. They do not always agree about what the important steps in this sequence are, but do agree that the audience has at least to pay attention to the communicators' message, understand the contents, and think about what was said (Eagly and Chaiken 1984). The audience's thoughts are critical in this process (Petty and Cacioppo 1981): the message will ultimately be accepted if

BOX 5.1 Characteristics of a communication likely to induce attitude to change

Finding	Factor
Experts are more persuasive than non-experts (Hovland and Weiss 1952). The same arguments carry more weight when delivered by someone who presumably knows all the facts.	Communicator
Popular and attractive communicators are more effective than unpopular and unattractive ones (Kiesler and Kiesler 1969).	Communicator
People who speak rapidly are more persuasive than people who speak slowly (Miller *et al.* 1976). One reason is that rapid speech conveys the impression the speaker knows what they are talking about.	Communicator
We are more easily persuaded if we think the message is not deliberately intended to persuade or manipulate us (Walster and Festinger 1962).	Message
Persuasion can be enhanced by messages that arouse fear in the audience (Leventhal *et al.* 1965). To persuade people to stop smoking, for instance, it may be useful to create a fear of dying from lung cancer by showing a cancerous lung to smokers.	Message
People with low self-esteem are persuaded more easily than people with high self-esteem (Janis 1954).	Audience
People are sometimes more susceptible to persuasion when they are distracted than when paying full attention, at least when the message is simple (Allyn and Festinger 1961).	Audience
When persuasion is difficult, i.e. when the audience is hostile, it is more effective to present both sides of the issues than just one side (Hovland *et al.* 1949).	Message and audience

it activates ideas favourable to it, whereas the communication will be rejected if the recipients argue strongly against it in their minds.

In the next three sections we look at each of the three links in the persuasion chain: the communicator, the message and the audience. It must be stressed however, that in any given context all three are operative. Some of the studies noted below do indeed study more than one of these three variables at a time, and often they interact – for example, we will note that whether an argument should present a one-sided or a two-sided case can depend on how intelligent the audience is considered to be.

The communicator

The Yale communication programme showed early on that there is a group of variables relating to characteristics of the source which can have significant effects on the acceptability of a message to an audience. A good level of expertise, good physical looks, and extensive interpersonal and verbal skills make a communicator more effective. Triandis (1971) has argued that a communicator who is an expert has knowledge, ability and skill; in turn, this increases our respect for that person. Further, there are people with whom we are familiar, or with whom we feel close, and to whom we are attracted. Such people are able to exert more influence on us than others. Again, there are others who have power and can therefore exert some control over the kinds of reinforcements we might receive. In all cases, such sources of influence are likely to have the best chance of persuading us to change our attitudes and behaviour.

Source credibility

This communicator variable has been found to have an important bearing on the acceptability of persuasive messages. Other source characteristics that affect whether recipients will accept or reject a persuasive message include attractiveness, likeability and similarity. In America, during the 1980s, actor Bill Cosby was used extensively in television commercials advertising everything from home computers to frozen ice-cream, while pop stars Michael Jackson and Tina Turner were used to advertise soft drinks. Recently, in Britain, Joanna Lumley has played a similar role. The logic behind these advertising campaigns is that attractive, popular and likeable spokespersons are persuasive. Attitude research generally supports this logic (Chaiken 1979, 1983). With regard to similarity, since people tend to like those who are similar to them, sources who are similar to a recipient should be more persuasive than sources who are dissimilar. However, it is not quite this simple (Petty and Cacioppo 1981). When the issue concerns a matter of taste or judgement (for example, who was Italy's greatest soccer player of all time?), similar sources are more accepted than are dissimilar sources, but when the issue concerns a matter of fact (for example, which European country won the greatest number of gold medals at the Barcelona Olympics?), dissimilar sources are more accepted (Goethals and Nelson 1973).

We have already noted that no one communication variable can be treated in total isolation, and that what 'works' in the persuasion process is an interaction of three categories of variables ('communication language' terms are given in parentheses):

1. The *source* (sender) – from whom does the communication come?

2. The *message* (signal) – what medium is used, and what kinds of argument are involved?
3. The *audience* (receiver) – who is the target?

Many experiments have focused on a single variable; others have two variables, one from each of two categories.

An example of the latter kind was a study by Bochner and Insko (1966) which dealt with source credibility in combination with the discrepancy between the opinion of the target and that of the source. With respect to credibility, Bochner and Insko expected that an audience should pay more attention to the opinion of the communicator who is more believable. They predicted that there is more room for attitude change when the target's opinion is more discrepant from that of the source.

The subjects were students who were initially asked how much sleep is required to maintain one's health. Most said eight hours. They were then exposed to two sources of opinion who varied in expertise. One was a Nobel Prize winning physiologist with expertise in sleep research (higher credibility) and the other a YMCA instructor (lower credibility). Discrepancy was manipulated in terms of the amount of variation between student opinion and that of the source. If the source said that five hours was enough, the discrepancy was three hours with respect to the typical view of eight hours – the pressure to shift should be higher than if the discrepancy was only one hour. However, what would happen if the source said two hours was sufficient? Look at the results in Figure 5.2. In terms of the discrepancy variable, more opinion

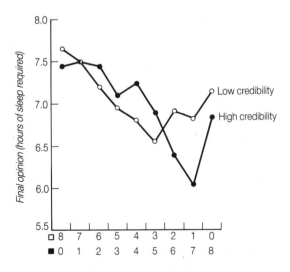

FIGURE 5.2 *The effect of communicator credibility and position discrepancy on opinion change. (Source: based on data from Bochner and Insko 1966.)*

change occurred at moderate levels of difference between the students and the source. It seems that extreme discrepancy is not a good tactic in influencing a target. The audience will resist if the difference is too great, and may look for ways of discrediting the communicator – 'They don't know what they are talking about.' However, this effect interacted with the variable of credibility. It was the expert who could induce the greatest amount of change, and this took place when discrepancy was marked. In Bochner and Insko's study the change was maximal when the highly credible source advocated one hour of sleep and students had suggested eight hours, a discrepancy of seven hours.

The message

Several message variables have been intensively investigated for their relative power in inducing attitude change. When, for example, would we choose to present both sides of an argument rather than just our own? This variable seems to react quite strongly with characteristics of the audience. If the audience is against the argument but also rated as fairly intelligent it is more effective to present both sides. It is better to present only one side, however, if the audience is already on one side and rather less intelligent (Lumsdaine and Janis 1953; McGinnies 1966). Examples of variables that have been studied are shown in Box 5.1.

Effects of repetition

In the advertising industry, it is a maxim that a message needs to be repeated often in order to be understood and to be recalled. It would be tempting to infer that advertising agencies wish to increase their profits by recommending to their client that frequent exposure of a message increases effectiveness. If we believe the advertising industry, however, this is not a major motive. According to Ray (1988), the main goal is to strive for repetition minimisation, that is, to have the maximum impact with the minimum exposures and therefore the most cost-effective expenditure. It seems that television advertising exposure reinforces preferences more than it motivates brand choices; and that the optimum rate is two to three times per week (Tellis 1987).

▶ Information processing
▶ Mere exposure effect

In general, the issue of message repetition invites a look at the topic of *information processing* and at how memory works. We shall see below that two recent models of attitude change which examine the process of message reception adopt a cognitive approach of this kind. Somewhat more startling is a finding by Arkes *et al.* (1991) that simple repetition of a statement makes it seem to be more true. According to the *mere exposure effect*, repeated exposure to an object clearly increases familiarity with that object. Repetition of a name can make that name seem famous (Jacoby *et al.* 1989), while an increase in familiarity with people can increase interpersonal liking (see Chapter 12).

Another variable which has received intensive study, because of the way in which it has been used by the media to induce people to obey the law or care for their health, is the use of fear.

Fear-arousing messages

Fear-arousing messages may enhance persuasion – but how fearful can a message become and still be effective? Many agencies in our community persist with forms of advertising which are intended to frighten us into complying with their advice or admonitions. Health workers may visit the local school to give the children a talk about how 'smoking is dangerous to your health'. To drive the point home they might show the children pictures of a diseased lung. Television advertising may remind you that 'if you drink, don't drive', and perhaps try to reinforce this message with graphic scenes of carnage on the roads. Does this work? The answer is a mixed one.

In an early study by Janis and Feshbach (1953), subjects were encouraged to take better care of their teeth in three different contexts. In a low-fear condition, they were told of the painful outcomes of diseased teeth and gums, and suggestions were made about how to maintain good oral health. In a moderate-fear condition, the warning about oral disease was more explicit. In a high-fear condition they were told that the disease could spread to other parts of their body and very unpleasant slides were presented showing decayed teeth and diseased gums. The subjects reported on their current dental habits and were followed up again after one week. Janis and Feshbach found an inverse relationship between degree of (presumed) fear arousal and change in dental hygiene practices. The low-fear subjects were taking the best care of their teeth after one week, followed by the moderate-fear group and then by the high-fear group.

A contradictory result was reported by Leventhal *et al.* (1967) in a study of how a fearful communication might aid in persuading people to stop smoking. The subjects were volunteers who wished to give up their habit. In a moderate-fear condition the subjects listened to a talk with charts used as illustrations to show the link between death from lung cancer and the rate at which cigarettes were used. In a high-fear condition they also saw a graphic film about an operation on a patient affected by lung cancer. Their results pointed to a greater willingness to stop smoking among people in the high-fear condition.

How do we explain the discrepancy between these results? Both Janis (1967) and McGuire (1969) suggested that an inverted-U curve hypothesis might be applied to conflicting results (see Figure 5.3). McGuire's analysis distinguishes two parameters which could control the way we respond to a persuasive message, one involving comprehension and the other involving the degree to which we yield to change. The more we can understand what is being presented to us, and can conceive of ways to implement advice, the more likely we are to go along with a particular message. In the case of the role of fear as a variable, when it is at a very low level an audience may be little motivated to attend to the message. As the fear content increases, so does arousal, interest and attention to what is going on. However, a very frightening way of

Note: The amount of attitude change increases as a function of fear up to a medium level of arousal. At high levels of fear, however, there is a fall-off in attitude change. This could be due to lack of attention to the stimulus, or to the disruptive effects of intense emotion, or to both.

FIGURE 5.3 *The inverted-U curve relationship between fear and attitude change.*

presenting an idea may arouse so much anxiety, even to a state of panic, that we become distracted and miss some of the factual content of the message. What we do not know is whether the high-fear condition in the Janis and Feshbach study aroused more fear than the one in Leventhal *et al.* study. If it did, then a curvilinear fit might be appropriate for the data.

Facts versus feelings

We noted in Chapter 4 that a distinction is commonly drawn between belief and affect as components of an attitude. In the advertising industry, a related distinction is sometimes made between *factual* and *evaluative* advertising. The former deals with claims of fact and is thought to be objective, whereas the latter reflects opinion and is subjective. A factually oriented advertisement is high on information and is likely to emphasise one or more attributes among the following: price, quality, performance, components or contents, availability, special offer, taste, packaging, guarantees or warranties, safety, nutrition, independent research, company-sponsored research, or new ideas. However, the simple recall of facts from an advertisement does not guarantee a change in brand purchased. Furthermore, if there is factual content in a message, it is important for people to be able to assimilate the general conclusion of the message (Albion and Faris 1979; Beattie and Mitchell 1985).

We noted in Chapter 4 that even if a distinction is made between beliefs and feelings, evaluating an object (say, judging whether it is good or bad) is not identical to experiencing affect, or an emotion. From this point of view, we can repeat the argument that attitudes are fundamentally evaluations, which is where Thurstone (1928) started out. Applying this to an advertising context means that an evaluation refers to couching a message in such a way that it makes the consumer feel generally 'good' about the product, rather than attempting to convey a set of facts or objective claims. A common method in evaluative advertising is to capitalise on the *transfer of affect*, which itself is based on associative learning. The tenor of evaluative advertising is caught in the following:

> Corporations pour millions of dollars into advertising aimed at convincing
> us that the lithest young women and the most athletic young men on the
> beach drink Coke (or Pepsi), the men who have the most fun in bars after
> work drink Bud (or Miller), and the fastest and smoothest cars, with the
> most beautiful drivers, are Pontiacs (or BMWs). (Sears *et al.* 1991, p. 172)

The distinction between facts and feelings does not imply that a given
advertisement contains only factual or only evaluative material. On the
contrary, modern marketing strategy favours using both approaches in any one
advertisement. A consumer can be led to *feel* that one product is superior to
another by subtle associations with music or colour, or through the use of
attractive models, and so forth. The same consumer can be led to *believe* that
the product is a better bet because it is of better value for money.

The medium and the message

Chaiken and Eagly (1983) have compared the relative effects on an audience of
presenting messages in video, audio and written forms. This has obvious
implications for advertising: which has more impact on the consumer –
television, radio or printed media? It depends. If the message is simple, as
much advertising is, the probable answer is: video more than audio more than
written. A mediating variable in this context is the relative ease or difficulty of
comprehension required in the audience. If the points of a message require
considerable processing by the target person, a written medium is likely to be
best. Readers have the chance to go back at will, mull over what is being said,
and then read on. If the material is quite complex, newspapers and magazines

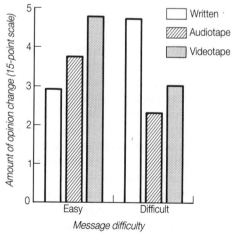

FIGURE 5.4 *The effects of source modality and message difficulty on opinion
change. (Source: based on Chaiken and Eagly 1983.)*

can come into their own. There is, however, an interesting interaction with the difficulty of the message. Look at the difference in effectiveness between various media in Figure 5.4. When the message was easy to comprehend, Chaiken and Eagly found that a videotaped presentation brought about the greatest degree of opinion change. When the message was difficult, however, opinion change was greatest when the material was written.

The audience

Hovland and his co-workers had noted that an audience can be more easily persuaded when it is distracted than when paying full attention, provided the message is simple; and that those low in self-esteem are more susceptible than people who are high on this attribute (see Box 5.1). McGuire (1968) suggested that the relationship between persuadability and self-esteem is actually curvilinear, that is, it follows an inverted-U curve of the kind shown in Figure 5.3 (substituting 'self-esteem' for 'fear'). Such a relationship suggests that people who are low or high on a measure of self-esteem are less persuasible than those in the middle range of self-esteem. He reasoned that those with low self-esteem would either be less attentive or else anxious when processing a message, whereas those high on self-esteem would be less susceptible to influence, presumably because they are more self-assured. (McGuire also proposed a similar curvilinear relationship between intelligence and persuasibility.) With respect to the self-esteem connection, a recent review by Rhodes and Wood (1992) tested McGuire's proposition and concluded that the evidence overall supports his view.

Another consistent but more controversial finding is that women are more persuasible than men (Cooper 1979; Eagly 1978). This effect was first reported by Crutchfield (1955) who found that women were more conforming and susceptible to social influence than males. Some researchers have proposed that this difference exists because females are socialised to be co-operative and non-assertive and are therefore less resistant than males to attempts to influence them (Eagly *et al.* 1981). However, Sistrunk and McDavid (1971) suggested another explanation, namely that women were more easily influenced than men only when the subject discussed was one with which men were more familiar. When the topic was female-oriented, men were more influenced than were women (see also Chapters 6 and 9). This finding led to the proposition that the consistent difference found in persuasibility had been due to a methodological bias. The persuasive messages used in attitude research had typically dealt with male-oriented topics, and the researchers were usually male. If the topics had not been sex-biased, the male/female differences would not have been found. Since the more recent studies are more sophisticated in both design and execution (for example, Eagly and Carli 1981), the conclusion they support is now widely accepted.

We consider now how the persuasion process works.

Message learning: two models of persuasion

Recent attitude research has focused on how the content of a message is understood. Although different approaches have been taken by Petty and Cacioppo (1986) and by Chaiken (1980, 1987; Chaiken *et al.* 1989), there are elements in common. The models considered below each draw on developments in research on memory from the field of cognitive psychology.

Elaboration-likelihood model

▶ Elaboration-
likelihood model

In Petty and Cacioppo's *elaboration–likelihood model*, when people receive a persuasive message, they think about the arguments it makes, though not necessarily deeply or carefully, since to do so requires considerable cognitive effort which is likely to be expended only if the issue is recognised as very important. Persuasion follows from either of two different processes, and the one selected depends upon the amount of elaboration or scrutiny required. If the arguments of the message are closely followed, a *central route* is used. We learn the arguments in a message, extract a point which meets our needs, and even indulge mentally in counter-arguments if we disagree with some of them. If the central route to persuasion is going to be used, the points in the message need to be convincingly put since we will be required to expend considerable cognitive effort, that is, to work hard, on them. Suppose, for example, that your doctor told you that you needed a fairly major piece of surgery. The chances are that you will take a fair amount of convincing, that you will listen carefully to what the doctor says, read what you can about the matter, and even seek a second medical opinion. On the other hand, when arguments are not well attended to, a *peripheral route* is followed. By using peripheral cues, we act in a less diligent fashion, preferring a consumer product on a superficial basis, such as an advertisement in which it is used by an attractive model. The alternative routes available according to the elaboration-likelihood model are shown in Figure 5.5.

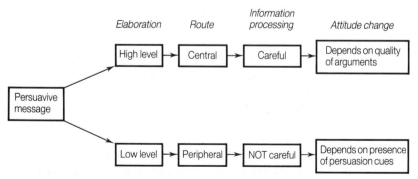

FIGURE 5.5 *The elaboration-likelihood model of persuasion. (Source: based on Petty and Cacioppo 1986.)*

Heuristic-systematic model

▶ Heuristic-
systematic model

In dealing with the same phenomena, Chaiken's *heuristic-systematic model* uses slightly different concepts, distinguishing between *systematic* processing and *heuristic* processing. Systematic processing occurs when people scan and consider the arguments. In the case of heuristic processing, we do not indulge in careful reasoning but instead use cognitive heuristics, or mental short-cuts, such as thinking that longer arguments are stronger. Persuasive messages are not always processed systematically. Chaiken has suggested that people will sometimes employ cognitive heuristics to simplify the task of handling information. You will recall that heuristics are a variety of simple decision rules or mental short-cuts that we use when we act like cognitive misers (see Chapter 2). So, when we are judging the reliability of a message we may resort to such truisms as 'statistics don't lie' or 'you can't trust a politician' as an easy way of making up our minds.

The emphasis on the strong role of cognition in relation to how we handle a persuasive message has been extended to cover the mediating role of transient states in the recipient. Mackie and Worth (1989), for example, have shown that the mere fact of being in a good mood may influence the way in which we attend to information. Being in a good mood makes it difficult to process a message systematically. Under time-limiting conditions, such as might apply in watching a television advertisement, a person already in a good mood appears to be more susceptible to peripheral heuristic processing.

In summary, when people are motivated to attend to a message and to deal with it *thoughtfully*, they use a central route to process it according to the elaboration-likelihood model (Petty and Cacioppo), or process it systematically according to the heuristic-systematic model (Chaiken). When attention is reduced so that people become cognitively *lazy*, they use a peripheral route (Petty and Cacioppo) or resort to heuristics, i.e. simple decision rules (Chaiken).

COMPLIANCE: INTERPERSONAL INFLUENCE

▶ Compliance

Sometimes, the literature dealing with social influence has used the term *compliance* (touched on briefly in Chapter 6) interchangeably with conformity. This can happen when conformity is broadly defined to include a change in behaviour, as well as beliefs, as a consequence of group pressure. In this chapter, compliance refers to a *behavioural* response to a *request by another individual*, while conformity refers to the influence of a group upon an individual.

We are daily confronted with demands and requests. Often they are put to us in a straightforward and clear manner, such as when a friend asks you to dinner, and nothing more is requested. At other times, requests have a 'hidden agenda', for example an acquaintance invites you to dinner to get you into the right mood to ask you to finance a new business venture. The result is often the same – we comply.

What are the factors and situations that make us more compliant, and why is it that we are more influenced on some occasions than on others? According to Penner (1986), people influence us when they use effective tactics or have a powerful attribute.

Tactics for enhancing compliance

To persuade people to comply with a request to buy certain products has been the cornerstone of many economies. It is not surprising, therefore, that over the years many different tactics for enhancing compliance have been worked out. Salespeople, especially, have designed and refined many indirect procedures for inducing compliance, since their livelihood depends on it. We have all come across these tactics.

▶ Ingratiation

One common tactic is *ingratiation*, in which a person attempts to influence others by agreeing with them and getting them to like her. Next, various requests are made. You would be using ingratiation if you: agreed with target people to appear similar, or to make them feel good you made yourself look attractive, gave compliments, dropped names of those held in high esteem, or physically touched target people. Smith *et al.* (1982) found that shoppers, when approached to sample a new food product, were more likely to sample and buy the item when they were touched in a socially acceptable way (though, they did not think the food tasted any better).

▶ Reciprocity principle

Reciprocity is another tactic, based on the social norm that 'we should treat others the way they treat us'. If we do others a favour then they feel obliged to reciprocate. Regan (1971) showed that greater compliance was obtained from people who had previously received a favour than from those who had received none. Similarly, *guilt arousal* also produces more compliance. Experimental studies have shown that when the researcher induces feelings of guilt in a subject, the latter is ready to comply with a later request – for example, participation in future experiments, or making a phone call to save native trees, or agreeing to donate blood (Carlsmith and Gross 1969; Darlington and Macker 1966; Freedman *et al.* 1967). Those who were not made to feel guilty, on the other hand, hardly ever complied.

Another very effective tactic is the *multiple request*. Instead of a single request, a two-step procedure is used, with the first request functioning as a set-up for the second, real request. Three common multiple-request tactics are: the foot-in-the-door, the door-in-the-face and (deriving from American baseball terminology) low-balling (see Figure 5.6).

▶ Foot-in-the-door
 tactic

The *foot-in-the-door tactic* is based on the notion that if you get someone to agree to a small request, the person will later be more willing to comply with a large request. Some telephone salespeople use this approach. At first they

Technique	Stage 1	Stage 2	Stage 3

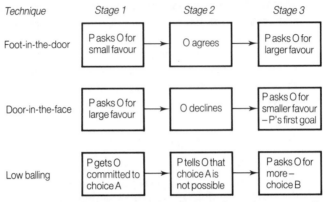

FIGURE 5.6 *Three techniques for inducing compliance.*

A multiple request technique. Foot-in-the-door: an effective technique for gaining compliance with a request. (Source: Andrew Lukey.)

might ask you to answer just a few questions 'for a small survey that they are doing', and then entice you to join 'the hundreds of other people in your area' who subscribe to their product. In a study by Freedman and Fraser (1966), subjects who had previously been contacted to answer a few simple questions about the kind of soap they use in the house were later more willing to comply with the much larger request of having six people come to make a thorough inventory of all the household items present. While only 22 per cent complied when they received the larger request 'cold', nearly 53 per cent complied when they had been softened up by the initial questions about their soap. DeJong (1979) suggested that the foot-in-the-door tactic can be understood in terms of self-perception theory (discussed later in this chapter). By complying with the small request people become committed to their behaviour and acquire a picture of themselves as 'giving' – the subsequent large request compels them to appear consistent.

The foot-in-the-door tactic may not always work. If the initial request appears too small or the second too large, the link between the multiple requests appears to break down (Zuckerman *et al.* 1979; Foss and Dempsey 1979). Nevertheless, a review by Saks (1978) suggested that if the technique is carefully tuned, people can be induced to act as donors for organ and tissue transplants. A refinement which involved students agreeing to a series of graded requests, rather than jumping from a small to large request, proved effective.

▶ Door-in-the-face
tactic

What happens if an attempt to get a foot in the door fails? Common sense suggests that this should reduce the likelihood of future compliance. Surprisingly, the opposite strategy of the *door-in-the-face tactic* can prove successful. Here, a person is asked a large favour first and a small request second. Politicians especially are masters of this art. To illustrate, say that the government warns you that student fees will go up 300 per cent. Would you be angry? Later, however, they officially announce that the increase is 'only' going to be 75 per cent, the actual figure planned. You would probably feel relieved and think 'that's not so bad', and consequently you are more accepting.

Testing this tactic, Cialdini *et al.* (1975) approached students with a huge request: 'would you serve as a voluntary counsellor at a youth offenders centre two hours a week for the next two years?' Virtually no-one agreed. However, when the researchers then asked for a considerably smaller request: 'would you chaperone a group of these offenders on a two-hour trip to the zoo?', 50 per cent agreed. On the other hand, when the second request was presented alone, less than 17 per cent complied. For the tactic to be effective, the researchers noted that the last request should be made by the same person who asked the initial favour. According to them, subjects perceive the scaled-down request as a concession by the influencer, and consequently they feel the pressure to reciprocate. If some other person were to make the second request, reciprocation would not be necessary.

According to Cialdini, the door-in-the-face technique may well capitalise on a contrast effect: just as lukewarm water feels cool after just having had your hand in hot water, a second request seems more reasonable and acceptable when it is contrasted with a larger request. This procedure is prevalent in sales settings. When you have informed a house agent that you would like to spend £20,000 on a small flat and she then shows you a few run-down and over-priced examples, so that the higher-priced flats (she really wants to show you) look like extremely good bargains, she has used the door-in-the-face tactic.

▶ Low-ball tactic

The other multiple request technique used in similar situations is the *low-ball tactic* (check the first focus question). Here, the influencer changes the rules halfway and manages to get away with it. Its effectiveness depends on inducing the customer to agree to a request, before revealing certain hidden costs. It is based on the principle that once people are committed to an action, they are more likely to accept a slight increase in the cost of that action. Suppose you shop around for a car and are confronted with the following chain of events. The car salesperson makes you a very attractive offer – a high trade-in price for your old car – and suggests a reduction on the marked purchase price of the car you have set your mind on. You decide to buy it and are ready to sign the papers. The salesperson then goes off to check the agreement with the boss, comes back, looks very disappointed, and informs you that the boss will not sanction it, since they would lose money on the deal. You can still have the car though, but at the marked price. What would you do? Surprisingly, many customers still go ahead with the deal. It seems that once you are committed, you are hooked and reluctant to back out. A commonplace example of low-balling is when someone asks 'could you do me a favour?', and you say 'yes', before actually knowing what will be expected of you.

The effectiveness of low-balling was demonstrated by Cialdini *et al.* (1978). They asked half of the subjects to be in an experiment that began at 7 a.m. In contrast, the other half were asked first to commit themselves to participating in an experiment, and then were informed that it would start at 7 a.m. The latter group, the low-balling situation, complied more (56 per cent) than the control group (31 per cent), and also tended to keep their appointments.

The above studies have shown us the circumstances in which compliance is likely to occur. In some situations, our decision to comply may be a rational choice, in which we weigh the pros and cons of our action. Often, however, we act before we think. It has been argued that many of our compliant responses are 'mindless', that is, we agree to many requests without even giving them a thought (Langer *et al.* 1978). Langer and her colleagues conducted experiments in which people were asked to comply with requests with little or no justification. In one of these experiments, a person about to use a photocopy machine was interrupted by an experimenter who requested to have first use of the copier, either (1) for no reason; (2) for a non-informative reason ('I have to make copies'); or (3) for a justifiable reason ('I'm in a rush'). Their findings indicated that as long as the request was a small one, people were likely to agree to it, even if a spurious reason had been provided. In contrast, they found that less compliance occurred when no reason at all was given.

▶ Mindlessness

Notwithstanding the fact that *mindlessness* may be a deciding factor in compliant behaviour, studies of power strategies indicate that this compliance frequently depends on the sources of power used.

Action research

At about the time that Hovland and his associates were studying attitude change in the American army, the German psychologist Kurt Lewin was undertaking another piece of practical wartime research on the home front for a civilian government agency. With the aim of conserving supplies in a time of food shortages and rationing, he tried to convince American housewives to feed their families unusual but highly nutritious foods such as beef hearts and kidneys rather than steak or roast beef.

▶ Action research

Lewin considered that attitude change could best be achieved if the recipients were somehow actively engaged in the change process rather than just being passive recipients. He referred to this involvement of the participants in the actual research process and its outcome as *action research*. Lewin demonstrated that an active discussion between 'housewives' about how best to present beef hearts and other similar foods to their families was much more effective than merely giving them a persuasive lecture presentation. His data showed that 32 per cent of the women in the first condition proceeded to serve the new food, compared with only 3 per cent in the second condition (Lewin 1943).

The emphasis on action by participants is not incompatible with the more passive approach to attitude change which characterised the work of Hovland and his associates. For instance, Janis and King (1954) investigated the effects of role-playing by their subjects. They found that those who gave a speech arguing against something that they believed in (that is, the subjects acted out a role) experienced more attitude change than when they listened passively to a speech arguing against their position. This early study of counter-attitudinal behaviour foreshadowed research on cognitive dissonance, discussed in the next section. One of Lewin's students was Festinger, who believed that humans are active processors and organisers of the information they receive from the world around them and of the cognitions (attitudes, beliefs, ideas, opinions) they have about the world. He accepted the consistency principle, and argued that people will even change their ideas to make them consistent with what they are feeling or with how they are acting (Festinger, 1980). This would be the basis of the theory of cognitive dissonance.

ATTITUDE/BEHAVIOUR DISCREPANCY AND COGNITIVE DISSONANCE

Cognitive dissonance is a prime example of the cognitive approach in social psychology, putting the emphasis on beliefs as a central component of an attitude. As we shall see, however, it also addressed the problem of attitude/behaviour discrepancy. It was developed by Festinger (1957) and became the most studied topic in social psychology during the 1960s. In essence, it states that cognitive dissonance is an unpleasant state of psychological tension generated when a person has two or more cognitions (bits of information) that are inconsistent or do not fit together. Cognitions are thoughts, attitudes, beliefs or states of awareness of behaviour. Festinger proposed that we seek harmony in our attitudes, beliefs and behaviours, and try to reduce tension from inconsistency among these elements. The theory holds that people will try to reduce dissonance by changing one or more of the inconsistent cognitions, by looking for additional evidence to bolster one side or the other, or by derogating the source of one of the cognitions. The greater the dissonance, the stronger the attempts to reduce it. When people are in a state of dissonance they become physically aroused. Changes in the electrical conductivity of the skin, typically associated with arousal, occur during dissonance.

▶ Selective exposure hypothesis

For dissonance to arise and consequently for attitudes to change, it is of course necessary that circumstances place one set of attitudes in contradiction to another set of attitudes (see Box 5.2). However, because dissonance is an unpleasant state of affairs, people often try to avert it in the first place, by avoiding exposure to information that might arouse dissonance. The *selective exposure hypothesis* states that people are remarkably selective in avoiding potentially dissonant information except when (1) their attitude or cognitive system is very strong and therefore they can integrate or argue against dissonant information, or (2) their attitude or cognitive system is very weak and therefore it seems better in the long run to discover the truth now in order to make appropriate attitudinal and behavioural changes (Frey 1986; Frey and

---

BOX 5.2 The impact of student exchange on national stereotypes

Student exchanges provide a wonderful opportunity for people to confront stereotypic attitudes about foreign nations with new information gleaned from personal experience as a sojourner in a foreign country. From a cognitive dissonance perspective one would expect (or hope) that pleasant personal experiences would conflict with ingrained negative attitudes towards a foreign nation, and would arouse cognitive dissonance which, under the circumstances, could only be resolved by changing the initial attitude. This idea is illustrated by a study by Stroebel *et al.* (1988) of American students on one-year exchanges in Germany and France. They found that in the case of sojourners in Germany, reality matched existing attitudes and consequently there was no dissonance and no attitude change over the year. Sojourners in France, however, found that realities were less pleasant than pre-existing attitudes led them to believe. There was dissonance, and consequently they departed from France with changed attitudes – unfortunately changed for the worse. These findings are consistent with other research into sojourner's attitudes (for example Klineberg and Hull 1979), and they foreshadow the complexity of studying the way in which stereotypes may change as a consequence of direct contact with an outgroup (see Chapter 10).

Rosch 1984). Potentially dissonant information can also be avoided when attitudinal change is likely to be very difficult. For example, Frey and Rosch (1984) gave subjects written profiles on the basis of which they had to form an attitude about whether to terminate or continue a 'manager'. Half the subjects were told that their attitude was reversible (they could change their mind later on) and half that their attitude was irreversible. They were then given the opportunity to select as many bits of additional information as they wished from a pool containing five items of consonant information (that is, information in support of their attitudinal position) and five items of dissonant information (in opposition to their position). As Figure 5.7 shows, subjects tended to choose more consonant than dissonant information, and the effect was greatly magnified in the irreversible condition.

One great virtue of cognitive dissonance theory is that it is stated in a broad and general way, which makes it applicable to many different situations in social psychology, particularly ones involving attitude or behaviour change. The following are just a few of the situations to which it has been applied:

1. People's feelings of regret and changes of attitude after making a decision.
2. People's patterns of exposing themselves to and searching for new information.
3. Reasons that people seek social support for their beliefs.
4. Attitude change in situations where a person has said or done something contrary to their customary beliefs or practice.

In Chapter 4 we noted that cognitive dissonance theory is often grouped with balance theory as one of a family of models which stress the human propensity for maintaining consistency in thought and action. However, a feature of dissonance theory which makes it unique is its ability to generate non-obvious predictions (Insko 1967). This arises from the manner in which the theory treats the way we make choices and decisions in conflict situations,

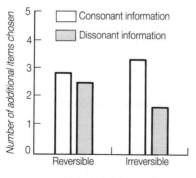

FIGURE 5.7 *Selection of consonant and dissonant information as a function of attitudinal irreversibility. (Source: based on data from Frey and Rosch 1984.)*

as will become clearer in the sections that follow. Three research paradigms can be distinguished in the many studies over the years since Festinger's original work (Worchel *et al.* 1988): effort justification, induced compliance and free choice.

Effort justification

▶ Effort justification

The moment we choose between two alternatives we bring about a state of dissonance. Suppose you need some fast food tonight. You make the momentous decision to go to the hamburger bar rather than to the fried chicken outlet. The two alternatives will be mulled over, even after making your choice. The thought of that hamburger is getting better already. In terms of dissonance theory, the chosen alternative will be evaluated more favourably, or perhaps the other one will become less attractive, or both – at least for tonight. The way the *effort justification* paradigm works is shown in Figure 5.8.

The notion of effort justification was explored in an early study by Aronson and Mills (1959). Female students volunteered to take part in a group discussion about sex, but were told that before they could join a group they first must pass a screening test for their capacity to speak openly. Those who agreed were assigned to one of two conditions. In a severe condition they were given a list of obscene words and explicit sexual descriptions to read aloud; in a mild condition they were to read words which included some such as 'petting' and 'prostitution'. After being initiated they then listened over headphones to a discussion held by a group, with a view to joining in during the following week. What they heard was quite tame, far short of the embarrassing material they had been led to expect. The discussion was in fact a tape recording in which the participants had been primed to mumble, be incoherent, and generally as boring as possible. As well as the severe and mild initiation conditions, there was also a control condition in which the subjects did not undergo the screening experience.

The hypothesis is that the severe condition should have caused some suffering to the subjects, and yet they had volunteered to participate in it. The act of volunteering to be embarrassed should cause dissonance. The predicted outcome is an increase in liking the thing for which you have suffered, namely to participate in the discussion group. To make this sequence consonant would require the subject to rate the group discussion as more interesting than it really was.

Aronson and Mills found that the subjects who had experienced the severe

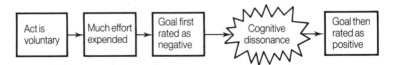

FIGURE 5.8 *The general model of the effort justification paradigm.*

initiation rated both the group discussion and the participants as much more interesting than those in the mild or control conditions. The results are shown in Figure 5.9.

Later studies have demonstrated that the effort justification effect can be particularly useful in inducing important behavioural changes relating to phobias and alcohol abuse. An interesting example assisting volunteers in a weight reduction programme was provided by Cooper and Axom (1982). The subjects were women who felt they needed assistance to lose body weight and were willing to try out a 'new experimental procedure'. To participate, all subjects were required to come to a laboratory where they were weighed and the procedure to be followed was explained to them. In a high-effort condition, some women were told they needed to participate in a variety of time-consuming, high-effort tasks, including the reading out loud of tongue twisters for a session period lasting forty minutes. It was reasoned by the investigators that the tasks used were based on psychological effort, that is no physical exercise was involved. In a low-effort condition the tasks were shorter and easier, and in a control condition the volunteers did not participate in any tasks at all but were simply weighed and asked to report again at a certain date. The subjects in the two experimental groups came to the laboratory for a total of five sessions over a period of three weeks, at which point all of the women were weighed again. The results are shown in Figure 5.10.

Cooper and Axom were encouraged to find that the weight loss effect in the high-effort group was not just an artefact of the interest shown in the women during the time of the five-week study. Without prior knowledge, the

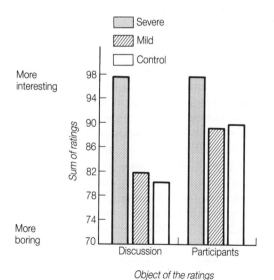

Object of the ratings

FIGURE 5.9 *Interest in a group discussion in relation to the severity of the initiation procedure. (Source: based on data from Aronson and Mills 1959.)*

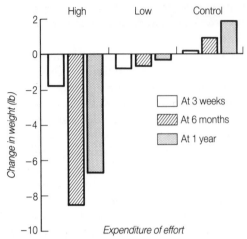

FIGURE 5.10 *Change in weight among overweight women after expending psychological effort. (Source: based on data from Cooper and Axom 1982.)*

participants were contacted again after six months and a year and agreed to be weighed again. The weight loss was much more marked after time had elapsed. After six months, a remarkable 94 per cent of the high-effort subjects had lost some weight while only 39 per cent of the low-effort subjects had managed to do so.

Induced compliance

▶ Induced compliance

Sometimes people are induced to act in a way which is inconsistent with their beliefs. An important aspect of the *induced compliance* paradigm is that the inducement should not be perceived in terms of being forced against one's will.

Festinger and Carlsmith (1959) carried out an often-quoted experiment in which students who had volunteered to participate in a psychology experiment were asked to perform an extremely boring task for an hour, believing that they were contributing to research on 'measures of performance'. Imagine that you are the volunteer and that in front of you is a board on which there are several rows of square pegs, each one sitting in a square hole. You are asked to turn each peg a quarter of a turn to the left and then a quarter of a turn back to the right. When you have finished turning all the pegs, you are instructed to start all over again, repeating the sequence over and over for twenty minutes. This was not designed to be fun. When the twenty minutes are up, the experimenter tells you that you have finished the first part and you can now start on the second part, this time taking spools of thread off another peg board and placing them all back on again, and again, and again. Finally the mind-numbing jobs are over. At this point the experimenter lets you in on a secret: you were a control subject, but you can now be of 'real' help. It seems that a confederate of the experimenter has failed to show up. Could you fill in? All you have to do is tell the next subject that the tasks are really very interesting. The experimenter explains that he was interested in the effects of preconceptions on people's work on a task. Later, the experimenter offers a monetary incentive if you would be willing to be on call to help again at some time in the future. Luckily, you are never called.

In the Festinger and Carlsmith study, subjects in one condition were paid the princely sum of $1 for agreeing to co-operate in this way, while others in a second condition were paid $20 for agreeing to help. The experimental design also included a control group of subjects who were not asked to tell anyone how interesting the truly boring experience had been, and were paid no incentive. On a later occasion, all subjects were asked to rate how interesting or otherwise this task had been.

According to the induced compliance paradigm, dissonance follows from the fact you have agreed to say things about what you have experienced when you know that the opposite is true. You have been induced to behave in a counter-attitudinal way. The variation in levels of incentive add an interesting twist. Subjects who had been paid $20 could explain their lie to themselves with the thought, 'I did it for the $20. It must have been a lousy task, indeed'. In other words, dissonance would probably not exist in this condition. (We should note that $20 was a sum of money not to be sneezed at by a student in the late 1950s.) On the other hand, the subjects who told the lie and had been paid only $1 were confronted with a dilemma: 'I have done a really boring task, then told someone else that it is interesting, and finally even agreed to come back and do this again for a measly $1.' Herein lies the dissonance. One way of

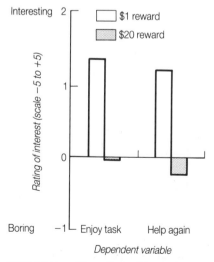

FIGURE 5.11 *The effect of incentives on evaluating a boring task in an induced compliance context. (Source: based on data from Festinger and Carlsmith 1959.)*

reducing the continuing arousal is to convince oneself that the experiment was really quite interesting after all. The results of this now–classic study are shown in Figure 5.11.

The interest ratings of the two reward groups confirmed the main predictions. The $1 subjects rated the task as fairly interesting, whereas the $20 subjects found it slightly boring (while control subjects found it even more so). The $1 subjects were also more willing to participate in similar experiments in the future. The main thrust of this experiment, which is to use a smaller reward to bring about a larger attitude change, has been replicated several times. To modify an old saying: 'if you are going to lead a donkey on, use a carrot, but make it a small one if you want the donkey to enjoy the trip'.

▶ Post-decisional conflict

Talking of carrots, what about the 'fried grasshoppers' focus question? An intriguing experiment carried out in a military setting by Zimbardo and his colleagues (Zimbardo *et al.* 1965) addressed this poser. The subjects were asked to comply with the aversive request of eating grasshoppers by an authority figure whose interpersonal style was either positive (warm) or negative (cold). According to the induced compliance variation of cognitive dissonance, *post-decisional conflict* (and consequent attitude change) should be greater when the communicator is negative – how else could one justify behaving voluntarily in a counter-attitudinal way? Read what happened in the Zimbardo *et al.* study reported in Box 5.3 and check the results in Figure 5.12.

Free choice

Suppose that your choices between alternative courses of action were fairly evenly balanced, and that you were committed to make some kind of decision.

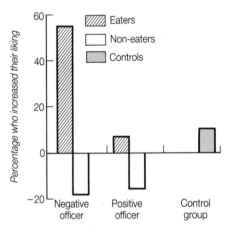

FIGURE 5.12 *Degree of liking fried grasshoppers as food by military cadets in relation to the interpersonal style of an officer. (Source: based on data from Zimbardo, et al. 1965.)*

BOX 5.3 An example of attitude change following induced compliance.

To know grasshoppers is to love them

Think back to the focus question. This issue has actually been researched in a famous study involving young military cadets (Zimbardo *et al.* 1965). Following a procedure established by Smith in 1961 (cited in Zimbardo *et al.* 1977), an officer in command suggested that the cadets might eat a few fried grasshoppers, and mild social pressure was put on them to comply. By administering a questionnaire about food habits earlier, it had been ascertained that all of the cadets thought there were some limits to what they should be expected to eat, and that a meal of fried grasshoppers was one such limit. The officer, however, proceeded to give a talk suggesting that soldiers in a modern army needed to be mobile in combat conditions and, among other things, should be ready to eat off the land. After finishing the talk, the cadets were each given a plate with five fried grasshoppers, and invited to try them out.

A critical feature of the experiment was the way in which the request was put. For half of the cadets the officer was cheerful, informal and permissive. For the other half, however, he was cool, official and stiff. There was also a control group who gave two sets of food ratings but were never induced to, or had the chance to eat grasshoppers. The social pressure on the experimental subjects had to be subtle enough so that they felt they had *freely chosen* whether to eat the grasshoppers. To be ordered to eat would not arouse dissonance because a subject could then justify his compliance by saying 'he made me do it'. The subjects with the positive officer might justify compliance to themselves by thinking 'I did it as a favour to this nice guy'. Those, however, who might eat the grasshoppers for the negative officer could not justify their behaviour in this way. The resulting experience should be dissonance, and the easy way to reduce this would be to change their evaluation of grasshoppers as a source of food.

In all, about 50 per cent of the cadets actually ate some grasshoppers. Those who complied ate, on average, two of the five hoppers sitting on their plate. The results in Figure 5.12 show the percentage of subjects who changed their ratings of liking or disliking grasshoppers as food. It is interesting to note that in both the negative and positive officer conditions, eaters were more favourable and non-eaters less favourable. This suggests that a degree of self-justification was required to account for an act which was voluntary but aversive. The most interesting result, however, concerned the negative officer condition. This is the case in which dissonance should be maximal and, in line with the theory, it was here that the biggest change towards liking the little beasties was recorded.

(Source: after Zimbardo *et al.* 1965.)

Reducing dissonance after free choice. 'I'm really pleased with my new car – I hope!' Dissonance reduction can ensure that someone feels even more positive about a product after freely parting with money for it. The situation depicted may represent free choice; it may also represent effort justification. How so? (Source: Andrew Lukey.)

This applies to numerous situations in our everyday life: whether to buy this product or that, go to one tourist spot or another for a holiday, take this job offer or some other one. Based on Festinger's (1964) blueprint of the process of conflict in decision-making, the pre-decision period is marked by uncertainty and dissonance, and the post-decision period by relative calm and confidence. *Free-choice* dissonance reduction is likely to be a feature of wagers made on the outcome of events such as sporting events, horse racing, gambling and so on. Once a person has made a choice between alternatives, dissonance theory predicts that the person making a bet will become more confident about a successful outcome. Younger *et al.* (1977) interviewed people at a Canadian National exposition who either were about to bet or had just placed their bets on games such as bingo and wheel of fortune, and asked them to rate their confidence in winning. They found that people who had already made their bet were more confident of winning (see Figure 5.13).

Alternative views to dissonance

Cognitive dissonance theory has had a chequered history in social psychology. Festinger's original ideas have been refined and sharpened. Dissonance was not as easy to create as Festinger originally believed, and in some cases other theories (such as self-perception theory) may provide a better explanation of attitude change than does cognitive dissonance. Nuttin and Beckers (1975)

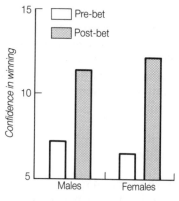

FIGURE 5.13 *Degree of confidence in winning before and after making a bet. (Source: based on data from Younger et al. 1977.)*

even proposed a rather radical reconceptualisation of the induced compliance studies, in which attitude change was explained in terms of implicit reinforcement of the expression of counter-attitudinal views. Despite all this, cognitive dissonance theory remains one of the most widely accepted explanations of attitude change and many other social behaviours. It has generated over one thousand research studies and will probably continue to be an integral part of social psychological theory for many years (Cooper and Croyle 1984).

▶ Self-perception theory

Some of the results of the dissonance experiments can also be explained by Bem's *self-perception theory* (Bem 1972). It has been suggested by some researchers that attitude change does not occur according to the basic mechanisms proposed by dissonance theory. There have been several experimental attempts to compare dissonance and self-perception theory. Both theories have been shown to be helpful in understanding behaviour (Fazio *et al.* 1977). To understand the uses of each theory, imagine that attitudes fall on a continuum, spread over a range of acceptable choices. The idea that there are latitudes of acceptance and rejection around attitudes forms the basis of social judgement theory (Sherif and Sherif 1967). If you are in favour of keeping the drinking age at 18, you might also agree to 17 or 19. There is a latitude of acceptance around your position. Alternatively, there is also a latitude of rejection: you might definitely be against a legal drinking age of either 15 or 21. Mostly we act within our own latitudes of acceptance. Sometimes we may go outside these, for instance, when we pay £20 for dinner at a restaurant rather than the planned £10. If you feel you chose freely you will experience dissonance about your decision: 'I wanted to pay only £10, was willing to go to £15 but actually paid £20.

The view which integrates self-perception and dissonance theories suggests that when your actions fall within your range of acceptance, self-perception theory best accounts for your response: 'I guess I was willing to pay more than

I thought'. However, when you find yourself acting outside your previous range of acceptance, dissonance theory gives a better account of your response. We reduce our dissonance only by changing our attitude: 'I paid £20, but that's okay because I really thought it was a great meal' (Fazio *et al.* 1977). Thus, attitudes may be changed either through a self-attributional process such as self-perception or through attempts to reduce the feeling of cognitive dissonance.

Cognitive dissonance: another look

Cooper and Fazio (1984) have attempted to counter some of the objections to cognitive dissonance theory which we have noted, particularly those that apply

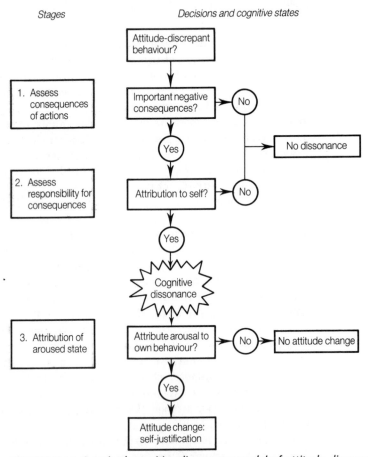

FIGURE 5.14 *A revised cognitive dissonance model of attitude-discrepant behaviour. (Source: based on suggestions by Cooper and Fazio 1984.)*

to the continuing controversy of how to defend retaining the concept of attitude in the case where a person's observed behaviour appears to run counter to that individual's own beliefs. According to this model, when behaviour is counter-attitudinal we try to figure out what the consequences might be. If these are thought to be negative and fairly serious, we must then check to see if our action was voluntary. If it was, we then accept responsibility, experience arousal from the state of dissonance which follows, and bring the relevant attitude into line, and so reduce dissonance. This revision, shown in Figure 5.14, also includes attributional processes, both in terms of whether we acted according to our freewill and of whether external influences were more or less important.

WHEN ATTITUDE CHANGE FAILS: RESISTANCE TO PERSUASION

By now you might be wondering just how susceptible are we to manipulation by others? You will be relieved to know that there is a limit to everything and that usually our attitudes are quite stable, and do not change from moment to moment. The emphasis to this point has been on factors that are conducive to us altering our attitudes, very often beyond a level of direct awareness. Yet, far more attempts at persuasion fail than ever succeed. Researchers have identified three major reasons: reactance, forewarning and inoculation.

Reactance

▶ Reactance

We noted in Box 5.1 that we can be more easily persuaded if we think the message is not deliberately intended to persuade or manipulate us. To do otherwise may set off a process referred to as *reactance*. Think back to the last occasion someone deliberately and obviously tried to change your attitudes. You might recall having an unpleasant reaction, and even hardening your existing attitude, perhaps becoming even more opposed to what that person was trying to convince you about. It was Brehm (1966) who coined the term reactance to describe this process, a psychological state that we experience when someone tries to limit our personal freedom. Research findings suggest that when we feel this way we often tend to shift in the opposite direction: an effect known as *negative attitude change*. The treatment a doctor recommends to a patient is sometimes responded to in this way (Rhodewalt and Strube 1985). What happened the last time you were told to ease up, go to bed and miss a social function you had really been looking forward to? Brehm felt that the underlying cause of reactance is a sense we might have of having our personal freedom infringed.

Forewarning

▶ Forewarning

Forewarning is basically prior knowledge of persuasive intent, that is telling someone you are going to influence them. Research evidence suggests that when we know in advance, persuasive effects are reduced (Cialdini and Petty 1979). Moreover, this seems to be especially true with respect to attitudes and issues that we consider important (Petty and Cacioppo 1979). It seems that what people do when they are forewarned that an attempt will be made to change their minds about an issue is to rehearse counter-arguments that can be used as a defence. From this point of view, forewarning can be thought of as a special case of inoculation.

Inoculation effect

▶ Inoculation

As the term suggests, inoculation is a form of protection. Whereas in biology one can inject a weakened or inert form of disease-producing germs into the patient to build up resistance to a more powerful form, so in social psychology we might seek a way to provide a defence against persuasive ideas (McGuire 1964). The technique is initiated by exposing a person to a weakened counter-attitudinal argument.

McGuire and his associates (for example, McGuire and Papageorgis 1961; Anderson and McGuire 1965) became interested in the technique following reports of the use of 'brainwashing' methods on American prisoners by Chinese forces during the Korean War of the early 1950s. Some of these soldiers made public statements denouncing the American government and saying that they wished to remain in China when the war had ended. McGuire reasoned that these soldiers were mostly inexperienced young men who had not been exposed before to attacks on the American way of life and were not forearmed with a defence against the subtleties of Marxist logic!

The biological analogy implies that a weak attack is mounted on the body's system which in turn mobilises its defences, effects a recovery and is reinforced by antibodies against a subsequent stronger attack. McGuire continued the metaphor by observing that there is another major way of heading off illness, namely by strengthening our bodies against disease through diet, exercise and so on. In the case of persuasive communications, this led him to distinguish between two major kinds of defence:

1. The *supportive defence* – a person's resistance could be strengthened by providing additional arguments which support the original beliefs.
2. The *inoculation defence* – perhaps more effectively, the person might learn what the counter-attitudinal arguments are and then hear these demolished.

Note that the inoculation defence picks up on the advantage of a two-sided presentation, discussed earlier in relation to characteristics of a persuasive message. In general terms, this defence starts with a weak attack on the person's position, since a strong one might be fatal. The person can then be told that the weak argument is not too strong and should be easy to rebut, or else an argument is to be provided that deals directly with the weak attack. It is thought that increased resistance to persuasion comes about because we both become motivated to defend our beliefs, and acquire some skill in doing this.

In a study by McGuire and Papageorgis (1961), both forms of defence were put to the test. Students were asked to indicate their extent of agreement on a fifteen-point scale for a series of truisms relating to health beliefs, such as:

1. 'It's a good idea to brush your teeth after every meal if at all possible'.
2. 'The effects of penicillin have been, almost without exception, of great benefit to mankind'.
3. 'Everyone should get a yearly chest X-ray to detect any signs of TB at an early stage'.
4. 'Mental illness is not contagious.'

Before the experiment began, many of the students thoroughly endorsed these propositions by checking 15 on the response scale. The main variables of interest were the effects of introducing defences and attacks on these health beliefs in the form of essays offering arguments for or against the truisms. Students who were in the defence groups were allocated to one of two conditions, the first being a *supportive* defence group (the students received support for their position) and the second an *inoculation* defence group (their position was subjected to a weak attack which was then refuted). There were also two control groups, one in which the students were neither attacked nor defended, and another who read essays that strongly attacked the truisms but none defending them.

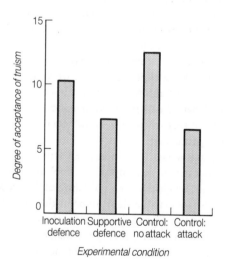

FIGURE 5.15 *Degree of acceptance of health truisms in modes of reading and writing as a function of supportive and inoculation defences. (Source: based on data from McGuire and Papageorgis 1961.)*

Not surprisingly, control subjects who had been neither attacked nor defended continued to show the highest level of acceptance of the truisms. In dealing with their central hypotheses, McGuire and Papageorgis found that providing a supportive defence helped just a little when compared with the controls who had been attacked without any defence. Subjects in the inoculation condition, however, were substantially strengthened in their defence against a strong attack, when compared with the same control group. The results are shown in Figure 5.15.

McGuire (1964) went on to argue that the supportive defence is not to be ignored but that it is most effective when attacks upon one's position are well understood, so that established and rehearsed supportive arguments can be called up. For example, try persuading committed visitors to your door that they are in error when they are intent on telling you about the wonders of their religion. The chances are that they have heard your counter-arguments before. On the other hand, McGuire favoured the inoculation defence when the audience will be exposed to a new argument. By having to deal with a mild, earlier attack on their position they will be better equipped to innovate when a stronger one is mounted.

SUMMARY

♦ The field of attitude change is vast and complex. Hovland headed the Yale approach to communication and persuasion which studied variables dealing with the communicator, the source of the message, the message itself and the context within which persuasion occurs.

♦ Two important areas of our lives which employ relevant principles from social-psychological research are advertising and political propaganda.

♦ Two recent models, each dealing with how a persuasive message is learned, draw on developments in research on memory. Petty and Cacioppo's elaboration-likelihood model proposes that, when people attend to a message carefully, they use a central route to process it; otherwise they use a peripheral route. Chaiken's heuristic-systematic model suggests that people use systematic processing when they attend to a message carefully; otherwise they use heuristic processing.

♦ A variety of techniques have been intensively studied which deal with ways of inducing another person to comply with one's requests. These techniques include ingratiation, reciprocity and guilt arousal. There are also multiple-request techniques (foot-in-the-door, door-in-the-face and low-balling) in which a first request functions as a set-up for the second, real request.

♦ Festinger's cognitive dissonance theory is a major approach to the topic of attitude change which addresses not only conflict between a person's beliefs but also discrepancy between behaviour and underlying attitudes. It includes three variations on the way in which dissonance is brought about: effort justification, induced compliance and free choice.

♦ Reactance is an increase in resistance to persuasion when the communicator's efforts to persuade are obvious. Techniques for building up resistance include forewarning and the inoculation defence.

FURTHER READING

Eagly, A. H. and Chaiken, S. (1992). *The Psychology of Attitudes*. San Diego, CA: Harcourt Brace Jovanovich.

McGuire, W. J. (1985). 'Attitudes and attitude change' in G. Lindzey and E. Aronson (eds), *The Handbook of Social Psychology* (3rd edn). New York: Random House.

Zimbardo, P. G. and Leippe, M. R. (1991). *The Psychology of Attitude Change and Social Influence*. New York: McGraw-Hill.

▶ KEY TERMS

action research
attitude change
audience
cognitive dissonance
compliance
door-in-the-face tactic
effort justification
elaboration-likelihood model
foot-in-the-door tactic
forewarning
heuristic-systematic model
induced compliance
information processing

ingratiation
inoculation
low-ball tactic
mere exposure effect
message
mindlessness
persuasive communication
post-decisional conflict
reactance
reciprocity principle
selective exposure hypothesis
self-perception theory
source

6 Social influence
....

FOCUS QUESTIONS

♦ If you wanted to persuade a friend to do you a rather large favour, say sacrifice a day to help fix your car, what sort of strategies do you think would be most effective?

♦ If someone ordered you to do something which might cause substantial suffering to another person, do you think you might obey?

♦ Why is it that people often yield to group pressure?

♦ Groups generally develop particular ways of doing things. Why do group members still conform to these group practices even when the others are not present?

♦ How is it that minorities can sometimes get their way and sway majority opinions in their direction?

TYPES OF SOCIAL INFLUENCE

▶ Social influence

Social psychology can be defined as 'an attempt to understand and explain how the thoughts, feelings, and behaviours of individuals are influenced by the actual, imagined, or implied presence of others' (Allport 1968, p. 3). This widely accepted and commonly quoted definition of social psychology (see Chapter 1) identifies a potential problem for the study of *social influence* – how does the study of social influence differ from the study of social psychology as a whole? There is no straightforward answer – instead, social influence research can be circumscribed by the sorts of issue addressed by social psychologists who consider themselves to be investigating social influence.

▶ Norms

Social life is characterised by argument, conflict and controversy in which individuals or groups try to change the thoughts, feelings and behaviours of others, by persuasion, argument, example, command, propaganda, force and so forth. Social life is also characterised by *norms* – that is, attitudinal and behavioural uniformities among people, what Turner has called '*normative social similarities and differences* between people' (1991, p. 2). One of the most interesting sets of issues in social influence, perhaps even in social psychology, is how people construct norms, how they conform to, or are regulated by, those norms, and how those norms change. Since norms are very much group phenomena, we discuss their structure, their origins, and some of their effects in Chapter 7, reserving for the present chapter discussion of the *process of conformity* to norms.

Compliance, obedience, conformity

▶ Compliance

We are all familiar with a clear difference between, on the one hand, yielding to direct or indirect social pressure from a group or an individual, and on the other being genuinely persuaded. For example, you may simply agree publicly with others' attitudes, comply with their requests, or go along with their behaviour, yet not feel privately persuaded at all. On other occasions, you may actually privately change your innermost beliefs in accordance with the views or behaviours of others. This has not gone unnoticed by social psychologists, who generally find it useful to distinguish between coercive compliance on the one hand and persuasive influence on the other.

Some forms of social influence produce public *compliance* – a surface change in behaviour and expressed attitudes, often as a consequence of coercion. Since compliance does not reflect internal change, it usually persists only while behaviour is under surveillance. For example, children may obey parental directives to keep their room tidy but only if they know that their parents are watching. An important prerequisite for coercive compulsion and compliance is that the source of social influence is perceived by the target of influence to have power – power is the basis of compliance (Moscovici 1976). It should be noted, however, that since evidence for internal mental states depends on observed behaviour, it can be very difficult to know whether compliant behaviour does or does not reflect internalisation (Allen 1965). People's strategic control over behaviour for self-presentation and communicative purposes can accentuate this difficulty.

In contrast to compliance, other forms of social influence produce private acceptance and internalisation. There is subjective acceptance and conversion (Moscovici 1976) which produces true internal change that persists in the absence of surveillance. Conformity is not based on power but rather on the subjective validity of social norms (Festinger 1950), that is, a feeling of confidence and certainty that the beliefs and actions described by the norm are correct, appropriate, valid and socially desirable. Under these circumstances the norm becomes an internalised standard for behaviour, and thus surveillance is unnecessary.

▶ Reference group
▶ Membership group

Kelley (1952) has made a useful distinction between *reference* groups and *membership* groups. Reference groups are groups that are psychologically significant for one's attitudes and behaviour, either in the positive sense that one seeks to behave in accordance with their norms, or in the negative sense that one seeks to behave in exact opposition to their norms. Membership groups are those groups to which one belongs (which one is *in*) by some objective criterion, external designation or social consensus. A positive reference group is a source of conformity (which will be socially validated if that group happens also to be one's membership group), while a negative reference group that is also one's membership group has enormous coercive power to produce compliance. For example, if I am a manual worker but I despise all the attributes of being a worker, and I would rather be a member of management because I value management norms so much more, then 'worker' is my membership group which is also a negative reference group, and 'management' is a positive reference group but not my membership group. I will comply with worker norms but conform to management norms.

▶ Dual process dependency model

The general distinction between coercive compliance and persuasive influence is a theme that surfaces again and again in different guises in social influence research. The distinction maps onto a general view that there are two quite separate processes responsible for social influence phenomena – hence Turner and colleagues refer to traditional perspectives on social influence as representing a *dual process dependency model* (Abrams and Hogg 1990a; Hogg and Turner 1987a; Turner 1991; Turner *et al.* 1987).

COMPLIANCE WITH REQUESTS

One of the most common forms of compliance is in response to direct pressure to comply with a request, for example when a friend asks a favour, a salesperson tries to induce us to buy a product, or a partner, spouse or housemate asks us to change some aspect of behaviour. Indeed, many researchers believe that attempts to gain compliance through direct requests are the most common form of social influence. As we saw in Chapter 5, research has tended to focus on the sorts of strategy that people can adopt to maximise the probability of compliance with a direct request. There are several effective strategies:

▶ Ingratiation

1. *Ingratiation* – if you can get someone to like you then she is more likely to comply.

▶ Reciprocity principle

2. *Reciprocity principle* – if you do someone a favour then she is very likely to comply with a subsequent request because there is a strong norm to reciprocate.

▶ Multiple requests

3. *Multiple requests* – what you want of someone in an ultimate request is prefaced by an initial 'softening up' request (Cialdini 1988 – see also Chapter 5).

Multiple requests can take different forms:

1. If you can secure compliance with a small preliminary request, then you increase the probability of subsequent compliance with a much larger focal request – the *foot-in-the-door tactic* (for example, Freedman and Fraser 1966).
2. If you first make an outrageous request that is sure to be refused, then you increase the probability of compliance with a scaled down but focal subsequent request – the *door-in-the-face tactic* (for example, Cialdini *et al.* 1975; Patch 1986).
3. If you can secure compliance by attaching attractive inducements to the request, then compliance will remain even once those inducements are subsequently removed – the *low-ball tactic* (for example, Cialdini *et al.* 1978).

Because research into compliance with direct requests has generally been conducted within an attitude-change framework, we have covered this topic in detail in Chapter 5.

BASES OF SOCIAL POWER

▶ Power

Compliance is not only influenced by the tactics used by the people making the request, but also by their perceived *power*. Power can be interpreted as the capacity or ability to exert influence; and influence is power in action. For example, French and Raven (1959) identified five bases of social power, and later Raven (1965) expanded this to six: reward power, coercive power, informational power, expert power, legitimate power and referent power (see Figure 6.1). That the power to administer reinforcements or punishments should influence behaviour is almost a truism in psychology. It is perhaps for this very reason that there has been virtually no attempt to demonstrate reward and coercive power (Collins and Raven 1969). One general problem is that reinforcement formulations, particularly of complex social behaviour, tend to have enormous difficulty specifying in advance what is a reward and what is a punishment, and yet find it very easy to do so after the event. As such, reinforcement formulations tend to be unfalsifiable. Thus, it may be more useful to focus on the cognitive and social processes that cause specific individuals in certain contexts to treat some things as reinforcement and others as punishment.

While information may have the power to influence, it is clearly not true that any information has such power. If I were to tell you that I had information that pigs really do fly, it is very unlikely that you would be persuaded. For you to be persuaded, other influence processes would also have to be operating; for instance the information might have to be perceived to be consistent with

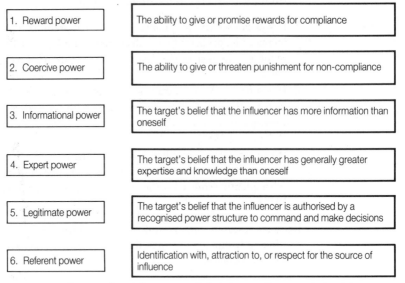

FIGURE 6.1 *Forms of social power and their bases. (Source: derived from Raven 1965.)*

normative expectations, or coercive or reward power might have to operate. Information can, however, be influential when it originates in an expert source. Bochner and Insko (1966) provided a nice illustration of expert power. They found that subjects more readily accepted information that people did not need much sleep when the information was attributed to a Nobel Prize-winning physiologist than to a less prestigious source. The information lost the power to influence only when it became intrinsically implausible – stating that almost no sleep was needed (see also Figure 5.2 in Chapter 5).

Legitimate power is based in authority, and is best illustrated by a consideration of obedience (see below). Referent power may operate through a range of processes (see also Collins and Raven 1969), including consensual validation, social approval and group identification – all of which are discussed below in the section on conformity.

In addition to power as the ability to influence, there are other perspectives on social power (Ng 1980). For example, Moscovici (1976) actually contrasts power with influence, seeing them as two very different processes. Power is the control of behaviour through domination that produces compliance and submission: if one has power, in this sense, one does not need influence, and if one can effectively influence then one need not resort to power. Power can also be considered as a role within a group that is defined by effective influence over followers, that is as a leadership position (Hollander 1985; see Chapter 8). Finally, power can also be treated as the exercise of legitimate authority (although leaders generally have legitimate authority, they need not).

OBEDIENCE TO AUTHORITY

In 1951 Asch published the results of a now classic experiment on conformity in which student subjects conformed to erroneous judgements of line lengths made by a numerical majority (see below for details). Some critics have been fairly unimpressed by this study: the task, judging line length, was trivial, and there were no significant consequences for self and others of conforming or resisting. As one of these critics, Milgram (1974, 1992) set out to replicate Asch's study but with a task that had important consequences attached to the decision to conform or to remain independent. He decided to have experimental confederates apparently administer electric shocks to another person, and see whether the true subject would conform. Before being able to start the study, Milgram needed to run a control group to obtain a base rate for people's willingness to shock someone *without* social pressure from confederates. For Milgram this became a crucial question in its own right. In fact he never actually went ahead with his original conformity study, and the control group became the basis for one of social psychology's most dramatic research programmes.

Milgram was also influenced by a wider social issue. Adolf Eichmann was the Nazi official most directly responsible for the logistics of Hitler's Holocaust in which six million Jews were systematically slaughtered. A book entitled *Eichmann in Jerusalem* (Arendt 1963) was published reporting his trial. The subtitle of this book, *A Report on the Banality of Evil*, captures one of the most disturbing findings that emerged from Eichmann's trial, and indeed from

Obedience: the power of a uniform. Although concerned at the arrest of one of their number these demonstrators may accept the legitimacy of police action. (Source: Andrew Lukey.)

the trials of other war criminals. These 'monsters' did not appear to be monsters at all. They were often mild-mannered, softly spoken, courteous people, who repeatedly and politely explained that they did what they did not because they hated Jews but because they were ordered to do it: they were simply obeying orders.

Milgram's obedience studies

These two strands came together in a series of experiments conducted during the 1960s by Milgram (1963, 1974). Subjects, recruited from the community by advertisement, reported to a laboratory at Yale University to participate in a study of the effect of punishment on human learning. They arrived in pairs, and drew lots to determine their roles for the study – one was the 'learner' and the other the 'teacher'. The learner's role was to learn a list of paired associates, and the teacher's role was to administer an electric shock to the learner every time the learner gave a wrong associate to the cue word. The teacher saw the learner being strapped to a chair and having electrode paste and electrodes attached to his arm, and overheard the experimenter explain that the paste was to prevent blistering and burning and the learner telling the experimenter that he had a slight heart condition. The experimenter also explained that although the shocks might be painful they would cause no permanent tissue damage.

The teacher was now taken into a separate room containing a shock generator (see Figure 6.2). He was told to administer progressively larger shocks to the learner every time he made a mistake – 15 V for the first mistake, 30 V for the next mistake, 45 V for the next, and so on. An important feature of the shock generator was the descriptive labels attached to the scale of increasing voltage. The teacher was given a sample shock of 45 V, and then the experiment commenced. The learner got some pairs correct but also made some errors and very soon the teacher had reached 75 V, at which point ·he learner grunted in pain. At 120 V the learner shouted out to the experimenter that the shocks were becoming painful. At 150 V the learner, or now more accurately the 'victim', demanded to be released from the experiment, and at 180 V he cried out that he could not stand it any longer. The victim continued

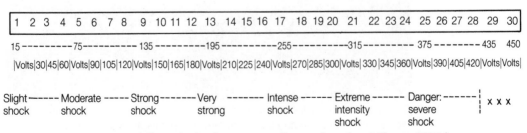

FIGURE 6.2 *Milgram's shock generator. (Source: based on Milgram 1974.)*

to cry out in pain at each shock, rising to an 'agonised scream' at 250 V. At 300 V the victim ceased responding to the cue words – the teacher was told to treat this as a 'wrong answer'.

Throughout the experiment the learner was agitated and tense, and frequently asked to break off. To such requests, the experimenter responded with an ordered sequence of replies proceeding from a mild 'please continue', through 'the experiment requires that you continue' and 'it is absolutely essential that you continue', to the ultimate 'you have no other choice, you *must* go on'. A panel of 110 experts on human behaviour, including 39 psychiatrists, were asked to predict how far a normal, psychologically balanced human being would go in this experiment. These experts believed that only about 10 per cent would exceed 180 V, and no-one would obey to the end (these predictions are shown schematically in Figure 6.3). Compare this with the actual behaviour of the subjects (Figure 6.3 also). In a slight variant of the procedure described above, in which the victim could not be seen or heard, but pounded on the wall at 300 V and 315 V and then went silent, almost everyone continued to 255 V, and 65 per cent continued to the very end – administering massive electric shocks to someone who was not responding, and who had previously reported having a heart complaint.

The subjects in this experiment were quite normal people: forty 20–50 year old males from a range of occupations. Unknown to them, however, the entire

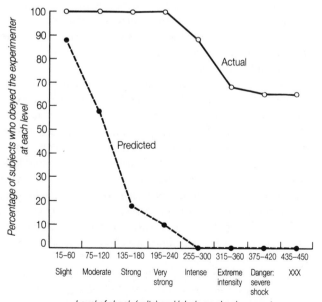

FIGURE 6.3 *Predicted and actual maximum shock levels administered in Milgram's obedience experiment. (Source: based on data from Milgram 1974.)*

experiment involved an elaborate deception in which they were always the teacher, and the learner/victim was actually an experimental stooge (an avuncular-looking middle-aged man) who had been carefully briefed on how to react. No electric shocks were actually administered – apart from the 45 V sample shock to the teacher.

Factors influencing obedience

Milgram (1974) conducted a total of eighteen experiments in which he varied different parameters to investigate factors influencing obedience. In all but one experiment the subjects were 20–50 year old male, non-university students from a range of occupations and socio-economic levels. In one study in which females were the subjects, exactly the same level of obedience was obtained as with male subjects. Milgram's experiment has been replicated in Italy, Germany, Australia, Britain, Jordan, Spain, Austria and the Netherlands (Smith and Bond 1993). Complete obedience ranged from over 90 per cent in Spain and the Netherlands (Meeus and Raaijmakers 1986), through over 80 per cent in Italy, Germany, and Austria (Mantell 1971), to a low of 40 per cent among Australian males and only 16 per cent among Australian females (Kilham and Mann 1974). Some studies have also used slightly different settings, for example Meeus and Raaijmakers (1986) used an administrative obedience setting.

One reason that people continue administering electric shocks may be that the experiment starts very innocuously with quite trivial electric shocks. Once having committed oneself to a course of action (that is, to give shocks) it can be difficult subsequently to change one's mind. The process may be similar to that involved in the foot-in-the-door technique of persuasion (Freedman and Fraser 1966; see Chapter 5).

An important factor in obedience is *immediacy* – the social proximity of the victim to the subject. Milgram (1974) varied the level of immediacy across a number of experiments. We have seen that 65 per cent of subjects 'shocked to the limit' of 450 V when the victim was unseen and unheard except for pounding on the wall. In an even less immediate condition, in which the victim was neither seen nor heard at all, 100 per cent of subjects went to the end. The baseline condition, that described in detail above, yielded 62.5 per cent obedience. As immediacy increased from this baseline, obedience decreased: when the victim was visible in the same room, 40 per cent obeyed to the limit, and when the teacher had actually to hold the victim's hand down onto the electrode to receive the shock obedience dropped to a still remarkably high 30 per cent.

Another important factor is the proximity/immediacy of the authority figure. Obedience was reduced to 20.5 per cent when the experimenter was absent from the room and relayed directions by telephone. When the experimenter gave no orders at all, and the subject was entirely free to choose when to stop, 2.5 per cent persisted to the end. Perhaps the most dramatic influence on obedience is group pressure. The presence of two disobedient peers (that is, others who appeared to revolt and refused to continue after giving shocks in the 150 V to 210 V range) reduced complete obedience to 10 per cent, while two obedient peers increased complete obedience to 92.5 per cent.

Group pressure probably has its effects because the actions of others helps confirm that it is either legitimate or illegitimate to continue administering the shocks. Another important factor is the legitimacy of the authority figure, which allows people to abdicate personal responsibility for their actions. For example, Bushman (1984, 1988) had confederates dressed in a uniform, neat attire or a shabby outfit stand next to someone fumbling for change for a parking meter. The confederate stopped passers by and 'ordered' them to give the person change for the meter. Over 70 per cent obeyed the uniformed confederate (giving 'because they had been told to' as the reason) and about 50 per cent obeyed the non-uniformed confederate (generally giving altruism as a reason). These studies suggest that merely the emblems of authority can create unquestioning obedience.

Milgram's original experiments were conducted by lab-coated scientists at prestigious Yale University, and the purpose of the research would quite clearly be the pursuit of scientific knowledge. What would happen if these trappings of legitimate authority were removed? Milgram ran one experiment in a run-down inner city office building. The research was ostensibly sponsored by a private commercial research firm. Obedience dropped, but only to a still remarkably high 48 per cent.

Some ethical considerations

Perhaps the most enduring legacy of Milgram's experiments is the heated debate it stirred up over research ethics (Baumrind 1964; Rosnow 1981). Recall that Milgram's subjects really believed that they were administering severe electric shocks that were causing extreme pain to another human being. Milgram was careful to interview and, with the assistance of a psychiatrist, follow up his subjects. There was no evidence of psychopathology, and 83.7 per cent of subjects who had taken part indicated that they were glad, or very glad, to have been in the experiment (Milgram 1992, p. 186). Only 1.3 per cent were sorry or very sorry to have participated.

The ethical issues, however, really revolve around three questions concerning the ethics of subjecting people to short-term stress:

1. Is the research important? If not, then such stress is unjustifiable. However, it can be very difficult objectively to assess the importance of research.
2. Is the subject free to terminate the experiment at any time? How free were Milgram's subjects? In one sense they were of course free to do whatever they wanted, but it was never made explicit to them that they could

terminate whenever they wished – in fact the very purpose of the study was to persuade them to remain.

3. Does the subject freely consent to being in the experiment in the first place? In Milgram's experiments the subjects did not give fully informed consent – they volunteered to take part, but the true nature of the experiment was not explained to them.

This raises the issue of deception in social psychology research. Kelman (1967) distinguishes two reasons for deceiving subjects: the first is to induce people to take part in an otherwise unpleasant experiment. This is, of course, an ethically highly dubious practice. The second reason is that in order to study the automatic operation of psychological processes subjects need to be naive regarding the hypotheses, and this can often involve a degree of deception concerning the true purpose of the study and the procedures used. The fall-out from this debate has been a code of ethics to guide psychologists in conducting research. The principal components of the code are:

1. Participation must be based on fully informed consent.
2. Subjects must be explicitly informed that they can withdraw, without penalty, at any stage of the study.
3. Subjects must be fully and honestly debriefed at the end of the study.

Although it is probably no longer possible to 'get away with' the impressively brazen deceptions that produced many of social psychology's classic research of the 1950s, 1960s and early 1970s, the use of minor and harmless procedural deceptions enshrined in clever cover stories is accepted as essential to preserve the scientific rigour of much experimental social psychology. The issue of research ethics in social psychology is discussed in Chapter 1.

CONFORMITY

Formation and influence of norms

▶ Conformity

While a great deal of social influence is reflected in compliance with direct requests and obedience towards authority, social influence can also operate in a less direct manner through *conformity* to social or group norms. For example, Allport (1924) observed that people in groups simply gave less extreme and more conservative judgements of odours and weights than when they were alone. It seemed as if, in the absence of direct pressure, the group could cause members to converge and thus become more similar to one another.

▶ Frame of reference
▶ Autokinesis

Sherif (1936) made a major step forward by explicitly linking this convergence effect with the development of *group norms*. Proceeding from the premise that people need to be certain and confident that what they are doing, thinking or feeling is correct and appropriate, Sherif argued that people use the behaviour of others to establish the range of possible behaviours – this we can call the *frame of reference*, or relevant *social comparative context*. Average, central or middle positions in such frames of reference are perceived to be more correct than fringe positions, and thus people tend to adopt them. Sherif believed that this explained the origins of social norms and concomitant convergence that accentuates consensus within groups. To test this idea, he conducted his classic *autokinetic* studies (see Box 6.1 for details), in which two- or three-person groups making estimates of physical movement quickly converged over a series of trials on the mean of the group's estimates, and remained influenced by this norm even when subsequently making estimates alone.

The origins, structure, function and effects of norms are discussed fully in Chapter 7. It is, however, worth emphasising that normative pressure is one of the most effective ways in which to change people's behaviour. For example, Lewin (1947) tried to encourage American housewives to change the eating habits of their families – specifically to eat more offal. Three groups of 13–17 housewives attended an interesting factual lecture that, among other things, stressed how valuable such a change in eating habits would be to the war effort

---

BOX 6.1 Sherif's (1936) autokinetic experiment: the experimental induction of a group norm

Norm formation

Muzafer Sherif (1936) believed that social norms emerge in order to guide behaviour under conditions of uncertainty. To investigate this idea, he took advantage of a perceptual illusion – the autokinetic effect. Autokinesis is an optical illusion where a fixed point of light in a completely dark room appears to move – the movement is actually caused by eye movement in the absence of a physical frame of reference (that is, objects). People asked to estimate how much the light moves find the task very difficult, and generally feel rather uncertain about their estimates. Sherif presented the point of light a large number of times (that is, trials), and had subjects who were unaware that the movement was an illusion estimate the amount the light moved on each trial. He discovered that subjects used their own estimates as a frame of reference: over a series of one hundred trials they gradually focused in on a narrow range of estimates, with different people adopting different ranges. Sherif also ran the experiment with subjects in groups of two or three taking it in turn to call out their estimates in a random sequence. Under these circumstances, subjects used others' estimates as the frame of reference, and converged very quickly indeed on the group mean, so that they gave virtually identical estimates. This norm seemed to have become internalised, because when subsequently making autokinetic estimates on their own, subjects remained strongly influenced.

(in 1943). Another three groups were given information but also encouraged to discuss among themselves and come to some consensus (that is, establish a norm) about buying the food. A follow-up survey revealed that the norm was far more effective than the abstract information in causing some change in behaviour: only 3 per cent of the information group had changed their behaviour while 32 per cent of the norm group had (see also Chapter 5). Subsequent research confirmed that it was the norm, not the attendant discussion, that was the crucial factor (Bennett 1955).

Yielding to majority group pressure

Like Sherif, Asch (1952) believed that conformity reflects a relatively rational process in which people construct a norm from other people's behaviour in order to determine correct and appropriate behaviour for themselves. Clearly, if one is already confident and certain about what is appropriate and correct, then others' behaviour will be largely irrelevant, and thus socially uninfluential. In Sherif's study, the object of judgement was ambiguous – subjects were uncertain and so a norm arose rapidly and was highly effective in guiding behaviour. Asch argued that if the object of judgement was entirely unambiguous (that is, one would expect no disagreement among judges) then disagreement, or alternative perceptions, would have no effect on behaviour – individuals would remain entirely independent of group influence.

To test this idea Asch (1951, 1952, 1956) created a classic experimental paradigm. Male students, participating in what they thought was a visual discrimination task, seated themselves around a table in groups of seven to nine. They took turns in a fixed and apparently random order to publicly call out which of three comparison lines was the same length as a standard line (see Figure 6.4). There were eighteen trials. In reality only one subject was a true naive subject, and he answered second to last. The others were experimental confederates instructed to give erroneous responses on twelve focal trials – on

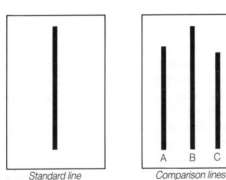

Standard line   *Comparison lines*

FIGURE 6.4 *Sample lines used in conformity experiment. (Source: based on Asch 1951.)*

six trials they picked a line that was too long, and on six a line that was too short. There was a control condition in which subjects performed the task privately with no group influence – since less than 1 per cent of control subjects' responses were errors, it can be assumed that the task was unambiguous.

The experimental results were intriguing. There were large individual differences, with about 25 per cent of subjects remaining steadfastly independent throughout, about 50 per cent conforming to the erroneous majority on six or more focal trials, and 5 per cent conforming on all twelve focal trials. The average conformity rate was 33 per cent – that is, the number of focal trials on which there was conformity divided by the product of the number of subjects and the number of focal trials.

After the experiment, Asch asked his subjects why they conformed. They all reported initially experiencing uncertainty and self-doubt as a consequence of the disagreement between themselves and the group, which gradually evolved into self-consciousness, fear of disapproval and feelings of anxiety, and even loneliness. Different reasons were given for yielding. The majority knew they saw things differently from the group but felt their perceptions may have been inaccurate and that the group was actually correct. Others did not believe the group was correct but simply went along with the group in order not to stand out. A small minority reported that they actually saw the lines as the group did. Independents were either entirely confident in the accuracy of their own judgements, or were emotionally affected but guided by a belief in individualism or in doing the task as directed (that is, being accurate and correct).

These subjective accounts suggest that one reason that people conform, even when the stimulus is completely unambiguous, may be to avoid censure, ridicule and social disapproval. This is a real fear. In another version of his experiment, Asch (1951) had sixteen naive subjects facing one confederate who gave incorrect answers. The subjects found the confederate's behaviour ludicrous, and openly ridiculed and laughed at him. Even the experimenter found the situation so bizarre that he could not contain his mirth and ended up laughing at the poor confederate. Perhaps, then, if subjects were not worried about social disapproval, there would be no subjective pressure to conform. To test this idea, Asch conducted another variation of the experiment in which the incorrect majority called out their judgements publicly, but the single naive subject wrote his down privately. Conformity dropped to 12.5 per cent.

This modification was taken further by Deutsch and Gerard (1955) who believed that they could entirely eradicate pressure to conform if the task was unambiguous, and the subject was anonymous, responded privately and was not under any sort of surveillance by the group. Why should anyone conform to an erroneous majority when there was an obvious, unambiguous and objectively correct answer, and the group had no way of knowing what you were doing? To test this idea, Deutsch and Gerard confronted a naive subject face-to-face with three confederates who made unanimously incorrect judgements of lines on focal trials – exactly as in Asch's original experiment.

In another condition the naive subject was anonymous, was isolated in a cubicle and responded privately – no group pressure existed. There was a third condition in which subjects responded face-to-face but with an explicit group goal to be as accurate as possible – group pressure was maximised. Deutsch and Gerard also manipulated subjective uncertainty by having half the subjects respond while the stimuli were present (the procedure used by Asch) and half respond after the stimuli had been removed (there would be scope for subjective uncertainty here). As predicted, the results showed that uncertainty and decreasing group pressure (that is, the motivation and ability of the group to censure lack of conformity) reduced conformity (Figure 6.5). Perhaps the most interesting finding is that people still conformed at a rate of about 23 per cent even when uncertainty was low (stimulus present) and responses were private and anonymous.

The discovery that subjects still conformed when isolated in cubicles has greatly facilitated the systematic investigation of factors influencing conformity. Crutchfield (1955) devised an apparatus in which subjects in cubicles believed they were communicating with one another by pressing buttons on a console that illuminated responses, when in reality the cubicles were not interconnected and the experimenter was the source of all communication. In this way, many subjects could be run simultaneously and yet all would believe they were being exposed to a unanimous group. The time-consuming, costly and risky practice of using confederates was no longer necessary, and data could now be collected much more quickly under more controlled and varied experimental conditions (Allen 1965, 1975).

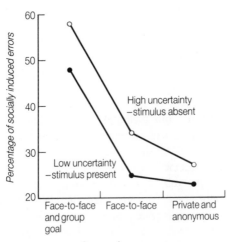

FIGURE 6.5 *Conformity as a function of uncertainty and perceived group pressure. (Source: based on data from Deutsch and Gerard 1955.)*

Who conforms? Individual and group characteristics

The existence of large individual differences in conformity has led some social psychologists to search for personality attributes that predispose some people to conform more than others. Those who conform tend to have low self-esteem, a high need for social support or social approval, a need for self-control, low IQ, high anxiety, feelings of self-blame and insecurity in the group, feelings of inferiority, feelings of relatively low status in the group, and a generally authoritarian personality (Costanzo 1970; Crutchfield 1955; Elms and Milgram 1966; Raven and French, 1958; Stang 1972). The existence of negative findings and evidence that people who conform in one situation do not conform in another suggest that situational factors may be more important than personality in conformity (Barocas and Gorlow 1967; Barron 1953; McGuire 1968; Vaughan 1964).

A similar conclusion can be drawn from research into sex differences in conformity. Females are typically found to conform slightly more than males in conformity studies. However, this can generally be explained in terms of the conformity tasks employed – ones with which females have relatively less familiarity and expertise, experience greater subjective uncertainty, and thus are influenced more than males (Eagly 1978, 1983; Eagly and Carli 1981; Eagly and Chrvala 1986). For example, Sistrunk and McDavid (1971) exposed male and female subjects to group pressure in identifying various stimuli. For some subjects the stimuli were traditionally masculine items (for example, identifying a special type of wrench), for some traditionally feminine items (for example, identifying types of needlework), and for others the stimuli were neutral (for example, identifying popular rock stars). As expected,

Conformity of group acceptance. Being different from one's peers can lead to disapproval. Dress and hairstyle provide one means of being accepted. (Source: *New Zealand Herald*)

females conformed more on masculine items, males more on feminine items, and both groups equally on neutral (non sex-stereotypic) items (see Figure 6.6).

Do cultural norms affect conformity? Smith and Bond (1993) tabulated thirty-one known published conformity studies using Asch's paradigm or a variant thereof. The level of conformity (that is, percentage of incorrect responses) ranges from a low of 14 per cent among Belgian students (Doms 1983) to a high of 58 per cent among Indian teachers in Fiji (Chandra 1973), with an overall average of 31.2 per cent. Interestingly, conformity was lower among subjects from 'individualist' cultures in North America and north-west Europe (25.3 per cent) than 'collectivist' cultures in Africa, Asia, Oceana and South America (37.1 per cent) – see Box 6.2.

Situational factors in conformity

The two situational factors in conformity that have been most exhaustively researched are group size and group unanimity (Allen 1965, 1975). Asch (1952) found that as the unanimous majority increased from one person to two, to three, to four, to eight, to 10–15, the conformity rate increased and then decreased slightly: 3, 13, 33, 35, 32, 31 per cent. Although some research finds a linear relationship between size and conformity (for example, Mann 1977), the most robust finding is that conformity reaches its full strength with a three-person to five-person majority, and additional members have little effect (for example, Stang, 1976). Campbell and Fairey (1989) suggest that group size may have a different effect depending on the type of judgement being made and the motivation of the individual. With matters of taste, where there is no objectively correct answer (for example, musical preference), and

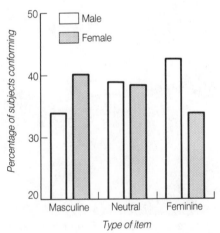

FIGURE 6.6 *Conformity as a function of sex of subject and sex-stereotypicality of task. (Source: based on data from Sistrunk and McDavid 1971.)*

BOX 6.2 Cultural influences on conformity

The Temne: no room for dissidents

Berry (1967) provides an intriguing insight into the way culture may
influence conformity. Using a variant of Asch's conformity paradigm,
Berry found that the Temne people of Sierra Leone conformed
significantly more strongly than the Eskimos of Canada, and traced
the cause of this difference to differences in economic practices. The
Temne subsist on a single crop which they harvest in one concerted
effort once a year. Since this requires enormous co-operation and co-
ordination of effort, consensus and agreement are strongly
represented in Temne culture. Berry quotes one of his subjects as
saying, 'When Temne people choose a thing, we must all agree with
the decision – this is what we call cooperation' (Berry 1967, p.417). In
contrast, Eskimo economy involves continual hunting and gathering
on a relatively individual basis, and thus consensus is relatively less
strongly emphasised in Eskimo culture.

---

where one is concerned to 'fit in', then group size will have a relatively linear
effect – the larger the majority the more you will be swayed. When there is a
correct response and one is concerned to be correct, then the views of one or
two others will usually be sufficient – the views of additional others will be
largely redundant.

Finally, Wilder (1977) observed that size does not refer to the actual number
of physically separate people in the group, but the number of seemingly
independent sources of influence in the group. For instance, a majority of three
individuals who are perceived to be independent will be more influential than a
majority of, say, five who are perceived to be in collusion and thus represent a
single information source. In fact, people may find it rather difficult to
represent more than four or five discriminable or independent pieces of
information and thus tend to assimilate additional group members into one or
other of these initial sources of information – hence the relative lack of effect
of group size above three to five members.

Asch's original experiment employed a unanimous erroneous majority to
obtain a conformity rate of 33 per cent. Subsequent experiments have shown
that conformity is greatly reduced if the majority is not unanimous (Allen
1975). Asch found that a correct supporter (that is, a member of the majority
who always gave the correct answer – and thus agreed with and supported
the true subject) reduced conformity from 33 per cent to 5.5 per cent. The
effectiveness of a supporter in reducing conformity is marginally greater if the
supporter responds before rather than after the majority (Morris and Miller
1975).

Support itself may not be the crucial factor in reducing conformity. Any sort of lack of unanimity among the majority seems to be effective. For example, Asch found that a dissenter who was even more incorrect than the majority was equally effective, and Shaw *et al.* (1957) found a dithering and undecided deviate was also effective. Allen and Levine (1971) conducted an experiment in which subjects who were asked to make visual judgements were provided with a supporter who had normal vision or a supporter who wore such thick glasses as to raise serious doubts about his ability to see anything at all let alone accurately judge lines. In the absence of any support, subjects conformed 97 per cent of the time. The 'competent' supporter reduced conformity to 36 per cent, but most surprising was that the 'incompetent' supporter reduced conformity as well, to 64 per cent (see Figure 6.7).

Supporters, dissenters and deviates appear to be effective in reducing conformity because they break the unanimity of the majority and thus raise or legitimise the possibility of alternative ways of responding or behaving. For example, Nemeth and Chiles (1988) confronted subjects with four confederates who all correctly identified blue slides as blue, or among whom one consistently called the blue slide 'green'. Subjects were then exposed to another group which unanimously called red slides 'orange'. The subjects who had previously been exposed to the consistent dissenter were more likely to correctly call the red slides 'red'.

Normative and informational influence

Social psychologists generally believe that there are two processes of social influence responsible for conformity, called *informational influence* and

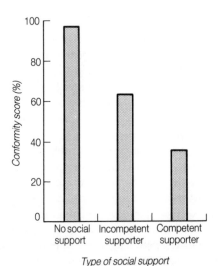

FIGURE 6.7 *Conformity as a function of presence or absence of support, and competence of supporter. (Source: based on data from Allen and Levine 1971.)*

normative influence (Deutsch and Gerard 1955; Kelley 1952). Informational influence is an influence to accept information from another as *evidence* about reality. People have a need to feel confident that their perceptions, beliefs and feelings are correct. Informational influence comes into play when people are uncertain, either because stimuli are intrinsically ambiguous or because there is social disagreement. Under these circumstances people initially make objective tests against reality, but if this is not possible then they make social comparisons (Festinger 1950, 1954). Effective informational influence causes true cognitive change.

▶ Informational influence

Informational influence was probably at least partially responsible for the effects found by Sherif (1936) in his autokinetic studies. Reality was ambiguous and subjects used other people's estimates as information to disambiguate reality and resolve subjective uncertainty. When subjects were told that the apparent movement was in fact an illusion, they did not conform (for example, Alexander *et al.* 1970) – presumably since reality itself was uncertain, their own subjective uncertainty was interpreted as a correct and valid representation of reality, and thus informational influence did not operate. Asch's stimuli were designed to be unambiguous in order to exclude informational influence. Asch (1952) found, however, that conformity increased as the comparison lines were made more similar to one another and the judgement task thus became more difficult.

▶ Normative influence

Normative influence is an influence to conform with the positive expectations of others. People have a need for social approval and acceptance that causes them to 'go along with' the group for instrumental reasons – to cultivate approval and acceptance, avoid censure or disapproval, or to achieve specific goals. Normative influence comes into play when the group is perceived to have the power and ability to mediate rewards and punishment contingent on one's behaviour. An important precondition is that one is under surveillance by the group. Effective normative influence creates surface compliance rather than true cognitive change.

Normative influence was, no doubt, the principal cause of conformity in the Asch paradigm – the stimuli were unambiguous (informational influence would not be operating) but subjects' behaviour was under direct surveillance by the group. We have seen above how privacy, anonymity and lack of surveillance reduced conformity in the Asch paradigm, presumably because normative influence was weakened. Deutsch and Gerard (1955) tried to remove normative influence entirely but, as we saw above, even under conditions in which neither informational nor normative influence would be expected to operate, they found residual conformity at an amazingly high rate of about 23 per cent. From this we can conclude one of the following:

1. That the conditions of the experiment were such that informational and/or normative influence were not completely eradicated.
2. That they were inoperative, but there is some third, as yet not specified, social influence process.

3. That social influence in groups needs to be explained in a somewhat different way.

Referent informational influence

▶ Referent informational influence

The distinction between informational and normative influence is only one among many different terminologies that have been used in social psychology to distinguish between two types of social influence. It represents what has been called by John Turner and his colleagues, a *dual process dependency model* of social influence (Abrams and Hogg 1990a; Hogg and Turner 1987a; Turner 1991; Turner *et al.* 1987). People are influenced by others because they are dependent on them either for information that disambiguates reality and thus establishes subjective validity, or for reasons of social approval and acceptance.

▶ Social identity theory
▶ Self-categorisation theory

This model has been challenged on the grounds that as an explanation of conformity it under-emphasises the role of group 'belongingness'. After all, an important feature of conformity is that we are influenced because we feel we belong, psychologically, to the group, and therefore the norms of the group are relevant standards for our behaviour. The dual process model has drifted away from group norms and group belongingness and focused on *interpersonal* dependency which could just as well occur between individuals as among group members. The challenge has come from *social identity theory* (Hogg and Abrams 1988; Tajfel and Turner 1979; Turner 1981b, 1982; see Chapter 10), which proposes a separate social influence process responsible for conformity to group norms, called *referent informational influence* (Hogg and Turner 1987a; Turner 1981b, 1982). Referent informational influence operates via the process of *self-categorisation* that self-categorisation theorists believe is responsible for group belongingness and group behaviour (Turner 1985; Turner *et al.* 1987; again see Chapter 10).

The categorisation of self and others present as members of the same social group (that is, psychological group belongingness) occasions the search for a relevant group norm to describe and prescribe the group's behaviour. The norm is constructed by the categorisation process in such a way as to simultaneously minimise perceived differences among members of the group and accentuate differences between the group and people who are not in the group (for example, outgroup members). The norm is internalised as a cognitive representation of the appropriate standard for behaviour as a group member. The self-categorisation process accentuates similarities between one's own behaviour and that prescribed by the group norm, thus causing one's own behaviour to conform to the norm. To the extent that all members of the group construct a very similar group norm, self-categorisation produces intragroup convergence on that norm and increases intragroup uniformity: the typical conformity effect.

Referent informational influence differs from normative and informational influence in a number of important ways. For example, people conform because they are group members, not to validate physical reality or to avoid social disapproval. People do not conform to other people, but to a norm – other people (usually ingroup members, but they could be outgroup members) are a source of information about the appropriate ingroup norm. Because the norm is an internalised representation, people can conform to it in the absence of surveillance by group members, or for that matter anybody else.

Referent informational influence has direct support from a series of four conformity experiments by Hogg and Turner (1987a). For example, under conditions of private responding (that is, no normative influence), subjects conformed to a non-unanimous majority that contained a correct supporter (that is, no informational influence) only if it was the subjects' explicit or implicit ingroup. Other support for referent informational influence comes from research into group polarisation – see Chapter 8).

MINORITY INFLUENCE AND SOCIAL CHANGE

▶ Minority influence

Our discussion of social influence, particularly conformity, has thus far been concerned with how individuals yield to direct or indirect social influence from a numerical majority – the usual Asch-type arrangement. Dissenters, deviates or independents have mainly been of interest indirectly, either as a means of investigating the effects of different types of majority or to investigate

An active minority: being visible. Active minorities can gain influence by acting in ways which attract attention to their views. These lesbians and gay men have their moment on centre stage at their annual Pride March. (Source: Nicola Horton.)

An active minority: being consistent and unanimous. Active minorities can counteract their lack of numbers by acting as one and being unwavering in their view. Greenpeace has consistently refused to compromise in its stand against what it perceives to be any form of pollution of the natural environment. (Source: Greenpeace Communications Photo Library, © Greenpeace/Hodson.)

conformist personality attributes. We are, however, all familiar with a very different, and very common, type of influence that can occur within a group: an individual or a numerical *minority* can change the views of the majority. Often such influence is based, in the case of individuals, on leadership or, in the case of subgroups, legitimate power (leadership is discussed in Chapter 8).

However, there is an entire class of events where a minority which has little or no legitimate power can be innovative and sway the majority to its own viewpoint. For example, Asch (1952) found that a single deviate (confederate) from a correct majority (true subjects) was ridiculed and laughed at. In another variant, however, Asch found quite a different response. When a correct majority of eleven true subjects was confronted by a deviant/incorrect minority of nine confederates, the majority remained independent (that is, continued responding correctly), but took the minority's responses far more seriously – nobody laughed. Clearly the minority had some influence over the majority, albeit not enough in this experiment to produce manifest conformity.

History illustrates the power of minorities. It could be argued that if the only form of social influence was majority influence then complete social homogeneity would have been reached tens of thousands of years ago – individuals and groups always being swayed to adopt the views and practices of the growing numerical majority. Minorities, particularly ones that are active and organised, introduce innovations that ultimately produce social change: without minority influence social change would be very difficult to explain. For example, the massive anti-war rallies during the 1960s in the United States had an effect on majority attitudes that hastened withdrawal from Vietnam. Similarly, the suffragettes of the 1920s gradually changed public opinion so that women were granted the vote, and the enormous CND rallies in western Europe in the early 1980s gradually shifted public opinion away from the 'benefits' of nuclear proliferation. An excellent example of an active minority is Greenpeace: the group is numerically small (in terms of 'activist' members) but has important and burgeoning influence on public opinion through membership of the organisation and wider publicity of its views.

The sorts of question that are important here are whether minorities and majorities gain influence via different social practices and, more fundamentally, whether the underlying psychology is different.

Critique of conformity research

▶ Conformity bias

Social influence research has generally adopted a conformity perspective in which individuals are dependent on majorities for normative and informational reasons. Moscovici and colleagues have launched an attack on this perspective (Moscovici 1976; Moscovici and Faucheux 1972; see Turner 1991). Moscovici believes there is a *conformity bias* which considers all social influence as serving an adaptive requirement of human life – to adapt to the status quo and thus produce uniformity and perpetuate stability. Clearly this is a valid and important need for individuals, groups and society. However, normative *change* is sometimes required to adapt to altered circumstances. Such change is difficult to understand from a conformity perspective – it requires an understanding of the dynamics of active minorities.

Moscovici and Faucheux (1972) suggested that in fact it is minority influence that Asch observed in his classic studies. The Asch paradigm appears to pit a lone individual (true subject) against an erroneous majority (confederates) on an unambiguous physical perception task. Clearly a case of majority influence in the absence of subjective uncertainty? Perhaps not. The certainty with which we hold views lies in the amount of agreement we encounter for those views – ambiguity and uncertainty are not properties of objects 'out there', but of other people's disagreement with us. This point is just as valid for matters of taste (if everyone disagrees with your taste in music then your taste is very likely to change) as for matters of physical perception (if everyone disagrees with your perception of length then, again, your perception is likely to change) – see Moscovici (1976, 1985a), Tajfel (1969) and Turner (1985). In this sense, Asch's lines were not 'unambiguous' because there was disagreement about their length. Furthermore, Asch's lone subject can be considered to be a member of a rather large majority (those people outside the experiment who would call the lines correctly – that is, the rest of humanity) confronted by a very small minority (the confederates who called the lines 'incorrectly') – see Tajfel (1972a). Asch's subjects were influenced by a minority – those who remained 'independent' can be considered to be the conformists. Independence in this sense is nicely described by Henry Thoreau in his famous quote from *Walden* (1854): 'If a man does not keep pace with his companions, perhaps it is because he hears a different drummer.'

In contrast to traditional conformity research, Moscovici (1976, 1985a) believed that there is disagreement and conflict within groups, and that there are three *social influence modalities* that define how people respond to such social conflict:

1. *Conformity* – majority influence in which the majority persuades the minority or deviates to adopt the majority viewpoint.
2. *Normalisation* – mutual compromise leading to convergence.
3. *Innovation* – a minority creates and accentuates conflict in order to persuade the majority to adopt the minority viewpoint.

Influence of behavioural style

▶ Genetic model

Moscovici originally developed a *genetic model* of minority influence. He called it genetic because it focused on the way in which the dynamics of social conflict can produce social change. People do not like social conflict: they try to avoid it or, if that is not possible, will often readily capitulate to resolve the situation. An active minority capitalises on this by going out of its way to create, draw attention to and accentuate conflict. Moscovici and colleagues believe that this can be an effective way of winning over the majority, but it hinges on just *how* the minority goes about its task – on the *behavioural style* it adopts.

The single most important behavioural style is consistency. A *consistent minority*, one in which all members repeatedly promulgate the same message, has the following effects:

1. It disrupts the majority norm and thus produces uncertainty and doubt.
2. It draws attention to itself as an entity.
3. It conveys the existence of an alternative coherent point of view.
4. It demonstrates certainty and unshakeable commitment to this point of view.
5. It shows that the only solution to the conflict that has arisen is espousal of the minority viewpoint.

The role of consistency is illustrated by Moscovici and his colleagues in a series of ingenious experiments often referred to as the blue/green studies (Maass and Clark 1984). In a modified version of the Asch paradigm, Moscovici *et al.* (1969) had four subjects confront two confederates for a colour perception task involving blue slides which varied only in intensity. The confederates were either consistent – always calling the slides green – or inconsistent – calling the slides green two-thirds of the time and blue one-third of the time. There was also a control condition with no confederates, just six true subjects. Figure 6.8 shows that the consistent minority had significantly more influence than the inconsistent minority. Although the conformity rate is much lower than with a consistent majority, it is

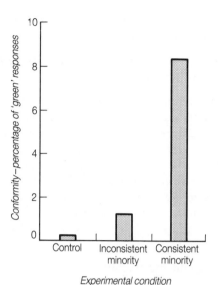

FIGURE 6.8 *Conformity to a minority as a function of minority consistency. (Source: based on data from Moscovici* et al. *1969.)*

nevertheless quite remarkable that four people (a numerical majority) were influenced by two people (a minority).

There are two other notable results from an extension of this experiment, in which subjects' real colour thresholds were tested privately after the social influence stage: (1) both experimental groups showed a lower threshold for green than the control group, that is they erred towards seeing ambiguous green/blue slides as green, and (2) this effect was greater among experimental subjects who were resistant to the minority, that is those that did not publicly call the blue slides green.

Moscovici and Lage (1976) employed the same colour perception task to compare consistent and inconsistent minorities with consistent and inconsistent majorities. There was also a control condition. As before, the only minority to produce conformity was the consistent minority (10 per cent conformity). Although this does not compare well with the rate of conformity to the consistent majority (40 per cent), it is comparable with the rate of conformity to the inconsistent majority (12 per cent). The most important finding, however, was that the *only* subjects in the entire experiment who actually changed their blue/green thresholds were those in the consistent minority condition.

There are two other properties of consistency that seem to be important:

1. It is perceived consistency, not merely objective repetition, that is important (Nemeth *et al.* 1974).

2. The presence of consistency between members of the minority (that is, consensus) is a crucial factor (Nemeth *et al.* 1977).

Aside from consistency, there are at least three other *behavioural style factors* that may affect minority influence:

1. *Investment* – minorities are more effective if they are seen to have made significant personal or material sacrifices for their cause.
2. *Autonomy* – minorities are more effective if seen to be acting out of principle rather than from ulterior motives.
3. *Rigidity/flexibility* – a minority which is too rigid risks being rejected as dogmatic, while one which is too flexible risks being rejected as inconsistent. There is a fine line to tread: a minority must be absolutely consistent with regard to its position but should adopt a relatively open-minded and reasonable negotiating style (Moscovici and Mugny 1983; Mugny 1982).

Group membership and social identity

Groups in society that promulgate minority viewpoints are generally widely stigmatised by the majority as social outgroups or are psychologised as deviant individuals. Their views are, at best, rejected as irrelevant, but are often ridiculed and trivialised in an attempt to discredit the minority (for example, the treatment of gays, environmentalists, feminists) – see Chapter 9 for a discussion of discrimination against outgroups. All this resistance on the part of the majority makes it even more difficult for minorities to have effective influence.

Research confirms that minorities exert mere influence when they are perceived by the majority as ingroup members (Maass *et al.* 1982; Martin 1988; Mugny and Papastamou 1982). This may be because minority influence changes self-referent attitudes and thus changes social identity (Mugny 1982; Turner 1991). This may be facilitated if the minority can be readily defined as an ingroup: for instance, straight males' attitudes towards homosexuality are more likely to become more liberal if such liberal attitudes are promulgated by ingroupers (that is, other straight males) rather than outgroupers (homosexual males).

Conversion

▶ Conversion effect

In 1980 Moscovici supplemented his earlier genetic model of social influence with a *dual process model* (Moscovici 1980). He argued that majorities and minorities exert influence through different processes. Majority influence brings about direct public compliance for reasons of normative or informational dependence. Majority views are accepted passively without much thought. In contrast, minority influence brings about indirect, often latent, private change in opinion due to the cognitive conflict and restructuring that deviant ideas produce. Minorities produce a *conversion effect* as a consequence of active consideration of the minority point of view. This distinction is very similar to that discussed earlier between normative and informational influence.

Conversion through minority influence would be expected to take longer to manifest itself than would compliance through majority influence. Indeed, as we have already seen, Moscovici *et al.* (1969), and Moscovici and Lage (1976) found evidence for private change in colour thresholds (that is, conversion) among subjects exposed to a consistent minority but who did not behave (or had not yet behaved) publicly in accordance with this change.

There is other evidence for the existence of two distinct processes. Nemeth and colleagues (Nemeth 1986; Nemeth and Wachtler 1983) have conducted a number of Asch type and blue/green experiments in which subjects exposed to majority or minority influence converged, with little thought, on majority responses, but minorities stimulated divergent, novel, creative thinking and more active information processing that increased the probability of correct answers. Maass and Clark (1983, 1986) report three experiments investigating people's public and private reactions to majority and minority influence regarding the issue of gay rights. In one of these experiments (1983), they found that publicly expressed attitudes conformed to the expressed views of the majority (that is, if the majority was pro-gay then so were the subjects), while privately expressed attitudes shifted towards the position espoused by the minority – see Figure 6.9.

Perhaps the most intriguing series of experiments is by Moscovici and Personnaz (1980, 1986), who employed the blue/green paradigm as before. Individual subjects, judging the colour of obviously blue slides that varied only

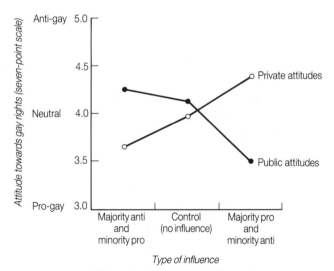

FIGURE 6.9 *Public and private attitude change in response to majority and minority influence. (Source: based on data from Maass and Clark 1983.)*

in intensity, were exposed to a single confederate who always called the slides green. Subjects were led to believe that most people (82 per cent) would respond as the confederate did, or that only very few people (18 per cent) would. In this way, the confederate was a source of majority or minority influence. Subjects publicly called out the colour of the slide and then (and this is the ingenious twist introduced by Moscovici and Personnaz) the slide was removed and subjects wrote down privately the colour of the after-image. Unknown to most people, including the subjects, the after-image is always the complementary colour. So, for blue slides the after-image is yellow, and for green slides it would be purple. There were three phases to the experiment: an influence phase where subjects were exposed to the confederate, preceded and followed by phases where the confederates were absent and so there was no influence. The results were remarkable – see Figure 6.10. Majority influence hardly affected the chromatic after-image: it remained yellow, indicating that subjects had seen a blue slide. Minority influence, however, shifted the after-image towards purple, indicating that subjects had actually 'seen' a green slide. The effect persisted even when the minority confederate was absent.

Although this remarkable finding, which clearly supports the idea that minority influence produces indirect, latent internal change while majority influence produces direct, immediate behavioural compliance, has been replicated by Moscovici and Personnaz, others have been less successful (for example, Doms and van Avermaet 1980; Sorrentino *et al.* 1980). Precisely why this may be remains unclear. There is also some concern (for example, Abrams and Hogg 1990a; Turner 1991) that the postulation of separate processes

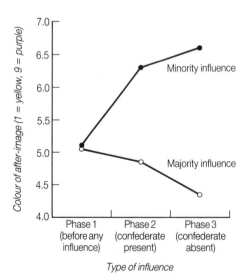

FIGURE 6.10 *Chromatic after-image as a result of majority and minority influence. (Source: based on data from Moscovici and Personnaz 1980.)*

to explain minority and majority influence has revived the opposition of informational and normative influence that has problems in explaining other social influence phenomena.

Attribution and minority influence

▶ Attribution

There are many aspects of minority influence that suggest the operation of an underlying *attribution* process (Kelley 1967; Hewstone 1989 – see Chapter 3). Effective minorities are consistent and consensual, distinct from the majority, unmotivated by self-interest or external pressures and flexible in style. This combination of factors encourages a perception that the minority has freely chosen its position. It is, therefore, difficult to explain away its position in terms of idiosyncrasies of individuals (though this is, as we saw above, a strategy that is attempted), or in terms of external inducements or threats. Perhaps then there might actually be some intrinsic merit to its position. This encourages people to take the minority seriously (though again social forces work against this) and at least consider its position: such cognitive work is an important precondition for subsequent attitude change.

Social impact and minority influence

▶ Social impact

Although majorities and minorities can be defined in terms of power, they also clearly refer to numbers of people. Although 'minorities' are often both less powerful and less numerous (for example, West Indians in Britain) they can be less powerful but more numerous (for example, until 1994 blacks in South Africa). Perhaps not surprisingly, an attempt has been made to explain minority influence purely in terms of social influence consequences of relative numerosity. Latané and Wolf (1981) draw on *social impact* theory (for example, Latané 1981) to argue that as a source of influence increases in size (numerosity) it has more influence. However, as the source of influence gets larger, the impact of each additional source is reduced. A good analogy is switching on a single light in a dark room – the impact is enormous. A second light improves things but only a little. If you have ten lights on, the impact of an eleventh will be negligible.

Evidence does support this idea: the larger the source of influence the more impact it has, but incremental changes due to additional sources decrease with increasing size (for example, Mullen 1983; Tanford and Penrod 1984). But how does this account for the fact that minorities actually can have influence? There is a sense in which the effect of a large majority on an individual majority member has reached a plateau – additional members or 'bits' of majority influence have relatively little impact. Although a minority viewpoint has relatively little impact, it has not yet attained a plateau – additional members or 'bits' of minority influence have a relatively large impact. In this way, exposure to minority positions can, paradoxically, have relatively greater impact than exposure to majority viewpoints.

This perspective can to some extent account for quantitative differences between majority and minority influence at the level of overt public behaviour. However, even Latané and Wolf (1981) admit that it cannot explain the qualitative differences that quite clearly exist, particularly at the private level of covert cognitive changes.

SUMMARY

♦ Social influence can produce surface compliance with requests, obedience of commands, or internalised conformity to group norms.

♦ People tend to be more readily influenced by reference groups, as they are psychologically significant for one's attitudes and behaviours, than by membership groups, as they are simply groups to which one belongs by some external criterion.

♦ Compliance is influenced not only by the specific tactics used to gain compliance but also by the perceived social power of the source of influence.

♦ Given the right circumstances we all have the potential blindly to obey commands, even if the consequences of such obedience include harm to others.

♦ Obedience is affected by the proximity and legitimacy of authority, by the proximity of the victim and by the degree of social support for obedience or disobedience.

♦ Group norms are enormously potent sources of conformity – we all tend to yield to the majority.

♦ Conformity can be reduced if the task is unambiguous and if one is not under surveillance, although even under these circumstances there is often residual conformity. Lack of unanimity among the majority is particularly effective in reducing conformity.

♦ People may conform in order to feel sure about the objective validity of their perceptions and opinions, to obtain social approval and avoid social disapproval, or in order to express or validate their social identity as a member of a specific group.

♦ Active minorities can sometimes influence majorities – this may be the very essence of social change.

♦ To be effective, minorities should be consistent but not rigid, should be seen to be making personal sacrifices and acting out of principle, and should be perceived as being part of the ingroup.

♦ Minorities may be effective because, unlike majority influence which is based on 'mindless' compliance, they cause latent cognitive change as a consequence of thought produced by the cognitive challenge posed by the novel minority position.

FURTHER READING

Baron, R. S., Kerr, N. and Miller, N. (1992). *Group Process, Group Decision, Group Action*. Buckingham: Open University Press.

Brown, R. J. (1988). *Group Processes: Dynamics Within and Between Groups*. Oxford: Blackwell.

Mugny, G. and Pérez, J. A. (1991). *The Social Psychology of Minority Influence*. Cambridge: Cambridge University Press.

Turner, J. C. (1991). *Social Influence*. Buckingham: Open University Press.

▶ KEY TERMS

attribution

autokinesis

compliance

conformity

conformity bias

conversion effect

dual process dependency model

frame of reference

genetic model

informational influence

ingratiation

membership group

minority influence

multiple requests

normative influence

norms

power

reciprocity principle

reference group

referent informational influence

self-categorisation theory

social identity theory

social impact

social influence

7 Group processes

FOCUS QUESTIONS

♦ When does a collection of people become a group?
♦ Do you find that you perform tasks better in front of an audience or on your own?
♦ Do groups work harder or do better than individuals?
♦ What is it, psychologically, that is responsible for group solidarity, and what are the effects of solidarity?
♦ Why do people join groups, how do they become members, and what is the process of group socialisation?
♦ How and why do group norms develop?
♦ Why do people in groups occupy different roles, and why are some roles more prestigious than others?

WHAT IS A GROUP?

▶ Group

Social groups occupy much of our day-to-day life. We work in groups, we socialise in groups, we play in groups, and we represent our views and attitudes through groups. Groups also largely determine the people we are, and the sorts of lives we live. Selection panels, juries, committees and government bodies influence what we do, where we live and how we live. The groups to which we belong determine what language we speak, what accent we have, what attitudes we hold, what cultural practices we adopt, what education we receive, what level of prosperity we enjoy, and ultimately who we are. Even the groups to which we do not belong, either by choice or by exclusion, have a profound impact on our lives. In this overwhelming matrix of group influences, the domain of the autonomous, independent, unique self may actually be very limited indeed.

Groups differ in all sorts of respects. Some have a large number of members (for example, a nation, a sex), and others are small (a committee, a family); some are relatively short-lived (a group of friends, a jury) and some endure for thousands of years (an ethnic group, a religion); some are concentrated (a yacht crew, a selection committee), others dispersed (radio hams, academics); some are highly structured and organised (an army, a flight crew), others more

Chance encounter. This audience has a common purpose: it waits to be entertained. But few of these people know each other, or will speak to or see each other again. Is an *ad hoc* collection of people a group? (Source: Andrew Lukey.)

informally organised (a supporters club, a community action group); some have highly specific purposes (an assembly line, an environmental protest group), others are more general (a tribal group, a teenage gang); some are relatively autocratic (an army, a police force), others relatively democratic (a university department, a commune); and so on.

Any social group can thus be described in terms of an array of features that highlight similarities to and differences from other groups. These can be very general features, such as membership size (for example, a religion versus a committee), but can also be very specific features, such as group practices and beliefs (for example, Catholics versus Muslims, liberals versus conservatives, Masai versus Kikuyu). However, this enormous variety of groups could be reduced by selecting a limited number of significant dimensions in order to produce a restricted taxonomy of groups. Social psychologists have tended to focus more on group size, group 'atmosphere', task structure and leadership structure than other dimensions.

Not all collections of individuals can necessarily be considered a group in a psychological sense. For example, people with green eyes, strangers in a dentist's waiting room, people on a beach, locals fishing off a pier – are these groups? Perhaps not. Perhaps these are simply social aggregates, collections of unrelated individuals, not groups at all. The important social psychological question is what distinguishes groups from aggregates, and it is by no means an easy question to answer. Social psychologists differ in their views on this issue. These differences are, to some extent, influenced by whether the researcher favours an individualistic or a collectivistic perspective on groups

(Hogg and Abrams 1988; Turner and Oakes 1986). Individualists believe that people in groups behave in much the same way as they do in pairs or by themselves, and that group processes are really nothing more than interpersonal processes among a number of people (for example, Allport 1924; Latané 1981). Collectivists believe that the behaviour of people in groups is influenced by unique social processes and cognitive representations that can only occur in and emerge from groups (for example, Abrams and Hogg 1988; McDougall 1920; Sherif 1936; Tajfel and Turner 1979).

Let us now return to definitions of the social group. Although there are almost as many definitions of the social group as there are social psychologists who research social groups, Johnson and Johnson (1987) have identified seven major emphases. The group is:

1. A collection of individuals who are interacting with one another.
2. A social unit consisting of two or more persons who perceive themselves as belonging to a group.
3. A collection of individuals who are interdependent.
4. A collection of individuals who join together to achieve a goal.
5. A collection of individuals who are trying to satisfy some need through their joint association.
6. A collection of individuals whose interactions are structured by a set of roles and norms.
7. A collection of individuals who influence each other.

Their definition incorporates all these emphases:

> A group is two or more individuals in face-to-face interaction, each aware of his or her membership in the group, each aware of the others who belong to the group, and each aware of their positive interdependence as they strive to achieve mutual goals. (Johnson and Johnson 1987, p. 8)

You will notice that this definition, and many of the emphases in the previous paragraph, either cannot encompass large groups and/or do not distinguish between interpersonal and group relationships. This is actually a relatively accurate portrayal of the social psychology of group processes, which is generally restricted, explicitly or implicitly, to small, face-to-face, short-lived, interactive, task-oriented groups. In addition, 'group processes' generally do not mean *group* processes but interpersonal processes among more than two people.

EFFECT OF THE GROUP ON INDIVIDUAL PERFORMANCE

Mere presence and audience effects: social facilitation

▶ Social facilitation

Perhaps the most basic and elementary *social* psychological question concerns the effect of the presence of other people on one's behaviour: 'what changes in

Winners, losers and the audience effect. The presence of an audience can cause people to perform well learned activities better and poorly learned activities worse – some even fall off. (Source: *New Zealand Herald.*)

an individual's normal solitary performance occur when other people are present?' (Gordon Allport 1954, p. 46). You are playing a musical instrument, fixing the car, reciting a poem or working out in the gym, and someone comes to watch – what happens to your performance? Does it improve or deteriorate?

This question intrigued Norman Triplett (1898), credited by some as having conducted the first social psychology experiment, though there has been controversy about this (see Box 1.1 in Chapter 1). From observing that people cycled faster when paced than when alone, and faster when in competition than when paced, Triplett hypothesised that competition between people energised and improved performance on motor tasks. To test this idea he had young children reeling a continuous loop of line on a 'competition machine', and confirmed his hypothesis: more children reeled the line more quickly when racing against each other in pairs than when performing alone. Floyd Allport (1920) termed this phenomenon *social facilitation* but felt that Triplett's narrowing of the effect to competition could be widened to allow for a more general principle: that an improvement in performance could be due to the *mere presence* of conspecifics (that is, members of the same species) as co-actors (doing the same thing but not interacting) or as a passive audience (passively watching).

▶ Audience effect
▶ Mere presence

Until the late 1930s an enormous amount of social facilitation research was conducted, much of it with an exotic array of animals. For example, we now know that cockroaches run faster, chickens, fish and rats eat more, and pairs of rats copulate more, when being 'watched' by conspecifics or when conspecifics are also running, eating or copulating. However, research has also revealed that social presence can produce quite the opposite effect: social inhibition, or a decrement in task performance. Contradictory findings such as these, in conjunction with imprecision in defining the degree of social presence (early research used a co-action paradigm while later research focused more on passive audience effects), led to the virtual demise of social facilitation research in about 1940.

Drive theory

▶ Drive theory

In 1965 Zajonc published a classic theoretical statement, called *drive theory* (see Figure 7.1), which revived social facilitation research and has kept it alive to the present day (see Geen 1989; Guerin 1986, 1993). Zajonc set himself the task of explaining what determines whether social presence (mainly in the form of a passive audience) facilitates or inhibits performance. Drive theory argues that because people are relatively unpredictable, there is a clear advantage to the species for their presence to cause us to be in a state of alertness and readiness. Increased arousal or motivation is thus an instinctive reaction to social presence. Such arousal functions as a drive that energises (that is, causes us to enact) those behaviours that are our dominant responses (that is, best learned, most habitual) in that situation. If the dominant response is correct (the task is subjectively considered to be easy), then social presence produces an improved performance; if it is incorrect (the task is considered to be difficult) then social presence produces an impaired performance.

Let us illustrate this with an example. You are a novice guitarist with a small repertoire of pieces to play. There is one piece which, when playing alone, you find extremely easy because it is very well learned – you almost never make mistakes. If you were to play this piece in front of an audience (say, your friends), drive theory would predict that because your dominant response is to make no mistakes your performance would be greatly improved. In contrast there is another piece which, when playing alone, you find extremely difficult because it is not very well learned – you almost never get it right. It would be a

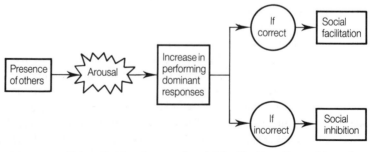

FIGURE 7.1 *Zajonc's drive theory of social facilitation. (Source: based on suggestions from Zajonc 1965.)*

rash decision indeed to play this in front of an audience—drive theory would predict that because the dominant response contains all sorts of errors your performance would be truly awful, much worse that when you play alone.

Evaluation apprehension

▶ Evaluation
apprehension
model

Although early research tends on the whole to support drive theory (Geen and Gange 1977; Guerin and Innes 1982), some social psychologists have questioned whether mere presence instinctively produces drive. Cottrell (1972) has proposed an *evaluation apprehension* model in which he argues that we quickly learn that the social rewards and punishments (for example, approval and disapproval) we receive are based on others' evaluations of us. Social presence thus produces an acquired arousal (drive) based on evaluation apprehension. In support of this interpretation, Cottrell *et al.* (1968) found no social facilitation effect on three well-learned tasks when the two-person audience was inattentive (that is, blindfolded) and merely present (that is, only incidentally present while ostensibly waiting to take part in a different experiment). This audience would be unlikely to produce much evaluation apprehension. However, a non-blindfolded audience that carefully attended to the subject's performance and had expressed an interest in watching, would be expected to produce a great deal of evaluation apprehension. Indeed, this audience did produce a social facilitation effect.

Other research is less supportive. For example, Markus (1978) had male subjects undress, dress in unfamiliar clothing (laboratory coat, special shoes), and then in their own clothing again. To minimise apprehension about evaluation by the experimenter, the task was presented as an incidental filler task. Subjects performed the task under one of three conditions: (1) alone; (2) in the presence of an incidental audience (low evaluation apprehension) – a confederate who faced away and was engrossed in some other task; (3) in the presence of an attentive audience (high evaluation apprehension) – a confederate who carefully and closely watched the subject dressing and undressing. The results (Figure 7.2) confirmed evaluation apprehension theory on the relatively easy task of dressing in familiar clothing – only an attentive audience decreased the time taken to perform this task. However, on the more difficult task of dressing in unfamiliar clothing mere presence was sufficient to slow performance down, and an attentive audience had no additional effect – this supports drive theory rather than evaluation apprehension.

Schmitt *et al.* (1986) conducted a similarly conceived experiment. Subjects were given what they thought was an incidental task that involved typing their name into a computer (a simple task), and then entering a code name by typing their name backwards interspersed with ascending digits (a difficult task). Subjects performed these tasks: (1) *alone* after the experimenter had left the room, (2) in the *mere presence* of only a confederate who was blindfolded, wore a headset, and was allegedly participating in a separate experiment on sensory deprivation, or (3) under the close *observation of the experimenter* who remained in the room carefully watching the subject's performance. The results of the

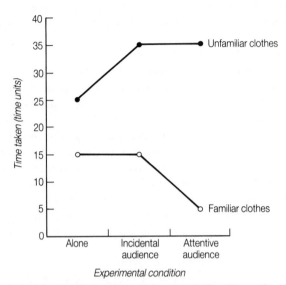

FIGURE 7.2 *Time taken to dress up in familiar and unfamiliar clothes as a function of social presence. (Source: based on data from Markus 1978.)*

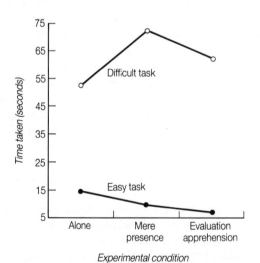

FIGURE 7.3 *Time taken for an easy and a difficult typing task as a function of social presence. (Source: based on data from Schmitt et al. 1986.)*

study show that mere presence produced a faster performance of the easy task and a slower performance of the difficult task, and that evaluation apprehension had little additional impact (Figure 7.3). Mere presence appears to be a sufficient cause of, and evaluation apprehension not .necessary for, social facilitation effects.

Guerin and Innes have suggested that social facilitation effects may occur only when people are unable to monitor the audience, and are therefore uncertain about the audience's evaluative reactions to their performance (Guerin and Innes 1982). In support of this idea, Guerin (1989) found a social facilitation effect on a simple letter-copying task only among subjects who were being watched by a confederate who they could *not* see. When the confederate could be clearly seen, there was no social facilitation effect.

Distraction-conflict theory

▶ Distraction-conflict theory

Another explanation of the link between social presence and drive has been proposed by Baron and others (Baron 1986; Sanders 1983; Sanders *et al.* 1978) – *distraction-conflict theory* (see Figure 7.4). They argue that people are a source of distraction that produces attentional conflict between attending to the task and attending to the audience or co-actors. While distraction alone impairs task performance, attentional conflict also produces drive that facilitates dominant responses. Together these processes impair the performance of difficult tasks and, because drive usually overcomes distraction, improve the performance of easy tasks.

In support of distraction-conflict theory, Sanders *et al.* (1978) had subjects perform an easy and a difficult digit-copying task either alone or co-acting with someone performing either the same or a different task. They reasoned that someone performing a different task would not be a relevant source of social comparison and so distraction should be minimal, whereas someone performing the same task would be a relevant source of comparison and therefore

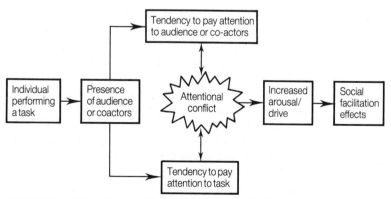

FIGURE 7.4 *Distraction-conflict theory of social facilitation. (Source: adapted from Baron and Byrne 1987.)*

highly distracting. As predicted, they found that subjects in the distraction condition made more mistakes on the difficult task and copied more digits correctly on the simple task, than in the other conditions.

Distraction/conflict theory has some other strengths. Experiments show that any form of distraction (noise, movement, flashing lights), not only social presence, can produce social facilitation effects. In addition, unlike an evaluation apprehension model, it can deal with results from studies of social facilitation in animals. It is difficult to believe that cockroaches eat more while other cockroaches are watching because they are anxious about evaluation; however, presumably even the lowly cockroach can be distracted. Distraction/conflict theory also has the edge on evaluation apprehension in an experiment by Groff *et al.* (1983). Whenever a tone sounded subjects had to rate the facial expressions of a person appearing on a television monitor, and at the same time, as an ostensibly incidental activity, squeeze as firmly as possible a bottle held in the hand (latency and strength of squeeze were measures of arousal/drive). Subjects undertook the experiment: (1) alone, (2) closely scrutinised by a confederate sitting off to one side – this would be highly distracting as the subject would need to look away from the screen in order to look at the observer, or (3) closely scrutinised by a confederate who was actually the person on the screen – no attentional conflict. As predicted from distraction/conflict theory, subjects squeezed the bottle much more strongly in the second condition.

Non-drive explanations of social facilitation

So far, we have discussed explanations of social facilitation that retain the notion of drive and differ only over whether drive is an innate response to mere presence, a learned response based on evaluation apprehension or a product of attentional conflict. Although, to date, these are the best established and most researched explanations of social facilitation, there are a number of other approaches that do not retain the notion of drive. After all, it is rather difficult to confirm or refute the existence of drive as a mediating mechanism. There are no unambiguous and direct ways to measure it: although physiological measures of arousal (for example, palmar sweating) presumably may access drive, the absence of physiological arousal is no guarantee that drive is not operating, as drive is defined in psychological not physiological terms.

One non-drive explanation of social facilitation is in terms of *self-awareness theory* (Carver and Scheier 1981; Duval and Wicklund 1972; Wicklund 1975). When people focus their attention on themselves as an object, they make active comparisons between actual self (their actual task performance) and ideal self (how they would like to perform). The discrepancy between actual and ideal self increases motivation and effort to bring actual into line with ideal, so on easy tasks there is improved performance. On difficult tasks the discrepancy is too great, so people give up trying, and thus there is a deterioration in performance. Self-awareness can be produced by a range of circumstances such as looking at oneself in a mirror or the presence of coactors or an audience.

Still focusing on the role of self in social faciliation, Bond (1982) believes that people are concerned with presenting to others the best impression possible of themselves. Since this is achievable on easy tasks, social presence produces an improved performance. On more difficult tasks people make or anticipate making errors, which creates embarrassment. This embarrassment impairs task performance.

Another way to explain social facilitation, without invoking self or drive, is in terms of the attentional consequences alone of social presence. Baron (1986) believes people have a finite attention capacity which can be overloaded by the presence of an audience. Attention-overload causes people to narrow attention and prioritise attentional demands to focus on a small number of central cues. Difficult tasks are ones that require attention to a large number of cues, and so attentional narrowing is likely to divert attention from cues that really ought to be attended to: thus social presence impairs performance. Simple tasks are ones that require attention to only a small number of cues, and so attentional narrowing actually eliminates distraction from attending to extraneous cues and focuses it onto central cues: thus social presence improves performance.

Manstead and Semin (1980) have suggested a similar model but with the emphasis on a distinction between automatic and controlled task performance. They argue that difficult tasks require a great deal of attention because they are highly controlled. An audience distracts vital attention from task performance which thus suffers. Easy tasks require little attention because they are fairly automatic. An audience causes more attention to be paid to the task which thus becomes more controlled and better performed.

Social psychologists have suggested and investigated a large number of different explanations of what initially may have appeared to be a rather basic and straightforward social phenomenon. Some explanations fare better than others, some have not yet been properly tested, and after almost one hundred years of research a number of questions remain unanswered. Nevertheless, the study of audience effects remains an important topic for social psychology, since much of our behaviour is in the physical presence of others as an audience. A survey administered by Borden (1980) revealed that people feared speaking in front of an audience more than heights, darkness, loneliness, and even death.

However, we should perhaps keep in perspective the actual degree of impact that mere presence has on behaviour. From a review of 241 social facilitation experiments involving 24,000 subjects, Bond and Titus (1983) concluded that mere presence accounted for only a tiny 0.3 per cent to 3.0 per cent of variation in behaviour. Bond and Titus used a technique called meta-analysis to arrive at these figures. This is a statistical technique that enables data from different individual studies to be analysed as if they came from one large study. In order to explain some of the remaining variation we now move from non-interactive contexts to more interactive contexts and true group processes.

Classification of group tasks

Social facilitation research distinguishes between easy and difficult tasks, but restricts itself to tasks that do not of necessity require interaction, inter-individual co-ordination, division of labour and so forth. While many tasks fall into this category (for example, dressing, washing the car, cycling), many others do not (for example, building a house, playing cricket, running a business). It is not unreasonable to assume that social presence will have entirely different effects on task performance, not only as a function of the degree of social presence (passive audience, co-actor, interdependent interaction on a group task) but also as a function of the specific task being performed. What is needed is a taxonomy of types of task based on a limited number of psychologically meaningful parameters.

▶ Task taxonomy

The pragmatic question of whether groups perform better than individuals has produced such a taxonomy (Steiner 1972, 1976). Steiner's *task taxonomy* has three dimensions that are best captured by asking three questions:

1. Is the task divisible or unitary?
   - A *divisible* task is one which benefits from a division of labour in which different people perform different subtasks.
   - A *unitary* task cannot sensibly be broken into subtasks. Building a house is a divisible task, and pulling a rope a unitary task.
2. Is it a maximising or an optimising task?
   - A *maximising* task is an open-ended task that stresses quantity – the objective is to do as much as possible.
   - An *optimising* task is one that has a predetermined standard to be met – the objective is to meet the standard, neither to exceed nor fall short of it. Pulling on a rope would be a maximising task, but maintaining a specified fixed force on the rope would be an optimising task.
3. How are individual inputs related to the group's product?
   - An *additive* task is one where the group's product is the sum of all the individual inputs, for example a group of people planting trees.
   - A *compensatory* task is one where the group's product is the average of the individuals' inputs, for example a group of people estimating the number of bars in Amsterdam.
   - A *disjunctive* task is one where the group selects as its adopted product one individual's input, for example a group of people proposing different things to do over the weekend will adopt one person's suggestion.
   - A *conjunctive* task is one where the group's product is determined by the rate or level of performance of the slowest or least able member, for example, a group working on an assembly line.
   - A *discretionary* task is one where the relationship between individual inputs and group product is not directly dictated by task features or social conventions; instead the group is free to decide on its preferred course of action, for example a group that *decides* to shovel snow together.

▶ Process loss

These parameters allow us to classify tasks. For example, a tug-of-war is unitary, maximising and additive; assembling a car is divisible, optimising and conjunctive; and many group decision-making tasks are divisible, optimising and disjunctive (or compensatory). As regards whether groups are better than individuals, Steiner believes that in general the actual group product is always less than the group's potential (based on the potential of its human resources). This shortfall is due mainly to a *process loss* (for example, losses due to the co-ordination of individual members' activities, disproportionate influence on the part of specific powerful group members, and various social distractors). However, against this background, Steiner's taxonomy makes predictions about what sorts of task favour group performance.

For additive tasks the group's performance is better than the best individual's performance. For compensatory tasks the group's performance is better than most individuals' (because the average is most likely to be correct). For disjunctive tasks the group's performance is equal to or worse than the best individual (the group cannot do better than the best idea proposed). For conjunctive tasks the group's performance is equal to the worst individual's performance, unless the task is divisible in which case a division of labour can redirect the weakest member to an easier task and so improve the group's performance.

▶ Co-ordination loss

Although Steiner emphasised the role of *co-ordination loss* in preventing a group from performing optimally in terms of the potential of its members, he also raised the possibility of an entirely different, and more fundamentally psychological, type of loss – motivation loss.

Social loafing and social impact

▶ Ringelmann effect

Ringelmann (1913), a French professor of agricultural engineering, conducted a number of experiments to investigate the efficiency of various numbers of people, animals and machines in performing agricultural tasks (Kravitz and Martin 1986). In one study he had young men, alone or in groups of two, three or eight pull horizontally on a rope attached to a dynamometer (an instrument that measures the amount of force exerted). He found that the force exerted per person decreased as a function of increasing group size: the larger the group the less strongly each person pulled (see Figure 7.5). This is termed the *Ringelmann effect*.

Our previous discussion suggests two possible explanations for this:

1. *Co-ordination loss* – due to jostling, distraction and the tendency for people to pull slightly against one another, subjects were prevented from reaching their full potential.
2. *Motivation loss* – subjects were less motivated: they simply did not try so hard.

To investigate these explanations, Ingham *et al.* (1974) replicated Ringelmann's study, but with two experimental conditions. One in which real groups of

Social loafing. When people work together on a task they often each put in a little less effort than they would if they had been working on their own. (Source: Andrew Lukey.)

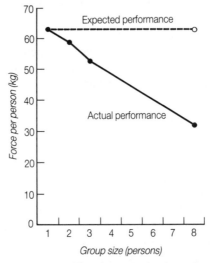

FIGURE 7.5 *Ringelmann's classic study of force per person as a function of group size. (Source: based on data from Ringlemann 1913.)*

varying size pulled on a rope, and the other involving pseudo-groups with only one true subject and a number of confederates. The confederates were instructed only to pretend to pull on the rope while making realistic grunts to indicate exertion. The true subject was in the first position and so did not know that the confederates were not actually pulling. The results (Figure 7.6) indicate a decrement in individual performance in pseudo-groups. Because

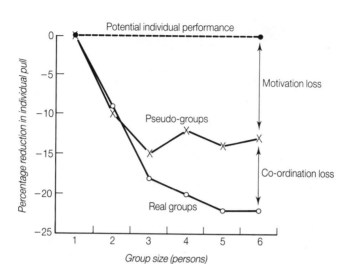

FIGURE 7.6 *Co-ordination and motivation losses in group rope-pulling. (Source: based on data from Ingham* et al. *1974.)*

there was no co-ordination, there can be no loss due to poor co-ordination: the decrement can be attributed only to a loss of motivation. In real groups there was an additional decrement in individual performance that can be attributed to co-ordination loss.

▶ Social loafing

This motivation loss has been termed *social loafing* by Latané *et al.* (1979), who replicated the effect with shouting, cheering and clapping tasks. For instance, they had subjects cheer and clap as loudly as possible alone or in groups of two, four or six. The amount of noise produced per person was reduced by 29 per cent in two-person groups, 49 per cent in four-person groups, and 60 per cent in six-person groups. For the shouting task subjects shouted alone or in two- or six-person real groups, or pseudo-groups (they wore blindfolds, and headsets transmitting continuous 'white noise'). As in Ingham *et al.*'s experiment, there was a clear reduction in effort for subjects in pseudo-groups, with additional co-ordination loss for real groups (see Figure 7.7).

Social loafing, then, is a tendency for individuals to work less hard (that is, loaf) on a task when they believe others are also working on the task. More formally, it refers to 'a reduction in individual effort when working on a collective task (in which one's outputs are pooled with those of other group members) compared to when working either alone or coactively' (Williams, *et al.* 1993, p. 131). A notable feature of loafing is that as group size increases the addition of new members to the group has a decreasingly significant impact on effort – the reduction of effort conforms to a negatively accelerating power function (see Figure 7.8). So, for example, the reduction in individual effort as the consequence of a third person joining a two-person group is relatively large, while the impact of an additional member on a twenty-person group is

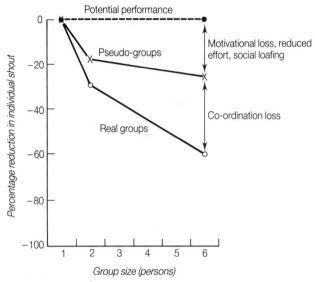

FIGURE 7.7 *Reduction in volume of individual shout in two-person and six-person real and pseudo-groups. (Source: based on data from Latané et al. 1979.)*

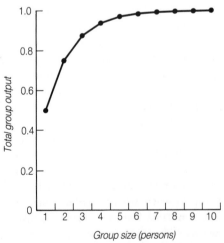

FIGURE 7.8 *Total group output as a negatively accelerating power function of group size.*

minimal. The range within which group size seems to have a significant impact is about one to eight members.

▶ Free-rider effect

Social loafing is related to the *free-rider effect* (Frohlich and Oppenheimer 1970; Kerr 1983) in research into social dilemmas and public goods (Chapter 10). A free-rider is someone who takes advantage of a shared public resource without contributing to its maintenance: for example a tax evader who uses the road system, visits national parks and benefits from public medical provisions is a free-rider. The main difference between loafing and free-riding is perhaps that although loafers reduce effort on co-active tasks they nevertheless do contribute to the group product (there is a *loss* of motivation); in contrast, free-riders exploit the group product while contributing nothing to it (there is a *different* motivation) – see Williams *et al.* (1993).

Social loafing is a pervasive and robust phenomenon across the almost eighty social loafing studies that have been conducted (see reviews by Geen 1991; Harkins and Szymanski 1987; Williams *et al.* 1993). The general paradigm is one in which individual or co-active performance is compared either with groups performing some sort of additive task (for example, brainstorming), or with the performance of pseudo-groups, in which people are led to *believe* they are performing collectively with varying numbers of others but in fact circumstances are arranged so that they are performing individually. Loafing has been obtained in the laboratory as well as in the field, on physical tasks (for example, shouting, clapping, rope-pulling, pumping air and swimming), on cognitive tasks (for example, generating ideas), on evaluative tasks (for example, quality ratings of poems, editorials and clinical therapists), and on perceptual tasks (for example, maze performance, vigilance performance), with a variety of subject populations from different cultures (for example, the United States, France, Poland, Japan, Taiwan, Thailand, India). Freeman *et al.* (1975) even found a loafing effect on restaurant tipping in the United States: roughly 20 per cent of people gave tips when seated alone, but only about 13 per cent when seated in groups of five or six.

Why do people loaf? Geen (1991) has suggested three explanations:

1. *Output equity* – people may loaf on collective tasks because they believe that people loaf in groups, thus expect their partners to loaf, and therefore loaf themselves in order to maintain equity (Jackson and Harkins 1985).
2. *Evaluation apprehension* – the presence of group members provides a cover to be anonymous and unidentifiable for people who are not motivated on a task (for example, an uninteresting, boring or tiring task) – Kerr and Bruun (1981). When performing individually or co-actively, rather than collectively, people are identifiable and thus apprehensive about performance evaluation by others, and therefore overcome their unmotivated state (Harkins 1987; Harkins and Szymanski 1987).
3. *Matching to standard* – people loaf because they have no clear performance standard to match. The presence of a clear personal, social or group

performance standard should reduce loafing (Goethals and Darley 1987; Harkins and Szymanski 1987; Szymanski and Harkins 1987).

▶ Social impact

Group size may have the effect it does due to *social impact* (for example, Latané, 1981 – see also Chapter 13). The experimenter's instructions to clap, shout, brainstorm or whatever (i.e. the social obligation to work as hard as possible) are a source of social impact upon the subjects. To the extent that there is one subject and one experimenter, the experimenter's instructions have maximal impact. If there are two subjects, the impact on each subject is halved, if three it is one-third, and so forth. There is a diffusion of individual responsibility that is greater the larger the group (see Chapter 13).

Loafing is not an inevitable consequence of group performance. Research has identified certain factors, apart from group size, that influence the tendency to loaf (see Geen 1991; Williams *et al.* 1993). For example, personal identifiability by the experimenter (Williams *et al.* 1981), personal involvement in the task (Brickner *et al.* 1986), partner effort (Jackson and Harkins 1985), intergroup comparison (Harkins and Szymanski 1989), and a highly meaningful task in association with expectation of poor performance by co-workers (Williams and Karau 1991) have all been shown to reduce loafing. In some circumstances people may even work harder collectively than co-actively in order to compensate for anticipated loafing by others on important tasks or in important groups (Williams and Karau 1991; Williams *et al.* 1993; Zaccaro 1984).

▶ Social compensation

This *social compensation* effect may be responsible for the results of an intriguing study by Zaccaro (1984). Zaccaro had male and female subjects construct 'moon tents' out of sheets of paper in two- or four-person co-active groups. The usual loafing effect emerged (see Figure 7.9). However, other subjects who believed they were competing against an outgroup, and for whom

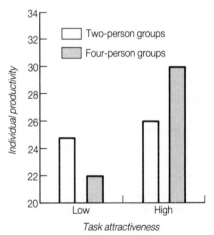

FIGURE 7.9 *Individual effort as a function of task attractiveness and group size. (Source: based on data from Zaccaro 1984.)*

the attractiveness and social relevance of the task was accentuated, behaved quite differently. The loafing effect was actually reversed – individuals performed at a higher rate in the larger group. This is an unusual finding. In contrast to the rather pessimistic view of some social psychologists that groups inevitably inhibit individuals from attaining their true potential (for example, Steiner 1972, 1976), this study indicates that group life may, under certain circumstances, cause people to exceed their individual potential.

BASIC ASPECTS OF GROUPS

Group cohesiveness

▶ Cohesiveness

One of the most basic properties of a group is its *cohesiveness* (solidarity, *esprit de corps*, team spirit, morale) – the way it 'hangs together' as a tightly knit, self-contained entity characterised by uniformity of conduct and mutual support among members. Cohesiveness is a variable property: it differs between groups, between contexts and across time. Groups with extremely low levels of cohesiveness appear hardly to be groups at all, and so the term may also capture the very essence of being a group – the psychological process that transforms an aggregate of individuals into a group. Cohesiveness is, thus, a descriptive term used to describe a property of the group as a whole; but it is

Putting it all together – group cohesiveness. Cohesive groups can get things done. These dragon boaters are amateurs, with little experience of this task, but their commitment to the team effort is paying off. (Source: *New Zealand Herald*.)

also a psychological term to describe the individual psychological process underlying the cohesiveness of groups. Herein lies a problem: it makes sense to say that a group is cohesive, but not that an individual is cohesive.

After almost a decade of informal usage, cohesiveness was formally defined by Festinger *et al.* (1950). They believed that a field of forces, deriving from the attractiveness of the group and its members and the degree to which the group satisfies individual goals, acts upon the individual. The resultant valence of these forces produces cohesiveness that is responsible for group membership continuity and adherence to group standards (Figure 7.10). Because concepts such as 'field of forces' are difficult to operationalise, and also because the theory was not precise about how to define cohesiveness operationally (that is, in terms of specific measures or experimental manipulations), social psychologists almost immediately simplified their conception of cohesiveness. For instance, in their own research into the cohesiveness of post-war student housing projects at the Massachusetts Institute of Technology, Festinger *et al.* simply asked students 'What three people ... do you see most of socially?' (1950, p. 37 – see Chapter 15 for details of this study).

Major reviews (for example, Cartwright 1968; Hogg 1992; Lott and Lott 1965) indicate that the bulk of research conceptualises cohesiveness in terms of attraction to group or interpersonal attraction, derives the cohesiveness of the group as a whole from summing (or some other arithmetical procedure) and operationalises cohesiveness accordingly. Not surprisingly, this research reveals that factors which increase interpersonal attraction (for example, similarity, co-operation, interpersonal acceptance, shared threat – see Chapter 12) generally elevate cohesiveness, and elevated cohesiveness produces or is associated with, for example, conformity to group standards, accentuated similarity, improved intragroup communication and enhanced liking.

It has been suggested (Hogg 1987, 1992; Turner 1982, 1984) that this perspective on group cohesiveness represents a much wider *social cohesion* or *interpersonal interdependence* model of the social group (see Figure 7.11), where

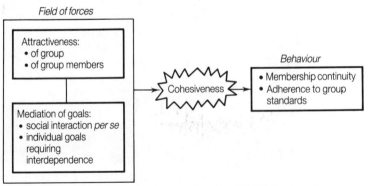

FIGURE 7.10 *Festinger, Schachter and Back's (1950) theory of group cohesiveness. (Source: adapted from Hogg 1992.)*

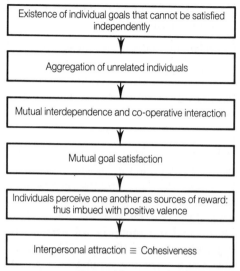

FIGURE 7.11 *General framework of the social cohesion/interpersonal interdependence model. (Source: adapted from Hogg 1992.)*

researchers tend to differ only in which components of the model they emphasise.

Because social psychologists have not really resolved the problem of knowing unambiguously how to operationalise cohesiveness (Evans and Jarvis 1980; Mudrack 1989), more recent research has tended to be in applied areas (Levine and Moreland 1990). In sports psychology, in particular, some quite rigorous scales have been devised, for example Widmeyer *et al.*'s (1985) eighteen-item *group environment questionnaire* to measure the cohesiveness of sports teams.

▶ Personal attraction
▶ Social attraction

A fundamental question that has been raised by social identity researchers (Hogg 1987, 1992; Turner 1984, 1985 – see Chapter 10) asks to what extent an analysis of group cohesiveness in terms of aggregation (or some other arithmetic integration) of interpersonal attraction really captures a *group* process at all. To all intents and purposes the group has disappeared entirely from the analysis and we are simply left with interpersonal attraction – about which we already know a great deal (Berscheid 1985 – see Chapter 12). Hogg (1992, 1993) suggests that a distinction should be made between *personal attraction* (true interpersonal attraction based on close relationships and idiosyncratic preferences) and *social attraction* (inter-individual liking based on perceptions of self and others in terms not of individuality but of group norms or prototypicality). Personal attraction is nothing to do with groups, while social attraction is the 'liking' component of group membership. Social attraction is merely one of a constellation of effects (ethnocentrism, conformity, intergroup differentiation, stereotyping, ingroup solidarity) produced by the process of self-categorisation specified in self-categorisation theory

(Turner *et al.* 1987 – see Chapter 10). This analysis has at least two major advantages over the traditional model:

1. It does not reduce group solidarity and cohesiveness to interpersonal attraction.
2. It is as applicable to small interactive groups (the only valid focus of traditional models) as large-scale social categories such as an ethnic group or a nation (people can feel attracted to one another on the basis of ethnic or national norms).

This perspective does appear quite promising. For example, Hogg and Turner (1985) aggregated people with others whom they ostensibly would like or dislike (the fact that the others were people they would like or dislike was irrelevant to the existence of the group), or explicitly categorised them as a group on the basis of the criterion that they would like one another or dislike one another. They found that interpersonal attraction was not automatically associated with greater solidarity (Figure 7.12). Rather, where interpersonal liking was neither the implicit nor explicit basis for the group (that is, in the random categorisation condition), group solidarity was unaffected by interpersonal attraction. In another study, Hogg and Hardie (1991) administered a questionnaire to an Australian Rules football team in Melbourne. Perceptions of team prototypicality and of norms were significantly related to measures of group-based social attraction, but not to measures of interpersonal attraction. This differential effect was strongest among members who themselves identified most strongly with the team. Similar findings have been obtained from studies of netball teams (Hogg and Hains 1994), laboratory

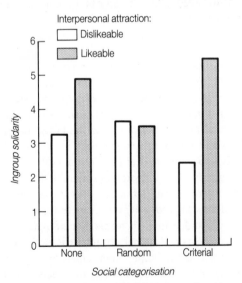

FIGURE 7.12 *Ingroup solidarity as a function of interpersonal attraction and social categorisation. (Source: Hogg and Turner 1985.)*

groups (Hogg *et al.* 1994), and of organisational and discussion groups (Hogg *et al.* 1993).

The social attraction perspective on group cohesiveness may also allow us to analyse the effects of intergroup relations on intragroup attraction. For example, one would predict that intergroup conflict would focus affective attention upon central group members with concomitant affective rejection of fringe members. Marques, in series of experiments on what he calls the black-sheep effect, has found some support for this idea (Marques 1990; Marques and Yzerbyt 1988; Marques *et al.* 1988).

Group socialisation

▶ Group socialisation

An obvious feature of many of the groups with which we are familiar is that new members join, old members leave, members are socialised by the group, and the group in turn is imprinted with the contribution of individuals. This dynamic aspect of groups often appears to be neglected in social psychology. To redress the balance, Moreland and Levine (1982, 1984; Moreland *et al.* 1993) have presented a model of *group socialisation* to describe and explain the passage of individuals through groups. They focus on the dynamic inter-relationship of group and individual members across the lifespan of the group.

There are three basic processes involved in group socialisation:

1. *Evaluation* refers to an ongoing comparison by individuals of the past, present and future rewards of the group with the rewards of potential alternative relationships (Thibaut and Kelley 1959) – see discussion of social exchange theory in Chapter 11. Simultaneously the group evaluates individuals in terms of their contribution to the life of the group. Behind this idea lies an assumption that people have goals and needs that create expectations. To the extent that expectations are, or are likely to be, met, social approval is expressed. Actual or anticipated failure to fulfil expectations invites social disapproval, and actions to modify behaviour or reject individuals or the group.
2. Evaluation affects *commitment* of the individual to the group and vice versa in a relatively straightforward manner. However, at any given time, commitment disequilibrium may exist such that the individual is more committed to the group or the group to the individual. This endows the least committed party with relatively greater power, and so is unstable. There is pressure towards commitment equilibrium. Commitment produces agreement on group goals and values, positive ties between individual and group, willingness to exert effort on the part of the group or the individual, and a desire for continuance of membership.
3. *Role transition* refers to discontinuities in the role relationship between individual and group. These discontinuities overlay a continuum of temporal variation in commitment, and are governed by groups' and

individuals' decision criteria for the occurrence of a transition. There are three general types of role: (1) non-member, including prospective members who have not joined the group and ex-members who have left the group; (2) quasi-member, including new members who have not yet attained full member status and marginal members who have lost that status; and (3) full member. Full members are those who are most closely identified with the group and who have all of the privileges and responsibilities associated with group membership. Role transitions can be smooth and easy where individual and group are equally committed and share the same decision criteria. However, commitment disequilibrium and unshared decision criteria can introduce conflict over whether a role transition should or did occur. For this reason, transition criteria often become formalised and public, and rites of passage become a central part of the life of the group.

▶ Initiation rites

Equipped with these processes, Moreland and Levine (1982, 1984) provide a detailed account of the passage of individual members through the group (Figure 7.13). There are five distinct phases of group socialisation, involving reciprocal evaluation and influence by group and individual, each heralded and/or concluded by a clear role transition (see Box 7.1). The occurrence of role transitions is considered an important aspect of group life. Indeed, Moreland and colleagues have conducted research on specific transitions; particularly those associated with becoming a member (Brinthaupt *et al.* 1991; Moreland 1985; Moreland and Levine 1989; Pavelchak *et al.* 1986). Generally, role transitions are ritualised public events – rites of passage or *initiation rites*.

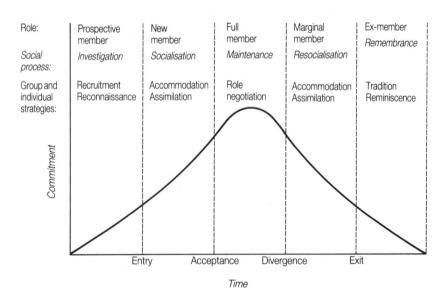

FIGURE 7.13 *Moreland and Levine's model of the process of group socialisation. (Source: Moreland and Levine 1982.)*

BOX 7.1 Phases of group socialisation

In their model of group socialisation, Moreland and Levine (1982, 1984; Moreland *et al.* 1993) identify five distinct phases of group socialisation (see Figure 7.13).

1. **Investigation.** The group recruits prospective members who in turn reconnoitre the group. This can be a formal process involving interviews and questionnaires (for example, joining an organisation or learned society), or more informal (for example, associating yourself with a student political society). Successful investigation leads to a role transition marking *entry* to the group.
2. **Socialisation.** The group assimilates new members by educating them in the ways of the group. In turn, new members attempt to get the group to accommodate to their own views. Socialisation can be unstructured and informal, but also quite formal (for example, induction programmes for new members of organisations). Successful socialisation is marked by *acceptance*.
3. **Maintenance.** Role negotiation among full members takes place. Role dissatisfaction can lead to a role transition called *divergence*, which can be unexpected and unplanned, but can also be an expected and quite ordinary feature of the group – for example, university students are expected to diverge as part of the process of graduating and leaving university.
4. **Resocialisation.** In the case of expected divergence there is little attempt at resocialisation. However, unexpected divergence marginalises the member into a deviant role and activates attempts at resocialisation. If successful, full membership is reinstated. If unsuccessful the individual leaves the group – *exit*. Exit may be marked by elaborate retirement ceremonies or the ritualistic stripping of insignia in a court martial.
5. **Remembrance.** After the individual has left the group, both parties engage in reminiscence. This can take the form of fond recall of the 'remember when ...' type, or the more extreme exercises in rewriting history engaged in by totalitarian regimes.

(Source: Moreland and Levine 1982).

These can be pleasant, marked by celebration and the giving of gifts (for example, graduation, a wedding), but more often than not they involve a degree of pain, suffering, degradation or humiliation (for example, circumcision, a wake). These rites may serve a number of functions:

1. *Symbolic* – to allow a consensual and public recognition of identity discontinuity.
2. *Apprenticeship* – some rites help individuals become accustomed to new roles and normative standards.
3. *Loyalty elicitation* – pleasant initiations involving gifts and special dispensations may elicit gratitude that should enhance commitment to the group.

▶ Cognitive dissonance In the light of this last function, the prevalence and apparent effectiveness of disagreeable initiation rites is puzzling. Surely people will avoid joining groups with severe initiations, and if unfortunate enough not to be able to do this then, at very least, they should subsequently hate the group and feel no sense of commitment. One way to explain this paradox is in terms of *cognitive dissonance* theory (Festinger 1957), which is described in Chapter 5. An aversive initiation creates subsequent dissonance between two cognitions: 'I knowingly underwent a painful experience to join this group' and 'some aspects of this group are not that good' (group life is usually a mixture of positive and negative aspects). Since the initiation cannot be denied (after all, it is usually a public event), dissonance can be reduced by revising one's opinion of the group (playing down negative aspects and focusing on more positive aspects). The consequence is a more favourable evaluation of the group, and thus greater commitment.

This analysis clearly predicts that the more unpleasant the initiation is, the more positive the subsequent evaluation of the group will be. The Aronson and Mills (1959) experiment described in Chapter 5 is an investigation of this idea. You will recall that Aronson and Mills recruited female students to participate in a group discussion of the psychology of sex. Before joining the group, they listened to and rated a short extract of the discussion (an extremely tedious and stilted discussion of the secondary sexual characteristics of lower animals). The discussion was quite rightly rated as such by control subjects, and also by a second group of subjects who had gone through a mild initiation in which they read out loud five words with vague sexual connotations. However, a third group who underwent an extreme initiation in which they read out loud explicit and obscene passages, rated the discussion as very interesting.

Gerard and Mathewson (1966) were concerned that the effect may have arisen because the severe initiation subjects were either sexually aroused by the obscene passage and/or relieved at discovering that the discussion was not as extreme as the passage. To discount these alternative explanations, they replicated Aronson and Mills' study. Subjects, who audited and rated a boring discussion they were about to join, were given mild or severe electric shocks either explicitly as an initiation or under some other pretext completely unrelated to the ensuing discussion. As predicted from cognitive dissonance theory, the painful experience enhanced evaluation of the group only when it was perceived to be an initiation (see Figure 7.14).

Norms

▶ Norms
▶ Stereotypes

Norms are shared beliefs about what is the appropriate conduct for a group member; they are both descriptive ('is' statements), and prescriptive ('ought' statements). As such, norms describe the uniformities of behaviour that characterise groups, while normative discontinuities provide the contours of different social groups. For example, the behaviour of students and lecturers in a university is governed by very different norms: knowing whether someone is a student or a lecturer establishes clear expectations of appropriate normative behaviours. Norms and *stereotypes* are closely related: the terms normative behaviour and stereotypical behaviour mean virtually the same thing. However, research traditions have generally separated the two areas: norms referring to behaviours that are shared in a group, and stereotypes (see Chapters 2, 9 and 10) to shared generalisations about other groups. Recently, however, self-categorisation theory (Turner 1985; Turner *et al.* 1987 – see Chapter 10) has tried to bridge this rather artificial distinction.

▶ Ethnomethodology

Norms can take the form of explicit rules that are enforced by legislation and sanctions (for example, societal norms to do with private property, pollution and aggression), or they can be the implicit, unobserved, taken-for-granted background to everyday life (Garfinkel 1967). Garfinkel believed that

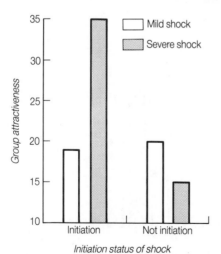

FIGURE 7.14 *Group attractiveness as a function of severity of electric shock and initiation status of the shock. (Source: based on data from Gerard and Mathewson 1966.)*

these latter norms are hidden because they are so integral to everyday life, and that they actually account for much behaviour that is often labelled native, instinctive and innate. Garfinkel devised a particular methodology, called *ethnomethodology*, to detect these background norms. One method involved the violation of norms in order to attract people's attention to them. For example, Garfinkel had students act at home for fifteen minutes as if they were boarders: that is, be polite, speak formally, and speak only when spoken to. Their families reacted with astonishment, bewilderment, shock, embarrassment and anger, backed up with charges of selfishness, nastiness, rudeness and lack of consideration. An implicit norm for familial interaction was revealed and its violation provoked a strong reaction.

Group norms can have a powerful effect on people. For example, Newcomb (1965) conducted a classic study of norms in the 1930s at a small American college called Bennington College. The college had progressive and liberal norms but drew its students from very conservative, upper-middle class families. The 1936 presidential election allowed Newcomb to conduct a confidential ballot. First year students strongly favoured the conservative candidate, while third and fourth year students had shifted their voting preference towards the liberal and communist/socialist candidates (Figure 7.15). Presumably, prolonged exposure to liberal norms had produced change in political preference.

Siegel and Siegel (1957) conducted a slightly better controlled study in which they took advantage of the random assignment of new students at a private American college to different types of student accommodation, called

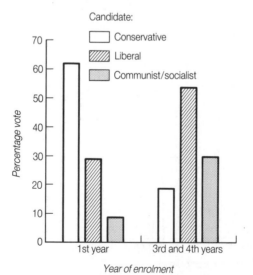

FIGURE 7.15 *Voting preference for 1936 presidential candidates as a function of exposure to liberal norms in Newcomb's Bennington study. (Source: based on data from Newcomb 1965.)*

sororities or dormitories. At this particular college, sororities had a conservative ethos and the dormitories had more progressive liberal norms. Siegel and Siegel measured the students' degree of conservatism at the beginning and the end of the year. Figure 7.16 clearly shows how exposure to liberal norms reduced conservatism.

▶ Reference frame

Norms serve a function for the individual. They specify a limited range of behaviours that are acceptable in a certain context and thus reduce uncertainty and facilitate confident choice of the 'correct' course of action. Norms provide a *reference frame* within which to locate one's own behaviour. You will recall that this idea was explored by Sherif (1936) in his classic experiments dealing with norm formation (see Box 6.1 in Chapter 6 for details). Sherif showed that when people made perceptual judgements alone, they relied on their own estimates as a reference frame; however, when they were in a group, they used the group's range of judgements to converge quickly on the group mean.

Sherif believed that subjects were using other members' estimates as a social frame of reference to guide them – he felt he had experimentally produced a primitive group norm. The norm was an emergent property of interaction among group members, but once created, acquired a life of its own. Members were later tested alone and still conformed to the norm. This same point was strikingly demonstrated in a couple of related autokinetic studies (Jacobs and Campbell 1961; MacNeil and Sherif 1976). The group comprised three confederates who gave extreme estimates, and one true subject. A relatively extreme norm emerged. The group went through a number of 'generations' in which a confederate would leave and another true subject would join until the membership of the group contained none of the original members. The original extreme norm still powerfully influenced the subjects' estimates. This is a very elegant demonstration that a norm is a true group phenomenon – it

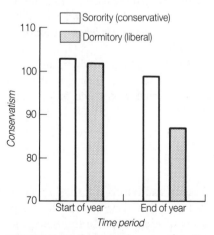

FIGURE 7.16 *Conservatism as a function of conservative or liberal norms of student residence. (Source: based on data from Siegel and Siegel 1957.)*

can only emerge from a group, and yet it can influence the behaviour of the individual in the physical absence of the group (Turner 1991). It is as if the group is carried in the head of the individual in the form of a norm.

Norms also serve functions for the group, in so far as they co-ordinate the actions of members towards fulfilment of group goals. In an early study of factory production norms, Coch and French (1948) describe a group that set itself a standard of fifty units per hour as it was the minimum level to secure job tenure. New members quickly adopted this norm. Those who did not were strongly sanctioned by ostracism, and in some cases had their work sabotaged.

Norms are inherently resistant to change – after all, their function is to provide stability and predictability. However, norms initially arise to deal with specific circumstances. They endure as long as those circumstances prevail, but ultimately change with changing circumstances. Norms vary in their 'latitude of acceptable behaviour' – some are very narrow and restrictive (for example, military dress codes) and others much wider and less restrictive (for example, dress codes for university lecturers). In general, norms that relate to group loyalty and to central aspects of group life have a very narrow latitude of acceptable behaviour, while norms to do with more peripheral features of the group are less restrictive. Finally, certain group members are allowed a greater latitude of acceptable behaviour than are others: higher status members (for example, leaders) can get away with more than can lower status members and followers. (This phenomenon is discussed in Chapter 8 when we talk about leadership.) There is evidence for the patterning and structure of different types of norms from Sherif and Sherif's (1964) pioneering study of adolescent gangs in American cities. Participant observers infiltrated these gangs and studied them over several months. The gangs had given themselves names, had adopted various insignia and had very strict codes about how gang members should dress. Dress codes were important as it was largely through dress that the gangs differentiated themselves from one another. The gangs also had strict norms concerning sexual mores and how to deal with outsiders (for example, parents, police). However, leaders were allowed some latitude in their adherence to these and other norms.

Norms are the yardstick of group conduct, and it is through norms that groups influence the behaviour of their members. The exact processes responsible are the subject matter of much of Chapter 6, which deals with social influence.

GROUP STRUCTURE

▶ Group structure

Cohesiveness, socialisation and norms refer mainly to uniformities in groups. However, we have just seen how there can also be a degree of patterning and differentiation of norms within groups. In this section we develop this theme. In very few groups indeed are all members equal, do all members perform identical activities, or do all members communicate freely with one another.

Group structure is clearly reflected with respect to roles, status and communication networks.

Roles

▶ Roles

Roles are very much like norms in so far as they describe and prescribe behaviour. However, while norms apply to the group as a whole, roles apply to a subgroup of people within the group. Furthermore, while norms may distinguish between groups they are not generally intentionally derived in order to benefit the framework of groups in a society. In contrast, roles are specifically designed to differentiate among people within the group for the greater good of the group as whole. Roles are not people but behavioural prescriptions that are assigned to people. They can be quite informal and implicit (for example, in friendship groups) or formal and explicit (for example, in aircraft flight crews).

Roles may emerge in a group for a number of reasons:

1. They represent a division of labour in the group – only in the most simple groups is there no division of labour.
2. They furnish clear-cut social expectations within the group, and information about how members relate to one another.
3. They furnish members with a self-definition and place within the group. Clearly, roles emerge to facilitate group functioning.

▶ Attribution
▶ Fundamental attribution error

Although we tend to adopt a dramaturgical perspective when we speak of people 'acting' or 'assuming' roles, we are probably only partly correct. Indeed, we can assume roles very much like actors taking different parts. However, many people only see us in particular roles and so assume that that is how we really are: professional actors are easily typecast in exactly the same sort of way. This tendency to attribute roles internally to dispositions of the role-player may be an example of the *fundamental attribution error* (Ross 1977; see Chapter 3). One practical implication of this is that you should avoid low status roles in groups, otherwise you will subsequently find it very difficult to escape their legacy. Perhaps the most powerful and well-known social psychological illustration of the power of roles to modify behaviour is Zimbardo's (1971; Banuazizi and Movahedi 1975) simulated prison experiment (see Box 7.2).

Status

▶ Status

All roles are not equal – some are consensually more valued and respected and thus confer greater *status* on the role occupant. The highest status role in most groups is the role of leader, which we discuss in Chapter 8. In general, higher status roles or their occupants tend to have two properties:

1. *Consensual prestige*.
2. A *tendency to initiate* ideas and activities that are adopted by the group.

BOX 7.2 Role behaviour in a simulated prison

Guards versus prisoners

Philip Zimbardo was interested to investigate the way in which people can adopt and internalise roles to guide behaviour. He was also interested to establish that it is largely the prescription of the role rather than the personality of the role occupant that governs in-role behaviour. In a famous role-playing exercise, twenty-four psychologically stable male Stanford University student volunteers were randomly assigned the roles of prisoners or guards. The prisoners were arrested at their homes and initially processed by the police, and then handed over to the guards in a simulated prison constructed in the basement of the Psychology Department at Stanford University. Zimbardo had planned to observe the role-playing exercise over a period of two weeks. However, he had to stop the study after six days. Although the students were psychologically stable and those assigned to the guard or prisoner role had no prior dispositional differences, things got completely out of hand. The guards continually harassed, humiliated and intimidated the prisoners, and used psychological techniques to undermine solidarity and to sow the seeds of distrust among them. Some guards increasingly behaved in a brutal and sadistic manner. The prisoners initially revolted but gradually became passive and docile as they showed symptoms of individual and group disintegration and an acute loss of contact with reality. Some prisoners had to be released from the study because they showed symptoms of severe emotional disturbance (disorganised thinking, uncontrollable crying and screaming) and, in one case, a psychosomatic rash all over his body.

For example, from his participant observation study of gangs in an American Italian immigrant community, Whyte (1943) reported that even the relatively inarticulate 'Doc', who described his assumption of leadership of the thirteen-member Norton gang in terms of whom he 'walloped', found that the consensual prestige that such wallopings earned him was insufficient alone to ensure his high status position. He admitted that his status also derived from the fact that he was the one who always thought of things for the group to do.

Status hierarchies in groups are not fixed: they can vary over time, and also from situation to situation. Take an orchestra; the lead violinist may have the highest status role at a concert, while the union representative has the highest status role in negotiations with management. One explanation of why status hierarchies emerge so readily in groups is in terms of social comparison theory (Festinger 1954; Suls and Miller 1977): status hierarchies are the expression and reflection of intragroup social comparisons. Groups furnish a pool of relevant others with whom to make social comparisons to assess the validity of one's opinions and abilities. Certain roles in the group have more power and influence and, because they are therefore more attractive and desirable, have many more 'applicants' than can be accommodated. Fierce social comparisons on behavioural dimensions relevant to these roles inevitably mean that the majority of group members, who are unsuccessful in securing the role, therefore cannot avoid the conclusion that they are less able than those who are successful. Thus arises a shared view that those occupying the attractive role are superior to the rest – consensual prestige and high status.

Status hierarchies can often become institutionalised so that individual members do not engage in ongoing systematic social comparisons. Rather, they simply assume that particular roles or role occupants are of higher status than their own role or themselves. Research into the formation of status hierarchies in newly created groups tends to support this view. For example, Strodtbeck *et al.* (1957) assembled mock juries to consider and render a verdict on transcripts of actual trials. They found that the high status role of jury foreman almost always went to people who had higher occupational status outside the context of the jury (for example, teachers or psychologists, rather than janitors or mechanics).

▶ Expectation states theory

One explanation of this phenomenon is in terms of *expectation states theory* (Berger *et al.* 1977; de Gilder and Wilke, in press). Status derives from two distinct sources:

▶ Specific status characteristics

▶ Diffuse status characteristics

1. *Specific status characteristics* – characteristics that relate directly to ability on the group task (for example, athletic ability in a sports team).
2. *Diffuse status characteristics* – characteristics that do not relate directly to ability on the group task but are nonetheless ones that are generally positively or negatively valued in society (for example, being male, being older, having a white–collar occupation, being white).

Diffuse status characteristics are associated with favourable expectations that are generalised to all sorts of situations, even ones that may not be very relevant to the group task at all. Group members simply assume that someone who rates highly on diffuse status (for example, a medical doctor) will be relatively more able than others to promote the group's goals (for example, analysing trial transcripts to render a verdict) and therefore has higher specific status.

According to a study by Knottnerus and Greenstein (1981), specific and diffuse status are independent and additive sources of status in a newly formed group. In their study, female subjects worked with a female confederate on two supposedly related tasks. Specific status was manipulated by informing subjects that they had performed better or worse than the confederate on the first task (a perceptual task). Diffuse status was manipulated by leading subjects to believe they were either younger or older than the confederate. The second task, a word construction task, allowed measures of yielding to the confederate's suggestions to be used as an index of effective status. The results (Figure 7.17) showed that subjects yielded more if they believed they were of lower specific or lower diffuse status than the confederate. Other factors shown to contribute to high status in a group include seniority, assertiveness, past task success and high group orientation.

Communication networks

▶ Communication network

People occupying different roles in a group need to co-ordinate their actions through communication, though not all roles need to communicate with one another. Thus, the structuring of a group with respect to roles entails an internal *communication network* that regulates who can communicate with whom (for example, Flament 1965). Although such networks can be informal, we are probably more familiar with the rigidly formalised ones in large organisations and bureaucracies (for example, a university or government office). What are the effects on group functioning of different types of communication network, and what factors affect the sort of network that evolves?

Bavelas (1968) suggested that an important consideration was the number of communication links to be crossed for one person to communicate with another. For example, if I can communicate with the dean of my faculty

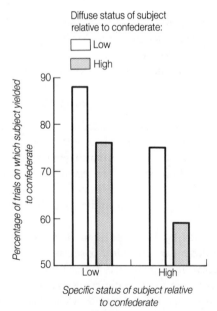

FIGURE 7.17 *Yielding as a function of specific and diffuse status of subjects relative to a confederate. (Source: based on data from Knottnerus and Greenstein 1981.)*

directly then there is one link, but if I have to go through the head of department then there are two. Figure 7.18 shows some of the communication networks that have been researched experimentally – those on the left are more highly centralised than those on the right.

It appears that for relatively simple tasks, greater centralisation improves group performance (for example, Leavitt 1951) – the hub person is quite able to receive, integrate and pass on information efficiently while allowing peripheral members to concentrate on their allotted roles. For more complex tasks a less centralised structure is superior because the quantity and complexity of information communicated would overwhelm a hub person who would be unable to integrate, assimilate and pass it on efficiently (for example, Shaw 1964). Peripheral members would thus experience delays and miscommunication. For complex tasks there are potentially serious co-ordination losses associated with overly centralised communication networks (Steiner 1972, 1976; see above). However, centralisation for complex tasks may pay off in the long run once appropriate procedures have been well established and well learned.

Another important consideration is the degree of autonomy felt by group members. Because they are dependent on the hub for regulation and flow of information, peripheral members have less power in the group and can feel restricted and dependent. According to Mulder (1960), having more power leads to a greater sense of autonomy and satisfaction, and so peripheral members can become dissatisfied while hub members, who are often perceived

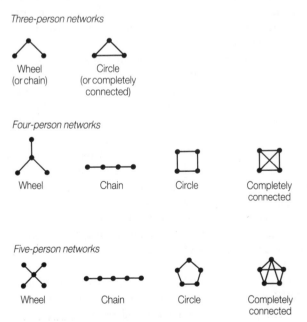

FIGURE 7.18 *Communication networks that have been studied experimentally.*

to be group leaders, feel a sense of satisfaction. Centralised communication networks can thus reduce group satisfaction, harmony and solidarity, and instead produce internal conflict.

WHY DO PEOPLE JOIN GROUPS?

This is not an easy question to answer. It depends on how one defines a group, and of course 'why' people join groups is not the same as 'how' people join groups. We also need to recognise that the groups to which we belong vary in the degree of free choice we had in joining. There is very little choice in what sex, ethnic, national or social class groups one 'joins' – membership is largely externally designated. There is a degree of choice, though possibly less than one might think, in what occupational or political group one joins, and of course there is a great deal of freedom in what clubs, societies and recreational groups one joins. Even in the most strongly externally designated social category memberships, such as sex and ethnicity, there can be a degree of choice in what the implications of membership in that group may be (for example, the group's norms and practices), and this may reflect the same sorts of motives and goals for choosing freely to join less externally designated groups (Hogg and Abrams 1993).

However, we can identify a range of circumstances, motives, goals, purposes and so forth that tend to cause, in more or less immediate ways, people to join or form groups (for example, aggregate, co-ordinate their actions, declare themselves members of a group). For example, physical proximity can promote group formation. We tend to get to like, or at least learn to put up with (Tyler and Sears 1977), people with whom we are in close proximity. This appears to promote group formation – we form groups with those around us. Festinger et al.'s (1950) classic study of a student housing programme, which we discussed earlier, concerned just this – the role of proximity in group formation, group cohesiveness and subsequent adherence to group standards. The recognition of similar interests, attitudes and beliefs can also cause people to become or join a group.

If people share goals that require behavioural interdependence for their achievement then this is another very strong and reliable reason for joining groups. This idea lies at the heart of Sherif's (1966) realistic conflict theory of intergroup behaviour, which is discussed in Chapter 10. For example, if you are concerned about degradation of the environment then you are likely ultimately to join an environmental conservation group because division of labour and interdependent action among like-minded people will achieve a great deal more than the actions of a lone protester.

We can join groups for mutual positive support and the mere pleasure of affiliation, for example to avoid loneliness (Peplau and Perlman 1982). We can join groups for self-protection and personal safety, for example adolescents can join gangs (Ahlstrom and Havighurst 1971), and mountaineers often climb in groups for this reason. We can join groups for emotional support in times of stress, for example support groups for AIDS sufferers and their relatives and friends fulfil this function. Oscar Lewis's (1969) account of a Catholic wake in Mexico in his novel *A Death in the Sanchez Family* describes the way in which people come together in stressful circumstances. Schachter (1959) has explored the same idea in controlled experimental circumstances. However, a word of qualification is needed. Extreme stress and deprivation (for example in concentration camps or after natural disasters) can sometimes produce social disintegration and individual isolation rather than group formation (Middlebrook 1980). This is probably because the link between stress and affiliation is not mechanical: if affiliation is not the effective solution to the stress then it may not occur. Indeed, Thomas Keneally's (1982) account in his powerful biographical novel *Schindler's Ark* of atrocities committed by the Nazis against Jews in the Polish city of Cracow supports this. Despite extreme stress, remarkably little affiliation occurred, for the reason that affiliation was difficult to sustain and would probably only exacerbate the situation.

One final, very important reason for joining a group is simply to obtain a social identity (Hogg and Abrams 1988; Tajfel and Turner 1979; Turner 1982). Groups provide one with a consensually recognised definition and evaluation of who one is, how one should behave and how one will be treated by others. There is thus a highly sought-after and satisfying reduction in subjective uncertainty. In addition, because we and others evaluate us in terms of the relative attractiveness, desirability and prestige of the groups to which we belong, we are motivated to join groups which are consensually positively evaluated (for example, high status) and which will furnish a positive social identity (Hogg and Abrams 1990; Tajfel and Turner 1979; see Chapter 10).

SUMMARY

♦ Although there are many definitions of the group, social psychologists generally agree that, at the very least, a group is a collection of people who define themselves as a group and whose attitudes and behaviours are governed by the norms of the group. Group membership often also entails shared goals, interdependence, mutual influence and face-to-face interaction.

♦ People tend to perform easy, well learned tasks better, and difficult, poorly learned tasks worse in the presence of other people than on their own.

♦ We may be affected in this way for a number of reasons. Social presence may instinctively drive habitual behaviours, we may learn to worry about performance evaluation by others, we may be distracted by others, or others may make us self-conscious or concerned about self-presentation.

♦ Tasks differ not only in difficulty but also in their structure and objectives. Whether a task benefits from division of labour and how individual task performances are interrelated have important implications for the relationship between individual and group performance.

♦ In groups, people tend to put less effort into task performance than when alone, unless the task is involving and interesting or their individual contribution is clearly identifiable.

♦ Members of cohesive groups tend to feel more favourably inclined towards one another as group members and are more likely to identify with the group and conform to its norms.

♦ Group membership is a dynamic process in which one's sense of commitment varies, one occupies different roles at different times, one endures sharp transitions between roles and one is socialised by the group in many different ways.

♦ Groups develop norms to regulate the behaviour of members, to define the group and to distinguish the group from other groups.

♦ Groups are internally structured into different roles that regulate interaction and best serve the collective interest of the group. Roles prescribe behaviour. They also vary in their desirability and thus influence status within the group.

♦ People may join or form groups to get things done that cannot be done alone, to gain a sense of identity, to obtain social support or simply for the pleasure of social interaction.

FURTHER READING

Baron, R. S., Kerr, N. and Miller, N. (1992). *Group Process, Group Decision, Group Action*. Buckingham: Open University Press.

Brown, R. J. (1988). *Group Processes: Dynamics Within and Between Groups*. Oxford: Blackwell.

Guerin, B. (1993). *Social Facilitation*. Cambridge: Cambridge University Press.

Hogg, M. A. and Abrams, D. (1988). *Social Identifications: A Social Psychology of Intergroup Relations and Group Processes*. London: Routledge.

Moreland, R. L. and Levine, J. M. (1994). *Understanding Small Groups*. Boston, Mass.: Allyn and Bacon.

▶ KEY TERMS

attribution	drive theory
audience effect	ethnomethodology
cognitive dissonance	evaluation apprehension model
cohesiveness	expectation states theory
communication network	free-rider effect
co-ordination loss	fundamental attribution error
diffuse status characteristics	group
distraction-conflict theory	group socialisation

group structure
initiation rites
mere presence
norms
personal attraction
process loss
reference frame
Ringelmann effect
roles

social attraction
social compensation
social facilitation
social impact
social loafing
specific status characteristics
status
stereotypes
task taxonomy

8 *Leadership and group decision-making*

··

FOCUS QUESTIONS

- Are some people simply better leaders than others, or does it depend very much on the situation or the particular task?
- Is it generally preferable to adopt a more democratic and person-oriented leadership style or a more directive and task-oriented style?
- Why is it that leaders can often get away with being a lot less conformist than other group members?
- Are groups more creative and better at recalling information than individuals?
- Do groups tend to make more or less cautious decisions than individuals?
- Juries are instructed to consider the evidence alone in coming to a verdict. Do you think that they are therefore largely free of group decision-making biases?

LEADERS AND GROUP DECISIONS

▶ Cohesiveness

As we have seen in Chapter 7, groups vary enormously in their size, composition, longevity and purpose. They also vary in cohesiveness, have different norms and are internally structured into roles in different ways. However, almost all groups, even those that are apparently most egalitarian, have some form of unequal distribution of power and influence whereby some people lead and others follow. Although leadership can take a variety of forms (for example, democratic, autocratic, informal, formal, intrusive, modest), it is, nevertheless, a fundamental aspect of almost all social groups.

We saw at the end of Chapter 7 that people can come together as a group for many different reasons and to perform many different activities. One of the most common reasons is to make decisions through some form of group discussion. In fact, many of the most important decisions that affect our lives are made by groups, often ones of which we are not members. This chapter continues the discussion of group processes that we began in Chapter 7. It focuses on two of the most significant social psychological group phenomena: leadership and group decision-making.

LEADERSHIP

▶ Leadership

In the many groups to which we may belong – teams, committees, organisations, friendship groups, gangs and so forth – we encounter leaders. People who seem to have the 'good' ideas that everyone else then agrees on, people whom everyone seems to follow, people who seem to have the power to make things happen. On a larger canvas, history and political news frequently comprises stories of the deeds of leaders and tales of leadership struggles.

To understand how leaders lead, what factors influence who is likely to be a leader in a particular context and what the social consequences of leadership may be, social psychology has embraced a range of different theoretical emphases and perspectives.

Personality traits

▶ Great person theory

Great or notorious leaders such as Lenin, Mao Tse Tung, Churchill, Hitler, Thatcher, Gandhi, Gorbachev, seem to have special and distinctive capabilities that mark them off from the rest of us. Not surprisingly, we tend to seek an

A great leader in the making. 'The time for the healing of wounds has come' – Nelson Mandela at his inauguration, May 1994. Mr Mandela's election as the first black president of South Africa in that country's first free elections is an event that will almost certainly ensure his place in history as a great leader. (Source: Popper Foto/Reuter.)

explanation in terms of unique properties of these people – an explanation in terms of personality characteristics that predispose certain people to lead. This *great person* type of explanation has a long and illustrious history that goes back to Plato and Classical Greece. More recently, in the nineteenth century, Francis Galton believed that good leaders were born, not made. He investigated the hereditary background of 'great men' in order to discover inherited capabilities of great leaders (Stogdill 1974).

Although social psychologists no longer believe that leadership potential is inborn, there is a tradition of research that pursues the possibility that it may be acquired early in life, and therefore that a constellation of personality attributes may well exist that imbues people with charisma and thus a predisposition to lead (Carlyle 1841; House 1977). The search for such characteristics has identified a handful of weak correlates of leadership. For example, leaders tend to be above average with respect to size, health, physical attractiveness, intelligence, self-confidence, talkativeness and need for dominance. Of these, intelligence (Mann 1959) and talkativeness (Mullen *et al.* 1989) are two of the most reliable correlates. Intelligence is important probably because leaders are expected to be able to think and respond quickly and to have more ready access to information than others; talkativeness because it attracts attention and renders the individual perceptually salient (Mullen *et al.* 1989).

In general, however, the search for reliable personality correlates of leadership has been relatively unsuccessful (Stogdill 1974; Yukl 1981). Correlations among traits, and between traits and effective leadership are simply very low, and there is little evidence for the great person theory of leadership. Nevertheless, folk wisdom generally prefers to interpret history in terms of the actions of great people: the French occupation of Moscow in 1812 was Napoleon's doing; the 1917 Russian Revolution was 'caused' by Lenin; Gandhi led India to independence in 1947; and the 1980s in Britain were the 'Thatcher years'. Folk wisdom also tends to attribute great leaps forward in science – what Kuhn (1962) calls *paradigm shifts* – to the independent actions of great people such as Copernicus, Darwin, Freud and Einstein.

This preference for great person theories may be explained in terms of fundamental characteristics of the way people construct an understanding of their world:

1. In the face of widespread, large-scale and complex phenomena (for example, the economy, war, revolution, famine, the meaning of life, plague), non-experts readily resort to explanations in terms of the actions of groups (for example, scapegoats – see Chapters 3, 9 and 10) or individuals (that is, leaders).
2. Having located an individual as the cause, we tend to attribute the behaviours internally to invariant dispositions of the leader (that is, we commit the fundamental attribution error – see Chapter 3).

Situational perspectives

In contrast to explanations of leadership exclusively in terms of personality traits are explanations that place an emphasis on the functional requirements of situations. The most extreme form of this perspective is to deny any influence at all to the leader. For example, much of Tolstoy's epic novel *War and Peace* is a vehicle for his critique of the great person account of history: 'To elicit the laws of history we must leave aside kings, ministers and generals, and select for study the homogenous, infinitesimal elements which influence the masses' (Tolstoy 1869, p. 977). Likewise, Karl Marx's theory of history places the explanatory emphasis on the actions of collectivities, not individuals.

Empirical tests of this extreme situationist perspective tend, however, to suggest that leaders do have a role. For example, Simonton (1980) analysed the outcome of three hundred military battles for which there was reliable archival data on the generals and their armies. Although situational factors such as size of the army and diversification of command structure were correlated with casualties inflicted on the enemy, some personal attributes of the leader, to do with experience and previous battle record, were also associated with victory. In other words, although situational factors influenced outcome, so did attributes of the leader.

A second form of the situational perspective is one in which the leader is attributed an important role in group achievement, but leadership is not seen as an invariant property of individual personality. Different situations call for different leadership properties, and therefore the most effective leader in a given context is the group member who is best equipped to assist the group in achieving its objectives (Bales 1950). From time to time, then, we are likely to find ourselves in situations in which we are leaders. An oft-cited illustration of this is the case of Winston Churchill. Although considered by many to be argumentative, opinionated and eminently unsuited to government, these were presumably precisely the characteristics needed in a great wartime leader. However, as soon as Second World War was over he was voted out of government as these were not thought to be the qualities most needed in a peacetime leader.

Social psychologists have found the same thing under more controlled conditions. For example, in their classic studies of intergroup relations at boys' summer camps in the United States (see Chapter 10 for details), Sherif *et al.* (1961; Sherif 1966) divided the boys into different groups, and found that in one group there was a leadership change under conditions of intergroup competition – the former leader was displaced by someone with greater physical prowess who was better equipped to lead the group successfully in the changed circumstances. In an experimental study, Carter and Nixon (1949) demonstrated the same point by having pairs of high-school students perform three different tasks: an intellectual task, a clerical task and a mechanical assembly task. Those who took the lead in the first two tasks rarely led in the mechanical assembly task.

All in all then, leadership seems to be a function of task or situational demands and is not purely a property of individual personality. Effective leadership is a matter of the right combination of personal characteristics and situational requirements. However, the discussion so far leaves some questions unanswered: what exactly do leaders do in order to lead; how do the 'person' and the 'situation' interact to produce effective leadership, and through what processes do leaders emerge in groups? These are the focus of the remainder of this discussion of leadership.

Behaviour of leaders

While one's personality may not be particularly important to leadership success, perhaps one's behaviour is. This idea forms the basis of one of the earliest and most influential studies of leadership, published by Lippitt and White in 1943. Lippitt and White used after-school activities clubs for young boys as an opportunity to investigate the effects of different styles of leadership on group atmosphere, morale and effectiveness. The leaders of the clubs were confederates of the researchers and they were trained in each of three distinct leadership styles:

▶ Autocratic
leadership
▶ Democratic
leadership

1. *Autocratic leaders* organised the club's activities, gave orders, were aloof and focused exclusively on the task at hand.
2. *Democratic leaders* called for suggestions, discussed plans and behaved as ordinary club members.
3. Laissez-faire leaders left the group to its own devices and generally intervened minimally.

Each club was assigned to a particular leadership style. One confederate was the leader for seven weeks and then the confederates were swapped around. This happened twice, so that each confederate adopted each leadership style, but each group was exposed to only one leadership style (but enacted by three different confederates). This important control allowed Lippitt and White to distinguish leadership behaviour *per se* from the specific leader who was behaving in that way, and therefore to rule out personality explanations.

What Lippitt and White found is illustrated in Figure 8.1. Democratic leaders were liked significantly more than autocratic or laissez-faire leaders, and created a friendly, group-centred, task-oriented atmosphere that was associated with relatively high group productivity that was unaffected by the physical absence or presence of the leader. In contrast, autocratic leaders created an aggressive, dependent and self-oriented group atmosphere that was associated with high productivity only when the leader was present. Laissez-faire leaders created a friendly, group-centred but play-oriented group atmosphere that was associated with low productivity that only increased if the leader was absent. Lippitt and White were able to use these finding to promote

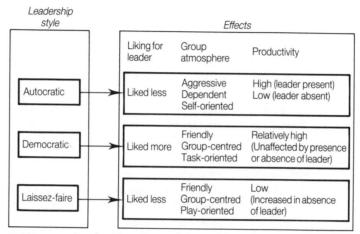

FIGURE 8.1 *Leadership styles and their effects. (Source: derived from Lippitt and White 1943.)*

their view that democratic leadership was more effective than other leadership behaviours.

Lippitt and White's distinction between autocratic and democratic leadership styles re-emerges in a slightly different form in later work. From his long series of studies of interaction styles in groups, Bales (1950) concluded that the two roles of task specialist and socio-emotional specialist (Slater 1955) were leadership roles in groups, but that no individual could occupy both roles simultaneously. Rather, the roles tend to devolve onto separate individuals, and the person occupying the task specialist role was more likely to be the supreme leader. Bales argued that task specialists tend to be centrally involved, often by offering opinions and giving directions, in the task-oriented aspects of group life. In contrast, socio-emotional specialists tend to respond to and pay attention to the feelings of other group members. Casual observation of groups and organisations tend to support this dual-leadership idea. For example, one theme which punctuated election struggles between the Labour and Conservative parties during the 1980s in Britain was to do with what sort of leader the country should have – Neil Kinnock was, among other things, heralded as a friendly and approachable leader concerned with people's feelings, and Margaret Thatcher as the hard-headed, task-oriented economic rationalist.

Another major research programme, the Ohio State leadership studies (for example, Fleishman 1973; Stogdill 1974), draws a similar distinction. Questionnaires concerning the behaviour and effectiveness of leaders administered to subordinates mainly in military and industrial groups revealed a distinction between *initiating structure* and *consideration*. Leaders rating high on initiating structure define the group's objectives and organise members' work towards the attainment of these goals: they are task-oriented. Leaders rating high on consideration are concerned with the welfare of subordinates and seek to promote harmonious relationships in the group: they are relationship-oriented. While this distinction is remarkably similar to Bales' (1950) distinction between task and socio-emotional leaders, there is one crucial difference. Bales considered his two dimensions to be inversely related: high scores on one entail low scores on the other. However, the Ohio State researchers considered, and obtained evidence for, the independence of their dimensions: a particular leader could be high on both initiating structure and consideration.

In fact, research reveals that the most effective leaders are precisely those who do score above average on both initiating structure and consideration (Stogdill 1974). For example, Sorrentino and Field (1986) conducted detailed observations of twelve problem-solving groups over a five-week period. Those group members who had been observed to score high on both the task and socio-emotional dimensions of Bales' (1950) system, were subsequently elected by groups to be their leaders.

Taken together, research on leadership behaviour does indicate the existence of a distinction between task and socio-emotional leadership orientations. However, this focus on leadership behaviour needs to be complemented by an analysis of the role of situational factors in determining leadership effectiveness. In particular we need to investigate the relationship between, and possible interaction of, leadership style and situational requirements.

Contingency theory

▶ Contingency theory

The need for an interactionist perspective gradually became apparent from observations that effective leadership was not simply a matter of the right mixture of task and socio-emotional orientation. The 'right mixture' seemed to depend rather heavily on the nature of the group – whether it was an aircrew in combat, an organisational decision-making group, a ballet company, a nation in economic crisis. This led Fiedler (1967, 1971, 1981) to propose an interactionist model of leadership effectiveness in which the effectiveness of particular leadership styles was contingent on situational factors – thus, *contingency theory*.

▶ Task-oriented leader
▶ Socio-emotional oriented leader

Fiedler accepts Bales' distinction between *task-oriented* and *socio-emotional oriented* leaders, and, like Bales, believes the dimensions to be inversely related, with people habitually adopting one or other leadership style. Fiedler considered task-oriented leaders to be authoritarian, to value group success and to derive self-esteem from task accomplishment rather than being liked by the group. Relationship-oriented leaders are relaxed, friendly, non-directive and sociable, and gain self-esteem from happy and harmonious group relations.

▶ LPC scale

Fiedler devised an instrument, called the least preferred co-worker *(LPC)* scale, to measure leadership style. Respondents think of all the people they have ever worked with and then describe on eighteen bipolar eight-point scales (for example, pleasant/unpleasant, boring/interesting, friendly/unfriendly) the one person with whom they found it most difficult to work. The scores are summed so that high scores (high LPC) indicate a favourable attitude towards this least preferred co-worker, and thus a relationship-oriented leadership style (relationships are more important than task performance), and low scores (low LPC) a negative attitude, and thus a task-oriented leadership style (task performance is more important than relationships). To recap: high LPC leaders are relationship-oriented because their attitude towards a group member remains positive despite the fact that the member was extremely difficult to work with, while low LPC leaders are task-oriented because their attitude towards a group member is unfavourable because the member was extremely hard to work with.

▶ Situational control

The effectiveness of either style of leadership is contingent on the requirements of a given leadership situation – specifically, the amount of control a situation allows the leader to have over the group. The *situational control* of a situation is influenced by three factors, the most important of which is the affective relationship between leader and followers. The next most important is the extent to which the group task is well or poorly structured, and the least important is the extent to which the leader, by virtue of her position, has legitimate power and authority over followers. Good leader/member relations, a well-structured task and legitimate power together make it easier for the leader to lead.

There is one further step in Fiedler's analysis of situational control. Suppose every leadership situation can be defined as high or low on each of the three dimensions of situational control, then there are eight possible combinations ranging from 'high, high, high' through intermediate combinations to 'low, low, low'. A high ranking on all three dimensions clearly indicates the most favourable situational control, while a low ranking on all three indicates the least favourable. But, how do we assess the relative overall favourability of intermediate combinations? Fiedler's *a priori* ranking of the importance of the three dimensions of situational control allows us to do this rather simply, as shown in Figure 8.2, to produce what is in effect an eight-point, or eight-category, scale.

Fiedler believed that low LPC, mainly task-oriented leaders would excel under conditions of extremely low or extremely high situational control. Where control is extremely low, leader/member relations are abysmal, the task is unstructured and the leader has little power. Under these conditions attempts to win over the group by being nice and supportive are unlikely to succeed and will in any case waste valuable time and hence reduce effectiveness. An autocratic style is the best bet. Where situational control is extremely high, leader/member relations are excellent, the task is clearly structured and the leader has power. Under these circumstances there is little need to waste time

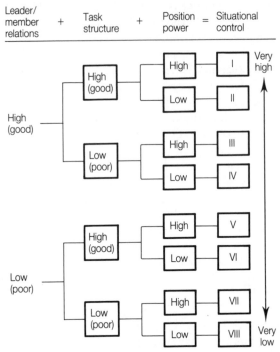

FIGURE 8.2 *Fiedler's eight-category situational control scale as a function of leader/member relations, task structure and position power. (Source: adapted from Fiedler 1967, 1971, 1981.)*

worrying about group morale. The leader has the means and power to be wholly task-directive. As regards intermediate levels of situational control, high LPC, mainly relationship-oriented leaders would be most effective because improvement in morale might compensate to some extent for a poorly defined task or a lack of authority.

This model makes the prediction that where situational control is extremely high or extremely low, group performance will be negatively correlated with LPC scores: that is, the lower the leader's LPC score, thus the more task-oriented his leadership style, the better the group will perform. Where situational control is intermediate, group performance will be positively correlated with LPC scores: that is, the higher the leader's LPC score, thus the more relationship-oriented he is, the better the group will perform. This prediction is shown in Figure 8.3, which also shows actual LPC/performance correlations reported by Fiedler (1965) from published studies. The results match the prediction remarkably well.

In general, the contingency model has accumulated a great deal of empirical support (for example, Strube and Garcia 1981), and, despite some continuing controversy (Peters *et al.* 1985), is considered the most useful approach to the

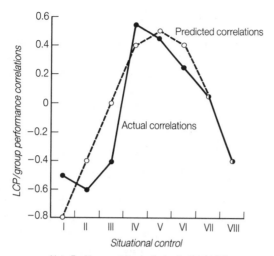

Note: Positive correlation indicates that high LPC, relationship-oriented leaders are more effective; negative correlation that low LPC, task-oriented leaders are more effective.

FIGURE 8.3 *Predicted and actual correlations between LPC scores and group performance as a function of situational control. (Source: based on data from Fiedler 1965.)*

analysis of leadership. There are, however, three points worth considering. The first concerns Fiedler's view that leadership style is a characteristic of the individual that is invariant across time and situation. This view is inconsistent with, for example: (1) current conceptualisations of personality and research showing substantial temporal and situational variation in personality (for example, Argyle and Little 1972; Mischel 1968); (2) evidence for relatively low test/retest reliability for LPC scores (Rice 1978), and (3) the ease with which Lippitt and White (1943) trained their confederates to adopt different leadership styles in the study described earlier.

The second question concerns the basis of Fiedler's assumptions concerning the *a priori* relative importance of leader/member relations, task structure and position power in the assessment of overall situational control. It would not be surprising if the relative order of importance might itself be a function of, among other things, contextual factors. Indeed, Singh *et al.* (1979) obtained a better fit between prediction and results under conditions where the situational favourability of the eight octants was based on subjective ratings by subjects rather than Fiedler's *a priori* classification.

Finally, although contingency theory explores the interaction between properties of the person and properties of the situation in the assessment of leadership effectiveness, it neglects examination of the group processes that are responsible for the rise and fall of leaders, and the situational complexion of leadership.

Leadership as a process

Explanations of leadership that focus on personality traits, situational demands, leadership behaviour or person/situation interaction leave an essential aspect of leadership unaddressed. Without followers there can be no leader. The role of leader is conferred on an individual by the members of the group, and it is the group that finally topples the leader. There is a dynamic interaction between leaders and their followers.

One basis of this process may be an interpersonal equity-based transaction (Walster *et al.* 1978). The distribution of skills and capabilities within a group almost inevitably means that certain individuals are relatively consensually seen to be contributing more than others to the achievement of group goals. These individuals can be considered to be rewarding other group members more than they themselves are being rewarded. A state of inequity exists. To redress the balance the group members reward the individual with social approval, praise, prestige, status and power – in other words, with the trappings of leadership. As the group's goals change this transactional process ought to confer leadership on a different individual (someone who is better equipped in terms of capabilities to fulfil group goals); however, the incumbent leader has been given power and so has the resources to resist being displaced. There is the familiar struggle for leadership among various contenders.

This analysis focuses on leadership as a product of interaction among group members. In so doing it reminds us that leaders are group members. Herein lies a paradox. On the one hand leaders epitomise and represent the group – they embody the ideal standards and norms of the groups. On the other hand they are the agents of change within the group – they steer the group in new directions because they can alter prevailing group norms. They are simultaneously conformist and deviant. How can a leader be both a loyal member who adheres faithfully to group norms, and an active deviate who influences the group to adopt new norms?

▶ Idiosyncrasy credit Hollander (1958; Hollander and Julian 1970) explained this paradox in terms of the notion of *idiosyncrasy credit*. Hollander argued that leaders initially need to build up 'credit' with the rest of the group. A good credit rating can be established by:

1. Initially conforming closely to established group norms.
2. Ensuring that the group feels it has democratically elected you as the leader.
3. Making sure that you are seen to have the competence to fulfil the group's objectives.
4. Being seen to identify with the group, its ideals and its aspirations.

A good credit rating gives a leader subsequent legitimacy to exert influence over the group and to deviate from existing norms: in other words, to be idiosyncratic.

Research tends to support this analysis. Merei (1949) introduced older children, who had previously shown leadership potential, into small groups of younger children in a Hungarian nursery. He reported that the most successful leaders were those who initially complied with existing group practices and who only gradually and later introduced minor variations. In another study, Hollander and Julian (1970) found that leaders of decision-making groups, who were led to believe they had been democratically elected, enjoyed more support from the group, felt more competent at the task, and were more likely to suggest solutions that diverged from those of the group as a whole. Finally, Kirkhart (1963) examined leadership choices in predominantly black college fraternity houses in the United States. Members who identified with the social group black were most likely to be selected, particularly in hypothetical situations involving black/white relations.

This last point reminds us of something important that is missing from all the perspectives on leadership that we have discussed. Fiedler's contingency theory is an advance on purely personality, situational or behavioural perspectives in so far as it recognises the interaction between personal and situational characteristics; however, it suffers from being rather a static view of leadership. Hollander's approach overcomes this problem by focusing on the forces in a group that render leadership a dynamic process. However, all these approaches neglect the intergroup dimension of leadership.

Leaders not only lead their groups, but in varying ways they lead their groups *against* other groups. The political and military leaders that are frequently invoked in discussions of leadership are of course leaders in a truly intergroup context – they lead their political parties, their nations or their armies *against* other political parties, nations or armies. It would be highly unlikely that the nature of intergroup relations did not influence leadership, by, for example, changing group goals or altering intragroup relations. Earlier we described how a leadership change in one of Sherif's groups of boys at a summer camp was produced by intergroup competition. More recently, Rabbie and Bekkers (1978) conducted a union/management bargaining simulation in which relatively insecure leaders (that is, they were likely to be deposed by their group) actively sought competitive bargaining situations, particularly when their group was in a strong bargaining position, in order to secure their leadership. Perhaps this captures the familiar tactic of political leaders experiencing unpopularity at home to pursue an aggressive foreign policy, for example Thatcher in the Falklands in 1982 and Bush in the Gulf War of 1991.

GROUP DECISION-MAKING

Groups perform a wide range of tasks, of which decision-making is probably one of the most important. The course of our lives is largely determined by decisions made by groups, for example selection committees, juries, parliament, committees of examiners, groups of friends. In addition, many of us spend a significant portion of our working lives engaged in group decision-making. Social psychologists have long been interested in the sorts of social process involved in group decision-making, and whether decisions made by groups are better than or different from decisions made by individuals. Another dimension of group decision-making comes into play when members of the decision-making group are formally acting as representatives of different groups. This is more properly called intergroup decision-making; it is dealt with in Chapter 10.

A variety of models has been developed to relate the distribution of initial opinions in a decision-making group to the final group decision (Stasser *et al.* 1989). Some of these are complex computer simulation models (Hastie *et al.* 1983; Penrod and Hastie, 1980; Stasser and Davis 1981), while others, although expressed in a rather formalised mathematical style, are more immediately related to real groups.

▶ Social decisions
schemes

Davis' *social decisions schemes* model identifies a small number of explicit or implicit decision-making rules that groups can adopt (Davis 1973; Stasser *et al.* 1989). Knowledge of the initial distribution of individual opinions in the group and what rule the group is operating under allows prediction, with a high degree of certainty, of the final group decision. These rules include:

1. *Unanimity* – discussion serves to pressurise deviants to conform.
2. *Majority wins* – discussion simply confirms the majority position, which is then adopted as the group position.
3. *Truth wins* – discussion reveals the position that is demonstrably correct.
4. *Two-thirds majority* – unless there is a two-thirds majority the group is unable to reach a decision.
5. *First shift* – the group ultimately adopts a decision consistent with the direction of the first shift in opinion shown by any member of the group.

For intellective tasks (ones where there is a demonstrably correct solution, for example a mathematical puzzle) groups tend to adopt the truth wins rule, and for judgemental tasks (no demonstrably correct solution, for example aesthetic preference) the majority wins rule (Laughlin 1980; Laughlin and Ellis 1986). Rules differ in their *strictness* – the degree of agreement required by the rule (unanimity is extremely strict and majority less strict) – and the *distribution of power* among members – authoritarian rules concentrate power in one member, while egalitarian rules spread power among all members (Hastie *et al.* 1983).

In general, the stricter the rule the less the power concentration – unanimity is very strict but very low in power concentration, while two-thirds majority is less strict but has greater power concentration. The type of rule adopted can have an effect, largely as a function of its strictness, not only on the group's decision itself but also on members' preferences, their satisfaction with the group decision, the perception and nature of group discussion, and members' feelings for one another (Miller 1989). For example, stricter decision rules can make final agreement in the group slower, more exhaustive and more difficult to attain, but can enhance liking for fellow members and satisfaction with the quality of the decision.

▶ Social transition scheme

Kerr's *social transition scheme* model focuses attention on the actual pattern of member positions that a group, operating under a particular decision rule, moves through en route to its final decision (Kerr 1981; Stasser *et al.* 1989). In order to do this, opinions have to be monitored during the process of discussion (Kerr and MacCoun 1985) either by periodically asking the discussants or by getting them to note every change in their opinion. These procedures can be rather intrusive, and so one issue concerns the extent to which they affect the natural ongoing process of discussion.

Brainstorming

▶ Brainstorming

An important part of the group decision-making process can be the generation of novel ideas. Indeed, some groups can come together almost exclusively for this purpose, the goal being to be as creative as possible in the generation of ideas. The technique of *brainstorming*, initially popularised by Osborn (1957), is now quite commonly used for this purpose. Group members are instructed to generate as many ideas as possible as quickly as possible. They are told not to be inhibited or concerned about quality (simply say whatever comes to mind), to be non-critical and to build on others' ideas when possible. Brainstorming, then, is a group performance technique designed to facilitate creative thinking and thus make the group more creative. Popular opinion is so convinced that brainstorming works that brainstorming is widely used in business organisations and advertising agencies.

However, although research reveals that groups which have been given brainstorming instructions do generate more ideas than groups that have not been so instructed, there is no evidence that individuals in brainstorming groups are more creative than when on their own (Diehl and Stroebe 1987; Mullen *et al.* 1991). On the contrary, *nominal* groups (that is, brainstorming groups in which individuals create ideas on their own and do not interact) are twice as creative as true interactive groups. The inferior performance of brainstorming groups has been attributed to three factors (Paulus *et al.* 1993):

1. *Evaluation apprehension* – despite explicit instructions designed to encourage the uninhibited generation of as many ideas as possible, members may still be concerned about making a good impression. This would introduce a degree of self-censorship and a consequent reduction in productivity.
2. *Social loafing* – there is a motivation loss because of the collective nature of the task (see Chapter 7).

▶ Production blocking

3. *Production blocking* – individual creativity and productivity are reduced due to interference effects from having to contend with others generating ideas at the same time as one is attempting to generate one's own ideas.

▶ Illusion of group
effectivity

Given the convincing evidence that brainstorming does not actually improve creativity, why do people so firmly believe that it does, and so continue to use it as a technique for generating new ideas in groups? Diehl and Stroebe have proposed an explanation of this paradox in terms of the existence of an *illusion of group effectivity* (Diehl and Stroebe 1991; Stroebe *et al.* 1992; see also Paulus *et al.* 1993). We all take part in group discussions from time to time, and therefore all have some degree of personal experience with idea-generation in groups. The illusion of group effectivity is an experience-based belief that we actually produce more and better ideas in groups than alone.

This illusion may be generated by at least three processes. First, although groups produce fewer non-redundant original ideas than the sum of individuals working alone, they do produce more ideas than any single member would produce alone. In groups, therefore, people are exposed to more ideas than if alone. People find it difficult to remember which ideas they produced, and which were produced by other people, and so tend to exaggerate their own contribution. They feel that they were individually more productive and were facilitated by the group, when in fact they were less productive. Stroebe *et al.* (1992) had subjects brainstorm in four-person nominal or real groups and asked them to estimate the percentage of ideas they had suggested, the percentage others had suggested but they had also thought of, and the percentage that others had suggested but they had not thought of. The results (Figure 8.4) show that subjects in real groups over-estimate the percentage of

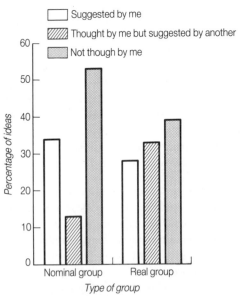

FIGURE 8.4 *Percentage of ideas assigned to self and others in nominal and real brainstorming groups. (Source: based on data from Stroebe et al. 1992.)*

suggestions that they either made or had but did not suggest, relative to subjects in nominal groups.

Second, brainstorming is generally great fun. People enjoy brainstorming in groups more than alone and so feel more satisfied with their performance. Third, people in groups know that they only call out some of the ideas they have because others have already been mentioned. Of course all group members are in the same position, but the subject is not privy to others' undisclosed ideas, and so attribute the relatively low overt productivity of others to their own relatively high latent productivity. The group is seen to have enhanced or confirmed their own high level of performance.

Group remembering and transactive memory

Another important component of group decision-making is the ability to recall information. For instance, juries need to be able to recall a great deal of testimony in order to be able to arrive at a verdict, and personnel selection panels need to recall information that differentiates among candidates in order to make an appointment. Group remembering can even be the principal reason for certain groups to come together, for example groups of old friends often meet mainly to reminisce.

Do groups remember more material than individuals? In summarising research on group remembering, Clark and Stephenson (1989) conclude that groups remember more material than individuals and more material than the best individual in the group. According to Lorge and Solomon (1955), groups recall more than individuals because members communicate unshared information and because the group recognises true information when it hears it. There is, however, some evidence that the superiority of groups over individuals varies depending on the memory task. On simplistic and artificial tasks (for example, nonsense words) group superiority is more marked than on complex and realistic tasks (for example, a story). One explanation of this is in terms of 'process loss' (Steiner 1976 – see Chapter 7). Faced by the task of recalling complex information, groups fail to adopt appropriate recall and decision strategies and therefore do not fully utilise all the human resources available in the group.

Group remembering is, however, more than simply collective regurgitation of facts. It is often a constructive process, characterised by negotiation of an agreed joint account of some part of experience. Some individuals' memories will contribute to the developing consensus while others' will not. In this way the group shapes a version of the truth that gains its subjective veracity from the degree of consensus. The group in effect constructs a version of the truth that guides individual members about what to store as a true memory and what to discard as an incorrect memory. The process of reaching consensus is subject to the entire range of social influence processes discussed in Chapter 6 as well as the group decision-making biases discussed in this chapter. The majority of research into group remembering tends to focus mainly on how much is remembered by individuals and by groups. Recently, however, Clark and Stephenson and their associates have begun looking at other aspects of group remembering (see Figure 8.5 and Box 8.1).

▶ Transactive memory

An entirely different perspective on group remembering has been proposed by Wegner and his colleagues (Wegner 1986; Wegner *et al.* 1991). Individuals in couples and groups have a *transactive memory* that is greater than their individual memories. This idea refers to the way in which couples and groups can share memory load so that each individual is responsible for remembering only part of what the group needs to know, but all members know who is responsible for each memory domain. Transactive memory is a shared system for encoding, storing and retrieving information.

For example, the psychology department at my university needs to remember an enormous amount of practical information to do with research, postgraduate supervision, undergraduate teaching, equipment and so forth. This is far too much information for a single individual to be able to remember. Instead, certain individuals are formally responsible for individual domains (for example, research), but all of us have a transactive memory in so far as we know who is responsible for which domains. Transactive memory is also very common in close relationships such as marriage, for example both partners know that one of them remembers financial matters and the other remembers directions.

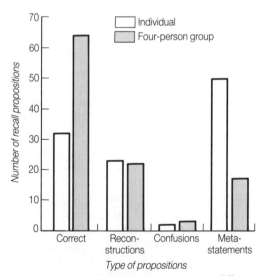

FIGURE 8.5 *Qualitative and quantitative differences between individual and collective remembering of police testimony. (Source: based on data from Clark and Stephenson 1989.)*

BOX 8.1 Differences between individual and collective remembering

Can two heads remember better than one?

Noel Clark, Geoffrey Stephenson and their associates have conducted a series of experiments on group remembering (for example, Clark *et al.* 1986; Stephenson *et al.* 1986a,b). Clark and Stephenson (1989) give an integrated overview of this research. Generally, students or police officers individually or collectively (four-person groups) recalled information from a five-minute police interrogation of a female who had allegedly been raped. The interrogation was real, or it was staged and presented as an audio recording or a visual transcript. The subjects had to recall freely the interrogation and answer specific factual questions (cued recall). The way in which subjects recalled the information was content-analysed to investigate:

1. The amount of correct information recalled.
2. The number of reconstructive errors made – that is, inclusion of material that was consistent with but did not appear in the original stimulus
3. The number of confusional errors made – that is, inclusion of material that was inconsistent with the original stimulus.
4. The number of metastatements – that is, inclusion of information that attributed motives to characters or went beyond the original stimulus in other ways.

Figure 8.5 shows that groups recalled significantly more correct information and made fewer metastatements than individuals, but did not differ in the number of reconstructions or confusional errors.

(Source: Clark and Stephenson 1989.)

▶ Group mind

Transactive memory is a group-level representation because, although it is represented in the mind of the individual, it can only emerge through psychological involvement in a group, and has no value or utility outside group membership. There can be no such thing as individual transactive memory. In this respect the concept of transactive memory is related to McDougall's (1920) notion of a *group mind* (Chapters 1 and 10) – a state of mind and mode of cognition found in groups that is qualitatively different from that found in individuals.

Wegner *et al.* (1991) describe the development of transactive memory. When groups or couples first form, the basis of transactive memory is usually social categorisation. People stereotypically assign memory domains to individuals on the basis of their category memberships. For example, members of hetero-sexual couples might initially develop a transactive memory in which there is sex-role stereotypic allocation of memory (the female remembers things to do with cooking and believes that information to do with the car can be obtained from the male, and vice versa). Category-based transactive memory is the default mode. In most cases, however, groups go on to develop more sophisticated memory assignment systems. Groups can negotiate responsibility for different memory domains, for instance couples can decide through discussion who will be responsible for bills, who for groceries, who for cars and so forth. Groups can assign memory domains on the basis of relative expertise, for instance a conference-organising committee might assign responsibility for the social programme to someone who has successfully discharged that duty before. Groups can also assign memory domains on the basis of access to information, for instance the conference-organising committee might assign responsibility for organising publicity to someone who has a good graphics package, a list of potential registrants and is friendly with some advertising people in the city.

There is a potential pitfall to transactive memory. The uneven distribution of memory in a couple or a group means that when an individual leaves there is a temporary loss of, or reduction in group memory. This can be very disruptive. Groups can often recover fairly quickly as there are other people (often already with some expertise and access to information) who can immediately take up the responsibility. In couples, however, partners are sually irreplaceable. Once one person leaves the couple, for example through death or separation, a whole section of group memory vanishes (see Chapter 12). It is quite possible that the depression usually associated with bereavement may, at least in part, be due to the loss of memory. Happy memories are lost, one's sense of who one is is undermined by lack of information, and one has to take responsibility for remembering a variety of things one did not have to remember before.

Groupthink

▶ Groupthink

Groups can sometimes employ poor decision-making procedures that produce poor decisions. The consequences of such decisions can be quite disastrous. Janis (1972) employed an archival method relying on retrospective accounts and content analysis to compare a number of American foreign policy decisions that had unfavourable outcomes (for example, the 1961 Bay of Pigs fiasco, the 1941 defence of Pearl Harbor) with others that had favourable outcomes (for example, the 1962 Cuban missile crisis). Janis coined the term *groupthink* to describe the group decision-making process that produced the poor decisions. Groupthink was defined as a mode of thinking in which the desire to reach unanimous agreement overrides the motivation to adopt proper rational decision-making procedures (Janis 1982; Janis and Mann 1977).

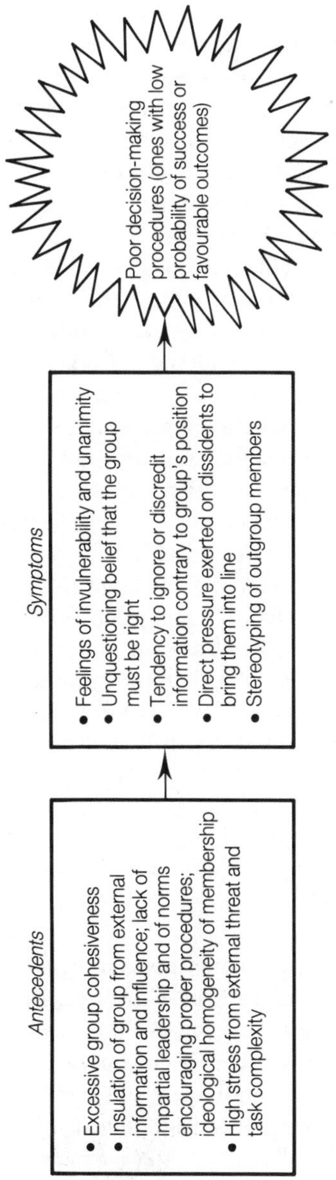

Antecedents

- Excessive group cohesiveness
- Insulation of group from external information and influence; lack of impartial leadership and of norms encouraging proper procedures; ideological homogeneity of membership
- High stress from external threat and task complexity

Symptoms

- Feelings of invulnerability and unanimity
- Unquestioning belief that the group must be right
- Tendency to ignore or discredit information contrary to group's position
- Direct pressure exerted on dissidents to bring them into line
- Stereotyping of outgroup members

Poor decision-making procedures (ones with low probability of success or favourable outcomes)

FIGURE 8.6 *Antecedents, symptoms and consequences of groupthink. (Source: derived from Janis and Mann, 1977.)*

The antecedents, symptoms and consequences of groupthink are displayed in Figure 8.6. The principal cause of groupthink is excessive group cohesiveness, but there are other antecedents that relate to basic structural faults in the group and to the immediate decision-making context. Together these factors generate a range of symptoms that is associated with defective decision-making procedures. For example, there is inadequate and biased discussion and consideration of objectives and alternative solutions, and a failure to seek the advice of experts outside the group.

Descriptive studies of groupthink (for example, Hart 1990, Hensley and Griffin 1986; Tetlock 1979) largely support the general model (but see Tetlock *et al.* 1992), while experimental studies tend to find little support for the role of cohesiveness. Experiments tend to establish background conditions for groupthink in four-person laboratory or quasi-naturalistic groups, and then manipulate cohesiveness (usually as friends versus strangers) and either a leadership variable (directiveness or need-for-power) or procedural directions for effective decision-making. Some have found no relationship between cohesiveness and groupthink (Flowers 1977; Fodor and Smith 1982); some have found a positive relationship only under certain conditions (Callaway and Esser 1984; Courtright 1978), and some a negative relationship (Leana 1985).

These problems have led people to suggest other ways to approach the explanation of groupthink (Hogg 1992; Turner *et al.* 1992). For example, group cohesiveness may need to be more precisely defined before its relationship to groupthink can be specified (Longley and Pruitt 1980; McCauley 1989): it currently ranges from close friendship to group-based liking. It has also been suggested that groupthink is merely a specific instance of 'risky shift' in which a group that already tends towards making a risky decision polarises through discussion to an even more risky decision (Myers and Lamm 1975 – see below). Others have suggested that groupthink may not really be a group process at all but really just an aggregation of individual coping responses to excessive stress (Callaway *et al.* 1985). Group members are under decision-making stress and thus adopt defensive coping strategies which involve suboptimal decision-making procedures that are symptomatic of groupthink. These behaviours are mutually reinforced by members of the group, and thus produce defective group decisions.

Group polarisation

Folk wisdom has it that groups, committees and organisations are inherently more conservative in their decisions than individuals. Individuals are likely to take risks, while group decision-making is very much a tedious averaging process that errs towards caution. This is quite consistent with much of what social psychologists know about conformity and social influence processes in groups (see Chapter 6). Sherif's (1936) autokinetic studies, which we discussed in Chapters 6 and 7, illustrate this averaging process very well.

◗ Risky shift

Imagine, then, the excitement with which social psychologists greeted the results of Stoner's (1961) unpublished master's thesis. Stoner had subjects play the role of counsellor/adviser to imaginary people faced by choice dilemmas (Kogan and Wallach 1964) in which there was a desirable but risky course of action contrasted with a less desirable but more cautious course of action (see Box 8.2). Subjects made their own private recommendations, and then met in small groups to discuss each dilemma and reach a unanimous group recommendation. Stoner found that groups tended towards recommending the risky alternative more than did individuals. This phenomenon has been called *risky shift*, but later research documented group recommendations that were more cautious than those of individuals, and caused the phenomenon to be treated as part of a much wider phenomenon of *group polarisation* (Moscovici and Zavalloni 1969).

BOX 8.2 An example of a choice dilemma

Giving advice on risk-taking

Suppose that the subject's task was to advise someone on a course of action which could vary between two extremes: risky and cautious. The following is an example of such a choice dilemma:

> Mr L., a married 30-year-old research physicist, has been given a five-year appointment by a major university laboratory. As he contemplates the next five years, he realises that he might work on a difficult long-term problem which, if a solution can be found, would resolve basic scientific issues in the field and bring him scientific honours. If no solution were found, however, Mr L. would have little to show for his five years in the laboratory, and this would make it hard for him to get a good job afterwards.
>
> On the other hand, he could, as most of his professional associates are doing, work on a series of short-term problems where solutions would be easier to find, but where the problems are of lesser scientific importance.
>
> Imagine that you (the subject) are advising Mr L. Listed below are several probabilities or odds that a solution would be found to the difficult, long-term problem that Mr L. has in mind.
>
> Please put a cross beside the LOWEST probability that you would consider acceptable to make it worthwhile for Mr L. to work on the more difficult, long-term problem.

The subject then responds on a ten-point scale, indicating the odds that Mr L. would solve the long-term problem.

(Source: Kogan and Wallach 1964.)

▶ Group polarisation

Group polarisation (Isenberg 1986; Myers and Lamm 1976; Wetherell 1987) is defined as a tendency for groups to make decisions that are more extreme than the mean of individual members' initial positions, in the direction already favoured by that mean. So, for example, group discussion among a collection of people who already slightly favour capital punishment is likely to produce a group decision that strongly favours capital punishment.

Although thirty years of research have produced many different theories to explain polarisation, they can perhaps be simplified to three major perspectives: persuasive arguments, social comparison/cultural values and self-categorisation theories.

Persuasive arguments

▶ Persuasive
  arguments theory

Persuasive arguments theory focuses on the persuasive impact of novel arguments in changing people's opinions (Burnstein and Vinokur 1977; Vinokur and Burnstein 1974). People tend to rest their opinions on a body of supportive arguments that they express publicly in group discussion. If the group contains people who hold similar positions tending in a certain direction, then among familiar arguments they will all also hear some arguments, not previously encountered, in favour of their initial positions. As a consequence, their initial opinions will become more entrenched and extreme, and thus the view of the group as a whole will become polarised.

Social comparison/cultural values

▶ Social comparison
▶ Cultural values
  theory

According to the *social comparison* or *cultural values theory* (Jellison and Arkin 1977; Sanders and Baron 1977), people are motivated to avoid social censure and to seek social approval. Group discussion reveals what views are socially desirable or culturally valued, and so group members shift in the direction of the group in order to gain approval and avoid disapproval. For example, favouring capital punishment and finding oneself surrounded by others who also favour capital punishment might be a strong basis for the, not necessarily accurate or valid, assumption that this is the socially valued attitude to hold. Social desirability considerations would cause people in the group to become more extreme in their support for capital punishment.

These two approaches are supported by some studies but not by others (Mackie 1986; Turner 1991; Wetherell 1987). For example, polarisation has been obtained under circumstances (for example, perceptual tasks) where arguments and persuasion are unlikely to play a role (Baron and Roper 1976), and under circumstances where lack of surveillance by the group should minimise the role of social desirability (Goethals and Zanna 1979; Teger and Pruitt 1967). In general it is not possible to argue that one perspective has a clear empirical advantage over the other. Isenberg (1986) has suggested that both are correct (they explain polarisation under different circumstances), and that we should seek to specify the range of applicability of each.

Self-categorisation

▶ Self-categorisation theory

This is a third perspective advanced by Turner and his colleagues (Turner 1985; Turner *et al*. 1987 – see also Chapter 10). Unlike persuasive arguments and social comparison/cultural values theories, self-categorisation theory treats polarisation as a regular conformity phenomenon (Turner and Oakes 1989). People in discussion groups actively construct a representation of the group norm from the positions held by group members in relation to those positions assumed to be held by people not in the group, or known to be held by people explicitly in an outgroup. Because such norms not only minimise variability within the group (that is, among ingroup members) but also distinguish the ingroup from outgroups, they are not necessarily the mean ingroup position – they can be polarised away from an explicit or implicit outgroup (see Figure 8.7). Self-categorisation, the process responsible for identification with a group, produces conformity to the ingroup norm, and thence, if the norm is polarised, group polarisation. If the norm is not polarised, self-categorisation produces convergence on the mean group position. Research tends to support this perspective in: (1) confirming how a norm can be polarised (Hogg *et al*. 1990); (2) showing that people are more persuaded by ingroup members than outgroup members or individuals, and (3) showing that group polarisation only occurs if an initial group tendency is perceived to represent a norm,

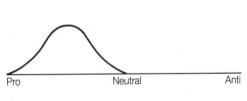

Stage 1:

Actual distribution of ingroup positions on an attitudinal dimension. Scale positions not under the bell curve are positions held by people not in the group.

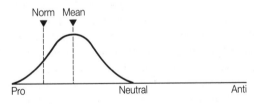

Stage 2:

Perceptual polarisation of the ingroup norm away from positions held by ingroup members.

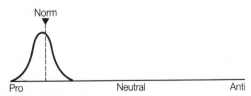

Stage 3:

Ingroup members conform to the polarised ingroup norm, causing the distribution of ingroup positions to be both homogenised and polarised.

FIGURE 8.7 *Group polarisation as self-categorisation-induced conformity to a polarised group.*

rather than an aggregate of individual opinions (Mackie 1986; Mackie and Cooper 1984; Turner *et al.* 1989).

Jury decision-making

Juries represent one of the most significant decision-making groups, not only because they are held up as a symbol of all that is democratic, fair and just in a society, but also because of the consequences of their decisions for defendants, victims and the community. A case in point is the devastating 1992 Los Angeles riots which were sparked by an unexpected 'not guilty' verdict delivered by an all-white jury in the case of the police beating of a black suspect (see Box 10.1 in Chapter 10). Juries are groups and thus potentially prey to all the deficiencies of group decision-making discussed in this chapter – for example, leadership, groupthink and group polarisation (Hastie 1993; Hastie *et al.* 1983; Kaplan 1977; Kerr, 1978; Kerr and Bray 1982).

In addition to these problems, research has identified a number of issues to do specifically with the task confronted by juries. Characteristics of the defendant and of the victim can affect the jury. Physically attractive defendants are more likely to be acquitted (Michelini and Snodgrass 1980) or to receive a lighter sentence (Stewart 1980), though biases can be reduced by furnishing sufficient factual evidence (Baumeister and Darley 1982), presenting the jury with written rather than spoken, face-to-face testimony (Kaplan and Miller 1978), or explicitly directing the jury to consider the evidence alone (Weiten 1980). Race can also affect the jury. In the United States, for example, blacks are more likely to receive prison sentences than whites (Stewart 1980), and people who murder a white are more likely than those who murder a black to receive the death penalty (11.1 per cent versus 4.5 per cent – Henderson and Taylor 1985).

Another issue is the influence of laws and penalties on the jury. Harsh laws with stiff penalties (for example, death penalty) tend to discourage juries from convicting (Kerr 1978) – quite the reverse of the intention of legislators who introduce such laws. Consider some of the pressures on an Australian jury discussing evidence relating to an Aboriginal defendant, given that there is a high incidence of suicide among Aborigines serving custodial sentences.

The jury foreman is important in guiding the jury to its verdict, as she occupies the role of leader. Research suggests that the foreman is most likely to be someone of higher socio-economic status, someone who has had previous experience as a juror or simply occupies the seat at the head of the table at the first sitting of the jury (Strodtbeck and Lipinski 1985). This is perhaps of some concern as diffuse status characteristics (Berger *et al.* 1977), which we discussed earlier this chapter, are influencing the jury process.

Research indicates that older, less educated and lower socio-economic status jurors are more likely to vote to convict, but that males and females do not differ, except that females are more likely to convict defendants in rape trials (Nemeth 1981). Jurors who score high on authoritarianism favour conviction when the victim is an authority figure (for example, police officer) while jurors who are more egalitarian favour conviction when the defendant is a police officer (Mitchell 1979).

SUMMARY

♦ Although certain personality traits are often associated with leadership, there are too many exceptions to support an explanation of leadership purely in terms of personality.
♦ Although almost all of us are suited to be leaders in the right circumstances, some individuals may have the edge over others.
♦ Leadership is best explained as an interaction of leadership style (task-oriented versus relationship-oriented) and task demands (depending on the nature of the task, one leadership style is more effective than the other).
♦ Leaders only exist in so far as there are followers. It is the followers who provide leaders with the trappings of power usually associated with leadership.
♦ Group decisions can sometimes be quite accurately predicted from the pre-discussion distribution of opinions in the group and from the decision-making rule that prevails in the group at that time.
♦ People believe that group brainstorming enhances individual creativity, despite evidence that groups do not do better than non-interactive individuals and that individuals do not perform better in groups than alone. This illusion of group effectivity may be due to distorted perceptions during group brainstorming, and the enjoyment people derive from group brainstorming.
♦ Groups, particularly established groups that have a transactive memory structure, are often more effective than individuals at remembering information.
♦ Highly cohesive groups with directive leaders are prone to groupthink – poor decision-making based on an over-zealous desire to reach consensus.
♦ Groups that already tend towards an extreme position on a decision-making dimension often make even more extreme decisions than the average of the members' initial positions would suggest.
♦ Juries are not free from the usual range of group decision-making biases and errors.

FURTHER READING

Baron, R. S., Kerr, N. and Miller, N. (1992). *Group Process, Group Decision, Group Action*. Buckingham: Open University Press.

Brown, R. J. (1988). *Group Processes: Dynamics Within and Between Groups*. Oxford: Blackwell.

Hogg, M. A. and Abrams, D. (1988). *Social Identifications: A Social Psychology of Intergroup Relations and Group Processes.* London: Routledge.

Moreland, R. L. and Levine, J. M. (1994). *Understanding Small Groups.* Boston, Mass.: Allyn and Bacon.

▸ KEY TERMS

autocratic leadership

brainstorming

cohesiveness

contingency theory

cultural values theory

democratic leadership

great person theory

group mind

group polarisation

groupthink

idiosyncrasy credit

illusion of group effectivity

leadership

LPC scale

persuasive arguments theory

production blocking

risky shift

self-categorisation theory

situational control

social comparison

social decisions schemes

social transition scheme

socio-emotional oriented leader

task-oriented leader

transactive memory

9 Prejudice

·················

FOCUS QUESTIONS

♦ Despite the rhetoric of, and legislation for equality, do minority groups in Britain now really receive equal treatment and have the same opportunities as the majority?

♦ What would your feelings be if someone less well qualified than you was to be given a job in preference to you because that person belongs to a historically disadvantaged social group?

♦ If you were frustrated in your ambitions or came from a harsh and repressive family background, do you think you might develop a tendency to vent your frustration and anger, from time to time, on minority social groups, rather than other targets?

♦ Most societies consider prejudice and discrimination unacceptable, and yet prejudice persists. Why?

NATURE AND DIMENSIONS OF PREJUDICE

These 'Ocean Men' are tall beasts with deep sunken eyes and beak-like noses... Although undoubtably men, they seem to possess none of the mental faculties of men. The most bestial of peasants is far more human... It is quite possible that they are susceptible to training, and could with patience be taught the modes of conduct proper to a human being. [The 'beasts' in question were Jesuit priests seen through the eyes of a Confucian scholar in the sixteenth century.] (cited in Vaughan 1988, p. 1)

▶ Prejudice
▶ Dehumanisation

This quotation illustrates perhaps the most worrying aspect of *prejudice*: the *dehumanisation* of an outgroup – see Chapters 11 and 15 for other examples of dehumanisation. Most people in liberal democratic societies consider prejudice a particularly unacceptable aspect of human behaviour, with terms such as racist, sexist and bigot being reserved as insults. Yet almost all of us experience prejudice from time to time in one form or another, ranging from relatively minor assumptions that people make about us, to crude and offensive bigotry or even violence. People make and behave in accordance with assumptions about our abilities and aspirations on the basis of, for example, age, sex, ethnicity or race, and we often find ourselves automatically making the same sorts of assumption about others. And herein lies a paradox: prejudice is socially undesirable and yet it pervades social life. Even in societies where prejudice appears to be institutionalised, sophisticated justifications are used to deny that it is prejudice that is actually being practised.

▶ Genocide

Prejudice is responsible for or associated with much of the pain and human suffering in the world, ranging from restricted opportunities and narrowed horizons to physical violence and *genocide*. It has always been with us, and it is a sobering thought that it may always remain with us as a fundamental part of the human condition. Nevertheless it is vitally important for humanity to gain an understanding of why and how people are prejudiced, in order to moderate its effects and, it is to be hoped, prevent its more extreme manifestations. It is social psychology which must rise to this challenge, as prejudice is a social psychological phenomenon. In fact, prejudice is doubly social: it involves people's feelings about and actions towards other people, and it is guided and given a context by the groups we belong to and the historical circumstances of specific intergroup relations in which these groups find themselves.

PREJUDICE AND DISCRIMINATION

Since the term prejudice literally means pre-judgement (from the Latin *prae* and *judicium*), it is usual to consider prejudice as an attitude (see Chapter 4) where the attitude object is a social group (for example, women, Americans, Muslims, West Indians, musicians, etc.). A traditional view (for example, Allport 1954) of prejudice is that it has three components:

1. *Cognitive* – a set of beliefs about the attitude object.
2. *Affective* – strong feelings (usually negative) about the attitude object and the qualities it is believed to possess.
3. *Conative* – a set of intentions to behave in certain ways towards the attitude object. It is important to note that the conative component is an *intention* to act in certain ways and is not the action itself.

We should note, however, that not all attitude theorists are comfortable with the *tripartite model* of attitude (see Chapter 4).

Box 9.1 provides a fictional illustration of how prejudice may arise and become the basis for discrimination. Although this is, of course, a fictional example, it does capture many of the principal features of prejudice that need to be explained. The first issue, which is essentially the attitude/behaviour relationship (see Chapter 4), is the relationship between prejudiced beliefs and the practice of discrimination. You will recall from Chapter 4 that LaPiere (1934), a social scientist, spent two years travelling around the United States with a young Chinese American couple. They visited 250 hotels, auto-camps, tourist homes and restaurants and were refused service in only one (that is, 0.4 per cent) – it would appear that there was very little anti-Chinese prejudice. After returning home, LaPiere contacted 128 of these establishments with the

BOX 9.1 Prejudice and discrimination: a fictional illustration

A new 'minority group'

A study by Joseph Forgas (1983) showed that students can have clear beliefs about different campus groups. One such target group is 'engineering students' who are often described in terms of their drinking habits (beer – and lots of it), their cultural preferences (sports and little else), and their style of dress (practical and conservative). This is, of course, a pre-judgement in so far as it is assumed that all engineering students are like this. If these beliefs (the cognitive component) are not associated with any strong feelings (*affect*) or any particular intentions to act (conation) then no real problem exists and one would probably not call this a prejudice – simply a harmless generalisation. However, if these beliefs were associated with strong negative feelings about engineering students and their characteristics then a pattern of *conations* would almost inevitably arise. If one hated and despised engineering students and their characteristics, then one would quite probably intend to avoid them, perhaps humiliate them whenever possible, and even dream of a brave new world without them.

This is now quite clearly prejudice, but it may still not be much of a social problem. Strong pressures would exist to inhibit expression of such views or the realisation of conation in action, and so people with such prejudices would quite probably be unaware that others shared their views. If, however, people became aware that their prejudices were widely shared then they might engage in discussion and form organisations to represent their views. Under these circumstances more extreme conations might arise, for example suggestions to isolate engineering students in one part of the campus and deny them access to certain resources on campus (for example, the bar, the pool, etc.). Individuals or small groups might now feel strong enough to discriminate against individual engineering students, though wider social pressures would probably present widespread discrimination. If, however, the students gained legitimate overall power in the university then they would be entirely free to put into action all their plans. They could indulge themselves freely in the dehumanisation of engineering students: deny them their human rights, degrade and humiliate them, herd them into ghettos behind barbed wire, and systematically exterminate them. Prejudice has become enshrined in, and legitimated by, the norms and practices of the community.

question 'will you accept members of the Chinese race as guests in your establishment?'. The responses included 92 per cent 'no', 7 per cent 'uncertain, depends upon circumstances' and 1 per cent 'yes' – it would appear that there was massive prejudice.

A controlled experiment was conducted later by Gaertner and Dovidio (1977). White female undergraduates waiting to participate in an experiment overheard a supposed 'emergency' in an adjoining room in which several chairs seemed to fall on a female confederate who was either white or black. The subjects were led to believe that they were alone with the confederate or that there were two other potential helpers. Ordinarily one would expect the usual bystander effect (see Chapter 13 for details) in which subjects would be less willing to go to the aid of the 'victim' when other potential helpers were available. Figure 9.1 shows that there was only a weak bystander effect when the victim was white, but that the effect was greatly amplified when the victim was black – the white subjects discriminated overtly against the black victim only when other potential helpers were present. There is an important lesson here: under certain circumstances prejudice may go undetected. If the 'two potential helpers' condition had not been included, this experiment would have revealed that white females were more willing to aid a black than a white victim. It was only with inclusion of the 'two potential helpers' condition that underlying prejudice was revealed. The absence of overt discrimination should always be treated with caution, as prejudice can be expressed in many indirect and subtle ways (see below).

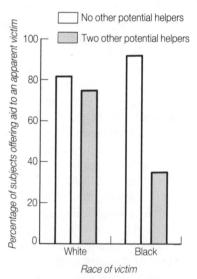

FIGURE 9.1 *Bystander apathy as a function of race and victim. (Source: data from Gaertner and Dovidio 1977).*

SOME CATEGORIES OF PREJUDICE

Human beings are remarkably versatile in being able to make almost any social group a target of prejudice. However, there are certain groups which can be considered the enduring victims of prejudiced attitudes; these include those based on sex, race, ethnicity, age, sexual preference, and physical and mental health.

Sexism

▶ Sexism

Social psychological research on *sexism* is important in at least two ways:

1. It tells us something about the social psychological mechanisms associated with prejudice in general.
2. It addresses a form of prejudice that may affect one in two human beings.

▶ Stereotypes

Research into sex stereotypes has revealed that both males and females believe that men score higher on traits reflecting competence and independence, and women score higher on traits reflecting warmth and expressiveness (Broverman *et al.* 1972; Spence *et al.* 1974). These beliefs have substantial cross-cultural generality: they prevail in Europe, North and South America, Australia and parts of the Middle East (Deaux 1985; Williams and Best 1982). These really are consensual social *stereotypes*. Knowledge of such stereotypes is not inevitably associated with a stereotype-consistent personal belief about the target group. In fact, it seems that such a correspondence between knowledge and belief only occurs among highly prejudiced individuals (Devine 1989).

Sex role and power. Who has the power here? Sexual harassment is still prevalent despite changing values and the creation of legislation outlawing its practice. (Source: Andrew Lukey.)

There is some evidence that, all things being equal, males and females do not actually describe themselves quite so strongly in sex-stereotypical terms (for example, Martin 1987), and that women deny feeling that they have been personally discriminated against: sexual discrimination is something experienced by *other* women (Crosby *et al.* 1989, 1993).

Presumably, dimensions reflecting competence, independence, warmth and expressiveness are all highly desirable and valued human attributes. If this were true there would be no differential evaluative connotation of the stereotype. Research, however, suggests that female stereotypic traits are significantly less valued than male stereotypic traits. Broverman *et al.* (1970) asked seventy-nine practising mental health clinicians (clinical psychologists, psychiatrists, social workers) to describe a healthy, mature, socially competent individual, who was either (1) a male, (2) a female or (3) a person. Both male and female clinicians described a healthy adult male and a healthy adult person in almost exactly the same terms (reflecting competency). The healthy adult female was seen to be significantly more submissive, excitable and appearance-oriented – characteristics not attached to either the healthy adult or the healthy male. It is ominous that females are not considered to be normal, healthy adult people.

▶ Sex role

Perhaps sex stereotypes accurately reflect sex differences in personality and behaviour? Perhaps males and females really do have different personalities? Bakan (1966) has, for example, argued that males are more 'agentic' (that is, action-oriented) than females, and females are more 'communal' than males (see also Williams 1984). This is a complicated issue. Traditionally, males and females have each occupied a different *sex role* in society (males pursue full-time out-of-home jobs, while females are 'homemakers'), and, as we saw in Chapter 7, roles constrain behaviour in line with role requirements. Sex differences, if they do exist, may simply reflect roles not sex, and role assignment may be determined and perpetuated by the social group which has more power (in almost all cases males). An alternative argument might be that there are intrinsic personality differences between males and females that suit the sexes to different roles – that is, there is a biological imperative behind role assignments. Clearly this is a debate that can be, and is, highly politicised.

Social psychological research indicates that there is a small number of systematic differences between the sexes, but that they are not very diagnostic: in other words, knowing someone's position on one of these dimensions is not a very reliable predictor of that person's sex (Parsons *et al.* 1984). For example, research on male and female military cadets (Rice *et al.* 1984) and male and female managers (Steinberg and Shapiro 1982) indicated that perceived stereotypic differences were an extreme exaggeration of very minor differences. In general, sex stereotypes are more myth than a reflection of reality (Eagly and Carli 1981).

▶ Gender

One reason that sex stereotypes persist is that role assignment according to *gender* persists. In general, women make up the overwhelming majority of restaurant servers, telephone operators, secretaries, nurses, babysitters, dental hygienists, librarians and elementary/kindergarten teachers, while most lawyers, dentists, truck drivers, accountants, top executives and engineers are male (Greenglass 1982). Certain occupations become labelled as 'women's work' and valued less accordingly. To investigate this idea, Eagly and Steffen (1984) asked male and female students to rate, on sex-stereotypic dimensions, an imaginary male or female, who was described as either being a 'homemaker' or being employed full-time outside the home. In a third condition, no employment information was given. Figure 9.2 shows that, irrespective of sex, homemakers were perceived to be significantly more feminine (in their traits) than full-time employees. This indicates that certain roles may be sex-typed, and suggests the possibility that as women increasingly enter masculine roles there will be substantial change in sex stereotypes. However, the converse may also occur: as a traditionally male role becomes increasingly occupied by relatively more women, that role may become less valued.

In any analysis of intergroup relations between the sexes we should not lose sight of the fact that in general males still have substantially more socio-political power than females to define the relative status of different roles in society. This analysis stems from *social identity theory* (Hogg and Abrams 1988; Tajfel and Turner 1979 – see below and Chapter 10). Not surprisingly, it is also the case that women often find it very difficult to gain access to higher status masculine roles/occupations. For example, female applicants for doctoral positions in American universities can be discouraged by condescending reactions from male peers and faculty members (for example, 'You're so cute, I can't see you as a professor of anything') (Harris 1970), and there are

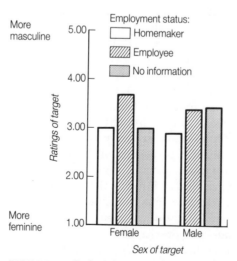

FIGURE 9.2 *Trait ratings as a function of sex and employment status of target. (Source: based on data from Eagly and Steffen 1984.)*

numerous studies, again from America, showing bias against hiring women for faculty positions in universities (for example, Fidell 1970; Lewin and Duchan 1971). Lest we wrongly infer that universities are bastions of male chauvinism, it should be noted that much research is conducted in universities because they are institutions that are eager to examine and improve their sex-role practices, and because other organisations are often difficult to gain access to, or are unwilling to co-operate in this sort of research.

It is quite probably on going to school that people first encounter gender, that is the set of societal definitions and expectations relating to the 'proper' conduct of males and females as distinct social categories in a systematic and powerful way. Lloyd and Duveen (1992; Duveen and Lloyd 1993) argue that gender categorisations and roles are implicit in the personal relationships prevailing in families, but that school, as a social institution, makes gender explicit in all sorts of subtle ways and thus legitimises it. Going to school is a crucial event in the development of gender identity and the internalisation of attitudes towards sex roles. Lloyd and Duveen report a study of 5-year olds first going to primary school in Britain to illustrate the ways in which this can happen. Children are primarily categorised in terms of sex (the register may be divided into boys and girls with boys' names called first, small groups are usually all boys or all girls, areas of the classroom become associated with one or other sex), activities and toys are clearly sex-stereotypical (boys' toys and games, and girls' toys and games), and types of behaviour are referred to sex-stereotypically (forceful/assertive behaviour is labelled as boys' behaviour, and passive/compliant behaviour as girls' behaviour).

▶ 'Face-ism'

One of the most powerful forces in the transmission and maintenance of traditional sex stereotypes is of course, the media. We are all very familiar with the obvious forms this may take: semi-clad women draped over boats, automobiles, motorcycles and other consumer products; the purely decorative role of women in TV game shows; the way in which women are often entirely extraneous to the plot of a drama and are presented only as sexual/romantic relief. Although the cumulative power of these images should not be under-estimated, there are some more covert forms that may be equally or even more powerful as they are more difficult to detect and thus combat. For example, Archer et al. (1983) have coined the term '*face-ism*' to describe the way in which depictions of males give greater prominence to the head while depictions of females give greater prominence to the body. Archer and colleagues analysed a large number of visual images of males and females (newspaper and magazine pictures as well as drawings made by students) and discovered that in almost all instances this was the case. Next time you watch, for example, a television interview or documentary, note how the camera tends to focus on the face of males but the face and upper body of females. Face-ism communicates the chauvinistic view that, relative to men, women are more important for their physical appearance than their intellectual capacity.

Sik Hung Ng has noted another subtle form of sexism, in the use of the generic masculine (Ng 1990; see also Wetherell 1986). This refers to the way in which when people are talking about people in general they tend to use terms such as 'mankind' and the masculine pronouns (he, him, his, etc.). This contains the clear implication that females are an aberration from the basic masculine mould of humanity. The sex-typing of occupations and roles is also maintained by terms such as 'housewife', 'chairman', and so on. Because it is largely through language that we represent our world (see Chapter 14) it is very important, in order to change sex-stereotypes, that the implicit meanings of words and phrases be considered, and those expressions that are clearly sexist (or prejudiced in other ways) be changed. For example, language codes such as the publication manual for the American Psychological Association (adhered to by psychologists around the world) have enshrined within them clear directions for non-sexist language use.

An area in which there is pervasive sex discrimination is performance evaluation. The quality of identical written work has been shown to be evaluated less favourably when attributed to a female than a male author (Goldberg 1968). In a similar study, Pheterson *et al.* (1971) found that works of art attributed to males or females were evaluated equally when experts had already evaluated them, but that in the absence of such adjudication those attributed to females were evaluated less favourably than those attributed to males. This implies that women are expected to be less competent than males until demonstrated otherwise.

▶ Attribution

There is now a great deal of evidence that success or failure is explained in different ways depending on the sex of the actor (see Chapter 3). In general, a successful performance by a male is attributed to ability, while an identical performance by a female is attributed to luck or the ease of the task (see Figure 9.3). For example, Deaux and Emswiller (1974) had students watch fellow students perform well on perceptual tasks which were male stereotypical (for example, identifying a tyre jack) or female stereotypical (for example, identifying types of needlework). On the masculine tasks, male success was attributed to ability more than was female success (see Figure 9.4). On feminine tasks there was no differential *attribution*. There are some circumstances when this bias may be overturned. For example, sex-stereotypical attributions disappear when the attention of the person who is evaluating

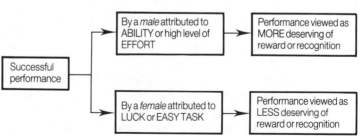

FIGURE 9.3 *Attribution of successful performance of an identical task performed by a male or a female.*

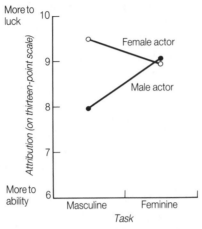

FIGURE 9.4 *Ability versus luck attribution for male or female success on masculine and feminine tasks. (Source: based on data from Deaux and Emswiller 1974.)*

performance is firmly directed onto the performance and away from the actor (Izraeli *et al.* 1985). There is also evidence that women who succeed in traditionally masculine activities (for example, becoming a top manager) are seen as more deserving than a similarly successful male (Taynor and Deaux 1973).

In general, however, sex-stereotypical attributions (on the part of both males and females) tend to create different evaluations of one's own worth as a male or a female. That is, for the same level of achievement women may consider themselves less deserving than men. Indeed, Major and Konar (1984) found this among male and female management students. The females' estimates of their realistic starting salaries were approximately 14 per cent lower than the males' estimates of their starting salaries, and 31 per cent lower with regard to estimated peak salaries.

While these forms of discrimination are very difficult, and thus slow, to change, there is some evidence that in western democratic societies some forms of blatant sex discrimination are on the wane – though sexual harassment in various forms persists (Gutek 1985). In 1893 New Zealand gave women the vote, followed closely by Australia. Other countries have been much slower in this regard: Britain in 1928, and Switzerland finally doing so only in 1971. In one canton (Appenzell Inner-Rhoden) in Switzerland, women were excluded from the cantonal vote until as recently as 1990. Societies are also increasingly passing anti-discrimination legislation and even (particularly in the United States) legislation for positive discrimination in favour of women (that is, against men) in certain occupations.

Social psychological research has perhaps detected some effects of these changes. For example, in the early 1970s Bartol and Butterfield (1976) found that female leaders in organisations were valued less relative to male leaders. By the early 1980s this effect had vanished (Izraeli and Izraeli 1985). In the mid-1960s Goldberg (1968) had women students evaluate identical pieces of written work attributed to a male (John T. McKay) or a female (Joan T. McKay), and found that those pieces ostensibly authored by a female were downgraded relative to those ostensibly authored by a male. A replication of this study in the late 1980s found no such effect (Swim *et al.* 1989). Finally, no sex discrimination was found in a study of performance evaluations of more than six hundred male and female store managers (Peters *et al.* 1984), or in a study of the compensation worth of predominantly male or predominantly female occupations determined by experts in employment compensation (Schwab and Grams 1985).

Racism

▶ Racism

Discrimination on the basis of race or ethnicity is historically responsible for some of the most appalling acts of mass inhumanity. While sexism is responsible for the continuing practice of selective infanticide in which female babies (and foetuses) are killed, this practice is now largely restricted to developing countries (Freed and Freed 1989). Genocide is universal: in this century it has been practised, for example, in Germany, Iraq, South Africa, Rwanda and the former Yugoslavia.

Most social psychological research on *racism* has been conducted in the United States concerning anti-black attitudes and behaviour. This research documents a dramatic reduction in anti-black attitudes since the 1940s (for example, Smedley and Bayton 1978). Much the same effect has occurred in other immigrant countries such as Australia and New Zealand where anti-Aborigine and anti-Maori attitudes have greatly improved over the past twenty-five years or so. The same trends can be observed in Britain and some other European countries, but against this general background there has, in the past ten years or so, been a revival of racist organisations and an increase in the incidence of overt racist acts.

From this, should we conclude that in general racial prejudice is gradually dying out in western industrial nations? Quite possibly not. Although explicit and blatant racism (derogatory stereotypes, ethnophaulisms or name-calling, abuse, persecution, assault and discrimination) is illegal and thus socially censured, and, it is now more difficult to find, social mores of respect and tolerance will hold little sway when a group of covert racists get together. But most people in most contexts simply do not behave in this way. Racism is now more difficult to detect as it is usually concealed, and expressed in subtle ways (Crosby *et al.* 1980). For example, racist attitudes persist in contexts of close social distance (such as marriage) though they may have disappeared in less close social relations (such as attending the same school) (Schofield 1986). In India, people who subscribe to the caste system will typically accept a lower caste person into their home, but will not consider marrying one (Sharma 1981).

Another context in which underlying prejudice can emerge is when prejudiced behaviour does not very obviously look like prejudice. Rogers and Prentice-Dunn (1981) had white or black confederates insult white subjects (in Alabama) who then had an opportunity to administer a shock to the confederate. Angered whites gave larger shocks to the black confederate. In another condition where no insults were forthcoming, subjects gave smaller shocks to the black than white confederate.

Prejudice can also surface inadvertently in people's relatively automatic cognition. For example, Duncan (1976) had white students in California observe on television what they thought was a live conversation between a black and a white male. The conversation degenerated into an argument in which one lightly shoved the other. When the white did the shoving the behaviour was interpreted as playful – only 13 per cent of subjects integrated it as violent. When the black did the shoving, 73 per cent of subjects interpreted the action as violent. Other evidence for well concealed prejudice comes from an experiment by Gaertner and McLaughlin (1983) in which subjects were given pairings of the social categories white or black with various positive or negative descriptive adjectives. Subjects had to decide whether the pairings were meaningful or not, and communicate their decision by pressing a button labelled yes or no. The latency of response is an index of the degree to which the pairing represents an existing attitude in the mind of the subject – faster responses indicate an existing attitude. The results (see Figure 9.5) show no tendency among subjects to pair negative words more strongly with black or white. However, subjects were much quicker at deciding whether positive words were meaningfully paired with white than black.

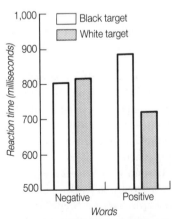

FIGURE 9.5 *Reaction time for deciding whether positive or negative words are meaningfully paired with the social categories black or white. (Source: based on data from Gaertner and McLaughlin 1983.)*

Another way in which racism can surface is via *symbolic racism* (Kinder and Sears 1981; Sears and Kinder 1985). This refers to a phenomenon in which negative feelings about blacks (based on early learned racial fears and stereotypes) blend with moral values embodied in the Protestant ethic. The result is behaviour which tends to have consequences that perpetuate racial disadvantage, not because self-interest is at stake but rather because of a more general racist ideology.

Finally, recent research shows how racism can very subtly and quite unintentionally be imbedded in the words we use, the way we express ourselves, and the way we communicate with and about racial outgroups (for example, Potter and Wetherell 1987; van Dijk and Wodak 1988; Wetherell and Potter 1992 – see Chapter 14). An example of the meticulous attention to detail to be found in some of this work is Teun van Dijk's (1987) lengthy analysis of spontaneous everyday talk among whites in the Netherlands and in southern California about other races (for example, blacks, East Indians, North Africans, Hispanics, Asians). One-hundred-and-eighty free-format interviews conducted between 1980 and 1985 were qualitatively analysed to show how racism is imbedded in and reproduced by everyday discourse.

Racial and ethnic prejudices are extremely pervasive if, as is almost always the case for most of us, we have been brought up in societies in which such prejudices have prevailed. Most of us are aware of the relevant stereotypes, and the task at hand is consciously to resist automatic stereotypic reactions – it would seem that less prejudiced people are more adept at this (Devine 1989). Pettigrew noted:

> Many Southerners have confessed to me ... that even though in their minds they no longer feel prejudice toward Blacks, they still feel squeamish when they shake hands with a Black. These feelings are left over from what they learned in their families as children. (Pettigrew 1987, p. 20)

In conclusion, although overt racism and ethnic prejudice is both illegal and morally condemned, and most people think and act accordingly, a long history of such prejudices cannot so easily be shrugged aside. The germs of racism still exist and racism can be detected in various subtle forms. Racial and cultural resentment and partiality still lurk beneath the surface – relatively dormant but nonetheless ready to be activated by a social environment (political regime) that might legitimise the expression of prejudice. The violence in Bosnia which began in 1992, and the genocide in Rwanda which began in 1994 are chilling illustrations of this.

A final important point to bear in mind is that although research suggests that overt discrimination may be on the wane in many western democracies, this does not mean that the social consequences of decades or even centuries of racism will change so quickly. For example, although attitudes towards blacks have improved dramatically in the past twenty years, the physical, material and cultural plight of blacks in Europe has not.

Ageism. Western industrial societies practise systematic discrimination against their most senior citizens. Being elderly can mean being without worth or power. (Source: Andrew Lukey.)

Ageism

▶ Ageism

In many cultures, particularly those in which the extended family thrives, older members of the community are revered – they are considered to be wise and knowledgeable teachers and leaders. In many other societies, largely those in which the nuclear family has displaced the extended family, this is often not the case (Oliver 1986). Countries such as Australia, Canada, the United States, the Netherlands and Britain fall into this latter category. In these societies, the qualities of youth are highly valued, and elderly people (a group that is rapidly increasing in relative number) attract unfavourable stereotypes (Brewer *et al.* 1981) and are treated as relatively worthless and powerless members of the community. They are denied many basic human rights, and their special needs go untended. Social psychologists have only recently begun systematically to investigate *ageism* (for example, Fox and Giles 1993; Hummert 1990; Kite and Johnson 1988 – see Chapter 14).

Discrimination against homosexuals

The Ancient Romans were relatively tolerant of all forms of sexual preference, and indeed there still is a great deal of cross-cultural variability in attitudes towards sexual preference (Gosselin and Wilson 1980). It was with the advent of Christianity that social norms regarding sexual behaviour became more restrictive. Homosexuality was seen as deviant and immoral, and the persecution of homosexuals became legitimate and quite acceptable. Prejudice against homosexuals is widespread, for example a survey in the United States showed that the majority of people believed that homosexuality was 'sick' and should be outlawed (Levitt and Klassen 1974). Discrimination against homosexuals is often even legal – in the mid 1980s the ultra right-wing state National Party in Queensland, Australia, actually passed legislation to prohibit the serving of liquor to 'perverts and deviants' (which included homosexuals) in bars, and it was only in 1973 that the American Psychiatric Association formally removed homosexuality from its list of mental disorders.

In general, since the late 1960s there has been a progressive liberalisation of attitudes towards homosexuals. However, the current HIV epidemic has, since the mid-1980s whipped up a frenzy of hysteria against homosexuals (Altman 1986; Herek and Glunt 1988; see Box 9.2). Against this background, continued liberalisation can often reveal deeply entrenched anti-homosexual prejudices in certain sectors of the community. For example, the departure of the National Party from power in Queensland in 1989 was accompanied by swift new legislation by the Labor Party to repeal a mass of restrictive laws, including those concerning homosexuality, and to pass new progressive legislation. This new legislation provoked a fierce public reaction from a number of religious groups. Similarly, in 1993 President Clinton met strong opposition to his proposal that homosexuals should be able to enlist in the American armed forces. The HIV epidemic has, however, focused the attention of social psychologists on homosexuality more strongly than in the past (for example, Abrams *et al.* 1989).

Discrimination on the basis of physical or mental handicap

Prejudice and discrimination against the physically handicapped has a long history in which such people have been considered repugnant and subhuman (Jodelef 1991). For example, most circuses had a side show alley in which various 'freaks' would be displayed (powerfully portrayed in Kevin Brownlow's movie *Freaks*), and many dramas hinge on the curiosity value of the physically handicapped (for example, David Lynch's *Elephant Man*, Fellini's *Satyricon* and Victor Hugo's *Notre-Dame de Paris*). Overt discrimination against people on the basis of physical handicap is now illegal and socially unacceptable in most western societies. The United States probably leads the world in this regard, with a whole range of legally required special provisions for people with various physical disabilities. The 1992 staging in Barcelona of the para-Olympics is another step in the normalisation of physical handicap. People generally no longer derogate the physically handicapped, but often are uncertain how to interact with them. This can quite unintentionally produce a patronising attitude that serves to emphasise and perpetuate handicap.

The dramatic improvement of attitude over the past twenty years concerning physical handicap has not generalised to mental/psychological handicap. In the Middle Ages female schizophrenics were labelled witches and burned at the stake; Hitler's 'final solution' did not apply only to the Jews but also the insane; and in Stalin's Russia, dissidents were labelled insane in order to justify their incarceration. Although Bedlam Hospital in London is long

BOX 9.2 The use of a fear surrounding AIDS to justify discrimination against homosexuals

AIDS and anti-gay prejudice

AIDS is a serious and, as far as is known, fatal illness that develops in people infected with the HIV virus. The virus is transmitted through exchange of certain bodily fluids, for example through blood transfusions, by needle-sharing among intravenous drug users, and by some sexual practices among gay men. Although AIDS is by no means a gay disease, the majority of people infected have tended to be gay (63 per cent of AIDS cases in the United States up to 1988 were gay – Herek and Glunt 1988), and so people assume a link between AIDS and being homosexual. Fear and ignorance of AIDS, in conjunction with knowledge of its association with gays, has activated latent prejudices against gays. In many ways, AIDS has provided moral justification (grounded in fear for self and society) for overt discrimination against gays – homophobics feel free to come out of the closet. The promotion of gay rights can be seen by such people as tantamount to the promotion of AIDS itself. Herek and Glunt's (1988, p.888) discussion of public reaction in the United States to AIDS provides telling evidence for the way AIDS has been linked to homosexuality and has been used to justify anti-gay attitudes. The epidemic was virtually ignored by the US media in the early 1980s because it was merely a 'story of dead and dying homosexuals', and was sometimes referred to as the 'gay plague'. Patrick Buchanan, a Republican columnist, wrote; 'There is one, only one, cause of the AIDS crisis – the wilful refusal of homosexuals to cease indulging in the immoral, unnatural, unsanitary, unhealthy, and suicidal practice of anal intercourse, which is the primary means by which the AIDS virus is being spread...' (1987, p.23). He felt that the 'Democratic Party should be dragged into the court of public opinion as an un-indicted co-conspirator in America's AIDS epidemic [for] seeking to amend state and federal civil rights laws to make sodomy a protected civil right, to put homosexual behaviour, the sexual practice by which AIDS is spread, on the same moral plane with being female or being black' (Buchanan 1987, p.23).

The Catholic Church used the apparent link between AIDS and homosexuality to argue against civil rights protection for gay people. Others were more extreme – a mayoral candidate for the city of Houston was heard publicly to joke that his solution to the city's AIDS problem would be to 'shoot the queers' (quoted in Herek and Glunt 1988, p.888).

closed down, very similar conditions prevail in asylums around the world – instances have only recently been exposed in, for example, Greece and Romania. In general, things may not be as bad as this, but ignorance and fear fuel strong prejudices and both institutionalised and face-to-face discrimination still prevail. Western societies still appear to want to overlook the existence of mental illness and to abdicate responsibility for the mentally ill. This is reflected in remarkably low funding for research into most mental illnesses – although most hospital beds are occupied by schizophrenics – and poor resourcing for the care and therapy of psychiatric patients. Recently there has been a policy in, for example, Britain, the United States and Australia to 'de-institutionalise' (actually, to 'give up on') chronic psychiatric patients and simply to release them onto the streets: that is, release them from hospital without providing adequate alternative community resources for their support.

▶ Self-esteem

Another facet of prejudice against the mentally ill is the way in which the 'mad' label is used to dehumanise and justify discrimination against minority status groups as a whole. 'Different' becomes labelled 'mad' (Szasz 1970). This is the serious side of what we regularly do in jest – 'You must be mad!' is a frequent exclamation on hearing someone outline a novel (read 'different') scheme. Research indicates that the stereotypic behaviours of women do not conform to what people consider to be the behaviours of a typical, well adjusted, adult human being (Broverman *et al.* 1970) – in this sense women are 'maladjusted' (Chesler 1972; Eichler 1980; Ussher 1991). A similar process in which cultural difference is made pathological by the dominant white middle class group occurs with respect to blacks, and other racial/ethnic minorities (Nahem 1980; Waxman 1977). There is a further twist to the story. Prejudice often tends to create brutal conditions of existence (poverty, poor health, low *self-esteem*, violence, etc.) that may actually produce certain types of psychiatric disorder within minority groups. In this way, fear and ignorance about psychiatric illness dovetails with and may amplify ethnic or racial prejudices.

SOME FORMS OF DISCRIMINATION

The preceding discussion has dealt with some of the principal targets of prejudice, and in so doing has inevitably spoken about different forms of discrimination. One important point that emerged is that a great deal of prejudice is expressed in subtle and often hidden ways – crude, overt discrimination is less frequent. In this section we deal with some other types of more subtle discrimination, specifically those that permit prejudiced people to indulge their prejudices without being detected.

Reluctance to help

Reluctance to help other groups to improve their position in society, by passively or actively declining to assist their efforts, is one way to make sure they remain disadvantaged. This strategy can be adopted by individuals (landlords may be reluctant to rent accommodation to ethnic minorities), organisations (organisations are reluctant to assist female employees by providing sensible maternity leave, flexible working hours or opportunities for job-sharing), or society as a whole (government resistance to legislate in favour of adequate maternity leave provisions). Studies show that reluctance to help is manifested only in certain conditions, specifically when such reluctance can be attributed to some factor other than prejudice. Gaertner and Dovidio's (1977) experiment that we described earlier in this chapter is an illustration of reluctance to help: white subjects were more reluctant to help a black than a white confederate faced with an emergency, but only when other potential helpers were thought to be present.

Tokenism

▶ Tokenism

As the term implies, *tokenism* refers to a relatively small or trivial positive act towards members of a minority group. The action is then invoked as a justification for declining to engage in larger and more meaningful positive acts or for subsequently engaging in discrimination – 'Don't bother me, haven't I already done enough?' For example, studies by Dutton and Lake (1973) and Rosenfield *et al.* (1982) found that white subjects who had performed a small favour for a black stranger were subsequently less willing to engage in more demanding forms of helping than were those who had not performed the small favour. Moreover, this effect was accentuated when the token action (the small favour) activated negative stereotypes about blacks, for example when the favour involved giving money to a black panhandler (beggar).

Tokenism can be employed by organisations and society as a whole. In the United States there has been criticism of the token employment of minorities (blacks, women, Hispanics) by organisations that then fail to take more fundamental and important steps towards egalitarianism. It would seem that such organisations may employ minorities as tokens in order better to deflect accusations of prejudice. Tokenism at this level can have damaging consequences for the self-esteem of those who are employed as token minorities (Chacko 1982 – see below).

Reverse discrimination

▶ Reverse
   discrimination

People with residual prejudiced attitudes may sometimes go out of their way to favour members of a group against which they are prejudiced more than if they were not members of that group. For example, Chidester (1986) had white students engage in a 'get-acquainted' conversation through audio equipment with another student who was ostensibly either black or white. The white students systematically evaluated black strangers more favourably than white strangers. Similar findings emerged from the Dutton and Lake (1973) study cited above. Initially, *reverse discrimination* appears to be the very opposite of what we usually think of as prejudice. It actually favours minority group members. On one level this certainly is true, and in the short term, reverse discrimin-ation can have beneficial effects. In the long run, however, it may have some harmful consequences for its recipients (Fajardo 1985 – see below). Reverse discrimi-nation can also signal over-sensitivity to category membership (for example, race, ethnicity): it is, after all, discrimination on the basis of minority group membership, and there is, as yet, no evidence that reverse discrimination reduces or abolishes the deep-seated prejudices of the discriminator.

SOME EFFECTS OF PREJUDICE

The effects of prejudice on the victims of prejudice are diverse, and range from relatively minor inconvenience to enormous suffering – Allport (1954) identified more than fifteen possible consequences of being a victim of pre-judice. Let's now examine some of these effects.

Self-esteem

In general, social groups that are the victims of prejudice and discrimination have relatively low status and little power in society, and find it difficult to avoid accepting society's consensual negative image of them. Members of these groups tend to internalise these evaluations and form an unfavourable self-image that can be manifested in relevant contexts as low self-esteem. For example, research reveals that women generally share men's negative stereotypes of women, often evaluate themselves in terms of such stereotypes, and under circumstances when sex is the salient basis of self-perception actually report a reduction in self-esteem (for example, Hogg 1985; Hogg and Turner 1987b; Smith 1985). Groups and their members are, however, extremely ingenious in finding ways to combat low status and consensual low regard, and so depressed self-esteem is by no means an inevitable consequence of prejudice (for example, Dion and Earn 1975; Dion *et al.* 1978). This is discussed in Chapter 10.

On a day-to-day basis, self-esteem can, of course, be damaged by crude expressions of prejudice (insults, denial of equality, violence). There is, however, evidence that more subtle forms of prejudice can also damage self-esteem. For example, Chacko (1982) asked women managers to rate the extent to which a number of factors (their ability, experience, education or sex) had influenced their being hired for the job. They also indicated their commitment to the organisation and their satisfaction with various aspects of the job. Subjects who felt that they had been hired only as token women reported less organisational commitment and job satisfaction than those who felt they had been hired on the basis of their ability (Figure 9.6). This is one way in which tokenism can have negative consequences.

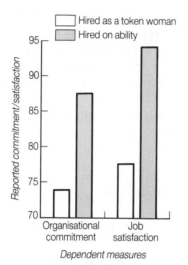

FIGURE 9.6 *Organisational commitment and job satisfaction as a function of perceived basis of being hired. (Source: based on data from Chacko 1982.)*

Reverse discrimination can also affect self-esteem. Fajardo (1985) had white teachers grade essays that were carefully designed to be poor, average or excellent in quality, and were attributed to either a black or a white student. The teachers evaluated identical essays more favourably when they were attributed to black than white students (Figure 9.7). Moreover, the reverse discrimination effect was more marked for average quality essays. In the short run this practice may furnish minority students with self-confidence. In the long run, however, some students may develop unrealistic opinions of their

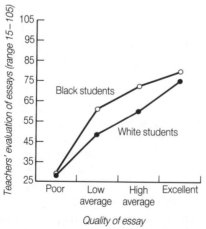

FIGURE 9.7 *White teachers' evaluations of student essays of varying quality as a function of student race. (Source: based on data from Fajardo 1985.)*

abilities and future prospects, resulting in severe damage to self-esteem when such hopes collide with reality. Reverse discrimination may also prevent students from seeking the help they may sometimes need early in their academic careers, with the consequence of perhaps contributing to educational disadvantage.

Failure and disadvantage

The victims of prejudice belong to groups that are denied access to those resources that society makes available for people to thrive and succeed – for example good education, health, housing, and employment. Discrimination thus creates clearly visible evidence of real disadvantage, and of manifest failure to achieve the high standards set by society. This sense of failure can be internalised by victims of prejudice so that they become chronically apathetic and unmotivated – they simply give up trying because of the obvious impossibility of succeeding. There is some evidence that in certain circumstances women tend to anticipate failure more than men and tend to lose motivation (for example, Smith 1985). As we saw earlier, when they do succeed they tend to attribute their success externally to factors such as luck or the ease of the task.

Self-fulfilling prophecies

▶ Self-fulfilling prophecy

Prejudiced attitudes covertly or overtly produce discriminatory behaviour that cumulatively, across time and individuals, creates disadvantage. In this way, a stereotypic belief can create a material reality that confirms the belief: it is a *self-fulfilling prophecy*. For example, Rosenthal and Jacobson (1968) administered an IQ test to elementary school children and told their teachers that the results of the test would be a reliable predictor of which children would 'bloom' (show rapid intellectual development in the near future). The teachers were given the names of the twenty 'bloomers' – in fact the twenty names were randomly chosen by the researchers, and there were no IQ differences between bloomers and non-bloomers. Very quickly the teachers rated the non-bloomers as being less curious, less interested and less happy than the bloomers: that is, the teachers developed stereotypic expectations about the two groups. Grades for work were consistent with these expectations. Rosenthal and Jacobson measured the children's IQ at the end of the first year, and at the start and end of the second year. They found that in both years the bloomers showed a significantly greater IQ gain than the non-bloomers – see Figure 9.8.

The process through which beliefs create reality has been researched systematically over a number of years by Snyder and his colleagues (Snyder 1981, 1984). One paradigm they have used involves creating an expectation in an observer that someone he is going to meet has an extrovert personality. The consequences for both the observer's and the actor's beliefs and behaviours are

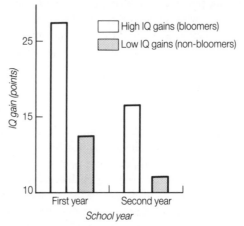

FIGURE 9.8 *IQ gain among elementary school children as a function of teachers' stereotypic expectations. (Source: based on data from Rosenthal and Jacobson 1968.)*

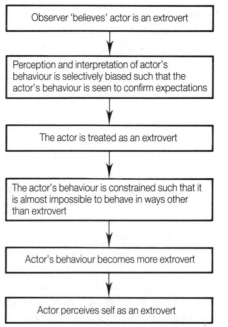

FIGURE 9.9 *How beliefs create reality. (Source: derived from Snyder, 1981, 1984.)*

carefully tracked through the entire interaction process to an end-point where the actor's behaviour and self-perception conform to the initial expectation – see Figure 9.9.

Violence and genocide

Much of the emphasis of this chapter has been on indirect or subtle forms of prejudice, and their effects. This reflects relatively accurately the current state of affairs in many western democracies where anti-discrimination legislation is in place. For example, there is a lively campaign to purge language of racist and sexist terminology. It is important, however, not to lose sight of the extremes of prejudiced behaviour. Prejudiced attitudes tend to have common themes: the targets of prejudice are considered, for example, to be dirty, stupid, insensitive, repulsive, aggressive and psychologically unstable (Brigham 1971; Katz and Braly 1933). This is a constellation that evaluates others as relatively worthless human beings who do not need or deserve to be treated with consideration, courtesy and respect. Together with fear and hatred, this is a potent mix. It dehumanises other people and, given certain social circumstances can permit individual violence, mass aggression or even systematic extermination.

In the absence of institutional or legislative support, dehumanisation usually sponsors individual acts of violence. For example, in Britain there are isolated attacks on Asian immigrants; in the United States the Ku Klux Klan is notorious for its lynchings of blacks (see the recent film *Mississippi Burning*); in Germany there are Nazi-style attacks on Turkish immigrants; and in India female infanticide is still practised, albeit covertly (Freed and Freed 1989). When prejudice is morally accepted and legally endorsed in a society then systematic acts of mass discrimination can be perpetrated. This can take the form of systems of apartheid in which target groups are isolated from the rest of the community. South Africa is the most recent example of this sort of system, but a similar system of segregation was practised in educational contexts in the United States until the mid-1950s, and the existence of reservations for native peoples in many countries (for example, Australia, United States) also attests to segregation. Apartheid and segregation often come equipped with a formidable array of social justifications in terms of benefits for the segregated group.

The most extreme form of legitimated prejudice is genocide (Staub 1989), where the target group is systematically exterminated. The dehumanisation process makes it relatively easy for people to perpetrate the most appalling acts of degradation and violence on others (see Thomas Keneally's biographical novel *Schindler's Ark*, or the film *The Killing Fields*). The most chilling, and best documented, recent instance of genocide is the Holocaust of the early 1940s in which six million Jews were systematically exterminated by the Nazis in death camps in central Europe. At the massive Auschwitz complex in Poland, two million Jews were gassed between January 1942 and the summer of 1944 (a rate of 2,220 men, women and children each day). There are more recent examples of genocide: Pol Pot's 'killing fields' in Kampuchea in the 1970s; Saddam Hussein's continuing extermination of Kurds in northern Iraq and Shi'ites in southern Iraq, Bosnian Serbs' campaign of 'ethnic cleansing' in Bosnia, and the massive scale of genocide in Rwanda in 1994.

Genocide can also be practised more indirectly by providing conditions of massive material disadvantage in which a group in effect exterminates itself through disease, and through suicide and murder based on alcoholism, drug abuse and acute despair. The plight of Australian Aborigines and Brazilian Indians falls squarely in this camp. Another form of genocide, though 'ethnic death' is a more appropriate term to distinguish it from the inhuman behaviours of the Holocaust, is cultural assimilation, in which entire cultural groups may disappear as discrete entities through widespread intermarriage and systematic suppression of their culture and language (for example, Taft 1973—see Chapter 14). This is particularly prevalent if societies do not practice multiculturalism (for example, England's treatment of the Welsh and the Scottish, and Indonesia's stance towards the people of East Timor).

EXPLANATIONS OF PREJUDICE AND DISCRIMINATION

▶ Mere exposure effect   Why are people prejudiced? Not surprisingly, theories of prejudice have tended to focus on the more extreme forms, in particular the aggression and violence that we have just discussed. At the turn of the century it was popular to consider prejudice to be an innate and instinctive reaction to certain categories of person (for example, certain races), much as animals would react in instinctive ways to one another (Klineberg 1940). This sort of approach is no longer popular, as it does not stand up well to scientific scrutiny. However, there may be an innate *component* to prejudice. There is some evidence that higher animals, including humans, have an inherent fear of the unfamiliar and unusual (Hebb and Thompson 1968), which might set the mould for negative attitudes towards groups that are considered different in certain ways. There is also evidence for a *mere exposure effect* (Zajonc 1968) in which people's attitudes towards various stimuli (for example, people) improve as a direct function of repeated exposure or familiarity with the stimulus, provided that initial reactions to the stimuli are not negative (Perlman and Oskamp 1971).

Another perspective rests on the belief that prejudices are learned. Indeed, Tajfel (1981b) argues that hatred and suspicion of certain groups are learned very early in life, before the child even knows anything about the target group, and that this provides an emotional framework that colours all subsequent information about and experience with the group. The role of parental attitudes and behaviour cannot be under-estimated in this very early learning phase (Aboud 1988; Goodman 1964; Katz 1976). The transmission of parental prejudices can occur through parental modelling (for example, the child witnesses parental expressions of racial hatred), instrumental/operant conditioning (for example, parental approval for racist behaviour and disapproval for non-racist behaviour), and classical conditioning (for example, a white child receives a severe parental scolding for playing with an Asian child). See also attitude formation in Chapter 4.

In the remainder of this section we discuss some major theories of prejudice. These approaches focus largely on prejudice as the mass expression of aggression against certain groups. In Chapter 10 we return to the issue of prejudice, but in a different guise – one that considers prejudice to be a form of intergroup behaviour based on social psychological processes associated with the categorisation of people into social categories.

Frustration-aggression

▶ Frustration-aggression hypothesis

The rise of anti-Semitism in Europe, particularly Germany, during the 1930s placed the explanation of prejudice high on social psychology's agenda. In 1939, Dollard and co-workers published their *frustration-aggression hypothesis* in which they argued that 'the occurrence of aggressive behaviour always presupposes the existence of frustration, and contrariwise, the existence of frustration always leads to some form of aggression' (Dollard *et al.* 1939, p. 1). The theory was grounded in the psychodynamic assumption that there is a fixed amount of psychic energy available for the human mind to accomplish psychological activities, and that the completion of a psychological activity is *cathartic*, that is, it dissipates the aroused energy and returns the system to psychological equilibrium.

▶ Scapegoat

Dollard *et al.* argued that personal goals entail arousal of psychic energy for their achievement, and that goal achievement is cathartic. If, however, goal achievement is impeded (that is, frustrated), psychic energy remains activated, and the system is in a state of psychological disequilibrium that can only be corrected by aggression. In other words, frustration produces an 'instigation to aggress', and the only way to achieve catharsis is through aggression. The target of aggression is usually the perceived agent of frustration, but in many cases the agent of frustration is amorphous (for example, a bureaucracy), indeterminate (the economy), too powerful (someone very big and strong wielding a weapon), unavailable (a specific individual bureaucrat), or someone you love (a parent). These, and many other circumstances, prevent or inhibit aggression against the perceived source of frustration, and cause the entire amount of frustration-induced aggression to be *displaced* onto an alternative target (a person or an inanimate object) that can legitimately be aggressed against without fear – in other words, a *scapegoat* is found.

Although this theory has been applied extensively, and relatively successfully, to the study of interpersonal aggression (see Chapter 11), Dollard *et al.*'s principal aim was to explain intergroup aggression – specifically the violence and aggression associated with prejudice. If a large number of people (a group) is frustrated in its goals by another group which is too powerful or remote to be aggressed against, the aggression is displaced onto a weaker group that acts as a scapegoat. Figure 9.10 shows how the frustration-aggression hypothesis could be used to explain the rise of anti-Semitism in Germany in the 1920s and 1930s. An archival study by Hovland and Sears (1940) provides some support for this sort of analysis. They correlated an economic index of frustrated ambitions (the price of cotton) with an index of racial aggression (number of lynchings of blacks) in the southern United States over a fifty-year period. The two indexes were negatively correlated: as the price of cotton fell (frustration) the number of lynchings increased (displaced aggression).

▶ Displacement

Much research on intergroup aggression has focused on the notion of *displacement* that lies at the heart of Dollard *et al.*'s account of displacement (that is, scapegoating) and thus prejudice and intergroup aggression. In one study (Miller and Bugelski 1948), young men at a summer camp eagerly anticipated a night out on the town but had their goals frustrated by the camp authorities who announced that they would have to stay behind to perform some uninteresting and difficult tests. In relation to a control group who were

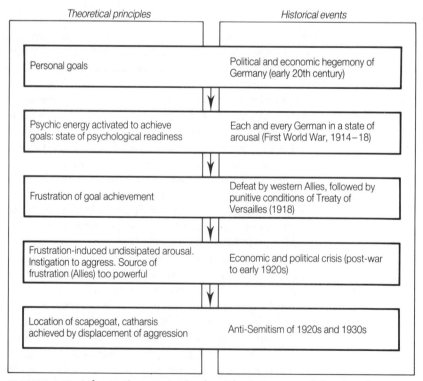

FIGURE 9.10 *A frustration-aggression hypothesis account of the rise of anti-Semitism in Germany in the 1920s and 1930s.*

not frustrated in this way, the young men's stereotypical attitudes towards two minority groups were found to deteriorate as a consequence of the frustration. Other research is inconclusive. For example, the frustration of doing badly on a test or experimental task has been shown to increase racial prejudice (Cowen *et al.* 1958), reduce prejudice (Burnstein and McRae 1962), or leave prejudice unaffected (Stagner and Congdon 1955), and there is no systematic evidence for an inverse correlation between international and intranational aggression (that is, aggression displaced onto another nation is not available to be vented intranationally) (Tanter 1966, 1969).

In some of this research it is very difficult to know whether aggression is displaced (that is, the entire quantity of aggression is vented on a specific scapegoat) or generalised (that is, anger towards the agent of frustration spills over onto irrelevant other stimuli). For example, in the Miller and Bugelski (1948) study, the subjects also felt angry towards the camp authorities. If both displacement and generalisation are operating, then it becomes difficult to predict the target of aggression. To address this problem, Miller (1948) suggested that displacement and generalisation might work against one another so that scapegoats are likely to be not too similar to the real source of frustration (displacement is based on inhibition of aggression against the real source of frustration, and such inhibition will be stronger for targets that are more similar to the real source), but not too dissimilar either (generalisation implies that the magnitude of aggression will decrease as the potential target becomes less and less similar to the real source). Although it is often possible with the advantage of hindsight to use this principle to account for the scapegoat, it is very difficult to predict it with any certainty (for example, Horowitz 1973).

The frustration–aggression hypothesis confronts another, rather major obstacle in the form of research showing that frustration is neither necessary nor sufficient for aggression: aggression can occur in the absence of frustration, and frustration does not necessarily result in aggression (Berkowitz 1962; Bandura 1973). The consequence is that the frustration–aggression hypothesis can address only a limited subset of intergroup aggression. Other constructs are needed to explain either other forms of intergroup aggression or prejudice and intergroup aggression as a whole. In an attempt to rescue the hypothesis, Berkowitz (1962) proposed three major changes:

1. The probability of frustration-induced aggression actually being vented is increased by the presence of situational cues to aggression, including past or present associations of a specific group (scapegoat) with conflict, dislike and so forth.
2. It is not objective frustration that produces an instigation to aggress but the subjective (cognitive) feeling of being frustrated.
3. Frustration is only one of a large number of aversive events (for example, pain, extreme temperatures and other noxious stimuli) that can cause an instigation to aggress.

▶ Collective
behaviour
▶ Relative
deprivation

This revamped frustration–aggression theory has attracted empirical support for the role of environmental cues and cognitive mediators in controlling the amount and direction of aggression (Berkowitz 1974; Konecni 1979). However, its main application has been in the explanation of *collective behaviour* (riots) and *relative deprivation* – these are discussed in Chapter 10.

Despite these modifications the frustration/aggression hypothesis has some other limitations as an explanation of mass intergroup aggression and prejudice. The phenomenon to be explained is one in which the attitudes and behaviour of a very large number of people are regulated and directed so that there is a great deal of uniformity as well as a clear logic to them. Critics have argued that the frustration–aggression hypothesis does not adequately explain this central aspect of prejudice, and that the reason for this is that it is a reductionist approach which arrives at group behaviour by aggregating individual psychological/emotional states in a communication vacuum (Billig 1976; Brown 1988; Hogg and Abrams 1988). For instance, the group members in this model do not speak to one another and are not exposed to mass communication or history. They are passive victims of individual frustration and anger rather than active participants in a social process involving construction, internalisation and the enacting of group norms (see Chapter 6). Aggression is only widespread and directed at the same target because a large number of people individually express aggression simultaneously, and coincidentally select the same target.

The authoritarian personality

▶ Authoritarian
personality

The liberation of Europe from the Nazis in 1945 revealed details of the Holocaust that were so appalling that it seemed that only people with dysfunctional personalities could perpetrate such atrocities. It was in this context that Adorno *et al.* (1950) developed their authoritarian personality explanation of prejudice. Unlike Dollard *et al.*, who believed that anyone could be prejudiced since it depended on the displacement of frustration-induced aggression, Adorno *et al.* believed that only people with prejudiced personalities could be prejudiced. They argued that certain people are bigots, who are prejudiced against all minorities. They have an *authoritarian personality* which is defined by a constellation of characteristics including respect for and deference to authority and authority figures, obsession with rank and status, a tendency to displace anger and resentment onto weaker others, intolerance of ambiguity and uncertainty, a need for a rigidly defined world, and problems with achieving intimacy.

This constellation originates in very early childhood. Adopting a psychodynamic perspective, Adorno *et al.* argue that children whose parents adopt excessively harsh and disciplinarian practices to secure emotional dependence and obedience develop an ambiguity in which they both love and hate their parents. This ambiguity is stressful and seeks resolution. Owing to guilt and fear, the hatred cannot be expressed, so it is *repressed* and finds expression through displacement onto weaker others, while the parents and the power and authority they represent are idealised. This resolution of ambivalence provides an enduring framework for future life, and is generalised to all authority figures.

For their original research, Adorno *et al.* (1950) distributed to two thousand members of organisations in California a questionnaire monitoring: (1) anti-Semitism, (2) general ethnocentrism, (3) political and economic conservatism, and (4) potential for fascism. A subset of respondents was administered projective tests and was interviewed about their childhood. The results were encouraging, but a number of methodological criticisms have been raised by Brown (1965). Among these, the most damning are:

1. The scales were scored in such a way that people's tendency to agree with items (acquiescence response set) would produce artificial correlation between the scales.
2. Because the interviewers knew both the hypotheses and the authoritarianism scores of the interviewees there is a danger of confirmatory bias (Rosenthal 1966).

Nevertheless, the authoritarian personality has, over the past forty years, attracted an enormous amount of interest (for example, Bray and Noble 1978; Christie and Jahoda 1954; Titus and Hollander 1957).

There are, however, a number of limitations to a personality explanation of prejudice (Billig 1976; Brown 1988; Hogg and Abrams 1988). The first is that powerful situational and socio-cultural factors are under-emphasised. For instance, Pettigrew (1958) tested the authoritarian personality theory in a cross-cultural comparison between South Africa, the southern United States, and the northern United States. He found that although whites from South Africa and the southern United States were significantly more racist than those from the northern United States, they did not differ in terms of how authoritarian their personalities were. Pettigrew concluded from this and other findings that while personality may predispose some people to be prejudiced in some contexts, a culture of prejudice that embodies societal norms legitimising prejudice is both necessary and sufficient. This conclusion is supported by other findings. For example, Minard (1952) found that the majority (60 per cent) of white miners in a West Virginian coal mining community quite readily shifted from racist to non-racist attitudes and behaviours as a function of situational norms encouraging or inhibiting prejudice, and Stephan and Rosenfield (1978) found that inter-racial contact was a more important determinant than parental background of change in racial attitudes among children.

For Adorno *et al.*, prejudice is laid down in childhood as an enduring personality style. This perspective is particularly troublesome in the light of everyday evidence for sudden and dramatic changes in people's attitudes and behaviours regarding social groups. For example, the extreme anti-Semitism in Germany between the wars arose in a short period of only ten years: far too short a time for a whole generation of German families to adopt new child-rearing practices giving rise to authoritarian and prejudiced children. Even more dramatic are sudden changes in attitudes and behaviours contingent on single events such as the Japanese bombing of Pearl Harbor in 1941, the Argentinian occupation of the Falkland Islands in 1982, the French sinking of the *Rainbow Warrior* in Auckland Harbour in 1985, and the Indonesian massacre of East Timorese in Dili in 1991. Personalities did not have time to change, yet attitudes and behaviours did.

Dogmatism and closed-mindedness

▶ Dogmatism
▶ Closed-mindedness

Another personality theory of prejudice has been proposed by Rokeach (1948, 1960). It is closely related to the authoritarian personality, but in the light of evidence that authoritarianism is not restricted to people who are politically and economically right wing (for example, Tetlock 1984), focuses on the cognitive style aspect. Rokeach argues for the existence of a more generalised syndrome of intolerance, called *dogmatism* or *closed-mindedness*. It is character-ised by isolation of contradictory belief systems from one another, resistance to belief change in the light of new information, and appeals to authority to justify the correctness of existing beliefs. Scales devised by Rokeach (1960) to measure these personality styles have good reliability, correlate well with measures of authoritarianism, and have been used extensively. However, the concept of dogmatism as an explanation of prejudice has the same limitations as the authoritarian personality theory: it is a concept that reduces a group phenomenon to an aggregation of individual personality predispositions, and largely overlooks the wider socio–cultural context of prejudice and the role of group norms (Billig 1976; Billig and Cochrane 1979).

Belief congruence

▶ Belief congruence
theory

At the same time as his personality theory of prejudice, Rokeach (1960) also proposed a separate *belief congruence theory*. Belief systems are important anchoring points for individuals, and therefore interindividual similarity or congruence of belief systems confirms the validity of one's own beliefs. Congruence is therefore rewarding and produces attraction and positive attitudes (Byrne 1971; Festinger 1954). The converse is that incongruence produces negative attitudes. For Rokeach, 'belief is more important than ethnic or racial membership as a determinant of social discrimination' (Rokeach 1960, p. 135) – prejudice is not an attitude based on group memberships, but an individual's reaction to perceived lack of congruence of belief systems.

Research using a paradigm in which subjects report their attitudes towards others (presented photographically or as verbal descriptions) who are of either the same or a different race, and whose beliefs are either similar to or different from those of the subject, shows that belief does indeed seem to be a more important determinant of attitude than race (for example, Byrne and Wong 1962; Hendrick *et al.* 1971; Rokeach and Mezei 1966). However, when it comes to more intimate behaviours such as friendship, then race is more important than belief (for example, Insko *et al.* 1983; Triandis and Davis 1965).

There are at least two problems with belief congruence as an explanation of prejudice. The first is that Rokeach (1960) hedges his theory with an important qualification. Under circumstances where prejudice is institutionalised or socially sanctioned, belief congruence plays no part: prejudice is a matter of ethnic group membership (see Figure 9.11). This is a rather restrictive exemption clause that excludes what we would consider to be the most obvious and distressing manifestations of prejudice; for example, racial prejudice in South Africa or religious prejudice in Northern Ireland would be excluded.

A second problem arises with the relatively small amount of prejudice that Rokeach has left himself to explain. His explanation of how belief congruence may influence prejudice in these circumstance may actually be an explanation of how belief similarity produces interpersonal attraction (Brown 1988; Brown and Turner 1981). The research paradigm used to test belief congruence theory has subjects rate their attitude towards a number of stimulus individuals presented in a repeated measures design. Some stimuli are of the same race and others of a different race (the race variable), and they all have different beliefs from one another (the belief variable). The absence of clear belief homogeneity within each group and belief discontinuity between groups may muddy intergroup boundaries and focus attention on differences among stimulus individuals rather than upon their racial or ethnic group member- ships. The research paradigm may have inadvertently diminished the

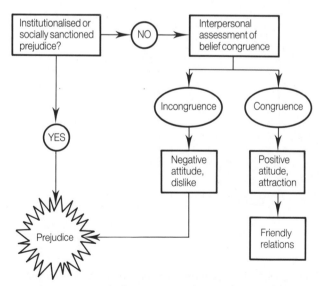

FIGURE 9.11 *Belief congruence theory. (Source: based on Rokeach 1960.)*

contextual salience of race or ethnicity such that subjects react to the stimulus individuals as individuals, not as members of racial or ethnic groups.

This interpretation has some support from experiments in which group membership is clearly differentiated from belief similarity. For example, Billig and Tajfel (1973) had children allocate rewards to anonymous other children who were either defined as having similar attitudes to them (on the basis of a bogus picture preference task) or for whom no information on similarity was provided, and who were either explicitly categorised as being members of the same group (simply labelled X-group) or for whom no categorisation information was provided. This research adopted the *minimal group paradigm*, which is described in more detail in Chapter 10. The focal outcome measure was *discrimination* in favour of some target individuals over others. Figure 9.12 shows that although belief similarity increased favouritism (as would be predicted from belief congruence theory), the effect of categorisation on favouritism was much stronger, and it was only in the two categorisation conditions that the amount of discrimination was statistically significant (that is, discrimination scores were significantly greater than zero). Belief congruence theory would not predict these last two effects. Similar findings emerged in a similar experiment by Allen and Wilder (1975).

Other explanations

There are two other major perspectives on the explanation of prejudice. The first concerns how people construct and use stereotypes. This is dealt with mainly in Chapter 2 as part of the discussion of social cognition and social

▶ Minimal group
   paradigm
▶ Discrimination

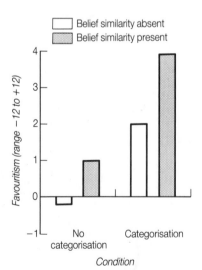

FIGURE 9.12 *Favouritism as a function of belief similarity and common group membership. (Source: based on data from Billig and Tajfel 1973.)*

thinking, but it also surfaces in Chapter 10. The second approaches prejudice and discrimination as an aspect of intergroup behaviour as a whole. This is dealt with in the next chapter.

Because Chapter 10 can be treated as an extension and continuation of the present chapter, we have reserved our discussion of prejudice reduction until the end of Chapter 10. The main practical reason for studying the social psychology of prejudice is to gain sufficient understanding of the phenomenon to be able to try to reduce its incidence and to alleviate conflict. Arguments about ways in which prejudice may be reduced rest on the particular perspectives on, and theories of prejudice to which one subscribes. The intergroup perspectives and theories dealt with in the next chapter suggest strategies which are different from those which derive from the person–centred explanations in the present chapter.

SUMMARY

- Prejudice can be considered to be an attitude about a social group, which may or may not be expressed in behaviour as overt discrimination.
- The most pervasive prejudices are based on sex, race, ethnicity, age, sexual preference, and physical and mental handicap. In most western nations, legislation and social attitudes have significantly reduced these prejudices (with the exception perhaps of the last two) in recent years, but there is still a long way to go.
- Legislation and social disapproval have inhibited the more extreme expressions of prejudice. Prejudice is more difficult to detect as it is expressed covertly or in restricted contexts, and may go almost unnoticed as it is embedded in ordinary, everyday assumptions, language and discourse.
- The victims of prejudice can suffer material and psychological disadvantage, low self-esteem, depressed aspirations and, of course, physical and verbal abuse.
- Prejudice may be a relatively ordinary reaction to frustrated goals, in which people vent their aggression onto weaker groups that act as scapegoats for the original source of frustration. By no means all prejudices can be explained in this way.
- Prejudice may be abnormal behaviour expressed by people who have developed generally prejudiced personalities, perhaps as a consequence of being raised in harsh and restrictive families. This may explain why some individuals are prejudiced, but the presence of a social environment encouraging prejudice seems to be a much stronger and more diagnostic determinant.
- These sorts of explanation of prejudice do not deal very well with the widespread collective nature of the phenomenon. They tend to overlook the

fact that people communicate with one another and are influenced by propaganda and mass communication.

FURTHER READING

Brown, R. J. (1988). *Group Processes: Dynamics Within and Between Groups.* Oxford: Blackwell.
Duckitt, J. (1992). *The Social Psychology of Prejudice.* New York: Praeger.
Hogg, M. A. and Abrams, D. (1988). *Social Identifications: A Social Psychology of Intergroup Relations and Group Processes.* London: Routledge.

▶ KEY TERMS

ageism
attribution
authoritarian personality
belief congruence theory
closed-mindedness
collective behaviour
dehumanisation
discrimination
displacement
dogmatism
'face-ism'
frustration-aggression hypothesis
gender
genocide

mere exposure effect
minimal group paradigm
prejudice
racism
relative deprivation
reverse discrimination
scapegoat
self-esteem
self-fulfilling prophecy
sexism
sex role
stereotypes
tokenism

10 Intergroup behaviour

FOCUS QUESTIONS
- Are the most disadvantaged groups the ones that are most likely to engage in intergroup conflict and collective protest?
- If two groups compete over a scarce resource, is conflict inevitable?
- What are the minimum conditions necessary for intergroup behaviour?
- Are people more antisocial in a crowd than alone?
- Is multiculturalism the most effective way to improve intergroup relations?

WHAT IS INTERGROUP BEHAVIOUR?

▶ Intergroup behaviour

International and intranational conflicts, political confrontations, revolutions, interethnic relations, negotiations between unions and managements and competitive team sports are all examples of *intergroup behaviour*. An initial definition of intergroup behaviour might, therefore, be that it is any behaviour which involves interaction between one or more representatives of two or more separate social groups. This sort of definition fairly accurately characterises much of the intergroup behaviour that social psychologists study; however, by focusing on face-to-face 'interaction', it might be a little restrictive.

A broader, and perhaps more accurate, definition would be that any perception, cognition or behaviour that is influenced by people's recognition that they and others are members of distinct social groups is intergroup behaviour. This broader definition has an interesting implication: it acknowledges that the real or perceived relations between social groups (for example, between the sexes, between ethnic groups) can have far-reaching and pervasive effects on the behaviour of members of those groups – effects that go well beyond situations of face-to-face intergroup encounters. This type of definition stems from a particular perspective in social psychology: an intergroup perspective which argues that a great deal of social behaviour is fundamentally influenced by the social categories to which we belong and the power and status relations between those social categories. A broad perspective such as this on the appropriate type of theory to develop is called a metatheory (see Chapter 1).

In many ways this chapter on intergroup behaviour brings together under one umbrella the preceding discussions of social influence (Chapter 6), group processes (Chapters 7 and 8), and prejudice and discrimination (Chapter 9). Social influence and group processes are generally treated as occurring within groups. But of course, wherever there is a group to which people belong (that is, an ingroup) there will be other groups to which those people do not belong (outgroups), and thus there is an intergroup, or ingroup/outgroup, context for whatever happens within groups. It is very unlikely that processes within groups will be unaffected by relations between groups. Prejudice and discrimination are, as we saw in Chapter 9, clear instances of intergroup behaviour (for example, between the sexes, between different races, between different age groups). One of the recurring themes of Chapter 9 was that personality or interpersonal explanations of prejudice and discrimination (for example, authoritarian personality, dogmatism, frustration/aggression) may have limitations precisely because they do not adequately consider the intergroup aspect of the phenomena.

In dealing with intergroup behaviour this chapter confronts important questions about the difference between individuals (and interpersonal behaviour) and groups (and intergroup behaviour), and the way in which harmonious intergroup relations can become conflicting and discriminatory, and vice versa. Social psychological theories of intergroup behaviour should therefore have clear applied utility, for example in the explanation of intergroup relations in employment contexts (Hartley and Stephenson 1992).

RELATIVE DEPRIVATION AND SOCIAL UNREST

Our discussion in Chapter 9 of the frustration–aggression hypothesis (Dollard *et al.* 1939) as an explanation of intergroup prejudice, discrimination and aggression, concluded with Berkowitz's (1962) modification of the original theory. Berkowitz argued that subjective (not objective) frustration is one of an array of aversive events (for example, heat, cold) that instigate aggression, and that the actual expression of aggression is strengthened by aggressive associations (for example, situational cues, past associations).

Berkowitz (1972a) used this analysis to explain collective intergroup aggression – riots. The best known application is to riots which have occurred during long periods of hot weather (defined as greater than 29°C) in the United States, for example the Watts riots in Los Angeles in August 1965 and the Detroit riots in August 1967 (see Figure 10.1). It is based on evidence that heat is an 'aversive event' that can facilitate or increase individual and collective aggression (for example, Anderson and Anderson 1984; Baron and Ransberger 1978; Carlsmith and Anderson 1979). Berkowitz (1972a) argues that under conditions of perceived relative deprivation (for example, blacks in the United

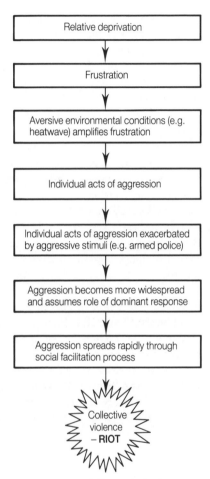

FIGURE 10.1 *A 'long, hot summer explanation' of collective violence. (Source: derived from Berkowitz 1972a.)*

States in the late 1960s) people feel frustrated. The heat of a long, hot summer amplifies the frustration (especially in poor, overcrowded neighbourhoods with little air conditioning or cooling vegetation) and increases the prevalence of individual acts of aggression, which are in turn exacerbated by the presence of aggressive stimuli (for example, armed police). Individual aggression becomes more widespread and is transformed into true collective violence by a process of social facilitation (Zajonc 1965 – see Chapter 7), in which the presence of other people facilitates dominant behaviour patterns (in this case aggression).

▶ Relative deprivation   A crucial precondition for intergroup aggression is *relative deprivation*. Deprivation is not an absolute condition but is always relative to other conditions: one person's new-found prosperity might be someone else's terrible deprivation. George Orwell captures this point very well in *The Road to Wigan Pier*, his essay on the plight of the British working class in the 1930s. 'Talking once with a miner I asked him when the housing shortage first became acute in his district; he answered, "When we were told about it", meaning that "till recently people's standards were so low that they took almost any degree of overcrowding for granted"'. (Orwell 1962, p. 57).

The concept of relative deprivation was introduced by Stouffer *et al.* (1949) in their classic wartime study of the American soldier. Its role in intergroup conflict and aggression was developed more formally by Davis (1959). Relative deprivation refers to a perceived discrepancy between attainments or actualities ('what is') and expectations or entitlements ('what ought to be'). In its most simple form, relative deprivation arises from comparisons between one's own experiences and one's expectations (Gurr 1970).

▶ J-curve

In his famous *J-curve* hypothesis (see Figure 10.2), Davies (1969) has suggested that people construct their future expectations from past and current attainments, and that under certain circumstances attainments may suddenly fall short of rising expectations. When this happens, relative deprivation is particularly acute, with the consequence of collective unrest – revolutions of rising expectations (see Box 10.1). The J–curve derives its name from the shape of the solid line in Figure 10.2. Some historical events do seem to fit this model. For example, the Depression of the early 1930s caused a sudden fall in farm prices that was associated with increased anti–Semitism in Poland (Keneally 1982, p. 95). In Australia the gold rush of the early 1850s was followed by a rapid decline in average annual takings per person (from \$780 in 1852, to \$216 in 1857) that was directly associated with a marked increase in mob violence, harassment and lynchings of Chinese workers in the goldfields

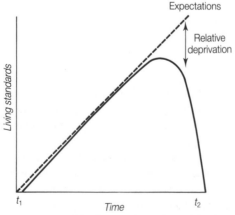

FIGURE 10.2 *The J-curve hypothesis of relative deprivation. (Source: Davies 1969.)*

BOX 10.1 Rising expectations and collective protest: the 1992 Los Angeles riots

An example of relative deprivation

The Los Angeles riots which erupted on 29 April 1992 resulted in more than 50 dead and 2,300 injured. The proximal cause was the acquittal by an all-white suburban jury of four Los Angeles police officers accused of beating a black motorist, Rodney King. Against a background of rising unemployment and deepening disadvantage, this was seen by blacks as a particularly poignant symbol of the low value placed by white America on American blacks.

The flashpoint for the riot was the intersection of Florence and Normandie Avenues in south central Los Angeles. Initially there was an outbreak of stealing liquor from a nearby liquor store, breaking of car windows and pelting of police. The police moved in en masse, but then withdrew to try to de-escalate the tension. This left the intersection largely in the hands of the rioters who attacked whites and Hispanics. Reginald Denny, a white truck driver who happened to be driving through, was dragged from his cab and brutally beaten – an incident watched live on television by millions and which has largely come to symbolise the riots.

South central Los Angeles is relatively typical of black ghettos in the United States. However, the junction of Florence and Normandie is not in the worst part of the ghetto by any means. It is, in fact, a relatively well-off black neighbourhood in which the poverty rate dropped during the 1980s from 33 per cent to only 21 per cent. That the initial outbreak of rioting would occur here, rather than in more impoverished neighbourhoods, is quite consistent with relative deprivation theories of social unrest.

(Yarwood and Knowling 1982, p. 168). Davies (1969) himself cites the French and Russian Revolutions, the American Civil War, the rise of Nazism in Germany, and the growth of black power in the United States in the 1960s. In all these cases a long period (twenty to thirty years) of increasing prosperity was followed by a steep and sudden recession. Systematic tests of predictions from Davies' (1969) theory are less encouraging. For example, from a longitudinal survey of American political and social attitudes, Taylor (1982) found little evidence that people's expectations were constructed from their immediate past experience, or that satisfaction was based on the degree of match between actualities and these expectations.

Runciman (1966) has made an important distinction between two forms of relative deprivation:

▶ Egoistic relative
deprivation

▶ Fraternalistic
relative deprivation

1. *Egoistic relative deprivation* which derives from the individual's sense of deprivation relative to other similar individuals.
2. *Fraternalistic relative deprivation* which derives from comparisons with dissimilar others or with members of other groups.

Studies that include measures of both types of relative deprivation provide some evidence that they are independent (for example, Crosby 1982). Research indicates that it is fraternalistic, particularly intergroup, relative deprivation that is associated with social unrest. Vanneman and Pettigrew (1972) conducted surveys in large cities in the United States to discover that whites who expressed the most negative attitudes towards blacks were those who felt most strongly that whites as a group were poorly off relative to blacks as a group. The deprivation is clearly fraternalistic, and, since whites were actually better-off than blacks, this illustrates the subjective nature of relative deprivation.

Abèles (1976) found that black militancy in the United States was more closely associated with measures of fraternalistic than egoistic relative deprivation, and Guimond and Dubé-Simard (1983) found that militant Francophones in Montreal felt more acute dissatisfaction and frustration when making intergroup salary comparisons between Francophones and Anglophones, rather than egoistic comparisons. In India, where there had been a rapid decline in the status of Muslims relative to Hindus, Tripathi and Srivasta (1981) found that those Muslims who felt most fraternalistically deprived (for example, in terms of job opportunities, political freedom) expressed the greatest hostility towards Hindus.

Finally, in a study of unemployed workers, Walker and Mann (1987) found that it was principally those who reported most fraternalistic deprivation who were prepared to contemplate militant protest such as demonstrations, law-breaking and destruction of private property. Those who felt egoistically deprived reported symptoms of individual stress, for example headaches, indigestion, sleeplessness. This study is particularly useful in showing how egoistic and fraternalistic deprivation produce different outcomes, and that it is the latter that is associated with social unrest as intergroup or collective protest or aggression.

Since fraternalistic relative deprivation depends on the particular ingroup/outgroup comparison that is made, it is important to be able to predict with whom one compares oneself (Martin and Murray 1983; Walker and Pettigrew 1984). From social comparison theory (Festinger 1954; Suls and Miller 1977) we would expect comparisons to be made with similar others – and some of the work cited above certainly supports this (for example, Abèles 1976; Runciman 1966). However, many intergroup comparisons, particularly those that lead to the most pronounced conflict, are made between markedly different groups (for example, black and white South Africans). One way to approach this issue is to consider the extent to which groups are involved in real conflict over scarce resources.

REALISTIC CONFLICT

A key feature of intergroup behaviour is ethnocentrism (Brewer and Campbell 1976; LeVine and Campbell 1972), described by Sumner as:

> a view of things in which one's own group is the centre of everything, and all others are scaled and rated with reference to it ... Each group nourishes its own pride and vanity, boasts itself superior, exalts its own divinities, and looks with contempt on outsiders. Each group thinks its own folkways the only right one ... Ethnocentrism leads a people to exaggerate and intensify everything in their own folkways which is peculiar and which differentiates them from others. (Sumner 1906, p. 13)

In contrast to other perspectives on prejudice, discrimination and intergroup behaviour which explain the origin of ethnocentrism in terms of individual or interpersonal processes (for example, frustration/aggression, relative deprivation, authoritarianism, dogmatism), Sherif believed that 'we cannot extrapolate from the properties of individuals to the characteristics of group situations' (Sherif 1962, p. 8) and that the origins of ethnocentrism lie in the nature of intergroup relations. For Sherif:

> *Intergroup relations* refer to relations between two or more groups and their respective members. Whenever individuals belonging to one group interact, collectively or individually, with another group or its members *in terms of their group identifications* we have an instance of intergroup behaviour. (1962, p. 5)

Sherif believed that where groups compete for scarce resources, intergroup relations become marked by conflict and ethnocentrism arises. To investigate this idea, Sherif and his colleagues conducted three famous field experiments in 1949, 1953 and 1954 at summer camps for young boys in the United States (Sherif 1966). The general procedure involved three phases:

1. The children arrived at the camp, which, unknown to them, was run by the experimenters. They engaged in various camp-wide activities through which they formed friendships.
2. The camp was divided into two separate groups that split pre-formed friendships. The groups were entirely isolated from each other: they had separate living quarters, engaged in separate activities, and developed their own norms and status differentiations. Although little reference was made to the outgroup, there was some embryonic ethnocentrism.
3. The two groups were brought together to engage in organised intergroup competitions embracing sports contests and other activities. This produced

strong competition and intergroup hostility that rapidly generalised to situations outside the organised competitions. Ethnocentric attitudes and behaviour were amplified and coupled with intergroup aggression and ingroup solidarity. Almost all intergroup encounters degenerated into intergroup hostility: for example, when the two groups ate together the meal became an opportunity for the groups to throw food at each other. Intergroup relations deteriorated so dramatically that two of the experiments were hastily concluded at this stage.

In one experiment, however, it was possible to proceed to a fourth stage:

▶ Superordinate goal

4. The two groups were provided with *superordinate goals* – goals they both desired but were unable to achieve on their own. The groups had to work together in co-operation.

As an example of a superordinate goal (also dealt with later in this chapter), the groups were told that the truck bringing a film they both wanted to watch had become bogged down and would need to be pulled, but that everyone would be needed to help as the truck was very heavy. Sherif and colleagues found a gradual improvement in intergroup relations as a consequence of a number of co-operative intergroup interactions in order to achieve superordinate goals.

There are some notable points about these experiments:

1. There was a degree of latent ethnocentrism even in the absence of intergroup competition (more of this below).
2. Prejudice, discrimination and ethnocentrism arose as a consequence of real intergroup conflict.
3. The boys did not have authoritarian or dogmatic personalities.
4. The less frustrated group (the winning group) was usually the one that expressed the greatest intergroup aggression.
5. Ingroups formed despite the fact that friends were actually outgroup members (see Chapter 7).
6. Simple contact between members of opposing groups did not improve intergroup relations (see below).

Realistic conflict theory

▶ Realistic conflict theory

To explain these phenomena, Sherif (1966) proposed a *realistic conflict theory* of intergroup behaviour, in which the nature of the goal relations among individuals and groups determines the nature of intergroup and inter-individual relations. He argued that individuals who share goals requiring interdependence for their achievement tend to co-operate and form a group (Figure 10.3), while individuals who have mutually exclusive goals (that is, a scarce resource that only one can obtain – for example, winning a chess game) engage in inter-individual competition that prevents group formation or contributes to the collapse of an existing group. At the intergroup level, mutually exclusive goals produce realistic intergroup conflict, ethnocentrism

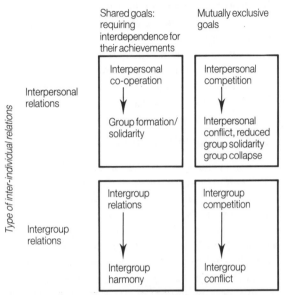

Goal relations

FIGURE 10.3 *Realistic group conflict theory. (Source: based on Sherif 1966.)*

and so forth, while shared goals requiring intergroup interdependence for their achievement (that is, superordinate goals) reduce conflict and encourage intergroup harmony.

Sherif's model is generally supported by other naturalistic experiments (Fisher 1990). For example, Blake and Mouton (1961) employed very similar procedures in a series of thirty studies, each run for two weeks, involving more than one thousand business people on management training programmes in the United States. Zimbardo's simulated prison experiment (Haney *et al.* 1973 – see Chapter 7) also illustrates the way in which mutually exclusive intergroup goals produce conflict and hostile intergroup relations. Sherif's studies have successfully been replicated in Lebanon (Diab 1970) and the Soviet Union (Andreeva 1984), but in Britain, Tyerman and Spencer (1983) were not so successful. Tyerman and Spencer used an established scout group as subjects and found that the different 'patrols' did not express anywhere near as much hostility as expected. Furthermore, it was very easy to increase inter-patrol co-operation even in the absence of a superordinate goal. Tyerman and Spencer attribute this to the fact that a well-established superordinate group already existed.

Realistic conflict theory makes good sense and is generally useful for understanding intergroup conflict, particularly in applied settings (Fisher, 1990). For example, Brewer and Campbell (1976 – see also Chapter 12) conducted an ethnographic survey of thirty tribal groups in Africa and found, among other things, greater derogation of tribal outgroups that lived close by and were thus likely to be direct competitors for scarce resources such as water and land. Realistic conflict theory does, however, suffer from one problem. Because so many variables are operating together in the various studies, how can we know that it is the nature of goal relations that ultimately determines intergroup behaviour, rather than, for example, the co-operative or competitive nature of interaction, or perhaps merely the existence of two separate groups (for example, Dion 1979; Turner 1981b)? These causal agents are confounded – an observation that we will pursue later in this chapter.

Co-operation, competition and social dilemmas

Realistic conflict theory focuses attention on the relationship between people's goals, the competitive or co-operative nature of their behaviour, and the conflicting or harmonious nature of their relations. One can study these relationships in highly abstract settings by designing 'games' with different goal relations for two or more people to play. Indeed, Von Neumann and Morgenstern (1944) introduced a model for analysing situations in which people are in conflict over some non-trivial outcome (for example, money, power). Variously called *decision theory*, *game theory* or *utility theory*, this initiated an enormous amount of research in the 1960s and 1970s. (This line of research is also dealt with in the context of interpersonal relations in Chapter 12.) The highly abstract nature of the research raised questions about its relevance (generalisability) to real-world conflict, and led to its decline in the 1980s (Apfelbaum and Lubek 1976; Nemeth 1970). Much of this research is concerned mainly with interpersonal conflict; however, much of it also has important implications for intergroup conflict, for example the prisoner's dilemma, the trucking game and the commons dilemma (for example, Liebrand *et al.* 1992).

The prisoner's dilemma

▶ Prisoner's dilemma

Introduced by Luce and Raiffa (1957; Rapoport 1976), the *prisoner's dilemma* is the most widely researched game. It is based on an anecdote. Two obviously guilty suspects are questioned separately by detectives who only have enough evidence to convict them of a lesser offence. The suspects are separately offered a chance to confess, knowing that if one confesses but the other does not, the confessor will be granted immunity and the confession will be used to convict the other on the more serious offence. If both confess, each will receive a moderate sentence. If neither confesses, each will receive a very light sentence. The dilemma faced by the prisoners can be summarised in the form of a *pay-off matrix* (Figure 10.4). Although mutual non-confession produces the best joint outcome, mutual suspicion and lack of trust almost always encourages both to confess. This finding has been replicated in literally hundreds of prisoner's dilemma experiments, using a variety of experimental conditions and pay-off matrices. The prisoner's dilemma is described as a two-person, mixed motive, non-zero-sum game. What this means is that two people are

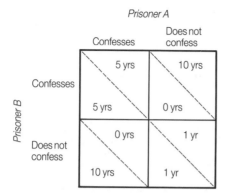

Prisoner A

Note: Each quadrant displays the prison sentence that A will receive (above diagonal) and B will receive (below diagonal) as a consequence of whether both, one or neither confesses.

FIGURE 10.4 *The prisoner's dilemma pay-off matrix.*

involved, they each experience a conflict between being motivated to co–operate and motivated to compete, and the outcome can be such that both parties gain or both lose (in contrast, a zero–sum game is one in which one party's gain is always the other's loss).

The trucking game

In this game, there are two trucking companies, Acme and Bolt, that have to transport goods from one place to another (Deutsch and Krauss 1960). Each company has its own private route, but there is a much quicker shared route that has a major drawback – there is a one-lane section (see Figure 10.5). Clearly the mutually beneficial solution is for the two companies to reach an agreement to take it in turns to use the one-lane section. Instead, research reveals again and again that subjects prefer to fight for use of the one-lane section: typically both enter and meet head on in the middle, and then waste time arguing until one backs up. Again, mutual mistrust has produced a suboptimal joint outcome.

These games elicit detrimental consequences of lack of trust that have clear real-world analogues. For example, mutual distrust between Iran and Iraq fuelled their recent conflict over which of them rightfully owned the Shatt al Arab waterway. When they laid down their arms in 1988, after horrific atrocities, over a million civilian and military casualties, and the devastation of their economies, the borders remained precisely where they were when the war began eight years earlier.

Game theory rests on a rationalistic characterisation of human kind as *homo oeconomicus* – a western model of human psychological functioning which derives from western thinking about work and industry (Stroebe and Frey 1982; see also the discussions of normative models and behavioural decision

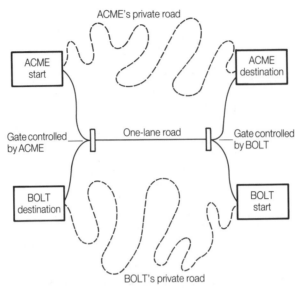

FIGURE 10.5 *The trucking game. (Source: Deutsch and Krauss 1960.)*

theory in Chapter 2). Possibly due to this perspective, a problem with game theory based research is that it may be relatively asocial. For example, it often overlooks the role of direct communication; and communication in two- and *n*-person prisoner's dilemma games actually tends to reduce conflict and increase co-operation in an enduring way (Liebrand 1984). Interactants' responses also tend to fulfil a communicative function, such that flexible and responsive partner's tend to raise the level of co-operation (Apfelbaum 1974). Similarly, subjective perceptions of the game are often overlooked. For example, the allocation or exchange of goods or resources always raises questions of perceived fairness and justice, and it would appear that interactants are more confident of fair solutions, behave more co-operatively and are more satisfied with outcomes if rules of fairness are explicitly invoked (McClintock and van Avermaet 1982; Mikula 1980). There is also some evidence that experimental games are spontaneously construed by subjects as competitive contexts and that when the game is introduced in different terms, for example as an investigation of human interaction or international conflict resolution, then people behave in a more co-operative manner (Abric and Vacherot 1976; Eiser and Bhavnani 1974).

The commons dilemma

▶ Commons dilemma Many other social dilemmas involve a number of individuals or groups exploiting a limited resource. These are essentially *n*-person prisoners' dilemmas, in that if everyone co-operates an optimal solution for all is reached, but if everyone competes then everyone loses. The *commons dilemma*, or 'tragedy of the commons' (Hardin 1968) gets its name from the common pasture that English towns used to have. People were free to graze their cattle on this land, and if all used it in moderation it would replenish itself and continually benefit them all. Imagine, however, one hundred farmers surrounding a common which could only support one hundred cows. If each grazed one cow, the common would be maximally utilised and minimally taxed. One farmer, however, might reason that if she grazed an additional cow her output would be doubled, minus a very small cost due to overgrazing – a cost borne equally by all one hundred farmers. So this farmer adds a second cow. If all one hundred farmers reasoned in this way they would destroy the common, thus producing the tragedy of the commons.

▶ Free-rider effect

Many of the world's most pressing environmental and conservation problems are commons dilemmas. They reflect a *free-rider effect* (Kerr 1983 – see also Chapter 7) in which people self-interestedly exploit a resource without caring for it. For example, if I own a cat it contributes fairly minimally to the disappearance of native fauna, but if all 56 million people living in Britain reason similarly, and hence own cats, annihilation is assured. Likewise, if I fail to fix my car exhaust or fail to plant trees in my garden it contributes minimally to noise, atmospheric and visual pollution, but if everyone living in my neighbourhood did likewise then it would become a horrible place to live.

Reflecting on the commons dilemma, Hardin observed:

> Ruin is the destination to which all men rush, each pursuing his own best interest in a society that believes in the freedom of the commons. Freedom in a commons brings ruin to all. (Hardin 1968, p. 162)

Experimental research on commons dilemmas finds that when self-interest is pitted against the collective good the usual outcome is competition and resource destruction (Edney 1979; Sato 1987). However, laboratory and field studies also obtain high levels of voluntary social co-operation (Caporael *et al.* 1989). A series of studies by Brewer and her colleagues (Brewer and Kramer 1986; Brewer and Schneider 1990; Kramer and Brewer 1984, 1986) identifies one condition under which this can occur. When individuals identify with the common good – in other words they derive their social identity (see below) from the entire group which has access to the resource – self-interest becomes subordinate to the common good. However, the same research indicates that when different *groups*, rather than individuals, have access to a public good then the ensuing intergroup competition ensures ethnocentric actions which are far more destructive than mere self-interest. International competition over limited resources such as rainforests, whales and wetlands, tragically accelerates their disappearance.

Groups often choose to have a leader manage a collective resource. Rutte and Wilke (1984) suggest that this is most likely to happen when: (1) the group, left to its own devices, has clearly failed to manage the resource properly, and (2) the group has allocated the resource unfairly such that there are large differences in outcomes among group members. Rutte and Wilke

(1985) confirmed this in an experiment in which they found that the default preference for groups was not to have a leader – if the group successfully managed the resource and the outcomes were fair there was little need to abdicate individual freedom to a leader. However, if the group was unsuccessful and a leader was needed, members initially preferred to nominate themselves, and once elected, leaders took care of group success and allocated outcomes fairly.

SOCIAL IDENTITY

Minimal groups

We have seen how realistic conflict theory (Sherif 1966) explains the origins and form of intergroup behaviour ultimately in terms of goal interdependence, and how research tends to confound a number of possible causal agents. Research seems, however, to suggest that ethnocentric attitudes and competitive intergroup relations are extremely easy to trigger and very difficult to suppress. For example, embryonic ethnocentrism was found in phase 2 of Sherif's summer camp studies, when groups had simply been formed but there was no realistic conflict between the groups (see also Blake and Mouton 1961; Kahn and Ryen 1972). Other researchers have found that competitive intergroup behaviour spontaneously emerges:

1. Even when intergroup goal relations are not interdependent (Rabbie and Horwitz 1969).
2. Under conditions of explicitly non-competitive intergroup relations (Ferguson and Kelley 1964; Rabbie and Wilkens 1971).
3. Under conditions of explicitly co-operative intergroup relations (Rabbie and DeBrey 1971).

▶ Minimal group paradigm

What, then, are the minimal conditions for intergroup behaviour, that is those conditions that are both necessary and sufficient for a collection of individuals to be ethnocentric and to engage in intergroup competition? Tajfel and his colleagues devised an intriguing paradigm to answer this question – the *minimal group paradigm* (Tajfel *et al.* 1971). British schoolboys, participating in what they believed was a study of decision-making, were assigned to one of two groups on a completely random basis, but allegedly on the basis of their expressed preference for paintings by the artists Kandinsky or Klee. The children only knew which group they themselves were in (Kandinsky group or Klee group), with the identity of fellow ingroup and outgroup members being kept hidden by use of code numbers. The children then had individually to distribute money between pairs of recipients identified only by code number and group membership. This paper-and-pencil task was repeated for a number of different pairs of ingroup and outgroup members, excluding self, on a series of distribution matrices carefully designed to tease out the sorts of strategy that were being used (see Box 10.2). The results indicated that, against a background of some fairness, the children strongly favoured their own group – they adopted the ingroup favouritism strategy (FAV) described in Box 10.2.

▶ Social categorisation

This is really a rather startling finding since the groups were indeed very minimal: they were created on the basis of a flimsy criterion, had no past history or possible future, the children did not even know the identity of other members of each group, and there was no self-interest involved in the money distribution task as self was not a recipient. Subsequent experiments were

---

BOX 10.2 The minimal group paradigm: distribution tasks and strategies

A. Sample distribution matrices

Subjects circle the column of numbers that represents how they would like to distribute the points (representing real money) in the matrix between ingroup and outgroup members.

1. Ingroup member:	7	8	9	10	11	12	13	14	15	16	17	18	19
Outgroup member:	1	3	5	7	9	11	13	15	17	19	21	23	25

2. Ingroup member:	18	17	16	15	14	13	12	11	10	9	8	7	6
Outgroup member:	5	6	7	8	9	10	11	12	13	14	15	16	17

B. Distribution strategies

From an analysis of responses on a large number of matrices it is possible to determine the extent to which the subjects' distribution of points is influenced by each of the following strategies.

- Fairness   F   Equal distribution of points between groups

- Maximum joint profit   MJP   Maximise total number of points obtained by both recipients together, irrespective of which group receives most

- Maximum ingroup profit   MIP   Maximise number of points for the ingroup

- Maximum difference   MD   Maximising the difference in favour of the ingroup in the number of points awarded

- Favouritism   FAV   Composite employment of MIP and MD

(Source: adapted from Hogg and Abrams 1988)

even more minimal. For example, Billig and Tajfel (1973) explicitly randomly categorised their subjects as X- or Y-group members, thereby eliminating any possibility that subjects might infer that people in the same group were interpersonally similar because they ostensibly preferred the same artist. Turner (1978) abolished the link between points and money – the task was simply to distribute points. Other studies have included, in addition to the point distribution task, measures of attitudinal, affective and conative aspects of ethnocentrism. The robust finding from scores of minimal group experiments conducted with a wide range of subjects is that the mere fact of being categorised as a group member seems to be necessary and sufficient to produce ethnocentrism and competitive intergroup behaviour (Brewer and Kramer 1985; Hogg and Abrams 1988; Tajfel 1982). More accurately, *social categorisation* is necessary but may not be sufficient for intergroup behaviour. People who have been categorised must then use the social category to define themselves as group members: they must psychologically identify with the minimal category (see below).

The minimal group paradigm has not gone unchallenged. For example, there has been a lively debate over the measures, procedures and statistics used (Aschenbrenner and Schaefer 1980; Branthwaite *et al.* 1979; Bornstein *et al.* 1983; Turner 1980, 1983). Another objection is that conditions of the experiments create a demand characteristic in which subjects conform to transparent expectations of the experimenters or simply to general norms of intergroup competitiveness (Gerard and Hoyt 1974). This interpretation seems rather unlikely in the light of evidence that discrimination can actually be reduced when adherence to norms would be expected to be more likely (Tajfel and Billig 1974), or under conditions of greater awareness of a norm of discrimination (Billig 1973). In fact, non-participating subjects tend to predict significantly less discrimination (that is, no norm of discrimination) than is actually expressed by those who do participate (St Claire and Turner 1982), and it can be almost impossible to encourage subjects to follow an explicitly co-operative norm in a minimal intergroup situation (Hogg *et al.* 1986).

Social identity theory

▶ Social identity
▶ Social identity
 theory

The inescapably central role of social categorisation in intergroup behaviour, as demonstrated by minimal group studies, led to the development by Tajfel, Turner and their colleagues of *social identity theory* (Abrams and Hogg 1990b; Hogg and Abrams 1988; Tajfel and Turner 1979; Turner 1981b, 1982). Based on the assumption that society is hierarchically structured into different social groups that stand in power and status relations to one another (for example, men and women, blacks and whites in South Africa, Catholics and Protestants in Northern Ireland, Malays and Chinese in Malaysia), the basic premise of this theory is that social categories (large groups such as a nation or church, or

Minority group assertion – social competition. When lesbians and gay men demonstrate for equal rights with heterosexuals they assert a challenge to the status quo of the intergroup relationship and to the majority group's power base. (Source: Nicola Horton.)

smaller groups such as an organisation or club) provide members with a *social identity*: a definition of who one is and a description and evaluation of what this entails. Social identities not only describe members but prescribe appropriate behaviour (that is, norms) for members. So, for example, being a member of the social category 'gypsy' means not only that one defines and evaluates oneself and one is defined and evaluated by others as a gypsy, but also that one thinks and behaves in characteristically gypsy ways.

Social identity is that part of the self-concept that derives from group membership. It is quite separate from personal identity, which is that part of the self-concept that derives from personality traits and idiosyncratic personal relationships one has with other people (Turner 1982). People have a repertoire of as many social and personal identities as they have groups with which they identify, or close relationships in terms of which they define themselves. These identities continually vary in their overall importance in the self-concept, and they become the relevant basis of self-perception and behaviour as a function of contextual factors. For example, talking with a close friend about a mutual acquaintance would most likely render a particular personal identity salient and cause one to consider oneself and one's partner in terms of that identity. Talking with the same close friend about the outcome of a football match in which you support opposing teams would very likely render the interaction an intergroup one based on a definition of self and other in terms of opposing supporters' groups.

▶ Authoritarian
personality
▶ Frustration-
aggression
hypothesis
▶ Reductionism

Social identity theory distinguishes social from personal identity as part of a self-conscious attempt to avoid explaining group and intergroup processes in terms of personality attributes or interpersonal relations. Social identity theorists believe that a major problem with many social psychological theories of group processes and intergroup relations is that they do not provide a complete answer because they try to explain the phenomena by simply combining the effects of personality predispositions or interpersonal relations – the *authoritarian personality* theory and the *frustration-aggression hypothesis* are examples of this type of explanation of prejudice and discrimination (Billig 1976 – see Chapter 9). To illustrate: if a social psychologist asks why people stick their arms out of car windows to indicate a turn, the question would remain unanswered by an explanation in terms of the biochemistry of muscle action. An explanation in terms of adherence to social norms would be more appropriate (though, of course, inappropriate to a biochemist asking the same question). It is the problem of *reductionism* (see Chapter 1 for details) that prompts social identity theory to distinguish between social and personal identity (Doise 1986; Israel and Tajfel 1972; Moscovici 1972; Taylor and Brown 1979; Turner and Oakes 1986).

▶ Ethnocentrism
▶ Ingroup
favouritism
▶ Intergroup
differentiation
▶ Stereotypes

Social identity is associated with group behaviour, which has some notable general characteristics: *ethnocentrism, ingroup favouritism, intergroup differentiation*; conformity to ingroup norms; and perception of self, outgroupers and fellow ingroupers in terms of relevant group *stereotypes*. Social identification produces these effects because it is associated with social categorisation, which, we have just seen, produces competitive intergroup behaviour. This is supported not only by the minimal group studies but also by more naturalistic investigations (but see Brown *et al.* 1986 for an alternative view). For example, Brown (1978), capitalising on competitive wage negotiations in Britain in the 1970s, found that shop stewards from one department in an aircraft engineering factory sacrificed as much as two pounds a week in absolute terms in order to increase their relative advantage over a competing outgroup to one pound. Relatedly, studies of nurses revealed that although nurses are supposed to be caring and self-sacrificing, ingroup identification was associated with just as much ingroup favouritism as among other less self-sacrificing groups (Oaker and Brown 1986; Skevington 1981; van Knippenberg and van Oers 1984).

Social categorisation has often been linked to stereotyping (for example, Allport 1954; Ehrlich 1973), and has also been shown empirically to accentuate perceived stereotypical similarities within groups and differences between groups (for example, Eiser and Stroebe 1972; McGarty and Penny 1988; Tajfel and Wilkes 1963 – see below and Chapter 2). Accentuation is considered to be an inevitable consequence of categorisation, which in turn is considered a basic human cognitive process that serves the important function of simplifying in meaningful ways the potentially limitless array of discernible stimuli in our environment (Doise 1978). Does this mean, then, that intergroup conflict is an inescapable consequence of an omnipresent and inevitable cognitive process?

▶ Positive self-esteem

Perhaps not. There is one final component of social identity theory. Drawing on social comparison theory (Festinger 1954; Suls and Miller 1977), it is assumed that people have a basic need to obtain, through comparison between themselves and others, a relatively positive evaluation of themselves – there is a need for *positive self-esteem*. In intergroup contexts, when social identity is salient and thus mediating self-evaluation, this need manifests itself by maintaining or securing a relatively positive social identity for the ingroup. For this reason, the accentuation of intergroup differences produced by social categorisation has two further features:

1. It occurs only on dimensions which favour the ingroup (hence it is ethnocentric, i.e. ingroup-favouring).
2. It is amplified under conditions where there is a strong need to differentiate the groups (for example, when intergroup boundaries are becoming unclear, in times of conflict, or among individuals with low self-esteem or for whom that particular ingroup is extremely important).

Researchers have found this positive social identity idea helpful in understanding a range of phenomena, for example delinquency. Emler and his colleagues have suggested that delinquency, particularly among boys, is strategic behaviour designed to establish and manage a favourable reputation among groups of peers (Emler and Hopkins 1990). Consistent with this view is the fact that delinquent behaviour is usually a group activity that occurs in public thus maximising its identity-confirming function (Emler *et al.* 1987). Furthermore, delinquent behaviour is particularly appealing to children who come from backgrounds that are unlikely to facilitate good academic performance at school – delinquency therefore offers an alternative source of positive identity (it is so attractive that most children toy with it to some extent at one time or another). Reicher and Emler (1985) have suggested that one reason that boys are much more likely than girls to become delinquent is that there is greater pressure on boys to perform well at school and therefore under-achievement is more poignantly felt – the motivation to establish an alternative positive social identity is so much stronger.

▶ Social mobility belief system

Experimental studies, however, of exactly how self-esteem motivates intergroup behaviour or how self-esteem is influenced by intergroup behaviour tend to produce rather inconsistent findings (for example, Abrams and Hogg 1988; Hogg and Abrams 1990, 1993; Hogg and Sunderland 1991; Crocker *et al.* 1993). In comparison with self-esteem, the role of positive social identity in intergroup relations is better understood (Figure 10.6). In pursuit of positive social identity, groups and individuals can adopt an array of different behavioural strategies, the choice of which is determined by people's beliefs about the nature of relations between their own and other groups (Hogg and Abrams 1988; Tajfel and Turner 1979; Taylor and McKirnan 1984). These beliefs, which may or may not accord with the reality of intergroup relations, hinge firstly on whether it is possible, as an individual, to 'pass' from a lower status group and gain acceptance in a higher status group. A *social mobility*

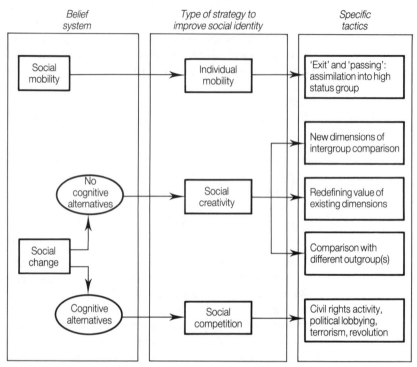

FIGURE 10.6 *Social identity theory: belief systems and strategies for improving social identity.*

belief system inhibits group action on the part of subordinate groups, and instead encourages individuals to dissociate themselves from the group and try to gain acceptance for themselves and their immediate family in the dominant group. The belief in social mobility is enshrined in western democratic political systems.

Where individuals believe that intergroup boundaries are impermeable to 'passing', a *social change belief system* exists, for example the Hindu caste system in India. Under these circumstances, positive social identity can only be achieved by forms of group action, and the sort of action taken is influenced by whether the status quo (the existing status and power hierarchy) is perceived to be secure or insecure. If the status quo is perceived to be stable, legitimate, and thus secure, it is difficult to conceive of an alternative social structure (that is, no cognitive alternatives exist), let alone a path to real social change. Groups tend to adopt *social creativity* strategies:

▶ Social change belief system

▶ Cognitive alternatives

▶ Social creativity

1. They can engage in intergroup comparisons on novel or unorthodox dimensions which tend to favour the subordinate group. For example, Lemaine (1966, 1974) had children engage in an intergroup competition

to build the best hut, and found that groups which were provided with poor building materials and thus no possibility of winning went on to emphasise how good a garden they had made.

2. They can attempt to change the consensual value attached to ingroup characteristics, for example the slogan 'black is beautiful'.

3. They can compare themselves with other low or lower status groups, for example 'poor white racism'.

▶ Social competition

Where social change is associated with a recognition that the status quo is illegitimate, unstable, and thus insecure, and where cognitive alternatives (that is, conceivable and attainable alternative social orders) exist, then direct *social competition* occurs – that is, direct intergroup conflict (for example, political action, terrorism, revolutions, war). Social movements typically emerge under these circumstances (for example, Milgram and Toch 1969).

The macrosocial aspect of social identity theory has been tested fairly successfully in a range of laboratory and naturalistic contexts (Ellemers *et al.* 1993; Hogg and Abrams 1988; van Knippenberg and Ellemers 1993), and has been elaborated and extended in many areas of social psychology (for example, the study of language and ethnicity – see Chapter 14). Social identity theory attributes the general form of intergroup behaviour (for example, ethnocentrism, stereotyping) to social categorisation and self-esteem processes, and the specific manifestation (for example, conflict, harmony) to people's beliefs about the nature of intergroup relations.

Haslam *et al.* (1992) capture this rather nicely in a recent study of subtle changes in Australians' stereotypes of Americans that occurred as a consequence of changes in intergroup attitudes caused by the 1991 Gulf War. They discovered that Australians who were making comparisons among Australia, Britain and the United States had a relatively unfavourable stereotype of Americans that deteriorated further during the course of the Gulf conflict, particularly on dimensions reflecting arrogance, argumentativeness and traditionalism. The authors argue that the reason that attitudes deteriorated on these particular dimensions rather than others was that these dimensions related directly to the perceived actions of Americans during the war in relation to other nations.

Self-categorisation theory

▶ Self-categorisation theory

Self-categorisation theory (Turner 1985; Turner *et al.* 1987) is a recent development of social identity theory, which stresses the role of self-categorisation in social identity phenomena (Hogg and McGarty 1990).

▶ Prototype
▶ Depersonalisation

Social identity regulates behaviour in the way it does because the underlying process is self-categorisation. In intergroup contexts people call up from memory or construct from the range of ingroup and outgroup people present a contextually appropriate cognitive representation of the defining features of each group. A *prototype* is a fuzzy set of features that define each group and describe appropriate behaviour for members of each group – prototypes are the way in which we represent social categories. Prototypes tend both to minimise intragroup differences and to exaggerate intergroup differences. When we categorise others as ingroup or outgroup members we accentuate their similarity to the relevant prototype, thus perceiving them stereotypically and ethnocentrically. When we categorise ourselves, we define, perceive and evaluate ourselves in terms of our ingroup prototype, and behave in accordance with that. Self-categorisation produces ingroup normative behaviour (conformity to group norms – see Chapter 6) and self-stereotyping (see Chapter 2), and is thus the process underlying group behaviour. Self-categorisation theorists believe that self-categorisation depersonalises perception and behaviour such that people, including ourselves, are perceived and behave not as unique individuals but as group members. *Depersonalisation* is not the same as dehumanisation, though it can produce dehumanisation if the outgroup is deeply hated and is stereotyped in terms that deny its members any respect or human dignity.

Self-categorisation theory has provided some important insights into the operation of social influence processes such as conformity (Chapter 6) and group polarisation (Chapter 8) – Abrams and Hogg (1990a), Turner (1991), Turner and Oakes (1989). It has also been applied to help understand group cohesiveness (Hogg 1992; Chapter 7), stereotyping (Oakes *et al.* 1994), the relationship between overt behaviour and self-categorisation (Abrams 1994, Terry and Hogg, in press), and the process of salience whereby an interaction between contextual and person factors render different self-conceptions the salient basis of behaviour (Oakes 1987; Oakes and Turner 1990).

SOCIAL COGNITION

While self-categorisation theory emphasises the role of cognitive processes and cognitive representations in intergroup behaviour, it is, nonetheless, a theory which articulates (Doise 1986 – see Chapter 1) with a more broadly social analysis. This is possible because of its explicit and formal relationship with social identity theory (Hogg and McGarty 1990). Social cognition (for example, Fiske and Taylor 1991 – see Chapter 2), however, provides a number of other, more purely cognitive explanations which focus on certain cognitive and perceptual biases that have important implications for intergroup behaviour.

Categorisation and relative homogeneity

▶ Accentuation
  effect
▶ Relative
  homogeneity effect

The most obvious bias is stereotyping. The categorisation of people (or objects) has been shown to cause an *accentuation effect* (Tajfel 1959): the perceptual accentuation of similarities among people within a category and differences between people from different categories, on those dimensions

A sexist billboard – social support for a stereotype. Educational and inter-individual attempts to change social stereotypes are unlikely to be successful when they are located within a wider social context that publicly promulgates, and thus seems to endorse, stereotypic values. (Source: Andrew Lukey.)

believed to be associated with the categorisation – that is, stereotypic dimensions (Doise 1978; Eiser and Stroebe 1972; Tajfel and Wilkes 1963). There is some evidence that people perceptually homogenise outgroup members more than ingroup members – '*they* all look alike, but *we* are diverse' (Brigham and Malpass 1985; Quattrone 1986). For example, Brigham and Barkowitz (1978) had black and white college students indicate for seventy-two photographs of black and white faces how certain they were that they had seen each photograph in a previously presented series of twenty-four photographs (twelve of blacks and twelve of whites). Figure 10.7 shows that subjects found it more difficult to recognise outgroup than ingroup faces. This effect is quite robust. It has emerged from other studies comparing Anglos with blacks (Bothwell *et al.* 1989), Hispanics (Platz and Hosch 1988) and Japanese (Chance 1985), and from studies of student eating clubs (Jones *et al.* 1981), college sororities (Park and Rothbart 1982), and artificial laboratory groups (Wilder 1984). The *relative homogeneity effect* is enhanced when groups are in competition (Judd and Park 1988).

The principal explanation for this effect is that because we are generally more familiar with ingroup than outgroup members, we have more detailed knowledge about them, and thus are better able to differentiate them (Wilder 1986). Although quite sensible, this may not be the entire story. For example, the outgroup homogeneity effect occurs when subjects report no greater familiarity with ingroup than outgroup (Jones *et al.* 1981), and when there is equally minimal information about both groups (Wilder 1984). Stephan (1977)

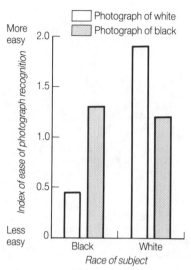

FIGURE 10.7 *Ease of recognition of faces as a function of race of subject and race of person in photograph. (Source: based on data from Brigham and Barkowitz (1978.)*

found that children in both segregated and integrated schools (that is, with lower or higher intergroup familiarity) actually rated their own group as more homogeneous than two outgroups. If outgroup homogeneity is not inevitable, then what factors influence the relative homogeneity effect?

One clue is that while most research has used majority or equal-sized groups, Stephan's (1977) groups were minority groups (chicanos and blacks). Also, the relative outgroup homogeneity affect is enhanced when the outgroup is perceived to be relatively small (Mullen and Hu 1989). To test the idea that relative homogeneity is influenced by the majority/minority status of the ingroup, Simon and Brown (1987) conducted a minimal group study in which relative group size was varied and subjects were asked to rate the variability of both ingroup and outgroup, and their identification with the ingroup. Figure 10.8 shows that while majorities rated the outgroup as less variable than the ingroup (the usual outgroup homogeneity effect), minorities did the opposite. In addition, this latter ingroup homogeneity effect was accompanied by greater group identification. This is quite consistent with self–categorisation and social identity theories: minorities categorise themselves more strongly as a group and are thus more strongly depersonalised (see above) in their perceptions, attitudes and behaviour.

Memory

Social categorisation is associated with category-based person memory effects (Fiske and Taylor 1991). For example, Taylor and co-workers (1978) had

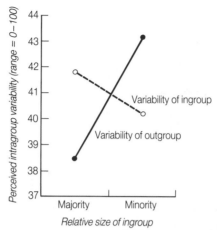

FIGURE 10.8 *Perceived intragroup variability of ingroup and outgroup as a function of relative majority or minority status of ingroup. (Source: based on data from Simon and Brown 1987.)*

subjects listen to taped mixed-sex or mixed-race discussion groups, and then later attribute various statements to the correct speaker. Subjects rarely attributed the statements to the wrong category, but within categories they were not very good at identifying the correct speaker: that is, they made few between-category errors, but many within-category errors. The category-based memory effect can be quite selective. For example, Howard and Rothbart (1980) had subjects attribute statements about behaviours to ingroup and outgroup members; some of the behaviours reflected favourably and others unfavourably on the actor. The subjects were equally accurate at recalling whether it was an ingroup or outgroup member who performed the favourable behaviours, but they were more accurate at recalling outgroup than ingroup actors who performed unfavourable behaviours (see Figure 10.9). These two experiments illustrate the way in which information about individuals can be cognitively represented and organised as category attributes which submerge individual differences between people within the same category. Furthermore, evaluative biases may also influence what information is associated with a particular category.

Distinctive stimuli and illusory correlation

A particularly important influence on what information is associated with which categories is the distinctiveness of the information. Anything that is out of the ordinary (objects, events and people who are statistically infrequent, rare, unusual, relatively vivid or conspicuous) tends to attract our attention and engage a disproportionate amount of cognitive activity (Taylor and Fiske

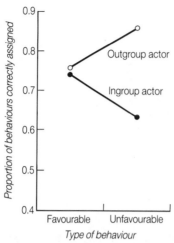

FIGURE 10.9 *Assignment of behaviours to actors as a function of item favourability and ingroup/outgroup status of actor. (Source: based on data from Howard and Rothbart 1980.)*

1978). So, for example, we tend to attend more to a single male in a group of females, a single black in a group of whites, or to a person who we understand to be a genius, a homosexual or a film star. Distinctive individuals can also disproportionately influence the generalised images we construct of groups. There is a tendency to generalise from distinctive individuals to the group as a whole, particularly when we have few prior expectations and/or are unfamiliar with the category (Quattrone and Jones 1980). For instance, on the basis of meeting one extremely stupid (that is, distinctive individual) Martian (that is, unfamiliar group), we are apt to stereotype the group as being stupid.

▶ Illusory correlation   Another effect of distinctiveness is that people tend to perceive an *illusory correlation* between co-occurring distinctive events. For example, Chapman (1967) presented subjects with word pairs (for example, lion/tiger, bacon/eggs, blossoms/notebook) and found that they over-estimated the frequency of presentation of pairs of distinctive words, for example blossoms/notebook because the two words were distinctively long. Illusory correlation due to paired distinctiveness has been used to explain some aspects of stereotyping (Hamilton 1979). People may develop negative stereotypes of outgroup members (particularly minority outgroups) through illusory correlation based on infrequent contact with outgroup members and the general infrequency of negative behaviour in most people's experiences. To test this idea, Hamilton and Gifford (1976) gave subjects a list of statements about group A and group B. Statements about group A were twice as numerous as those about group B, and positive statements were twice as numerous as negative statements. Within the experiment, then, group B and negative statements were more distinctive due to their statistical infrequency. Subjects over-estimated the number of co-occurrences of group B with negative statements – that is, an illusory correlation. Hamilton and Gifford (1976) replicated the experiment with positive statements as the more infrequent ones. Subjects over-estimated co-occurrence of group B with positive statements.

Distinctiveness-based illusory correlation is a robust empirical effect which is stronger for negative behaviours and under conditions of high memory load (Mullen and Johnson 1990), and when people are aroused (Kim and Baron 1988). Once an illusory correlation between a group and a negative attribute in one domain (for example, intellectual) has been established, there is a tendency to generalise the negative impression to other domains (for example, social) – Acorn *et al.* (1988). Illusory correlation effects can also be based on expectations (Hamilton and Rose 1980).

Optimal distinctiveness

▶ Optimal
distinctiveness

Distinctiveness enters into intergroup behaviour in rather a different way in Brewer's (1991, 1993) theory of *optimal distinctiveness*. Brewer (1988) argues that the default mode for processing information about others is in terms of their category membership (satisfying a need to recognise similarities among people). However, if one feels ego-involved in the task, or related to or interdependent with the stimulus person, then information processing is based on highly specific and personalised information about the stimulus person (this satisfies a need to recognise differences among people). In most contexts people strive to achieve a satisfactory level of distinctiveness for others and for themselves, in order to resolve the tension between the needs for similarity and difference. In intergroup behaviour this manifests itself as a degree of differentiation among group members, including self, against a background of homogenisation. A related phenomenon was earlier identified by Codol (1975), called the *primus inter pares* effect, in which individuals within a group seemed to differentiate themselves from one another in competition to be the most representative or best group member.

One implication of optimal distinctinctiveness theory is that people should be more satisfied with membership of mid-size groups than groups which are very large (the need for differences is unsatisfied) or very small (the need for similarity is unsatisfied). This idea is usually tested in the laboratory with a rather restricted range of relative group sizes. To investigate groups which varied enormously in relative size, Abrams (1994) analysed survey data on political identity from over four thousand 18- to 21-year-olds in England and Scotland. He found that small parties (Greens, Social Democrats, Scottish Nationalists) did indeed provide members with a more solid and distinct identity than did the large parties (Labour, Conservatives).

COLLECTIVE BEHAVIOUR AND THE CROWD

▶ Collective behaviour

The term *collective behaviour* usually refers to instances in which large numbers of people who are in the same place at the same time behave in a uniform manner which is volatile, is characterised by strong emotions and is often in violation of social norms (Graumann and Moscovici 1986; Milgram and Toch 1969; Moscovici 1985b). Some social psychologists interpret this to include the study of rumours (see Chapter 3), fads and fashions, social movements and cults, and contagions of expression, enthusiasm, anxiety, fear and hostility. Contagions include some of the most bizarre behaviours imaginable (Klapp 1972). In the 1630s, tulip mania swept north-west Europe, with people trading small fortunes for a single, ultimately worthless bulb; in the fifteenth century there was an epidemic in Europe in which nuns bit each other; in the eighteenth century there was an epidemic of nuns meowing like cats; between the tenth and fourteenth century in Europe there were frequent episodes of dancing mania with people continually dancing from town to town until they dropped and even died; and in the mid and late 1980s there were epidemics in China of men complaining hysterically about shrinkage of the penis and an overwhelming fear of impending death.

Usually, however, the study of collective behaviour is a far more sober affair. It is the study of crowd behaviour. The crowd is a very vivid social phenomenon for both those who are involved and those who witness the events firsthand or through literature and the media. Consider the Tian'anmen Square protest in 1989, the Los Angeles riots of 1992, the Nazi rallies of the 1930s, the celebrations at the removal of the Berlin Wall in 1990, the huge anti-war demonstrations of the late 1960s, the enormous rock festivals of the 1970s, and the crowd scenes in Richard Attenborough's film *Gandhi* or the novels of Emile Zola or Victor Hugo.

Crowd behaviour, in its full manifestation, can be difficult to research in the laboratory, though attempts have been made. For example, French (1944) locked his subjects in a room and then wafted smoke under the door while sounding the fire alarm. Ethics aside, the study was not very successful as an attempt to create panic in the laboratory: one group kicked open the door and knocked over the smoke generator, and another group calmly discussed the possibility that its reactions were being observed by the experimenters.

Early theories

One of the earliest theories of collective behaviour was proposed by LeBon (1908). LeBon, who lived in France during a period of great social turmoil, observed and read accounts of the great revolutionary crowds of the French Revolution of 1848 and the Paris Commune of 1871 – accounts such as those to be found in Zola's novels *Germinal* and *La Débacle*, and Hugo's *Les Misérables*. He was appalled by the 'primitive, base and ghastly' behaviour of the crowd, and the way in which people's civilised conscious personality seemed to vanish and be replaced by savage, animal instincts. He believed that:

> by the mere fact that he forms part of an organised crowd, a man descends several rungs in the ladder of civilisation. Isolated, he may be a cultivated individual; in a crowd he is a barbarian – that is, a creature acting by instinct. (1908, p. 12)

LeBon believed that crowds produce primitive and homogeneous behaviour because (see Figure 10.10):

1. Members are anonymous and thus lose personal responsibility for their actions.
2. Ideas and sentiments spread rapidly and unpredictably through a process of contagion.
3. Unconscious antisocial motives ('ancestral savagery') are released through suggestion (a process akin to hypnosis).

LeBon is still important (see Apfelbaum and McGuire 1986; Hogg and Abrams 1988; Reicher 1987) mainly due to the enormous influence of his perspective, in which crowd behaviour is considered to be pathological/abnormal, on later theories of collective behaviour (for example, Freud 1921; McDougall 1920; Zimbardo 1970). Freud, for example, argued that the crowd 'unlocks' the unconscious. Society's moral standards maintain civilised behaviour because they are installed in the human psyche as the super-ego. However, in crowds, the super-ego is supplanted by the leader of the crowd who now acts as the hypnotist who controls unconscious and uncivilised id-impulses. Crowd leaders have this effect because of a deep and primitive instinct in all of us to regress, in crowds, to the 'primal horde' – the original, brutal human group at the dawn of existence. Civilisation is able to evolve and thrive only to the extent that the leader of the primal horde, the 'primal father', is rebelled against. This analysis has been used to explain how 'Reverend' Jim Jones had such enormous power over his cult followers that

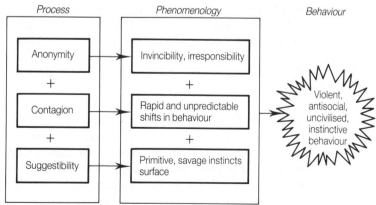

FIGURE 10.10 *LeBon's model of the crowd. (Source: adapted from Hogg 1992.)*

over nine hundred of them participated in collective suicide – the massacre at Jonestown in Guyana in 1978 (Ulman and Abse 1983).

Another important early theorist is McDougall (1920). He characterised the crowd as:

> excessively emotional, impulsive, violent, fickle, inconsistent, irresolute and extreme in action, displaying only the coarser emotions and the less refined sentiments; extremely suggestible, careless in deliberation, hasty in judgement, incapable of any but the simpler and imperfect forms of reasoning, easily swayed and led, lacking in self-consciousness, devoid of self-respect and of a sense of responsibility, and apt to be carried away by the consciousness of its own force, so that it tends to produce all the manifestations we have learnt to expect of any irresponsible and absolute power. (1920, p. 45)

McDougall believed that the most widespread instinctive emotions are the simple primitive ones (for example, fear, anger), and that therefore these would be the most common and widely shared emotions in any human aggregate. More complex emotions would be rare and less widely shared. Stimuli eliciting the primitive simple emotions would therefore cause a strong consensual reaction, while those eliciting more complex emotions would not. Primary emotions spread and strengthen very rapidly in a crowd as each member's expression of the emotion acts as a further stimulus to others – a snowball effect dubbed 'primitive sympathy'. This effect is not easily modulated, as individuals feel depersonalised and have a lowered sense of personal responsibility.

Deindividuation and self-awareness

▶ Deindividuation

More recent explanations of collective behaviour discard some of the specifics of earlier approaches (for example, the emphasis on instinctive emotions, the psychodynamic framework), but retain the overall perspective. People usually refrain from exercising their basically impulsive, aggressive and selfish nature because of their identifiability as unique individuals in societies that have strong norms against 'uncivilised' conduct. In crowds these restraints are relaxed and we can revert to type and embark upon an orgy of aggressive, selfish, antisocial behaviour. The mediating mechanism is *deindividuation*.

The term deindividuation, coined by Festinger *et al.* (1952), originates in Jung's definition of 'individuation' as 'a process of differentiation, having for its goal the development of the individual personality' (Jung 1946, p. 561). It was Zimbardo (1970), who developed the concept most fully. He believed that being in a large group provides people with a cloak of anonymity that diffuses personal responsibility for the consequences of one's actions. This leads to a loss of identity and a reduced concern for social evaluation: that is, a state of deindividuation that causes behaviour to become impulsive, irrational, regressive and disinhibited because it is not under the usual social and personal controls.

Research on deindividuation has tended to focus on the effects of anonymity on behaviour in groups. Festinger *et al.* (1952) found that subjects dressed in grey laboratory coats and seated in a poorly lit room for a group discussion of their parents made more negative comments about their parents than did subjects in a control condition (see also Cannavale *et al.* 1970). Similarly, subjects dressed in laboratory coats used more obscene language when discussing erotic literature than did more easily identifiable individuals (Singer *et al.* 1965). Zimbardo (1970) conducted a series of experiments in which subjects were deindividuated by wearing cloaks and hoods (reminiscent of the Ku Klux Klan). In one such experiment deindividuated female students gave electric shocks to a female confederate in a paired associate learning task, that were twice the duration of those given by conventionally dressed subjects. In another classic study, in which a simulated prison was constructed in the basement of the psychology department of Stanford University, Zimbardo (Zimbardo *et al.* 1982 – see Chapter 7) found that student subjects who were deindividuated by being dressed as guards were extremely brutal to other students who were deindividuated as prisoners. There is also evidence that people are more willing to lynch someone (Mullen 1986) or bait a disturbed person to jump from a building if it is dark, and if they are in a larger group (Mann 1981 – see Chapter 11).

Finally, Diener *et al.* (1976) conducted a clever study which took advantage of halloween, when the streets are filled with children, disguised and thus anonymous, who are trick-or-treating. The researchers observed the behaviour of 1,352 children, alone or in groups, who approached twenty-seven focal homes in Seattle where they were warmly invited in and told to 'take *one* of the candies' on a table. Half the children were first asked their names and where they lived, to reduce deindividuation. Groups and deindividuated children were more than twice as likely to take extra candy: the transgression rate varied from 8 per cent of individuated individuals to 80 per cent of deindividuated groups.

Although in general anonymity seems to increase the incidence of aggressive antisocial behaviour (Dipboye 1977) there are problematic findings. Zimbardo (1970) employed his deindividuation paradigm with Belgian soldiers, and found that they gave shorter duration electric shocks when dressed in cloaks and hoods. Zimbardo suggests this might be because the soldiers were an intact group (that is, already deindividuated), and the 'cloak and hood' procedure had the paradoxical effect of decreasing deindividuation. However, other studies have also found a reduction in aggression as a consequence of anonymity or group membership (Diener 1976). Johnson and Downing (1979) had subjects administer shocks to confederate 'learners' in a paired associate learning task. Subjects were deindividuated by either wearing a robe resembling a Ku Klux Klan outfit or a robe resembling a nurse's uniform – the experimenter highlighted the situational norms by explicitly commenting on the resemblance. Although all subjects wore the special clothing, half also wore a large badge displaying their name in order to individuate them (reduce deindividuation). Deindividuation failed to increase aggression, even among those dressed as Ku Klux Klan members (see Figure 10.11). Those dressed as nurses were significantly less aggressive than those dressed as Ku Klux Klan members, and deindividuated nurses were the least aggressive of all. These studies tell us two important things:

1. Aggression and antisocial behaviour are not automatic and inevitable consequences of anonymity.
2. Normative expectations surrounding situations of deindividuation may influence behaviour.

Regarding this second point, Jahoda (1982) has noted the similarity between Zimbardo's method of deindividuation (that is, hood and robe), and the wearing of the *chadoor*, full-length veil, by women in certain Islamic countries. Far from setting free antisocial impulses, the chadoor very precisely specifies one's social obligations.

More recently, Diener (1980) has assigned Duval and Wicklund's (1972) notion of objective self-awareness (awareness of oneself as an object of attention) a central role in the deindividuation process:

> A deindividuated person is prevented by situational factors present in a group from becoming self-aware. Deindividuated persons are blocked from awareness of themselves as separate individuals and from monitoring their own behaviour. (Diener 1980, p. 210)

Factors present in crowds reduce self-awareness and create a psychological

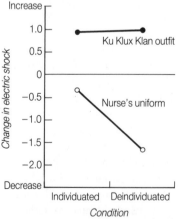

FIGURE 10.11 *Administration of electric shocks as a function deindividuation and type of uniform. (Source: based on data from Johnson and Downing 1979.)*

state of deindividuation that has specific consequences for behaviour (Figure 10.12). Although these consequences do not inevitably include aggression, they tend to facilitate the emergence of antisocial behaviour. In support of Diener's model, Prentice-Dunn and Rogers (1982) found that subjects who were prevented from becoming self-aware, by being subjected to loud rock music in a darkened room while working on a collective task, subsequently administered more intense electric shocks to a 'learner' than did subjects who had been working individually in a quiet, well-illuminated room under instructions to concentrate on their own thoughts and feelings.

Another perspective on deindividuation distinguishes between public and private self-awareness (Carver and Scheier 1981; Scheier and Carver 1981). Reduced attention to one's private self (feelings, thoughts, attitudes and other private aspects of self) is equated with deindividuation, but does not necessarily produce antisocial behaviour unless the appropriate norms are in place (Figure 10.13). It is reduced attention to one's public self (how one wishes others to view one's conduct) that causes behaviour to be independent of social norms and thus become antisocial.

Emergent norm theory

▶ Emergent norm theory

Emergent norm theory takes a very different approach from the explanation of collective behaviour (R. Turner 1974; Turner and Killian 1957). Rather than treating collective behaviour as pathological or instinctual behaviour, it focuses

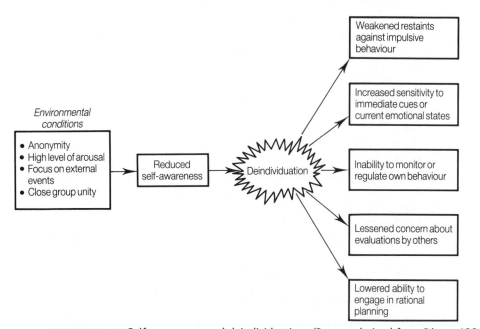

FIGURE 10.12 *Self-awareness and deindividuation. (Source: derived from Diener 1980.)*

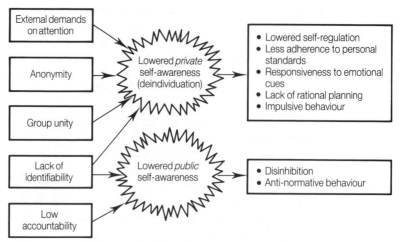

FIGURE 10.13 *Private and public self-awareness and deindividuation. (Source: adapted from Hogg and Abrams 1988.)*

on collective action as norm-governed behaviour, much like any other group behaviour. Turner believes that what is distinct about the crowd is that it has no formal organisation or tradition of established norms to regulate behaviour, and so the problem of explaining crowd behaviour is to explain how a norm emerges from within the crowd (hence, 'emergent norm theory') – see Figure 10.14. People in a crowd find themselves together under circumstances in which there are no clear norms to indicate how to behave. Their attention is attracted by distinctive behaviours (or the behaviour of distinctive individuals). These behaviours imply a norm and consequently there is pressure against non-conformity. Inaction on the part of the majority is interpreted as tacit confirmation of the norm, which consequently amplifies pressures against non-conformity.

By focusing on norms, emergent norm theory acknowledges that members of a crowd may communicate with one another in the elaboration of appropriate norms of action. However, the general nature of crowd behaviour is influenced by the role of distinctive behaviours, which are presumably behaviours that are relatively rare in most people's daily lives, for instance antisocial behaviours. Two other critical observations have been made. Diener (1980) correctly observes that a norm-regulated crowd would have to be a self-aware crowd (there is no need for people to comply with norms unless they are identifiable and thus individuated and self-aware), and yet evidence indicates that self-awareness is very low in crowds. Indeed, an experiment by Mann and his associates (1982) supports Diener's view: irrespective of whether a norm of leniency or aggressiveness had been established by a confederate, subjects were more aggressive when anonymous than when identifiable. However, anonymous subjects were more aggressive when the aggressive norm was in

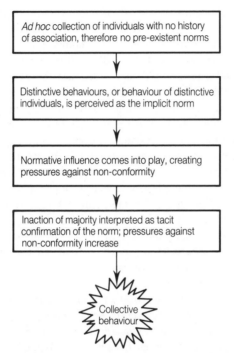

FIGURE 10.14 *Emergent norm theory. (Source: derived from Turner and Killian 1957.)*

place. The second critical observation comes from Reicher (1982, 1987) who reminds us that crowds rarely come together in a normative vacuum. More often than not, members of a crowd congregate for a specific purpose and thus bring with them a clear set of shared norms to regulate their behaviour as members of a specific group, for example a crowd of people welcoming the Queen, watching a football match, demonstrating outside parliament or protesting on campus. The lack of tradition of established norms that Turner refers to may be more myth than reality. There is a logic to the crowd, Reicher argues, that is not adequately captured by emergent norm theory.

Social identity theory

An important feature of crowd behaviour that is usually ignored is that it is actually very much an *intergroup* phenomenon (Reicher and Potter 1985). Many crowd instances involve, for example, a direct collective confrontation between police and rioters, or rival gangs or team supporters, and even where no direct confrontation occurs there is symbolic confrontation in that the crowd event symbolises a confrontation between, for instance, the crowd (or the wider group it represents) and the state. A second point is that far from losing identity, people in the crowd actually assume the identity provided by the crowd – there is a change from idiosyncratic personal identity to shared social identity as a crowd member. These points have been made by Reicher (1982, 1984, 1987), who applies social identity theory (Hogg and Abrams 1988; Tajfel and Turner 1979; Turner 1982 – see above) and self-categorisation theory (Turner 1985; Turner *et al.* 1987 – see above) to collective behaviour.

Individuals come together, or find themselves together, as members of a specific social group for a specific purpose (for example, conservationists protesting environmental destruction). There is a high degree of shared social identity that promotes social categorisation of self and others in terms of that group membership. It is this wider social identity that provides the limits for crowd behaviour. For example, for certain groups violence may be legitimate (for example, neo-Nazi groups in Germany) while for others it may not (for example, supporters at a cricket match). While these general group norms provide the limits for acceptable crowd behaviour, there are often few norms to indicate how to behave in the specific context of the crowd event. Crowd members look to the identity-consistent behaviour of others, usually central group members, for guidance. Self-categorisation produces conformity to these context-specific norms of conduct. This explains why different groups in a crowd event often behave differently. For example, the police act in one way while the protesters act in a different way because, despite being exposed to the same environmental stimuli, their behaviours are being controlled by different group memberships.

This analysis does seem to be consistent with what actually goes on in the crowd. For example, Fogelson's (1970) analysis of American race riots of the 1960s showed that one noteworthy feature was that the violence was not arbitrary and without direction, and Milgram and Toch (1969) report accounts from participants in the Watts riot in which a sense of positive social identity is strongly emphasised. Reicher (1984; Reicher and Potter 1985) uses his analysis to explain a specific riot which occurred in the spring of 1980 in the St Pauls district of Bristol (this was a forerunner of subsequent widespread rioting in other cities in Britain during the early 1980s). Three important points that emerged from this analysis were:

1. The violence, burning and looting were not unconstrained – the crowd was 'orderly' and the rioters were selective. Aggression was directed only at symbols of the state – the bank, the police, and entrepreneurial merchants in the community.
2. The crowd remained within the bounds of its own community – St Pauls.
3. During, and as a consequence of, the riot, rioters felt a strong sense of positive social identity as members of the St Pauls community.

All this makes sense when it is recognised that the riot was an anti-government protest on the part of the St Pauls community, an economically deprived area of Bristol with very high unemployment during a time of severe national unemployment.

IMPROVING INTERGROUP RELATIONS

Different theories of prejudice and intergroup behaviour spawn different emphases in the explanation of prejudice and conflict reduction. From the perspective of personality theories (for example, authoritarian personality, dogmatism – Chapter 9), prejudice reduction is a matter of changing the personality of the prejudiced person. More precisely, it would involve ensuring that particular parental strategies of childrearing were avoided in order to prevent the creation of bigoted people. From the perspective of frustration-aggression theory (Chapter 9) or relative deprivation theory (this chapter), prejudice and intergroup conflict can be minimised by preventing frustration, lowering people's expectations, distracting people from realising that they are frustrated, providing people with harmless (non-social) activities through which to vent their frustration, or ensuring that aggressive associations are minimised among frustrated people. For realistic conflict theory (this chapter) it is the existence of superordinate goals and co-operation for their achievement that gradually reduces intergroup hostility and conflict. The avoidance of mutually exclusive goals would also help. Finally, from the perspective of social identity theory (this chapter) prejudice and overt conflict will wane to the extent that intergroup stereotypes become less derogatory and polarised and there exist mutually legitimised non-violent forms of intergroup competition.

Propaganda and education

Propaganda messages, in the form of official exhortations that people should not be prejudiced, are usually formulated with reference to some absolute standard of morality (for example, humanism). This may be effective for those people who subscribe to the standard of morality that is being invoked. It may also suppress more extreme forms of discrimination because it communicates social disapproval of discrimination.

Since prejudice is at least partly based in ignorance, education, particularly formal education of children, may reduce bigotry. This can involve teaching children about the moral implications of discrimination, or teaching them facts about different groups. One problem with this strategy is that formal education will only have marginal impact if children are massively exposed to prejudice outside the classroom, for example bigoted parents, chauvinistic advertising and the material consequences of discrimination.

Another educational strategy which may be more effective is to allow children to experience being a victim of prejudice. Jane Elliot, an Iowa schoolteacher, made a short film called *The Eye of the Storm* of a classroom demonstration in which she divided her class of very young children into those with blue and those with brown eyes. For one day the 'brown eyes', and then for one day the 'blue eyes', were assigned inferior status – they were ridiculed, denied privileges, accused of being dull, lazy and sloppy, and made to wear a special collar. It was hoped that the experience would be unpleasant enough to make the children think twice about being prejudiced against others.

One problem about prejudice is that it is *mindless*, a metaphorical kneejerk reaction to others as stereotypes. Perhaps if people, particularly when they are children, are taught to be mindful of others – to think about others not as stereotypes but as complex whole individuals – then stereotypic reactions would be reduced. Langer *et al.* (1985) explored this idea in the context of young children's attitudes towards the handicapped. They found a definite improvement in attitudes towards and treatment of handicapped children by children who had been trained to be *mindful* of others.

Intergroup contact

A core feature of prejudice and conflict is the existence of unfavourable stereotypic outgroup attitudes. Such attitudes are enshrined in widespread social ideologies and are maintained by lack of access to information which may disconfirm or improve negative attitudes. In most cases, such isolation is reinforced by real physical isolation of different groups from one another. In other words, there is simply a chronic lack of intergroup contact and little opportunity to meet real members of the outgroup. The groups are kept apart by educational, occupational, cultural and material differences, as well as by intergroup fear and anxiety (Stephan and Stephan 1985). It is this state of affairs which spawns the popular view that if there was greater intergroup contact then social harmony would prevail.

The contact hypothesis. Japanese tourists are a common sight at scenic locations. Contact between people from different cultures can sometimes improve intergroup relations. However, the circumstances of the contact will permit generalisation of positive attitudes to the group only if the range of contexts is wide. (Source: Andrew Lukey.)

▶ Contact hypothesis   This view, called the *contact hypothesis*, was proposed scientifically in 1954 by Allport, in the same year as the United States Supreme Court paved the way for the racial desegregation of the American education system. Contact is only likely to be effective under certain conditions (Allport 1954):

1. It should be prolonged and involve co-operative activity rather than casual and purposeless interaction. It was precisely this sort of contact that improved relations in Sherif's (1966) summer camp studies.
2. It should occur within the framework of official and institutional support for integration. Although legislation against discrimination or for equal opportunities will not in itself abolish prejudice, it will provide a social climate which is conducive to the emergence of more tolerant social practices.
3. It should involve people (or groups) of equal social status. Unequal status contact is more likely to confirm stereotypes and thus entrench prejudices.

Cumulative research over the years confirms that contact under these sorts of conditions does improve intergroup relations (Amir 1976). For instance, a recent review of research on intergenerational contact also generally supports this conclusion (Fox and Giles 1993).

Research carried out in New Zealand by Vaughan (1978a,b) has bearing on the role of intergroup contact and, because of its time span of ten years, is an illustration of the power of a social change belief system, discussed earlier in this chapter. The groups studied were the Maori, New Zealand's indigenous Polynesian people who make up about 10 per cent of the population and the Pakeha (that is, caucasian). Ingroup (ethnic) preferences were studied among children, aged 6–12 years, who came from either urban or rural backgrounds. Data were collected at various times during the 1960s, a period of considerable social change in many western countries. The results shown in Figure 10.15 define ingroup preference above, and outgroup preference below, the 50 per cent line. Urban Pakeha preferred their own group, but were less ethnocentric than rural Pakeha, and rural Maori showed more marked outgroup preference than urban Maori. The most notable change was that between 1961 and 1971 urban Maori, with a trend away from the outgroup towards the ingroup. This coincided with a rise in New Zealand of a Brown (Maori) Power movement modelled on the American Black Power movement of the 1960s. Intergroup perceptions may be less ethnocentric in the city for a number of reasons, including the nature of interethnic contact. Maori who moved to the city were often cut off from the traditional Polynesian extended family (and from other aspects of Maori culture), and found they had to compete with Pakeha for work. There was a gradual realignment of ethnic power relations and greater possibility of more equal status interethnic contact. This is likely to have contributed to some extent to reduced prejudice on the part of Pakeha and elevated ethnic pride on the part of Maori.

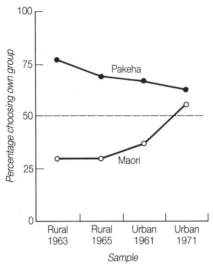

FIGURE 10.15 *Intergroup choices among Pakeha (caucasian) and Maori children as a function of social change (time and nature of intergroup contact). (Source: based on Vaughan 1978b.)*

There are, however, three issues concerning precisely how contact has its effect (Hewstone and Brown 1986; Johnston and Hewstone 1990; Miller and Brewer 1984). These are looked at next.

Similarity

It has long been believed that prejudice is based in ignorance and the perception of irreconcilable intergroup differences (Pettigrew 1971; Stephan and Stephan 1984). Contact causes people to recognise that they are in fact a great deal more similar than they had thought, and hence get to like one another (Byrne 1971). There are some problems with this perspective:

1. Because groups are often very different indeed, contact is likely to bring to light more profound or more widespread differences, and hence reduce liking further and produce a deterioration in intergroup attitudes (for example, Bochner 1982).
2. Since groups are actually so different, it may be misleading to promulgate the view that they are similar – it will establish false positive expectations that are disconfirmed by contact.
3. Research indicates that intergroup attitudes are not merely a matter of ignorance or unfamiliarity, rather they reflect real conflict of interest between groups, and are often maintained by the very existence of social categories. New knowledge made available by contact is unlikely to change attitudes.

Generalisation

Contact between representatives of different groups is supposed to improve attitudes towards the group as a whole, not just the specific outgroup members involved in the encounter. Weber and Crocker (1983) suggested three models of how this might happen:

1. Bookkeeping – the accumulation of favourable information about an outgroup gradually improves the stereotype.
2. Conversion – dramatically counter-stereotypic information about an outgroup causes a sudden change in attitudes.
3. Subtyping – stereotype-inconsistent information produces a subtype so that the outgroup stereotype becomes more complex but the superordinate category remains unchanged.

In general, research indicates that contact improves attitudes towards the participants, but it does not generalise to the group as a whole (Amir 1976; Cook 1978). One explanation is that most intergroup contact is actually *interpersonal* contact, i.e. contact between individuals as individuals, not group members. There is no good reason why an attitude towards one person should generalise to other people who are not categorically related. This raises an interesting paradox: perhaps intergroup contact is more likely to generalise if people's group affiliations are made *more* not less salient during contact. There is some support for this idea. Wilder (1984) had subjects from rival colleges come into contact over a co-operative task in which the outgroup person, who was either highly typical or highly atypical of that college, behaved in a pleasant or unpleasant manner. The subjects evaluated the other college as a whole after the contact. Figure 10.16 shows that relative to a no-contact control, it was only where contact was both pleasant and with a typical outgroup member that there was generalised improvement of attitude (see also Rothbart and John 1985; Weber and Crocker 1983).

Miller and co-workers (1985) have a different perspective. They argue that contact which draws attention to people's group affiliations will rapidly degenerate into conflict, and thus a deterioration of generalised attitudes. Instead, they recommend interpersonal encounters that stress socio-emotional aspects and avoid group- or task-related aspects of the encounter. This does seem to work, but as yet the idea has been tested only in abstract experimental settings where intergroup relations lack the powerful emotions and personal investments associated with 'real' intergroup relations. Where real intergroup conflict exists (for example, between Catholics and Protestants in Northern Ireland) it may be almost impossible to distract people from their group affiliations.

Contact policy in multicultural contexts

Initially, it might seem that the most non-discriminatory and unprejudiced way to approach interethnic relations is simply to be 'colour-blind': that is, to ignore completely group differences (Berry 1984; Schofield 1986). This is a

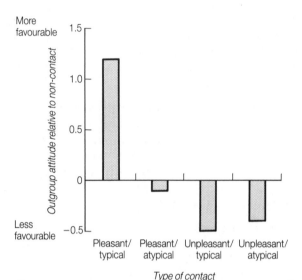

FIGURE 10.16 *Outgroup attitude as a function of pleasantness of contact and outgroup typicality of target. (Source: based on data from Wilder 1984.)*

melting pot policy where all groups are ostensibly treated as equal. There are at least three problems with this approach:

1. It ignores the fact that discrimination has disadvantaged certain groups (for example, regarding education or health) and that unless positive steps are taken to rectify the problem the disadvantage will simply persist.
2. It ignores the reality of ethnic/cultural differences (for example, Muslim dress code for women).
3. The melting pot is not really a melting pot at all, but rather a 'dissolving' pot, where ethnic minorities are dissolved to be assimilated by the dominant social group, thus minority groups are stripped of their cultural heritage and cease to exist.

The alternative approach is pluralism or multiculturalism – an approach which draws attention and responds to the reality of group differences in an attempt to improve negative attitudes and redress disadvantage, at the same time as the cultural integrity of different groups is preserved. This approach aims to achieve a multicultural society in which intergroup relations among the constituent groups is harmonious.

Superordinate goals

In his summer camp studies, Sherif (1966) managed to improve intergroup relations between the warring factions by allowing them to co-operate in order to achieve a number of superordinate goals (shared goals that were unachievable by either group alone). The effectiveness of providing a superordinate goal has been confirmed by other studies (Brown and Abrams 1986; Worchel 1979; Ryen and Kahn 1975; Turner 1981b). One particularly effective superordinate goal is resistance against a shared threat from a common enemy (Dion 1979; Wilder and Shapiro 1984). This is the basis of alliances that can temporarily improve relations between erstwhile opponents: for example, for almost forty-five years the existence of the Soviet Union provided a common foe to unite western nations.

However, there is an important qualification: superordinate goals do not reduce intergroup conflict if the groups fail to achieve the goal. For example, Worchel and co-workers (1977) created competitive, co-operative or independent relations between two groups and then provided a superordinate goal which the groups either failed or succeeded to achieve. The superordinate goal improved intergroup relations in all cases except where previously competitive groups failed to achieve the goal. In this condition relations actually deteriorated. Unsuccessful intergroup co-operation to achieve a superordinate goal appears to worsen intergroup relations only when the failure can be attributed, rightly or wrongly, to the actions of the outgroup (Worchel and Novell 1980). Where there is sufficient external justification, and the outgroup is not blamed, there is the more usual improvement in intergroup relations. For example, the 1982 Falklands conflict provided a superordinate goal to reduce factional conflict within Argentina. The co-operative exercise failed (Argentina lost the war), and, because the actions of the junta could easily be blamed, there was renewed factional conflict that almost immediately overthrew the junta (Latin American Bureau 1982).

There is another pitfall of superordinate goals. Intense or prolonged co-operation to achieve a shared goal can tend gradually to blur intergroup boundaries (Gaertner *et al.* 1989). Although this may seem to be an ideal solution to intergroup conflict, it can backfire. Although the groups may have superordinate goals they may also wish to maintain their individual identities and so resist the perceived threat of becoming a single entity. New conflicts can thus arise to maintain intergroup distinctiveness. This effect has been observed in a chemical plant (Blake *et al.* 1964), an engineering factory (Brown 1978), and the laboratory (Brown and Wade 1987; Deschamps and Brown 1983). It will be interesting to see if the current pressures in Europe for international co-operation in the service of superordinate economic goals (the European Union) increase international conflict on other dimensions to maintain national distinctiveness.

Communication

Groups in conflict can try to improve intergroup relations by directly communicating about the conflict and attempting to resolve it. This can be attempted through bargaining, mediation or arbitration.

Bargaining

▶ Bargaining

Intergroup negotiations are generally between representatives of the opposing groups: for example, union and management may try to resolve disputes by direct negotiation between representatives. One of the most significant intergroup negotiations of this century was the 1945 meeting in Yalta in the Crimea between Stalin, Churchill and Roosevelt, as representatives of the victorious allies of the Second World War: the Soviet Union, Britain and the United States. The negotiation of international differences at that meeting has determined the nature of the world to the present day. Social psychological research indicates that when people are *bargaining* on behalf of social groups to which they belong they tend to bargain much more fiercely and less compromisingly than if they were simply bargaining for themselves (Benton and Druckman 1974; Breaugh and Klimoski 1981). The effect is enhanced when negotiators are aware that they are being observed by their constituents, either directly or through the media (Carnevale *et al.* 1979).

This rather 'bullish' strategy of relative intransigence is actually less likely to secure a satisfactory compromise than a more interpersonal orientation in which both parties make reciprocal concessions (Esser and Komorita 1975; Komorita and Esser 1975). Direct negotiation between group representatives is therefore quite likely to reach an impasse in which neither group feels it can compromise without losing face.

Morley and Stephenson (1977) have explored the interplay of intergroup and interpersonal factors in bargaining. They demonstrate that bargaining often follows a sequence of stages. The first stage is an intergroup one in which representatives act very much in terms of group memberships and assess each group's power and the strength of each group's case. The second stage is more interpersonal, with individuals trying to establish harmonious interpersonal relations with one another in order to be able more easily to solve problems. The final stage is again more intergroup, with negotiators making sure that the final decision is consistent with the historical aims of their own group. Close interpersonal relations, which are encouraged by more informal bargaining procedures and contexts, can facilitate negotiation. However, close interpersonal relations also have a drawback – the group as a whole can become fearful of a 'sell out' and can resort or return to more confrontational intergroup behaviours which hinder the negotiation process.

There is a potentially important limitation of much social psychological research on bargaining – the wider intergroup context is often neglected as researchers focus only on the specific bargaining event as a form of social change (Morley *et al.* 1988). In reality, bargaining is often a way to maintain the status quo. Groups in conflict isolate from the wider context of intergroup relations a specific and circumscribed point of disagreement – one that can be solved. The solution of the specific problem then allows broader intergroup issues to remain unchanged.

Mediation

▶ Mediation

To break the deadlock, a third party can be brought in to *mediate* between the groups (Pruitt 1981). To be effective, mediators should have power, must be seen by both groups to be impartial (Lim and Carnevale 1990), and the groups should already be fairly close in their positions (Rubin 1980). Biased mediators are ineffective because they are not trusted, and weak mediators are ineffective because there is little pressure for intransigent groups to be reasonable.

Although mediators have no power to impose a settlement, they can help in several important ways:

1. They are able to *reduce emotional heat* associated with deadlock (Tetlock 1988).
2. They can help *reduce misperceptions*, encourage understanding and establish trust.
3. They can propose *novel compromises* that allow both groups to appear to win, that is change a zero-sum conflict (one in which one group's gains are precisely the other group's losses, the more one gains the more the other loses) into a non-zero-sum conflict (that is, both groups can gain).
4. They can help both parties make a *graceful retreat*, without losing face, from untenable positions.
5. They can *inhibit unreasonable claims* and behaviours by threatening to expose publicly the group as being unreasonable.
6. They can *reduce intragroup conflict* and thus help a group clarify its consensual position.

Recent history provides instances of effective mediation. For example, Henry Kissinger's shuttle diplomacy of the mid-1970s, which involved meeting separately with each side over a period of two years after the 1973 Arab–Israeli conflict, produced a number of significant agreements between Israel and its Arab neighbours (Pruitt 1981). In the late 1970s, using a slightly different strategy, Jimmy Carter secluded Egypt's President Sadat and Israel's Prime Minister Begin at Camp David in the United States, and after thirteen days an agreement was reached that ended a state of war that had existed between Israel and Egypt since 1948.

Arbitration

▶ Arbitration

Many intergroup conflicts are so intractable, the underlying interests so divergent, that mediation is ineffective. The last resort is *arbitration*, in which the mediator or some other third party is invited to impose a mutually binding settlement. Research shows that arbitration really is the very last resort for conflict resolution (McGillicuddy *et al.* 1987). The prospect of arbitration can backfire because both groups adopt outrageous final positions in the hope that arbitration will produce a more favourable compromise (Pruitt 1986). One way to combat this is through *final-offer arbitration*, where the third party chooses one of the final offers. This tends to encourage more reasonable final positions.

Conciliation

▶ Conciliation

Although direct communication may help improve intergroup relations, tensions and suspicions often run so high that direct communication is all but impossible. Instead, conflicting groups threaten, coerce or retaliate against one another, and if this behaviour is reciprocated there is an escalation of the conflict. For example, during the Second World War Germany believed it could move Britain to surrender by bombing its cities, and the Allies believed they could break Germany's will by bombing their cities. Similarly, Japan believed it could dissuade the United States from interfering in its imperial expansion in Asia by bombing Pearl Harbor, and the United States believed it could bring North Vietnam to the negotiation table by sustained bombing of cities and villages. There are uncountable examples of the terrible consequences of threat, coercion and retaliation. Can this cycle be broken by one group adopting an unconditionally co-operative strategy in the hope that the other group will reciprocate? Laboratory research suggests not: unilateral unconditional co-operation simply invites retaliation and exploitation (Shure *et al.* 1965).

A more effective alternative, that is both *conciliatory* (that is, not retaliatory) and strong enough to discourage exploitation, has been suggested by Osgood (1962). Called 'graduated and reciprocated initiatives in tension-reduction' (with the acronym GRIT), it invokes social psychological principles to do with the norm of reciprocity and the attribution of motives. GRIT involves at least two stages:

1. One party announces its conciliatory intent (allowing a clear attribution of non-devious motive), clearly specifies a small concession it is about to make (activates reciprocity norm) and invites its opponent to do likewise.
2. The initiator makes the concession exactly as announced, and in a publicly verifiable manner. There is now very strong pressure on the other group to reciprocate.

Laboratory research provides evidence for the effectiveness of this procedure. For example, a *tit-for-tat* strategy which begins with one co-operative act and proceeds by matching the other party's last response is both conciliatory and strong, and can improve interparty relations (Axelrod and Dion 1988). Direct laboratory tests of GRIT by Linskold and his colleagues (for example, Linskold 1978; Linskold and Han 1988) confirm that announcement of co-operative intent boosts co-operation, repeated conciliatory acts breed trust, and maintenance of power equality protects against exploitation. GRIT-type strategies have been used effectively from time to time in international relations: for example, between the Soviet Union and the United States during the Berlin Crisis of the early 1960s, and between Israel and Egypt on a number of occasions.

SUMMARY

♦ Intergroup behaviour can be defined as any behaviour that is influenced by group members' perceptions of an outgroup.

♦ Group members may engage in collective protest to the extent that they subjectively feel deprived as a group relative to their aspirations or to other groups.

♦ Competition for scarce resources tends to produce intergroup conflict. Co-operation to achieve a shared goal reduces conflict.

♦ Social categorisation may be the only necessary precondition for being a group and engaging in intergroup behaviour – provided people identify with the category.

♦ Self-categorisation is the process responsible for psychologically identifying with a group and behaving as a group member (for example, conformity, stereotyping, ethnocentrism, ingroup solidarity). Social comparison and the need for self-esteem motivate groups to compete in different ways (depending on the nature of intergroup relations) for relatively positive social identity.

♦ Crowd behaviour may not represent a loss of identity and regression to primitive antisocial instincts. Instead, it may be group behaviour which is governed by local contextual norms that are framed by a wider social identity.

♦ Prejudice, discrimination and intergroup conflict are very difficult to reduce. Education, propaganda and shared goals, together may help, but simply bringing groups into contact with one another is unlikely to be very effective. Other strategies can include bargaining, mediation, arbitration and conciliation.

FURTHER READING

Brown, R. J. (1988). *Group Processes: Dynamics Within and Between Groups*. Oxford: Blackwell.

Hogg, M. A. and Abrams, D. (1988). *Social Identifications: A Social Psychology of Intergroup Relations and Group Processes*. London: Routledge.

▶ KEY TERMS

accentuation effect
arbitration
authoritarian personality
bargaining
cognitive alternatives

collective behaviour
commons dilemma
conciliation
contact hypothesis
deindividuation

depersonalisation
egoistic relative deprivation
emergent norm theory
ethnocentrism
fraternalistic relative deprivation
free-rider effect
frustration-aggression hypothesis
illusory correlation
ingroup favouritism
intergroup behaviour
intergroup differentiation
J-curve
mediation
minimal group paradigm
optimal distinctiveness
positive self-esteem

prisoner's dilemma
prototype
realistic conflict theory
reductionism
relative deprivation
relative homogeneity effect
self-categorisation theory
social categorisation
social change belief system
social competition
social creativity
social identity
social identity theory
social mobility belief system
stereotypes
superordinate goal

11 Aggression
··················

FOCUS QUESTIONS

♦ Are we born with a tendency to want to harm others?

♦ If it is learned, is it not an inevitable part of the way people live, and impossible to control?

♦ Some people say you should not let feelings like that remain bottled up. You should release them, at least part of the time, should you not?

♦ Why does so much violence occur in intimate relationships?

♦ Is it true that violence in films and on television can really affect the behaviour of children; and do 'blue' movies make men violent towards women?

AGGRESSION IN OUR LIVES

Aggression and violence dominate the lives of most of us (see Table 11.1). Some of us are victims of physical assault, abuse, rape and verbal aggression by strangers, 'friends', partners, relatives or family. Many of us witness aggression from time to time or on a regular basis, and almost all of us regularly see evidence and symbols of aggressive acts or aggressive people: graffiti, vandalism, violent arguments, weapons, belligerent dress. All of us are continually bombarded by reports of aggression in newspapers, magazines and on television: rapes, muggings, child abuse, assaults, robberies, wars and gang violence. In most cases the victims of aggression are those who in a particular context have less power or are disadvantaged: women, the very young, the old, the sick and people from different ethnolinguistic backgrounds. Most of us are aggressive from time to time, and some find pleasure in 'playing' aggressive games: shooting, hunting, fighting, video games. It is not surprising, then, that virtually all of us feel our behaviour is constrained in various ways by aggression: we are frightened to walk in certain areas at certain times, to visit certain places or to engage in certain activities. Jones and colleagues (1994) report statistics from a survey of ten thousand women in the UK that showed that 1 in 5 (20 per cent) felt 'very unsafe' when walking out at night, although

TABLE 11.1 Percentage of people reporting being victims of violent crime (burglary and assault) in the United States and selected European countries in 1988

Burglary		Assault	
USA	3.8	USA	3.0
France	2.4	Netherlands	2.0
Netherlands	2.4	W. Germany	1.5
Belgium	2.3	Norway	1.4
UK	2.1	France	1.2
Spain	1.7	Spain	1.2
W. Germany	1.3	Switzerland	0.9
Switzerland	1.0	Belgium	0.7
Norway	0.8	UK	0.6

Source: Jones *et al.* 1994.

in fact fewer than 1 in 150 (0.7 per cent) reported actually having been attacked in the last year.

▶ Homicide

Aggression is part of the human condition, but many people feel that the world is each year becoming a more aggressive place. It is difficult to assess the accuracy of an observation such as this. There is little doubt that much of the feeling that aggression and violence are on the increase can be attributed to the fact that more people are more frequently exposed to a greater number of more vivid media reports of violence. Aggression is simply more salient (see Chapter 2). However, crime statistics from various countries do indicate that *homicide* and other violent crimes may be on the increase. This is particularly the case in the United States, but even in New Zealand proven violent offences (murder, manslaughter, assault, rape/attempted rape) per head of population increased over the twenty-five years between 1960 and 1985 by a massive 593 per cent (Roper Report 1987). This may actually be an under-estimation of violence since much domestic violence (assault, rape and incest) which may account for as much as 80 per cent of all violent offences remains unreported.

Jones *et al.* (1994) report some figures for the UK. Over the thirteen years from 1979 to 1992 there has been a 120 per cent increase in the number of reported crimes – a figure which will double again by 2004. The most marked increase seems to be in violent and aggressive crimes. From 1991 to 1992, violent crimes (violence against the person, sexual offences, robbery) and criminal damage increased 7.2 per cent and 9.9 per cent, respectively, which is above the 6 per cent increase for all offences taken together.

For virtually all people, even if they are not so immediately touched, there are more indirect and insidious effects of violence at the societal level, which does appear to be escalating. Increasingly, we are changing aspects of our lifestyle because of fear of attack; more people carry weapons of some kind, take special precautions to avoid vulnerability or take lessons in self-defence.

The media report a constant, depressing barrage of violent behaviour at the interpersonal, societal and international level. At the individual level, it is likely that most of us experience feelings of aggression towards others quite regularly, although our response may stop short of acting out those feelings in aggressive behaviour.

It would, therefore, seem reasonable to conclude that aggression is both omnipresent and an integral part of human nature. Indeed, some theorists (for example, Ardrey 1961) have claimed that aggression is a basic human instinct, an innate fixed action pattern comparable with other animals (see also the bodily expression of emotions, Chapter 14), and therefore an inevitable and inescapable aspect of our lives. Other theorists are more optimistic about our ability to prevent and control violence and aggression, but nonetheless agree that aggression will continue to be an aspect of human behaviour. We will explore these different emphases concerning the origins of aggression in a later section. The challenges for psychologists are to identify the reasons that people aggress against others, and to find ways of reducing the harmful effects of aggression on both the victims and the aggressors. First, however, how are we to define 'aggression'?

DEFINITIONS AND MEASUREMENT

Defining aggression

Definitions are to an extent determined by theoretical perspectives, which are discussed later in this chapter. There is a special problem for social psychologists in defining aggression which arises within empirical research. The study of aggressive behaviour, whether in experimental or in naturalistic settings, requires some agreement in describing and explaining the phenomenon. Here we have a problem: although most of us might talk about aggression in everyday speech with a reasonably clear idea of what we mean, there is still no consensus within or across the sciences about its components. To an extent, what is considered to be aggressive is determined by the social and cultural standards of the perceiver. There are cultures and subcultures which regard violence as ordinary and even necessary, an analysis which Elkin (1961) has applied to Australian Aborigines. On the other hand, there are others who consider that most western societies are unacceptably violent.

There is no shortage of definitions of aggression in the social psychological literature. Here are a few:

1. Behaviour that results in personal injury or destruction of property (Bandura 1973).
2. Behaviour intended to harm another of the same species (Scherer *et al.* 1975).
3. Behaviour directed towards the goal of harming or injuring another living being who is motivated to avoid such treatment (Baron 1977).

4. The intentional infliction of some type of harm on others (Baron and Byrne 1991).

Conceptual differences between these definitions are apparent. In Baron's case, it is interesting to see how he has simplified his later definition. Now check the kinds of behaviour listed in Box 11.1. Should they be included as components in a satisfactory definition? Although most textbooks offer a

---

BOX 11.1 Applying two definitions of aggression

What is aggression?

Consider these two attempts fo define aggression:

1. **Behaviour that results in personal injury or destruction of property.** (Bandura 1973)
2. **The intentional infliction of some type of harm upon others.** (Baron 1977)

Now compare and evaluate these two definitions in relation to the following kinds of behaviour. Can you decide which ones are *necessary* components of aggression? Also, which ones in combination are *sufficient* to define aggression?

- Actual harm (though not unsuccessful hostility, even if it was intended).
- Physical injury (though not psychological harm, such as verbal abuse).
- Any kind of harm to a person (though not to an animal or to property).
- Harm to a person in a rule-governed context (such as a boxing match).
- Intention to do harm (though not careless or negligent harm, or accidental injury caused by self-serving behaviour).
- Belief by the victim that harm has occurred (though not sadomasochistic injury).
- Injury in the victim's 'best interests' (such as smacking a child).
- Harm to another (though not self-injury, such as self-mutilation or suicide).

This list is not exhaustive. You may think of other elements of behaviour which may or may not render it aggressive, according to your perspective. Discuss some of these issues with a friend. This should give you some idea of how difficult it is to achieve consensus on a definition.

definition of aggression, there is none that is generally agreed. In reviewing various attempts, Carlson *et al.* (1989) have argued that more common ground is achieved, across findings and contexts, by defining aggression as 'the intent to harm'. After you have checked Box 11.1, you may well agree that this definition is a major compromise.

Measuring aggression

In practice, researchers tend to use definitions which correspond to their own social values. As a result, the behaviour studied may differ in crucial ways from one researcher to another, and yet be given the same label 'aggression'. For example, are bodily cues of anger directed towards someone else the same as actually fighting? Are protests by indigenous peoples about their traditional lands comparable with acts of international terrorism; or is smacking a child comparable with the grisly deeds of the Yorkshire Ripper?

▶ Operational
definition
▶ Analogue

Since problems of definition are as yet unresolved, we must ask how aggression has been operationalised. We noted in Chapter 1 that the scientific social psychologist should offer a definition of a social process in such a way that it is rendered capable of measurement, that is, the definition should be an *operational definition*. The difficulty is that different researchers have used different measures for the same term. Look at some examples drawn from different researchers shown in Box 11.2. Collectively, each of these measures has been used as a substitute, or an *analogue*, for the 'real thing'. The major reason for this is ethical (see Chapter 1), since it is very difficult to justify inducing an actual physical assault against a person in an experimental setting. Consequently, the extent to which a study's findings can be generalised is usually limited.

Since this chapter explores just some of an extensive range of behaviours which are labelled aggressive, it should become clear that it is inappropriate to attempt any single definition for all of a variety of complex, and perhaps qualitatively different, phenomena.

BOX 11.2 Experimental analogues of aggression

- Punching an inflated plastic doll (Bandura *et al.* 1963).
- Pushing a button which is supposed to deliver an electric shock to someone else (Buss 1961).
- Pencil-and-paper ratings by teachers and classmates of a child's level of aggressiveness (Eron 1982).
- Written self-report by institutionalised teenage boys as to their prior aggressive behaviour (Leyens *et al.* 1975).
- A verbal expression of willingness to use violence in an experimental laboratory setting (Geen 1978).

MAJOR THEORETICAL POSITIONS

▶ Nature/nurture
controversy

Trying to understand why humans aggress against their own kind, and the factors which make them behave with viciousness and brutality towards one another in ways and degrees unparalleled in other animals, has produced supposition since ancient times (Geen and Donnerstein 1983). Explanations of aggression fall into two broad classes – the biological and the social – though the compartments are not rigid. A debate about which of the two is the crucial component is an example of the *nature/nurture controversy*: is human action determined by our biology or by our social environment? (A further instance of this debate involves the origins of prosocial behaviour – see Chapter 13.)

Our interest is social psychological and favours a treatment of social factors, and therefore a class of theories which incorporates a learning component. Interest in the biological thread, however, cannot be ignored. After all, violence is a reaction of our bodily system. Of even more interest is that some theories are so thoroughly biological that they might seem to constitute a threat to any form of theory which is social. We shall deal with each class in turn.

Biological explanations

▶ Instinct

The starting point for these explanations is that aggression is an innate tendency for action. Although modification of the consequent behaviour is possible, the wellspring is not. Aggression is an instinct, that is, a predetermined pattern of responses that are genetically controlled. As such, it should show certain characteristics of an instinct. According to Riopelle (1987), an *instinct* is:

1. *Goal-directed*, and terminates in a specific consequence, that is, an attack.
2. *Beneficial* to the individual and to the species.
3. *Adapted* to a normal environment (though not to an abnormal one).
4. *Shared* by most members of the species (though its manifestation can vary from individual to individual).
5. *Developed* in a clear way as the individual matures.
6. *Unlearned* on the basis of individual experience (though it can become manifest in relation to learned aspects within a context).

Three major views have shared most, if not all, of these biological attributes in their treatment of human aggression. All argue cogently that aggressive behaviour is an inherent part of human nature, that we are programmed at birth to act in that way. The oldest is the Freudian position, dating back to the earlier part of this century. This was followed a little later by the ideas propounded by the ethologists, based on their studies of animal behaviour. The third is a much more modern and somewhat startling view put forward by the sociobiologists.

Freudian theory

▶ Neo-Freudians

In his later theory, Freud (1930) proposed that human aggression stemmed from an innate death instinct, *thanatos*, which was in opposition to a life instinct, *eros*. *Thanatos* is initially directed at self-destruction, but later in development becomes redirected outwards at others. Freud's theory was influenced heavily by his background as a physician, and his notion of *thanatos* was partly a response to the large-scale destruction of the First World War. Like the sexual urge which stems from *eros*, an aggressive urge from *thanatos* builds up from bodily tensions, and needs to be expressed. This is essentially a one-factor theory: aggression builds up naturally and must be released. His ideas were revised by later theorists known as *neo-Freudians*, who viewed aggression as a more rational, but nonetheless innate, process whereby people sought a healthy release for primitive survival instincts which are basic to all animal species (Hartmann *et al.* 1949).

Ethological theory

▶ Ethology

In the 1960s, three books made a strong case for the instinctual basis of human aggression, on the basis of a comparison with animal behaviour: Lorenz's *On Aggression* (1966), Ardrey's *The Territorial Imperative* (1966), and Morris' *The Naked Ape* (1967). The general perspective which underpins this explanation of aggression is referred to as *ethology*, a branch of biology devoted to the study of instincts, or fixed action patterns, among all members of a species when living in their natural environment.

▶ Releasers

Like the neo-Freudians, ethologists stressed the positive, functional aspects

The release of an appeasement gesture. Intra-species aggression in the animal kingdom is usually limited because of a rich repertoire of appeasement gestures designed to signify an end to aggression. Lorenz argued that humans may have forgotten 'how to stop' being aggressive. (Source: Andrew Lukey.)

of aggression, but also recognised that while the potential or instinct for aggression may be innate, actual aggressive behaviour is elicited by specific stimuli in the environment known as *releasers*. Lorenz invoked evolutionary principles to propose that aggression has survival value. An individual animal is considerably more aggressive towards other members of its species, which serves to distribute the individuals and/or family units in such a way as to make the most efficient use of available resources, such as sexual selection and mating, food and territory. Most of the time, intra-species aggression may not result in actual violence, since one animal will display instinctual threat gestures which are recognised by another animal, which can then depart the scene. Even if fighting does break out it is unlikely to result in death, since the losing animal can display instinctual appeasement gestures which divert the victor from killing. Over time, in animals such as monkeys which live in colonies, appeasement gestures can help to establish dominance hierarchies, or 'pecking orders'. This is a two–factor theory: (1) there is an innate urge to aggress, which (2) depends upon appropriate stimulation by the environmental releasers.

▶ Fighting instinct

Lorenz extended the argument to humans who must also have an inherited *fighting instinct*. Unfortunately, however, its survival value is much less clear than is the case for other animals. This is largely because humans lack well-developed killing appendages, such as large teeth or claws, so that clearly recognisable appeasement gestures seem not to have evolved. There are two implications from this approach: (1) once we start being violent we do not seem to know when to stop; (2) in order to kill we generally need to resort to weapons. Unfortunately, the advanced technology of our times has produced frightful devices which allow for the slaughter of people in large numbers. Furthermore, this can be accomplished at a great distance, so that even the visual and auditory feedback cues of the victim's anguish are not available to persuade the victor to desist.

Sociobiology

▶ Sociobiology

A recent and influential theory which assumes an innate basis for aggression is *sociobiology* (Krebs and Miller 1985; Wilson 1978), an ambitious approach which has been put forward to highlight the biological basis of all social behaviour (including altruism – see Chapter 13). Based on Darwinian evolutionary theory, the sociobiological argument is a provocative one; specific behaviours have evolved because they promote the survival of genes that allow the individual to live long enough to pass the same genes on to the next generation. Aggression is adaptive since it must be linked to living long enough to procreate. As such, it is helpful to the individual and to the species. In common with the ethological view, being aggressive also increases access to resources. For humans, the goals for which aggressive behaviour is adaptive include social and economic advantage, either to defend the resources that one already has or to acquire new ones.

Shortcomings of biological arguments

Generally, biological explanations of aggression have considerable appeal in our community, picking up as they do on the popular assumption that violence is part of human nature. The seventeenth century philosopher Thomas Hobbes was one who saw fit to remark that people's lives are 'short, nasty and brutish'. Biological explanations also allow for our common experience of the power of strong bodily reactions that accompany some emotions, in this case, anger. Broadly speaking, however, social scientists (Goldstein 1987; Ryan 1985) reject the sufficiency of the explanation of aggression when it is based totally on the cornerstone of instinct, on the grounds that this concept:

1. Depends on energy that is unknown, unknowable and immeasurable.
2. Is supported by only limited and biased empirical observation of actual human behaviour.
3. Has little utility in the prevention or control of aggression.
4. Relies on circular logic, proposing causal connections for which there is no evidence.

Social and biosocial explanations

▶ Biosocial theories

Social psychologists generally do not favour theories of aggression defined in terms of an instinct, preferring instead to emphasise learning processes and factors within the social context which appear to be linked to aggressive behaviour. Even though most social psychologists do not accept that aggression is necessarily innate and instinctual, there are some who have regarded it as a general drive that can be either innate or learned, and which is elicited by social events or circumstances. Since these approaches incorporate a biological element, we refer them to as *biosocial theories*. The two outlined below each consider that a drive (or state of arousal) is a precondition for aggression, although they differ in the ways in which internal and external factors are thought to interact to promote aggressive reactions.

Frustration and aggression

▶ Frustration-
aggression
hypothesis

The *frustration/aggression hypothesis* is a famous theory which linked aggression to an antecedent condition of frustration. It derived from the work of a group of psychologists at Yale University in the 1930s, and we have noted that it has been used in an attempt to explain prejudice (see Chapter 9). The anthropologist Dollard and his psychologist colleagues (Doob, Miller, Mowrer and Sears) proposed that aggression was always caused by some kind of frustrating event or situation; conversely, in a later formulation, frustration did not invariably lead to aggression (Dollard *et al.* 1939). The theory had considerable appeal for a period, in as much as it was decidedly different from the Freudian approach. According to Goldstein (1980), 'it was a theory with no psychoanalytic mumbo jumbo. No need to bother about such phantoms as ids, egos, superegos, and ego–defence mechanisms' (pp. 262–63). Later research was to show that the basic hypothesis was simplistic and far from a complete explanation for aggressive behaviour. One major flaw is the theory's loose definition of 'frustration', and the difficulty in predicting which kinds of frustrating circumstance may lead to aggression. As we shall see, there are many factors other than frustration which can cause violence between people.

Excitation-transfer

▶ Excitation-transfer model

A later approach to aggression which features a drive concept is Zillmann's (1979, 1988) *excitation-transfer model*. This suggests that the expression of aggression (or any other emotion, for that matter) is a function of three factors:

1. Some learned aggressive behaviour.
2. Some arousal or excitation from another source.
3. The person's interpretation of the arousal state, such that an aggressive response seems appropriate.

Zillmann suggests that this residual arousal transfers from one situation to another in such a way that it promotes or contributes to the likelihood of the person interpreting a situation in an aggressive way, especially if aggressive behaviour is well established within that person's usual behaviour patterns. According to Zillmann, any experience which markedly increases the level of overall excitation can lead to unintended consequences. Look at the example shown in Figure 11.1. Imagine that a student (not you, of course) has been working out at the gym, and is still in a state of physical arousal when driving to the local supermarket. Here, another customer's car sneaks forward into the parking space that the student was trying to reverse into. Although this could ordinarily be mildly annoying, the residual excitation from the workout (now forgotten) triggers some verbal abuse from the student.

It is not difficult to think of instances where heightened arousal can lead people to react more aggressively than they usually might: aggressive acts while

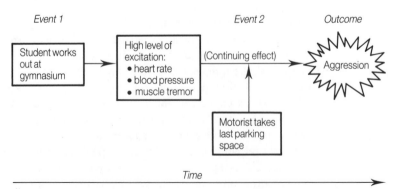

FIGURE 11.1 *The excitation-transfer model of aggression. (Source: adapted from Zillman 1979.)*

driving a car in stressful conditions; the greater tendency to yell angrily at someone when we are already upset about something quite unrelated; the mother who smacks a child for accidentally getting lost; the fights that break out so readily among children on exciting occasions. All of these instances make some sense in terms of Zillmann's theory. We can also note that it can be applied to the experience of sexual arousal as well (see the section on erotica below), or indeed any kind of former stimulation whose effects linger over time.

Aggression can be learned

▶ Social learning
theory

Social learning theory is a wide-ranging behavioural approach in psychology which features the processes responsible for:

1. The *acquisition* of a behaviour or a behavioural sequence.
2. The *instigation* of overt acts.
3. The *maintenance* of the behaviour.

Its most famous proponent is Bandura (1977; Bandura and Walters 1963), who also applied it specifically to the understanding of aggression (Bandura 1973). Of course, if antisocial behaviour can be learned, so too can prosocial behaviour. Indeed, this view has been advanced (see Chapter 13). Although Bandura acknowledges the role of biological factors in relation to aggression, the emphasis is on the role of experience, which can be direct or vicarious. Through socialisation, the child learns to aggress because either it is directly rewarding or because someone else is seen to be rewarded for their actions.

Vicarious experience – learning to be aggressive. Sanitised violence on television. Bandura argued that children can learn violence by observing an admired model, especially one who is reinforced for acting aggressively. (Source: Andrew Lukey.)

▶ Learning by direct
experience

▶ Learning by
vicarious
experience

The idea of *learning by direct experience* is based on Skinner's operant reinforcement principles: a behaviour is maintained by rewards and punishments experienced by the child. For example, if Xiao Heng takes Xiao Ling's biscuit from her, and no-one intervenes, then he is reinforced by now having the biscuit. The idea of *learning by vicarious experience* is a contribution made by the social learning theorists. In this mode, learning occurs through the processes of modelling and imitation from other people. We should note that the concept of imitation *per se* is not new in social theory. The French sociologist Tarde (1890), for example, devoted a whole book to the subject and asserted that 'society is imitation'. What is unique in social learning theory is the proposition that the behaviour to be imitated must be seen to be rewarding in some way. Some models are more appropriate for the child than others: parents, siblings and peers. The learning sequence of aggression can be extended beyond interactive contexts to include media images such as television. It can also be applied to learning in later life by an adult.

According to Bandura, whether a person is aggressive in a particular situation will depend upon several factors:

1. The person's previous experiences of aggressive behaviour, including that of both the individual and others.
2. The degree of success of aggressive behaviour in the past.
3. The current likelihood of the aggression being either rewarded or punished.
4. The complex array of cognitive, social and environmental factors in the situation.

▶ Modelling

Bandura's studies used a variety of experimental settings to show that

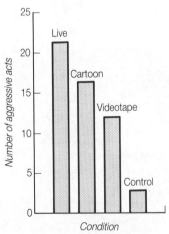

FIGURE 11.2 *Learning aggression through mere observation: the effects on children of watching a violent model. (Source: based on data from Bandura and Walters 1963.)*

children will quite readily mimic the aggressive acts of others. In particular, an adult makes a potent model, no doubt because children perceive their elders as responsible and authoritative figures (also see Chapters 4 and 13). The early findings pointed to a clear *modelling* effect when the adult was seen acting aggressively in a live setting. Even more disturbing, this capacity to 'acquire' aggression was also demonstrated when the adult model was seen acting violently on television (see Figure 11.2 and Box 11.3).

The social learning approach has had a major impact on research into aggression, stimulating many other studies. It has also touched a chord in our community about the causes of aggression, and has directly increased research into the effects of violence in the visual media on both children and adults. If violence is learned, exposure to aggressive and successful models leads people to imitate them. Being aggressive can become an established pattern of behaving, even a way of life which is likely to repeat itself by imitation across generations (Huesmann *et al.* 1984). This does not necessarily mean that change is impossible since, if aggression can be learned, presumably it can also be modified. This is the basis of behaviour modification programmes, such as anger management, used by clinical and community psychologists to help people find peaceful ways of dealing with others.

Does theory have any point?

Social psychology is replete with theory, as each chapter in this book attests. In the case of aggression, theories are not only numerous but are vigorously debated. There is no sign of change, and little wonder, since it is part of a community's everyday experience, and of every person's wish to explain it. Despite this, Geen and Donnerstein (1983) argue that little theoretical progress has been made. Many investigations have been criticised for being aimless and contributing little to our understanding of the nature of aggression and violence (Lubek 1979).

Some of this criticism relates to problems involving both definitions and ethics described at the beginning of this chapter. Some critics have concluded that theory based on case studies and on experimentation has doubtful validity. This criticism applies in some degree to all of the theories we have considered, and all have some difficulty in accounting for the diverse dimensions of aggression. No available theory can provide a complete explanation for the origins and occurrence of aggression, and even when the precipitating factor for an aggressive act may be apparent, there will invariably be several other contributing factors which are not so obvious. Examples of this are the cultural values and social pressures which may contribute to a pub brawl involving unemployed immigrants, even though drunkenness may appear initially to be the cause; or the underlying effects of poverty, chronic frustration and social disadvantage which cumulatively often lead to acts of domestic violence. Some of these factors are considered next.

BOX 11.3 Bandura's view of the role of vicarious experience in learning aggressive behaviour

Sock it to the Bobo doll!

Can the mere observation of a behaviour be sufficient to learn that behaviour? Albert Bandura and his colleagues addressed this question in a series of experiments at Stanford University. This work had a considerable impact on the acceptance of social factors within the narrower field of experimental research on learning, but also had a long-term effect on wider thinking about the origins of aggression. According to the social learning theory of observational learning, observing a behaviour produces a cognitive representation in the observer who then experiences vicarious reinforcement. This kind of reinforcement refers to a process whereby the outcome for the model, whether rewarding or punishing, becomes a remote reinforcement for the observer. If this is so, then aggression is likely to be one of many social behaviours which can be learned.

Bandura *et al.* (1963) tested this idea in one study of four- and five-year-old children who watched a male or female adult play with a commercially popular inflated Bobo doll. There were four conditions:

1. *Live* – the adult model came into the room where the child was playing. After playing with some Tinker Toys, the adult then began to act aggressively towards the Bobo doll. The acts included sitting on the doll, hitting its nose, banging it on the head with a mallet, and kicking it around the room. The words were: 'sock him in the nose', 'pow', 'kick him', 'hit him down' and the like. After this, the child was left to play with the Bobo doll.
2. *Videotape* – this was the same as the live sequence, but had been filmed on videotape for the child to view.
3. *Cartoon* – the model acted in the same way, but was dressed in a cat costume, and the room was decorated as if it were in a cartoon.
4. *Control* – the child skipped all of these conditions and went directly to play with the Bobo doll.

The results in Figure 11.2 show that the children who watched an adult behave aggressively in any condition also behaved more aggressively later. The most effective condition for modelling aggressive behaviour was the live sequence. However, the finding that the cartoon and videotaped conditions also increase imitative aggression in children provided fuel for critics who argued that graphic presentations of violence in films and television could have serious consequences for children's later behaviour.

PERSONAL AND SITUATIONAL FACTORS

Although it is possible conceptually to distinguish between the person and the situation when dealing with any social behaviour, common sense suggests that an interaction of both determines how people behave. Ross and Nisbett (1991) have cogently argued in this way. Like an echo of Lewin's early field-theory doctrine of a tension between the person and the environment (see Chapter 1), people bring their unique characteristics to any situation, and their individual way of construing it. When we apply such thinking to the study of aggression, the separation of person variables from situation variables is a matter of convenience, and even of over-simplification. It reflects the way most research has been done and belies the reality that the 'causes' of aggression are complex and interactive.

Consider some contexts in which people may show aggression. It could be in response to teasing, a hangover from a near traffic accident, a continuing way of responding to the burden of poverty, a male mechanism for dealing with an insistent spouse, a mother's control over a fractious child. Some of these instances appear to be situational variables, but closer inspection shows that some go with the person, or with a category of person (the poor, the male, the mother). What is more, not all people in that category respond in that way. With that caveat in mind we will plunge on.

Person variables

Personality

It is an attractive proposition that people aggress because they have an 'aggressive personality'. It is probably not too difficult for you to rate your friends according to how much or how little they typically tend towards aggressive behaviour, and this ability to evaluate people in terms of their aggressiveness is an important part of some psychometric (psychological test-based) and clinical assessments (Sundberg 1977) – for example in determining the likelihood of re-offending amongst violent offenders (Mullen 1984). It is, of course, simplistic to think of people as somehow naturally aggressive, but for a variety of reasons, including one's age, gender, culture, personal experiences and so on, some people are more typically aggressive in their behaviour than are others.

▶ Type A personality

Research in recent years has suggested the existence of a behaviour pattern called *Type A personality* (Matthews 1982). This syndrome is associated with susceptibility to coronary heart disease. Persons showing this pattern are over-active and excessively competitive in their encounters with others. A study by Carver and Glass (1978) found that Type A people were also more aggressive towards others who were perceived to be competing with them on an important task. According to Dembroski and MacDougall (1978), Type A people prefer to work alone rather than with others when they are under stress, as if to avoid exposure to incompetence in others and to feel in control of the situation. Although Type A people may have found that behaving in this way was rewarding at certain points in their life, it can have some very destructive effects for themselves and for those who are close to them. For example, Type A personalities were reported to be more prone to engage in child abuse (Strube *et al*. 1984). In an organisational setting, Baron (1989) found that managers who were classified as Type A experienced more conflict with peers and subordinates, though not with their supervisors. They apparently know when to draw the line.

Gender

Another learned source of individual difference lies in the differential socialisation of the sexes, which occurs in extremely subtle ways such that males in our society are encouraged from early childhood to be more aggressive than females, who in turn are actively discouraged from such behaviour (Condry and Ross 1985). A wealth of research has now confirmed this male/female difference in many societies and across socio-economic groups, although the size of the difference appears to vary according to the mode of aggressiveness; for example, males are more likely than females to be physically violent and hold more aggressive attitudes, but females are almost as likely as males to use verbal attack in similar contexts, although the degree to which they aggress may be less (Eagly and Steffen 1986).

Frustration

The consequences of being frustrated figured large in the account of the frustration-aggression hypothesis (see above and Chapter 9). There is a difficulty in measuring frustration empirically, but you can probably bring to mind many personal instances where you have become angry and lashed out verbally or physically because of some circumstance which gets in the way of your goals – for example, thumping a photocopier machine, fuming at another motorist who slows you down, kicking a reluctant lawn-mower, or chastising a family member for causing you to be late in leaving home for an engagement. Although there is little doubt that frustration may lead to aggression, there is a great deal of unpredictability in the frustration-aggression formula. However, two factors help to predict whether frustration will result in aggression: the intensity of the frustrating event, and how apparently legitimate, reasonable or unavoidable it is (Kulik and Brown 1979).

Catharsis

▶ Catharsis

An instrumental reason for aggression which has been suggested is *catharsis*, which refers to the use of a behaviour as an outlet or release for pent-up emotion. Although associated with Freud, the idea can be traced back to Aristotle and ancient Greek tragedy: by acting out their emotions, people can purify their feelings (Scherer *et al*. 1975). The idea makes sense, arguing that we have a need to 'let off steam' from frustration in order to get back to a stable level of functioning, and that acting aggressively will help to get rid of the stressful emotion. In Japan, some companies have acted on this hypothesis by providing a special room with a toy replica of the boss onto which employees can relieve their tensions 'by bashing the boss' (see Middlebrook 1980). However, research in this area shows that the relationship between frustration and catharsis is quite complex; catharsis has appeared to reduce feelings of aggression in some studies, but actually increased it in others (Konecni and Ebbesen 1976). It seems that other factors, such as the individual's normal level of aggressiveness, whether or not the catharsis is a sufficient release for the person's feelings, whether it induces guilt feelings, and the further consequences of the aggression, all contribute to whether the person then feels less or more aggressive (Geen and Quanty 1977).

Direct provocation

▶ Reciprocity principle It is probably obvious that we might aggress when directly provoked, even at times when the provocation appears to be quite mild. Laboratory research has shown that this is so for both verbal and physical provocation (Geen 1968), and you may recall past incidents of responding aggressively to being teased or taunted. Moreover, provocation can readily escalate into quite vicious fighting, as occurs in brawls in bars or in sports, and sometimes in street demonstrations. This suggests that a *reciprocity principle* is operating, that is we tend to strike back rather than to turn the other cheek. (See also how reciprocity can operate in relation to interpersonal attraction in Chapter 12 and to prosocial behaviour in Chapter 13.) Of course, there will always be other contributing factors, such as whether we have viable alternative responses, the likely consequences of aggression in the particular situation, and factors such as age and gender. For example, young children, especially boys, are more likely to reciprocate with aggressiveness than are older people (Eagly and Steffen 1986). In real life, aggression in the form of self-defence might save a life, and this is recognised in law as a form of justification for some cases of homicide.

Alcohol

It is often assumed that alcohol befuddles the brain. This is a particular form of the *disinhibition hypothesis* (see below): that is, alcohol detracts from cortical control and increases activities of more primitive brain areas. In an experiment by Taylor and Sears (1988), eighteen male students were assigned to either an alcohol or a placebo condition. They were placed in a competition involving reaction time with another subject. In each pair, the person who responded more slowly on a given trial would receive an electric shock from the opponent. The level of shock to be delivered could be at various intensity levels and was selected by each person before that trial commenced. In reality, the opponent's shock settings, which were always low intensity (that is, fairly passive), and the win/loss frequency (50 per cent) was determined by the experimenter. The results in Figure 11.3 show the proportions of high-intensity shocks given by

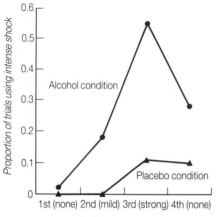

FIGURE 11.3 *The effects of alcohol and social pressure upon males' willingness to deliver electric shocks to a passive opponent. (Source: adapted from Taylor and Sears 1988.)*

subjects who were either in an alcohol or a placebo condition. In four sequential stages (none, mild, strong, none), social pressure, by way of encouragement to give a shock, was sometimes exerted on the subject by a confederate who was watching the proceedings. The results show an interaction between taking alcohol and being pressured to aggress: subjects who had imbibed were more susceptible to influence, and continued to give high-intensity shocks even after the pressure was withdrawn.

The analogy to real life is the context of social drinking, such as at a party or at a bar, where others may goad the drinker to be aggressive. Actual statistics concerning the connection between alcohol and aggression are suggestive but not clear-cut. Although alcohol consumption is disproportionately associated with physical violence, the causal pathways are complex. Research on the links between violent offending and drinking patterns show that stress and lifestyle factors appear to contribute to high levels of both alcohol consumption and aggressiveness, and that drinking and violence coincide as much because violent people also tend to drink a lot, as because alcohol actually promotes violent behaviour (Bradbury 1984).

Disinhibition

▶ Disinhibition

▶ Deindividuation

▶ Dehumanisation

Another cognitive social phenomenon which will often lead to aggression, even where such reactions are not typical of the aggressor, is *disinhibition*, which refers to any kind of reduction in the usual social forces which operate to restrain us from acting aggressively. There appear to be several ways in which people may lose their normal inhibitions from aggressing against others. In Box 11.4 we consider the case in which the *aggressor* experiences a state of *deindividuation*. This process (discussed in more detail in Chapter 10) involves

---

BOX 11.4 How disinhibition can lead to violence

Reduced likelihood of punishment

A dramatic example of how a real, or perceived, reduction in the likelihood of punishment can enhance aggression and violence was seen in the My Lai incident in the war in Vietnam, where American soldiers slaughtered an entire village of innocent civilians. In the official inquiry it was revealed that the same unit had previously killed and tortured civilians without any disciplinary action; that the area was a designated 'free-fire zone', so that it was considered legitimate to shoot at anything that moved; and indeed that the whole ethos of the war was one of glorified violence (Hersh 1970).

In addition, there was a sense of anonymity, or *deindividuation*, from being part of a large group which further enhanced the perception of the men that they would not be punished as individuals (see also the effects of deindividuation in Chapter 6). This sense of anonymity is thought to contribute to translating aggressive emotion into actual violence, and it may occur either through being part of a large group or gathering, as in the crowd which baits a suicide to jump (Mann 1981) or a pack rape at a gang convention, or through something which protects anonymity in another way, such as the white hoods worn by Ku Klux Klan members (Middlebrook 1980), the stocking worn over the face of an armed robber, or the halloween masks which prompt children to steal candy and money from others (Diener *et al.* 1976). A study by Malamuth (1981) found that almost one-third of male students questioned at an American university admitted there was a likelihood that they would rape if they were certain of not getting caught.

---

changes controlled by situational factors impacting on the aggressor, such as the presence of others or lack of identifiability. In Box 11.5 we look at how other factors which focus on how the aggressor perceives the victim, such as being less than human (*dehumanisation* – see also Chapters 9 and 15), can increase the probability of a hostile act following.

▶ Collective aggression   Mann applied the concept of deindividuation to a particular context relating to *collective aggression*: 'the baiting crowd'. The typical situation is where a person is threatening to jump from a high building, a crowd gathers below and some begin to chant 'jump, jump'. In one dramatic case in New York in 1938, thousands of people waited at ground level, some for eleven hours, until a man jumped to his death from a seventeenth-storey hotel ledge. Mann proceeded to analyse twenty-one cases of suicides reported in newspapers in the 1960s and 1970s. He found that, in ten out of the twenty-one cases where there had been a crowd watching, baiting had occurred. He examined other features of these

---

BOX 11.5 Deindividuation in an aggressor brought about by dehumanising the victim

A variation of deindividuation in the aggressor can occur when the victim, rather than the aggressor, is anonymous or dehumanised in some way, so that the aggressor cannot so easily see the personal pain and injury suffered by the victim. This can weaken any control by feelings of shame and guilt.

Terrible examples of this phenomenon have been documented, such as the violent treatment of psychiatric patients and prisoners kept either naked or dressed identically so that they are indistinguishable as individuals (Steir 1978); and having faceless and deindividuated victims in violent films and television programmes has been shown to have a disinhibiting effect on some people, thus encouraging them to play down the injury and be more likely to imitate the violent acts (Bandura 1986). An extreme and inhumane instance of disinhibition was the dropping of a second atomic bomb on Nagasaki in 1945. Cohen (1987) has presented a revealing analysis of the ways in which military personnel 'sanitise', and thereby justify, the use of nuclear weaponry by semantics which dehumanise the likely or actual victims, referring to them as 'targets', 'the aggressed', or even 'collateral damage'. The same semantic strategies have been used by American military personnel during the Vietnam War to rationalise and justify the killing of Vietnamese civilians, who were known as 'gooks' (Sabini and Silver 1982).

In 1993, Bosnian Serbs in what was once part of Yugoslavia have referred to acts of genocide against the Muslim population as 'ethnic cleansing'. The media as well can unwittingly lessen the impact of the horror of large-scale killing. A phrase used often on television during the Allied bombing campaigns in Iraq in 1991 was the 'theatre of war', inviting the audience to sit back and be entertained.

---

reports which distinguished between crowds that bait and those that do not. Baiting was more likely to occur at night and when the crowd was quite large (more than three hundred people). Also, the crowd was typically a long way from the victim, usually at ground level. These features are likely to produce a state of deindividuation in the individual. Furthermore, the longer the crowd waited the more likely that baiting would start, perhaps arising from feelings of irritability and frustration (see Figure 11.4).

Since the early 1970s, European, but particularly British, soccer has become strongly associated with hooliganism – which popular hysteria tends to characterise in terms of the familiar stereotyped images of soccer fans on the

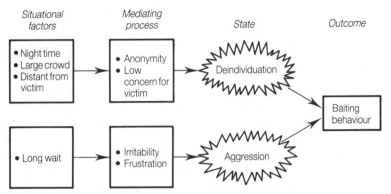

FIGURE 11.4 *The baiting crowd: an exercise in deindividuation and frustration.
(Source: based on suggestions from Mann 1981)*

rampage (Murphy *et al.* 1990). It is tempting to apply an explanation in terms of deindividuation in a crowd setting, but a study of soccer hooliganism by Marsh *et al.* (1978) suggests a different cause. According to their analysis, violence by football fans is actually orchestrated far away from the stadium and long before a given match. What might appear to be a motley crowd of supporters on match day can actually consist of several groups of fans with different status. By participating in ritualised aggression over a period of time, a faithful follower can be 'promoted' into a higher group and can continue to pursue a 'career structure'. Rival fans who follow their group's rules quite carefully can avoid real physical harm to themselves or others. For example, chasing the opposition after a match ('seeing the others off') need not necessarily end in violence since part of the agreed code is not to actually catch anyone. Seen in this light, soccer hooliganism is a kind of staged production and is not the example of an uncontrollable mob sometimes depicted by the media. When real violence does take place it tends to be both unusual and attributable to particular individuals.

Soccer hooliganism can also be understood in more societal terms. For example, Murphy *et al.* (1990) describe how soccer arose in Britain as an essentially working class sport, and that by the 1950s working class values to do with masculine aggression had already become associated with the game. Attempts by the government (seen as middle class) to control this aspect of the sport can backfire because they enhance class solidarity and encourage increased violence that generalises beyond matches. This sort of explanation points towards an analysis in terms of intergroup relations and the subcultural legitimation of aggression (see Chapter 10).

Other factors

There is a diversity of other factors which have sometimes been implicated in aggression for some individuals. For example, having a greater need for personal space has been found to predispose prisoners to greater violence in crowded prison conditions (Walkley 1984 – see more on crowding in prisons in Chapter 15). One's personal beliefs and attitudes about the acceptability of aggressiveness will naturally also be an important source of individual difference in levels of aggressive behaviour. Although there is a correlation between some psychological disturbances and interpersonal violence, it seems that mental abnormality *per se*, contrary to common myth, does not predispose people to aggression (Mullen 1984). Another myth that can be laid to rest is the notion that having an extra Y chromosome – XYY rather than XY – can predispose men to be violent. An extensive survey by Witkin and colleagues (1976) reported that XYY male prisoners showed rates of violence and criminality that were similar to those of XY prisoners. It also seems doubtful that brain tumours or unusual hormonal levels in some people can be linked directly to levels of aggression (Montague 1973; Valenstein 1975), while there is no evidence of a simple control centre for violence in the brain (Simmel *et al.* 1983).

Situation variables

Physical environment

Various aspects of our physical environment have been shown also to contribute to violence. For example, research has pointed to a connection between *temperature* and collective violence (Carlsmith and Anderson 1979; Harries and Stadler 1983), showing that riots are significantly more likely to occur in temperatures which are hotter than normal, but not excessive (see the discussion of collective behaviour in Chapter 10, and the effects of heat as a stressor in Chapter 15).

The effect of *crowding* and invasion of personal space on aggressiveness have already been mentioned. At peak hours in some large taverns there may be several hundred people in various stages of intoxication so that only a small incident might lead to a brawl. In a context such as this there may be a series of contributory factors: heat, crowding, alcohol, provocation and disinhibition. A challenge for architects and designers is to take such environmental variables into account in the planning of spaces which encourage quiet social interaction in the context of drinking alcohol (see Chapter 15).

Disadvantaged groups

▶ Relative deprivation

At a societal level of analysis, the general social conditions in which people live can lead to the perception by some groups that they are not so well off (Davies 1962). *Relative deprivation* (see Chapter 10 for details) is applied to the situation in which people compare their socio-economic circumstances with relevant reference groups in their community, and feel discontented with the outcome. They might see not only that they are disadvantaged relative to others, but also that the chance of improving their own conditions is slight. In such a context, if hope of improvement cannot be achieved legitimately, a deprived person or group might act aggressively. At an individual level this could include vandalism, assault or burglary; at an intergroup level it could extend to collective violence such as violent protest or rioting. The Los Angeles race riots of 1992 were ostensibly triggered by a jury verdict which acquitted white police officers of extended physical battery of a black motorist. Underlying this incident, however, there was a probable undercurrent of dissatisfaction with the lot of many black people in downtown and suburban Los Angeles (see Box 10.1 in Chapter 10).

There is a reasonable level of support for the validity of the concept of relative deprivation, from both experimental sources and historical analyses, and it provides a plausible, partial explanation for some recent events in Europe, such as increased violence against Turkish immigrants in what was formerly East Germany where unemployment is now running at historically high levels.

Criminality and women

An interesting variation of large-scale social disinhibition is the idea that the emancipation of women in recent decades may have been criminogenic: that is, by removing some of the restraints on women from being assertive or aggressive, the women's movement may have contributed inadvertently to the substantial increase in violent crime amongst women which has occurred in many countries the past decade or so (Hall 1984). This notion still requires more investigation, since although violent offending by women is more common now, the trend is more pronounced in lower socio-economic groups, and it could be argued that such women are the least likely to have been influenced by the women's movement. Nevertheless, the re-definition of male and female roles in most western societies in the past twenty years can be linked to a rise in alcohol and drug abuse among women. The return of women to the workforce has coincided more recently with widespread unemployment, a further trigger to an increase in offences against persons (and, of course, property). It should be stressed that although female convictions for violent offending have increased more rapidly than for males over the past ten years or so, male criminal violence is still enormously more prevalent.

Cultural variation

One outcome of the ideology of democracy which characterises the western world, and especially the increased awareness of and pressure for human rights in the twentieth century, is the development of an ethic of non-violence, which has been manifested in organisations, and training courses, as diverse as Men For Non-Violence, Amnesty International, Women Against Rape, assertiveness training and self-defence programmes, and consciousness-raising concerning child abuse.

▶ Cultural norm
▶ Value

It is important to recognise this emphasis on non-violence for what it is: a socio-cultural artefact, and not a universal morality. Throughout history there have always been differences in *cultural norms* and *values* which have shaped some societies as more or less aggressive than others, and usually it has not been hard to trace the reasons. Historical factors such as repeated invasions, geographical factors which made some societies more competitive or more vulnerable than others, and even bio-evolutionary factors which simply permitted some groups to be more aggressive by virtue of their greater size, all have played a part in shaping the social philosophies of particular societies. Moreover, these philosophies are dynamic, and can change very rapidly with a change in context. Examples of this in recent years are the development of aggressive Zionism following the Jewish Holocaust in the Second World War, altering a religious philosophy of pacifism which had endured for centuries; and in Australia the emergence of black activism amongst Aborigines, whose generally low level of aggression towards outsiders probably contributed to their initial exploitation (Rowley 1971). Conversely, the ethic of non-violence in our own society is relatively recent and at variance with the norms of earlier days when the violence of soldiery, and physical pursuits for schoolboys such as boxing and football, were not only approved but even considered an essential element of masculinity (Phillips 1987).

While most societies in the world do show forms of interpersonal violence (Rohner 1976), there are some which still actively practise a lifestyle of non-aggression, including the Hutterite and Amish communities in the United States, and the Pygmies of Central Africa. Although this appears to support Bandura's claims that aggression is learned, rather than instinctual, it is noteworthy that all of these societies which remain peaceful in the twentieth century are both small and relatively isolated, suggesting that these may be necessary preconditions for peaceful coexistence (see Gorer 1968 for a social anthropological review of peaceful societies).

The fact remains that different societies view aggressive behaviour in different ways according to historical, normative and social-contextual factors, and sometimes this can lead to damaging misunderstandings in this age of increasingly multicultural societies. An example from New Zealand concerns the very different attitudes of Samoan people to violent drunken behaviour, which is viewed as a bout of sickness rather than aggression; and rape is seen as an offence against the victim's whole family, not just the woman personally (Kinloch 1985). Both of these differences have important implications for police intervention with Samoan offenders in New Zealand.

Cross-cultural differences in perspectives on aggression and more broadly on issues to do with human rights are increasingly becoming a source of conflict between western nations and newly industrialising countries. For example, recent western outrage over capital punishment for drug trafficking in Malaysia and Thailand, over corporal punishment in Singapore, and over state suppression of democratisation in China and in Indonesia have all invited strident accusations from these countries of ethnocentrism and cultural imperialism.

▶ Subculture of
violence

A different kind of evidence in support of social learning theory comes from the study of the *subculture of violence* (Toch 1969). Within societies there are often smaller groups or minority subcultures in which violence is specifically valued and given legitimisation as a lifestyle, initially perhaps because this is seen as a way of improving their status and power within the larger society. The beliefs, values and norms of the group reflect an approval of aggressiveness, and there will be both social rewards for violent behaviour and negative sanctions for not going along with the group's violent activities. These groups are often labelled and self-styled as 'gangs', and the value of violence is reflected in their appearance as well as in their behaviour. Violence is a way of life for such groups, both towards the greater society and amongst themselves. A graphic example of the traditional initiation rite for the Sicilian Mafia was given by Nieburg (1969). After a long lead-up period of observation, the new Mafia member would attend a candlelit meeting of other members and be led to a table showing the image of a saint, an emblem of high religious significance. Blood taken from his right hand would be sprinkled on the saint and he would swear an oath of allegiance binding him to the brotherhood. In a short time, he would then prove himself worthy by executing a suitable person selected by the Mafia.

Such a subculture exists within many prison communities, where the factions often parallel gang membership. Violence in most prisons in western society is actually institutionalised (a term discussed in a later section) in ways that are informal but clearly recognised by both inmates and prison staff. Paradoxically, this staunchness is believed actually to account for much of the control and discipline within prisons (Calkin 1985).

Interactionism

▶ Levels of
explanation or
analysis

By now it should be evident that aggression is never a simple act resulting from one specific cause, and there will be contributing factors at each of the *levels of explanation* (personal, social, situational and cultural) discussed above (see Chapter 1 for further discussion of the way in which levels of explanation are used across different theoretical approaches in psychology). While the most obvious cause often may appear to be some aspect of the immediate situation, a fuller explanation for the behaviour will always require a search for underlying social and cultural factors as well. Part of this picture is the role of the mass media. We have chosen to treat this separately in the following section since so much attention has focused on the idea that films, television, books and newspapers might increase the likelihood of violence. This is a controversial view, with protagonists arguing for and against, both at the research level and in everyday discussion within our community. We return again to the concept of 'levels' in relation to explanations of war later in this chapter.

MASS MEDIA

The impact of the various *mass media* and especially the visual media on aggressive behaviour has been a controversial area of research and theory in the past two decades or more. There are myriad reported examples of individuals emulating violent acts such as assault, rape and murder in almost identical fashion to what they have viewed in some film or television programme, as well as the disinhibitory effects on the general population from watching an excessive amount of sanitised violence on the screen. Attempts by laboratory researchers to establish a causal link between viewing violence and acting aggressively have been fraught with flaws of both methodology and theory. For example, much of the work on the effects of desensitisation to media violence has involved exposure to rather mild forms of television violence for relatively short periods of time. (Freedman 1984; Geen and Donnerstein 1983). Despite this, it seems likely that watching violence on the screen can contribute to higher levels of aggressive behaviour in some people. Bandura (1973, 1986) has demonstrated how film and television violence distort the perceived outcomes of violence by sanitising both the aggressive acts and the injuries received by the victim. This suggests to the viewer that the aggression is not harmful. Moreover, the aggressor is often portrayed as the 'good guy' in the situation and is rarely punished for his acts of violence. Social learning theory (Bandura 1973) has taken a strong position on this point: children can readily mimic the behaviour of a model who is reinforced for aggressing, or at least escapes punishment.

Sheehan (1983) presents evidence of a correlation between Australian children's television viewing habits and their levels of aggressive behaviour. His samples were upper middle-class boys and girls aged 5 to 10 years at primary schools in Australia in 1979–81. Some of these samples were age cohorts tested more than once across different years. The behaviour variable consisted of ratings by peers of each child's acts that physically injure or irritate another person. Other data relating to the use of aggressive fantasies by the children, and parental variables, were also gathered. Correlations between viewing violent programmes and peer-rated aggression were consistently significant only among older children (approximately 8 to 10 years), mostly close to $r = 0.25$, and were stronger among boys than among girls. However, Sheehan also carried out multiple regression analyses to try to determine cause-and-effect relationships. From this he was not able to show a direct connection between early (younger age) viewing habits and later (older age) aggression. The best predictors, according to these longitudinal regressions, turned out to be ratings of aggression for the same child (from younger to older), parental characteristics (income, rejection of child, use of punishment, television viewing habits), and the use of aggressive fantasies by the child. In other words, there were multiple links involving several factors between the viewing of television violence and aggressive behaviour in children. As opposed to the use of experimental techniques, it is difficult in a field study to confirm causal relationships between variables, a point which Sheehan noted.

Several other non-experimental studies have demonstrated a generalised connection between mass media violence and both intrapersonal and interpersonal aggression (see Phillips 1986 for a comprehensive review). The effect is not simply one of the imitation of violence modelled on the screen or read about in newspapers and magazines, nor just of desensitisation and disinhibition; there is evidence that seeing and reading about violence in general can promote greater aggression in some people. However, it remains to be seen which individuals are most susceptible to this kind of influence.

A cognitive interpretation

▶ Neo-associationist
  analysis
▶ Priming

Recent views about the idea that the media can trigger violence have featured the manner in which people process information and, in this case, automatically react to aggressive scenes or descriptions (Berkowitz 1984; Huesmann 1988). Berkowitz's *neo-associationist analysis* picked up on old themes in psychology, including the nineteenth-century notion of ideomotor responses – that merely thinking about an act can facilitate its performance (see Box 1.2 in Chapter 1). According to neo-associationism, real or fictional images of violence that are presented to an audience can translate later into antisocial acts. Conversely, exposure to images of people helping others can lead later to prosocial acts (see Figure 11.5). Berkowitz drew on cognitive psychological literature in which memory is treated as a collection of networks, each of which consists of nodes. A node can include substantive elements of thoughts and feelings, connected through associative pathways. When a thought comes into focus, its activation radiates from that particular node via the associative pathways to other nodes, which in turn can lead to a *priming* effect (see also Chapter 2). Consequently, if you have been watching a film depicting a violent

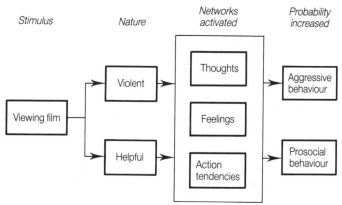

FIGURE 11.5 *'Unconscious' effects of the media: a neo-associationist analysis. (Source: based on suggestions from Berkowitz 1984.)*

gang 'rumble' someone, then other semantically related thoughts can be primed, such as *punching, kicking, shooting a gun* and so on. This process can be mostly automatic, without much conscious thinking involved. Similarly, feelings associated with aggression, such as some components of the emotion of anger, may likewise be activated. The outcome is an overall increase in the probability that an aggressive act will follow. Such action could be of a generalised nature or may even be very similar to what was specifically portrayed in the media – in which case, it could be an example of a 'copy-cat crime' (Phillips 1986).

Erotica and aggression

If exposure to erotica, such as in magazines and films, can lead to sexual arousal, might it also be related to later aggression? The answer must be yes, if only because of the possibility of the excitation-transfer effect (see Figure 11.1). This phenomenon, however, depends on the person experiencing some later frustrating event which acts as a trigger to aggress. So, the next question is whether sexual arousal from erotica *per se* is sufficient to cause aggression. It should be stressed here that we are talking about non-violent erotica. The evidence points to a U-function, depending on the kind of erotica viewed. Looking at pictures of attractive nudes, for example, seems to reduce aggression when compared with a control condition of neutral pictures, pointing to a distracting effect caused by mild erotica (Baron 1979; Ramirez *et al.* 1983). On the other hand, the viewing of highly erotic materials such as explicit lovemaking can increase aggression (Baron and Bell 1977; Zillman 1984). Zillman and Bryant (1984) reported higher levels of aggression by both males and females against an annoying person following massive exposure to violent pornography. We should note that these are experimental effects and could be explained as instances of excitation-transfer – the design typically involves a later provoking event, such as an irritating confederate in an experiment.

Following their long exposure to violent pornography, Zillman and Bryant's subjects became more callous about what they had seen – they viewed rape more tolerantly and became more lenient about prison sentences which they would recommend as a function of the amount of pornography which they had viewed (see Figure 11.6).

Linz *et al.* (1988) reported that when women were depicted to be enjoying violent pornography, men were later more willing to aggress against women, though, interestingly, not against men.

Perhaps just as telling are other consequences of such material. It can perpetuate the myth that women actually enjoy sexual violence. It has been demonstrated that portrayals of women apparently enjoying such acts reinforces rape myths and weakens social and cognitive restraints over violence towards women (Malamuth and Donnerstein 1982). Zillman and Bryant (1984) pointed out that massive exposure to violent pornography

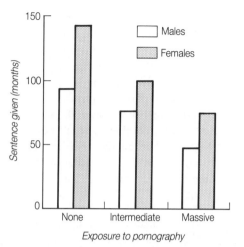

FIGURE 11.6 *Effect of viewing pornographic films on lenience in giving prison sentences. (Source: based on data from Zillmann and Bryant 1984.)*

trivialises rape by portraying women as 'hyperpromiscuous and socially irresponsible'.

There has been a growth of resistance to such materials by women's movements in recent years. A *feminist perspective* emphasises two concerns about continual exposure of males to media depicting violence and/or sexually explicit material involving women:

1. That exposure to violence will cause males to become callous or desensitised to violence against female victims.
2. That exposure to pornography will contribute to the development of negative attitudes towards women.

Some feminist writers (see Gubar and Hoff 1989) maintain that pornography is a blight when it depicts women as subordinate to men and existing solely to satisfy men's sexual needs.

DOMESTIC VIOLENCE

Behind closed doors

Domestic violence has been a topic of much concern in our community and has prompted considerable research in recent years. However, it is difficult to assess whether domestic violence is actually increasing or whether supporting data reflect a higher level of vigilance and reporting, more media publicity or even unreliable statistics. People are often reluctant to report or admit to violence within their homes, so that it is difficult to know how commonly it occurs (Haines 1987). A survey of more than two thousand families in the United States revealed that some kind of physical assault with intent to injure had occurred in 28 per cent of the married couples sampled, and in 16 per cent of the cases within the past year. These were not trivial acts, but behaviours such as pushing, hitting with fist, slapping, kicking, throwing something, and beating up. Seven per cent reported being threatened with a gun or knife (Straus *et al.* 1980). Moreover, more than 70 per cent of parents reported using slaps and spankings on children, and 20 per cent admitted to hitting children with some object. The phenomenon extends with equal or greater frequency to intimate relationships outside of families (Sigelman *et al.* 1984), and the difference between the sexes appears to relate to the degree of violence of the acts but not to the frequency with which they occur (Straus *et al.* 1980).

There is also evidence to a link between the experience of being a victim of violence and lack of adequate prosocial behaviours towards others. When abused toddlers were compared with other pre-school children who had affectionate and caring parents, they were found to be quite unsympathetic towards age-mates in distress (Zahn-Waxler *et al.* 1979).

Why do people remain silent about the physically and psychologically traumatic attacks they suffer? Personal pride, fear of reprisals either on oneself or another family member (Fergusson *et al.* 1986), fear of blame or social ridicule, and the perceived and actual failure of the police and others to provide any real help – these have all been found to prevent people from telling others about the violence which occurs behind closed doors. Thus the majority of instances go unreported, and therefore unpunished and without constructive or protective intervention.

Hurting the ones we 'love'

It has been suggested that assault, rape and incest within intimate relationships may account for as much as 80 per cent of all violent offending. Why do people want to hurt those closest to them? Again, there are no simple answers, but some of the most influential factors are:

▶ Abuse syndrome
1. *Learned patterns of aggression*, imitated from parents, together with low competence in other non-aggressive ways of responding; the generational cycle of child abuse is a well-established phenomenon (Straus *et al.* 1980), and the chronic repetition of violence within some families has been identified now as an *abuse syndrome*.
2. The *proximity* of family members, which makes them more likely to be sources of annoyance or frustration, and targets when these feelings are generated externally.
3. *Stresses*, especially financial difficulties, unemployment and illnesses, which

partly account for domestic violence being much more common in poorer families.

4. The division of *power* within traditional nuclear families, favouring the male, which makes it easier for less democratic styles of interaction to predominate.

The interaction of these factors, heightened by the normal stresses of day-to-day living which we all encounter, means that those we live closest to are, ironically, the likely targets of our aggression. A further irony is that domestic violence seems to be most common in, if not endemic to, the so-called civilised societies, and relatively uncommon in the so-called primitive ones (Steinmetz and Straus 1973); which suggests that factors associated with the 'civilisation' process, such as urbanisation, population increase and density (see Chapter 15) and competition for resources may play an important part in starting the cycle of domestic abuse. In spite of substantial efforts in recent years to provide preventive and protective interventions, it is uncertain whether these various social programmes and legal measures have actually been successful in reducing the incidence of domestic abuse, either in general or in individual cases (Clarkson *et al.* 1985; Ney and Herron 1985).

INSTITUTIONALISED AGGRESSION

Role of society

Aggression has not been universally defined by all societies as necessarily bad. In our society, an emphasis on non-violence is an outcome of historical and socio-cultural factors; it is an ethic which derives from a combination of politics, religions and events in recent history, including the atrocities of the Second World War and the Vietnam War, and the threat of nuclear annihilation. As mentioned earlier, the point to remember is that it constitutes a socio-cultural value judgement about aggression, and that each society views various kinds of aggression in different ways.

▶ Social order
▶ Norms
▶ Institutionalised aggression

We noted at the outset that biological theories usually argue that aggression is functional, that is it has useful properties. Can we find examples of human aggression, apart from personal self-defence, that seem reasonable? To an extent, issues of definition reappear: there are ways in which aggression has been used, at both interpersonal and societal levels, in an attempt to bring about positive outcomes for individuals or particular groups, which have in common the characteristic of preserving the *social order* (see Kelvin 1970). In the first instance, human societies depend for their continuity on social *norms*; those that are well established may become embedded in values that are widely shared in a community, such as 'caring for one's fellows'. Ultimately, protection for a social system is provided by law. Occasionally, the mechanisms of social order may even sanction the use of violence. Table 11.2 sets out some

Institutionalised aggression. By its nature, a contact sport presents a problem in distinguishing between play which is fair but rough and that which is foul. A difficulty in drawing a line is that some forms of violence can be legitimised by the rules of the game. (Source: *New Zealand Herald.*)

'legitimate' functions of *institutionalised aggression*, but also suggests that they can have either socially desirable or undesirable effects, depending on the degree of violence used and the motives underlying the acts. Moral issues underlie the judgements that we might make, as they do when we debate issues such as suicide, abortion and euthanasia – all of which can be made to fit a definition of aggression. Since the end of the Cold War we have also witnessed a moral debate about the conditions under which the United Nations, NATO or the United States should use military force to impose peace and humanity

TABLE 11.2 Social control functions of aggression

Bona fide or intended function	'Desirable' effects (?)	'Undesirable' effects (?)
• National defence	• US forces in Vietnam	• My Lai massacre
• Policing; law and order	• Use of 'bouncers' in night clubs	• Death penalty for drug trafficking
• Behaviour control	• Smacking young children	• Caning in schools
• Protection of civilians	• US soldiers hold northern Iraq for Kurdish refugees	• British occupation of Northern Ireland
• Self-defence	• Martial arts (for example, karate)	• Legal, domestic ownership of guns

on international 'trouble spots', for example Somalia, Bosnia, Rwanda and Haiti.

War: aggression on a grand scale

Large-scale aggression and war, which can be linked to the topics of prejudice and discrimination (discussed in Chapters 9 and 10) continue as part of the human condition, and an increasingly technologically oriented civilisation seems no better equipped than a more simple one in eliminating these phenomena.

One way of glimpsing the continuing tragedy is to consider the incidence and severity of wars. In the First World War (1914–18) four million died directly from the conflict. The figure was fifteen million in the Second World War (1939–45), even disregarding acts of genocide such as the six million Jews exterminated during the Holocaust, deaths in concentration camps, or civilians killed in bombing raids in Europe. Table 11.3 includes interstate wars between 1946 and 1981, and only those in which more than one thousand deaths have

TABLE 11.3 Interstate wars 1946–81 with deaths exceeding one thousand

War	Period	Deaths
Palestine	1948–49	16,000
Korea	1950–53	2,000,000
Hungary	1956	39,000
Sinai	1956	4,000
Sino-India	1962	5,000
First Kashmir	1947–49	1,000
UK–India	1946–48	800,000
Yugoslavia	1946–48	45,000
Egypt	1948–59	8,000
Indo-China	1946–54	105,000
Madagascar	1947–49	1,000
Laos	1953–73	10,000
Algeria	1954–62	115,000
Tibet	1956–59	14,000
Suez	1957	3,500
Lebanon	1958–81	45,000
Vietnam	1961–75	1,000,000
Second Kashmir	1965	14,000
Six-day (Israeli)	1967	21,000
Honduras–Salvador	1969	2,000
Bangladesh	1971	17,000
Cambodia	1975–79	2,500,000
Angola	1961–75	38,000
Angola	1979	6,000
China–Vietnam	1979	70,000

Source: Vaughan 1988.

been documented. Even these estimates (Dupuy and Dupuy 1977; Hartman and Mitchell 1984; Singer and Small 1972) are conservative; and the list does not include fatal casualties in civil wars and wars of independence during the period covered.

Role of the state

The worst acts of inhumanity are committed against humanity itself. Warfare is not possible without a supporting psychological structure involving the beliefs and emotions of a people. If such a structure is lacking, national leaders can create one by way of propaganda, as we noted in Chapter 5. In times of war, both the soldiers who are fighting and the people at home need to have 'good morale'. We noted in Chapter 9 that genocide can be thought of as a kind of legitimised prejudice, carried through into behaviour. Some political regimes have fostered beliefs in genetic differences between groups of people to justify oppression and slaughter. An ideology of racial inferiority was a cornerstone in the Nazi programme directed against Jews. Open antagonism expressed by Hitler led to German citizens avoiding all Jews, sometimes neighbours and friends. This climate paved the way for the enactment of the Nürnberg laws of discrimination. It was an easy step to the burning of synagogues and attacks on Jews. The horrific last link in the chain was the killing of millions of people. The role of the state, then, can be to suggest to its citizens that aggression is reasonable in certain circumstances. Our earlier treatment of authoritarianism (Chapter 9) linked obedience to a set of personality characteristics, although this research has been found wanting as a major explanation of prejudice and of aggressive behaviour. However, a political structure which is a powerful autocracy is one which constrains its citizens to obey without question.

People as agents

In this context, Milgram's (1974) experiment on blind destructive obedience (covered in detail in Chapter 6) is worthy of further mention. We noted then that subjects from all walks of life were, in a series of experiments, willing to give apparently lethal shocks to a stranger when ordered to do so by a 'scientist'. Milgram gave lie to an explanation that these people were psychopaths: on the contrary, his results suggested that many of us might have responded in the same way. Although his work was criticised for its supposed artificiality with respect to 'real life', as well as for his deception of subjects to induce an 'immoral act', Milgram defended himself on the grounds of his contribution to the understanding of ordinary people's willingness to aggress when obeying a legitimate authority. A few years after the original experiment (Milgram 1963) came the news of a massacre of men, women and children at a village called My Lai in Vietnam in 1969. This war scarred the American psyche more than any other, and this incident has acquired a uniqueness by exploding the myth that atrocities are only committed by the 'enemy'.

▶ Agentic mode

Milgram generalised from the theatre of war to the everyday life of citizens in any country: people are taught from childhood to obey both the laws of the state and orders of those who represent its authority. In so doing, citizens enter an *agentic mode* of thinking and distance themselves from personal responsibility for their actions.

Levels of explanation

▶ Levels of explanation or analysis

We noted earlier in this chapter that different *levels of explanation* may be adopted to account for aggression, and, in Chapter 1, for a wide variety of social behaviours. In the context of war, psychological explanations have varied in degree from being heavily person-centred to those that are group-centred. Studies of authoritarianism have stressed that prejudice, discrimination, violence and war atrocities reside in extreme or deviant personalities. Milgram moved a step away from this by suggesting that individuals experience a psychological condition of becoming agents of the state and will carry out orders which can harm others when the voice of authority seems legitimate. Sherif (Sherif and Sherif 1953) moved well away from an individual level of explanation by relating large-scale conflict to the nature of *intergroup relations*, suggesting that discriminatory acts against an outgroup will flower only when the objective interests of the ingroup are threatened. Tajfel refined this group-centred approach by pointing to the very existence of groups as the essential cause of prejudice, discrimination and conflict. Outgroups provide a reference and must be kept at bay. These issues are examined in detail in Chapter 10.

The contrast between a person-based and a group-based account of aggression has been summed up by Tajfel (1974) in Box 11.6. The first account is an individualist perspective offered by Berkowitz (1962). The second account by Tajfel has taken Berkowitz's own words and made crucial substitutions of terms which implicate society as the 'cause'.

REDUCING AGGRESSION

With the development of behavioural technologies based on social learning theory, and the increased attention given to the social costs of apparently increasing violence, there has been more effort put into the prevention and control of aggression. The effectiveness of interventions to reduce aggressive behaviour on both interpersonal and intergroup levels is a contentious issue and can involve political decisions about the costs involved. To make an impact on the underlying causes of violence requires significant changes at the societal level to improve the conditions of those sectors of our society which are plagued by stresses which exacerbate the cyclic repetition of violence. At the family level, parents can contribute to raising more peaceful children by not rewarding acts of violence, by rewarding behaviour that is not compatible with violence, and by avoiding the use of punishing behaviour themselves.

At the interpersonal level there is probably more optimism, and there are

BOX 11.6 Two different levels of explanation of aggression and war

Individual versus social levels of explanation

We have noted that an explanation of prejudice and discrimination was once offered by Adorno *et al.* (1950) in terms of person characteristics, namely, the authoritarian personality. The use of a similar individual level of explanation is clear in the views of Berkowitz (1962) in his account of the causes of aggression:

> Granting all this, the present writer is still inclined to emphasise the importance of individualistic considerations in the field of group relations. Dealings between groups ultimately become problems of the psychology of the individual. Individuals decide to go to war; battles are fought by individuals; and peace is established by individuals. It is the individual who adopts the beliefs prevailing in his society, even though the extent to which these opinions are shared by many people is a factor governing his readiness to adopt them, and he transmits these views to other individuals. Ultimately, it is the single person who attacks the feared and disliked ethnic minority group, even though many people around him share his feelings and are very important in determining his willingness to aggress against this minority. (Berkowitz 1962, p.167).

Tajfel regarded this view as typical of the restricted level of explanation offered by American social psychology. In an unpublished paper written in 1974, he deliberately rewrote Berkowitz's words as follows, using words in italics to emphasise where an individual focus is replaced by a societal one:

> Granting all this, the present writer is still inclined to emphasise the importance of *considering the field of group relations in terms of social structure*. Dealings between groups *cannot be accounted for* by the psychology of the individual. *Governments* decide to go to war; battles are fought by *armies*; and peace is established by *governments*. The *social conditions* in which groups live largely determine their beliefs and the extent to which they are shared. Ultimately, a single person's attack on an ethnic minority group that he dislikes or fears would remain a trivial occurrence had it not been for the fact that he acts in *unison with others* who share his feelings and are very important in determining his willingness to aggress against this minority.

(Source: Vaughan 1988.)

techniques of behaviour modification, social skills training, non-aggressive modelling, anger management and assertiveness training that have been shown to be effective in teaching people personal self-control in this area.

▶ Peace studies

Mass violence such as genocide and war is quite a different matter. The introduction of *peace studies* into the education system may well help to cause some people to think twice before acting in ways which might support intergroup aggression: for example, one can cast one's vote in such a way as to exclude from office political parties which endorse war. However, these sorts of provision may only be available to prosperous democratic countries with highly developed educational systems. Mass aggression is intergroup aggression and, as we discussed in Chapter 10, it is very difficult to reduce intergroup aggression without dealing directly with the underlying social identities, prejudices, group stereotypes, real conflicts of interests between groups and histories of intergroup relations.

We cannot wave a magic wand and banish violence. At a community level, aggression is maintained to a large degree by inequitable relationships between groups (see Chapters 9 and 10). At an interpersonal level, it is linked to the way people handle frustration. There is room at both of these levels for social psychologists and others to work towards harmony in a world of increasing stress and dwindling resources.

SUMMARY

- 'Aggression' has had a wide number of definitions which reflect differences in underlying theories about its nature and its causes. One recent, and simple, definition is 'the intentional infliction of some type of harm on others'.
- There have been two major classes of theory about the origins of aggression, one stressing its biological origins and the other stressing social influences.
- Biological explanations can be traced to Darwinian theory and include the views of Freud, the ethologists and, more recently, the sociobiologists. These approaches share an emphasis on genetically determined behaviour patterns shared by a species.
- Social explanations usually stress the role of societal influences and/or learning processes. Some incorporate a biological component as well, such as the frustration-aggression hypothesis and excitation-transfer theory. Social learning theory is a developmental approach which stresses reinforcement principles and the influence that models have on the young child.
- Some research into causes has concentrated on factors thought to be 'part' of the person, such as personality correlates and gender. Other work has looked at transitory states: the experience of frustration, the role of catharsis, the effects of provocation and of alcohol, and the experience of disinhibition.
- Other studies have focused on situational factors. These include stressors in the physical environment, such as heat and crowding. A major societal

variable is the perceived disadvantage which some groups have in relation to those holding power. This analysis is basic to relative deprivation theory.

♦ A social approach to aggression allows for the possibility of change in patterns over time and cultural context. A challenging possibility in recent times is that aggression is increasing in women. Less surprising are data showing that rates of physical aggression vary across cultures, reflecting long-standing differences in norms and values.

♦ The role of the mass media, particularly television, is controversial. It is fashionable to argue that the continued portrayal of violence at the very least desensitises young people to the consequences of violence. A stronger argument is that it provides a model for future behaviour – a debate which still continues.

♦ Reports of domestic violence against spouse and children now have a high profile in our community. Whether these trends are now more common is a moot point. The rise of the women's refuge movement is a direct response to increased awareness of the magnitude of the problem.

♦ War is a continuing massive blight on humanity. Arguments about its causes and its prevention which are defined purely in political terms miss a crucial point: the role of intergroup relations themselves, and the perpetuation across generations of outgroup stereotypes and prejudice.

FURTHER READING

Averill, J. R. (1982). *Anger and Aggression*. New York: Springer-Verlag.
Baron, R. A. and Richardson, D. R. (1991). *Human Aggression* (2nd edn). New York: Plenum.
Zillman, D. (1979). *Hostility and Aggression*. Hillsdale, NJ: Erlbaum.

▶ KEY TERMS

abuse syndrome
agentic mode
analogue
biosocial theories
catharsis
collective aggression
cultural norm
dehumanisation
dindividuation
disinhibition
ethology
excitation-transfer model

fighting instinct
frustration-aggression hypothesis
homicide
instinct
institutionalised aggression
learning by direct experience
learning by vicarious experience
levels of explanation or analysis
modelling
nature/nurture controversy
neo-associationist analysis
neo-Freudians

norms
operational definition
peace studies
priming
reciprocity principle
relative deprivation
releasers

social learning theory
social order
sociobiology
subculture of violence
Type A personality
value

12 Affiliation, attraction and love

··

FOCUS QUESTIONS

◆ Have you ever taken your mother and father for granted? Join the team. We are told from our early years that we owe them a great deal, but would you believe that their role as caretakers is crucial to your intellectual and social development, setting you on the path to proper functioning as a human being?

◆ Why do we need to interact with other people? Can we not just be islands unto ourselves?

◆ You have just been introduced to an attractive stranger. How fairly can you judge this person's other attributes, such as their intelligence?

◆ How do romance and companionship differ?

◆ If a relationship ends, the ending can come out of the blue – true or false?

WHY AFFILIATE?

The need to affiliate underlies the way in which we form interpersonal relationships. Most people need to be with and to interact with others. At times we may appear to behave in a contrary way and wish simply to enjoy our own company. Most of us do not have the opportunity to do this for more than some hours, so that it is interesting to consider instances where people have been isolated for long periods of time.

▶ Need to affiliate

In the early part of this century, an attempt was made to explain affiliative behaviour in terms of instinct. McDougall (1908), for example, put it down to a gregarious propensity, that is, an inborn tendency to gather together. In this respect, he thought, we have something in common with other animals who live in herds or colonies. Simplistic instinct theories fell out of favour with the advent of the behaviourist revolution spearheaded by Watson (1913), who argued that simply accounting for a behaviour like herding by calling it a herding instinct is no explanation at all. An attempt to find some biological base for social behaviour still persists among sociobiologists, however, and examples of this approach are touched in relation to aggression (see Chapter 11) and to prosocial behaviour (see Chapter 13).

In apparent opposition to affiliation is the need we all show at times to avoid interacting with others. In Chapter 15 we argue that this conflict of motives is really a balancing act in an attempt to regulate our privacy: in a busy world we sometimes want some 'space' to ourselves, while at other times we seek out company.

▶ Affiliative behaviour   In the following sections we look first at the effects of being isolated, as a form of indirect evidence that being with others fulfils a number of important functions. At the same time we can examine several proposals of the reasons underlying *affiliative behaviour*. From there we turn our attention to the attraction process, focusing on why we choose some persons rather than others as the ones with whom we would prefer to interact. The question of attraction leads naturally to the area of long-term relationships and the nature of love.

No-one is an island

One way of learning what it means to affiliate is to ask what happens when people are prevented from being with others. We shall see that even relatively short-term separation from other people can be a nasty experience. Even more compelling, long-term separation can have serious consequences and, in the case of the young, permanently damaging outcomes.

Stories from the field

There have been many situations in which people have been isolated and then returned to the company of others to tell their stories, for example, prisoners in solitary confinement and shipwreck survivors. However, in these situations, the experience of isolation has also been accompanied by deprivation of another form, such as food, or it has been enforced as punishment. For this reason, the experiences of Admiral Byrd are perhaps the most interesting example we have as his isolation was voluntary and planned, so he had adequate supplies to cater to his physical needs.

Admiral Byrd volunteered to spend six months alone in an Antarctic weather station observing and recording conditions. Although he had radio contact with the main base of the expedition, he had no other contact with people. He reported looking forward to the experience as he wanted to 'be by myself for a while and to taste peace and quiet and solitude long enough to find out how good they really are' (Byrd 1938, p. 4). However, after twenty-four days he began to write of the loneliness he felt and how this caused him to feel 'lost and bewildered' (p. 95). He began embroidering his experience by imagining that he was among familiar people. After sixty-three days he became preoccupied with religious questions and dwelt on the 'meaning of life'. His thoughts turned to ways of believing that he was not alone: 'The human race, then, is not alone in the universe. Though I am cut off from human beings, I am not alone' (p. 185). After three months, he became severely depressed and apathetic. He was beset with hallucinations and bizarre ideas.

The effects of 'wintering over' among both navy and civilian personnel in the Antarctic have been detailed recently by Taylor (1987), which we take up again in the context of the effects of the physical environment on social functioning in Chapter 15.

Although this evidence is based on reports from people who have left the trappings of 'normal civilisation' behind, it is supported by other accounts of those for whom long periods of isolation is part of their annual experience of seasonal cycles. For example, Eskimos go fishing in groups to prevent hallucinations and thereby avert disasters, such as drowning. Young males of the American Plains Indians deliberately isolated themselves for several days to await a visitation from benevolent spirits, for them a positive experience. However, westerners who experience hallucinations generally seem to have found them, and the other correlates of isolation, an extremely stressful experience. Some never recover. Lilly (1956) reviewed some of the autobiographies of people who had endured isolation and concluded that they displayed many, if not all, of the symptoms of the mentally ill.

Short-term sensory deprivation

▶ Brainwashing
▶ Sensory
deprivation

A dramatic experiment of not only social but also nearly total sensory isolation was carried out at McGill University in Canada by Bexton *et al.* (1954). This work grew out of interest in the way in which enforced isolation was thought to contribute to the phenomenon of *brainwashing*, an experience which received media publicity following reports of the solitary confinement, sleep deprivation and intensive interrogation of western prisoners during the Korean War of the 1950s. The subjects in the McGill experiment were twenty-two paid volunteer students who were surprised to find that their task was to lie on a bed, wearing opaque goggles, cardboard cuffs, heavy gloves, and do nothing. The location was in a sound-deadened cubicle, there was a masking hum, and there was a foam pillow fitted around the person's ears. After nearly three days of this severe reduction in sensory input, subjects reported fuzzy vision, difficulties in focusing, the appearance of the visual environment as two-dimensional, and deterioration on a number of cognitive tasks. In a follow-up study by Bexton (cited in Kubzansky 1961), subjects were also persuaded to change their views on psychic phenomena after listening to a long and monotonous recorded propaganda message.

We should note that the effects reported in this research follow from short-term sensory and social isolation, and that the outcomes are transitory, even if immediate. Nevertheless, *sensory deprivation* studies of human volunteers provide an interesting example of the power of the social context over the individual. We come to understand something of the importance of having others near us by experimentally impoverishing the environment, that is, taking these others away. We return to this theme in dealing with the topic of loneliness.

Clinical studies of infants

▶ Hospitalism

According to child psychiatrist Bowlby (1988), the release of two films had a profound effect on research workers in the 1950s, one by René Spitz, *Grief: A Peril in Infancy* (1947), and the other by James Robertson, *A Two-Year-Old Goes to Hospital* (1952). Survival, it transpired, depends on physical needs, but also on a quite independent need for care and intimate interaction. Reminiscent of recent discoveries in Romania, Spitz (1945) reported on babies who had been left in an overcrowded institution for a two-year period by mothers unable to look after them. These babies were, in essence, deprived of a caregiver during this time. They were, of course, fed but were rarely handled, and were confined to their cots for most of their sleeping and waking hours. Not only were they later found to be less advanced, mentally and socially, when compared with other institutionalised children who had been given adequate care, but the mortality rate was extremely high. Spitz coined the term *hospitalism* to describe the psychological condition in which he found these children.

▶ Attachment behaviour

Systematic research of infant behaviour would seem to support this view. Bowlby (1969) and his colleagues studied the attachment of infants to their mothers, noting that young children maintain physical proximity with their mothers or restore it if disrupted. Behaviours observed were signal behaviours such as crying and smiling and also behaviours which physically maintained proximity such as clinging or following, all of which Bowlby attributed to an innate affiliative drive. Innate predispositions, of course, are anathema to

The effects of being in a day centre. The child whose parents work need not be socially deprived. One recipe for a well-adjusted youngster appears to be a high rate of contact with peers and with compassionate adults combined with reduced contact, though of good quality, with the parents. (Source: Andrew Lukey.)

learning theorists who would prefer to argue that infants come to associate their mothers with need-reduction and pleasure, and therefore seek them out on this basis. Whatever its basis, the tendency to affiliate is both strong and observable. For Bowlby, *attachment behaviour* is not limited to the mother/infant experience, but can be observed throughout the life-cycle, especially in emergencies. In a study by Feeney and Noller (1990), different attachment styles shown in childhood, such as secure, avoidant and anxious, can be picked up in the way romantic relationships are formed in later life.

That isolation can cause such extreme effects leads to the general proposition that all of us need people, that affiliation is important. Why we have a need to affiliate is a more complex question. Physical survival needs could answer the question if we were concerned only with infants. The infant has no resources of its own to feed, protect or provide itself with shelter. All these needs must be met by another person. The only resource at the infant's disposal is a rather loud signal (crying) which is easily perceived by older humans as registering a need. The infant uses this tool to summon other people to identify and meet its needs. Adults can take care of most of their own physical needs, yet still we need to affiliate. It is possible that this is a residual learned response from childhood, but the strength of reactions to isolation places doubt on this.

▶ Feral children

There have been several documented cases of children who were virtually totally deprived of human contact over a period of several years. They are sometimes referred to as *feral children*, a term suggesting that they behave as if reared in the wild, by animals. Davis (1949) reported the cases of two children, Anna and Isabelle, each of whom had been kept in nearly total seclusion for the first few years of their life. Anna was kept in a room without windows, seated in a chair, with her hands tied, her punishment for being illegitimate. When discovered by the authorities, she was thought to be deaf and blind. Later care showed that these senses were intact; and she learned to communicate in short phrases, and before her death at ten years of age, could look after her bodily needs and understand simple directions. Isabelle spent her first years in a darkened room. Although she had the company of her mother, the latter was a deaf mute. When first examined by specialists, she was thought to be both deaf and mentally retarded. She not only learned to talk, however, but accelerated through several stages of cognitive and social development, and completed high school.

We cannot be sure, of course, that Anna and Isabelle were not substantially different from each other in intellectual capacity at birth; but it is interesting to note that Isabelle made the greater progress, especially in terms of language mastery, after her release from isolation; and it was she who had the company of another person, albeit a deaf mute, during her first years.

Developmental studies of the kind referred to so far point to the need of the young child to receive a modicum of care and attention for adequate socialisation to take place. What is not indicated is that this care must come from a *parent*. A study of kibbutz children in Israel, a context in which child-care is group-centred rather than parent-centred, has not pointed to any intellectual or social deficit (Kohen-Raz 1968). Likewise, an American study of the children of working mothers has reported that adequate development can take place in day-care centres. Moreover, the daily periods of maternal separation were not found to interfere with a child's attachment to its mother which had built up in its baby years (Farran and Ramey 1977). What we can conclude is that close contact with other humans is important for the young child, a role normally (but not necessarily) played by the parents.

Studies of animals

▶ Maternal deprivation We have noted in the last section that the young 'prisoner' Isabelle made social as well as intellectual progress when she was placed into society. This change is an example of socialisation. We can think of this as the process by which society moulds an individual's behaviour to follow certain rules which, if generally obeyed, make it acceptable to others in the community (see Moreland and Levine's (1982) theory of group socialisation in Chapter 7). Those deprived socially may not only appear to be 'strange' to other people, but may also be unable to use and harness the range of resources available around them. For most of us, the earliest socialising influence is provided by our parents. Some of the most penetrating insights into factors which are crucial to normal social development have been provided by Harlow in studies of relationships between newborn rhesus monkeys and their mothers (Harlow 1958; Harlow and Harlow 1965; Harlow and Zimmermann 1959). His work on *maternal deprivation* was carried out at the University of Wisconsin at the same time that Bowlby was carrying out his research in London, each being aware of the other's ideas. Bowlby (1988) has discussed Harlow's work in a way that showed he was not fussed that one set of studies was carried out on human infants and the other on monkeys. The principles uncovered have much in common.

In one of Harlow's experiments, baby monkeys were separated from their mothers at birth and raised in isolation for up to twelve months. Each baby's home was a wire cage, which contained an artificial mother. In one condition, the mother surrogate was no more than a wire frame; in a second condition, this frame was covered with towelling cloth, and topped with a primitive face. As a further variable, each 'mother' was either equipped or not with a lactating nipple. The results are shown in Figure 12.1.

Lactation turned out to have little effect on the number of hours per day which a baby spent in contact with the surrogate mother. The critical determinant was the provision of the soft cloth covering, something which the baby could cling to. The results in Figure 12.1 point clearly to a preference by the baby monkey for a soft, dry (non-lactating) surrogate over a wire, nursing (lactating) surrogate. At these extreme limits of 'motherhood', contact comfort proved to be a major factor in forming an affectional bond between baby and

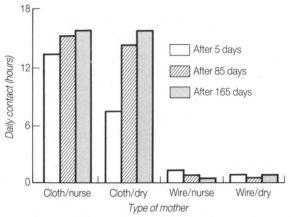

FIGURE 12.1 *Baby monkeys' preference for 'mothers' who differ in their softness and their capacity to nurse. (Source: based on data from Harlow 1958.)*

mother. Follow-up research showed that the baby monkey would spend more time on a rocking mother than on a stationary mother; and, in the early days of life, on a warm mother than on a cold mother.

A monkey mother, however, provides more than contact, food, rocking and warmth: she is the first link in the chain of the baby's experience of socialisation. Harlow's investigation was extended to babies who were totally isolated from contact with any living thing for up to twelve months. He found that such long periods of solitary confinement had drastic consequences. The infant monkeys would sometimes huddle in a corner, rock back and forth repetitively, and bite themselves. When later exposed to normal peers, they did not enter into the rough-and-tumble play of the others, and failed to defend themselves from attack. As adults, they were sexually incompetent; as parents, a state achieved by artificial insemination, there was an absence of adequate parenting behaviour. There were also examples of violent 'child abuse', such as a mother biting her baby to death. In all, there was a marked failure by monkeys who had been reared in total isolation to make a satisfactory or acceptable adjustment to the needs of living a normal social life. Harlow's study is an example of an artificially contrived laboratory situation for monkeys which would not occur in their natural habitat. In the wild, motherless young animals are either adopted or killed very quickly. However, its relevance to humans is clear enough when we think back to the sad cases of Anna and Isabelle.

In sum, studies of baby monkeys and of humans show that long-term social isolation is very damaging to the individual involved, and that the effects can be permanent. Up to this point, we have considered the question of an underlying need to affiliate against a background of what happens when we are deprived of social relationships. In the next section we take a different approach to explanation, one which features a transitory experience for humans.

Reducing anxiety: a short-term motive

▶ Shared stress

The quest for explanation of the purpose behind affiliative behaviour can include a passing motive state. Such a case is provided by the research of Schachter into the role played by anxiety reduction. In a famous experiment (1959) dealing with a condition sometimes referred to as *shared stress*, female psychology students were led to believe that they were to receive electric shocks. One group was told that the shocks would be painful (high anxiety condition), while another group was told that the shocks would not be at all painful (low anxiety condition). Subjects were then told that there would be a delay while the equipment was set up. They were given the option of either waiting alone or with another subject. Once this choice was made, the experiment was terminated (see Case A in Figure 12.2). Results supported Schachter's hypothesis that a greater preference for company would occur among high-anxious subjects: twenty of the thirty-two high-anxious subjects elected to wait with others, while only ten of the thirty low-anxious subjects chose this option.

▶ Social comparison

Schachter also asked why it is that anxious people prefer company (see Case B in Figure 12.2). It could be hypothesised either that the presence of another person provided a distraction from the anxiety-provoking stimulus, or that subjects wanted company for *social comparison*, that is, a yardstick against which to validate their reactions. If a distraction was desired, then any person would suffice for company. However, if company was desired for social-comparison purposes, the other person would need to be in a similar situation for the comparison to be valid. Subjects in this experiment were all told that they were to receive painful electric shocks, so they were all in a high-anxiety condition. They were given the choice of either waiting alone or waiting with others. The characteristics of the others formed the independent variable in this situation because some subjects were to choose between waiting alone and waiting with others involved in the same experiment, while for other subjects the choice was between waiting alone and waiting with other students who were not involved in the experiment, but merely waiting to see their teachers.

The results for Case B in Figure 12.2 showed that the preference for company could not be accounted for by a desire for distraction: those who were able to choose to wait with others involved in the experiment did so, whereas those who could choose to wait with uninvolved students preferred to wait alone. This points quite strongly to social comparison as the motive for affiliation in times of fear, specifying, however, that not any old company will do. It seems that if we have something to worry about we prefer to wait with another worrier. Putting this into a practical situation, it suggests that patients awaiting surgery would prefer to be with others like themselves who are awaiting surgery rather than, for example, with friends on their way to watch a football match.

In summary, the need to affiliate can be affected by temporary states, such as fear. It is not just any old person that we want to be with, but somebody specific. The reduction of anxiety is only one condition which invokes the process of social comparison. In a broader context, we make these comparisons whenever we look to the views of a special group, our friends. How people

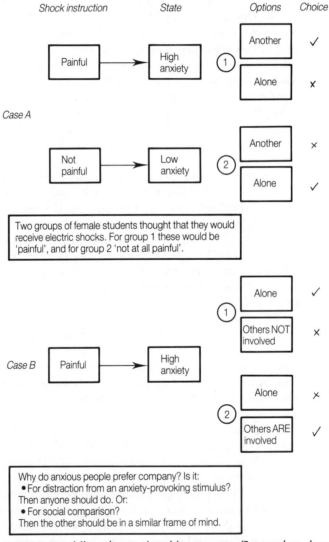

FIGURE 12.2 *Misery loves miserable company. (Source: based on data from Schachter 1959.)*

come to be part of this special group is looked at in the next section dealing with why some people attract us more than others.

WHY ARE SOME PEOPLE ATTRACTIVE?

Attraction occurs when a person feels positively towards another. This usually makes us want to know that person, to spend some time with them, and is how friendships begin. However, we meet many people who do not become friends. Some of the reasons for our friendship choices are discussed below.

Physical attractiveness

You will be familiar with the saying 'beauty is in the eye of the beholder', which suggests that what is regarded as physically attractive is a matter of personal preference. Another view is that what is beautiful is a matter of fashion, a function of a particular society and its history. Some have also hinted at a more sociobiological dimension to physical attractiveness. For example, Cunningham (1986) argued that American men found women with 'cute' faces more attractive, and defined 'cute' as being a function of childlike appearance (the eyes are large and set well apart, and the nose and chin are small). 'Childlike' appearance in women might signal youth and hence greater childbearing potential.

The first thing we notice about others is usually how they look, and this tends to form the basis of the first evaluation we make. Although you might think that evaluating someone on the basis of their physical attractiveness is a superficial strategy, evidence shows that we frequently do it. An attractive person, for example, is less likely to be judged to be maladjusted or disturbed (Cash *et al.* 1977; Dion 1972) more likely to be offered a job on the basis of interview (Dipboye *et al.* 1977) and more likely to receive higher evaluations of written work.

In an experiment by Landy and Sigall (1974), male students were asked to grade two essays of different quality. (The same essays were also rated independently without knowledge of the authors' identity.) The students were provided with a photograph of the supposed writer, a female student. In a first condition, the good essay was paired with an attractive, and then with a relatively unattractive, photograph; in a second condition, the poor essay was paired with each of the photographs. Sad to relate, better grades were given to the attractive female (see Figure 12.3).

In another study, attractive people were rated as being happier and more successful, having a better personality and being more likely to get married than less attractive people (Dion *et al.* 1972). In a legal setting, jurors were found to be easier on attractive women defendants (Sigall and Ostrove 1975). With attractiveness such an asset, those who spend a lot of money on cosmetics and fashion could be making a real investment in their looks. Short

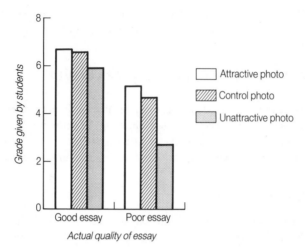

FIGURE 12.3 *Effect of perceived attractiveness on grades given to essays of varying quality. (Source: based on data from Landy and Sigall 1974.)*

of this, just a smile can also work wonders. Forgas and his colleagues (1983) found that students who smile were punished less after a misdemeanour than those who do not.

Proximity

▶ Proximity

Mundane as it might seem, the physical *proximity* (sometimes referred to as propinquity) of one person to another is a potent factor which facilitates attraction. Chance occurrences, such as who is allocated the adjoining room in the hostel, or who catches the same bus home, play an important role in determining friendships. In a study carried out in a housing complex, more people chose for their friends others living on the same floor rather than on a different floor or in more distant buildings (Festinger *et al.* 1950). This study (also discussed in Chapters 7 and 15) showed that subtle architectural features, such as the location of a staircase, can affect the process of making acquaintances and, therefore, of choosing one's friends.

Why is this so? A variety of studies point to several factors which hinge on the simple fact of being physically close.

Familiarity

▶ Familiarity

Proximity generally leads to repeated exposure and, therefore, more liking. This is a way of saying that a friend becomes like your favourite pair of shoes, something that you feel comfortable about! Zajonc (1968) has found that the repetitive presentation of a variety of stimuli increases liking for them. Familiarity extends to the faces of strangers, which are more liked as they are seen more often (Jorgensen and Cervone 1978), and to some discomfort when the familiar seems different. An example of this is that people do not usually like mirror reversals of photos of their own or other's appearance (Mita *et al.* 1977).

Availability

People who live close by are easily accessible, so that interaction with them requires little effort. Therefore, rewards of social interaction are available at a low cost. This notion of cost is considered in more detail below in terms of social exchange theory. Think what happens when a friend shifts to a distant place. Do you keep up the often-promised contact?

Expecting continued interaction

In line with Heider's (1958) balance theory (see Chapter 4), we can predict that it would be an uncomfortable experience not to get on with one's neighbours. More specifically, this includes the process of being aware that neighbours are people with whom further interaction is anticipated. An experiment by Berscheid *et al.* (1976), for example, showed that college students who thought they might actually date someone seen only on a videotape liked that person more than someone else with whom they were led to believe they might not have a continued interaction.

Reciprocity

▶ Reciprocity principle Liking, and disliking, often follow the *reciprocity principle*, that is, we tend to like those who like us and dislike those who dislike us. (See also how reciprocity can operate in the field of aggression in Chapter 11). Dittes and Kelley (1956) led students in small discussion groups to believe, by way of anonymous written evaluations (actually written by the experimenters), that other group members either liked or disliked them. Results showed that students who believed they were liked were more attracted to the group than those who believed they were disliked.

Reciprocity, however, may not operate uniformly between people. An influential variable seems to be the level of self-esteem. Dittes (1959) found that for those with high self-esteem, liking did not seem to be affected by acceptance or rejection. In contrast, those with low self-esteem liked the group a lot when they were accepted, but when rejected, they disliked the group a lot. Dittes carried out an experiment in which the subjects were classified as high or low on self-esteem. They were placed in a satisfying condition, where the group's behaviour towards them was positive, or a frustrating condition, where it was negative. For subjects who were low in self-esteem, attraction to the group depended on how the group behaved, whereas for those high in self-esteem the difference in attraction was not significant. These results are shown in Figure 12.4.

It could be argued that people who have high self-esteem do not need the bolster of assurances from others, whereas those who are low in self-esteem

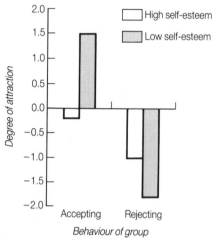

FIGURE 12.4 *Attraction to groups showing acceptance or rejection as a function of a member's self-esteem. (Source: based on data from Dittes 1959.)*

are in need of social support. An alternative explanation suggests a reverse causality. In a study by Minahan (1971), teenage schoolgirls with higher self-esteem gave more favourable ratings to their bodies, in terms of perceived physical attractiveness, than those lower in self-esteem. The higher self-esteem girls had more dates with boys and expected to marry earlier. The line of inference is that girls who were judged as more attractive by boys in turn judged themselves to be more attractive, leading to a more favourable self-image.

▶ Gain/loss hypothesis   The effects of reciprocity can interact with the nature of the situation. If reciprocity is based on the power of praise as a social reward, the outcome can vary along with the value of how the praise is perceived. For example, if praise comes from a flatterer with ulterior motives, its value will not be high and we will not respond with liking. We also attach lower value if the praise comes from a friend rather than a stranger, since we expect praise from our friends. The pattern in which the praise is received is also influential. An interesting example of this is the *gain/loss hypothesis*: we tend to like most those who initially dislike us, but then warm to us; and we dislike most those people who initially like us, but turn cold (Aronson and Linder 1965). This phenomenon is slightly puzzling as it runs counter to a reinforcement model: the person who is constantly praised receives more rewards but likes the praiser less. Aronson and Linder have suggested two explanations. The first involves anxiety reduction: when experiencing rejection, anxiety arises; when rejection changes to acceptance, the anxiety is reduced so that we experience the pleasure of being liked. Alternatively, it is possible that we regard those who like us from the beginning as undiscriminating, and this reduces the value of their praise. However, those who dislike us to begin with, but then re-evaluate as they get to know us better, are discerning people so their praise is worth more.

Aronson and Linder (1965) carried out an experiment designed to test the effect of the order in which we receive feedback from another person. Subjects heard feedback about themselves, across seven meetings, from a confederate. The quality of the feedback was either all negative or all positive for the first three meetings. Then, depending on the condition, the quality was either reversed or remained the same. Of the four conditions, liking for the confederate was greatest when the order was negative–positive, and least when it was positive–negative. The results are shown in Figure 12.5, indicating that we are most likely to be attracted to another when that person shifts from early dislike to showing liking for us.

Similarity

▶ Similarity of attitudes or values

Similarity of attitudes or values is one of the most important determinants of attraction to have been identified. In a classic study students were given rent-free accommodation in return for filling out numerous questionnaires about their attitudes and values (Newcomb 1961). The first questionnaires were filled out before the students arrived at the university. Over the course of a semester, attraction between the students and attitude changes were measured. Results showed that in the first few weeks, attraction was related to proximity. However, as the semester progressed, attraction related most closely to similarity of pre-acquaintance attitudes. Byrne (1971) confirmed the effect of attitude similarity on attraction in a series of laboratory experiments. A high degree of consistency in his results led him to formulate a 'law of attraction': this stated that attraction towards a person bears a linear relationship to the proportion of attitudes associated with the person (Clore and Byrne 1974). Clore (1976) has pointed out that the law is actually intended to be more general than simply applying to attitudes in common between two people.

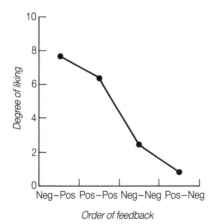

FIGURE 12.5 *The gain/loss hypothesis: negative and positive feedback on liking for another person. (Source: based on data from Aronson and Linder 1965.)*

Anything that other people do which agrees with your perception of things is reinforcing. The more they agree, the more reinforcing they are and the greater your attraction to them. The most obvious case is that of shared attitudes.

Cross-cultural research has offered evidence on a wider scale that similarity increases liking. In an extensive study of thirty different tribal groups in East Africa, Brewer (1968) found that perceived similarity was one of several factors which determined liking. Her fifteen hundred interviews highlighted three variables affecting inter-tribal attraction. In order of importance, they were:

1. Perceived similarity.
2. Physical distance between tribes.
3. Perceived educational and economic advancement.

When another tribe was thought to have quite different attitudes, social contact was avoided; if they were perceived as quite similar, intimate contact was possible. The physical distance factor meant that neighbours were generally liked more than those much further away. The more advanced a tribe was seen to be also increased liking, but this appeared to play a role only when a tribe was judged to be dissimilar in attitudes. The most disliked tribe would be one that was dissimilar and backward.

Need complementarity

▶ Need complementarity

In contrast to the theory of similarity, Winch (1958) has formulated a theory of complementarity of needs. Winch hypothesised that we seek others who can best satisfy our needs, for example the pairing of apparent opposites, as when a dominant person is attracted to a submissive partner. Although Winch found some support for his theory, later studies have been less encouraging (for example, Levinger *et al.* 1970). One reason that has been put forward to explain the seemingly contradictory evidence is that *need complementarity* may be more important at a particular stage in the development of a relationship. One study found that social-status factors were the most important predictors early in a dating relationship. Later, similarity of values became more important, which, in turn was followed by need complementarity (Kerckhoff and Davis 1962). However, this pattern has not been replicated by other studies. A second reason, put forward by Levinger (1964), is that studies in need complementarity tend to take global measures of personality characteristics, such as whether a person has a general need for dominance, rather than specific measures of needs relevant to close relationships. Support for this theory comes from Lipetz *et al.* (1970), who found that complementarity of needs relating to marriage did correlate with marital satisfaction, in spite of there being no correlation between complementarity of general psychological needs and marital satisfaction.

The dating game

One common piece of advice, especially to females, is that by pretending to be somewhat distant or aloof, you can attract the partner you desire. Presumably, the hypothesis guiding this behaviour is that by ensuring that a potential partner's early advances seem less than successful one can increase one's 'value' as a mate and thus appear more desirable. However, research suggests that this is not as simple as it first appears (see Box 12.1).

THEORIES OF ATTRACTION

Rarely in psychology does a theory account for the totality of a phenomenon. More frequently, several theories will contribute different perspectives, which focus on different aspects of the same process. Theories of attraction are no exception. At the broadest level, theories of attraction can be divided into those that view human nature as striving to maintain cognitive consistency, and those that invoke explanations in terms of behaviourism and reinforcement principles. In this section we deal with a major contribution of one approach based on consistency: balance theory. Behaviouristic theories have been put forward with a number of important variations. We look at two which favour a fairly traditional reinforcement approach and two more which are based on an economic model of people's behaviour.

Balance theory

Balance theory focuses on people's mental processes rather than objective reality (see also Chapter 4). It suggests that we like people who are similar to ourselves because agreement is an affirming experience involving positive affect. When two people like each other but find that there is something on which they disagree, whether it be an attitude or belief about an object or person, negative psychological tension arises, bringing about a state of imbalance. To reduce this tension and restore balance, one or both will alter their cognitions, resulting in agreement. If people perceive dissimilarity when they first meet, they will not like each other and a state of non-balance will exist which neither person will try to change, as there is no balance to be restored.

This theory does not, however, hold for every interaction we have. There are times when we like to be regarded as dissimilar, as this can make us feel unique and special. It has also been found that if the threat of rejection by the dissimilar other is removed, by knowing in advance that they are willing to discuss other points of view, the dissimilarity is no longer a barrier to interaction and attraction (Broome 1983; Sunafrank and Miller 1981).

BOX 12.1 Strategic subtleties in the dating game

Playing 'hard to get'

One common piece of advice, especially to females, is that playing 'hard-to-get' will help you to attract the partner that you desire. However, research suggests that this is not as simple as it first appears.

Walster *et al.* (1973), reported negative results on several studies which look at the 'hard to get' hypothesis. The first experiment involved college males who were recruited ostensibly to help improve a computer-dating service. They filled out a questionnaire and returned two weeks later to pick up the phone number of their prospective dates. They were asked to call her from the office so their first impressions could easily be recorded. To those in the *easy to get* condition, the confederate responded with delight at the phone call and being asked out. In the *hard to get* condition, the confederate reluctantly accepted a date, conveying the impression that she had many other dates. The subject's evaluations of the confederate were uniformly high across conditions, and therefore, did not support the hypothesis.

The second study was a field experiment whereby a prostitute conveyed the impression either that she was welcoming of all clients, or that she had to be selective about who she could see. The clients' evaluations were rated in three ways: the prostitute's own estimation of how much they liked her, how much the client paid her, and how

▶

Reinforcement theories

A rather simple reinforcement model of attraction was proposed by Lott and Lott (1972, 1974), according to which we may like people who happen to be present when we receive a reward, even if they have nothing to do with the rewarding event. In a study by Griffit and Guay (1969), a subject's creativity was supposedly evaluated by the experimenter while another person was in the room. The subjects liked both people better following a positive evaluation than a negative one. Furthermore, there was no difference in liking for the two people, even though only one of them had been involved in the reinforcement.

A simple reinforcement explanation, however, is not conclusive; usually, an alternative cognitive explanation can be offered as well. For example, in the Griffit and Guay study the subjects may have believed that the second person shared the experimenter's opinion of their creativity. Despite this, we should soon afterward the client called for a second appointment. Again the hypothesis was not supported, as clients in both conditions responded in the same way, though it should be noted that two of the ratings in this experiment are confounded by financial factors and the third is a subjective measure which could easily be influenced by other factors.

Faced with this lack of support, the experimenters took another look at the factors involved, such as how relaxing each type of woman would be on a date. They came up with a reworked hypothesis which proposed that the maximally rewarding date would be one who was easy for the subject to get, but hard for anyone else to get.

This hypothesis was tested using the computer dating system again. Subjects filled out questionnaires then returned several weeks later. On their return they were told that the computer had come up with five possible dates for them. The subjects were able to read biographies of these five so they could indicate their preference. With the biography was also a supposed evaluation, made by the woman, of the dates the computer had matched for her. These evaluations were manipulated so that one woman appeared easy to get as she rated all her dates highly. Another woman appeared hard to get as she did not rate any of her dates particularly highly. A third woman appeared selectively hard to get by having rated only the subject highly. The other two women constituted a control condition whereby they had not made any evaluations. The results showed strong support for the revised hypothesis. The women in all conditions were liked equally except for the selectively hard-to-get woman who was uniformly the most popular.

stress that a different theoretical account does not render the first one useless. In general, deductions from a variety of learning (and reinforcement) theories have had considerable impact in this area of social psychology. An example of enlightening research was a study by Lott *et al.* (1969). Applying the principle that immediate reinforcement is sometimes stronger than delayed reinforcement, they found that children liked a person who was associated with immediate reward for task completion, rather than with reward after a ten-second delay.

▶ Reinforcement-affect model

Another variation derived from learning theory was the *reinforcement-affect model* of Byrne and Clore (1970). As the name suggests, reinforcement is supplemented by a feeling component. The logic is drawn from classical (Pavlovian) conditioning. Just as a dog learns to associate the sound of a bell with the positive reinforcement of food, so humans can associate another person with other positive features of the environment on that occasion. The way the model works is shown in Figure 12.6.

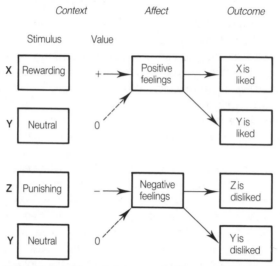

FIGURE 12.6 *The reinforcement-affect model: attraction is influenced by conditioning. (Source: derived from Clore and Byrne 1974.)*

The reinforcement-affect model includes the following features:

1. People identify stimuli as *rewarding* or *punishing*, and then seek out the former while avoiding the latter.
2. Positive *feelings* are associated with rewarding stimuli and negative feelings with punishing stimuli.
3. A stimulus is evaluated in terms of the feelings it arouses. An *evaluation* is good if the feelings are positive, and bad if the feelings are negative.
4. Any background *neutral* stimuli which happen to be associated with reward will elicit positive feelings, while those associated with punishment will elicit negative feelings.

Consequently, people can be liked or disliked depending on whether they are associated with positive or negative feelings. In a study by Griffit and Veitch (1971), statements by strangers were presented to subjects who were in either physically uncomfortable conditions (hot and crowded), or physically comfortable conditions. Results indicated that in the more uncomfortable conditions, the stranger was liked less. It was concluded that the stranger's statements (the neutral stimulus) had become associated with the negative feelings about physical comfort in the uncomfortable condition.

Social exchange theory

▶ Cost/reward ratio

Although social exchange theory can be considered a member of the general family of behaviourist theories, as an approach to the topic of interpersonal relationships it goes beyond reinforcement theory by taking an interactive approach. It focuses on the fact that there are at least two people in a relationship and, as its name suggests, is concerned with how these people proceed to exchange rewards. One major proponent was Homans (1961), a sociologist who made it clear that he was adapting the blueprint from Skinner's operant psychology. As a model of behaviour, it proposes several economic concepts, wedded to behaviourism, to account for our interpersonal relationships. Whether we like someone else is determined by the *cost/reward ratio*: 'What will it cost me to get a positive reward from that person?' Social exchange theory, however, takes an extra step in arguing that two participants' outcomes are *jointly* determined by their actions.

Even though the consequences of this may not be dramatic, the process is ongoing in much of our everyday behaviour. We seek to obtain, preserve or exchange things of value with other human beings. We bargain over what we are prepared to give to another in exchange for what they will give us. Some of these exchanges can be very brief and perhaps without deep meaning, while others are ongoing and long term, and may be extremely important to us. In all

---

BOX 12.2 Stages in the development of social exchange relationship

Building a relationship: steps along the way
When we are attracted to others we hope that they feel the same way about us. Thibaut and Kelley (1959) suggested four stages in the development of a relationship:

1. **Sampling.** When people consider a new relationship they check its potential costs and rewards, and compare it with other relationships available.
2. **Bargaining.** As an interaction takes place, there is a giving and receiving of rewards that test whether a deeper relationship is worthwhile.
3. **Commitment.** Sampling and bargaining are reduced, and the focus is now on one other person. Most relationships are between people equal in status (Homans 1961), or in popularity (Jennings 1943), both of which assist predictability in a relationship. Attraction will increase further if the costs of interacting are lowered. You are less likely to misunderstand your partner's intentions as you get to know them better. In addition, the ability to predict allows each partner to know how to elicit rewards from the other.
4. **Institutionalisation.** Finally, norms are developed that recognise the legitimacy of a particular relationship and the specific pattern of rewards and costs for each partner.

cases, we experience outcomes or pay-offs which are dependent on the behaviour of others. Over time, individuals will try to develop a pattern of interaction that is rational and mutually beneficial. We can think of social exchange as a give-and-take relationship between people, and relationships as business transactions. So far, you might be thinking that this is a fairly dry approach to the study of important relationships. If so, you are right. Its proponents would argue, however, that this does not detract from its validity. An example of how social exchange theory might be applied to the development of a relationship is shown in Box 12.2.

At a broad level, Foa and Foa (1975) set out six kinds of interpersonal relationship, each involving an exchange of resources:

1. *Goods* – any products or objects.
2. *Information* – advice, opinion or instructions.
3. *Love* – affectionate regard, warmth or comfort.
4. *Money* – any coin or token that has some value.
5. *Services* – activities of the body or belonging to the individual.
6. *Status* – an evaluative judgement which conveys high or low prestige.

▶ Minimax strategy

Any of these resources can be exchanged in a relationship between people. In most relationships, according to this point of view, we try to use a *minimax strategy*, that is, we aim to minimise costs and to maximise rewards, although we may not be conscious of doing so and would probably object to the idea that we do.

▶ Profit

Along with Homans, the social psychologists Thibaut and Kelley (1959) also provided impetus to social exchange theory in a major work, *The Social Psychology of Groups*, that underpinned much subsequent research. They argued that one must understand the *structure* of a relationship in order to deal with the behaviour that takes place, since it is the structure that defines the rewards and punishments available. A relationship between people is a series of trading interactions or business transactions. We have already noted that a guiding aim, according to the minimax strategy, is that a relationship is unsatisfactory when the costs exceed the rewards. In practice, people exchange resources with one another in the hope that they will earn a *profit*, that is, the rewards will exceed the costs. This is a novel way of defining a 'good relationship'. Rewards from interacting with someone can include satisfaction, gratification or pleasure. Costs include effort, embarrassment, time wasted and money spent. This is a deliberate and explicitly economic approach to human behaviour and relationships. In common with other theories which stress the importance of behavioural principles, exchange theory argues that socially significant behaviour is repeated only if it has been suitably reinforced.

▶ Comparison level

A final important concept in social exchange theory is each person's *comparison level*. This is a standard against which all of one's relationships are judged. People's comparison levels are the product of their past experiences with other parties in the exchange, their past experiences in other similar exchanges, and their general views of what can reasonably be expected from the exchange.

If the final result in a particular exchange is positive, that is, a person's profit exceeds that person's *comparison level* (CL) then the relationship will be perceived as satisfying and the other person will seem attractive. However, if the final result is negative (that is, the profit is smaller than the CL), then dissatisfaction will follow. The CL concept is helpful in accounting for why some relationships might be acceptable at some times but not at others. See Box 12.3 for a further discussion of comparison level.

BOX 12.3 Using a comparison level in a relationship: an exercise in social exchange theory

What do you get from a relationship?

An individual's comparison level (CL) is an idiosyncratic judgemental point, since each person has had unique experiences. Your CL is the average value of all outcomes of relationships with others in your past, and also of outcomes for others about whom you may have heard. It can vary across different kinds of relationship, so that your CL for your doctor will be different from that for a lover.

Your entry point into a new relationship is seen against a backdrop of the other people you have known (or know about) in that context, along with the profits and losses you have encountered in relating to them. This running average constitutes a baseline for your relationships in that particular sphere. A new encounter could only be judged as satisfactory if it exceeds this baseline.

Take as an example a date that you may have had with another person. The outcome is defined as the rewards (having a nice time, developing a potential relationship) minus the costs (how much money it cost you, how difficult or risky it was to arrange, whether you feel you blew your chance to make a good impression, and so on). The actual outcome will be determined in terms of how it compares with other dates you have had in similar circumstances and perhaps how well you have seen or heard other people's dates go.

To complicate matters a little, your CL can change as time goes by. Although age may not make you any wiser, it could lead you to expect more of some future commitment to another person than when you were younger.

Furthermore, there is an additional concept – the *comparison level for alternatives*. Suppose you are in an already satisfying relationship but then meet someone new, an enticing stranger. As the saying goes, 'the grass always looks greener on the other side of the fence'. In social exchange language, there is the prospect here of an increase in rewards over costs. This, of course, further complicates the mental computations. And so on ...

A strong feature of exchange theory is that it accommodates the extent of *individual differences*, which are apparent in interpersonal relationships, in two ways: (1) differences between people in perceiving what are rewards and what are costs; (2) differences within the person based on variations in comparison levels, both over time and across different contexts.

The notion of equity in a relationship

It can be argued that western society is actually founded on a system of social exchange within which we strive for equity, or balance, in our relationships with others (Walster *et al.* 1978). Accordingly, people generally believe that outcomes for participants in a social exchange should be fair and just. This view is reinforced by societal laws and norms, which provide both internal and external pressure to comply with the 'rules'.

▶ Equity theory

Equity theory is a more specific model within social exchange theory which asks how people decide when an exchange is fair, and what they do if they decide it is not. It was popularised in social psychology by Adams (1965), and dealt with two main social situations:

1. A mutual exchange of resources (for example, a marriage relationship).
2. An exchange in which limited resources must be distributed (for example, a judge awarding compensation for injury).

In both situations, an equity model predicts that people expect resources to be given out *fairly*, that is, in proportion to their contribution. (The idea of equity can also be extended to an understanding of *altruism* – see the work of Piliavin and colleagues in Chapter 13. If we help others, that is act altruistically, then it is fair to expect them to help us.) According to Adams (1965), equity exists between two persons, A and B, when A's outcomes plus A's inputs equal B's outcomes plus B's inputs.

▶ Distributive justice

An individual first estimates the *ratio* of what has been put into a relationship to what has been received from it. This ratio is then compared with the ratio applying to the other person. If these ratios are equal, people feel they are being treated fairly or equitably. If the ratios are not equal (in either direction) people feel treated unfairly or inequitably (see Figure 12.7). Equity in a relationship, therefore, is defined as a situation where all participants' outcomes (rewards minus costs) are proportional to their inputs or contributions to the relationship. This is usually referred to as the rule of *distributive justice*, another concept originally propounded by Homans.

It is obvious that equity theory is applicable to many areas of social life. A wide variety of applications to exploitative relationships, helping relationships and to intimate relationships have been summarised by Walster *et al.* (1978). The more inequitably people are treated, the more distress they will feel. People who believe they are getting less than their fair share will experience distress, though people who are aware that they are receiving more can also experience distress (Adams 1965). Most distress, however, is felt when people

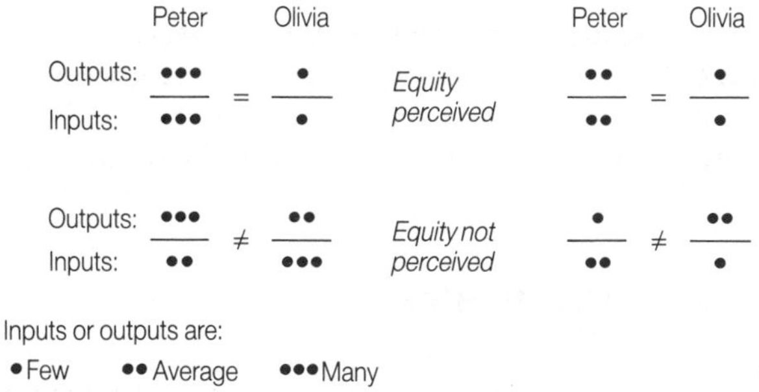

	Peter	Olivia		Peter	Olivia
Outputs:	•••	•	*Equity*	••	•
	=		*perceived*	=	
Inputs:	•••	•		••	•

	Peter	Olivia		Peter	Olivia
Outputs:	•••	••	*Equity not*	•	••
	≠		*perceived*	≠	
Inputs:	••	•••		••	•

Inputs or outputs are:

•Few ••Average •••Many

FIGURE 12.7 *Equity theory applied to two equitable and two inequitable relationships. (Source: adapted from Baron and Byrne 1987.)*

feel they are victims, rather than beneficiaries, of inequitable relationships (Lane and Messé 1971).

Whenever we experience inequity, we are motivated in either of two ways to do something about it. We can:

1. alter our inputs to, or outcomes from, the exchange; or
2. restructure our perceptions of inputs and outcomes so that the ratios no longer appear inequitable.

Generally, only one method is used to restore equity in a given situation. If neither method works, and if the ratio is below an individual's comparison levels, the relationship is likely to end (Adams 1965). The special case of how relationships can end is dealt with at the end of this chapter.

As we have noted, the process of deciding what is a fair allocation of resources is often complex and difficult. A fundamental issue is how an allocation can be worked out to everyone's satisfaction. In practice, a society operates according to a set of standards, or *norms*, which guide social behaviour. We can then be guided by common rules of practice, such as the following:

1. An *equity norm*, such as the rule of distributive justice.
2. A *social welfare norm*, or rule that the amount of resources allocated to people should be proportional to their needs.
3. An *equalitarian norm*, or rule that everyone should get an equal amount.

According to Adams (1965), people always prefer the equity norm when allocating resources, but more recently this has been questioned (Deutsch 1975; Mikula 1980). It now seems probable that different norms are preferred in different situations. When allocations are made on the basis of inputs, people may evaluate a friend's inputs differently from a stranger's. Strangers tend to allocate resources on the basis of *ability*, whereas friends allocate on the basis of both *ability* and *effort* (Lamm and Kayser 1978).

Individual differences, such as gender, can also play a role. Women are more likely to allocate resources on the basis of an equality norm, whereas men tend to use an equity norm (Kahn *et al.* 1980; Major and Adams 1983; Major and Deaux 1982). The reasons for these differences are not clear, although Kahn *et al.* attribute it to a traditional female role of maintaining group harmony and peace, which might best be achieved through treating people equally.

LOVE RELATIONSHIPS

Liking and loving: are they different?

We have discussed the general process of interpersonal attraction in terms of a powerful need to affiliate with others, and have extended our discussion to deal with the way we choose our acquaintances and friends. Can we further extend these principles to the important topic of the very special people whom we love? What, indeed, is love, and is it a qualitatively different experience from liking? Intuition tells us: yes. Let us explore this further.

There is not a great deal known as yet about what we call 'love'. We use terms such as passion, romance, companionship, infatuation and sexual attraction, but what are the differences between these states? Couple this with the way love is regarded as somewhat magical and, therefore, non-comprehensible in terms of our usual reasoning processes, and it is almost impossible to take the phenomenon into the laboratory. Not surprisingly, most research that has been carried out in this area has been conducted through survey and interview methods.

▶ Passionate or romantic love

▶ Companionate love

Rubin (1973) maintained that 'liking' referred to a quite different state from 'loving', and developed scales to measure each separately. Hatfield and Walster (1981) distinguished between *passionate love* (or romantic love) and *companionate love*:

> Passionate love is an intensely emotional state and a confusion of feelings: tenderness, sexuality, elation and pain, anxiety and relief, altruism and jealousy. Companionate love, on the other hand, is a less intense emotion, combining feelings of friendly affection and deep attachment. It is characterised by friendship, understanding, and a concern for the welfare of the other. (Hatfield 1987, p. 676)

Such a distinction appeals to common sense since there are many people, of both sexes, with whom we may find it pleasant and comforting to share time, without the suggestion that we are 'in love' with them. Argyle and Henderson (1985) have extended the distinction to couples who have been married for some time, noting that people report that their passion evolves into a relationship marked more by attachment and affection, but reduced sexual excitement.

Does love go with marriage like 'a horse and carriage', as the popular song once claimed? In western culture there appears to have been a change over time, even across a generation. Simpson *et al.* (1986) compared responses across three time samples, from the 1960s to the 1980s. Would you be surprised to learn that young people in a later generation expected a causal connection more than they did twenty years before? The respondents answered the same question: 'If a man (woman) had all the qualities you desired, would you marry this person if you were not in love with him (her)?' Those who answered no increased over time, especially the women (see Figure 12.8). Presumably, marrying for conferred status or security is not favoured by modern young people.

Romantic love

Though many songwriters have attempted to answer the elusive question 'What is love?', social psychologists tend to stick more to descriptions of behavioural and cognitive tendencies which are indicative of the state of being 'in love'. Such things may be thinking of the lover constantly, wanting to spend as much time as possible with him or her and often being unrealistic in judgements about the lover (Murstein 1980). This usually results in the lover becoming the focus of the person's life, to the exclusion of other friends (Milardo *et al.* 1983). It is perceived as a very intense emotion, and, moreover, one over which the individual has very little control. We speak of 'falling' in love as though it is some sort of accident, something that happens to us rather than some process in which we actively participate. It is interesting that we perceive love in this manner, because one of the most widely accepted claims about love among social psychologists is that a prerequisite for falling in love is that one must be raised in a culture that believes in the concept and teaches it to young people, both in fiction and real-life depictions. If it really was an

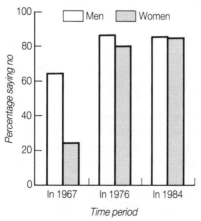

FIGURE 12.8 *Generational changes in the willingness to marry without love. (Source: based on data from Simpson* et al. *1986.)*

The look and the touch of love. They might be Romeo and Juliet, but hopefully without the tragic ending. Love, young and passionate, has stirred art in its manifest forms. Its nature defies control and, therefore, the experimental scientist. What methods remain to study love? (Source: Andrew Lukey.)

accident that happened to us, we would expect people from all cultures to fall in love, but this is not the case.

As with many other situations in life, our beliefs determine what happens to us. Not only do you need to have a concept of love before it happens to you, but the more you think about love, the more likely you are to fall in love (Tesser and Paulhus 1976); and if you believe that 'love at first sight' is possible, the chances are that it will happen to you (Averill and Boothroyd 1977).

Is love just a label?

▶ Three-factor theory of love

Now, we don't want to spoil your fun, but some social psychologists have argued that romantic love is a label we apply to the product of interacting variables. According to Hatfield and Walster (1981), there are, in the *three-factor theory*, three variables which underlie the experience of love (see Figure 12.9). The first is the cultural determinant to which we referred earlier. The second is that there needs to be an appropriate love–object present. In our society this has usually been an attractive member of the opposite sex of similar age, though the majority of love patterns at any time do seem to follow beliefs about what types of partner are appropriate. The third is emotional arousal, labelled 'love', that is felt when interacting with, or even thinking about, an appropriate love object. Label or not, most who have been smitten report feeling powerful effects!

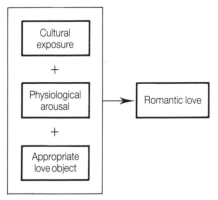

FIGURE 12.9 *Hatfield and Walster's three-factor theory of romantic love.*

Although this notion of labelling arousal may not seem intuitively appealing, it has a basis in research. Our physiological reactions do not seem to be very well differentiated across the emotions – very similar reactions seem to occur regardless of whether we describe ourselves as angry, fearful, joyful or sexually aroused (Fehr and Stern 1970). Taking this into account, Schachter and Singer (1962) proposed that when events elicit internal physiological arousal, we look for external cues in the world around us to discover the reason for the arousal. We then label the arousal as an emotion consistent with what we see as possible cues. For example, if we feel arousal following insult, we are likely to label the arousal as anger. However, if we experience arousal while interacting with an attractive member of the opposite sex, we are likely to label the arousal sexual attraction, liking or love. Mixed evidence, some of which provides support for the proposal (for example, Schachter and Singer 1962), and some of which does not (for example, Marshall and Zimbardo 1979) means that we cannot say with confidence that we exclusively label arousal according to external cues. It is probable that the relationship is rather more complex and that external cues are one factor in our perception of arousal (see Chapter 3 on attribution and the cognitive labelling of arousal).

The effects of arousal in love can also be looked at from the perspective of the reinforcement-affect model, discussed earlier in this chapter. According to this model, any positive arousal experienced while with a possible love-object is associated with or attributed to that person. In this way, the belief of being in love can grow.

Regardless of whether we accept the mislabelling hypothesis and/or the reinforcement-affect model, according to the three-factor theory love depends on past learning of the concept, presence of someone to love, and arousal. It would be difficult to dispute the involvement of these factors in love. However, though they may be necessary for the state of love to occur, they do not seem to be sufficient. If they were, love could easily be taken into the laboratory. The ingredients required would be that Peter's culture includes a concept of love, and Olivia provides arousal by being attractive, or by chasing Peter around the room, or by paying him a compliment – and hey presto, 'love'. It is at this point that we run into problems with Schachter's mislabelling hypothesis. Although love can be accompanied by sexual arousal, the latter itself is not a reliable indicator of love. Anecdotal evidence provides the best support for this. For example, sometimes when a person is called to account for an extramarital affair by a spouse, the classic response is 'but, dear, it didn't mean anything.'

▶ Social matching

What process is it that sometimes leads us to be both aroused and to fall in love? Or, how is it that we feel sexual attraction (lust) for, without any glimmerings of love towards, someone else? Although conclusive answers are not available, several contributing factors can be identified. A major variable highlighted by research has been the degree of appropriateness of another person as a partner. Field research (Silverman 1971) has shown that the couples who seem happiest with their dating partners are those who are fairly well matched with regard to physical attractiveness. Elder (1969) tracked down female students who had been rated for attractiveness in the 1930s. He found that the more attractive the female had been, the 'better' she had achieved in marriage with regard to social status. This supported the belief that couples match themselves on some sort of social desirability scale: in the latter case, the females 'trading' the attractiveness which made them desirable for the social status which made their partners desirable. This process of *social matching*, which we can see is an example of equity theory discussed earlier, has been supported by research (Walster *et al.* 1978).

We also bring our previously held beliefs to the situation. Beliefs about appropriate characteristics such as gender, physique, socio–economic class and religion. Although there will be great similarity of these beliefs in any society, individual variations are extensive. For example, most people would regard a sibling as an inappropriate love-object; however, a brother and sister in Britain were reported as being prepared to go to prison to defend their love (Russell 1987). Again, many people will not fall in love with others who are already involved in a relationship, on the basis that these others are judged to be unavailable from the outset.

Furthermore, we bring various ideals or images to the situation. A person can fall out of love fairly quickly if the partner is not what (or who) they were first thought to be. The initial state of love was not for the partner, but for some *ideal image* that the person had formed of this partner, such as 'the knight in shining armour'. Where these images come from we do not know, but possible sources are previous lovers, characters from fiction or childhood love-objects such as parents. A physical characteristic similar to one of the image can start a chain of belief whereby other characteristics from the image are transferred onto the partner. It is this area of images that seems best to differentiate love from liking (though not love from sexual arousal). Love seems to be inexorably tied up with fantasy. The clinical psychologist Reik has postulated that it is when we are dissatisfied with ourselves that we are vulnerable to love because this is the time when we fantasise about having our needs met. We then go on to drape these fantasies around another person (Berscheid and Walster 1978).

Evidence which supports Reik's hypothesis comes from work on deprivation. For example, Leiman and Epstein (1961) showed that when people are sexually aroused, they usually have sexual fantasies. Further evidence shows that we do mix up these fantasies with the reality of another person. Stephan *et al.* (1971) proposed that when we are sexually aroused, fantasising occurs and this affects our perceptions of reality. The study asked college men to give their impressions of a blind date who had been picked for them. While they were waiting, they were given something to read. For one condition, this reading material was designed to dampen sexual feelings, being a boring account of the sex life of the herring gull. Those in the other condition were given a story of sexual seduction designed to stimulate their sexual feelings. The same date, a pretty blonde who was active, intelligent and easy to get on with, was described to all the subjects. The men in the aroused condition thought the date more beautiful and more likely to be receptive to sexual advances. It was also found that the more sexually inexperienced subjects found the date more attractive (supposedly a reflection of their greater need) than those who reported having had sexual experience frequently and recently. These results demonstrate that arousal does alter the perception of a member of the opposite sex. However, the results are limited as the study only takes account of male subjects and looks at sexual arousal and assumptions about sexual response rather than love.

Liking and loving also differ in how logical they are as processes with regard to reinforcement theory. Whereas liking can be accounted for in terms of reinforcers, love frequently seems to go its own way. Many people seem to choose love objects who only bring suffering – the dilemma 'I can't live with him and I can't live without him' is fairly common. That such ambivalence can exist makes it very difficult to explain loving only in terms of liking.

No greater love

Sternberg (1988) has offered a model of love in which commitment and intimacy are factors as crucial as passion to some experiences of love. *Passion* is roughly equivalent to sexual attraction; *intimacy* refers to feelings of warmth, closeness and sharing; *commitment* is our resolve to maintain the relationship, even in moments of crisis. In an Australian study, Forgas and Dobosz (1980) found that women tended to show higher levels of commitment than men.

▶ Consummate love

An interesting notion in Sternberg's proposal is that romance is exceeded by one other experience, *consummate love*, which includes all three factors. By systematically creating combinations in terms of the presence or absence of each factor we can distinguish eight cases, ranging in the degree of bonding from no love at all to consummate love. Out of such logic some interesting relationships emerge. Fatuous love is characterised by passion and commitment

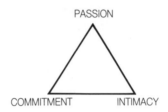

	Passion	Commitment	Intimacy
No love	X	X	X
Infatuation	✓	X	X
Empty love	X	✓	X
Liking	X	X	✓
Fatuous love	✓	✓	X
Romantic love	✓	X	✓
Companionate love	X	✓	✓
Consummate love	✓	✓	✓

FIGURE 12.10 *Sternberg's triangle of love.*

but no intimacy, for example the 'whirlwind Hollywood romance'. Do you recognise some of the relationships in Figure 12.10?

Maintaining relationships

The relevant literature has dealt mostly with marriage, since it has been assumed that it is the most obvious relationship to be preserved. However, in view of what we have discussed in the last section, marriage is only one of a number of love relationships. Marriage also involves other factors which make it unlike most others: it is a contractual arrangement; it can be a financial partnership with accumulating assets; it usually involves parenting; and the nature of the initial attraction transforms over a lengthy period of time. External influences, such as pressure from in-laws, are yet other factors beyond love which can perpetuate a marriage relationship.

It is an interesting question whether a love relationship is *ever* maintained. Some works of literature lead us to believe that 'love endures', while long-running television soap operas often focus on relationship break-ups. The reason for their appeal is intriguing in a society where marriage 'till death do us part' is still the ideal.

In previous generations, love was taken as the prerequisite for marriage in western societies. In a study by Burgess and Wallin (1953), one thousand young people who were engaged to be married were asked: 'Do you think that a person should ever marry one whom he or she does not love?' The results

Till death do us part. Despite a marked increase in divorce rates in western cultures during the 1980s and beyond, a traditional wedding ceremony is still very popular. One facet of the western ceremony is its continued insistence on a stereotype of true love for ever and a day. (Source: Andrew Lukey.)

showed that: 82 per cent of men and 80 per cent of women said no; only 12 per cent of men and 15 per cent of women said yes. The remainder were undecided.

Despite the precondition put on love, there is general agreement that a relationship which survives time is one in which the partners adapt and change with respect to what they expect of each other. What counts in maintaining a relationship is companionate love, which we have noted earlier. Such love involves deep friendship and caring, and arises from the sharing of lives and a myriad of experiences which only time can provide. From such a starting point, we can get a glimmering of how both the western 'love' marriage and the eastern arranged marriage could each result in a similar perception of powerful bonding between partners.

In companionate love, the ambivalence of feeling that 'I can't live with him and I can't live without him' recedes. However, even companionate love cannot guarantee a lasting relationship. *Security* is a critical variable which can exert influence in several different ways. When one partner feels insecure, the emotion of *jealousy* can follow, a state expressed by extreme possessiveness and suspicion, that accelerates the deterioration of the relationship. On the other hand, feeling secure in a relationship can bring its own problems. Companionate love might imply that the 'magic' of romantic love has disappeared. In this case, security can lead to boredom and a consequent search for new stimulation, often away from the partner. Despite this risk, security can also enhance a relationship if the search for new stimulation is undertaken together.

▶ Role complementarity   *Role complementarity* is a major factor in maintaining any relationship. Any change in a relationship requires a renegotiation of roles. For example, if one person has been ill for a long time and then recovers, the partner may feel down even though he believes he should be happy about it. This can be because his role of care-giver may be almost redundant, so it becomes difficult for him to see where he fits in.

Even without a radical change in roles, people do change over time and if this change occurs in different directions or at different rates, a breakdown of the relationship is often the result. The latter half of the twentieth century is witnessing a relatively dramatic redefinition of the role of women in society so that they have greater economic and social equality with men. This has impinged on interpersonal relationships between men and women so that many couples experience role strain which can sometimes lead to a broken relationship (see Box 12.4).

BOX 12.4 The changing role of women

Role change can strain a relationship

The manner in which role relationships are defined is especially important for the way males and females respond to each other. Traditional gender role stereotypes have been going through a process of change in our society for about a generation, with the larger degree of reconstruction taking place for women. In what is perhaps a surprising result, Carmichael (1983) found in a study of 18–34 year olds that young women (57 per cent) were less likely than young men (78 per cent) to endorse the item 'people should consider needs of spouses and children as more important than their own.'

Women taking assertiveness training courses have become less prepared to play a *submissive role*. This will inevitably put a strain on their relationship if their male partner expects to continue in a dominant role. His traditional role of breadwinner has been eroded to differing degrees for different couples. Social security provisions lessen the extent to which women need to be directly dependent on men for the financial means of caring for children.

Participation by women in the workforce enables a degree of financial independence which in many cases raises self-esteem and changes perceptions of equity. Economic factors, allied with the changed status and work expectations of women compared with a generation ago, mean that in many families the female is working while the male is unemployed. This reversal of the breadwinner role can be difficult to reconcile to the traditional roles a husband and wife may have played.

Ending a relationship

Deterioration of a relationship involves the perception by one or both partners that it is not as desirable as it once was. Levinger (1980) points to four factors which usually mean the ending of a relationship:

1. A new life seems to be the only solution.
2. Alternative partners are available.
3. There is an expectation that the relationship will fail.
4. There is a lack of commitment to a continuing relationship.

Most research in this area deals with heterosexual relationships, but a study by Schullo and Alperson (1984) has shown these factors to be valid for homosexual relationships as well.

Rusbult and Zembrodt (1983) believe that once deterioration is identified, it can be responded to in any of four ways:

A partner can take a *passive* stance and show:
1. *Loyalty*, by waiting for an improvement to occur.
2. *Neglect*, by allowing the deterioration to continue.

Alternatively, a partner can take an *active* stance and show:
3. *Voice behaviour*, by working at improving the relationship.
4. *Exit behaviour*, by choosing to end the relationship.

It is not easy to determine whether the passive or the active approach leads to more pain at the final break-up since many other factors are involved, such as previous levels of attraction, amount of time and effort invested, and the availability of new partners. It can also depend on the person's general level of social contact. It is often loneliness which adds to the pain and makes life seem unbearable, and if it is minimised, recovery from the end of a relationship can be quicker.

▶ Relationship dissolution model

Duck (1988, 1992) has offered a detailed *relationship dissolution model* of four phases that partners will pass through when a break-up occurs. Each phase culminates in a threshold which, when reached, leads to the behaviours shown in Figure 12.11.

1. The *intra-psychic phase* starts as a period of brooding with little outward show, perhaps in the hope of putting things right. This can give way to needling the partner and seeking out a third party to be able to express one's concerns.
2. The *dyadic phase* takes the person to the point of deciding that something needs to be done, short of leaving the partner, an act which is usually easier said than done. Arguments will show, and differences between the pair in attributing responsibility for what is going wrong will emerge. With luck, they may talk their problems through.

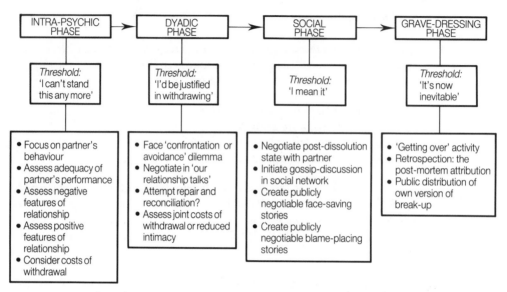

FIGURE 12.11 *When things go wrong: phases in dissolving an intimate relationship. (Source: adapted from Duck 1982.)*

3. The *social phase* involves a new element: in saying that the relationship is near an end, the partners may negotiate with friends, both as a means of social support for an uncertain future and for reassurance of being right. The social network will probably take sides, pronounce on guilt and blame and, like a court, sanction the dissolution.

4. The final *grave-dressing phase* can involve more than leaving a partner, to include the division of property and of access to children, and also a further working towards an assurance for one's reputation. In the individual's community it will probably be important to emerge with a self-image of relationship reliability for the future. The partners know that the relationship is dead. Its burial is marked by erecting a tablet. This 'grave-dressing' activity seeks a socially acceptable version of the life and death of the relationship.

In the case of the institution of marriage, divorce is now so common that post-marital relationships can be anticipated. According to Noller and Callan (1990), divorce occurs so frequently that it has been over-estimated by people who were asked to imagine a normal family with two children. Divorce can no longer be viewed as deviant or pathological, but is an institution in its own right (Ahrons and Rodgers 1987).

Loneliness and bereavement

One way of defining loneliness is as dissatisfaction with one's relationships. This can come about when the desired rate of interaction that we have with

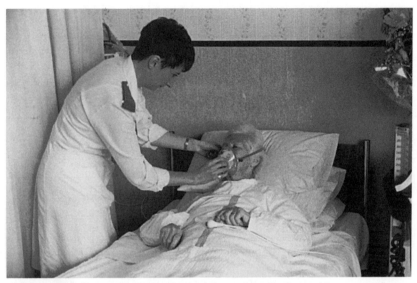

The winter of discontent. Even a long and committed relationship must end. An effective support network can be crucial to the emotional welfare of a surviving partner. (Source: Andrew Lukey.)

others is not satisfied by the actual rate that we experience (see Altman's privacy regulation model as discussed in Chapter 15). Williams and Solano (1983), however, have argued that the inadequate *quality* of relationships, defined as a lack of closeness, contributes to feeling lonely. In a study of first-year university students, they found that there was no difference between lonely and non-lonely persons in terms of the number of best friend's they listed or in the number of persons who reciprocated the best friend's choice. Instead, lonely students perceived a lack of intimacy with their friends. Maxwell and Coebergh (1986) isolated four predictors of loneliness: how close people are to the closest person in their life, how many close friends they have, how satisfied they are with their relationships, and whether they have daily contacts with others. On balance, it is probable that two factors are involved:

1. A person's social network in global terms, including the rate at which contact with others is maintained and controlled by the person.
2. The degree of perceived intimacy in at least some relationships.

▶ Transactive memory

When a relationship ends, through separation or death, loneliness is only one possible consequence. There can also be serious disruption of *transactive memory*. Transactive memory refers to the way in which, for instance, a couple divides up responsibility for remembering different things but each member of the couple knows who has responsibility for which memories (Wegner *et al.* 1991; see Chapter 8 for details). The end of a relationship, therefore, leads to an often debilitating loss of memory for each partner.

Another consequence of the end of a relationship can be depression. The evidence suggests that it is men who suffer more (Stroebe and Stroebe 1983, 1987), possibly because they are less likely than women to have or to establish quickly a support network. Social support, particularly social support from a close relationship partner, can have an important function in preventing depression. From an extensive study of the mental health and close relationships of 458 women in south London, Brown and Harris (1978) found that of

---

BOX 12.5 Health risks among the bereaved

Dying of a broken heart

> 'I care for you,' she said, 'but what if we lose one another?'
> 'Well,' he said, 'that is the price we must pay.'
> (Raphael 1985, p.402)

The media often report cases of elderly couples who die within a short time of each other. While it is possible that these events could occur by chance, there is other evidence suggesting a causal link (Stroebe *et al.* 1982).

Death of a loved one can lead to a prolonged period of grief in which the first six months after the loss is a particularly critical period. Although some deaths among bereaved spouses could be attributed to a tendency to neglect one's body, there is some evidence that there may be a related deterioration in the immune system following an extended period of grieving (Jemmott and Locke 1984). Care-givers who help to support the terminally ill are well aware of the *broken heart effect* and continue to support the family of the bereaved for a time following the patient's death (Youngson 1989). This post-death care of others deliberately targets the first of several of a bereaved person's anniversaries, such as birthdays, Christmas, the marriage and the actual death.

In a study carried out by Raphael (1985), fifty-six widows who were judged to be both lacking a supportive network and also at risk of poor resolution of their spouse's death were allocated randomly to either an intervention or a non-intervention group. The intervention group received on average four two-hour counselling sessions, usually in their homes. These were distributed over a thirteen-month period, in order to cover all first anniversaries. A comparison of the two groups, carried out by an independent rater, showed that the intervention group were coping significantly better with their loss. The non-intervention group showed a substantial health impairment.

those who had had a stressful life experience during the past year, only 10 per cent who had a supportive husband experienced depression while 41 per cent who did not have a supportive husband experienced depression.

The end of a relationship, particularly through death, can have even more extreme consequences. Stroebe and colleagues (1982) have calculated figures to show that the death rate among bereaved spouses is three times higher than for other people of similar age, and in the 20–29 years age group it is a staggering ten times higher (see Box 12.5).

SUMMARY

♦ Studies of isolation show that long-term separation from others can have disturbing intellectual and social outcomes. Young children who are deprived for a long period of physical and social contact with others, especially adults, may suffer irreversible psychological damage.

♦ Various researchers have emphasised a need to affiliate which is clearly not satisfied by prolonged periods of isolation.

♦ According to Schachter's shared-stress model, being in the company of others who are experiencing a similar psychological state to ourselves helps to reduce anxiety.

♦ Variables which play a significant role in determining why people are attracted to each other include: how physically attractive they are, whether they live or work close by, whether they reciprocate positive reinforcers, and how similar they are in terms of attitudes and values. In a long-term relationship, it can also be important that the needs of the parties are complementary.

♦ Theories of attraction include balance theory (which is also a consistency theory of attitude), reinforcement theories (stressing mutual reinforcement), and social exchange theories (which use a costs/benefits analysis).

♦ Love is distinguished by some theorists (such as Hatfield and Walster, and Sternberg) from mere liking. In turn, different kinds of love have been distinguished, particularly romantic and companionate love.

♦ The break-up of long-term relationships can be traced through a series of stages. Duck's relationship dissolution model noted four phases: intra-psychic, dyadic, social and grave-dressing phases.

♦ Loneliness is a serious problem for people who have ended a relationship or who have suffered a bereavement. Its effects on both physical and psychological health can be profound. There is a need for a social support network to help most people through this experience.

FURTHER READING

Berscheid, E. and Walster, E. H. (1978). *Interpersonal Attraction* (2nd edn). Reading, MA: Addison-Wesley.
Duck, S. (1992). *Human Relationships* (2nd edn). London: Sage.
Forgas, J. P. (1985). *Interpersonal Behaviour: The Psychology of Social Interaction*. Sydney: Pergamon.

▸ KEY TERMS

affiliative behaviour
attachment behaviour
brainwashing
companionate love
comparison level
consummate love
cost/reward ratio
distributive justice
equity theory
familiarity
feral children
gain/loss hypothesis
hospitalism
maternal deprivation
minimax strategy
need complementarity

need to affiliate
passionate or romantic love
profit
proximity
reciprocity principle
reinforcement-affect model
relationship dissolution model
role complementarity
sensory deprivation
shared stress
similarity of attitudes or values
social comparison
social matching
three-factor theory of love
transactive memory

13 *Prosocial behaviour*

································

FOCUS QUESTION
- You turn the corner of a city street to see a man sprawled across the footpath in front of you. What do you do? Probably it depends. Before you read this chapter make a brief checklist of the things you might want to know more about before deciding on your action. When you have finished your reading, look back at this list and see how you fared against the experts!

BACKGROUND

Researchers typically refer to acts that benefit another person as either prosocial behaviour, helping behaviour or altruistic behaviour. These terms are not interchangeable, although many people often use them that way, and there are considerable differences in the way these terms are used in the literature.

▶ Prosocial behaviour

Prosocial behaviour as a very broad category refers to acts that are positively valued by society. In our culture, helping others is socially valued. Thus helpful responses are a form of prosocial behaviour. Wispé (1972) defined prosocial behaviour as behaviour that has positive social consequences, and that contributes to the physical or psychological well-being of another person. Behaviours that fall into this category include altruism, aiding, attraction, bystander intervention, charity, co-operation, friendship, helping, rescue, sacrifice, sharing, sympathy and trust. It is important to remember, however, that the determining factor is the perspective of the society being considered. Aggression, for example, is typically considered to be antisocial behaviour, but if it were valued by society, such as fighting an enemy, it could also be considered prosocial behaviour.

▶ Helping behaviour

Helping behaviour is a term most commonly used in this field of literature to denote a subcategory of prosocial behaviour. It can be defined as an intentional act which benefits another living being. The intention to benefit is the important aspect of this definition. If you accidentally drop ten pounds and someone finds it, you have not performed a helping behaviour. However, if you decide to give ten pounds to someone who needs it, this would clearly be helping.

Altruistic behaviour (*altruism*) is a subcategory of helping behaviour and refers to an act which is motivated by the desire to benefit another rather than oneself (Batson and Coke, 1981; Macaulay and Berkowitz 1970). If we cannot determine whether an act stems from a long-term ulterior motive (such as ingratiation), then altruism is difficult to demonstrate (Rushton and Sorrentino

▶ Altruistic behaviour

▶ Altruism

BOX 13.1 The Kitty Genovese murder: a stimulus to research on helping behaviour

A sad night in New York City

Kitty Genovese was attacked by a man with a knife on her way home from work late at night in March 1964. The area in which the attack took place was Kew Gardens in the Queens area of New York City, a respectable neighbourhood. Her screams and struggles drove off the attacker at first, but seeing no-one come to the woman's aid, the man attacked again. Yet her screams were to no avail, and she was soon cornered again. She was stabbed eight more times and then sexually molested. In the half hour or so that it took the man to kill Kitty Genovese, not one of the neighbours helped her. About half an hour after the attack began, the local police received a call from an anonymous witness. He reported the attack, but would not give his name because he did not want to 'get involved'. The next day when the police interviewed the area's residents, thirty-eight people openly admitted to hearing the screaming. They had all had time to do something but had failed to act. It is perhaps understandable that some of these people had not rushed out into the street for fear of being attacked themselves, but why did they not at least call the police?

This tragic and horrific event received national media attention in America, all asking why none of the neighbours helped. Not surprisingly, this resulted in the heightened interest of social psychologists, including Latané and Darley:

> This story became the journalistic sensation of the decade. 'Apathy,' cried the newspapers. 'Indifference,' said the columnists and commentators. 'Moral callousness,' 'dehumanization,' 'loss of concern for our fellow man,' added preachers, professors, and other sermonizers. Movies, television specials, plays and books explored this incident and many like it. Americans became concerned about their lack of concern. (Latané and Darley 1976, p.309).

1981). Staub (1977) noted that there may also be 'private' rewards associated with acting prosocially, such as feeling good or virtuous.

The Kitty Genovese murder

Social psychological research into helping behaviour began in the late 1950s. As a result of over a thousand articles dealing with altruism and helpfulness (Dovidio 1984), in the past two decades or so social psychologists have learned a great deal about why we sometimes turn our backs on persons requiring assistance, and also why we often go out of our way to help those in need. However, one single event is credited with providing a major impetus to this area, the murder of a young woman in New York in 1964, the reporting of which appalled thousands of its residents (see Box 13.1).

Prosocial behaviour is difficult to explain with traditional theories of human behaviour. Most psychologists have conceptualised human behaviour as *egoistic*, emphasising self-interest. Prosocial behaviour is unusual because it seems to be independent of reinforcement. It highlights an optimistic and positive view of human beings. How can effort and sacrifice for another person be reinforcing in the usual sense?

▶ Nature/nurture controversy

A recurring theme in psychology is the nature/nurture controversy, the debate of biological versus learned determinants of behaviour. We saw it in relation to aggression in Chapter 11, and it crops up again here in dealing with prosocial behaviour.

WHY DO PEOPLE HELP?

The question of why people help others is obviously basic, and has been studied from two major viewpoints: a biological approach and a social learning approach. This distinction is significant and represents important differences among psychologists generally, as well as social psychologists. A third approach combining aspects of both biological and social learning approaches has also been developed recently.

The biological approach

The biological position is that just as humans have innate tendencies to eat and drink, so they have innate tendencies to help others. This may seem strange at first, but suggesting such a need to help others is seen as one reason that human beings have been so successful in an evolutionary sense. Recently there has been a great deal of interest in the possibility that altruism might be a trait that has evolutionary survival value (Campbell 1975; Krebs and Miller 1985; Wilson 1978).

▶ Sociobiology

This explanation of helping is primarily the product of a branch of biology called *sociobiology*. Sociobiologists approach human social behaviour from quite a different perspective from most social psychologists. They view many social behaviours as being caused by our human genetic heritage – that is, they are inborn or innate and not learned (see how sociobiologists approach the question of aggression in Chapter 11). The basic contention is that we may be biologically predisposed to respond with aid to the suffering of others (Barash 1977). Sociobiology proposes that the essence of life is gene survival, and that our genes drive us in ways that maximise their chance of survival so that when we die they live on. Sociobiologists believe there is such a thing as strong altruism which occurs in the absence of any benefit for the helper. They argue that since such behaviour is not affected by rewards and punishments, it can only be explained in terms of a species-wide genetic predisposition. Stories such as the following are seen as showing strong altruism caused by certain genetic characteristics.

A small child, Margaret, and her friend Red were seated in the back seat of Margaret's parents' car. Suddenly the car burst into flames. Red jumped from the car, but realised Margaret was still inside. He jumped back into the burning automobile, grabbed Margaret by the jacket and pulled her to safety (Batson 1983). Should we view these actions as caused by an altruistic impulse inherited from our ancestors? The answer is still being debated, but the fact that Red was an Irish Setter – a dog – tends to add weight to the argument that there is a genetic aspect to altruism and prosocial behaviour. Sociobiologists point out that such acts of altruism are commonly observed in a variety of animals. These behaviours are not learned, they consider, but are inborn, and the same argument applies to humans. For humans, modifications of Darwin's theory of evolution are used to explain why altruism is a positive evolutionary trait. Sociobiologists such as Wilson (1975, 1978) have argued that genes responsible for self-sacrificial behaviour might be selected for over generations because, in the long run, self-sacrifice in certain circumstances increases the probability that the species will survive.

The idea that we have a biological predisposition to help others is a fascinating one and has generated a great deal of debate between psychologists and sociobiologists (Vine 1983). In general, social psychologists have not accepted biological explanations of human social behaviour. Sociobiology has been accepted to some extent, but also heavily criticised. The major criticisms are that no good studies with humans have supported the biological explanation of helping and that sociobiologists have ignored the social learning theorists' extensive research on the causes of helping in humans. The Kitty Genovese case, for instance, is difficult to explain from a biological perspective.

Learning to be helpful

Most social psychologists reject the idea that helping is due to innate drives.

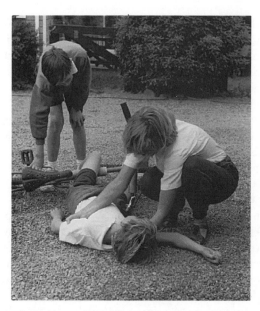

Learning to be helpful. Helping behaviour is heavily influenced by socialisation. This child notes that helping is a 'natural' act to offer someone in distress, and perhaps, learns some elementary procedures appropriate to this kind of accident. (Source: Andrew Lukey.)

They contend that this social behaviour originates in the socialisation process, that is, it is learned by people, not inborn. They propose that classical conditioning, instrumental conditioning and observational learning all play a role in the development of human prosocial behaviour.

The focus of research here has been mostly on how children learn prosocial behaviour, but research with adults investigating under what conditions it is acquired or displayed has also been carried out. Childhood has, however, been considered an important learning period for such behaviours. There are several ways for this learning to take place.

Giving instructions

Simply telling children to be helpful to others does increase their helpfulness (Grusec *et al.* 1978). Telling a child what is appropriate behaviour establishes an expectation about the desired behaviour and may later guide the child's behaviour. Simply preaching about being good to others is of doubtful value (Rushton 1980), unless a fairly strong form is used (Rice and Grusec 1975). Further, telling children to be generous is probably useless unless the 'preacher' behaves consistently. 'Do as I say, not as I do' does not work. When an adult acted selfishly, but urged children to be generous, the children were actually less generous.

Using reinforcement

When a behaviour is rewarded, people are more likely to repeat that behaviour. When young children in natural settings are rewarded by others for offering to help, they are more likely to offer again later. Similarly, if they are not rewarded they are less likely to offer again (Grusec 1982). When children in an experiment are praised or reinforced with bubblegum for their sharing, they will learn to share what they have with other children (Fischer 1963).

Rushton and Teachman (1978) studied children who saw a second person behaving generously by donating tokens to a third person (see Figure 13.1). Most children tended to imitate, by also donating tokens in a later play situation. Next, the second person either rewarded or punished the child for behaving generously. Both tactics had strong effects on how children behaved, both immediately and after a two-week follow-up. This study employed not only reinforcement principles but also the effects of watching a model.

Exposure to models

▶ Modelling

People can also learn to be helpful by observing another person engaging in a helping act. Laboratory research has shown that setting an example has a strong effect on helping behaviour. Learning to be helpful through observation is a particular case of *modelling*, a process which we have noted can help account for the learning of attitudes (Chapter 4) and of aggressive behaviour (Chapter 11). Children who win tokens in games, and who then see an adult model donating tokens to help a needy child, are more likely to be generous themselves (Grusec and Skubiski 1970). In studies of the effects of viewing prosocial behaviour on television in America, the general finding has been that children's attitudes towards prosocial behaviour are improved (Coates *et al.* 1976; Rushton 1979). There was less direct effect on actual prosocial behaviours, and less effect over longer time periods.

Adults are also capable of being influenced by helpful models. Consider the example described in Box 13.2.

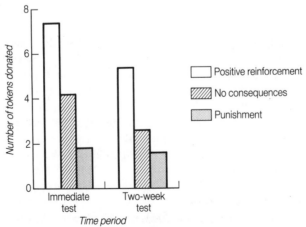

FIGURE 13.1 *The effects of reward and punishment on children's willingness to behave generously. (Source: based on data from Rushton and Teachman 1978.)*

BOX 13.2 The case of the helpful motorist

Flat tyres to fix

A model shows us how to perform a helpful act, reminds us that helping is appropriate, increases our confidence in being able to help, and gives us information about the consequences of helping others (Rushton 1980).

In a study of the *modelling effect*, Bryan and Test (1967) investigated whether a model would influence the number of people who might stop to help a woman fix a car tyre. There were two conditions:

1. In the *experimental* condition, motorists first passed a woman whose car had a flat tyre; another car was pulled to the side of the road, and the male driver was apparently helping her to change the tyre. This condition provided a helping model for subjects who shortly came upon another car with a flat tyre. This time, the woman was alone and needed assistance.
2. In the *control* condition, only the second car and driver were present; there was no model.

The results were clear. The motorists who were exposed to a prosocial model were over 50 per cent more likely to help when compared with those in the no-model condition.

(Source: based on data from Bryan and Test 1967.)

▶ Social learning theory

▶ Learning by vicarious experience

When a person observes a model and behaves in kind, is this just a matter of mechanical imitation? The work of Bandura (1973) suggested otherwise (see also Chapter 11). According to his *social learning theory*, it is knowing what happens to the model which largely determines whether the observer will also help. As with direct learning experience, positive outcomes should increase a model's effectiveness in influencing the observer to help, while negative outcomes should decrease the model's effectiveness. Hornstein (1970) conducted an experiment where people saw a model returning a lost wallet. They either appeared pleased to be able to help, displeased at the bother of having to help, or showed no strong reaction. Later, the subject also came across another 'lost' wallet. Those who had witnessed the pleasant consequences helped the most; others who saw the unpleasant consequences helped the least. Observing the outcomes for another person is called *learning by vicarious experience* (see also Chapter 11); it can increase the rates at which both selfishness and selflessness take place (Midlarsky and Bryan 1972).

Through attribution processes

The attributions people make about their own helping or non-helping behaviour and about persons who are in need of help can play a role. Even if a person is helpful on a first occasion, in order for helpfulness to continue the idea of helpfulness must be internalised. Attribution theory (see Chapter 3) suggests that this occurs through developing self-attributions of helpfulness. A child who decides 'I am a helpful person' makes an attribution that will guide future behaviour in situations where helping is an option. Self-attributions of helpfulness are even more powerful than reinforcement for helping behaviour in young children: those who were told they were 'helpful people' donated more marbles to a needy child than those who were reinforced with verbal praise, and this effect persisted over time (Grusec and Redler 1980). Indeed, children may experience self-criticism and bad feelings when they fail to live up to the standards implied by their attributions (Perry *et al.* 1980).

▶ Just-world hypothesis   Attributions about the person in need are also important, and are likely to determine whether help is offered. Under some conditions people do not help, and may even blame an innocent victim. According to the *just-world hypothesis* (Lerner and Miller 1978), people have a need to believe – perhaps for their own security – that the world is a just place where people get what they deserve. If, for instance, someone has an accident, it may have been deserved (Bulman and Wortman 1977). Consequently, if some victims deserved their fate (which means that blame is attributed to them), the bystander is less likely to help. Some of the witnesses in the Kitty Genovese case may well have believed that it was her fault for being out so late. This is a familiar response to many crimes. A rape victim, for example, might have 'deserved' what happened because her clothing was tight or revealing. Accepting that the world must necessarily be a just place begins in childhood, and is a learned attribution.

Fortunately, evidence of people's undeserved suffering can undermine this belief in a just world, and one way to re-establish justice is to compensate, or in this case, help the victim. Miller (1977), however, argued that a necessary precondition of actually helping is the belief that such help will be effective. He distinguished two kinds of need which may convince a would-be helper: (1) need extent, and (2) need persistence. Each of these should operate at a fairly low level if the giving of help is likely to be judged as effective. An example of this line of thinking is a study carried out by Warren and Walker (1991) which showed that if the needs of a person in distress can be evaluated, they can be used by others to determine if giving help is justified. In a field study of 2,648 adults in Perth in Western Australia, letters were mailed soliciting donations for a refugee family from Sudan. Covering letters with slightly different wording were used. A higher rate of giving was recorded when the letter highlighted that: (1) the donation was restricted to this particular family rather than being extended to other people in Sudan; and (2) the family's need was only short term. In short, the case was just and action would be effective.

Through normative influences

▶ Norms

Often we help others simply because 'something tells us' we should. We ought to help that little old lady to cross the street, we ought to return a wallet we found, we ought to help a child in distress. An important influence on the development and maintenance of prosocial behaviour is that of a cultural norm. *Norms* provide a background form of social influence on human social behaviour (see Chapters 6 and 7), and are learned rather than innate. A norm is a standard of action that specifies what standard of behaviour is expected, or 'normal', and what behaviour is abnormal. Norms are social expectations, prescribing proper social behaviour. Almost every culture has a norm that concern for others is good and that selfishness is bad. The unwritten rule in most societies is that when the cost is not very great and another person is in need, one should do all that one can to help that person. The universality of some types of norm of social responsibility indicates that this standard has functional value and that it operates to facilitate social life. One way of accounting for helping others, therefore, is to say that it is normative, and that there are social rewards for behaving in accord with the norm and sanctions for violating it. Sanctions may range from mild disapproval to incarceration or worse, depending on the threat posed to the existing social order.

Two specific social norms have been proposed as a basis for altruism:

▶ Reciprocity principle

1. The *reciprocity norm* – we should help those who help us. Gouldner (1960) argued that this norm, which is also referred to as the *reciprocity principle*, is as universal as the incest taboo. Nevertheless, the extent of one's obligation to reciprocate varies according to circumstance. We feel deeply indebted when someone freely makes a big sacrifice for us, but much less so if the sacrifice is smaller and expected (Tesser *et al.* 1968; Wilke and Lanzetta 1970). Additionally, in terms of the concept of social exchange (see Chapter 12), people might only give help in return for help given in the past or anticipated in the future.

▶ Social responsibility norm

2. The *social responsibility norm* – help should be freely given to those in need, without regard to future exchanges (Berkowitz 1972b; Schwartz 1975). Members of a community are often willing to help needy people, even when they remain anonymous, and there is no expectation of social reward (Berkowitz 1972b). Charitable donations given to callers at the front door are an example. In practice, people usually apply this norm selectively, such as to those in need through no fault of their own. Consistent with the just-world hypothesis, the social responsibility norm dictates that we should give to people in line with what they deserve. If they are victims of a natural disaster, by all means help, but if they are drunk and injure themselves falling over, then they should suffer what they deserve. The application of the norm depends on the attribution of causes of the need for help. Ironically, it can run counter to a norm that we should not interfere in other people's lives.

Teger (1970) has suggested that a norm of helping is often endorsed verbally, but really is an ideal rather than an actual behaviour, and not a very compelling force at that. As an ideal norm, the prosocial ethic is an expression of people paying lip service to being responsible citizens. The question, then, is when and why do people actually adhere to such social norms? Schwartz (1977) has identified certain conditions that determine whether a person is sensitive to internalised norms or feelings of moral obligation. This, however, brings us to the area of situational influences on prosocial behaviour, which is covered later in this chapter.

Empathy and arousal

As with other social behaviours, both genetic and environmental factors seem to be involved in helping others, and there have been attempts to offer a compromise between sociobiological and social learning approaches in explaining altruism. For example, Vine (1983) and Hoffman (1981) argued that a motive to help has evolved through natural selection, but also that it is sensitive to environmental influences. Biological mechanisms may predispose a person to act, but how a person ultimately responds is affected by past experiences and immediate circumstances.

▶ Empathy

Several theorists believe that a state of *arousal* is necessary before we act prosocially, and that it is *empathy* which then motivates us to help others (Gaertner and Dovidio 1977; Hoffman 1981; Hornblow 1980). Empathy is an emotional response to someone else's distress, a reaction to witnessing a disturbing event. There is considerable evidence that both adults and children respond empathically to the distress of another person, suggesting that it is unpleasant to watch someone else suffer. Even infants of one or two days of age can respond to the distress of another infant (Sagi and Hoffman 1976; Simner 1971). When we actually help, however, we are trying to reduce the unpleasant feelings that their distress or pain arouses in us. The extra ingredient, though, is empathy, or the ability to identify with another's experiences, particularly their feelings (Krebs 1975).

A major model of prosocial behaviour put forward by Piliavin *et al.* (1975) proposed that people will intervene in an emergency because they find it unpleasantly arousing and seek relief. As a result, 'altruism' is a misnomer because it is really motivated by self-interest. A person helps out of a desire to deal with an unpleasant emotion. Helping is an act that will most rapidly and completely reduce the unpleasant feelings. Piliavin *et al.*'s approach is dealt with in a later section.

One factor which mediates empathy is *similarity*: we are more likely to feel empathy towards someone whom we perceive as similar to ourselves. Krebs has demonstrated that people show a physiological response when they see someone like themselves being shocked; the greater the similarity the greater the arousal, and also the greater the later altruism to the victim.

If it is true that prosocial behaviour is based only on self-interest, is there such a thing as an altruist? Batson *et al.* (1981) argued that an act is truly altruistic only if people seek to help even when they will no longer be troubled by observing the suffering of another person (for example, turning back to help after passing a stranded motorist). This approach could offer a different perspective to the Genovese case, with the bystanders feeling disturbed, but not sufficiently so to act: perhaps they could not identify with the victim.

SITUATIONAL MODELS OF HELPING

▶ Bystander intervention

▶ Bystander effect

We noted at the outset that social psychologists were curious and concerned about the lack of involvement of witnesses or bystanders during the Kitty Genovese murder. As a result, research was undertaken to identify when people will help in an emergency. More recently, the question has been broadened to ask: When will people help in non-emergencies by performing such deeds as giving money, donating blood, or contributing time or effort? The focus here is on the situational factors that affect *bystander intervention* in real-life situations in the real world, rather than on the origins or learning of helping behaviour. Furthermore, there has been an attempt to develop models of the helping process, largely from a cognitive viewpoint. The initial emphasis was on helping in emergencies, but this has now widened to prosocial behaviour in general. Perhaps the most influential and thoroughly studied factor that affects prosocial behaviour and responding is whether the potential helper is alone or in the company of others. What is now known is that a lone bystander is more likely to help than any of several bystanders, a phenomenon known as the *bystander effect*. A number of general models attempt to explain situational influences on bystander intervention. We will consider two, the first by Latané and Darley (1970) and the second by Piliavin *et al.* (1981).

Latané and Darley's cognitive model

▶ Emergency situation

Directly stemming from the wide public discussion and concern about the Genovese case, Latané and Darley began a programme of research (Darley and Latané 1968), now considered a classic in its field. Surely, these researchers asked, empathy for another's suffering, or at the very least a sense of civic responsibility, should lead to intervention in a situation of danger; in any event, when several bystanders are present there should be a correspondingly greater probability that someone will help. Before dealing with this question, consider first the elements of an *emergency situation*:

1. It can involve danger, for person or property.
2. It is an unusual event.
3. It can differ widely in nature, from a bank on fire to a pedestrian being mugged.

4. It is not foreseen, so that prior planning of how to cope is improbable.

5. It requires instant action, so that leisurely consideration of options is impossible.

At this juncture, we can note a similarity between the nature of an emergency and that of the autokinetic phenomenon used by Sherif in his study of the way in which social norms develop (see Chapters 6 and 7): both involve uncertainty, ambiguity and a lack of structure in terms of a proper cause for judgement or for action. Consequently, there should be a greater probability in each case that the individual will look to others for guidance on how to think and act. If so, a major prediction about an emergency is that a particular individual will react quite differently according to whether others are present or absent.

BOX 13.3 Steps in Latané and Darley's cognitive model

Deciding whether to help

- Does the bystander even notice an event where helping may be required, such as an accident?
- How is the event interpreted? We are most likely to define a situation as an emergency, and most likely to help, when we believe that the victim's condition is serious and is about to deteriorate rapidly. Shotland and Huston (1979) showed in a field experiment that people were more likely to help in emergencies (for example, someone needs an insulin shot for diabetes) than in non-emergencies (e.g. needing some allergy medicine). Verbal distress cues (for example, screaming) are particularly effective and increase the likelihood of bystander intervention (Clark and Word 1972, 1974; Gaertner and Dovidio 1977): the act of screaming can lead to receiving help 75 per cent or more of the time. These studies suggest that bystander apathy is markedly reduced once people interpret a situation as an emergency.
- Does the bystander accept personal responsibility for helping? Sometimes a person witnessing an emergency knows that there are other onlookers but cannot see their reactions. This was clearly the case in the Genovese incident. Sometimes the decision to assume responsibility is determined by how competent the bystander feels in the particular situation. For both the second and third steps the influence of other people is clearly a determining factor.
- What does the bystander decide to do?
- Is help given? If we doubt whether the situation is an emergency, or what to do if it is, the behaviour of others around us can influence what we do.

Latané and Darley noted that it would be easy simply to label the failure to help a victim in an emergency as apathy – an uncaring response to the problems of others. They reasoned, however, that the apparent lack of concern of the witnesses in the Genovese case could conceal other processes. An early finding was that failure to help occurred more frequently when the group size of witnesses increased. Their cognitive model of bystander intervention proposes that whether a person helps depends on the outcomes of a series of decisions. At any point along this path a decision could be made which would terminate helping behaviour. The steps in this model are described in Box 13.3, and the decision process is illustrated in Figure 13.2. In the following sections, a series of experiments are outlined to illustrate how this model works.

'Where there's smoke there's fire'

In an illustrative experiment (Latané and Darley 1970), male students were invited to an interview to discuss some of the problems involved in life at a large university. While they were filling out a preliminary questionnaire smoke began to pour into the room from a wall vent. This continued for six minutes until the room was full of smoke. Subjects were either alone, with two other subjects they did not know or with two confederates who ignored the smoke. The issue was what the subject did about this, and how long he took. The authors hypothesised that people in such situations look to others around them to decide what to do. The results supported this. Subjects who were alone were more likely to report the smoke than were subjects with other strangers. While 75 per cent of the subjects who were alone took positive action, only 38 per cent of the two-stranger groups intervened. Subjects in the presence of two passive confederates, who had been instructed to ignore the smoke, were even less likely to report the situation, taking action only 10 per cent of the time.

Latané and Darley's interpretation was that the presence of others can inhibit people from responding to an emergency: the more people the slower the response. Even worse, many of the people who did not respond were persuaded by the passive behaviour of others that the situation was not an

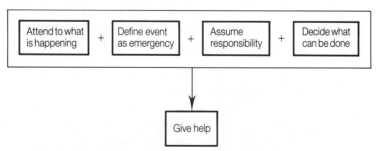

FIGURE 13.2 *The decision process in Latané and Darley's cognitive model. (Source: based on suggestions by Latané and Darley 1970.)*

emergency. Some later reported that they believed there was no danger from the smoke. In a real emergency this could easily have proved fatal.

A lady in distress

Latané and Rodin (1969) replicated these results and extended the argument to situations where others might be in danger. Again, male subjects were alone or in pairs filling out a questionnaire, and heard a woman in another room struggle to open a filing cabinet. They then heard a loud crash followed by a cry of pain, and moans and groans. Subjects who were alone helped 70 per cent of the time, and when in pairs only 40 per cent of the time. Subjects with a passive confederate who suggested the situation was not critical helped only 7 per cent of the time. One further refinement was added, and it was found that pairs of friends helped more often, 70 per cent of the time.

'He's having a fit'

Must bystanders be physically present to reduce the probability of a person giving help? Darley and Latané (1968) devised an experiment where students could communicate with each other only with microphones while in separate cubicles. They were led to believe that the group consisted of either two people (self and a victim), four or six people. The 'victim' told the others over the intercom system that he was an epileptic. Later he was heard to choke and gasp, apparently having a seizure, and then became quiet. The important question was whether the number of presumed bystanders who might help influenced how long the subject took to help. The results showed that the more bystanders that people thought there were, the less likely they were to help. Before the end of the fit, 85 per cent of the subjects who were alone helped, but only 62 per cent of the subjects who believed that two other people were present helped, and 31 per cent of those who thought there were four others present helped. Within six minutes after the event began, the respective figures were 100 per cent, 81 per cent and 62 per cent.

Processes contributing to bystander apathy

Let us take stock. To respond to an emergency, people must stop whatever they were doing and engage in some unusual, unexpected behaviour. The lone bystanders will usually do just that, often without hesitation. However, when several bystanders are present there is a clear tendency to hold back, and perhaps not to respond at all. Multiply this effect across each individual and a whole group of onlookers may fail to intervene. What is it, then, about a group that can produce this effect?

As the results of their own and others' experiments were being gathered, Latané and Darley (1976) puzzled about which of several possible social processes could underlie the reluctance of groups to help a victim. Three major explanations were available. In distinguishing between them, we can use the analogy of the nature of the communication channel open to the onlookers.

Three questions can be asked:

1. Is an individual aware that others are present?
2. Can an individual actually see or hear the others, and be aware of how they are reacting?
3. Can these others monitor the behaviour of the individual?

Each of the following processes is distinctive in terms of how these questions are answered:

▶ Diffusion of responsibility

1. *Diffusion of responsibility* – think back to the phenomenon of social loafing (discussed in Chapter 7) in which an individual who is part of a group often tends to offload responsibility for action onto others. In the case of an emergency situation, the presence of other onlookers provides the opportunity to transfer the responsibility for acting, or not acting, onto them. The communication channel does not imply that the individual can be seen by the others, or can see them. It is only necessary that they be available, somewhere, for action. People who are alone are most likely to help a victim because they believe they carry the entire responsibility for action. If they do not act, nobody else will. Ironically, the presence of just one other witness allows responsibility to be diffused among all present.

▶ Fear of social blunders

2. *Audience inhibition* – other onlookers can make the individual self-conscious of an intended action; one would not want to appear foolish by over-reacting. In the context of prosocial behaviour, anticipated embarrassment is sometimes referred to as a *fear of social blunders*. Have you felt a dread of being laughed at for misunderstanding little crises involving others? What if it is not like it seems? What if someone is playing a joke? Am I on *Candid Camera*? The communication channel implies that the others can see or hear the individual, but it is not necessary that they can be seen.

3. *Social influence* – other onlookers provide a model for action. If they are passive and unworried, the situation may seem to be less serious. The communication channel implies that the individual can see the others, but not vice versa.

The three-in-one experiment

We will consider the most complicated of Latané and Darley's experiments which was designed specifically to detect the operation of each of the three processes just outlined. By the use of television monitors and cameras, subjects were induced to believe that they were in one of four conditions, with respect to other onlookers. They could: (1) see and be seen; (2) see, but not be seen; (3) not see, but be seen; or (4) neither see nor be seen. This complexity was necessary in order to allow for the consequences of sequentially adding social influence and audience inhibition effects to that of diffusion of responsibility. We should note here that diffusion of responsibility must always be involved if a bystander is, or is thought to be, present. However, the additive effect of another process can be assessed and then compared with the effect of diffusion acting on its own. You will get a good idea of how this was achieved by studying Box 13.4.

The results measured in seconds the amount of time which elapsed before the subject moved to help the prostrate experimenter. Figure 13.3 shows the cumulative number of subjects who intervened as time went by. It also distinguishes between the 'alone' and three sets of bystander results. The investigators collapsed the results for two of these (diffusion of responsibility plus either audience inhibition or social influence) since they did not differ significantly, and each involved one-way communication.

The results in Figure 13.3 show that the probability of help being offered decreases as the amount of communicated information increases. Simple diffusion of responsibility (no communication) reduces helping behaviour, and the latter declines further when either social influence or audience inhibition is added (one-way communication). When all three processes are allowed to operate (two-way communication), the least help is given.

BOX 13.4 The conditions in the three-in-one experiment

A shocking experience

The subjects were students who had agreed to take part in a study of repression. Their supposed task was to rate whether the way in which a target person responded to verbal stimuli indicated if they had received an electric shock or not. When certain words were presented, the target person would receive a shock from the experimenter. The subject would watch this on closed circuit television in another room, and judge when shocks had been delivered by studying the target person's overall behaviour. The experiment was carried out at night in a deserted building at Princeton University. Subjects were to work in pairs (except in the 'alone' condition), though in fact the second rater in each case was a confederate of the experimenter.

Each pair of subjects was initially taken to a control room, where there was an antiquated shock generator. Commenting on it, the experimenter said that the parts were from army surplus and were not reliable. In front of the generator was a chair, with a television camera pointing at it. The experimenter then noted that the target person was late, and that time could be saved by filling out a background questionnaire. They were ushered to their individual cubicles, each of which contained two television monitors and a camera. Monitor 1 was operating and showed the control room

▶

which they had just left, with the shock generator in clear view. The experimenter apologised for the presence of monitor 2, and for the camera, saying that these belonged to another, absent staff member and could not be touched. Both items were operating. This extra, supposedly superfluous, equipment provided the basis for several experimental conditions. Monitor 2 could show the neighbour in the next cubicle, and the camera could show the subject to the neighbour. There were five conditions:

1. *Alone* – this is a baseline condition in which no other person is present with the real subject. The camera in the real subject's room is pointing at the ceiling, and monitor 2 shows a shot of the ceiling of the second cubicle, but no sign of anybody else.
2. *Diffusion of responsibility* – like the remaining conditions, there are two people, but here there is no communication. Monitor 2 shows only the ceiling of the other cubicle (where the camera is pointing). The camera in the real subject's room is also pointing at the ceiling. It is different from the 'alone' condition, however, since the subject knows that there is a bystander present.
3. *Diffusion plus social influence* – The subject sees the other's response, but not vice versa. One camera is trained on someone, in this case on the bystander. The confederate can be seen working on a questionnaire on monitor.
4. *Diffusion plus audience inhibition* – the other sees the subject's response, but not vice versa. One camera is trained on someone, in this case on the subject. Although the bystander cannot be seen, presumably the subject can be.
5. *Diffusion plus social influence plus audience inhibition* – the two persons see each other. Both cameras are trained on them, and they can be seen on the respective monitors.

The emergency was created when the experimenter left the subject in the cubicle and returned to the control room to adjust the shock generator, visible in monitor 1. On the screen, the experimenter could be seen to pick up some wires.

They must not have been the right wires, because the experimenter screamed, jumped in the air, threw himself against the wall, and fell to the floor out of camera range with his feet sticking up. About fifteen seconds later he began to moan softly, and he continued until help was received or for about six minutes. (Latané and Darley 1976, p.327).

What will the real subject do in each condition? See the results in Figure 13.3.

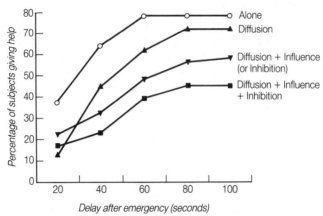

FIGURE 13.3 *The effects of three processes upon willingness to help a victim. (Source: adapted from Latané and Darley 1976.)*

Limits to these effects

Bystanders who are strangers inhibit helping even more because communication between them is slower. When bystanders are known to each other there is much less inhibition of prosocial behaviour than in a group of strangers (Latané and Rodin 1969; Rutkowski *et al.* 1983). Gottlieb and Carver (1980) showed, however, that, even among strangers, inhibition is reduced if they know there will be an opportunity to interact later and possibly to explain their actions. Overall it can be concluded that the bystander effect is strongest when those involved are anonymous strangers who do not expect to meet again, which could have been the situation in the Genovese case.

Piliavin et al.'s bystander-calculus model

▶ Bystander-calculus model

Whereas Latané and Darley's approach is purely cognitive, the *bystander-calculus model* is a mixture of cognitive and physiological processes. According to Piliavin *et al.* (1981), when bystanders perceive someone in trouble, they work their way through three stages before they respond to the person. This process involves a set of calculations, hence the notion of calculus. At first, they become physiologically aroused by the sight of another's distress. Next, this arousal is labelled as an emotion. Finally, the consequences of helping or not are evaluated.

Physiological arousal

When we see another person in distress, our first reaction is physiological, an empathic response. However, Piliavin *et al.* (1981) showed that there is often a decline in physiological responses when someone first sees an emergency; for example, heart rate decreases. This is an *orienting reaction*, which is designed to allow us to figure out what is going on. It is quickly followed by a dramatic increase in physiological reactions, a *defence reaction*, which prepares an observer to act. This pattern of arousal is typical when people encounter a strong stimulus; in the case of an emergency involving another person, it is an empathic response since it is caused by something that happened to someone else.

The greater the arousal in emergencies, the greater the chance a bystander will help (Piliavin *et al.* 1981). Gaertner and Dovidio (1977) found a strong correlation between the speed of subjects' responses and their heart rate, when subjects helped a woman who had been hurt by falling chairs. The strength of a bystander's empathic physiological reaction is also influenced by non-social factors. For example, as the severity and clarity of the victim's plight increases, so does the strength of a bystander's physiological arousal (Geer and Jarmecky 1973).

Labelling the arousal

Being aroused is one thing, but feeling a specific emotion (fear, anger, love, etc.) is another. Generally, arousal does not automatically produce specific emotions; people's cognitions or thoughts about the arousal play a critical role in determining the nature of emotions they feel (Schachter and Singer 1962). When another person is distressed, the situational cues trigger two distinct sets of responses, personal distress and empathic concern (Batson and Coke 1981; Davis 1980; Piliavin *et al.* 1981). Personal distress is an experience of anxiety when someone else is upset. Empathic concern is a response to another person in which the bystander feels compassion.

According to Piliavin, physiological arousal is often labelled by a bystander as a *personal distress*. If you believe that someone is hurt then you feel aroused, that is, tense and anxious. You label this as personal distress: 'I feel upset because of this'. This is more likely to occur if you do not have a close personal relationship with the victim, or if the situation involves a highly arousing emergency. Piliavin proposed that helping others reduces a bystander's personal distress (see also Gaertner and Dovidio 1977).

▶ Empathic concern   This unflattering idea that helping is motivated by self-serving needs of the bystander, and not because it serves the needs of the victim, has been disputed by others. Batson and his associates (Batson and Coke 1981; Batson *et al.* 1981; Toi and Batson 1982) have suggested that when bystanders believe they are similar to a victim, and identify with that person, they experience *empathic concern*. The difference here is that helping is motivated by concern for the other, not from a desire to reduce personal distress in a bystander. Helping that is motivated by empathic concern could, therefore, be accurately called altruistic.

Evaluating the consequences

Piliavin went on to argue that bystanders evaluate the consequences of acting before helping a victim. They weigh the costs of either direct helping or indirect helping. They then choose the action that will reduce their personal distress to the lowest cost (note the strong social exchange flavour here – see Chapter 12). The two main costs of helping are time and effort: the greater these costs, the less likely a bystander is to help (Batson *et al.* 1978; Darley and Batson 1973). So, in the Genovese case, the fear of being attacked may have reduced the likelihood of the bystanders helping (McGovern 1976; Midlarsky and Midlarsky 1973).

▶ Empathy costs of not helping

Now, not helping can also involve costs. Piliavin distinguished between *empathy costs of not helping* and *personal costs of not helping*. A critical intervening variable is the relationship between the bystander and the victim. We have already seen that empathic concern was one motive for helping a distressed person; conversely, not helping when you feel empathic concern results in empathy costs. This consists of continued unpleasant feelings (tension, anxiety) in response to the other's plight. Thus, the clarity of the emergency, its severity and the closeness of the bystander to the victim will increase the costs of not helping. Anything that increases the impact of the victim's state on the bystander will increase the empathy costs, if help is not given.

You will remember that Latané and Darley (1970) noted that helping was influenced by the number of other people witnessing an emergency. A review by Latané and Nida (1981) of more than fifty studies dealing with the effect of group size on helping concluded that the higher the number of bystanders the less likely that anyone will intervene to help. A Piliavin interpretation is that the presence of others reduces the cost of not helping, a subtly different perspective on the concept of diffusion of responsibility.

▶ Personal costs of not helping

Personal costs of not helping are many and varied, such as public censure or self-blame. Certain characteristics of the person in distress also affect the costs of not helping, for instance, the greater the victim's need for help, the greater the costs of not helping (Piliavin *et al.* 1981). If you believe a victim might die if you do not help, the personal costs are likely to be high. If a tramp in the street asked you for money to buy alcohol, the personal costs of refusing might not be high, but if the request was for money for food or medicine the costs might be quite high.

Other things being equal, the more similar the victim is to the bystander, the more likely the bystander is to help (Gross *et al.* 1975; Krebs 1975; Pandey and Griffitt 1974). Similarity causes greater physiological arousal in bystanders and thus greater empathy costs of not helping. Similar victims may also be friends, for whom the costs of not helping would probably be very high. Recall the sociobiological position that preservation of one's genes is the basis of protecting one's kin. The Piliavin model would simply note the high level of similarity between bystander and victim, thereby increasing the cost of not helping to an excruciating level. Think of the agony if one did not enter a blazing house to rescue one's own child.

Piliavin *et al.* (1981) used the reward/cost matrix shown in Figure 13.4 and Box 13.5 to describe how these costs will affect bystanders' responses in an emergency.

Let us take an experimental example (Piliavin *et al.* 1975). Each subject saw a person fall over and apparently require help. In a high-cost condition, this person had an extensive birthmark, and in a low-cost condition, did not. You might think this a little strange, but it seems that many people find physical disfigurement aversive. There was also a second bystander. For half of the subjects, the other bystander was dressed like a medical intern, and for the other half dressed ordinarily. In the low-cost (no birthmark) condition, people helped equally, regardless of how the other bystander was dressed. In the high-cost (birthmark) condition, it depended on dress: with the ordinary person, 72 per cent of subjects helped, but with an intern present only 48 per cent helped. The Piliavin interpretation is that, in the high-cost condition, the first bystander could more easily refer responsibility for helping to the intern, thereby lowering the costs of not helping.

With regard to the Genovese case, the bystander–calculus model suggests that, although the onlookers would have been aroused and felt personal distress and empathic concern, the empathy costs and personal costs were not sufficient. Personal costs, in particular, may have deterred people from inter-vening. What if they got killed? In terms of the matrix in Figure 13.4, the costs of helping directly would be high; the costs of not helping could be either high or low, depending on how individuals interpreted the situation: for example, was it just a marital dispute? In this case, the outcome is contained in the two right-hand cells of the matrix. People either ignored the problem or denied it existed, or lowered the costs of not helping (perhaps help was not really needed; maybe someone else has done something by now). If someone were to have called the police, this would have been an instance of indirect intervention.

Perhaps you can now see some of the complications involved in asking why did the people not help in the Genovese murder. Most of the research on situational influences on helping among adults has focused on the bystander effect. Check the various points made by comparing the step-by-step decision approach of Latané and Darley in Figure 13.2 with the rewards/costs matrix approach of Piliavin *et al.* in Figure 13.4.

Lest we conclude this section with the feeling that Piliavin's model is unaccept-ably mechanistic, consider a recent view expressed by Piliavin and Charng:

> There appears to be a 'paradigm' shift away from [an] earlier position that behaviour that appears to be altruistic must, under close scrutiny, be revealed as reflecting egoistic motives. Rather, theory and data now being advanced are more compatible with the view that true altruism – acting with the goal of benefiting another – does exist and is part of human nature.
> (Piliavin and Charng 1990, p. 27)

THE PERSON IN THE EQUATION

With so many situational factors affecting prosocial behaviour, we might wonder if aspects of the person have much effect. Let us re-establish some

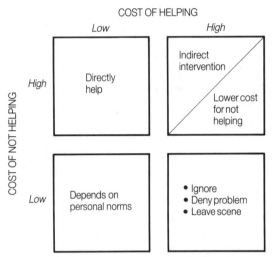

COST OF HELPING

Low   High

High   Directly help   Indirect intervention / Lower cost for not helping

COST OF NOT HELPING

Low   Depends on personal norms   • Ignore • Deny problem • Leave scene

FIGURE 13.4 *Piliavin et al.'s model of how costs affect bystanders' responses to the problems of a victim. (Source: adapted from Piliavin et al. 1981.)*

balance by noting the psychological maxim that 'behaviour is a product of the individual and the environment'.

Are there personal characteristics which are relatively independent of the situation? Research has concentrated on two areas: transitory psychological states and personality characteristics. The former includes passing mood and feelings, which all of us may experience; the latter implies relatively permanent attributes.

Transitory psychological states

We have all experienced days where everything seems to go either perfectly well or totally wrong, and know that this can affect how we interact with other people. Prosocial research has shown that people who feel good are much more likely to help someone in need than are people who feel bad (Bierhoff 1988).

Good moods

A typical experimental approach is to get subjects to believe that they have succeeded or failed at a task they are asked to perform. It then transpires that those who believe they have been successful are more helpful than those who believe they have failed or those who have received no feedback. Isen (1970) found that teachers who were more successful on a task were more likely later to contribute to a school fund-raising drive. Those who had done well, in fact, donated seven times as much as the others. So, such momentary feelings as success in a relatively innocuous task can dramatically affect prosocial behaviour.

BOX 13.5 Differences in costs in Piliavin *et al.*'s model

The Costs of helping or not helping

Referring to Figure 13.4:

- *Lower right cell* – the costs of helping are high and the costs of not helping are low. For example, suppose fifty people witness a knife fight between two drunks outside a pub at closing time. Fear of being injured would be an obvious high possible cost for intervening. The costs of not helping are low because: (1) you can diffuse responsibility for not helping to all the others present; (2) the victims are not deserving of help as they brought it on themselves. In such instances, bystanders are likely to leave the scene or ignore a victim's plight.
- *Lower left cell* – both types of cost are low. Personal norms are likely to guide whether help is offered. Such a situation might be helping a market researcher on the street with a brief survey.
- *Upper left cell* – the cost of helping is low and the cost of not helping is high. For example, giving aid to a child accident victim lying on the side of the road after a car crash. Most people would directly intervene.
- *Upper right cell* – both kinds of cost are high. Here, bystanders may engage in indirect intervention, for example calling the police, ambulance or fire engine. This action could help the victim and also involves a low cost. If such indirect intervention is not possible (for example, no telephone is at hand), bystanders may resolve their dilemma by lowering the costs of not helping, for example, deciding that the situation does not really require their help (reinterpretation) or that the victim deserved what is happening (derogation).

Isen suggested that doing well creates a 'warm glow of success' which makes people more likely to help. (You can compare this effect with the *reinforcement-affect model* of interpersonal liking in Chapter 12.) When people feel good they are less preoccupied with themselves and are more sensitive to the needs and problems of others. Being in a good mood means that people are more likely to focus on positive things (Isen *et al.* 1976), to have a more optimistic outlook on life, and to see the world in pleasant ways (Isen and Stalker 1982). People who hear good news over the radio show greater attraction toward strangers and greater willingness to help compared with people who hear bad news (Holloway *et al.* 1977); people are in better moods and are more helpful on sunny, temperate days than on overcast, cold days (Cunningham 1979). Even experiences such as reading aloud statements expressing elation or recalling pleasant events from one's childhood can increase the rate of helping. The evidence consistently demonstrates that good moods produce helpful behaviour under a variety of circumstances.

Bad moods

In contrast, people who feel bad, sad or depressed are inner-focused. They concentrate on themselves, their problems and worries (Berkowitz 1970), are less concerned with the welfare of others, and help others less (Weyant 1978). Berkowitz (1972b) showed that self-concern lowered the rate and amount of helping among students awaiting the outcome of an important exam. Likewise, Darley and Batson (1973) led seminary students, who were due to give a speech, to think they were either quite late, just in time or early. They then had the opportunity to help a man who had apparently collapsed in an alley. The percentages who helped were: quite late 10 per cent, just in time 45 per cent, and early 63 per cent.

However, not all bad moods produce the effect of lowered helping. Isen *et al*. (1973) have shown that some kinds of self-concern may cause people to be more helpful. Guilt is one such feeling (see Box 13.6).

Overall, the research on mood or similar psychological states is complex and indicates that experiencing success and having good moods generally lead to prosocial helping behaviour, but that bad moods may or may not lead to helping, depending on whether they are moderated by self-concern. Nevertheless, a common feature derived from providing help is that the helper ends up 'feeling good' (Williamson and Clark 1989) and experiences, at least for a while, a more positive self-evaluation.

Attributes of the person

Special interpersonal relationships can increase the feeling of personal responsibility that a bystander in an emergency will experience. This is more likely, for example, if there is a special bond with or commitment to the victim (Geer and Jarmecky 1973; Moriarty 1975; Tilker, 1970) or if the victim is especially dependent on her (Berkowitz 1978).

However, are there other intrapersonal factors that can make people more helpful, even temporarily? Indeed, are there factors that make some people consistently more helpful than others? Famous figures such as Florence Nightingale, Mahatma Gandhi, Albert Schweitzer and Mother Theresa come to mind. This area of research has been described as the attempt to identify or profile the 'Good Samaritan'. In reaction to earlier work, Huston and Korte (1976) argued that there had been an over-emphasis on situational factors in

---

BOX 13.6 The case of the guilty helper

'Oh dear, You've smashed my camera ...'

People who have accidentally broken something or injured someone show increases in helping behaviour. When subjects believed they had ruined an experiment, cheated on a test, broken expensive equipment, or inflicted pain on another, they were much more likely to help the person against whom they had transgressed (Cialdini *et al.* 1973; Katz *et al.* 1979). Regan *et al.* (1972) led a group of female subjects to believe that they had broken an expensive camera. Later, when they had the chance to help another female who had dropped some groceries, 50 per cent of the 'guilty' subjects intervened to help, while only 15 per cent of a control group did so.

One explanation offered to account for the guilty helper is the image-reparation hypothesis: people want to make amends. If you have hurt someone, you can restore self-esteem by making it up. However, the complication is that the guilty party will actually help anyone in need, not just the person towards whom they feel guilty. It is difficult to see how their self-esteem can be threatened in this way. According to Cialdini's negative relief state model (Cialdini *et al.* 1973, 1981; Cialdini and Kenrick 1976) hurting another person, or even seeing this happen, causes a bystander to experience a negative affect state. This motivates them to do something to relieve this feeling. We come to learn that helping can alleviate negative moods. Consequently, people are motivated to *feel* good rather than to *look* good. If so, this process is better described as hedonism rather than altruism, since it is motivated by self-interest. This view gains support from the finding that people who have inflicted, or who have witnessed, harm or pain and then receive an unexpected monetary reward or social approval immediately afterwards, are less helpful than subjects who are left in a bad mood (Cialdini *et al.* 1973; McMillen, 1971).

---

helping, and that personal factors have been neglected. Has their confidence in individual–level predictors been justified?

Demographic variables

Several studies (see Huston and Korte 1976) have attempted to identify why some individuals are likely to be helpers. The results are inconclusive. Latané and Darley (1970) found that fairly obvious demographic variables, such as father's occupation and number of siblings, were not correlated with helping behaviour. However, there was the intriguing suggestion that size of home town might be connected. Subjects from small-town backgrounds were more likely to help than those from larger cities. This finding was replicated by Gelfand *et al.* (1973). We deal with this point again in relation to a more comprehensive study by Amato (1983) of the role of the physical environment – see Chapter 15.

Personality variables

Latané and Darley (1970) reported that none of several personality test measures predicted helping behaviour. Such measures included authoritarianism, alienation, trustworthiness, machiavellianism (the tendency to manipulate others) and need for approval.

On the other hand, positive relationships between helping behaviour have been noted with: belief that one's fate lies within one's control; mature moral judgement; need for social approval or self-esteem; and the tendency to take responsibility for others' welfare (Eisenberg-Berg 1979; Schwartz and Clausen 1970; Staub 1974). None of this evidence, however, is strong enough clearly to distinguish the Good Samaritans from the rest of humanity, and there is some doubt whether the attempt is meaningful (Bar-Tal 1976; Schwartz 1977), or even useful. Even the strongest reported correlates of helping are weak predictors. Gergen *et al.* (1972) summarised this situation by concluding that the characteristics of the situation and of the request for help can interact in complex ways with personality characteristics. An individual's personality and background are bound to interact and influence how they interpret a situation and how they respond to it.

Competence: 'have skills, will help'

While it is clear that many situational cues and characteristics influence whether prosocial behaviour occurs, at another level the reactions of all bystanders are those of individuals. Each person must interpret, process and react to the situation. As we noted above, the bystander effect is diminished if the bystanders are friends or know each other well. The interpretation of the situation is critical: anything that makes the situation less ambiguous decreases the bystander effect (Clark and Word 1972).

An important individual factor which affects the likelihood of helping is the feeling of competence to deal with the emergency (Korte 1971), an awareness that 'I know what I'm doing'. Since costs are determinants of helping, people who feel competent to deal with potential costs for helping are more likely to intervene than are people who feel unable to handle the situation.

Feelings of competence for a specific task have been shown clearly to increase helping:

1. People who were told they had a high tolerance for electric shock were more willing to help others move electrically charged objects (Midlarsky and Midlarsky 1976).

Competence in an emergency. 'Trust us – we know what we're doing,' People with the appropriate knowledge, skills, equipment and expertise are much more likely to help someone in difficulty. (Source: *New Zealand Herald*.)

2. People who were told they were good at handling rats were more likely to help recapture a possibly dangerous laboratory rat (Schwartz and David 1976).

There is some evidence that the competence effect may even generalise beyond being specifically linked to the nature of the prosocial act. Kazdin and Bryan (1971) found that subjects who were led to believe they had done well either on a creativity task or on a health examination were later more willing to donate blood.

Certain 'packages' of skills, of course, should be perceived as being relevant to many emergencies. In a study of reactions to a stranger who was bleeding, people with first-aid training intervened more often than those who were untrained (Shotland and Heinold 1985). Pantin and Carver (1982) similarly 'created' competence by giving female students a series of films on first-aid and emergencies, and three weeks later provided an opportunity to help a confederate who was apparently choking. The bystander effect was reduced by seeing the films: this simple educational experience reduced the inhibiting consequence of the presence of others. It could be argued that these results might depend on a transitory state of feeling skilled. Pantin and Carver, however, reported that the increase in helping persisted over time.

The role that skills can play should be easily tested by comparing the degree of help offered by professionals and novices. An experiment by Cramer *et al.* (1988) provided such evidence. Their subjects were female students, half of whom were actually registered nurses (high competence) and half general course students (low competence). In the main condition, each subject waited with a non-helping confederate. The nurses were more likely than the general students to help a workman, seen earlier, who apparently had fallen off a ladder in an adjoining corridor (a rigged accident, with pre-recorded moans). In responding to a post-experimental questionnaire, the nurses specified that they felt they had the skills to help.

To sum up how competence relates to helping: a situational role which highlights that a person possesses clearly relevant skills implies that they

---

BOX 13.7 Counteracting diffusion of responsibility: the role of acting like a leader

'Who's in charge around here?'

A major requirement of effective leadership is to guide decision-making for a group (see Chapter 8) and, in an emergency, provide control and direction for action. In an experiment by Baumeister *et al.* (1988) thirty-two male and female students were led to believe that they had been allocated to four-person groups, in which one member was thought to be randomly assigned to act as leader. The students were told that their task was to decide which survivors of a nuclear war should be allowed to join the group in its bomb shelter. The assistants could make recommendations, but the final decision would be made by their designated leader.

Subjects were actually tested individually, half as leaders and half as followers, and group discussion was simulated using tape recordings over an intercommunication system. At a critical point, each subject was then exposed to a simulated emergency, when the recorded voice of a male group member faltered, and said 'Somebody come to help me, I'm choking!' He then had a fit of coughing and went silent.

Subjects who came out of the test room to help were met by the experimenter who told them that were was no problem. All were later debriefed.

Those who had been designated as leaders were much more likely than assistants to help: as many as 80 per cent (12 of 15) of leaders helped, but only 35 per cent (6 of 16) of assistants did so.

Now, the leaders in this study were randomly allocated to their role, so that the outcome cannot be explained in terms of them just having a set of personal skills. In Baumeister's view, acting as a leader brings with it a generalised responsibility which both goes beyond the immediate requirement of the group task to involve external events, and provides a buffer against the usual process of diffusion of responsibility to which ordinary members are prone and which can mediate the seeming indifference of helping a victim.

should be used. The self-percept is: 'I know what to do, so I have the responsibility to act'. Competence may be situation-specific, but there is the tantalising possibility that it may not only last over time, but also generalise to non-related situations.

Leaders and followers

A variation on the theme of competence is the instance of acting as a leader. Of course, we might think that a leader is, by definition, more generally competent than followers, and more likely to initiate all kinds of action, including helping in an emergency. The skills component of leadership probably could be used to account for some helping outcomes. Even so, a study by Baumeister and his colleagues (1988) specified an additional feature of the leadership role (see also Chapter 8) which goes beyond the 'have skills, will help' explanation: being a leader acts as a cue to generalised responsibility. In an emergency situation, Baumeister hypothesised, the leader does not experience the same degree of diffusion of responsibility as ordinary group members. Read how they tested for this in Box 13.7.

Male/female interactions

Are men meant to be gallant? It seems that males are more likely to help females than vice versa (Latane and Dabbs 1975). Typically such a situation involves helping a motorist in distress or of offering a ride to a hitchhiker. When the person in need of such help is female, passing cars are much more likely to stop than for a male or a male/female pair (Pomazal and Clore 1973;

Bystander intervention and gallantry. Research suggests that this young woman is more likely than a man to receive assistance – from a young male. (Source: Andrew Lukey.)

Snyder *et al.* 1974; West *et al.* 1975). Those who stop are typically young males driving alone. It is interesting that the male tendency to be more helpful to females stands up in a meta-analysis of research findings, despite a baseline difference of women showing more empathy generally than men (Eagly and Crowley 1986).

A question is whether men might be motivated by sexual attraction to help women in trouble. Benson *et al.* (1976) and West and Brown (1975) found that those who are physically attractive are more likely to get help, suggesting that sexual cues may be important. Przybyla (1985) clarified the motivation involved by manipulating the sexual arousal of subjects. Male and female students saw either an erotic (sexually explicit) videotape, a non-erotic videotape or none at all. When leaving the laboratory, the subjects passed either a male or a female confederate who accidentally knocked over a stack of papers. The results are shown in Figure 13.5. Almost all the male subjects who had seen an erotic tape were motivated to help a female stranger. They also spent more time helping a female (a relaxed six minutes) than they spent helping a fellow male (about thirty seconds).

Przybyla noted that both males and females reported degrees of arousal in response to viewing the sexually explicit tape. In the case of males, the more aroused the male felt, the longer he spent helping a female, an effect not extended to another male. In contrast, the more aroused females spent less time helping anyone. Thus it seems that male altruism towards females is confounded with a desire to be romantic. On the other hand, females are less likely to initiate such interactions with strangers (especially males), perhaps due to socialisation experiences.

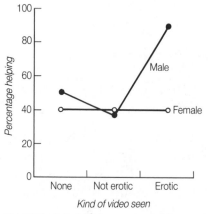

FIGURE 13.5 *Helping an opposite-sex stranger as a function of sexual arousal. (Source: based on data from Przybyla 1985.)*

APPLIED CONTEXTS

Helping to prevent crime

An interesting line of research has focused on the causes and prevention of petty and non-violent crime, such as property theft and shoplifting; and of misdemeanours, such as classroom cheating. Preventing crime can involve a class of prosocial behaviours. The development of neighbourhood watch schemes and accompanying media campaigns are examples of the promotion of prosocial behaviour. People are most likely to engage in non-violent crime if the benefits are high and the costs are low. Fraud (Lockard *et al*. 1980) and tax evasion (Hassett 1981) are often perceived this way by offenders.

A riskier crime is property theft, which is statistically more common among younger males. As individuals mature, their assessment of the costs and benefits change. Older persons are more likely to deceive a customer or lie about a product or service than actually to steal something. Research on property theft, however, illustrates two important phenomena related to prosocial behaviour: responsibility and commitment.

People are most likely to be helpful to others if they have a feeling of *responsibility* for providing assistance. We have seen earlier, for example, that individuals feel responsible if they are the only witness to a crime or accident, or if they have been trained in dealing with emergencies. Feeling responsible for providing aid increases the likelihood of prosocial behaviour.

▶ Prior commitment

Prior commitment is a specific form of responsibility that can be experimentally manipulated to induce a prosocial act. Consider the study by Moriarty (1975) in Box 13.8.

Cheating, stealing, lying, and other unethical acts have also been of interest to social psychologists. Massive American surveys (Gallup 1978; Hassett 1981) have revealed that about two-thirds of the population had cheated in school at least once. In a study of over 24,000 people, Hassett found that surprisingly high numbers of people had broken various rules of ethical conduct. About 25 per cent had cheated on an expense account, 40 per cent had driven while drunk, and 65 per cent had stolen office supplies from their employers. Understanding the types of situation that can induce such behaviours, or the types of people most likely to commit such acts, could give clues to reduce their occurrence and even to replace them with prosocial alternatives.

Shoplifting

Stealing goods from shops is a petty crime that has been of interest to psychologists investigating prosocial behaviour (Gelfand *et al*. 1973). Bickman and Rosenbaum (1977) showed that most people would report a thief to the management, if reminded by an experimental confederate. In contrast, it is clear that posters or other mass media messages have not been effective in reducing shoplifting. It is possible that impersonal reminders like these influence attitudes about shoplifting and about reporting thieves, but do not

---

BOX 13.8 Preventing theft as a consequence of prior commitment

Being responsible: the committed minder
In a real-life series of encounters, Moriarty chose individuals who were sitting alone on a crowded beach, and then sat next to them with a radio and blanket. Shortly afterwards he talked to the subjects and either simply asked for a match, or, to create commitment, asked them to watch his things while he went for a short walk. All subjects agreed to the second request, thereby committing themselves to be *responsible bystanders*. Then a confederate came along and took the radio and walked away. Of subjects who were simply asked for a match, only 20 per cent did anything about this, compared with 95 per cent for those specifically asked to be responsible. These subjects even ran after and grabbed the confederate until the experimenter returned.

The powerful effects of such prior commitments have been similarly demonstrated in other ways, for example watching a stranger's suitcase in an automat (Moriarty 1975), watching another student's books in a library (Shaffer *et al*. 1975) and a stranger's books in a classroom (Austin 1979). The results were similar, with a high likelihood of prosocial interventions following explicit prior commitment.

(Source: Moriarty 1975.)

---

actually change the behaviour itself (Bickman and Green 1977). A specific programme was developed to reduce shoplifting by informing people about its nature and its costs, in both financial and human terms. The most effective method for increasing prosocial interventions in shoplifting was found to be a lecture stressing not only how and why to report this crime but also the reasons that bystanders are sometimes inhibited from taking action (Klentz and Beaman 1981).

Exam cheating

Are there personality correlates? Cheating in examinations has been well researched by social psychologists. One very early study of the character and disposition of cheaters was carried out by MacKinnon (1933) – see Box 13.9.

There have been more recent studies which have also pursued links between cheating and personality. The following links have been reported. Students who cheat tend to be low in the ability to delay gratification (Yates and Mischel 1979), high in sociopathic tendencies (Lueger 1980), high in need for approval (Milham 1974), low in interpersonal trust (Rotter 1980), high in chronic self-

Cheating in examinations. Despite regulations and the vigilance of examiners, cheating is a quite common event. Does cheating imply that a student is lacking in ethical standards? (Source: Andrew Lukey.)

destructive tendencies (Kelley *et al.* 1985), low in adherence to the work ethic and in the desire to perform tasks industriously (Eisenberger and Shank 1985), and high in the belief that transgressions are not automatically punished (Karniol 1982). Persistent cheaters have been found to be emotionally and morally immature individuals who are not committed to hard work, are unable to give up immediate pleasures in order to obtain future goals, and who believe that they are likely to get away with breaking the rules.

Despite these findings, correlations are typically modest, so that situational factors are thought to be more important.

An area of some interest has been the influence of *arousal* or, more specifically, the feelings of excitement or the thrills that occur when people take a chance and cheat, at least when there is little risk of being caught (Scitovsky 1980).

Lueger (1980) took a different line by suggesting that any type of arousal is distracting and makes us less able to regulate our behaviour. In his study, subjects either saw an arousing film or a relaxing one and then had the chance to cheat while undergoing an intelligence test. In the relaxed condition 43 per cent cheated, but 70 per cent in the aroused condition cheated. It is possible that the build-up of arousal could account for the finding that warning examination students of the penalties for being caught cheating can, paradoxically, increase cheating (Heisler 1974).

Of course, the object of much of this research has been to be able to *discourage cheating*. A traditional reaction has been to increase the severity of punishments available. The efficacy of a punitive approach, however, can be diminished by the arousal that accompanies its publicity, and by the fact that only about one in five self-reported cheaters are ever caught (Gallup 1978). Consider again the early research results shown in Box 13.9. These suggest an alternative. Would something which increases feelings of guilt lead to a

---

BOX 13.9 An early study of dispositional features associated with cheating

An old look at exam cheats

As far back as 1933, MacKinnon investigated the role of personality in cheating. In this experiment subjects were required to solve a series of problems, knowing that the answers were in books next to them. They were allowed to look at only a few examples from this book and then had to work the rest out themselves, not knowing that they were being observed. The question was, who would cheat and look up more answers than was permitted?

The subjects were divided into cheaters and non-cheaters. Cheaters tended to express anger towards the task more than non-cheaters, non-cheaters blamed themselves for not solving the problems more than cheaters did, non-cheaters tended to verbalise the problem and develop other strategies to help solve them, cheaters were more destructive or aggressive (kicking the table leg or pounding their fists on the table), non-cheaters behaved more nervously and fidgeted more.

Several weeks later, the students were asked if they had cheated. Those who had not readily said so; but those who had cheated either denied it, or admitted it but said they felt no guilt about it. Further research showed that such guilt feelings were a critical variable in determining whether a person cheated or not: 84 per cent of the non-cheaters said they would feel guilty if they were to cheat. The most guilt associated with the idea of cheating was reported by those who did not cheat. Such feelings were, however, relatively rare among those who had cheated.

This early example of research assumed that cheating was dispositional, that is, a personality characteristic and something inherent in a 'cheater'. Since this research, many other psychologists have considered that cheating is more influenced by situational variables, and that research should concentrate on these factors, especially if methods to deter it are to be developed. Guilt, however, has been identified in a number of ways as leading to prosocial behaviour.

(Source: MacKinnon 1933.)

decrease in cheating? Most people agree that cheating is wrong, and those who do cheat disapprove as strongly as those who do not (Hughes 1981). Some schools have introduced programmes to raise the ethical awareness of their students, and hence promote prosocial behaviour in a variety of ways (see Britell 1981; Dienstbier *et al.* 1980; Hechinger 1980). Dienstbier *et al.* (1980) reported some success with a programme that compared externally oriented guilt with internally oriented guilt. Cheating was lower in the internally oriented guilt condition, which suggests that the problem is not a lack of morality and ethical standards, but rather how to make ethical standards salient. This also reflects an emphasis on situational rather than dispositional causes of cheating and is a fairly optimistic view of human beings.

In summary, it is clear that a large number of people readily confess to a wide variety of unethical or illegal behaviours at one time or another. Non-violent crimes such as fraud, tax evasion and insurance fraud are prevalent in our society (as well as violent crime, of course), and social psychologists have become interested in the causes of such behaviour in an attempt to promote prosocial and behaviour campaigns such as neighbourhood watch schemes. Shoplifting is another area of interest. Research has concentrated on cheating in school students in an attempt to understand the situational and dispositional causes of these behaviours. Such research provides an interesting and potentially useful application of social psychology to real-life problems, especially in terms of devising advertising campaigns and interventions to increase prosocial behaviour in our communities.

Receiving help

We have focused this chapter around the psychology of the 'helper': when will we help, why do we hesitate, how can we improve the rate of helping in our community? There is another perspective which we should give a little time to. Does the recipient always want help? Just as we have noted that there can be psychological costs in helping (Piliavin *et al.* 1981), is it possible to expand this argument to the person who is seen to need help? Nadler (1986) believes it can. He noted that western society encourages people to be self-reliant and to achieve as individuals. To ask for help, then, confronts an individualist with a dilemma: the benefits of being aided are tempered by the costs of appearing dependent on others.

A cultural variation

Nadler introduced a socio-cultural dimension to this issue by comparing the help-seeking tendencies of Israeli high-school students living in kibbutzim with those dwelling in cities. In Israel, socialisation in a kibbutz stresses collectivist values, a lifestyle in which having a communal and egalitarian outlook is important, and being co-operative with peers is crucial. Kibbutz dwellers rely on being comrades, depending heavily on group resources and treating group goals as paramount. On the other hand, the Israeli city context is typically western, with an emphasis on individualist values, including personal independence and achievement. If values are as important as we would like to think, they should affect the way we behave (see also Chapter 4). Box 13.10 describes how Nadler tested this idea.

Help-seeking has a strong socio–cultural component. Nadler found that requesting aid was treated in dramatically different ways by the two groups. If it was clear that the situation affected the outcome for a group as a whole, kibbutz dwellers were much more likely than city dwellers to seek help, and

---

BOX 13.10 The design of Nadler's study of the relationship between socio-cultural values and the tendency to seek help

'For my comrades' sake, will you help me?'

Nadler's (1986) subjects were 110 male and female high-school students in Israel. Half grew up and lived with their families on various kibbutzim and attended a high school catering for the needs of kibbutz dwellers. The city dwellers grew up and lived with their families in two middle-sized towns in northern Israel, attending their local high schools, and were mostly of middle-class background. The study was conducted in the students' classrooms.

The task consisted of solving twenty anagrams, and its importance was made salient by suggesting that performance could predict success in other domains in life. The subjects were told that several of the problems had not been solved by people in the past. However, they were also told that, if they could not solve certain anagrams, they would have the opportunity to seek help from the investigator. The dependent variable was the percentage of occasions that a student sought help. For example, if help was asked for on five anagrams out of ten unsolved ones, the help-seeking score was 50 per cent.

In a two-by-two design, half of each of the kibbutz and city groups were tested after receiving a group-oriented instruction, and the remaining half after an individual-oriented instruction. In the group condition, the students believed that their scores would be compared with the average scores of other classes. In the individual condition they would be compared with other individuals. In terms of a cost/benefit analysis, Nadler hypothesised that help-seeking by these two groups would vary according to the nature of the instruction. Kibbutz dwellers would seek help more often if it was group-oriented, whereas city dwellers would look for help if it were individual-oriented.

The results are shown in Figure 13.6.

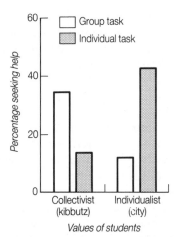

FIGURE 13.6 *Effects of collectivist versus individualist values on the tendency to seek help on two kinds of task. (Source: based on data from Nadler 1986.)*

vice versa if the benefit was defined in individual terms. There were no differences between males and females in these trends. The results are shown in Figure 13.6.

An inter-racial context

In Chapter 12 we noted that a reinforcement approach to the study of interpersonal attraction investigated how liking for one's workmates can be affected by whether help is received when the individual has trouble doing a job properly (Cook and Pelfrey 1985). A variable in this study compared own-race with mixed-race workgroups. The subjects were eighty-four white male airforce trainees, selected for their negative orientation towards blacks, and who came from geographical regions in the United States where racial prejudice was quite high. Each group consisted of an experimental subject and two confederates, and their task was to run a simulated freight business. The group interacted over five days. Each member had specific duties as either shipping officer, equipment officer or communications officer, and needed to collaborate with the others to run the business successfully. The task was structured so that the unfortunate subject (as victim) experienced a task overload in trying to deal with his duties as shipping officer.

The confederate who was the communications officer 'noticed' the subject's difficulties, and reacted as a 'helper' in one of three ways: (1) voluntarily offering help; (2) giving help, but only after being instructed to do so by the experimenter; (3) making no effort to help.

In an additional condition, the helper was also either a white person or a black person. At the end of five days, the subjects reported privately on their degree of liking for their workmates.

There was a strong, and not surprising, effect for subjects to show greatest liking for confederates who volunteered help. Even helpers who were instructed to act were liked more than those who did not help at all. The most interesting outcome, however, was that this applied equally to black helpers when compared with white helpers. This was particularly interesting in view of the likely high level of racial prejudice in the white participants of this study.

A health support network

▶ Social support
network

The very use of the term 'victim' so often in this chapter reaches out to another field, the function of a *social support network* (see Callan *et al.* 1991). We shall look at just one example from this extensive literature: a study by Dakof and Taylor (1990) dealing with cancer patients. A victimising event such as cancer has profound effects on how significant others (family, friends, workmates, medical staff) might interact with a patient: an initial reaction of aversion can give way to a facade projecting good cheer. Not surprisingly, the victim can feel stigmatised and unwanted. Dakof and Taylor have argued that the reactions of members of a support network are moderated by the nature of the relationship that people have with the victim and, in a wider sense, by the cultural constraints imposed on social interactions. In most nuclear families, those close to a cancer victim are more likely to be over-protective rather than withdrawing. Their study concentrated on how a victim views the nature of help, and how this interacts with its source.

Dakof and Taylor's subjects were fifty-five cancer patients, mostly caucasians, in Los Angeles. In terms of the source of help, most valued helpful acts by intimate providers (family, friends) related to the victim's self-esteem and emotional support, such as concern, empathy and affection. In contrast, helpful acts by medical staff and other cancer patients were informational and tangible support, such as prognosis and technical or medical care. When either group stepped out of the appropriate role, the act became misguided and unhelpful. In the case of nursing staff, helpful acts tended to be closer to those appreciated among people intimate to the victim.

SUMMARY

♦ Prosocial behaviour is a broad category that refers to all acts positively valued by society, and includes helping and altruistic behaviours. Helping behaviour refers to intentional acts designed to benefit another person. Altruistic behaviour refers to behaviours motivated by the desire to benefit another with no expectation of personal gain or reward. It is difficult to clearly identify purely altruistic behaviour because motives or rewards may be entirely internal.

♦ The Kitty Genovese murder stimulated and heavily influenced the entire study of prosocial behaviour in human beings, and research into bystander intervention specifically.

♦ There have been two major developmental approaches attempting to explain the origin and nature of prosocial behaviour in humans: a biological approach known as sociobiology, and a social learning theory approach. Most social psychologists reject the sociobiological approach. Recently, a third, integrative approach has attempted to combine aspects of both of these, focusing on arousal and empathy.

♦ Attempts to understand situational effects on bystander intervention have focused on explaining the bystander effect, that is, that there is less help given, or it takes longer to give, when a crowd of bystanders is present than when a single bystander is present to witness an emergency. Two major models have been developed, one by Latané and Darley, and the other by Piliavin *et al.*

♦ Individual characteristics influencing prosocial behaviour have tended to be overlooked with the greater emphasis on situational determinants. However, such factors as mood, background, personality characteristics and competence can have an influence in certain circumstances. For example, people who feel guilty about transgressing show an increased desire to help others in need.

♦ Other strands of research into prosocial behaviour have been developed that are less influenced by the Genovese case, and are interesting examples of applied social psychology. These include research into male/female differences in helping behaviour (especially with the 'stranded motorist' paradigm), research into preventing or reporting theft or shoplifting, and research into cheating in examinations.

FURTHER READING

Eisenberg, N. and Mussen, P. H. (1989). *The Roots of Prosocial Behaviour in Children*. Cambridge: Cambridge University Press.

Piliavin, J. A., Dovidio, J. F., Gaertner, S. L. and Clark, R. D., III (1981). *Emergency Intervention*. New York: Academic Press.

Rushton, J. P. (1980). *Altruism, Socialisation, and Society*. Englewood Cliffs, NJ: Prentice Hall.

▶ KEY TERMS

altruistic behaviour (or altruism)	empathy
bystander-calculus model	empathy costs of not helping
bystander effect	fear of social blunders
bystander intervention	helping behaviour
diffusion of responsibility	just-world hypothesis
emergency situation	learning by vicarious experience
empathic concern	modelling

nature/nurture controversy
norms
personal costs of not helping
prior commitment
prosocial behaviour

reciprocity principle
social learning theory
social responsibility norm
social support network
sociobiology

14 *Language and communication*
....

FOCUS QUESTIONS

♦ Does language determine thought, or is language the expression of thought?
♦ What influences how well someone learns to speak a second language?
♦ Why is it that some ethnic groups fight to promote their language and culture while others do not?
♦ Have you ever been 'talked down' to? Why does this happen, and why did it make you feel the way you did? How did you respond?
♦ How important is body language in communication? What sort of information are non-verbal channels best designed to communicate? How much awareness of and control over them do we have?

COMMUNICATION

▶ Communication

Communication is the essence of social interaction. What mostly goes on during social interaction is communication. Indeed, it is almost impossible to conceive of a social interaction which is free of communication. People constantly communicate information, intentionally or unintentionally, about their perceptions, thoughts, feelings, intentions and identity. They do this through direct contact or the written word, and with spoken words, expressions, gestures or signs. Communication is social in a variety of ways, for instance:

1. It involves interrelationships among people.
2. It requires that people acquire a shared understanding of what particular sounds, words, signs, gestures and so forth mean.
3. It is the means whereby people influence others and are in turn influenced by them.

At the very least, communication requires a sender, a message, a receiver and a channel of communication. However, any communicative event is enormously complex – the sender is also the receiver, and vice versa, and there may be multiple, sometimes contradictory, messages communicated simultaneously through an array of different verbal and non-verbal channels.

Communication has also been considered by some social psychologists to be the missing dimension from social cognition. Social cognition (that is, socially influenced/determined thought – see Chapter 2) has generally focused on individual information processing and storage and has under-emphasised the important role of communication in structuring cognition (Forgas 1981; Markus and Zajonc 1985; Zajonc 1989).

▶ Language

The study of communication is potentially an enormous undertaking which can draw on a wide range of disciplines: for example, psychology, social psychology, sociology, linguistics, sociolinguistics, philosophy, literary criticism. Social psychologists have tended broadly to distinguish between the study of *language* and the study of *non-verbal communication*. Recently some social psychologists have focused on *discourse*. The structure of this chapter reflects the existence of these three overlapping areas of research.

LANGUAGE

▶ Phoneme
▶ Morpheme

Spoken languages are based on a rule-governed and meaningful structuring of elementary sounds. In most languages there are about forty-five elementary and meaningless sounds called *phonemes*. Linguistic rules determine their combination into about one hundred thousand basic units of meaning, called *morphemes* – these are elementary words or parts of words that have meaning. The grammatical rules for the construction of words are called *morphological rules*, and those for the construction of sentences are called *syntactic rules*. Semantics is the study of the meanings attached to words, sentences and entire utterances. Language is a powerful medium for communication because shared knowledge of morphological, syntactic and semantic rules permits the generation and comprehension of almost limitless meaningful utterances.

▶ Utterance
▶ Locution
▶ Illocution

Meaning can be communicated by language at a number of levels, ranging from a simple *utterance* (a sound made by one person to another) to a *locution* (words placed in sequence – for example, 'It is stuffy in this room') to an *illocution* (the locution and the context in which it is made – 'It is hot in this room' may simply be a statement, or a criticism of the institution that does not provide ventilated rooms, or a request to turn on the electric fan, or a plea to move to another room, and so forth) – Austin (1962). A complete mastery of language also requires knowledge of the cultural rules determining what it is appropriate to say when, where, how and to whom – this has spawned a whole field of sociolinguistics (Fishman 1972 – see also Forgas 1985a), and more recently an emphasis in social psychology on the study of discourse as the basic unit of analysis (Potter and Wetherell 1987 – see also below). Finally, Searle (1979) identifies five sorts of meaning that people can intentionally use language to communicate:

1. Say how something is.
2. Get someone to do something.
3. Express feelings and attitudes.
4. Make a commitment.
5. Accomplish something directly.

Language is a distinctly human form of communication. Although young apes (the chimpanzee Washoe and gorilla Koko) have been taught to combine basic signs in order to communicate meaningfully (Gardner and Gardner 1971; Patterson 1978), even the most precocious ape cannot match the complexity of hierarchical language structure used by a normal 3-year-old child (Limber 1977). The species specificity of language has caused some theorists to believe that there must be an innate component to language – in particular, Chomsky (1957) argued that the most basic universal rules of grammar are innate (called a language acquisition device) and are activated by interaction to form the basis for 'cracking the code' of language. Others argue that the basic rules of language do not have to be innate, but can easily be learned through prelinguistic interaction between a child and its parents (Lock 1978, 1980), and that the meanings of utterances are so dependent on social context that they are unlikely to be innate (Bloom 1970; Rommetveit 1974).

▶ Linguistic relativity

Language is clearly social in all sorts of ways – as a system of symbols, it lies at the very heart of social life (Mead 1934). It may, however, be an even more important social influence on people – that is, if thought itself is determined by language. We tend to perceive and think about the world in terms of linguistic categories, and thinking frequently involves a silent internal conversation with ourselves. Vygotsky (1962) argues that inner speech is the medium of thought, and it is mutually interdependent with external speech (the medium of social communication). This interdependence suggests that cultural differences in language and speech are reflected in cultural differences in thought. A more extreme version of this idea has been proposed by Sapir and Whorf in their theory of *linguistic relativity* (Whorf 1956).

The strong version of this theory is that language entirely determines thought, and so people who speak different languages see the world in entirely different ways, and in effect live in entirely different cognitive universes. Eskimos have a much more textured vocabulary for snow than other people – does this mean they actually see more differences than we do? In English we differentiate between living and non-living flying things while the Hopi of North America do not – does this mean that they actually see no difference between a bee and an aeroplane? Japanese personal pronouns differentiate between interpersonal relationships more subtly than do English personal pronouns – does this mean that English speakers cannot tell the difference between different relationships?

The strong form of the Sapir–Whorf hypothesis is now considered to be too extreme, and a weak form seems to accord better with the facts (Hoffman *et al.* 1986). Language does not determine thought, but rather permits one to communicate more easily about those aspects of the physical or social environment that are important for the community. If it is important to be able to communicate about snow then it is likely that a rich vocabulary concerning snow will develop. If you want or need to discuss wine in any detail and with any ease, it is very useful to be able to master the arcane vocabulary of the wine aficionado. Although language may not determine thought, it certainly can constrain thought so that it is more or less easy to think about some things than others. If there is no simple word for something, it is more difficult to think about it. Nowadays, of course, there is, for this reason, a great deal of borrowing of words from other languages – for example English has borrowed *Zeitgeist* from German, *raison d'être* from French, *aficionado* from Spanish, and *verandah* from Hindi. This idea is powerfully illustrated in George Orwell's novel *1984*, in which is described a fictional totalitarian regime, based on Stalin's Russia. The regime develops its own highly restricted language, called Newspeak, designed specifically to inhibit people from even thinking non-orthodox or heretical thoughts (see Chapter 3).

Paralanguage and speech style

▶ Paralanguage

Language does not communicate in terms only of *what* is said, but also of *how* it is said. *Paralanguage* refers to all the non-linguistic accompaniments of speech – volume, stress, pitch, speed, tone of voice, pauses, throat-clearing, grunts, sighs and so forth (Knapp 1978; Trager 1958). Timing, pitch and loudness (the *prosodic* features of language – Argyle 1975) are particularly important as they can change dramatically the meanings of utterances – a rising intonation at the end of a statement transforms it into a question or communicates uncertainty, doubt or need for approval on the part of the speaker (Lakoff 1973). Prosodic features are important cues to underlying emotions – low pitch can communicate sadness or boredom while high pitch can communicate anger, fear or surprise (Frick 1985). Scherer (1974) systematically varied, by means of a synthesiser, a whole range of paralinguistic features of short neutral utterances and then had subjects identify the emotion that was being communicated. Table 14.1 shows the way in which different paralinguistic features communicate information about the speaker's feelings.

▶ Speech style

In addition to these paralinguistic cues, something can be said in different accents, different language varieties and, of course, different languages altogether. These are important *speech style* differences that have been the subject of an enormous amount of research in social psychology (Giles and Coupland 1991). In general, the social psychology of language tends to be more concerned with how something is said, rather than what is said – with speech style rather than speech content.

TABLE 14.1 Emotions displayed through paralinguistic cues

Acoustic variable	Quality	Perceived as
Amplitude variation	Moderate	Pleasantness, activity, happiness
	Extreme	Fear
Pitch variation	Moderate	Anger, boredom, disgust, fear
	Extreme	Pleasantness, activity, happiness, surprise
Pitch contour	Down	Pleasantness, boredom, sadness
	Up	Potency, anger, fear, surprise
Pitch level	Low	Pleasantness, boredom, sadness
	High	Activity, potency, anger, fear, surprise
Tempo	Slow	Boredom, disgust, sadness
	Fast	Pleasantness, activity, potency, anger, fear, happiness, surprise
Duration (shape)	Round	Potency, boredom, disgust, fear, sadness
	Sharp	Pleasantness, activity, happiness, surprise
Filtration (lack of overtones)	Low	Pleasantness, happiness, boredom, sadness
	Moderate	Potency, activity
	Extreme	Anger, disgust, fear, surprise
	Atonal	Disgust
Tonality	Tonal-minor	Anger
	Tonal-major	Pleasantness, happiness
Rhythm	Not rhythmic	Boredom
	Rhythmic	Activity, fear, surprise

Source: Scherer 1974.

Social markers in speech

There are few significant or reliable interpersonal differences in speech style (Giles and Street 1985). On the contrary, people generally have a repertoire of speech styles, and they automatically or deliberately modify the way they speak to the context of the communicative event. For instance, we tend to speak slowly and use short words and simple grammatical constructions when we speak to foreigners and children (Clyne 1981; Elliot 1981), and longer and more complex constructions, or more formalised language varieties or standard accents, when we are in a formal context such as an interview.

Brown and Fraser (1979) chart many of the different components of a communicative situation that may influence speech style (see Figure 14.1). This is an objective classification of situations, and so it is important to bear in mind that different individuals may not define the same objective situation in the same way – what seems a formal context to one person may seem quite informal to another. It goes without saying that it is the subjective perception of the situation that influences speech style. Furnham (1986) goes one step further in pointing out that not only do we modify speech style to perceived situational demands, but we can also seek out situations that are appropriate to a preferred speech style – if one wants to have an informal chat one is likely to choose a pleasant café rather than a seminar room as the venue.

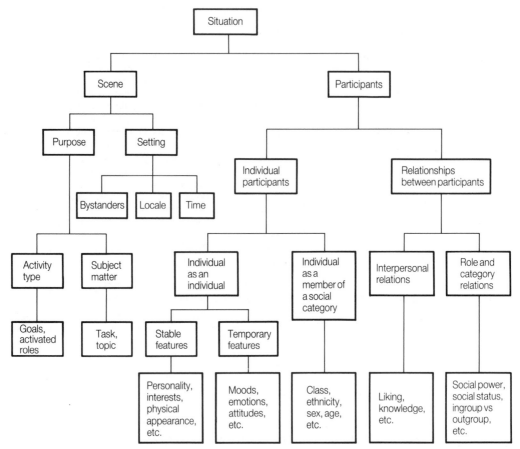

FIGURE 14.1 *Components of communicative situations. (Source: Brown and Fraser 1979.)*

▶ Social markers

Contextual variation in speech style means that speech style itself can tell us something about the context: in other words, speech contains clues to who is speaking to whom, in what context, about what, and so forth. Speech contains *social markers* (Scherer and Giles 1979), and some of the most researched markers are of group memberships such as social class, ethnicity, sex and age. Social markers are often clearly identifiable and act as very reliable clues to group membership, for instance most Britons can quite easily identify Americans, Australians and South Africans from speech style alone. Speech style alone can thus be sufficient to elicit a listener's attitudes towards the group that the speaker represents. You will recall the lengths to which Eliza Doolittle went in the film *My Fair Lady* to acquire a standard English accent in order to conceal her cockney origins.

▶ Matched-guise technique

This idea is the basis of one of the most widely used research paradigms in the social psychology of language: the *matched-guise technique*. Lambert *et al.*

(1960) devised this technique to investigate language attitudes – people's attitudes towards a person as a function of speech alone. The method involves people rating short extracts of speech that are identical in all paralinguistic, prosodic and content respects, and differ only in speech style (accent, dialect, language, etc.). All the speech extracts are spoken by the same person (someone who is fluently bilingual). The speaker is rated on a number of evaluative dimensions which frequently fall into two distinct clusters:

1. *Status* variables – for example, intelligent, competent, powerful.
2. *Solidarity* variables – for example, close, friendly, warm.

▶ Received
pronunciation (RP)

The matched-guise technique has been used extensively in a wide range of cultural contexts to investigate the social evaluation of speakers of standard and non-standard language varieties. The standard language variety is the one that is associated with high economic status, power and media usage – in Britain it is what is called received pronunciation (RP) English. Non-standard varieties include regional accents (for example, Yorkshire), non-standard urban accents (for example, Birmingham), and minority ethnic languages (for example, Hindi in Britain). Research reveals that standard varieties are more favourably evaluated on status and competence dimensions (for example, intelligence, confidence, ambition) than non-standard varieties (Giles and Powesland 1975). There is also a tendency for non-standard speakers to be more favourably evaluated on solidarity dimensions. For example, Gallois and her associates (1984) found that both white Australians and Australian Aborigines upgraded Aboriginal accented English on solidarity dimensions: and Hogg *et al.* (1984) found that Swiss Germans upgraded speakers of non-standard Swiss German relative to speakers of High German, on solidarity dimensions.

Language and ethnicity

Matched-guise and other studies suggest that how one speaks (one's accent or even language) can affect the way in which one is evaluated by others. This is very unlikely to be because certain speech styles are intrinsically more pleasing than others, but rather because speech styles are associated with particular social groups that are consensually evaluated more or less positively in society. Use of a speech style that is associated with a lower status group may cause people to regard you in terms of their evaluation of that group – with all sorts of potential implications for how you may perceive yourself, your group and other groups, and how you may act in society. This idea suggests that language behaviour may be affected by processes associated with intergroup relations and group membership.

▶ Social identity
theory

Giles and Bourhis and their colleagues have employed and extended principles from *social identity theory* (for example, Hogg and Abrams 1988; Tajfel and Turner 1979; Turner 1982 – see Chapter 10), to develop an intergroup perspective on the social psychology of language (Giles *et al.* 1977;

▶ Ethnolinguistic
group
▶ Ethnolinguistic
identity theory

Giles and Johnson 1981, 1987). Because the analysis focuses mainly on ethnic groups that differ in speech style, the theory is called *ethnolinguistic identity theory*. Ethnic groups can differ from one another in terms of their appearances, their dress, their cultural practices, their religious beliefs, and of course their language or speech style. Language or speech style is often one of the most distinct and clear markers of ethnic identity: for instance, the Welsh and the English in the UK are most distinctive *ethnolinguistic groups* in terms of accent and language. Speech style, then, is an important and often central stereotypical or normative property of group membership – one of the most powerful ways to display your Welshness is to speak Welsh.

Language or speech style cues ethnic identity. Therefore, whether people accentuate or de-emphasise their ethnic language will to some extent depend on the degree to which they see their ethnic identity as being a source of self-respect and pride. This perception will in turn be influenced by the real nature of the power and status relations between ethnic groups in society. Almost all societies are multicultural to some degree, containing a single dominant high status group whose language is the lingua franca of the nation, and a number of other ethnic groups whose languages are subordinate. However, it is in immigrant countries such Australia, Canada and the United States that the biggest variety of large ethnic minorities occur. Not surprisingly, much of the research into ethnicity and language has come from these countries, in particular Australia (see Box 14.1) and Canada.

▶ Ethnolinguistic
vitality
▶ Subjective vitality

Giles *et al.* (1977) introduced the term *ethnolinguistic vitality* to describe those objective features of an interethnic context that influence language behaviour (see Figure 14.2). Ethnic groups which are high on status, demographic and institutional support variables have high ethnolinguistic vitality. This encourages continued use of the language and thus ensures its survival, and the survival of the ethnolinguistic group as a whole as a distinct entity in society. Low vitality is associated with declining use of the ethnic language, its gradual disappearance, and often the disappearance of the ethnolinguistic group as a distinct entity – that is, there is language death or language suicide. Objective ethnolinguistic vitality configurations can be calculated for different groups (Giles 1978; Saint-Blancat 1985), but it is *subjective vitality*, that is individuals' subjective perception of the vitality of their group, that more directly influences language usage (Bourhis *et al.* 1981). In general there is a correspondence between objective and subjective vitality, but the two need not be identical: ethnic minorities may consider their language to have more or less vitality than objective indexes indicate. Under some circumstances a dominant group may actively encourage a minority to under-estimate the vitality of its language in order to inhibit ethnolinguistic revival movements that may threaten the status quo.

Inter-ethnic relations, and subjective perceptions of these relations, may thus influence language behaviour. In Canada, the past twenty years has witnessed a strong French revival in the province of Quebec which can be understood in terms of changes in subjective vitality (Bourhis 1984; Sachdev and Bourhis 1990). Other language revivals include Hebrew (which was considered a dead language half a century ago) in Israel, Flemish in Belgium, Welsh in the UK, and Hindi in India (Fishman 1989). Language death also

---

BOX 14.1 Ethnic communication differences and academic performance

A communication mismatch

Australia is a multicultural society where English is the lingua franca but there are large Italian-, Greek-, and Vietnamese-Australian communities. Not surprisingly, a great deal of research into ethnicity and language has been conducted in Australia (for example, Gallois and Callan 1986; Giles *et al.* 1985; Hogg *et al.* 1989; McNamara 1987; Smolicz 1983).

For example, Chinese ethnic students have recently become the largest single ethnic group of overseas students enrolled in Australian tertiary institutions. Due to cultural differences in communication styles, these students frequently find it difficult to adjust to Australian communication norms that encourage students to speak out in class and to interact with academic staff. Gallois and her associates (1992) have studied this phenomenon. They prepared twenty-four carefully scripted videotapes of communications between a student and a lecturer, in which the student adopted a submissive, assertive or aggressive communication style to ask for help with an assignment or to complain about a grade. The student was either a male or a female Anglo-Australian or ethnic Chinese (the lecturer was always Anglo-Australian and the same sex as the student).

Gallois and colleagues had Australian students, ethnic Chinese students (that is, from Hong Kong, Singapore or Malaysia), and lecturers view the videotaped vignettes and rate the students on a number of behavioural dimensions and on the effectiveness of their communication style. All subjects agreed that the aggressive style was inappropriate, ineffective, and atypical of students of any ethnic background. Consistent with stereotypes, submissiveness was considered more typical of Chinese students. Chinese students felt that the submissive style was more effective than the assertive style. However, lecturers and Australian students interpreted the submissive style as less effective and as indicating less *need* for assistance. There is a clear possibility that this assumption that a submissive style indicates lack of need and interest could nourish the stereotype that Chinese students are less talented than their Australian counterparts.

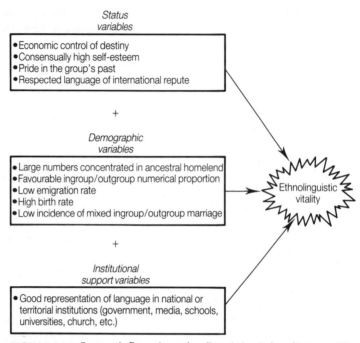

FIGURE 14.2 *Factors influencing ethnolinguistic vitality. (Source: Giles* et al. *1977; based on Hogg and Abrams 1988.)*

occurs – for example, in Canada Italian- and Scottish-Canadians generally consider themselves Anglo-Canadian (Edwards and Chisholm 1987), and third generation Japanese in Brazil have entirely lost their Japanese culture (Kanazawa and Loveday 1988). In Australia there are very different vitality configurations for first and second generation Greek-, Italian- and Vietnamese-Australians, and this has implications for the extent to which these cultural groups will maintain or lose their ethnolinguistic identity (Clyne 1985; Currie and Hogg 1994; Hogg *et al.* 1989).

Speech accommodation

▶ Speech
accommodation
theory

Social categories, such as ethnic groups, may develop and maintain or lose their distinctive languages or speech styles as a consequence of intergroup relations. However, categories do not speak. People speak, and they speak to one another, usually in face-to-face interaction. As described above, when people speak they tend to modify their speech style to the context – the situation, and in particular the listener. This idea is the basis of *speech accommodation theory* (Giles 1984; Giles *et al.* 1973) which explains the ways in which people accommodate their speech style to those who are present, in terms of specific motivations. The sorts of motive that may be involved include a desire to help the listener understand what you are saying or a desire to promote a specific impression of oneself in order to obtain social approval.

▶ Speech convergence
▶ Speech divergence

Based on the assumption that most talk involves people who are potentially of unequal status, speech accommodation theory describes the type of accommodation that might occur as a function of the sort of social orientation that the interactants may have towards one another (Table 14.2). Where a simple interpersonal orientation exists (for example, between two friends) bilateral *convergence* occurs: higher-status speakers shift their accent or speech style 'downwards' towards that of lower-status speakers, who in turn shift 'upwards'. In this context, convergence satisfies a need for approval or liking. Convergence increases interpersonal speech style similarity and thus enhances interpersonal approval and liking (Bourhis *et al.* 1975) particularly if the convergence behaviour is clearly intentional (Simard *et al.* 1976). Where an intergroup orientation exists and the lower-status group has low subjective vitality coupled with a belief in social mobility (that is, that one can pass, linguistically, into the higher-status group), there is unilateral upward convergence on the part of the lower-status speaker, and unilateral *divergence* on the part of the higher-status speaker. In intergroup contexts, divergence achieves psycholinguistic distinctiveness – it differentiates the speaker's ingroup on linguistic grounds from the outgroup. Where an intergroup orientation exists and the lower status group has high subjective vitality coupled with a belief in social change (that is, that one cannot pass into the higher-status group), bilateral divergence occurs. Both speakers pursue psycholinguistic distinctiveness.

Speech accommodation theory has been rather well supported empirically (Giles and Coupland 1991). For example, Bourhis and Giles (1977) found that Welsh adults accentuated their Welsh accent in the presence of RP English speakers (that is, the standard non-regional variety of English). Bourhis *et al.* (1979) obtained a similar finding in Belgium with Flemish speakers in the presence of French speakers. In both cases there was a language revival under way at the time, and thus an intergroup orientation with high vitality was

TABLE 14.2 Speech accommodation as a function of status, social orientation and subjective vitality

Speaker status	Social orientation and vitality of lower status group		
	Interpersonal	*Intergroup*	
		Low vitality (Social mobility)	High vitality (Social change)
Higher	Downward convergence	Upward divergence	Upward divergence
Lower	Upward convergence	Upward convergence	Downward divergence

salient. In a low vitality social mobility context, Hogg (1985) found that female students in Britain shifted their speech style 'upwards' towards that of their male partners.

Accommodation in intergroup contexts reflects an intergroup or social identity mechanism in which speech style is dynamically governed by the speakers' motivations to adopt ingroup or outgroup speech patterns. These motivations are in turn formed by perceptions of:

1. The *relative status* and *prestige* of the speech varieties and their associated groups.
2. The *vitality* of their own group.

▶ Stereotype

What may actually govern changes in speech style is conformity to stereotypical perceptions of the appropriate speech norm (see Chapter 6). Thakerar *et al.* (1982) have recognised this in distinguishing between objective and subjective accommodation. People converge on or diverge from what they perceive to be the relevant speech style. Objective accommodation may reflect this, but in some circumstances it may not – for instance, subjective convergence may look like objective divergence if the speech style *stereotype* is different from the actual speech behaviour of the other speaker.

▶ Communication accommodation theory

Recently, speech accommodation theory has become extended in recognition of the role of non-verbal behaviours in communication (non-verbal behaviour is discussed below). Now more accurately called *communication accommodation theory* (Giles *et al.* 1987), it acknowledges that convergence and divergence can occur non-verbally as well as verbally. For instance, Mulac *et al.* (1987) found that women in mixed-sex dyads converged towards their partner's gaze. While verbal and non-verbal channels are often accommodatively synchronised, this does not necessarily have to be the case. Bilous and Krauss (1988) found that females in mixed-sex dyads converged towards males on some dimensions (for example, total words uttered and interruptions) but diverged on others (such as laughter).

Bilingualism and second language acquisition

As already remarked, most countries are bilingual or multilingual to some extent. They contain a variety of ethnolinguistic groups with a single dominant group whose language is the lingua franca. Very few countries are monolingual (Portugal is an example). Bilingualism or second language acquisition for most people is not simply a recreational activity, it is vital for survival. For example, in Germany Turkish immigrants have to learn German in order to be educated and to be able to participate in employment, culture and day-to-day life in the country. The acquisition of a second language is thus not so much a matter of acquiring basic classroom proficiency, but rather the wholesale acquisition of a language imbedded in its cultural context (Gardner 1979). Second language acquisition requires native-like mastery, and this hinges very much on the motivations of the second language learner rather than linguistic aptitude or pedagogical factors.

Building on earlier models by Gardner (1979) and Clément (1980), Giles and Byrne (1982) proposed an intergroup model. There are five *socio-psychological dimensions* that influence a subordinate group member's motivational goals in learning the language of a dominant group (see Figure 14.3):

1. Ethnolinguistic identification.
2. Number of alternative identities available.
3. Number of high status alternative identities available.
4. Subjective vitality.
5. Social belief system regarding whether it is possible to pass linguistically into the dominant group.

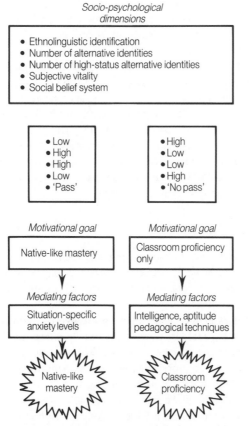

FIGURE 14.3 *Intergroup model of second language acquisition. (Source: derived from Giles and Byrne 1982.)*

Low identification with the ethnic ingroup, low subjective vitality and a belief that one can 'pass' linguistically, coupled with a large number of other potential identities of which many are high-status, are conditions which motivate the individual to acquire native-like mastery in the second language. Proficiency in the second language is seen to be economically and culturally useful: it is considered *additive* to one's identity. Realisation of this motivation will be facilitated or inhibited by the extent to which one is made to feel confident or anxious about using the second language in specific contexts. The converse set of socio-psychological conditions (see Figure 14.3) motivates people to acquire only classroom proficiency. Predicated on a fear of assimilation, the second language is considered *subtractive* in that it may attract ingroup hostility and accusations of ethnic betrayal. Acquisition of classroom proficiency will be affected by intelligence and aptitude. This model has been broadly supported by Hall and Gudykunst (1986) in a study conducted in Arizona. They found that the English language ability of over two hundred international students from a wide range of cultural and linguistic backgrounds could be explained in terms of Giles and Byrne's (1982) intergroup model. The model is, however, still being developed and modified in recognition of the enormous complexity of accurately modelling second language learning in multicultural contexts (Garrett *et al.* 1989; Giles and Coupland 1991). For instance, Lambert *et al.* (1986) have proposed a *multiculturalism hypothesis*. Secure ethnolinguistic minorities do not inevitably consider native-like mastery to be subtractive; on the contrary, they can sometimes consider it to be additive. Examples of this process would include English language mastery among Japanese (San Antonio 1987) and Hong Kong Chinese (Bond and King 1985), and Italian language mastery among Valdotans (a French-speaking community in northern Italy – Saint-Blancat 1985). These groups acquire native-like mastery in the dominant language and yet maintain their own cultural and ethnolinguistic heritage.

Sex, age and language

Much of the social psychology of language focuses on ethnicity and language. The analyses are, however, generally intended to deal with intergroup aspects of language behaviour, and so are intended, all things being equal, to apply to any intergroup context.

Sex differences in speech style have been investigated principally in western countries (Smith 1985). In these countries there are quite strong stereotypes about sex differences in speech (Haas 1979 – see Chapter 9). For example, women are said to be more talkative, polite, emotional, positive, supportive and tentative, less assertive, and more likely to talk about home and family. Real speech differences are very much smaller than stereotypes lead one to believe, and such differences are highly context-dependent. Even paralinguistic differences that are grounded in physiology (women's voices have a higher pitch, softer volume, greater variability, and more relaxed and pleasant tone) are influenced by context and show great within-sex variability (Montepare and Vega 1988).

Because speech style has become stereotypically sex-typed, it is not surprising to discover that both men and women can adopt more or less masculine or feminine speech styles depending on whether they have a more or less traditional sex-role orientation (Smith 1985). Non-traditional men tend to eschew more masculine speech styles, and non-traditional women eschew more feminine speech styles. Speech style can also vary as a function of the immediate communicative context, in accordance with the principles of speech accommodation theory. Women tend to adopt a more masculine speech style when speaking to male strangers or acquaintances (Hall and Braunwald 1981; Hogg 1985), but a more feminine style when speaking to intimate male friends (Montepare and Vega 1988). There is some evidence that women often adopt a 'powerless' form of speech when addressing men or in the company of men (Wiemann and Giles 1988). Powerless speech involves greater use of *intensifiers* (for example, 'very', 'really', 'so'), *hedges* (for example, 'kind of', 'sort of', 'you know'), *tag questions* (for example, '... didn't they?'), rising *intonation* which transforms a declarative statement into a question, and *polite forms of address* (Lakoff 1975).

Through life we all move into and out of a sequence of age groups – infant, child, teenager, youth, young adult, adult, middle aged, old. Society has stereotypic beliefs and expectations about the attitudes and behaviours associated with these categories. In western society, for instance, old people are generally considered to be frail, incompetent, low status, and largely worthless (Baker 1985 – see Chapter 9). This attitude is reflected in an intergenerational speech accommodation strategy where younger people (in the United States) adopt a sort of 'baby talk' to communicate with both institutionalised and non-institutionalised elderly people (Caporael *et al.* 1983; Ryan *et al.* 1986). The elderly find this rather insulting, though some see it as nurturant.

Because age categories are so pervasive, we all know what is expected of us once we reach a particular age. Furthermore, 'age group' is one of the most salient and frequently used social categorisations – almost every official form you complete asks your age and sex. Together these are likely to make it very difficult for elderly people not to 'act their age'. The social costs of not acting one's age can be quite extreme – as was amusingly illustrated in the film *Cocoon*. Perhaps, then, elderly people talk a great deal about their age, make painful disclosures about their health, and exhibit other symptoms of elderly speech not so much because of their age but because they are constrained to conform to social expectations (Coupland *et al.* 1988; Giles and Coupland 1991).

NON-VERBAL COMMUNICATION

▶ Non-verbal
communication

Verbal communication through the articulation of language (that is, speech) rarely occurs in isolation from non-verbal cues. Even on the telephone people tend quite automatically to use all sorts of gestures that cannot possibly be seen by the person at the other end of the line. Similarly, telephone conversations can often be difficult precisely because many *non-verbal* cues are not accessible. However, non-verbal channels do not necessarily work in concert with speech to facilitate understanding. Sometimes the non-verbal message can starkly contradict the verbal message: for instance, threats, cutting sarcasm, and other negative messages accompanied by a smile (Bugental *et al.* 1971; Noller 1984). The importance of non-verbal behaviour for communication is now well recognised in social psychology (Argyle 1988; Rimé 1983). Doing research in this area is, however, a major challenge. People can produce about twenty thousand different facial expressions (Birdwhistell 1970) and about one thousand different paralanguage variations (Hewes 1957). All in all there are about seven hundred thousand different physical gestures, facial expressions and movements (Pei 1965). Even the briefest interaction can involve the fleeting and simultaneous use of a large number of these communicative devices, making it enormously difficult even to code behaviour, let alone analyse the causes and consequences of particular non-verbal communications.

Non-verbal behaviours can serve a variety of purposes (Patterson 1983):

1. They can provide information about feelings and intentions – for example, non-verbal cues are often reliable indicators of whether someone likes you.
2. They can be used to regulate interactions – for example, non-verbal cues can signal the approaching end of an utterance or that someone else wishes to speak.
3. They can be used to express intimacy – for example, touching and mutual eye contact.
4. They can be used to establish dominance or control – for example, non-verbal threats.
5. They can be used to facilitate goal attainment – for example, pointing.

These functions will be evident in our discussion of specific non-verbal behaviours: gaze, facial expressions, body language, touch, and interpersonal distance.

One final general point about non-verbal behaviours. People acquire, without any formal training, consummate mastery of a rich repertoire of non-verbal behaviours very early in life. Perhaps partly because we acquire non-verbal behaviours unawares, we also tend to be unaware that we are using non-verbal cues or that we are being influenced by others' use of such cues – non-verbal communication goes largely unnoticed, yet has enormous impact.

This is not to say that non-verbal behaviours are completely uncontrolled. On the contrary, social norms can influence their expression: for example, even if delighted at the demise of a foe, we are unlikely to smile at his or her funeral. There are also individual and group differences, with some people being better than others at noticing and using non-verbal cues. For instance, research shows that women are generally more adept than men at detecting and sending non-verbal communications, though they differ less in terms of conscious awareness of precisely what information has been communicated by which non-verbal channel (Brown 1986; Eagly 1987; Hall 1979). This difference is usually attributed to sex-specific child-rearing strategies that encourage girls more than boys to be emotionally expressive and attentive. Finally, there is scope for all of us to improve our non-verbal skills. Since this can be very useful for improving interpersonal communication, detecting deception, presenting a good impression, hiding our feelings, and so forth, practical books and courses on communication skills are very popular.

Gaze and eye contact

▶ Gaze

The eyes are often considered to be the windows of the soul, and so it is not surprising to learn that people spend a great deal of time gazing at each other's eyes – in dyads, people spend 61 per cent of the time gazing, and a *gaze* lasts about three seconds (Argyle and Ingham 1972). Eye contact, an older term for this non-verbal channel, refers more precisely to mutual gaze – people in dyads spend on average 31 per cent of the time engaging in mutual gaze, and a mutual gaze lasts less than a second. In many respects, gaze is perhaps the most information-rich and important of the non-verbal communication channels (Kleinke 1986). We are inexorably driven to seek out the information communicated by others' eyes, even though under certain circumstances (for example, passing a stranger in the street) eye contact itself is uncomfortable and even embarrassing. Absence of eye behaviour can be equally unnerving. Consider how disorientating it can be to interact with someone whose eyes you cannot see (for example, someone wearing opaque or dark glasses) or someone who continually avoids eye contact. Conversely, obscuring your own eye behaviour from others can increase your own sense of security and privacy: for example, female tourists visiting notably chauvinistic societies are often encouraged to wear dark glasses and to avoid eye contact with male strangers. In many societies women secure privacy in public places by wearing a veil.

The amount and pattern of gazing is a rich source of information about people's feelings, their relative status, their credibility and honesty, and their competence and attentiveness (Kleinke 1986). People tend to look more at people they like than those they dislike. Likewise, intimacy is communicated by greater gaze, particularly mutual gaze. This appears to be such common knowledge that even false information about how much someone has looked at you can influence your liking for that person. Kleinke *et al.* (1973) gave mixed-sex couples, who had engaged in a ten-minute conversation, false feedback on gaze. Individuals who were told they had been gazed at less than average were less attracted to their partners. Above-average gaze increased males' liking for their female partners, but did not affect females' liking for their male partners.

Gaze can communicate status. From studies using experimentally manipulated or real-life status differences between interactants, it has been found that lower status individuals gaze at their partners more than do higher status individuals (for example, Exline 1971; Dovidio and Ellyson 1985). To the extent that the traditional power difference between men and women casts women in a lower status position, this may explain why women engage in more eye contact than men (Duncan 1969; Henley 1977; Henley and Harmon 1985). Dovidio *et al.* (1988) investigated this idea by having mixed-sex pairs discuss three topics of conversation – one where the male had more expertise, one where the female had more expertise, and one where both partners had equal expertise. The percentage of speaking time, and separately of listening time, spent gazing was recorded. Figure 14.4 shows that both men and women in a position of relatively high expertise displayed their power non-verbally (gazing almost as much or more while speaking as listening), while men and women in a position of relatively lower expertise exhibited the usual lower status pattern (gazing more while listening than speaking). The interesting finding is that under conditions of equal expertise, women displayed a lower status non-verbal pattern and men a higher status pattern.

Gaze regulates interaction. Mutual gaze, making eye contact, is an important means of initiating conversation (Argyle 1971; Cary 1978), and we tend to avoid eye contact if we do not wish to be drawn into conversation. Gaze plays an important role in regulating the course of a conversation once started. White adults spend on average 75 per cent of the time gazing when listening, and 41 per cent of the time gazing when speaking (Argyle and Ingham 1972), and thus a listener can decrease gaze in order to signal an intention to gain the floor, while a speaker can increase gaze to indicate an intention to stop speaking. LaFrance and Mayo (1976) have shown that this pattern is reversed among North American blacks, who gaze more when speaking than listening.

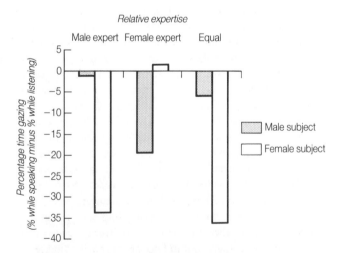

Note: A gaze pattern is more dominant to the extent that someone gazes more while speaking than listening – the more positive (less negative) the scores, above, the more dominant the pattern.

FIGURE 14.4 *Gaze as a function of sex and relative expertise. (Source: based on data from Dovidio* et al. *1988.)*

This produces some very complicated communication problems in interracial interactions. For example, a white speaker may interpret a black listener's *low* rate of gaze as lack of interest, rudeness, or an attempt to butt in and take the floor, while a black speaker may interpret a white listener's *high* rate of gaze in the same way. From the perspective of the listener, a white may interpret a black speaker's high rate of gaze as arrogance and/or an invitation to take the floor, while a black may interpret a white speaker's low rate of gaze in the same way. It is easy to see how smooth and harmonious interaction may be hindered by non-verbal miscommunication such as this. It is obviously important for people to be aware of cultural differences in non-verbal communication.

▶ Visual dominance behaviour

Gaze exercises control. People gaze more when they are trying to be persuasive or trying to ingratiate themselves (Kleinke 1986). A stern stare can also express disapproval, dominance and threat. It can stop someone talking or even cause flight. For instance, Ellsworth *et al.* (1972) found that drivers waiting at an intersection departed much more rapidly when stared at, than not stared at, by a person standing on the corner. Higher status people, who, as described above, generally gaze less than lower status people at a partner, can adopt a specific pattern of gaze behaviour in order to exert control. This *visual dominance behaviour* is a tendency to gaze fixedly at a lower status speaker. Leaders who adopt this visual dominance pattern tend to be given higher leadership ratings than leaders who do not (Exline *et al.* 1975 – see also Chapter 7).

Finally, gaze can facilitate the accomplishment of various tasks. A gaze can be used secretly to communicate information (for example, surprise at an outrageous statement) to a partner in the presence of a third party. A gaze can be used to signal a routine activity in an established working relationship (for example, sailing a boat) or a noisy environment (for example, a production line). A gaze can also serve to communicate something that is too complex, difficult or long-winded to explain in words in that context (for example, a dental patient).

Facial expression

The scientific study of facial expression has largely focused on the way in which facial expressions communicate emotions. Darwin (1872) believed that there is a small number of universal emotions and associated with these emotions are universal facial expressions. Subsequent research generally identified six basic emotions (happiness, surprise, sadness, fear, disgust and anger), from which more complex or blended emotions are derived (Ekman 1982; Scherer 1986 – see also Ortony and Turner 1990). Basic emotions are associated with quite distinctive patterns of facial muscle activity: for instance, surprise is associated with raised eyebrows, dropped jaw, horizontal wrinkles across the forehead, raised upper eyelid, and lowered lower eyelid (Ekman and Friesen 1975). Figure 14.5 shows posed versions of the six basic emotions. See if you can identify the emotions intended by our models.

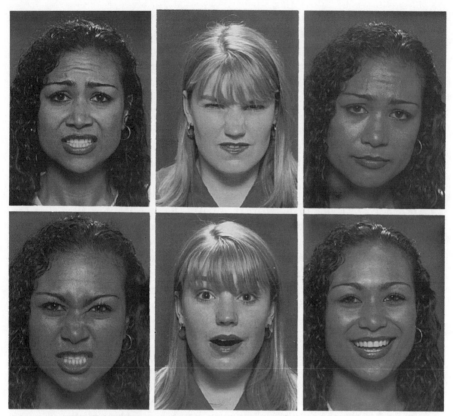

FIGURE 14.5 *Facial expression of six fundamental emotions: anger, happiness, surprise, fear, sadness and disgust. But which is which? (Photo: Max Osborne.)*

Recently, researchers have developed a computer program which can simultaneously vary different facial components (for example, roundness of eyes, thickness of lips, curve of eyebrows, distance between mouth and eyes) to reproduce on a computer screen recognisable emotional expressions (Katsikitis *et al.* 1990).

The facial expressions associated with basic emotions appear to be fairly universal. Ekman and colleagues showed subjects a series of photographs of faces expressing the six basic emotions, and had them report the emotions being expressed (Ekman 1971; Ekman and Friesen 1971; Ekman *et al.* 1987). Subjects from a variety of western cultures (Argentina, Brazil, Chile, Greece, Germany, Italy, Japan, Scotland, the United States), Asian cultures (Hong Kong, Sumatra, Turkey) and tribal cultures (Borneo, New Guinea) were remarkably accurate in identifying the six emotions from facial expression by people from both the same and different cultures. Krauss *et al.* (1983) used a more naturalistic technique in which, rather than showing static and largely decontextualised photographs, people identified emotions as they occurred on videotapes of Japanese and American soap operas. Again there was remarkable cross-cultural agreement. The apparent universality of facial expressions of emotion may reflect universals of ontogeny (that is, cross-cultural commonalities in early socialisation), or may reflect phylogeny (that is, an innate link between emotions and facial muscle activity). The contribution of phylogeny has some support from research with people born deaf, blind and without hands. Although these people have limited access to the normal cues one would use to learn which facial expressions go with which emotions, they express basic emotions in much the same way as people who are not handicapped in this way (Eibl-Eibesfeldt 1972).

▶ Display rules

Despite the apparent universality of facial expressions associated with particular basic emotions, there are marked cultural and situational rules, called *display rules*, governing the expression of emotions. These rules exist because of the important communicative function of facial expressions (Gallois 1993). For instance, the expression of emotion is encouraged for women and in Mediterranean cultures but discouraged for men and in northern European and Asian cultures (Argyle 1975). In Japan, people are taught to control facial expressions of negative emotion, and to use laughter or smiling to conceal anger or grief. In our own culture it is considered impolite to display happiness at beating an opponent in, say, squash by laughing, and yet laughter is quite acceptable to display happiness at a party. Similarly, tears are an acceptable display of sadness at a funeral but not on hearing disappointing news in a business setting.

The distinction between expressive and communicative functions of facial expression has been investigated by Kraut and Johnston (1979). In a series of

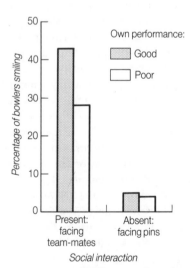

FIGURE 14.6 *Smiling as a function of social interaction and quality of performance. (Source: based on data from Kraut and Johnston 1979.)*

naturalistic studies of smiling, these investigators observed the frequency of smiling in a range of settings, including bowling alleys, hockey arenas and public sidewalks. They found that people were most likely to smile when talking to others than alone, and that whether they were really happy or not seemed to have little influence on whether they smiled – smiling seemed to be more important as a communication of happiness than an expression of happiness. Figure 14.6 shows the percentage of bowlers in a bowling competition who smiled when facing their team-mates (social interaction) or facing the pins (no social interaction), as a function of whether they had scored well or poorly.

Focusing on cross-cultural differences in emotional expression, Ekman (1973) monitored facial expressions of American students in America and Japanese students in Japan watching a very stressful film in private and talking about it to the experimenter afterwards. In private, both groups displayed negative emotions, but in public only the Americans gave facial expressions indicating negative emotions. In public, the Japanese students' facial expressions were indicative of positive emotions. This finding clearly reflects the existence of different cultural display rules.

Body language: postures and gestures

▶ Kinesics
▶ Illustrators
▶ Emblems

In addition to the eyes and the face, the head, hands, legs, feet and torso also communicate information. Birdwhistell (1970) has embarked on a very ambitious attempt to construct an entire linguistics of body communication, called *kinesics*. From extensive observations mainly in the United States, he identified sixty or seventy basic units of body movement (for example, flared nostrils), and described rules of combination that produce meaningful units of body communication (for example, the combination of a shoulder shrug, raised eyebrows and upturned palms). While some scholars feel that this may be somewhat ambitious, there is general agreement with Ekman and Friesen's (1972) distinction between *illustrators* and *emblems*.

▶ Postures
▶ Gestures

Body movements and *postures* that accompany spoken language are illustrators: for example, the use of your hands to help explain directions to someone. The communicative importance of illustrators becomes apparent when conversing on the phone, when of course they cannot be used. Emblems, on the other hand, are *gestures* that replace or stand in for spoken language: for example, a wave of the hand in greeting, or less friendly hand signals. Some emblems are widely understood across cultures, but many are culture-specific. The same thing can be indicated by different gestures in different cultures, and the same gesture can mean different things in different cultures. For instance, we refer to 'self' by pointing at our chest while the Japanese put a finger to the nose (DeVos and Hippler 1969). A sideways nod of the head means 'no' in Britain, but 'yes' in India, and in Turkey 'no' is indicated by moving the head backwards and rolling the eyes upwards (Rubin 1976). In Britain we invite people to approach by beckoning with an upturned finger, while Indians use all four downturned fingers. If you were to draw your finger across your throat it would mean, in Britain, that you'd 'had it'. The same gesture would be interpreted in Swaziland as 'I love you'. Cross-cultural differences in the meaning of gestures can have serious consequences. Argyle (1975) recounted the tale of a missionary girl who tried to shake hands with an African chieftain, who interpreted this as an attempt to throw him to the ground.

Body language can also serve other functions apart from illustrating or replacing spoken language. The relative status of interactants can be very evident from body cues (Mehrabian 1972). Higher-status individuals adopt a relaxed, open posture with arms and legs asymmetrically positioned, and a backward lean to the body. Lower-status individuals adopt a more rigid, closed and upright posture with arms close to the body and feet together. Status differences between men and women in society may explain why, all things being equal, men tend to adopt a higher-status body posture, and women a lower-status posture (Henley 1977). Finally, posture communicates information about attraction. People who like one another tend to lean forward, maintain a relaxed posture and face one another (Mehrabian 1972).

Touch

Touch is perhaps the earliest form of communication we learn. Long before we learn language, and even before we are adept at using body illustrators or gestures, we give and receive information by touch. There are many different types of touch (for example, brief, enduring, firm, gentle) of different parts of the body (for example, hand, shoulder, chest). The meaning of a touch varies as a function of the type of touch, the context within which the touch occurs, who touches whom, and what the relationship is between the interactants (for example, husband and wife, doctor and patient, strangers). From analysis of fifteen hundred bodily contacts between people, Jones and Yarbrough (1985) identified five discrete categories of touch:

1. *Positive affect* – to communicate appreciation, affection, reassurance, nurturance or sexual interest.
2. *Playful* – to communicate humour and playfulness.
3. *Control* – to draw attention or induce compliance.
4. *Ritualistic* – to satisfy ritualised requirements (for example, greetings and departures).
5. *Task-related* – to accomplish tasks (for example, a nurse taking one's pulse, or violin teacher positioning one's hand).

To these can be added, *negative affect* (gently pushing an annoying hand away) and *aggressive touches* (slaps, kicks, shoves, punches) (Burgoon *et al.* 1989).

Even the most incidental and fleeting touches can have significant effects.

Crusco and Wetzel (1984) found that both male and female customers in a restaurant gave larger tips when they had been incidentally touched on the hand by their waitress than when there was no touch. In another study, by Fisher *et al.* (1976), university library clerks briefly touched the hand of students checking out books. Females who had been touched indicated greater liking for the clerk and even the library than those who had not been touched. Male students were unaffected. This sex difference has been explored by Whitcher and Fisher (1979), who arranged for patients to be touched or not touched by a nurse during a pre-operative teaching interaction. Although the touches were brief and 'professional', they had significant effects on post-operative physiological and questionnaire measures. Female patients who had been touched reported less fear and anxiety, and had lower blood pressure readings, than those who had not been touched. Male patients who had been touched were more anxious and had higher blood pressure.

In general, men touch women more often than women touch men, and people are more likely to touch members of the opposite than same sex (Henley 1973). Women derive greater pleasure from being touched than do men (Major 1981), but the circumstances of the touch are very important. Heslin (1978) asked men and women how much they would enjoy being 'squeezed and patted' in various parts of the body by strangers or close friends of the same or the opposite sex. Figure 14.7 shows that both sexes agreed that being touched by someone of the same sex was relatively unpleasant, and that being touched by an opposite-sex close friend was relatively pleasant, but disagreed about the pleasantness of being touched by an opposite sex stranger – while females did not enjoy being touched by strange males, males enjoyed being touched by strange females. Heslin (1978) also found that males were much more likely than females to read sexual connotations into touch, with all sorts of obvious implications for miscommunication and misinterpretation (Heslin and Alper 1983).

Apparent sex differences in touch may reflect more general status differences in touch – people who initiate touch are perceived to be of higher status than those who receive a touch (Major and Heslin 1982). Major (1981) has argued that the usual sex differences in touch (women react more positively than men) occur only when status differences between interactants are ambiguous or are negligible – under these circumstances wider societal assumptions about sex-linked status differences come into play. When the toucher is clearly higher in status than the recipient, then both men and women react positively to being touched.

In addition to sex and status differences in touch, there is a great deal of cross-cultural variation in the amount of actual use made of touch. People from Latin American, Mediterranean and Arab countries touch a great deal, while people from Australia, North America, northern Europe and Asia do not (Argyle 1975). From a study of the touching behaviour of couples in cafés in different countries, Jourard (1966) observed, in a one-hour period, no touching in London, 2 touches in Florida, 110 touches in Paris, and 180 in

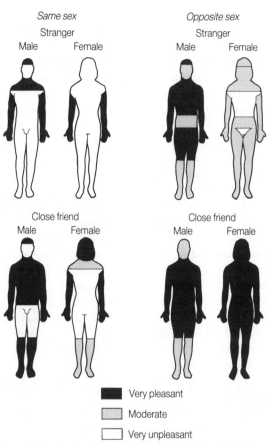

Very pleasant

Moderate

Very unpleasant

FIGURE 14.7 *Males' and females' reported pleasantness of being touched on different parts of the body by same-sex or opposite-sex strangers or close friends. For example, the two figures at the top left show that males find it very pleasant to be touched by same-sex strangers on the arms, shoulders and head, while females find it very unpleasant to be touched by same-sex strangers anywhere except on the arms. (Source: Burgoon et al. 1989.)*

Puerto Rico. Clearly a Londoner in Puerto Rico or a Puerto Rican in London would feel very uncomfortable.

Interpersonal distance

▶ Proxemics

The forms of communication discussed so far involve parts of the body as a means of transmitting messages. In this section we consider the distance between bodies as a communication channel. The study of interpersonal distance is often called *proxemics*. The closer two people are to one another, the greater the number of non-verbal cues that can be detected, and so non-verbal communication can become richer. One implication is, therefore, that interpersonal distance can be used to regulate privacy and intimacy – the greater the distance the more private you can be. On the basis of extensive observational studies, mainly in the United States, Hall (1966) has identified the existence of four discrete *interpersonal distance zones* – an intimate zone, a personal zone, a social zone and a public zone – each a little more removed from the individual's body. We return to this topic in Chapter 15 (see Table 15.1).

Interpersonal distance can be used to communicate intimacy and associated information about liking (Hayduk 1983) and status. For instance, Rosenfeld (1965) had female students talk to a female confederate with the goal of either appearing friendly or of avoiding the appearance of friendliness. The friendly subjects placed their chairs on average 4.75 feet (1.5 metres) from the confederate, while those who did not want to appear friendly placed their chairs 7.34 feet (2.25 metres) away. Dean *et al.* (1975) found that navy personnel maintained greater interpersonal distance when interacting with someone of a different rank than with someone of the same rank, and the effect was stronger as the difference in rank increased.

Interpersonal distance is such a potent cue to intimacy that it can be very disconcerting to find oneself at an inappropriate distance to someone. Argyle and Dean (1965) have proposed an intimacy-equilibrium theory that predicts that when intimacy signals are increased in one modality they are decreased in other modalities (for example, eye contact). For instance, on approaching a stranger on the street people are quite content to gaze, but as soon as the approaching stranger crosses into one's social zone (about 3.5 metres) then people avert their gaze – or feel compelled to engage in some form of ritualised recognition (a smile or mumbled greeting). Intimacy-equilibrium theory is nicely illustrated by how people behave in lifts – interpersonal distance is inappropriately close and so people reduce intimacy cues in other modalities by assiduously avoiding eye contact (Zuckerman *et al.* 1983). Life behaviour is only one example of the way in which physical space can enforce inappropriate levels of intimacy. Inappropriate seating arrangements can have a similar effect (Sommer 1969). Seating people in a large diameter circle facing each other would be an inappropriate way to promote a friendly relaxed atmosphere – interpersonal distance is inappropriately large and there is a confrontational orientation between people across the circle. There are, however, also examples of appropriate seating – for instance, in some transport lounges where people are forced to be overly close to strangers, seats are designed to inhibit eye contact (for example, television screens are used to distract attention, or seats are oriented away from one another – see Chapter 15, Figure 15.6).

Inappropriate interpersonal distance can be very stressful. Middlemist *et al.* (1976) conducted a rather memorable study in which a male confederate loitered outside a male urinal until someone entered. The confederate followed the subject into the urinal and stood in another cubicle which varied in distance from the subject. The closer the distance, the longer the subject took to begin urinating and the quicker the act was completed.

Interpersonal distance violations can also occur as a consequence of interaction between people who have different interpersonal distance zones. There are notable differences in interpersonal distance zones as a function of culture, age and sex. For instance, Aiello and Jones (1971) found that black children and working class children in the United States tend to stand closer to people than do white or non working class children. Other research reveals that southern Europeans prefer closer interactions than northern Europeans, children tolerate closer distances than adults, and females interact more closely, especially with other females, than do males.

Impression management and deception

Although non-verbal communication is often 'subliminal' and automatic, in that we are relatively unaware that we or others are using it, we do have some control and awareness, and can use non-verbal cues strategically to form an impression of ourselves or to influence other people's beliefs, attitudes and behaviour. We can also sometimes detect others' strategic use of non-verbal cues. This raises the possibility that people may try to hide their true feelings or communicate false feelings or information by controlled use of appropriate non-verbal cues. In general, such attempts at deception are not completely successful since there is information leakage via non-verbal channels. As Freud (1905) so eloquently remarked: 'He that has eyes to see and ears to hear may convince himself that no mortal can keep a secret. If his lips are silent he chatters with his fingertips; betrayal oozes out of him at every pore.'

Research indicates that people are relatively good at controlling the verbal content of a message to conceal deception. Liars try to avoid saying things that might give them away, and so they tend to make fewer factual statements, are prone to making vague sweeping statements and leave gaps in the conversation (Knapp *et al.* 1974). There is also a tendency for attempts at deception to be accompanied by a slightly raised vocal pitch (Ekman *et al.* 1976). Facial expressions are generally not very 'leaky' – people tend to make a special and concerted effort to control facial cues to deception. However, with so much attention diverted to facial cues, other channels of non-verbal communication are left unguarded. For example, deceivers tend to touch their face more often (Ekman and Friesen 1974), or fiddle with their hands, their glasses or other external objects (Knapp *et al.* 1974). Some people are better than others at concealing deception. For instance, people who habitually monitor their own behaviour very carefully tend to be better liars (Siegman and Reynolds 1983). People who are highly motivated to deceive, because, for instance, they believe it to be necessary for career advancement, tend to be very adept at controlling verbal channels (DePaulo *et al.* 1983) but, ironically, rather poor at controlling other channels. This is often their downfall.

However, people are generally rather poor at detecting deception. Even those whose jobs are, in essence, the detection of deception (for example, in the customs, police, legal and intelligence professions) are often not significantly better than the general population (Kraut and Poe 1980). Even people who do detect deception tend only to feel generally suspicious but are not sure of exactly what the false information is that is being communicated (DePaulo and Rosenthal 1979; DePaulo and DePaulo 1989). Interestingly, although women are superior to men at reading other people's non-verbal cues (Hall 1978), they are no better than men at detecting deception (Rosenthal and DePaulo 1979). Does this discussion of deception lead to the conclusion that, all things being equal, one is more likely to be able to get away with a lie than be detected? Zuckerman *et al.* (1981) have reviewed research on deception and conclude that, overall, receivers have the edge: they are slightly better at detecting deception than senders are at concealing deception.

CONVERSATION AND DISCOURSE

Although language and non-verbal communication have been considered separately in this chapter, they usually occur together in communication. Non-verbal and paralinguistic behaviours can influence the meaning of what is said, and can also serve particularly important functions in regulating the flow of conversation.

Conversation and body cues. How do these people manage a four-way conversation? A major role is played by paralinguistic cues. Facial expression, eye contact, hand gestures and body orientation also help to regulate turn-taking. (Source: Andrew Lukey.)

Conversation

Conversations have distinct phases (for example, opening and closing) and an array of complex cultural rules that govern every phase of the interaction (Clark 1985). For instance, there are ritualistic openings (for example, 'hello') and closings (for example, 'well, I must go'). We can signal the end of a face-to-face conversation non-verbally by moving apart and looking away (looking at one's watch is a common but unsubtle way of doing this), and a telephone conversation by lengthening pauses before responding. During a conversation it is important to have rules about turn-taking otherwise there would be conversational chaos. Argyle (1975) describes a number of signals that people use to indicate they are ending their turn and giving the listener an opportunity to take the floor:

1. Coming to the end of a sentence.
2. Raising or lowering the intonation of the last word.
3. Drawing out the last syllable.
4. Leaving a sentence unfinished to invite a continuation (for example 'I was going to go to the beach, but, uh ...'
5. Body motions such as ceasing hand gestures, opening the eyes wide or lifting the head with the last note of a question, sitting back or looking directly at the listener.

▶ Back-channel communication

Attempts to butt in before the speaker is ready to yield the floor invite *attempt-suppressing* signals: the voice maintains the same pitch, the head remains straight, the eyes remain unchanged, the hands maintain the same gesture, the speaker may speak louder or faster and may keep a hand in mid-gesture at the end of sentences. At the same time, listeners may regularly signal that they are still listening and not seeking to interrupt. This is done by using *back-channel communication*: the listener nods or says 'mm-hmm' or 'okay' or 'right'.

The course of conversation differs depending on how well the interactants know one another and on their relationship – see Box 14.2. Close friends are more interpersonally responsive, and tend to raise more topics and disclose more about themselves (Hornstein 1985). Under these circumstances, women are more likely than men to talk about and self-disclose relational and personal topics (Davidson and Duberman 1982; Jourard 1971), but both sexes adhere to a reciprocity norm governing intimacy of self-disclosure (Cozby 1973). The reciprocity norm is relaxed in longer-term relationships (Morton 1978).

In marriage, one of the most intimate of relationships, communication is a central process. Indeed, effective communication is one of the strongest correlates of marital satisfaction (Snyder 1979), and marital therapists identify communication problems as one of the major features of marital distress (Craddock 1980). Noller (1984) has analysed communication between married partners in detail, by asking people to imagine situations in which they have to communicate something to their partners and to verbalise the communication (that is, encode what they intend to communicate). The partner then has to

---

BOX 14.2 Power and status imbalance in doctor/patient communication

Effective communication is of paramount importance in the doctor/patient consultation. In order to make a correct diagnosis and to provide proper treatment, the communicative context should be one in which the doctor can obtain as much relevant information as possible. To do this, the doctor ought to develop rapport with the patient, appear empathic, encourage the patient to speak frankly and openly, and generally do a substantial amount of listening. Is this your experience of visiting the doctor?

Research in America reveals a marked conversational imbalance, with the doctor controlling the conversation (Fisher and Todd 1983; West 1984). The doctor does most of the talking, initiates 99 per cent of utterances, leaves only 9 per cent of questions to be asked by the patient, asks further questions before the patient has finished answering the last one, interrupts the patient more, determines agenda and topic shifts, and controls the termination of the consultation.

This communication pattern reflects a power and status imbalance between doctor and patient which resides in social status differences, unshared expertise and knowledge, and uncertainty and to some extent anxiety on the part of the patient. This is all accentuated by the context of the consultation – the doctor's surgery. Far from encouraging communicative openness, this conversational imbalance may inhibit it, and may actually in many instances be counterproductive as far as diagnosis and treatment are concerned.

---

decode the communication to discover what was intended – a number of choices are given, and only one can be selected. Using this paradigm, Noller was able to discover that couples who scored high on a scale of marital adjustment were much more accurate at encoding their own, and decoding their partner's communications than were couples who scored low. In general, women were better than men at encoding messages, particularly positive ones. Maritally dissatisfied couples tended to spend more time arguing, nagging, criticising and being coercive, and were poor and unresponsive listeners. On balance it seems, from Noller's (1984) research, that poor marital communication may be a symptom of a distressed relationship rather than something brought to the relationship by partners. People who have problems encoding and decoding messages within the marriage may have absolutely no such problems in their non-marital relationships with others.

Discourse

▶ Discourse

The social psychology of language and communication tends to analyse speech styles and non-verbal communication rather than the actual text of the communication. It also tends to break the communicative act down into component parts, and then reconstructs more complex communications from the interaction of different channels. This approach may have some problems. For example, a great deal of language research has rested on the use of the matched-guise technique (Lambert *et al.* 1960; see above) to isolate the text of a speech from the speech style (that is, non-text), in order to see how the speaker is evaluated on the basis of the group which is marked by the speech style. However, the text of a speech is rarely truly neutral – that is, rarely carries no information on group membership (for example, older and younger people talk about different things). Furthermore, the meaning of the text can itself be changed by speech style. Thus text and non-text features of utterances are inextricable and together convey meaning that influences attitude (Giles *et al.* 1990). This suggests that we might need to look to the entire *discourse* (what is said, in what way, by whom and for what purpose) in order to understand the contextualised attitudes that may emerge (Billig 1987; Giles and Coupland 1991; Potter and Wetherell 1987).

▶ Social representations

This idea has been taken up by a number of researchers in the study of racism and sexism as they are embedded in and created by discourse (Potter and Wetherell 1987; van Dijk 1987; Wetherell and Potter 1992 – see Chapter 9), in the study of youth language (Widdicombe and Wooffitt 1994), and in the study of intergenerational talk (Giles and Coupland 1991). The entire discourse is considered the unit of analysis, and it is through discourse that categories of meaning are constructed by people. For instance, 'the economy' does not really exist for most of us. It is something that we bring into existence through talk (see discussion of *social representations* in Chapters 3 and 4).

One can go a step further by arguing that many social psychological concepts such as attitude, motivation, cognition, identity and so forth may likewise be constituted through discourse and therefore any discussion of them as causal processes or structures is misguided. If accepted in its extreme form, this idea necessarily rejects much of social psychology, and invites a new social psychology that focuses on talk, not people, groups, cognition and so forth, as the basic social psychological unit. This is an interesting and provocative idea that forms the core of a recent *discourse analysis* approach to social psychology (for example, Potter and Wetherell 1987; Potter *et al.* 1990). It has its origins in post-structuralism (Foucault 1972), ethnomethodology (Garfinkel 1967), ethogenics (Harré 1979) and dramaturgical perspectives (Goffman 1959). Critics believe, however, that it can be extreme in its rejection of cognitive processes and structures (Abrams and Hogg 1990c; Zajonc 1989), and that it may be more profitable to retain cognition and theorise how it articulates with language (Giles and Coupland 1991).

SUMMARY

♦ Language is a shared, rule-governed and meaningfully structured system of elementary sounds. Speech is the articulation of language.

♦ Language does not determine thought, but makes it easier to think about things which have communicative importance in one's social and physical environment.

♦ The way one speaks carries information about one's feelings and motives, one's membership of social groups (for example, sex, ethnicity, religion, age), and who one is talking to and in what context.

♦ Ethnic groups may gradually abandon or may actively promote their own languages, depending on the degree of vitality they consider their ethnolinguistic group to possess in a multi-ethnic context.

♦ People automatically or consciously modify their speech style to the communicative context. Minority ethnic groups tend to converge on higher-status speech styles unless they consider the status hierarchy illegitimate and the vitality of their own group to be high.

♦ For ethnolinguistic minority groups, vitality considerations provide the motivational framework for the acquisition of native-like mastery as opposed to classroom proficiency in the dominant group's language as a second language.

♦ Non-verbal channels of communication (for example, gaze, facial expression, posture, gesture, touch, interpersonal distance) carry important information about our feelings and emotions, as well as relative status.

♦ We have less awareness of and control over non-verbal communication than spoken language. For this reason, non-verbal cues can often give away a lie.

♦ Non-verbal cues play an important role in regulating turn-taking and other features of conversation.

♦ As with language and speech style, there are large cross-cultural differences in non-verbal communication.

♦ A great deal of information about communication can be learned from an analysis of what is said, in what way, by whom and in what context, by focusing on complete communicative events (that is, discourse).

FURTHER READING

Argyle, M. (1988). *Bodily Communication* (2nd edn). London: Methuen.

Burgoon, J. K., Buller, D. B. and Woodall, W. G. (1989). *Nonverbal Communication: The Unspoken Dialogue*. New York: Harper & Row.

Giles, H. and Coupland, N. (1991). *Language: Contexts and Consequences*. Milton Keynes: Open University Press.

Smith, P. M. (1985). *Language, the Sexes and Society*. Oxford: Blackwell.

▶ KEY TERMS

back-channel communication

communication

communication accommodation
   theory

discourse

display rules

emblems

ethnolinguistic group

ethnolinguistic identity theory

ethnolinguistic vitality

gaze

gestures

illocution

illustrators

kinesics

language

linguistic relativity

locution

matched-guise technique

morpheme

non-verbal communication

paralanguage

phoneme

postures

proxemics

received pronunciation (RP)

social identity theory

social markers

social representations

speech accommodation theory

speech convergence

speech divergence

speech style

stereotype

subjective vitality

utterance

visual dominance behaviour

15 The physical environment and social behaviour

....

FOCUS QUESTIONS

♦ How do we regulate social interaction, that is, the amount of time we actually spend with other people?

♦ You might feel annoyed if someone sat fairly close to you in the library, but not feel this way if you sat even closer at a rock concert. Why?

♦ What do architects and town planners need to take into account when creating an environment in which to work or to live?

♦ Does the bustle of city living have a harmful effect on the quality of people's lives?

ENVIRONMENTAL PSYCHOLOGY

Its origins

▶ Environmental psychology

Environmental psychology is the study of the interaction between the physical world and human behaviour. It is an extremely practical area of psychology because of its application to the design of the built environment. As such, environmental psychology interfaces with architecture and urban planning.

Its origins as a subdiscipline can be traced to the work in the United States of Barker and Wright in 1947 at the Midwest Psychological Field Station in Kansas (Holahan 1982). Their research subjects were people in everyday life, and the contexts which they investigated were natural rather than those contrived in the laboratory. Their basic unit of study was the behaviour setting, a term which has now become part of the wider psychological dictionary. It refers to the dynamic relationship between a pattern of behaviour and the spatial and temporal environment within which it occurs. The observed behaviour is typical of the physical context, and not peculiar to specific people. The behaviour setting of a musical concert, for example, consists of the characteristics of the venue (say a hall or a stadium), the time (warm weather, at night), and of a densely populated crowd of people. How any particular individual behaves at the concert is heavily determined by these factors – in interaction, we must add, with the social rules for the local culture. To drive home the importance of this field of inquiry, Barker and Wright referred to it as ecological psychology. This reinforced a biological perspective – the new field's goal was the understanding of how naturally occurring behaviour is influenced by natural settings (Barker 1965). Ecological psychology can now be seen as a precursor to environmental psychology: the latter includes the study of behaviour in both natural and artificial settings and is typically interdisciplinary in nature, with social psychology as one of its components (McAndrew 1993).

The interaction which takes place between an individual and the immediate physical environment will mostly involve other people and the way in which they are responding Wicker (1979) has pointed out that traditional models in social psychology can be applied to understand the outcomes of such an interaction. In Chapter 13 (see Figure 13.4), for example, we used a social exchange model to throw light on the process of whether or not a person might help in an emergency situation. Let us take an example in relation to environmental psychology. Suppose that a male patient in a psychiatric institution were to act in either of two ways – in a relatively normal manner or in a really bizarre fashion – in the hospital cafeteria. The cafeteria staff could respond in two basic ways – let the patient stay or try to eject him from that area. In social exchange terms, this can be expressed in a 2 × 2 matrix, as shown in Figure 15.1. The issue underlying this example is whether the patient's actions are seen to be appropriate for the behaviour setting. There are four possible outcomes, only one of which is beneficial to both the patient and the staff. If he responded in a fairly normal way, this is in keeping with the setting; but it would be unfortunate if he were ejected, perhaps because visitors 'might be upset'. If he starts 'acting up', the staff may deem it best for other users to have him removed, even though permitting him to stay could be seen as helping him progress in his therapy.

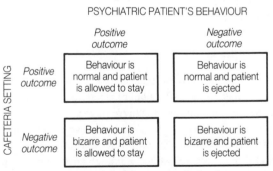

PSYCHIATRIC PATIENT'S BEHAVIOUR

FIGURE 15.1 *A social exchange analysis of a person and a behaviour setting. (Source: adapted from Wicker 1979.)*

A planning disaster

A particular event which heightened interest in environmental psychology in the late 1960s was a major American planning catastrophe, the Pruitt-Igoe housing project in St Louis, Missouri (Holahan 1982). The estate comprised forty eleven-storey buildings, built in the 1950s, with nearly three thousand apartments for low-income families. They were set in spacious grounds, and the planners were optimistic that finally the problem of the 'slums' had been solved. However, within three years of completion, the broken windows and urine-stained stairwells made it clear that the project had not been a success. The rate of occupancy ran as low as 30 per cent. This encouraged criminals and juvenile delinquents to become squatters, which further rendered the project undesirable and unsafe. Despite the fact that the project received a variety of design awards, it was destroyed in 1972. Here was a fiasco on a grand scale: something which was planned to be a pleasant place to live turned out to be an environmental nightmare.

What went wrong? In a series of interviews conducted among the residents, Yancey (1971) demonstrated that the root cause was that the design had never been connected to the way that a community of people actually behaves. Although the architects had provided 'galleries' as places for informal meetings, they had placed these a long way from the apartments and hallways. Consequently, the backyard 'chat' of older slum neighbourhoods was not able to take off at Pruitt-Igoe, and the residents quickly became isolated and lonely. Parents experienced difficulty in supervising their children, since they were unable to keep an eye on them through their apartment windows as they had been able to do in their former neighbourhoods. The hiding places created by corridors and stairwells were not only problems for the parents of mischievous children, but they also exposed residents to attacks from muggers (Newman 1973).

In our own lives, we may take our neighbourhood for granted, and adapt fairly easily to the physical environment even when we shift houses. We do not really attend to the effects that urban planning can have on our lives until something goes badly awry, as it did at Pruitt-Igoe and indeed at countless other similar building projects from the 1950s and 1960s in large industrial cities in Britain and in Europe.

Perceiving the environment

We judge the spaces around us to have certain characteristics, such as friendly, spacious, quiet, peaceful. The characteristics relate to physical properties of the space. Sometimes they are directly related and can be measured (for example, as quiet is related to noise level), but what are the requisites for a characteristic such as friendly? Researchers began looking for a set of universal dimensions by which we judge such things. They would ask people to give their reactions to a space, such as a room, each time changing a particular attribute of it, for example, whether it was tidy or messy. Other inputs into studies dealing with such questions have come from the field of human factors (an American label) or ergonomics (a British label) (Bennett 1977).

> ▶ Architectural
> features
> ▶ Ambient
> conditions

Two main categories of variables have been investigated: the ambient conditions and *architectural features* of a space. *Ambient conditions* refer to the physical properties of the atmosphere such as temperature, sounds, light and humidity. Perception of these conditions usually occurs only with deviation from the norm. Most conditions have a fairly wide 'comfort band' and we only notice the condition when it goes above or below this. Studying the perception of architectural features is more complex. Not only are there many dimensions such as size, shape, colour and texture, which have almost infinite ranges, but also, most importantly, all these dimensions interact within their ranges and with the other dimensions. For example, the colour of a wall is perceived of itself and also in relation to the effect it has on the other colours in the room. Furthermore, perceptions of size can be mediated by other dimensions, such as how many windows there are, how much furniture there is, and also by the colours used for walls, floors and ceilings. To cope with such complexity of variables we select and simplify. We form an impression, just as we do with people. This impression tends to be an evaluative one. Canter (1969) found that impressions are favourable when a room is considered interesting, friendly, soft and bright; and Acking (1971) reported that people like a room which is stimulating, informal, harmonious, soft and beautiful. People often form impressions of rooms on the basis of friendliness. In addition to the 'background' variables mentioned above, another major factor is the way in which the furniture is arranged. Chairs positioned to facilitate interpersonal interaction increase the degree to which the room itself is perceived as friendly (Wools and Canter 1970).

Perception of larger environments, such as a city, become even more complex. The number of dimensions which could be used for evaluation is immense. The type of dimension used probably varies among different groups of people. For example, older people may judge an area on its accessibility to public transport and how quiet it is, whereas younger people may judge on the basis of how many other young people are in the area and its accessibility to entertainment.

Our perceptions of a setting change over time because we adapt to the stimulation it provides. What once seemed a very noisy environment will in time become the norm and the noise will no longer be noticed. Adaptation can be a result of physiological mechanisms or it can occur because other properties of the environment have demanded our attention.

Because of adaptation, our standards for evaluation change over time. This means that physical settings tend to have their greatest effects on newcomers. Evans *et al.* (1982) have documented this effect with regard to smog and air pollution. People new to cities often rate smog as a major problem whereas long-term residents will rank it low on a list of community problems.

Cognitive mapping

▶ Cognitive maps

Our perceptions of the environment form mental images that we call *cognitive maps*. Typically these involve a physical setting with which we are acquainted and the area surrounding it, whether it be our home, our neighbourhood, our city or country. Cognitive maps do not conform to physical scale; the areas we know best are represented in the most detail and as the largest part of the map (Altman and Chemers 1980). We use cognitive maps as a sort of shorthand for orientation, and as such the places in which we spend a lot of time are central to us and tend to take the central place in the map.

Kevin Lynch's (1960) book *The Image of the City* was based on the mental representations that people held of the cities of Boston, Jersey City and Los Angeles. In an open-ended approach, Lynch compared the cognitive maps that people had of their city, when asked to describe its features in an interview, with the actual features (including their size, location and nature) determined in a field reconnaissance. He found five groups of elements that could be used to classify the city images:

1. *Paths* – paths, streets, bus lines.
2. *Nodes* – intersections, junctions, strategic areas.
3. *Edges* – shores, borders, boundaries which both separate and join areas.
4. *Landmarks* – physical objects used as reference points because of their visibility.
5. *Districts* – such as a commercial quarter or an entertainment area.

In a more structured approach to cognitive mapping, Milgram (1977a) showed New Yorkers colour slides of their city and asked them to identify the locations. He found that people had a very 'uneven' map of their city, with a much more accurate feel for Manhattan than for other boroughs (for example, the Bronx). He suggested that what the urban dweller probably does is to build up enough of a map which 'assuages the panic of disorientation', that is, serves to get one by.

Cognitive maps are in essence personal as they reflect experience-based individual perspectives. However, when cognitive maps are widely shared (say by a nation) and are externalised by being printed (for example as an atlas) then the shared personal perspectives of one nation can mould the perspectives of other people for whom such a perspective may be inappropriate, inaccurate or even belittling. We are all familiar with the map of the world as it appears in atlases, with Europe in the centre, looking larger than South America or Australia. This is, however, only one perspective on the relative sizes and positions of countries – usually a variant of a projection devised by the sixteenth-century German cartographer Mercator. It is a perspective that shows Britain and western Europe as figural and dominant against the background of the rest of the world. It is a perspective that has clearly evolved from western Europe's historical, political and economic role in the world, and a perspective that continues to communicate this to other countries (which all use the same atlases). A more accurate projection which is not Euro-centric is the German historian Arno Peters' equal-area projection, which accurately portrays the relative sizes of the nations of the world. You have probably seen it. Britain and Europe look very small indeed against the true enormous areas of Australia (which is actually larger than western Europe), South America (three times larger than western Europe) and Africa (five times larger).

INFLUENCES ON SOCIAL BEHAVIOUR

▶ Stress

Properties of the environment affect the way we feel, the way we function and our health. Sometimes the environment is purposely manipulated to have such effects. For example, the hard plastic seats in fast food outlets mean that customers do not linger after finishing their meal. However, more often the effects are unintended and are just by-products of some other activity which is occurring. Most often studied are those factors in the environment which affect us negatively by causing *stress*. Stress occurs when stimuli are perceived as some sort of threat with which we must cope. Disasters such as volcanoes and earthquakes naturally fall into the stress-producing category, but so do many other less dramatic factors such as noise and temperature. The following sections deal with two features of the ambient environment that we often talk about: noise and heat. When either of these is experienced at a relatively extreme level we can be irritated. Our focus here, however, is more subtle. Each can have severe consequences on social functioning, that is on the way we relate to other people.

▶ Environmental stressors

Before dealing with these well-researched *environmental stressors*, however, think back to the topics of isolation and sensory deprivation covered in Chapter 12. A monotonous environment can create a considerable challenge to maintaining harmonious relationships for groups which need to work together for extended periods of time (see Box 15.1).

Noise as a stressor

Noise is a predominant feature of urban and industrial society, and as such has been studied fairly extensively. Here is an interesting definition by an environmental psychologist: noise is a 'sound that the listener does not want to hear' (Holahan 1982, p. 134). Even a low intensity sound can be obtrusive, such as a dripping tap when you are trying to get to sleep. Within certain limits, we learn to adapt to noises of different intensities. In a comparison of sound in different everyday contexts, Beranek (1966) recorded the following decibel levels: a quiet office 40 dB; home 46 dB; conversation 60 dB; noisy office 76 dB; street 80 dB; aeroplane 106 dB. (These differences are perhaps less extraordinary than a decibel measure seemingly indicates, since the scale is exponential: 20 dB is four times louder than 1 dB, whereas 100 dB is one

BOX 15.1 Living in the Antarctic: the effects of a monochrome environment

White-out!

By the 1960s, the World Health Organization had been alerted to 'socio-psychological problems' which people can experience when they live for extended periods of time in polar regions (Vuori, cited in Taylor, 1987). The physical harshness of the climate, the eternal night conditions of the so-called winter season and the invariant white background are major environmental factors beyond the experience of most humans. Nowhere is this more extreme than at the South Pole.

In a book with the challenging title, *Antarctic Psychology*, Taylor (1987) reported a series of studies by himself and other researchers of various groups of men who have 'wintered over' in the Antarctic. Various national groups have been studied in this way, including Australians, New Zealanders, Americans, French, Japanese and Russians; no cross-cultural variations in response to stress have been reported. Some of the stressors which these men are forced to confront include: physical harm from the environment, social isolation, confinement, the continuous presence of other men in the living quarters, monotony and heterosexual deprivation.

With respect to the physical environment in particular, one individual who was accustomed to the outdoor life in his home environment was moved to remark about how the Antarctic affected him as follows:

> It's hard to define ... like being locked in a prison ... came down expecting wide open spaces ... I get angry and tired ... I miss the green and blue something terrible ... it makes me unhappy ... I would like to see some free water and the sea ... there is nothing but endless white and endless black. (Taylor 1987, p.49)

Although no long-term changes in mental health have been found during or after the wintering experience, some fluctuations in the men's success in coping have been noted, such as mood swings, headaches, sleep disturbances and fits of depression. Interpersonal conflicts arose over trivial issues and could be difficult to resolve, due in part to the impossibility of the men being able to withdraw from one another.

The challenge for those living in these extreme conditions, then, is two-fold:

1. Handling a truly tough and relentless physical environment.
2. Living for months in the constant company of the same people.

thousand times louder than 1 dB.) The essential point is that we can learn to deal with the noisy office if we work there, but could become quickly stressed if this level of noise invaded our home.

Laboratory studies

Researchers can now give a general idea of what sorts of task are *not* affected by noise. A simple guideline for this has been proposed by Broadbent:

> Almost any task in which a person has to react only at certain definite times, receives a clear warning of the need for reaction, and receives an easily visible stimulus will show no effect in continuous loud noise. (1979, p. 17)

Tests of visual functioning fit into this category, with tasks such as contrast detection (Broussard 1979), distance judgement, dark vision, and speed of changing focus (Stevens 1972) being unaffected by noise. A second category of tasks which are not affected are those requiring practised and repetitive dexterous movements, such as fitting together nuts and bolts (Harris 1973).

It is not quite so simple to delineate which tasks are affected by noise. Most tasks are affected at the onset or cessation of noise because of the change in level of stimulation from the environment. Complex tasks which require a person to process data from multiple inputs can be affected by continuous noise. Research suggests that noise causes an increased attentional focus on the primary data source, at the expense of the others. The types of test used in this research have included visual monitoring tasks presented with auditory secondary tasks (for example, Boggs and Simon 1968) and tasks which require memorising a particular stimulus prior to presentation, and recalling a second stimulus which had been presented at the same time (for example, Hockey and Hamilton 1970). In the Boggs and Simon study, subjects performed a *primary task* which was either a simple or a complex reaction-time (RT) test, and then a *secondary task* which was a test of making responses to number sequences.

Errors on the secondary task increased when noise was introduced into both the simple and complex RT tests. This increase points to noise interference, and was more dramatic in the complex condition. The results are shown in Figure 15.2.

▶ Tolerance of frustration

▶ Environmental after-effect

Deleterious effects of noise have also been found in task performance after the exposure. An experiment by Glass and Singer (1972) demonstrated this phenomenon. The first part of the experiment involved subjects working for about half an hour on simple problems of addition and verbal reasoning. During this time subjects were exposed to either soft or loud noise (108 dB) which was either predictable or unpredictable. A further condition was that some subjects were provided with a button they could press to stop the noise if it became intolerable, making the noise controllable. Results showed that the noise had no effect on the performance of the tasks and that although physiological arousal was evident at the beginning, this decreased as subjects adapted. The second phase involved the subjects in a quiet room, working on

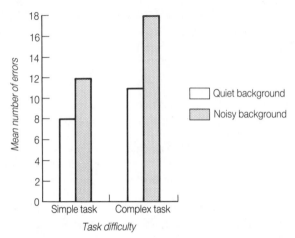

FIGURE 15.2 *Errors on a second task as a function of noise during performance of simple and complex primary tasks. (Source: based on data from Boggs and Simon 1968.)*

four puzzles, two of which were insoluble. The length of time that subjects persisted with the puzzles was recorded as an indication of their frustration tolerance. Following the puzzles, they proof-read a manuscript. Those with the least *tolerance of frustration* on the puzzles, and who identified the least number of errors in the manuscript, were also those who had been subjected to unpredictable and uncontrollable loud noise. Thus, although noise did not affect performance on simple tasks, it produced an *environmental after-effect*, causing a deterioration in later performance. It must be noted that such after-effects have been found after exposure to other unpredictable and uncontrollable stressors, such as electric shock. This suggests that the effect is not related to the noise itself but to the cognitive factors involved in the predictability of, and the capacity to control, environmental stressors.

Field studies
Correlational field studies looking at the scholastic achievement of children whose schools are in noisy areas have brought some serious problems to notice. A school board contracted research to support a lawsuit against the Seattle-Tacoma airport. Results showed that children with low aptitude test scores attending schools in the airport's flight paths showed lower scholastic achievement compared with control groups of children from quiet schools. (Maser *et al.* 1978). Greene (1979) reported a positive correlation between school noise level and the percentage of children whose test achievement scores were one or more years below the expected level. A similar finding was reported in a study by Bronzaft and McCarthy (1975) of a school located next to a railway line. Children whose classrooms were situated on the noisy side of

the school showed less achievement on a reading test than children whose classrooms were on the quiet side of the building.

Because performance on intellectual tasks is generally not impaired during short-term exposure to noise, it is thought that the lower levels of achievement are the result of noise interfering with the actual learning process. Research which looks at children who learn in a noisy environment but are tested in a quiet environment provides support for this. Children who lived in apartment buildings over busy expressways were later tested in a quiet environment. They performed more poorly on auditory discrimination tasks and reading tests than did children who had been living in quiet apartments (Cohen *et al.* 1973). In another study, children whose school was under the flight path of a busy airport performed more poorly than counterparts from a quiet school on both a simple and a difficult puzzle-solving task. They were also more likely to 'give up' on the task, showing less tolerance for frustration (Cohen *et al.* 1980).

There is little doubt that the scholastic achievement of children whose schools are in noisy areas is often impaired. Possible ways that the noise could be interfering in the teaching/learning process have been suggested. Noise may force teachers to interrupt their speech by having to pause frequently, or it may make communication difficult between teacher and student because speech is being 'drowned-out' (Crook and Langdon 1974). Children's information processing strategies might be influenced by the noise (Cohen *et al.* 1973), their feelings of personal control altered, or their level of arousal interfered with (Cohen *et al.* 1980).

Effects on social behaviour

▶ Altruism

Noise affects not only performance but also social behaviour, most noticeably *altruism* or helping behaviour. Research in this area has focused on sensitivity for others. In one experiment (Mathews and Canon 1975) the researcher dropped a box of books to study the helping behaviour of passers-by. In half of the incidents, the experimenter's arm was in a cast to indicate injury. The noise condition was provided by a noisy lawnmower nearby which was running during some of the incidents. The results showed that when the mower was quiet, people gave more help when the experimenter was wearing the cast. This suggests that they were responding to the social cue of the cast, as meaning that more help was required. However, when the lawnmower was running, less help was given and the cast made no difference. It could be that the noise of the mower created a discomfort which discouraged people from stopping, but the fact that the cast made no difference in the noisy condition would suggest that stimulus overload was occurring. The concept of overload (discussed again later in this chapter) is derived from information-processing theories, whereby stimulation occurs at a faster rate than the person can process it. In an attempt to reduce the stimulation to a manageable level, people narrow their attention, thus failing to perceive, or ignoring, some cues such as the experimenter's cast which indicated that help was genuinely required.

A field study of traffic noise showed a correlation with the level of social interaction in residential streets (Appleyard and Lintell 1972). Three streets in San Francisco, which formed part of a neighbourhood of moderate income, differed in noise level: one had a light amount of traffic, the second a moderate amount, and the third a heavy amount. Casual social interaction occurred far more frequently on the street with light traffic, while on the street with heavy traffic virtually no sidewalk activity occurred. Residents were surveyed about their feelings for the neighbourhood. Those on the street with heavy traffic described it as a lonely place, while residents of the street with light traffic thought it a friendly and sociable area. Although differences between the types of people who lived on the streets cannot be ruled out, the results do suggest that noise not only decreases helping behaviour and invalidates some social cues, but it also decreases casual social interaction.

Because of the arousal qualities of noise, some researchers suggested that it might increase aggression. In one study, subjects were shown either aggressive or non-aggressive films, and then given the opportunity supposedly to shock another person while they were in a noisy or quiet room. As predicted, subjects in the noisy rooms gave more shocks (Geen and O'Neal 1969). In another study, half of the subjects were initially angered by a confederate, in each of three conditions: in the first condition, the environment was quiet, while in the second and third it was noisy. In one of these, the noise could be stopped by pressing a button. Angered subjects exposed to noise gave greater shocks, except when they had a control button (Donnerstein and Wilson 1976) (see Figure 15.3). This result can be compared to a finding by Glass and Singer (1972), that the perception of having control negates the effects of a stressor.

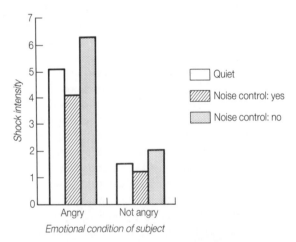

FIGURE 15.3 *Intensity of shocks delivered to a victim as a function of anger and of control over noise. (Source: based on data from Donnerstein and Wilson 1976.)*

Heat as a stressor

The ambient air temperature is another stressor of the urban environment. During the hottest part of the day we shut ourselves up in buildings or cars which often provide insufficient air-flow to cool us. Extreme heat and humidity in a city may lead to increased violence. In an analysis of more than four thousand cases of aggravated assaults for the year 1980 in Dallas, Texas, Harries and Stadler (1983) demonstrated a relationship between violence and 'thermal discomfort', that is heat plus humidity.

Laboratory studies (for example, Griffit 1970) have examined the relationship between interpersonal attraction and heat: because a hot and humid room is unpleasant, attraction to a stranger is less than when conditions are comfortable. This effect has been qualified by a result which showed that temperature had no effect on liking if the stranger had recently complimented or insulted the subject (Bell and Baron 1974).

Altruism is also affected by heat in the laboratory. Even when temperature was mild when help was needed, subjects exposed to hot conditions were less likely to help others (Page 1978). Cunningham (1979) found that pedestrians were more willing to be interviewed in winter months when the temperature was rising, but less willing when temperature was rising in summer months. This indicates that people are more willing to help when temperature is moderate than when it is extreme. The finding of greater altruism during moderate temperatures may not apply at the other extreme of the scale. A field study by Fisher *et al.* (1984) reported that altruism was more pronounced during very harsh winter temperatures.

A study of archival data and an experimental field study have shown that as heat increases, so does aggression. Crimes such as murder and rape have been studied in relation to temperature. A positive relationship was found between the daily rates of these two crimes and the daily average temperature, over a two-year period (Anderson and Anderson 1984). Another study gauged motorists' responses to a car blocking the road at a green light by recording the amount of horn-honking. Again, the relationship was positive. As the temperature rose, so did the amount of honking (Kenrick and MacFarlane 1986).

What can we do about the effect of heat on aggression? Outdoor temperatures are not under our control – we cannot keep the city as a whole bathed in a mild clime in the interests of crime prevention. However, institutions such as schools and prisons can reduce excessive heat with an appropriate cooling system and adequate ventilation.

INTERACTION AND THE DESIGNED ENVIRONMENT

▶ Built environment

Often, we fail to notice the *built environment* around us unless it is in some way peculiar or perceived to be threatening. To the uninitiated, a visit to a coalmine, or a noisy timber mill with buzzing saws can suggest a high level of danger, leading to a fairly high level of stress. There is growing evidence that the built environment can cause us stress even when threat is not consciously perceived. In the context of a work setting, stress can follow if the design of the setting does not fulfil the person's needs, whether these needs are recognised or not. The consequences of stress will vary in severity according to the degree of misfit between the person and the environment, and also in terms of the strategies available to the person for coping (Baum *et al.* 1981a). An office worker who needs a quiet place to complete a task may be able to control the degree of noise by shutting an office door. If the office is open plan, there may be a quiet place provided for such tasks. We noted in the Donnerstein and Wilson (1976) study that the sense of control which an individual has over a stressor can affect how aggressively a person may respond. A similar argument can be mounted here: stress in the workplace can be reduced by specific design features which enhance individual control. In an inflexible work environment we can only resort to an interpersonal coping strategy, such as taking work home to finish, or even abandoning the task.

A further complication arises from an interaction between the design of an environment and the rules of the system in which it operates. A rule which constrains our options also constrains our choice for coping. For example, the office door is useless in creating a quiet place if company policy is that the door must not be shut.

Effects on friendship choices

▶ Sociometric choice
▶ Functional distance

We noted in Chapter 12 that the physical proximity of one person to another is an important determinant of the chance for interaction to take place and can have a major outcome in terms of liking and attraction. A classic study of the relationship between proximity and *sociometric choice* by Festinger *et al.* (1950), was carried out in a housing project for married students on a university campus. The results showed that residents living in a complex of seventeen apartment buildings were more likely to become friends with those on the same floor than with those living on other floors or in other buildings. A typical layout of one block is shown in Figure 15.4. An interesting, fine-grained variable emerged in this research: residents in apartments 1 and 5 in this figure gave and received more sociometric choices from people living on the upper floor than did any other lower-floor residents. If you look carefully at the layout you will see that the people in numbers 1 and 5 are close to the staircases that the upper-floor people must use, hence increasing the probability of physically meeting. By way of comparison, friendships occurred more frequently among 1 and 6, than 2 and 7; and likewise among 5 and 10 than 4 and 9. Now, the physical distance between each of these pairs is the same, but the interactive behaviours vary. Festinger and his colleagues referred to the active variable here as *functional distance*, that is, the number of contacts that a location or an architectural design permits during the process of becoming acquainted with others.

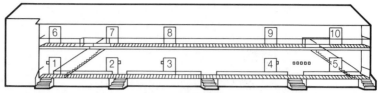

FIGURE 15.4 *Friendship choice as a function of physical proximity: the effect of housing design. (Source: Festinger* et al. *1950.)*

Controlling social interaction

One of the most frequently studied areas of design/person fit deals with the way we wish to control the frequency and nature of our interactions with others. This is not surprising when events occur, such as a prison mutiny, which can be partly attributable to crowding and the consequent lack of privacy (Andelman 1980), and when a large housing complex is dynamited by the city, partly because its design seemed to cause alienation and crime (Rainwater 1966).

These incidents represent cases where the design did not fit the needs of the inhabitants for control over their social interactions. On a less dramatic scale, such a misfit can cause anxiety, depression, *anomie* (breakdown of social norms) and crime when there are no effective coping strategies available.

The concepts of privacy, personal space and territorial behaviour help us to understand how the designed environment can interfere with our social needs.

Privacy and its regulation

Altman has developed a theoretical framework which encompasses personal space and territoriality and has privacy as its core concept. He defined privacy as the:

> central regulatory process by which a person (or group) makes himself more or less accessible and open to others and ... the concepts of personal space and territorial behaviour are mechanisms that are set in motion to achieve desired levels of privacy. (1975, p. 3)

The regulatory process is a dynamic process by which the boundaries between people change. Desired privacy refers to an ideal level of interaction with others, though what is ideal changes from moment to moment. Achieved privacy is the actual amount of interaction occurring. If the achieved privacy either falls short of or exceeds the level of desired privacy, the person will be dissatisfied and may take measures to change the situation.

Altman has theorised that the central function of privacy is the definition of the 'self'. The other intermediate goals of privacy help to build up relationships with the social world and the interface of the self and social world, that is, the boundary between the self and the environment. From a developmental

Privacy and personal space. This office worker has some control over her personal space and can regulate her privacy to an extent. However, the lack of solid boundaries associated with open planning presents several problems (see later in chapter). (Source: Andrew Lukey.)

perspective, a young child first must learn that it has a self which is separate from the environment; next, the child must find ways to meet its needs by manipulating the boundary. According to Altman, satisfactory self-definition can take place only if the child acquires the skills which permit control over the boundary. Self-definition also requires the capacity to evaluate oneself. Crucial to this ongoing process is time to make comparisons with other people, an activity which occurs more often when we are actually with others. Social comparison is not a new idea, and we have noted (see Chapter 6) that Festinger (1954) proposed that it acted to validate one's opinions and attitudes. Altman, however, throws additional light on how comparisons with others become consolidated: we need to get away from others – time and space to be alone, to relax, to reflect and to assimilate ideas.

▶ Privacy regulation   It is our culture that defines how we adjust the boundaries to regulate our social contact. Altman cited studies reported by several investigators of other cultures where privacy in the contemporary western sense does not seem to exist. For example, in Java one's home has the privacy of a public square, in that people wander through quite freely. The walls of the house are very thin and often there are no doors. However, because physical boundaries are lacking, contact is regulated by psychological ones. Relationships are restrained and people speak softly and resist showing emotion (Geertz, cited in Altman 1975). The level of privacy familiar to people in northern Europe has not always prevailed. For example, historians recount how it was not until the Elizabethan age in the late sixteenth century that the very public 'great hall' of medieval times began to be supplemented by long galleries with special provision for more private conversation. And it was not until the late seventeenth century that the concept of the even more private 'withdrawing' room (what we now call the drawing room) came into being.

Altman's model of privacy, and of *privacy regulation*, is shown in Figure 15.5. Note in part A how our desired level of contact with others can vary across time (and, of course, across situations). Privacy regulation in part B of this model now makes social isolation and the feeling of being crowded (discussed in a later section) the opposite sides of the same coin.

In western culture, we use a variety of mechanisms to regulate contact. Verbally, both the content and structure of our comments can either promote or deter interaction. Our non-verbal behaviour, or body language, becomes very important when people come too close physically (see also Chapter 14). In one study, several confederates sat close to people working in a library. The closer a confederate would sit, the more the person would show defensive and

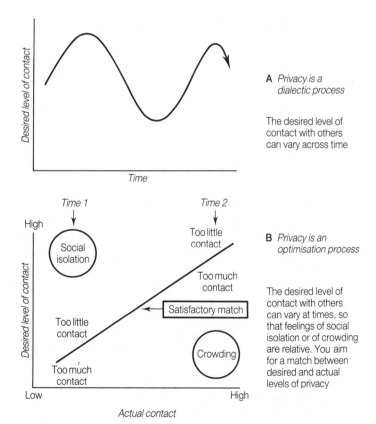

FIGURE 15.5 *Dialectic and optimisation properties of privacy. (Source: Altman 1975.)*

territorial behaviour, such as glaring, placing hands or elbows between their body and the confederate's, and turning their body away from the confederate (Patterson *et al.* 1971).

▶ Territory

Closing a door in our culture means 'don't come in', especially when that door happens to be the bathroom door (Bossard and Boll 1950; Schwartz 1968). Doors are not the only physical barrier we use; fences and hedges also announce that the *territory* they enclose is not open to all.

Privacy mechanisms in our society also hinge on rank. The manager of an organisation has a more private office than other workers, as well as more barriers to interaction such as passageways and secretaries. A similar situation occurs within the family. While children rarely open closed doors to their parents' bedroom (Altman *et al.* 1972), parents do not regard children's bedroom doors as any such barrier (Bates 1964).

▶ Dehumanisation

This reduction in control of privacy for low-status people is very destructive for residents in mental institutions. Goffman (1961) observed that such people have little control over their personal selves. Their clothing and possessions are often taken away to be made available again with staff permission (*dehumanisation* is also discussed in Chapters 9 and 11). Belongings are often subjected to spot checks, and staff also have the right to examine the person's body at any time. Schedules further reduce the person's control: such things as having a hair cut and using the toilet have to concur with a timetable which suits the staff. Such measures take away the people's capacity to regulate their privacy, and detract from people's control of self. The importance of self-regulation of interpersonal boundaries in mental-health therapy has been recognised (Osmond 1957), but this issue still seems to be neglected in many institutions.

Baum and Valins (1977) compared two types of college accommodation, exploring whether the traditional dormitory design might provide sufficient opportunity to regulate social contact. The traditional corridor, in this instance, had one lounge and one bathroom, shared by the inhabitants of the thirty-three bedrooms. All bedrooms opened straight onto the corridor, with no buffer between the private space of the bedroom and the public space of the corridor. The second design was a suite where three bedrooms opened onto a lounge. Each suite also had its own bathroom. Here, when the students left their bedrooms, the only people they were likely to see were one or more of their five suite mates.

In the corridor condition, however, students could see any of the sixty-five others who shared the corridor. In effect, this meant that the corridor residents were exposed to more unpredictable and uncontrollable social contact. Indeed, the corridor students reported that they experienced more unwanted interaction than the suite students, especially those who lived near the bathroom. Other differences were that suite students reported having a greater sense of control over what happened on their floors, whereas the corridor students spent more time in their rooms when in the dormitory, but overall spent less time in the dormitory at all. While the differences between these conditions were dramatic, there were some confounding factors in this design. For example, it is likely that just providing one bathroom per five bedrooms was appreciated by the suite students. After all, would you like to share a bathroom with sixty-five other people?

Personal space

▶ Personal space

Personal space is one of the mechanisms involved in privacy because distance between people determines the types of communication which are possible. For example, at a distance of fifteen centimetres even tiny changes of facial expression are observable whereas at a distance of one metre only larger changes can be observed.

The first important work on personal space was presented by the anthropologist Edward Hall (1966) in *The Hidden Dimension*. Hall noted the importance of distance in communication and how distance norms varied across cultures. His observations of Americans led him to describe four zones of space used in social interaction (see Table 15.1).

Altman saw these zones as boundaries around the self that people manipulate to indicate their degree of openness to others. We open up or shut off channels of communication simply by moving closer or further away.

If a person moves into another's personal space, thereby opening possibilities for communication, but the other person does not want that communication, typically she will move away. Other shutting-off behaviours are: leaning away, drawing in arms and heads, turning away or placing physical barriers such as a pile of books between oneself and the intruder (Felipe and Sommer 1966). Subjects were more aroused (according to their galvanic skin response, or sweating) when approached to a distance of less than one metre than they were at three metres, and when the approach was made from the front rather than the side (McBride *et al.* 1965).

Reaction to intrusion also depends on the situation. For example, pedestrians reacted less when intrusions occurred while they were waiting at traffic lights than when waiting at a bus stop (Dabbs 1972). This was presumably due to the very temporary nature of waiting at traffic lights.

Individual differences affecting personal space

Many researchers have looked for differences in personal space dimensions and reactions to intrusions. *Children* learn space requirements gradually, as they do any other social skill (Hall 1966). Girls develop stable personal space boundaries earlier than boys, but by the age of sixteen these differences no longer exist (Guardo and Meisels 1971).

Schizophrenics and other *mentally ill* people show greater than usual variability in their personal space boundaries. Prison inmates with a history of high aggression had larger body buffer zones (Kinzel 1970). These results are

TABLE 15.1 Four zones of space in social interaction

Zone	Distance (m)	Description
Intimate distance	Up to 0.5	At this distance, which may involve physical contact, much is exposed about a person. Cues can come from sight, sound, smell, body temperature and depth and pace of breath
Personal distance	0.5–1.25	This is the transitional area between intimate contact and formal behaviour. It is the normal distance for everyday interactions with friends and acquaintances. Touching is still possible at this distance. Although a lot of cues are still available, the effects of body temperature, smell and breathing are greatly reduced
Social distance	1.25–4	This is the typical distance for casual interactions with people who are not well known, and for business interactions. Many cues are lost at this distance but verbal contact is still easily maintained. Furniture arrangement usually falls within this distance. For example, the typical office desk is about 0.75 metres deep. Allowing for chair space on either side, people interacting on either side of the desk are usually 1.25 metres away. (Differences attributable to rank are also observable with personal space: managers usually have much wider and deeper desks)
Public distance	4–8	At this distance communication cues become quite gross. The distance is common for lecturers, public speakers, and celebrities. In a lecture hall, lecterns are usually placed about four metres back from the first row of seats. Courtrooms also use this spacing to remove the judge from easy communication. In these situations interaction is often not wanted and the distance conveys this message

Source: Hall 1966.

interesting because there may be a direct relationship between personal space and aggression. If a person reacts aggressively to intrusion of personal space, and has larger than usual boundaries, he will appear more aggressive as he will inevitably be intruded upon more frequently.

Our personal space requirements change not only between friend and stranger but also between so-called normal people and those with *stigmata*, such as amputees, epileptics and mental patients (Kleck *et al.* 1968). In a study of stigmata (Wolfgang and Wolfgang 1968), people known to have some non-visible stigma, such as epilepsy or a diagnosed mental illness, tended to be kept at a greater distance by a normal person than those with a visible stigma. Among the latter groups, people with broken arms were allowed closest, followed by amputees and clubfoots, while obese figures were placed farthest away. Since our personal space distances imposed on others have consequences for interaction possibilities, these results point to a lonely life for the obese.

Partly because of the difficulty of operationally defining personality factors, there has not been a comprehensive set of studies linking these with personal space behaviour. However, several studies have shown that anxious people tend to put greater distance between themselves and others (for example, Bailey *et al.* 1972).

Sex differences in interaction tend to receive a lot of attention; however, in the study of personal space, this attention has only been half-hearted as researchers often examine sex differences as a secondary variable to some other aspect. This has resulted in little clear knowledge about differential behaviour between the sexes. In spite of this, there are a few trends which have come to light:

1. Males have larger personal space zones than females, a finding which holds up across different measures such as seating selection (Leibman 1970) and face-to-face interaction (Mehrabian and Diamond 1971).
2. Males show greater discomfort than females when their personal space is invaded (Garfinkel 1964; Patterson *et al.* 1971).

In the light of these larger area requirements and the greater reaction to invasion, it is not surprising that people maintain greater distances from males (Hartnett *et al.* 1970). There is a suggestion in one study that this may not hold for homosexual males (Kuethe and Weingartner 1964). No data are currently available for a homosexual female population.

Even more complex than studies of sex differences are those relating to *cultural differences*. Some studies have shown differences where expected, for example between Arabs and Americans (Watson and Graves 1966) whereas others have not, for example between American, English and Swedish groups (Sommer 1968). This issue becomes even more confusing when studies look at ethnic groups residing in the same country. In this situation, it is very important to rule out socio-economic factors before any differences are attributed to culture. When differences are found, it appears that they cannot be generalised across situations as social norms do not necessarily follow the same patterns across cultures. For example, Baxter (1970) found that Mexican-Americans interacted most closely in outdoor settings while African-Americans were the closest in indoor settings. Further research in this area which helps to reduce confusion would be worthwhile. Personal and group-level interactions with people from other cultures would undoubtedly be facilitated with knowledge of each other's space norms since the chances of giving offence or unintentionally causing discomfort would be reduced.

Territoriality

▶ Territoriality

The concept of *territoriality* differs from that of personal space in that it usually refers to a geographical area that is fixed rather than an area of space which moves around with you. Altman proposes that by regulating social interaction, territorial behaviour helps to smooth out contact between people

A territorial marker. Territorial boundaries are often defined by territorial markers – gang graffiti in this case. (Source: Nicola Horton.)

and therefore helps to avoid social conflict and miscommunication. This regulation occurs because territorial behaviour involves personalising a place with a marking device which serves as a boundary and communicates ownership.

▶ Primary territory
▶ Secondary territory
▶ Public territory

Altman (1975) distinguished between three kinds of territory: primary, secondary and public (see Table 15.2). A *primary territory*, such as a home, usually relates to our primary group, such as a family. It is the most central to our privacy regulation and is therefore the most clearly marked and the most actively defended when invaded. A *secondary territory* is like a buffer between primary and public. It often involves partial ownership, such as with club-rooms or the foyer of an apartment building. Neighbourhood bars can be secondary territories. Regulars may regard the bar as their personal domain and use groups of people near the door to deter outsiders (Cavan 1963, 1966). In Cavan's studies, strangers coming in were treated as intruders, being subjected to hostile looks and insulting or mocking statements. In such a situation there is no 'ownership' *per se*, so conflict over boundaries arises. A *public territory* is one to which everybody has access and occupancy rights. Occupancy is temporary and usually not exclusive, for example just because you are first at the beach does not mean you can stop other people coming to swim. Some territories are exclusive for the time of occupancy, such as a seat in a restaurant or a telephone booth, but you have no rights over them once you leave.

▶ Territorial markers

People use *territorial markers* to deter encroachment on their territory. A house-owner might use fences, hedges, signs (for example 'beware of dog') as

TABLE 15.2 Three types of human territory

Type	Occupants	Use	Control and privacy	Examples
Primary	Individual Family Other primary group	Regular and frequent use Long-term occupancy Personal or important activities	High by members	Private room Residence Flat Private office
Secondary	Secondary group	Regular use for varying periods	Moderate by non-members	A local hotel Church Park Apartment building Hostel
Public	Individual or group	Temporary use for a limited period	Limited	Table at a restaurant Bench at bus stop Theatre seat

Source: Altman 1975.

a deterrent. In a shared office, a worker could use emblems such as calendars, posters and photos partly as an assertion of personal identity but also as markers of one's territory. Even temporary occupancy of a public territory can be 'marked', such as leaving one's bag and books on a desk at the library.

▶ Territorial invasion   The reaction to *territorial invasion* varies with the type of territory. Primary territories, such as homes, usually involve legal ownership so the police can be called in to deal with encroachment here. Encroachments onto secondary territories are more difficult to cope with as ownership is not always obvious, as with an apartment building foyer, or it has no legal claim, as in the neighbourhood bar. Public territory encroachment is down to the individual or group to deal with unless it involves physical abuse. As with personal space, the reaction is often to leave and establish a new territory. Alternatively, the original occupants may try to drive away the intruders with behaviour ranging from physical abuse to just making the environment unpleasant with direct and indirect verbal insults. In general, the type of territory and the options available for re-establishing balance help to determine the severity of the occupier's reaction when his territory is encroached upon.

Planning the environment

Building design

The extent to which encroachment on one's personal space or one's territory occurs in a public area can depend on the skills of the designer. For example, if bus seats are made too narrow, people inevitably encroach on one another's territory, to the point of touching. An insufficient number of lifts in a large building can have the same effect. Tables set too closely in a restaurant can lead to the noise of one group disturbing the conversation of another. Rows of telephone booths with insufficient sound-proofing have a similar result. Although this is not a bodily encroachment, one person's noise is still moving into the 'sound' territory of another or their personal space, and this can provoke reaction on a similar scale.

Newman (1973, 1975) has suggested that secondary territory is also at the mercy of designers. He related the crime rates in apartment blocks to the lack of secondary territory provided by the designers. He suggests that building designs need clearly to indicate responsibility for spaces to encourage residents to form social networks and to place a value on their space. This, in turn, would facilitate the recognition and challenge of intruders. He offers three guidelines for designers to create this sort of 'defensible space'. They should:

1. Provide natural surveillance of common space, for example where kitchen windows overlook entrances, thereby facilitating awareness of intruders.
2. Provide paving differences or low walls to create symbolic markers which help establish territoriality.
3. Improve the appearance of housing to instil identification and pride in residents.

Newman's proposals were initially based on analyses of public housing which compared designs and crime rates across housing situations which had similar groupings of residents. Newman's work has been criticised (Patterson 1977), and in a study of one of his renovations, not all of his predictions were fulfilled (Kohn *et al.* 1975). In fact, the central one of crime level was reversed: unfortunately, it increased following the renovations. Before we get too pessimistic, however, it is worth noting that few, if any, isolated field studies can control all variables which may affect an outcome. Newman's propositions require further testing to determine if they may have some restricted validity, rather than simply to be abandoned.

A review of research dealing with design in relation to the health sector pointed to a disappointing level of awareness by planning authorities of the needs of hospital users, especially patients, visitors and non-medical staff (Reizenstein 1982). In a present age of 'consumer evaluation', the hospital environment should be one which encourages a positive response in the patient, as part of the process of getting well, and also one which avoids dehumanising the patient.

Activity spaces

Another area which has been studied is the facilitation of casual interaction. Design can make such interaction personally costly by reducing spaces where people naturally have contact in their daily activities.

In a study of shared housing for the elderly, it was found that the location of a lounge determined its frequency of use (Howell *et al.* 1976). Lounge areas situated near entrances and along main hallways were frequently used, while distant ones were neglected. The authors suggested that one reason for this was the differing degree of social commitment involved. If, on arriving at a distant lounge, the person decides that interaction with those already present is disagreeable, it would be difficult to leave without some plausible reason for having visited the lounge at all. However, the same situation in a lounge on a main hallway need not be so difficult to leave as a 'passing-through' explanation could be valid. This gives people greater choice and control over their social interaction. Optimum facilitation of casual interaction through the use of activity nodes requires that they are centrally located and equally accessible to all and that they are close to necessary functions to ensure that lots of people pass them (Bechtel 1977). A further requisite is that they offer a wide range of access and exposure so that people's differing needs for both can be met (Archea 1977).

▶ Open planning

The 1970s saw the introduction of *open planning* in offices and schools, partly because it was believed that communication, and therefore social networks would be improved, and partly because they provided flexibility at a very low cost. The facilitation of communication may have been an admirable goal, but user evaluations of both schools (Evans and Lovell 1979) and offices (Wineman 1980) have shown that the activities of one person or group frequently interfere with the activities of others in such a way that privacy needs go unfulfilled. Although this can occur because of visual distractions, it is predominantly the intrusion of noise. Hearing the noise created by others, along with their conversations, can be disruptive to a work routine. There is the additional problem of being overheard in an intimate discussion. In sum, the lack of solid boundaries between activities and people may increase user communication, but at some cost.

Furniture arrangements

▶ Sociofugal layout
▶ Sociopetal layout

Very often, room layouts allow some flexibility in how chairs, tables and room dividers (including screens and even large pot plants) are placed, which in turn can have subtle effects on the way in which people interact. Burgoon *et al.* (1989) distinguished between room layouts which are *sociofugal* and those which are *sociopetal*. The former bring people together, encouraging them to interact; the latter push them apart, discouraging interaction. The trick is to use the appropriate layout for the function of a room or space. If you were in a doctor's waiting room you may not feel like engaging in conversation with another patient, whereas at a social function you would no doubt want to feel at ease, when seated, to engage in conversation. Furniture arrangement, then, provides cues to the users of a space about what kinds of social encounter are expected. Whereas sociopetal layouts suggest that a space is public, sociofugal layouts suggest that it is private. Look at the arrangement of furniture in

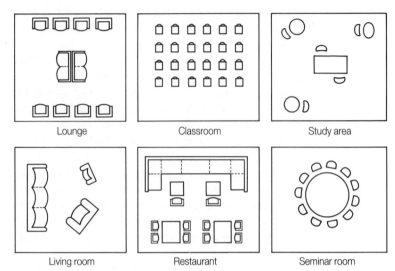

FIGURE 15.6 *Sociofugal versus sociopetal arrangements of furniture. (Source: Burgoon et al. 1989.)*

Figure 15.6, and check this against the purpose of the particular space. Which arrangements are sociofugal? Which are sociopetal?

CROWDING

As Insel and Lindgren (1978) have noted, the very word 'crowding' is difficult to avoid but hard to define. Sometimes it is used in an extreme way:

> In the year 1799, Daniel Boone left his home in the raw frontier state of Kentucky and moved to uncharted land west of the Mississippi river, saying 'Too crowded! I want more elbow room!' (Insel and Lindgren 1978, p. 15)

We should establish at the outset that crowding has psychological properties and can be distinguished conceptually from *population density*, which consists of one or more physical variables. Even though densely populated areas often lead to crowded living conditions, a connection between the two is not inevitable.

▶ Population density   *Population density* has been used in a variety of ways (Galle *et al.* 1972; Galle and Gove 1979). It describes:

1. Number of persons per room.
2. Number of rooms per housing unit.
3. Number of housing units per structure.
4. Number of residential structures per hectare or per acre.

Crowding and stress in the city. Urban bustle can lead to the subjective state of feeling crowded. Note that little or no eye contact takes place between people. (Source: Nicola Horton.)

Galle and Gove compared the relative effects of population density on one hand and of 'social structural' variables (such as ethnicity, income, education, occupation) on the other. They reported that each made a contribution to the level of stress (discussed further below), but that 90 per cent of the variance was attributable to an interaction between density and social structure.

▶ Crowding

In contrast to density, *crowding* is an experiential state which often arises from an interaction of relatively high densities of people with other social and environmental variables (Choi *et al*. 1976).

Early research on crowding did not attempt to disentangle it from the effects of very high population density. An example is an animal study by Calhoun (1962) who built accommodation which could comfortably house forty-eight rats. The colony was allowed to grow to eighty rats and, although adequate food and water were provided, pathological behaviour soon became evident. Nest-building, courting, mating and rearing of the young were areas affected by behavioural abnormalities. Some male rats became aggressive and killed their fighting partners, disregarding the signals of submission which normally ended a fight. Female rats often neglected their young to the extent that the infant mortality rate rose to as high as 75 per cent. Physiological symptoms of prolonged stress were evident in the autopsies which revealed signs such as enlarged adrenal glands.

Christian *et al*. (1960) carried out a naturalistic study of density among sika deer on an island. At one stage, the population rose to a peak of three hundred, which averaged about one deer per acre. Although food was plentiful, 50 per cent of the deer died in the winter two years later. The following year more deer died, until the herd stabilised at about eighty animals. As with the Calhoun study, autopsies revealed enlarged adrenal glands.

The severe effects of crowding reported from such research confirmed what many people believed to be common sense: that population density can affect behaviour. Early research with humans seemed to confirm this view, pointing to a correlation between the number of persons per acre, on one the hand, and crime and mental illness on the other (Zlutnick and Altman 1972). It is simplistic, however, to attribute physical and behavioural pathology in the urban environment solely to population density. Taken at face value, the density/pathology link overlooks the fact that the densely populated areas of a city usually accommodate its poor; therefore, confounding variables associated with poverty could account for any consequent pathology. When variables such as occupation, income, education, ethnicity and quality of housing were statistically controlled, the density relationship disappeared (Winsborough 1965).

Possible explanations for the differences in animal and human responses to crowding are that animals are genetically predetermined to respond to crowding (Calhoun 1971), whereas humans are influenced by social and cognitive factors. Furthermore, humans can usually get away from an overcrowded environment, an option that the animals involved in the studies did not have.

The fact that the initial studies of human behaviour in the crowded environment showed no negative effects when confounding variables were removed did not stop researchers looking at the phenomenon. Crowding was having effects in some situations, such as specific building structures. In prisons, as the population rises, disciplinary infractions and the death rate increase (Cox et al. 1984). Inmates of dormitory cells have higher numbers of illness complaints than those in single cells (McCain et al. 1976).

Why does crowding have an effect in some situations and not others? The difference seems to arise from what we actually call crowding. Density of people relates to the number of people in a given space. Crowding only occurs in a dense situation when there is a negative psychological response. For example, most people who attend rock concerts do not feel crowded, even though the density of people is such that they would feel crowded in another situation, such as a classroom. Density becomes crowding and causes the negative psychological response when it interferes with our goals (Schopler and Stockdale 1977), provides information overload (Cohen 1978; Milgram 1977b) or prevents us from predicting future events or controlling significant outcomes (Baron and Rodin 1978; Baum and Valins 1979).

Epstein (1981) has suggested that, this being so, the effects of residential crowding should be less severe in families than other residential groups because the co-operative nature of the family minimises interference with an individual's goals, information overload and loss of control.

Studies of families have found no evidence of a correlation between density and pathology (Freedman 1975; Freedman *et al.* 1975), whereas studies of other residential groups such as prison inmates (Cox *et al.* 1984) and students living in dormitories (Karlin *et al.* 1978) find negative effects of density. Epstein also suggested that, although families in general should not suffer effects from density, children might, since their position in the family gives them less freedom to use coping mechanisms. For example, their goals would not usually take priority and they do not have the control to manipulate other people's behaviour to fulfil their own needs or to leave the situation at will. Studies looking at children's social behaviour in America (Rodin 1976) and task performance in Israel (Shapiro 1974) offer support for Epstein's proposition.

Research shows that negative effects of crowding occur in residential groups other than families, where effects have only been found with children. This supports the hypothesis that density turns to crowding where it results in interference with goal achievement and loss of control.

Laboratory studies support the control explanation. Where subjects in a crowded environment are offered a button which, if pressed, will signal the experimenter to remove them from the environment, adverse reactions to crowding are reduced through the sense of control offered by the button (Sherrod 1974). Perception of control by subjects standing beside the control panel of a densely packed elevator, meant that they felt less crowded and perceived the elevator as larger than those who were standing away from the control panel (Rodin *et al.* 1979).

Several other issues which have been addressed in the laboratory but not in field studies are task performance, adverse after-effects and sex differences.

It was believed that because crowding caused stress, task performance in a crowded environment ought to be adversely affected. Even when subjects were kept working for several hours on tasks such as rudimentary arithmetic problems and crossing out certain letters in a printed text, no relationship between density and performance emerged. However, recent research introduced more complex tasks and the expected density/performance relationship was found. This was for tasks such as tracing three-dimensional mazes (Paulus *et al.* 1976), doing two things at once (Evans 1979) and assembling things in cramped quarters where other people might get in the way (Heller *et al.* 1977).

Adverse after-effects of crowding were found in an experiment which was modelled on Glass and Singer's experiment with noise. Groups of eight women worked on tasks in either a small or a large room. A 'sense of control' condition was added by telling some of the women that they were free to leave at any time. Results of this part of the experiment indicated that neither density nor control had affected task performance. However, following this the women worked on another task in a spacious room. At this time, those who had been in the crowded and lack of control condition did worst on measures of tolerance for frustration (Sherrod 1974). Although short-term crowding may not appear to have adverse effects, it can affect performance on a later task.

Stokols *et al.* (1973) found that males and females react differently in a crowded room. Groups of eight men or eight women worked on a task in either a large or a small room. The small room created crowding in both groups, but the women reacted positively to one another in that they made fewer hostile comments, whereas the men reacted negatively to one another by making more hostile comments than when they were in conditions of low density.

Coping with crowding

▶ Social withdrawal

On an intrapersonal level, a common method of coping with crowding is withdrawal, either from the situation or from involvement with those present. This can easily be observed on a crowded rush-hour bus where, although sitting or standing very close to one another, people will look out of different windows to avoid possible eye contact. *Social withdrawal* has even been found with those who are anticipating being crowded. In a study by Baum and Greenberg (1975), subjects thought they were about to participate in a group setting in which there would be either four or ten participants. They were told to choose one from a stack of chairs and to sit where they wanted. When the expected group was thought to be larger, many more subjects chose a corner position, an outcome which suggested that they wish to avoid being crowded (see Figure 15.7).

A large factor in determining when density becomes crowding is the perception of loss of control. One way to avoid the negative psychological reaction of crowding is, therefore, to give the perception of control. This can be done by informing people what to expect before the crowded situation (Baum *et al.* 1981b). In limited spaces such as classrooms or aeroplanes,

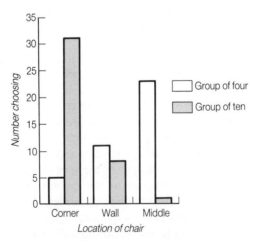

FIGURE 15.7 *The tendency to choose peripheral seating (corner chair) in anticipation of being crowded. (Source: based on data from Baum and Greenberg 1975.)*

perception of control can be increased by having an adequate amount of well-marked and easily accessible exits.

Alterations to the environment to avoid crowding are not always possible, but sometimes even simple changes can be effective. Rohner (1974) reported that dormitory residents prefer bunk beds to twin beds as this provides more space and means that room-mates are out of sight at night. In another study by Baum and Davis (1980), a long corridor dormitory was divided into two by constructing a wall. This led to a perception of an increase in privacy and a decrease in crowding, while fewer social problems were reported. A 43 per cent reduction in the enrolment at a junior high school improved both grades and attitudes about the school among students, while there was less absenteeism among teachers (McCain *et al.* 1985). Reducing total population as in this study is probably the most effective way of avoiding crowding, as in the animal study referred to at the beginning of this section. Our standards of 'humaneness', however, preclude this as a large-scale measure for humans. Furthermore, in institutions it is often a long-term goal, but interim measures must be used to cope in the short term. An issue which has attracted media attention in several countries in recent years is crowding in prisons, though the causes of prison riots and solutions to various reported incidents may be complex (see Box 15.2).

PEOPLE IN CITIES

▶ Prosocial behaviour

Urban settings are characterised by intense stimulation: the sights, sounds, smells and crowds of people. In such a situation, we would expect a human's

---

BOX 15.2 Crowding in prisons

Recent years have seen outcries from those involved in the prison system, both inmates and officers, that prisons are grossly overcrowded. Research in the United States has pointed to possible outcomes of this situation. Cox *et al.* (1984) report that as the population of a prison increases, so do the death rate and the number of disciplinary infractions. They report that in one institution where the population doubled, the rate of serious infractions increased sixfold and the suicide rate increased threefold. Inmate reaction to this in the United States was for some to institute law suits against the state for the crowding, which they call 'cruel and unusual punishment'.
Reaction in the New Mexico Penitentiary was a mutiny which involved many fatalities. In Britain in 1990, a protracted protest over poor living conditions occurred at the Strangeways Prison. Protests such as these are likely to continue as long as there is overcrowding in prisons.

amazing powers of adaptation to come into play. They probably do, but it seems that we also try to screen out many stimuli to enable our information-processing capacities to cope (discussed further below). City dwellers adopt a norm of *non-involvement*, and appear to be less helpful and less friendly than the small-town dweller (Krupat and Guild 1980; note that many variables can affect the rate of *prosocial behaviour* – see Chapter 13).

Amato (1983) studied helping behaviour in fifty-five cities and towns in Australia, with such acts as picking up fallen envelopes, giving a donation to charity, giving a favourite colour for a student project, correcting inaccurate directions which are overheard, and helping a stranger who had hurt a leg and had collapsed on the footpath. With the exception of picking up the fallen envelope, the results showed that, as population size increased (that is, in the bigger towns and cities), acts of helping decreased. The results for four of the helping measures are shown in Figure 15.8. Best-fitting regression lines for each set of data points are shown. You can see that there is a consistent trend for helping a stranger to diminish as population levels increase.

Research has also looked at friendliness towards strangers and found similar results. Milgram (1977b) looked at willingness to return the friendly handshake of a stranger and found that small-town dwellers more readily reciprocated than city dwellers. One study of the avoidance of eye contact in commuters included both urban and suburban train passengers. The investigators recorded the number of people leaving the trains who returned their gazes, finding that eye contact was avoided at a higher rate in the city environment (McCauley *et al.* 1977).

These studies have looked at social contact with strangers. Those which look at social contact with friends show quite a different pattern of results. People

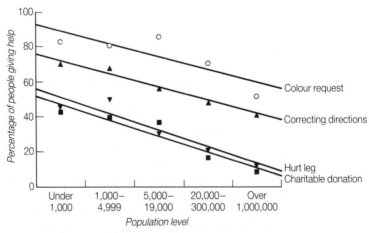

Note: The graph shows regression lines for each helping measure.

FIGURE 15.8 *The effect of population level on willingness to help a stranger. (Source: adapted from Amato 1983.)*

who move into cities usually take longer to make friends than those who move into small towns (Franck 1980), but after a few months, an equal number of ties are formed. Furthermore, there is no difference in the quality of ties or frequency of contact (Fischer 1982; Glenn and Hill 1977).

Although the concept of stimulus overload emphasises the negative aspects of urban stimulation, there are many people who choose to live in the city because of the amount of stimulation available, though the quality of this stimulation can also be an important variable. Some people may even emigrate to the anticipated excitement of a large city like London, Paris or New York in the quest for a higher level of stimulation.

Coping with city living

Urban arousal

People who come from rural or small-town settings often do not react well to city visits:

> When I first came to New York it seemed like a nightmare. As soon as I got off the train at Grand Central I was caught up in pushing, shoving crowds on 42nd street. Sometimes people bumped into me without apology; what really frightened me was to see two people literally engaged in combat for possession of a cab. (From an informant, quoted by Milgram 1977b, p. 24)

▶ Stimulus overload

Nevertheless, some people prefer the sights, sounds and smells of the city to the quiet of the countryside. Milgram applied the concept of *stimulus overload* (from systems analysis) to describe how many people control the way they react in a big city. When a person receives more stimuli (or inputs) from a busy environment than can be dealt with, some will be kept in abeyance or sacrificed altogether, thereby easing the strain of processing information. The urban dweller generally meets more people in a day than rural dwellers do, with the result that much of the interchange that takes place is superficial in nature.

Milgram has indicated several *adaptive responses* to the overload of dealing with many people:

1. Allocate *less time* to each person encountered – this leads to brief and superficial encounters with others.
2. Disregard *low-priority persons* – for example, ignoring a drunk sick on the street, by carefully navigating between other pedestrians.
3. *Shift responsibility* in a social transaction to the other party – for example, requiring bus passengers to have the exact fare.
4. *Block contact* with others – for example, using an unlisted telephone number.
5. *Reduce involvement* – by avoiding both self-revelation and revelation by others.
6. Availability of *specialised institutions* – a 'social welfare department' is an urban invention. Other examples are the telephone information services.

Milgram also argued that urban life is less likely to favour prosocial behaviour, not because urban dwellers are callous but because urban social norms are biased towards emotional and social privacy, since physical privacy is difficult to attain.

Most of us spend the greater part of our lives living and working in an urban environment. Can the research literature tell us anything about maximising the satisfaction we can gain from an urban lifestyle? A study by Amato and McInnes (1983) has suggested that the high level of stimulation provided in a city does not always need to be equated with stress. They isolated the important variable of the specific environmental setting, which can interact with city living: more friendly and affiliative behaviour is triggered by certain settings than by others. In a study of twelve cities, Amato and McInnes classified settings into four kinds using two dimensions: high or low *arousal* (complex, stimulating) and high or low *pleasantness*. An inner city pedestrian mall was rated as both arousing and pleasant, whereas a construction site was arousing and unpleasant. Members of the public who were walking by in these settings were greeted in a friendly way by a male or female investigator. Their responses were coded in terms of affiliative behaviour (smiling, head nods, eye contact, speech). The results in Figure 15.9 show that pleasant but stimulating conditions encouraged the highest level of reciprocating friendly behaviour – see also Box 15.3. The moral is that we do not necessarily have to give up on the city simply because it is an arousing environment; friendly settings will induce friendly behaviour. There is a challenge here for urban planners to provide friendly settings that are accessible to the urbanite.

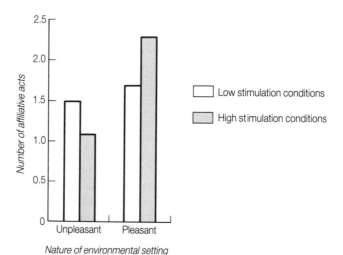

FIGURE 15.9 *Number of affiliative responses made to a friendly stranger as a function of stimulation and pleasantness of the environment. (Source: based on data from Amato and McInnes 1983.)*

BOX 15.3 Amato and McInnes' view that living in a city can vary according to both level of stimulation and pleasantness

City living: stimulation or stress?

At what point is urban stimulation enhancing, and when is it an overload? Amato and McInnes (1983) have suggested that a pleasantness variable must be considered. If an urban environment is both stimulating (that is, complex and arousing) and pleasant, then it can encourage friendly behaviour between its citizens. Amato and McInnes tested this proposition by classifying twelve city settings into four categories:

1. Arousing and pleasant.
2. Arousing and unpleasant.
3. Not arousing and pleasant.
4. Not arousing and unpleasant.

The measure of friendliness towards a stranger was the amount of eye contact, smiling, nodding and speech when greeted by a male or female investigator. Results supported the 'pleasantness' hypothesis. Friendly behaviour was most frequently exhibited in the pleasant and arousing condition. This suggests that stimulation and stress are not directly related to the totality of such a complex environment as a city. The environment needs to be broken down into its components and then studied before accurate predictions can be made.

Hall (1966) had some timely advice for urban planners:

1. Find ways of measuring the human scale for a city.
2. Allow for the ethnic enclave. In the United States, for example, this must take in groups such as African Americans, Hispanics and so on. Their spaces must reinforce their cultures.
3. Conserve large, accessible outdoor spaces. Cities such as London, Paris and Stockholm provide examples.
4. Preserve useful and satisfying older buildings and suburbs. They provide a sense of continuity and a link with the past.

Crowding in the urban home

We have already dealt with the topic of crowding, and the related measure of population density. Galle *et al.* (1972) found that symptoms of emotional problems were associated only with one measure of density, the number of *people per room*.

By definition, living in a city is associated with high population density. Take as an example the city of Hong Kong, an area of extremely high density. In a study by Mitchell (1971), 41 per cent of its citizens said that they slept in a bed with two or more others. The size of the bed was not reported. Mitchell reported that those in the most 'packed' dwellings were less happy and more worried. More specifically, however, emotional illness was associated with two variables: (1) living with others who were unrelated – this applied to 40 per cent of Mitchell's sample – and (2) living on the sixth or higher storey of a high-rise apartment building.

In a British study (Rutter *et al.* 1975), a comparison was made between ten-year-old children living in an inner London borough and those living on the Isle of Wight. The London children rated less favourably in terms of reading ability and mental health; their parents had experienced more marital difficulties and more often had served time in prison. Both groups of children had adverse environmental difficulties to deal with, but a crucial difference between the two samples was living in a crowded home. Within both samples, there were more problem parents and problem children in houses occupied by large families.

From these examples, the issue which matters most in relation to emotional stress is that of population density within the home unit, and the crowding effect that is hard to combat when people's individual privacy is violated by being forced to live in very close circumstances.

▶ Social support network

Population density alone, however, may not lead inevitably to stress; and when it is implicated, it may be in combination with other factors. In a recent study by Kearns and his colleagues (Smith *et al.* 1993), density (that is, space per person) was included as one of several housing stressors which might cause psychological distress. They found that *global dissatisfaction* with a house is related to distress, and that several variables may be involved, for example density, access to utilities, state of repair, heating, prevalence of pests. As long as the level of dissatisfaction is not too high, the availability of relatives as a *social support network* (discussed in Chapter 12) had a buffering effect and helped to reduce the overall perceived distress.

SUMMARY

♦ Environmental psychology is the study of the interaction between the physical world and human behaviour. It has connections with the study of the built environment and provides a connection between psychology and both architecture and urban planning.

♦ The ambient conditions and architectural features of an environment have major, if subtle, effects on both the way people feel and how they interact with others.

♦ Within limits, people adapt to the stimulation that the physical environment provides, such as background noise. When stimulation is extreme or beyond the control of the individual, however, the common reaction is stress. Over extended periods of time, this can lead to both intellectual impairment and emotional maladjustment.

♦ The layout of buildings and connecting spaces have significant effects on the way people respond to others and can influence choices in the early phase of forming friendships.

♦ An important feature of any specific environment is the degree to which its design allows people to control their social interactions and to experience the level of privacy that they desire at any moment in time.

♦ Personal space is a mechanism involved in privacy regulation. It refers to the interpersonal distance that an individual wishes to maintain in a given interaction. Intrusions on one's personal space cause irritation and sometimes stress. There are important individual differences (for example, cultural) in the way that people perceive their personal space.

♦ Territories are geographical areas over which an individual feels some sense of ownership. In order, they can be primary, secondary or public, each with a decreasing sense of personal ownership. A primary territory is highly personalised and, when occupied, difficult to distinguish from personal space.

♦ The designs of large-scale dwellings in urban areas should take account of territoriality. If a public area can be redefined psychologically as a secondary area (with a sense of shared ownership), the risk of vandalism is reduced.

♦ Room layouts have sociofugal or sociopetal properties. The former bring people together, encouraging them to interact, whereas the latter push them apart, discouraging interaction.

♦ Crowding is a psychological state and can be distinguished from population density, which has physical properties. Prolonged periods of crowding can be both intellectually and emotionally damaging.

♦ A large city can be a crowded, confusing and socially unhelpful environment. This is not inevitable, however, and the challenge is for urban planners to provide friendly settings that are accessible to the urbanite.

FURTHER READING

Holahan, C. J. (1982). *Environmental Psychology*. New York: Random House.
Krupat, E. (1985). *People in Cities: The Urban Environment and Its Effects*. Cambridge: Cambridge University Press.
McAndrew, F. (1993). *Environmental Psychology*. Monterey, CA: Brooks/Cole.

▶ KEY TERMS

altruism	built environment
ambient conditions	cognitive maps
architectural features	crowding

dehumanisation
environment psychology
environmental after-effect
environmental psychology
environmental stressors
functional distance
open planning
personal space
population density
primary territory
privacy regulation
prosocial behaviour
public territory

secondary territory
social support network
social withdrawal
sociofugal layout
sociometric choice
sociopetal layout
stimulus overload
stress
territorial invasion
territorial markers
territoriality
territory
tolerance of frustration

Glossary
·············

Associative meaning	2	Illusory correlation in which items are seen as belonging together because they 'ought' to, on the basis of prior expectations.
Associative network	2	A model of memory in which nodes or ideas are connected by associative links along which cognitive activation can spread.
Attachment behaviour	12	The tendency of infants to maintain close physical proximity with their mothers.
Attitude	4	1. A relatively enduring organisation of beliefs, feelings and behavioural tendencies towards socially significant objects, groups, events or symbols. 2. A general feeling or evaluation – positive or negative – about some person, object or issue.
Attitude change	5	Any significant modification of an individual's attitude. In the persuasion process, this can involve several variables: the communicator, the communication, the medium used and the characteristics of the audience. Attitude change can also occur by inducing a person to perform an act which is counter to an existing attitude.
Attitude formation	4	The process of forming an attitude. Our own experiences, the influences of others and our emotional reactions are the main determinants.
Attribution	2	Process of assigning a cause to one's own or others' behaviour.
Attributional style	3	An individual (personality) predisposition to make a certain type of causal attribution for behaviour.
Audience	5	The intended target of a persuasive communication.
Audience effect	7	Impact on individual task performance of the presence of others.
Authoritarian personality	10	Personality syndrome originating in childhood that predisposes individuals to be prejudiced.
Autocratic leadership	8	Leadership style based on giving orders to followers.
Autokinesis	6	Optical illusion in which a point of light shining in complete darkness appears to move about.
Automatic activation	4	According to Fazio, an attitude which has a strong evaluative association with an attitude object is more likely to be automatically activated from memory.
Availability	2	A heuristic in which the frequency or likelihood of an event is based on how quickly instances or associations come to mind.
Averaging	2	A method of forming positive or negative impressions by averaging the valence of all the constituent person attributes.
Back-channel communication	14	Verbal and non-verbal ways in which listeners let speakers know they are still listening.
Balance theory	4	According to Heider, people prefer attitudes that are consistent with each other, and avoid those which are inconsistent. A person (P) tries to maintain consistency in attitudes to, and relationships with, other people (O) and to elements of the environment (X).
Bargaining	10	Process of intergroup conflict resolution where representatives reach agreement through direct negotiation.
Base-rate information	2	Pallid, factual, statistical information about an entire class of events.

Behaviour	1	What people actually do that can be objectively measured.
Behavioural decision theory	2	The set of normative models (ideal processes) for making accurate social inferences.
Behaviourism	2	An emphasis on explaining observable behaviour in terms of reinforcement schedules.
Belief congruence theory	9	Theory that similar beliefs promote liking and social harmony and dissimilar beliefs disliking and prejudice.
Belief in a just world	3	Belief that the world is a just and predictable place where good things happen to 'good people' and bad things to 'bad people'.
Biosocial theories	11	In the context of aggression, theories which emphasise an innate component, though not the existence of a full-blown instinct.
Bogus pipeline technique	4	A measurement technique which leads people to believe that a 'lie detector' can monitor their emotional responses, thus measuring their 'true' attitudes.
Bookkeeping	2	Gradual schema change through the gradual accumulation of schema-inconsistent information.
Brainstorming	8	Uninhibited generation of as many ideas as possible in a group, in order to enhance group creativity.
Brainwashing	12	The experience of extensive social isolation, broken sleep and intensive interrogation. An outcome is said to be a high level of susceptibility to political propaganda.
Built environment	15	Physical structures with a clear function designed by people.
Bystander–calculus model	13	In attending to an emergency, the bystander calculates the perceived costs and benefits of providing help compared to those that accrue for not helping.
Bystander effect	13	People are much less likely to help in an emergency when they are with others than when alone. The greater the number, the less likely it is that any one will help.
Bystander intervention	13	This occurs when an individual breaks out of the role of a bystander and helps another person in an emergency.
Case study	1	In-depth analysis of a single case (or individual).
Catharsis	11	A dramatic release of pent-up feelings, the idea that aggressive motivation is 'drained' by acting against a frustrating object or a substitute, or else by a vicarious experience.
Causal schemata	3	Experience-based beliefs about how certain types of cause interact to produce an effect.
Central traits	2	Traits that have a disproportionate influence on the configuration of final impressions, in Asch's configural model of impression formation.
Closed-mindedness	9	Theory that people who have a cognitive style that is rigid and intolerant are predisposed to be prejudiced.
Cognition	4	The knowledge, beliefs, thoughts and ideas that people have about themselves and their environment. It may also refer to mental processes through which knowledge is acquired, including perception, memory and thinking.
Cognitive algebra	2	An approach to the study of impression formation which focuses on how people combine attributes that have valence into an overall positive or negative impression.

Cognitive alternatives	10	A belief that the status quo is unstable and illegitimate, and that social competition with the dominant group is the appropriate strategy to improve social identity.
Cognitive consistency	2	A model of social cognition in which people are motivated to reduce inconsistency, which they find aversive, among their cognitions.
Cognitive consistency theories	4	A group of attitude theories stressing that people try to maintain an internal consistency, order and agreement among their various beliefs.
Cognitive dissonance	5,7	A state of psychological tension, produced by holding two simultaneous and opposing cognitions, that motivates the individual to reduce the tension, often by changing or rejecting one of the cognitions. Festinger proposed that we seek harmony in our attitudes, beliefs and behaviours, and try to reduce tension from inconsistency among these elements.
Cognitive maps	15	Mental representations of our physical environments.
Cognitive miser	3	A model of social cognition in which people are assumed to use the least complex and demanding cognitions that are able to produce generally adaptive behaviours.
Cognitive theories	1	These attempt to explain behaviour in terms of the way people actively interpret and represent their experiences, and then plan action.
Cohesiveness	7,8	Essential property of a group that makes it act like a group.
Collective aggression	11	Unified aggression by a group of individuals, who may not even know each other, against another individual or group.
Collective behaviour	10	The behaviour of people en masse, such as in a crowd, protest or riot.
Commons dilemma	10	A social dilemma in which co-operation by all benefits all, but competition by all harms all.
Communication	14	Transfer of meaningful information from one person to another.
Communication accommodation theory	14	Modification of verbal and non-verbal communication styles to the context (for example, listener, situation) of a face-to-face inter-individual interaction; an extension of speech accommodation theory to incorporate non-verbal communication.
Communication network	7	Set of rules governing the possibility or ease of communication between different roles within a group.
Companionate love	12	Caring and affection for another person which usually arises from sharing time together.
Comparison level	12	A standard that develops over time which allows one to judge whether a new relationship is profitable or not.
Compliance	6	Superficial, public and transitory change in behaviour and expressed attitudes in response to requests, coercion or group pressure.
Conciliation	10	Process whereby groups make co-operative gestures to one another in the hope of avoiding escalation of conflict.
Configural model	2	Asch's Gestalt-based model of impression formation, in which central traits have a disproportionate role in configuring the final impression.
Conformity	6	Deep-seated, private and enduring change in behaviour and attitudes due to group pressure.

Conformity bias	6	Tendency for social psychology to treat group influence as a one-way process in which individuals or minorities always conform to majorities.
Confounding	1	Where two or more independent variables covary in such a way that it is impossible to know which has caused the effect.
Consensus information	3	Information about the extent to which other people react in the same way to a stimulus X.
Consistency information	3	Information about the extent to which a behaviour Y always co-occurs with a stimulus X.
Conspiracy theory	3	Tendency to explain widespread, complex and worrying events in terms of the premeditated actions of small groups of highly organised conspirators.
Consummate love	12	Sternberg argues that this is the ultimate form of love, involving passion, intimacy and commitment.
Contact hypothesis	10	View that bringing members of opposing social groups together will improve intergroup relations and reduce prejudice and discrimination.
Contingency theory	8	Fiedler's interactionist theory that the effectiveness of particular leadership styles depends on situational and task factors.
Conversion	2	Sudden schema change as a consequence of gradual accumulation of schema-inconsistent information.
Conversion effect	6	When minority influence brings about a sudden and dramatic internal and private change in the attitudes of a majority.
Co-ordination loss	7	Deterioration in group performance in comparison to individual performance due to problems in co-ordinating behaviour.
Correlation	1	Where increases or decreases on one variable can be reliably predicted by changes on another variable.
Correspondent inference	3	Causal attribution of behaviour to underlying dispositions.
Cost/reward ratio	12	A tenet of social exchange theory according to which the degree of liking for another is determined by calculating what it will cost to be reinforced by that person.
Covariation model	3	Harold Kelley's theory of causal attribution: people assign the cause of behaviour to the factor that covaries most closely with the behaviour.
Crowding	15	The perception that the actual level of contact with others exceeds one's desired level.
Cultural norm	11	A norm whose origin is part of the tradition of a culture.
Cultural values theory	8	The view that people in groups use members' opinions about the position valued in the wider culture, and then adjust their views in that direction for social approval reasons.
Data	1	Publicly verifiable observations.
Deindividuation	10, 11	A process whereby people lose their sense of socialised individual identity and engage in unsocialised, often antisocial behaviours.
Demand characteristics	1	Features of an experiment that seem to 'demand' a certain response.
Democratic leadership	8	Leadership style based on consultation and obtaining agreement and consent from followers.

Dependent variable	1	That which changes as a consequence of changes in the independent variable.
Depersonalisation	10	The perception and treatment of self and others not as unique individual persons but as prototypical embodiments of a social group.
Diffuse status characteristics	7	Information about a person's abilities that are only obliquely relevant to the group's task, but derive mainly from large-scale category memberships outside the group.
Diffusion of responsibility	13	The tendency of an individual to assume that others will take responsibility – as a result no-one does. This is an hypothesised cause of the bystander effect.
Discounting	3	If there is no consistent relationship between a causal contender and a specific behaviour, the contender is discounted in favour of some other causal candidate.
Discourse	14	Entire communicative event or episode located in situational and socio-historical context.
Discrimination	9	The behavioural expression of prejudice.
Disinhibition	11	A breakdown in the learned controls (social mores) against behaving impulsively and can be a precursor to aggression. For some people, alcohol has a disin-hibiting effect.
Displacement	9	Psychodynamic concept referring to the transfer of negative feelings onto an individual or group other than that which originally caused the negative feelings.
Display rules	14	Cultural and situational rules governing the contextual appropriateness of expressing emotions.
Distinctiveness information	3	Information about the extent to which a person's reaction is distinctive to a stimulus X, or is a common reaction to many stimuli.
Distraction/conflict theory	7	The physical presence of members of the same species causes drive because people are distracting and produce conflict between attending to the task and to the audience.
Distributive justice	12	A concern with whether the outcome of a decision in distributing resources has been fair.
Dogmatism	9	A cognitive style that is rigid and intolerant and predisposes people to be prejudiced.
Door-in-the-face tactic	5,6	Multiple request technique to gain compliance, in which the focal request is preceded by a larger request that is bound to be refused.
Double-blind	1	Procedure to reduce experimenter effects, in which the experimenter is unaware of the experimental conditions.
Drive theory	7	Zajonc's theory that the physical presence of members of the same species instinctively causes arousal that motivates performance of habitual behaviour patterns.
Dual process dependency model	6	General model of social influence in which two separate processes operate: interindividual dependency for social approval and for information about reality.
Effort justification	5	A special case of cognitive dissonance: inconsistency is experienced when a person makes a considerable effort to achieve a modest goal.
Egoistic relative deprivation	10	Sense of personally having less than one feels one is entitled to relative to one's aspirations or to other individuals.

Elaboration-likelihood model	5	Petty and Cacioppo's model of attitude change: when people attend to a message carefully, they use a central route to process it; otherwise they use a peripheral route. This model competes with the *heuristic-systematic model*.
Emblems	14	Gestures that replace or stand in for spoken language.
Emergent norm theory	10	Collective behaviour is regulated by norms based on distinctive behaviour that arise in the initially norm-less crowd.
Empathic concern	13	An element in Batson's theory of helping behaviour. In contrast to personal distress (which may lead to us fleeing from the situation), it includes feelings of warmth and compassion for a person in need.
Empathy	13	The ability to sense another person's experiences; identifying with and experiencing another person's emotions, thoughts and attitudes.
Empathy costs of not helping	13	Piliavin *et al.*'s view that failing to help can cause distress to a bystander who empathises with a victim's plight.
Environmental after-effect	15	A deterioration in performance subsequent to exposure to a stressor, such as noise, shock, density.
Environmental psychology	15	The study of the interaction between the physical world and human behaviour.
Environmental stressors	15	Background factors, often not consciously attended to, which can induce stress symptoms and can inhibit or even disrupt performance.
Equity theory	12	A special case of social exchange theory that defines a relationship as equitable when the ratio of profit to contribution is perceived to be the same by each partner.
Ethnocentrism	10	Evaluative preference of all aspects of one's own group relative to other groups.
Ethnolinguistic group	14	Social group defined principally in terms of its language.
Ethnolinguistic identity theory	14	Application and extension of social identity theory to deal with language behaviour of ethnolinguistic groups.
Ethnolinguistic vitality	14	Concept describing objective features of an inter-ethnic context that influence language, and ultimately the cultural survival or disappearance of an ethnolinguistic group.
Ethnomethodology	7	Method devised by Garfinkel involving the violation of hidden norms to reveal their presence.
Ethology	11	Animal behaviour should be studied in both the species' natural physical and social environment. Behaviour is genetically determined and is controlled by natural selection.
Evaluation apprehension model	7	The argument that the physical presence of members of the same species causes drive because people have learned to be apprehensive about being evaluated.
Excitation-transfer model	11	This suggests that the expression of aggression is a function of learned behaviour, some excitation from another source and the person's interpretation of the arousal state.
Exemplars	2	Specific instances of a member of a category.
Expectancy-value model	4	Direct experience with an attitude object informs a person how much that object should be liked or disliked in the future.
Expectation states theory	7	Theory of the emergence of roles as a consequence of people's status-based expectations about others' performance.

Experimental method	1	The intentional manipulation of independent variables in order to investigate effects upon one or more dependent variables.
Experimental realism	1	Psychological impact of the manipulations in an experiment.
Experimenter effects	1	Effects that are produced or influenced by clues to the hypotheses under examination, inadvertently given by the experimenter.
External (or situational) attribution	3	Process of assigning the cause of one's own or others' behaviour to external or environmental factors.
External validity	1	Similarity between circumstances surrounding an experiment and circumstances encountered in everyday life.
Face-ism	9	Media depiction that gives greater prominence to the head and less prominence to the body for males, but vice versa for females.
False consensus effect	3	Tendency to see one's own behaviour as being more typical than it really is.
Familiarity	12	As one becomes more familiar with a stimulus (even another person), one feels more comfortable with it and shows more liking for it.
Family resemblance	2	The defining property of category membership.
Fear of social blunders	13	The dread of acting inappropriately or of making a foolish mistake witnessed by others. The desire to avoid ridicule inhibits effective responses to an emergency by members of a group.
Feral children	12	An apparent animal-like condition of children deprived of contact with adults for years from early in their infancy.
Fighting instinct	11	An innate impulse to aggress which ethologists claim is shared by humans as well as other animals.
Foot-in-the-door tactic	5,6	Multiple request technique to gain compliance, in which the focal request is preceded by a smaller request that is bound to be accepted.
Forewarning	5	Advance knowledge that one is to be the target of the persuasion attempt. Forewarning often produces resistance to persuasion.
Frame of reference	6	Complete range of subjectively conceivable positions that relevant people can occupy in that context on some attitudinal or behavioural dimension.
Fraternalistic relative deprivation	10	Sense that one's group has less than it is entitled to relative to its aspirations or to other groups.
Free-rider effect	7,10	Result of a group member avoiding costly obligations of group membership, and allowing other members to incur the costs.
Frustration-aggression hypothesis	9,11	Theory that all frustration leads to aggression, and all aggression comes from frustration. Used to explain prejudice and intergroup aggression.
Functional distance	15	The effect of a design on the probability that people will interact with others.
Fundamental attribution error	3,7	The bias in attributing another's behaviour more to internal rather than to situational causes.
Fuzzy set	2	Categories are considered to be fuzzy sets of features organised around a prototype.
Gain/loss hypothesis	12	The paradox of liking people more if they initially dislike us and then later like us; and of liking them less if the sequence is reversed.

Gaze	14	Looking at someone's eyes.
Gender	9	Sex-stereotypical attributes of a person.
Genetic model	6	Moscovici's early focus on how social conflict between minority and majority can change the attitudes and behaviours of the majority.
Genocide	9	The ultimate expression of prejudice by exterminating an entire social group.
Gestalt psychology	2	A perspective in which the whole influences constituent parts rather than vice versa.
Gestures	14	Meaningful body movements and postures.
Great person theory	8	Perspective on leadership that attributes effective leadership to innate or acquired individual characteristics.
Group	7	Two or more people who share a common definition and evaluation of themselves, and behave in accordance with such a definition.
Group mind	8	William McDougall's idea that people adopt a qualitatively different mode of thinking when in a group than when not in a group.
Group polarisation	8	A tendency for group discussion to produce more extreme group decisions than the mean of members' pre-discussion opinions, in the direction favoured by the mean.
Group socialisation	7	Dynamic relationship between the group and its members that describes the passage of members through a group, in terms of commitment and of changing roles.
Group structure	7	Division of a group into roles that often differ with respect to status and prestige.
Groupthink	8	A mode of thinking in highly cohesive groups in which the desire to reach unanimous agreement overrides the motivation to adopt proper rational decision-making procedures.
Guttman scale	4	A scale that contains either favourable or unfavourable statements arranged hierarchically. Agreement with a strong statement implies agreement with the weaker ones. Disagreement with a weak one implies disagreement with stronger ones.
Hedonic relevance	3	Refers to behaviour that has important consequences for self.
Helping behaviour	13	Acts that intentionally benefit someone else.
Heuristics	2	Cognitive short-cuts that provide adequately accurate inferences for most of us most of the time.
Heuristic-systematic model	5	Chaiken's model of attitude change: when people attend to a message carefully, they use systematic processing; otherwise they process information by using heuristics, or 'mental short-cuts'. This model competes with the *elaboration-likelihood model*.
Homicide	11	Usually refers to the unlawful killing of another human being, including acts of murder and manslaughter.
Hospitalism	12	The state of apathy and depression noted among institutionalised infants deprived of close contact with a care-giver.
Hypotheses	1	Empirically testable predictions about what goes with what, or what causes what.
Ideology	4	A systematically interrelated set of beliefs whose primary function is explanation. It circumscribes thinking, making it difficult for the holder to escape from its mould.

Idiosyncrasy credits	8	Hollander's transactionist theory that followers reward leaders for achieving group goals by allowing them to be relatively idiosyncratic.
Illocution	14	Words placed in sequence and the context in which this is done.
Illusion of control	3	Belief that one has more control over one's world than one really does.
Illusion of group effectivity	8	Experience-based belief that we produce more and better ideas in groups than alone.
Illusory correlation	10	Cognitive exaggeration of the degree of co-occurrence of two stimuli or events, or the perception of a co-occurrence where none exists.
Illustrators	14	Body movements and postures that accompany spoken language.
Implicit personality theories	2	Idiosyncratic and personal ways of characterising other people and explaining their behaviour.
Independent variable	1	That which changes of its own accord, or can be manipulated by an experimenter, to have effects on a dependent variable.
Induced compliance	5	A special case of cognitive dissonance: inconsistency is experienced when a person is persuaded to behave in a way that is contrary to an attitude.
Information integration theory	4	The idea that a person's attitude can be estimated by averaging across the positive and negative ratings of the object.
Information processing	4,5	The evaluation of information; in relation to attitudes, the means by which people acquire knowledge and form and change attitudes.
Informational influence	6	An influence to accept information from another as evidence about reality.
Ingratiation	5,6	A strategic attempt to get someone to like you in order to obtain compliance with a request.
Ingroup favouritism	10	Behaviour that favours one's own group over other groups.
Initiation rites	7	Often painful or embarrassing public procedure to mark group members' movements from one role to another.
Inoculation	5	A way of making people resistant to persuasion. By providing them with a diluted counter-argument they can build up effective refutations to a later stronger argument.
Instinct	11	An innate drive or impulse, genetically transmitted.
Institutionalised aggression	11	Aggression that is given formal or informal recognition and social legitimacy by being incorporated into rules and norms.
Instrumental	11	Having some constructive intention or purpose.
Intergroup attribution	3	Process of assigning the cause of one's own or others' behaviour to group membership.
Intergroup behaviour	10	Behaviour among individuals that is regulated by those individuals' awareness of and identification with different social groups.
Intergroup differentiation	10	Behaviour that emphasises differences between one's own group and other groups.
Internal (or dispositional) attribution	3	Process of assigning the cause of one's own or others' behaviour to internal or dispositional factors.
Internal validity	1	Psychological impact of the manipulations in an experiment.

J-curve	10	A graphical figure which captures the way in which relative deprivation arises when attainments suddenly fall short of rising expectations.
Just-world hypothesis	13	According to Lerner, people need to believe that the world is a just place where we get what we deserve. Since evidence of undeserved suffering undermines this belief, people may conclude that victims deserve their fate.
Kinesics	14	Linguistics of body communication.
Laboratory	1	A place, usually a room, in which data are collected, usually by experimental methods.
Language	14	System of sounds that convey meaning because of shared grammatical and semantic rules.
Leadership	8	Getting other people to achieve the group's goals.
Learning by direct experience	11	The acquisition of a behaviour when the performance of an act leads to reinforcement.
Learning by vicarious experience	11	The acquisition of a behaviour following the observation that an act performed by another leads to reinforcement.
Levels of analysis (or explanation)	3	The types of concept, mechanism and language used to explain a phenomenon.
Likert scale	4	A scale that evaluates how strongly people agree/disagree with favourable/ unfavourable statements about an attitude object. Initially, many items are tested. After item analysis, only those items which correlate with each other are retained.
Linguistic relativity	14	The view that language determines thought and therefore people who speak different languages see the world in very different ways.
Locution	14	Words placed in sequence.
Low-ball tactic	5,6	A technique for inducing compliance in which a person who agrees to a request can feel committed even after finding that there is a hidden cost.
LPC scale	8	Fiedler's scale for measuring leadership style in terms of favourability of attitude towards one's least preferred co-worker.
Matched-guise technique	14	Research methodology to obtain people's attitudes towards a speaker based solely on speech style.
Maternal deprivation	12	An extended period of separation of an infant from its principal care-giver. The consequences can lead to irreversible damage to both intellectual and social functioning.
Mediation	10	Process of intergroup conflict resolution where a neutral third party intervenes in the negotiation process to facilitate a settlement.
Membership group	6	Harold Kelley's term for a group to which one belongs by some objective external criterion.
Mere exposure effect	4,5,9	When repeated exposure to an object results in greater attraction to that object.
Mere presence	7	Refers to an entirely passive and unresponsive audience that is only physically present.
Message	5	A communication from a source directed to an audience.
Metatheory	1	Set of interrelated concepts and principles concerning which theories or types of theory are appropriate.

Mindlessness	5	The act of agreeing to a request without giving it a thought. A small request is likely to be agreed to, even if a spurious reason is provided.
Minimal group paradigm	9	Experimental methodology to investigate the effect of social categorisation alone on behaviour.
Minimax strategy	12	In relating to others we try to minimise the costs and maximise the rewards that accrue.
Minority influence	6	Social influence processes whereby numerical or power minorities change the attitudes of the majority.
Modelling	4,11, 13	The tendency for a person to reproduce the action, attitudes and emotional responses exhibited by a real-life or symbolic model. Also called *observational learning*.
Moderator variable	4	One which qualifies an otherwise simple hypothesis with a view to improving its predictive power.
Morpheme	14	Basic units of meaning; elementary words or parts of words that have meaning.
Motivated tactician	2	A model of social cognition which characterises people as having multiple cognitive strategies available, which they choose among on the basis of personal goals, motives and needs.
Multiple-act criterion	4	A term for a general behavioural index based on an average or combination of several specific behaviours.
Mundane realism	1	Similarity between circumstances surrounding an experiment and circumstances encountered in everyday life.
Naive scientist (or psychologist)	2,3	A model of social cognition that characterises people as using rational, scientific-like, cause/effect analyses to understand their world.
Nature/nurture controversy	13	The classic argument about whether biology or the environment is more important in determining how people behave. Most scientists accept that it is neither one nor the other, but an interaction of both.
Need complementarity	12	Winch's theory that we seek our apparent opposites, as they can best satisfy our needs.
Need to affiliate	12	The motive to form connections and contact with other people.
Neo-associationist analysis	11	A view of aggression according to which mass media may provide images of violence to an audience which later translate into antisocial acts.
Neo-behaviourism	1	An attempt to explain observable behaviour in terms of contextual factors and of unobservable intervening constructs such as beliefs, feelings and motives.
Neo-Freudians	11	Psychoanalytic theorists who modified the original theories of Freud.
Non-common effects	3	Effects of behaviour that are relatively exclusive to that behaviour.
Non-verbal communication	14	Transfer of meaningful information from one person to another by means other than written or spoken language (for example, gaze, facial expression, posture, touch).
Normative influence	6	An influence to conform with the positive expectation of others, to gain social approval or to avoid social disapproval.
Normative models	2	Ideal processes for making accurate social inferences.
Norms	6,11 13	Attitudinal and behavioural uniformities that define group membership and differentiate between groups.
One-component attitude model	4	An attitude consists of affect or evaluation towards the object.

Open planning	15	The removal of barriers, such as walls and partitions, to encourage communication among users of an area. This can lead to feelings of intrusion into one's territory and personal space.
Operational definition	1	One which defines a theoretical term in a manner that renders it susceptible to measurement.
Optimal distinctiveness	10	People strive to achieve a balance between conflicting motives for inclusiveness and separateness – expressed in groups as a balance between intragroup differentiation and intragroup homogenisation.
Overjustification effect	3	In the absence of obvious external determinants of our own behaviour we tend to assume that we freely chose the behaviour because we enjoy it.
Paired distinctiveness	2	Illusory correlation in which items are seen as belonging together because they share some unusual feature.
Paralanguage	14	The non-linguistic accompaniments of speech (for example, stress, pitch, speed, tone, pauses).
Passionate (or romantic) love	12	A state of intense absorption in another person involving physiological arousal.
Peace studies	11	A multi-disciplinary movement dedicated to both the study and promotion of peace.
Peripheral traits	2	Traits that have an insignificant influence on the configuration of final impressions in Asch's configural model of impression formation.
Personal attraction	7	Liking for someone based on idiosyncratic preferences and interpersonal relationships.
Personal constructs	2	Idiosyncratic and personal ways of characterising other people.
Personal costs of helping	13	Piliavin *et al.*'s view that helping a victim in distress can be costly to a bystander, such as experiencing blame.
Personalism	3	Refers to behaviour that appears to be directly intended to benefit or harm oneself rather than others.
Persuasive arguments theory	8	The view that people in groups are persuaded by novel information that supports their initial position, and thus become more extreme in their endorsement of their initial position.
Persuasive communication	5	A message intended to change an attitude and related behaviours of an audience.
Phoneme	14	Elementary and meaningless sounds that are combined in various ways to produce more meaningful sound units.
Population density	15	The number of people in a given space.
Positive self-esteem	10	The holding of positive feelings about and evaluations of oneself.
Positivism	1	Non-critical acceptance of science as the only way to arrive at true knowledge – science as religion.
Post-decisional conflict	5	The dissonance associated with behaving in a counter-attitudinal way. Dissonance can be reduced by bringing the attitude into line with the behaviour.
Postures	14	Meaningful positionings of parts of the body (for example, hands, head, arms).
Power	6	The capacity to influence others while resisting their attempts to influence.
Prejudice	9	Unfavourable attitude towards a social group and its members.
Primacy	2	An order of presentation effect in which earlier presented information has a disproportionate influence on social cognition.

Primary territory	15	An area associated with the primary group, usually family, and is central to our regulation of social contact or privacy process.
Priming	2	The procedure of recalling accessible categories or schemata that we already have in mind.
Prior commitment	13	An individual's agreement in advance to be responsible if trouble occurs, for example committing oneself to protect the property of another person against theft.
Prisoner's dilemma	10	A two-person game in which both parties are torn between competition and co-operation, and depending on mutual choices both can win or both can lose.
Privacy regulation	15	The process by which people make themselves more open or less open to contact with other people.
Process loss	7	Deterioration in group performance in comparison with individual performance due to the whole range of possible interferences among members.
Production blocking	8	Reduction in individual creativity and productivity in brainstorming groups due to interruptions and turn-taking.
Profit	12	This flows from a relationship when the rewards that accrue from continued interaction exceed the costs.
Prosocial behaviour	13	Acts that are positively valued by society.
Prototype	2	Cognitive representation of the typical/ideal defining features of a category.
Proxemics	14	Study of interpersonal distance.
Proximity	12	The factor of living close by is known to play an important role in the early stages of forming a friendship.
Public territory	15	An area accessible to all and over which any person has only temporary rights of occupancy.
Racism	9	Prejudice and discrimination against people based on their ethnicity or race.
Radical behaviourism	1	An attempt to explain observable behaviour in terms of reinforcement schedules, without recourse to any intervening unobservable (for example, cognitive) constructs.
Reactance	5	Brehm's theory that people try to protect their freedom to act. When they perceive that this freedom has been curtailed, they will act to regain it.
Realistic conflict theory	10	Sherif's theory of intergroup conflict that traces the complexion of intergroup behaviour to the nature of goal relations between groups.
Received pronunciation (RP)	14	Standard, high status spoken variety of English.
Recency	2	An order of presentation effect in which later presented information has a disproportionate influence on social cognition.
Reciprocity principle (or norm)	5,6, 11,12 13	The law of 'doing unto others as they do to you'. It can refer to an attempt to gain compliance by first doing someone a favour, or to mutual aggression or mutual attraction.
Reductionism	1	Explanation of a phenomenon in terms of the language and concepts of a lower level of analysis, usually with a loss of explanatory power.
Reference frame	7	Complete range of subjectively conceivable positions that relevant people can occupy in that context on some attitudinal or behavioural dimension.
Reference group	6	Harold Kelley's term for a group that is psychologically significant for one's behaviour and attitudes.

Referent informational influence	6	An influence to conform with a self-referent group norm that defines oneself as a group member.
Regression	2	Tendency for initial observations of instances from a category to be more extreme than subsequent observations.
Reinforcement-affect model	12	A model of attraction which postulates that we like people who are around when we experience a positive feeling (which itself is reinforcing).
Relationship dissolution model	12	Duck's proposal of the sequence through which most long-term relationships proceed if they finally break down.
Relative deprivation	9,10	Sense of having less than that to which one feels entitled.
Relative homogeneity effect	10	Tendency to see outgroup members as all the same and ingroup members as more differentiated.
Releasers	11	Specific stimuli in the environment thought by ethologists to trigger aggressive responses.
Representativeness	2	A heuristic in which instances are assigned to categories or types on the basis of overall similarity or resemblance to the category.
Reverse discrimination	9	The practice of publicly being prejudiced in favour of a minority group in order to deflect accusations of prejudice and discrimination.
Ringelmann effect	7	A reduction of individual effort as a function of increasing group size.
Risky shift	8	A tendency for group discussion to produce more risky group decisions than the mean of members' pre-discussion opinions, but only if the pre-discussion mean already favoured risk.
Role complementarity	12	A successful relationship requires role negotiation, some 'give and take'.
Roles	2	Patterns of behaviour that distinguish between different activities within the group, and that interrelate to one another for the greater good of the group.
Salience	2	A property of a stimulus that makes it stand out in relation to other stimuli and which attracts attention.
Scapegoat	9	Individual or group that becomes the target for anger and frustration caused by a different individual or group or some other set of circumstances.
Schema	2	A cognitive structure that represents knowledge about a concept or type of stimulus, including its attributes and the relations among those attributes.
Science	1	Method for studying nature that involves the collecting of data to test hypotheses.
Script	2	A schema about an event.
Secondary territory	15	An area that is not personally owned but is not accessible to all others either.
Selective exposure hypothesis	5	People tend to avoid potentially dissonant information.
Self-categorisation theory	2	John Turner and associates' theory of how the process of categorising oneself as a group member produces social identity and group and intergroup behaviours.
Self-esteem	9	Feelings about and evaluations of oneself.
Self-fulfilling prophecy	9	Expectations and assumptions about a person that influence one's interaction with that person and eventually change that person's behaviour in line with one's expectations.

Self-handicapping	3	Publicly making advance external attributions for one's anticipated failure or poor performance in a forthcoming event.
Self-perception theory	4,5	Bem's argument that, since we infer other people's attitudes from their behaviour, we infer our own attitudes from our own behaviour. In the absence of a clear external cause, we assume that the behaviour reflects our true attitude.
Self-rating scale	4	An attitude measure that asks for agreement or disagreement with an attitude position.
Self-serving bias	3	Attributional distortions that protect or enhance self-esteem or the self-concept.
Semantic differential	4	An attitude measure that asks for a rating on a scale composed of bipolar (opposite) adjectives. (Also a technique for measuring the connotative meaning of words or concepts.)
Sensory deprivation	12	An experience of an impoverished environment leading to reduced sensory input.
Sensory overload	15	Stimulation occurs at a faster rate than it can be processed, leading to a narrowing of attention.
Sex role	9	Behaviour deemed sex-stereotypically appropriate.
Sexism	9	Prejudice and discrimination against people based on their sex.
Shared stress	12	A condition noted by Schachter according to which anxiety can be reduced by sharing the experience in common with others.
Similarity of attitudes or values	12	One of the most important positive determinants of attraction.
Situational control	8	Fiedler's classification of task characteristics in terms of how much control effective task performance requires.
Social attraction	7	Liking for someone based on common group membership and determined by the person's prototypicality of the group.
Social categorisation	10	Classification of people as members of different social groups.
Social change belief system	10	Belief that intergroup boundaries are impermeable. Therefore, a lower status individual can improve social identity only by challenging the legitimacy of the higher-status group's position.
Social cognition	2	Cognitive processes and structures that influence and are influenced by social behaviour.
Social comparison	8	The process of comparing one's behaviours and opinions with those of others in order to establish the correct or socially approved way of thinking or behaving.
Social compensation	7	Increased effort on a collective task in order to compensate for other group members' actual, perceived or anticipated lack of effort or ability.
Social competition	10	Group-based behavioural strategies that improve social identity by directly confronting the dominant group's position in society.
Social creativity	10	Group-based behavioural strategies that improve social identity but do not directly attack the dominant group's position.
Social decisions schemes	8	Explicit or implicit decision-making rules that relate individual opinions to a final group decision.

Social facilitation	7	An improvement in the performance of well-learned/easy tasks and a deterioration in the performance of poorly learned/difficult tasks in the mere presence of members of the same species.
Social identity	10	That part of the self-concept that derives from one's membership of social groups.
Social identity theory	2	Theory of group membership and intergroup relations based on self-categorisation, social comparison and the construction of a shared self-definition in terms of ingroup defining properties.
Social impact	6	The degree of effect that other people have on one's attitudes and behaviour, usually as a consequence of factors such as group size, and temporal and physical immediacy.
Social influence	6	The process whereby attitudes and behaviour are influenced by the real or implied presence of other people.
Social judgeability	2	Belief, based on social convention, that it is or is not legitimate to make an impression-based judgement of another person.
Social learning theory	11	The view championed by Bandura that human social behaviour is not innate but learned from appropriate models.
Social loafing	7	A reduction in individual effort when working on a collective task (in which one's outputs are pooled with those of other group members) compared with when working either alone or coactively.
Social markers	14	Features of speech style that convey information about mood, context, status and group membership.
Social matching	12	Accounts for the way people are attracted to partners of approximately the same level of social desirability.
Social mobility belief system	10	Belief that intergroup boundaries are permeable. Therefore, it is possible for an individual to pass from a lower-status into a higher-status group in order to improve social identity.
Social order	11	The balance and control of a social system, regulated by norms, values, rules and law.
Social psychology	1	Scientific investigation of how the thoughts, feelings and behaviour of individuals are influenced by the actual, imagined or implied presence of others.
Social representations	3	Collectively elaborated explanations of unfamiliar and complex phenomena that transform them into a familiar and simple form.
Social responsibility norm	13	The idea that we should help people who are dependent and in need. It is contradicted by another norm that discourages interfering in other people's lives.
Social support network	13, 15	People who know and care about us and who can provide back-up during a time of stress.
Social transition scheme	8	A method for charting incremental changes in member opinions as a group moves towards a final decision.
Social withdrawal	15	Avoidance of social contact such as speech, touching or eye contact.
Socio-cognitive model	4	A recent theory of attitude highlighting an evaluative component. Knowledge of an object is represented in memory along with a summary of how to appraise it.
Socio-emotional oriented leader	8	Leader who is concerned with group members' feelings and relationships rather than with the group task.

Sociobiology	11	A biological view that aggression, altruism and some other social behaviours serve to protect the survival of one's genes.
Sociofugal layout	15	Arranging a room in order bring people together.
Sociometric choice	15	A measure of the extent to which people both like and wish to interact with others.
Sociopetal layout	15	Arranging a room in order push people apart.
Source	5	The point of origin of a persuasive communication.
Specific status characteristics	7	Information about a person's abilities that are directly relevant to the group's task.
Speech accommodation	14	Modification of speech style to the context (for example, listener, situation) of a face-to-face inter-individual conversation.
Speech convergence	14	Accent or speech style shift towards that of the other person.
Speech divergence	14	Accent or speech style shift away from that of the other person.
Speech style	14	The way in which something is said (for example, accent, language) rather than the content of what is said.
Statistical significance	1	An effect is statistically significant if statistics reveal that it, or a larger effect, is unlikely to occur by chance more often than one in twenty times.
Statistics	1	Formalised numerical procedures performed on data to investigate the magnitude and/or significance of effects.
Status	7	Consensual evaluation of the prestige of a role or role occupant in a group, or of the prestige of a group and its members as a whole.
Stereotype	2	Widely shared and simplified evaluative image of a social group and its members.
Stimulus overload	15	In a busy environment we screen out many stimuli to enable our information-processing capacities to cope. In a bustling city these stimuli can include people.
Stress	15	A state of physiological arousal which occurs when a stimulus is perceived as a threat for which the coping resources are inadequate.
Subculture of violence	11	A grouping in a society within which a higher level of violence is accepted as the norm.
Subject effects	1	Effects which are non-spontaneous due to demand characteristics and/or subjects wishing to please the experimenter.
Subjective vitality	14	Individual group members' representation of the objective ethnolinguistic vitality of their group.
Subtyping	2	Schema change as a consequence of schema-inconsistent information causing the formation of subcategories.
Summation	2	A method of forming positive or negative impressions by summing the valence of all the constituent person attributes.
Superordinate goal	10	A goal that both groups desire but that can only be achieved by both groups co-operating together.
t-test	1	Statistical procedure to test the statistical significance of an effect in which the mean for one condition is larger than the mean for another.
Task-oriented leader	8	Leader who is concerned with the group task rather than relationships among members.

Task taxonomy	7	Group tasks can be classified according to whether a division of labour is possible, whether there is a predetermined standard to be met, how an individual's inputs can contribute.
Territorial invasion	15	An intrusion into one's territory.
Territorial markers	15	The use of fixtures, items and emblems to declare ownership of a territory.
Territoriality	15	Behaviours used by an owner to control activity that occurs in or near a territory.
Territory	15	A geographical area with known boundaries and an owner.
Theory	1	Set of interrelated concepts and principles that explain a phenomenon.
Theory of planned behaviour	4	A modification by Ajzen of the *theory of reasoned behaviour*. It suggests that predicting a behaviour from an attitude measure is improved if people believe that they have control over that behaviour.
Theory of reasoned action	4	Fishbein and Ajzen's model of the links between attitude and behaviour. A major feature is the proposition that the best way to predict a behaviour is to ask if the person intends to do it.
Three-component attitude model	4	An attitude consists of cognitive, affective and behavioural components. This threefold division has an ancient heritage, stressing thought, feeling and action as basic to human experience.
Three-factor theory of love	12	Hatfield and Walster distinguished three components of what we label 'love': a cultural concept of love, an appropriate person to love and emotional arousal.
Thurstone scale	4	Originally, an eleven-point scale with twenty-two items, two for each point. Each item has a value, determined by judges, ranging from very unfavourable to very favourable. Subjects check the items with which they agree. Their attitude is the average scale value of these items.
Tokenism	9	The practice of publicly making trivial concessions to a minority group in order to deflect accusations of prejudice and discrimination.
Tolerance of frustration	15	The ease with which subjects give up on a performance task.
Transactive memory	8,12	A shared system for encoding, storing and retrieving information in a group.
Two-component attitude model	4	An attitude consists of a mental readiness to act. It also guides evaluative (judgemental) responses.
Type A personality	11	The 'coronary-prone' personality – a behavioural correlate of heart disease characterised by striving to achieve, time urgency, competitiveness and hostility.
Ultimate attribution error	3	Tendency to internally attribute bad outgroup and good ingroup behaviour and externally attribute good outgroup and bad ingroup behaviour.
Uni-dimensionalilty	4	On a Guttman scale, this refers to it being cumulative, for example agreement with the highest-scoring item implies agreement with all lower-scoring items.
Unobtrusive measures	4	Observational approaches that neither intrude on the processes being studied nor cause people to behave unnaturally.
Utterance	14	Sound made by one person to another.
Value	4,11	A higher-order concept thought to provide a structure for organising attitudes.
Visual dominance behaviour	14	Tendency to gaze fixedly at a lower-status speaker.

Vividness	2	An intrinsic property of a stimulus on its own that makes it stand out and catch attention.
Völkerpsychologie	1	Early precursor of social psychology, as the study of the collective mind, in Germany in the mid to late nineteenth century.
Weighted averaging	2	A method of forming positive or negative impressions by first weighting and then averaging the valence of all the constituent person attributes.

References

....

Abèles, R. D. (1976). 'Relative deprivation, rising expectations, and black militancy'. *Journal of Social Issues*, **32**, 119–37.

Abelson, R. P. (1968). 'Computers, polls and public opinion – some puzzles and paradoxes'. *Transaction*, **5**, 20–27.

Abelson, R. P. (1972). 'Are attitudes necessary?' in B. T. King (ed.), *Attitudes. Conflict and Social Change*. New York: Academic Press.

Abelson, R. P. (1981). 'The psychological status of the script concept'. *American Psychologist*, **36**, 715–29.

Abelson, R. P., Aronson, E., McGuire, W. J., Newcomb, T. M., Rosenberg, M. J. and Tannenbaum, P. H. (eds) (1968). *Theories of Cognitive Consistency: A Sourcebook*. Chicago: Rand McNally.

Aboud, F. (1988). *Children and Prejudice*. Oxford: Blackwell.

Abrams, D. (1994). 'Political distinctiveness: an identity optimising approach'. *European Journal of Social Psychology*, **24**, 357–65.

Abrams, D. (1994). 'Social self-regulation'. *Personality and Social Psychology, Bulletin*, **20**, 473–83.

Abrams, D. and Hogg, M. A. (1988). 'Comments on the motivational status of self-esteem in social identity and intergroup discrimination'. *European Journal of Social Psychology*, **18**, 317–34.

Abrams, D. and Hogg, M. A. (1990a). 'Social identification, self-categorisation, and social influence'. *European Review of Social Psychology*, **1**, 195–228.

Abrams, D. and Hogg, M. A. (eds) (1990b). *Social Identity Theory: Constructive and Critical Advances*. London: Harvester Wheatsheaf.

Abrams, D. and Hogg, M. A. (1990c). 'The social context of discourse: let's not throw out the baby with the bath water'. *Philosophical Psychology*, **3**, 219–25.

Abrams, D., Carter J. and Hogg, M. A. (1989). 'Perceptions of male homosexuality: an application of social identity theory'. *Social Behaviour*, **4**, 253–64.

Abramson, L. Y., Seligman, M. E. P. and Teasdale, J. D. (1978). 'Learned helplessness in humans: critique and reformulation'. *Journal of Abnormal and Social Psychology*, **87**, 49–74.

Abric, J. C. and Vacherot, C. (1976). 'The effects of representations of behaviour in experimental games'. *European Journal of Social Psychology*, **6**, 129–44.

Acking, C. A. (1971). 'Factorial analysis of the perception of an interior' in B. Honikman (ed.), *Proceedings of the Architectural Psychology Conference at Kingston Polytechnic*. London: RIBA Publications and Kingston Polytechnic.

Acorn, D. A., Hamilton, D. L. and Sherman, S. J. (1988). 'Generalisation of biased perceptions of groups based on illusory correlations'. *Social Cognition*, **6**, 345–72.

Adair, J., Dushenko, T. W. and Lindsay, R. C. L. (1985). 'Ethical regulations and their impact on research practice'. *American Psychologist*, **40**, 59–72.

Adams, J. (1965). 'Inequity in social exchange' in L. Berkowitz (ed.), *Advances in Experimental Social Psychology* (vol. 2, pp. 267–99). New York: Academic Press.

Adorno, T. W., Frenkel-Brunswik, E. Levinson, D. J. and Sanford, R. M. (1950). *The Authoritarian Personality*. New York: Harper.

Ahlstrom, W. and Havighurst, R. (1971). *400 Losers: Delinquent Boys in High School*. San Francisco, CA: Jossey-Bass.

Ahrons, C. and Rodgers, R. (1987). *Divorced Families*. New York: Norton.

Aiello, J. R. and Jones, S. E. (1971). 'Field study of the proxemic behaviour of young children in three subcultural groups'. *Journal of Personality and Social Psychology*, 19, 351–56.

Ajzen, I. (1989). 'Attitude structure and behaviour' in A. R. Pratkanis, S. J. Breckler and A. G. Greenwald, (eds). *Attitude Structure and Function* (pp. 241–74). Hillsdale, NJ: Erlbaum.

Ajzen, I. and Fishbein, M. (1980). *Understanding Attitudes and Predicting Social Behaviour*. Englewood Cliffs, NJ: Prentice Hall.

Ajzen, I. and Madden, T. J. (1986). Prediction of goal directed behaviour: attitudes, intentions and perceived behavioural control. *Journal of Experimental Social Psychology*, 22, 453–74.

Albion, M. S. and Faris, P. W. (1979). *Appraising Research on Advertising's Economic Impacts*. Report no. 79–115. Cambridge, MA: Marketing Science Institute.

Alexander, C. N., Zucker, L. G. and Brody, C. L. (1970). 'Experimental expectations and autokinetic experiences: consistency theories and judgemental convergence'. *Sociometry*, 33, 108–22.

Allen, V. L. (1965). 'Situational factors in conformity' in L. Berkowitz (ed.), *Advances in Experimental Social Psychology* (vol. 2, pp. 133–75). New York: Academic Press.

Allen, V. L. (1975). 'Social support for non-conformity' in L. Berkowitz (ed.), *Advances in Experimental Social Psychology* (vol. 8, pp. 1–43). New York: Academic Press.

Allen, V. L. and Levine, J. M. (1971). 'Social support and conformity: the role of independent assessment of reality'. *Journal of Experimental Social Psychology*, 7, 48–58.

Allen, V. L. and Wilder, D. A. (1975). 'Categorisation, belief similarity, and group similarity'. *Journal of Personality of Social Psychology*, 32, 971–77.

Alloy, L. B. and Tabachnik, N. (1984). 'Assessment of covariation by humans and animals: the joint influence of prior expectations and current situational information'. *Psychological Review*, 91, 112–49.

Allport, F. H. (1920). 'The influence of the group upon association and thought'. *Journal of Experimental Psychology*, 3, 159–82.

Allport, F. H. (1924). *Social Psychology*. Boston, MA: Houghton-Mifflin.

Allport, G. W. (1935). 'Attitudes' in C. M. Murchison (ed.), *Handbook of Social Psychology* (pp. 789–844). Worchester, MA: Clark University Press.

Allport, G. W. (1954). *The Nature of Prejudice*. Reading, MA: Addison-Wesley.

Allport, G. W. (1968). 'The historical background of modern social psychology' in G. Lindzey and E. Aronson (eds), *Handbook of Social Psychology* (2nd edn, vol. 1, pp. 1–80). Reading, MA: Addison-Wesley.

Allport, G. W. and Postman, L. J. (1945). 'Psychology of rumour'. *Transactions of the New York Academy of Sciences*, 8, 61–81.

Allport, G. W. and Vernon, P. E. (1931). *A Study of Values*. Boston: Houghton-Mifflin.

Allyn, J. and Festinger, L. (1961). 'The effectiveness of unanticipated persuasive communications'. *Journal of Abnormal and Social Psychology*, 62, 35–40.

Altman, D. (1986). *AIDS and the New Puritanism*. London and Sydney: Pluto Press.

Altman, I. (1975). *The Environment and Social Behaviour*. Monterey, CA: Brooks/Cole.

Altman, I. and Chemers, M. (1980). *Culture and Environment*. Monterey, CA: Brooks/Cole.

Altman, I., Nelson, P. A. and Lett, E. E. (1972). *The Ecology of Home Environments. Catalogue of Selected Documents in Psychology*. Washington, DC: American Psychological Association.

Amato, P. R. (1983). 'Helping behaviour in urban and rural environments: field studies based on a taxonomic organisation of helping episodes'. *Journal of Personality and Social Psychology*, 45, 571–86.

Amato, P. R. and McInness, I. R. (1983). 'Affiliative behaviour in diverse environments: a consideration of pleasantness, information rate, and the arousal-eliciting quality of settings'. *Basic and Applied Social Psychology*, 4, 109–22.

American Psychological Association (1982). *Ethical Principles in the Conduct of Research with Human Participants*. Washington, DC: American Psychological Association.

Amir, Y. (1976). 'The role of intergroup contact in change of prejudice and ethnic relations' in P. A. Katz (ed.), *Towards the Elimination of Racism* (pp. 245–308). Elmsford, NY: Pergamon Press.

Andelman, D. L. (1980). '10 reported killed after inmates seize New Mexico prison'. *The New York Times*, 3 February.

Anderson, C. A. and Anderson, D. C. (1984). 'Ambient temperature and violent crime: tests of the linear and curvilinear hypothesis'. *Journal of Personality and Social Psychology*, 46, 91–97.

Anderson, C. A. and Slusher. M. P. (1986). 'Relocating motivational effects: a synthesis of cognitive and motivational effects on attributions for success and failure'. *Social Cognition*, 4, 250–92.

Anderson, J. and McGuire, W. J. (1965). 'Prior reassurance of group consensus as a factor in producing resistance to persuasion'. *Sociometry*, 28, 44–56.

Anderson, J. R. (1990). *Cognitive Psychology and Its Implications* (3rd edn). New York: Freeman.

Anderson, N. H. (1965). 'Adding versus averaging as a stimulus combination rule in impression formation'. *Journal of Experimental Psychology*, 70, 394–400.

Anderson, N. H. (1971). 'Integration theory and attitude change'. *Psychological Review*, 78, 171–206.

Anderson, N. H. (1978). 'Cognitive algebra: integration theory applied to social attribution' in L. Berkowitz (ed.), *Cognitive Theories in Social Psychology* (pp. 1–126). New York: Academic Press.

Anderson, N. H. (1980). 'Integration theory applied to cognitive responses and attitudes' in R. E. Petty, T. M. Ostrom and T. C. Brock (eds), *Cognitive Responses in Persuasion*. New York: Erlbaum.

Anderson, N. H. (1981). *Foundations of Information Integration Theory*. New York: Academic Press.

Andreeva, G. (1984). 'Cognitive processes in developing groups' in L. H. Strickland (ed.), *Directions in Soviet Social Psychology* (pp. 67–82). New York: Springer-Verlag.

Apfelbaum, E. (1974). 'On conflicts and bargaining'. *Advances in Experimental Social Psychology*, 7, 103–56.

Apfelbaum, E. and Lubek, I. (1976). 'Resolution vs. revolution? The theory of conflicts in question' in L. Strickland, F. Aboud and K. J. Gergen (eds), *Social Psychology in Transition* (pp. 71–94). New York: Plenum.

Apfelbaum, E. and McGuire, G. R. (1986). 'Models of suggestive influence and the disqualification of the social crowd' in C. F. Graumann and S. Moscovici (eds), *Changing Conceptions of Crowd Mind and Behaviour* (pp. 27–50). New York: Springer-Verlag.

Appleyard, D. and Lintell, M. (1972). 'The environmental quality of city streets: the residents' viewpoint'. *Journal of the American Institute of Planners*, 38, 84–101.

Archea, J. (1977). 'The place of architectural factors in behavioral theories of privacy'. *Journal of Social Issues*, 33, 116–38.

Archer, D., Iritani, B., Kimes, D. D. and Barrios, M. (1983). 'Face-ism: five studies of sex differences in facial prominence'. *Journal of Personality and Social Psychology*, 45, 725–35.

Ardrey, R. (1961). *African Genesis*. New York: Delta Books.

Ardrey, R. (1966). *The Territorial Imperative*. New York: Atheneum.

Arendt, H. (1963). *Eichmann in Jerusalem: A Report on the Banality of Evil*. New York: Viking.

Argyle, M. (1971). *The Psychology of Interpersonal Behaviour*. Harmondsworth: Penguin.

Argyle, M. (1975). *Bodily Communication*. London: Methuen.

Argyle, M. (1980). 'The development of applied social psychology' in R. Gilmour and S. Duck (eds), *The Development of Social Psychology*. New York: Academic Press.

Argyle, M. (1988). *Bodily Communication* (2nd edn). London: Methuen.

Argyle, M. and Dean, J. (1965). 'Eye-contact, distance and affiliation'. *Sociometry*, 28, 289–304.

Argyle, M. and Henderson, M. (1985). *The Anatomy of Relationships*. London: Heinemann and Harmondsworth: Penguin.

Argyle, M. and Ingham, R. (1972). 'Gaze, mutual gaze, and proximity'. *Semiotica*, 6, 32–49.

Argyle, M. and Little, B. R. (1972). 'Do personality traits apply to social behaviour?' in N. S. Endler and D. Magnusson (eds), *Interactional Psychology and Personality*. New York: Wiley.

Argyris, C. (1975). 'Dangers in applying results from experimental social psychology'. *American Psychologist*, 12, 8–12.

Arkes, H. R., Boehm, L. E. and Xu, G. (1991). 'Determinants of judged validity'. *Journal of Experimental Social Psychology*, 27, 576–605.

Aronson, E. (1984). *The Social Animal* (4th edn). New York: Freeman.

Aronson, E. and Linder, D. (1965). 'Gain and loss of esteem as determinants of interpersonal attractiveness'. *Journal of Experimental Social Psychology*, 1, 156–71.

Aronson, E. and Mills, J. (1959). 'The effects of severity of initiation on liking for a group'. *Journal of Abnormal and Social Psychology*, 59, 177–81.

Aronson, E., Ellsworth, P. C., Carlsmith, J. M. and Gonzales, M. H. (1990). *Methods of Research in Social Psychology* (2nd edn). New York: McGraw-Hill.

Asch, S. E. (1946). 'Forming impressions of personality'. *Journal of Abnormal and Social Psychology*, 41, 258–90.

Asch, S. E. (1951). 'Effects of group pressure upon the modification and distortion of judgements', in H. Guetzkow (ed.), *Groups. Leadership and Men* (pp. 177–90). Pittsburg, PA: Carnegie Press.

Asch, S. E. (1952). *Social Psychology*. Englewood Cliffs, NJ: Prentice Hall.

Asch, S. E. (1956). 'Studies of independence and conformity: a minority of one against a unanimous majority'. *Psychological Monographs: General and Applied*, 70, 1–70 (whole no. 416)

Aschenbrenner, K. M. and Schaefer, R. E. (1980). 'Minimal group situations: comments on a mathematical model and on the research paradigm'. *European Journal of Social Psychology*, 10, 389–98.

Ashmore, R. D. (1981). 'Sex stereotypes and implicit personality theory' in D. L. Hamilton (ed.), *Cognitive Processes in Stereotyping and Intergroup Behaviour* (pp. 37–81). Hillsdale, NJ: Erlbaum.

Assael, H. (1981). *Consumer Behaviour and Marketing Action*. Boston: Kent.

Atkin, C. K. (1977). 'Effects of campaign advertising and newscasts on children'. *Journalism Quarterly*, 54, 503–508.

Atkin, C. K. (1980). *Effects of the Mass Media*. New York: McGraw-Hill.

Augoustinos, M. (1991). 'Consensual representations of social structure in different age groups'. *British Journal of Social Psychology*, 30, 193–205.

Augoustinos, M. and Innes, J. M. (1990). 'Towards and integration of social representations and social schema theory'. *British Journal of Social Psychology*, 29, 213–31.

Austin, J. L. (1962). *How to Do Things with Words*. Oxford: Clarendon Press.

Austin, W. (1979). 'Sex differences in bystander intervention in a theft'. *Journal of Personality and Social Psychology*, 37, 2110–20.

Averill, J. R. and Boothroyd, P. (1977). 'On falling in love in conformance with the romantic ideal'. *Motivation and Emotion*, 1, 235–47.

Axelrod, R. and Dion, D. (1988). 'The further evolution of cooperation'. *Science*, 242, 1385–90.

Bailey, K. G. Hartnett, J. J. and Gibson, S. W. (1972). 'Implied threat and the territorial factor in personal space'. *Psychological Reports*, 30, 263–70.

Bains, G. (1983). 'Explanations and the need for control' in M. Hewstone (ed.), *Attribution Theory: Social and Functional Extensions* (pp. 126–43). Oxford: Blackwell.

Bakan, D. (1966). *The Duality of Human Existence*. Chicago, IL: Rand McNally.

Baker, P. M. (1985). 'The status of age: preliminary result'. *Journal of Gerontology*, 40, 506–08.

Baldwin, J. M. (1897). *Social and Ethical Interpretations in Mental Development*. New York: Macmillan.

Bales, R. F. (1950). *Interaction Process Analysis: A Method for the Study of Small Groups*. Reading, MA: Addison-Wesley.

Bandura, A. (1973). *Aggression: A Social Learning Analysis*. Englewood Cliffs, NJ: Prentice Hall.

Bandura, A. (1977). *Social Learning Theory*. Englewood Cliffs, NJ: Prentice Hall.

Bandura, A. (1986). *Social Foundations of Thought and Action: A Social Cognitive Theory*. Englewood Cliffs, NJ: Prentice Hall.

Bandura, A. and Walters, R. H. (1963). *Social Learning and Personality Development*. New York: Holt, Rinehart and Winston.

Bandura, A. Ross, D. and Ross, S. A. (1963). 'Imitation of film-mediated aggressive models'. *Journal of Abnormal and Social Psychology*, **66**, 3–11.

Banuazizi, A. and Movahedi, S. (1975). 'Interpersonal dynamics in a simulated prison: a methodological analysis'. *American Psychologist*, **30**, 152–60.

Barash, D. P. (1977). *Sociobiology of Behaviour*. New York: Elsevier.

Bargh, J. A. (1984). 'Automatic and conscious processing of social information' in R. S. Wyer, Jr and T. K. Srull (eds), *Handbook of Social Cognition* (vol. 3, pp. 1–44). Hillsdale, NJ: Erlbaum.

Bargh, J. A. and Pratto, F. (1986). 'Individual construct accessibility and perceptual selection'. *Journal of Experimental Social Psychology*, **22**, 293–311.

Bargh, J. A. and Tota, M. E. (1988). 'Context-dependent automatic processing in depression: accessibility of negative constructs with regard to self but not others'. *Journal of Personality and Social Psychology*, **54**, 925–39.

Bargh, J. A., Lombardi, W. J. and Higgins, E. T. (1988). 'Automaticity of chronically accessible constructs in person X situation effects on person perception: it's just a matter of time'. *Journal of Personality and Social Psychology*, **55**, 599–605.

Bar-Hillel, M. (1980). 'The base-rate fallacy in probability judgements'. *Acta Psychologica*, **44**, 211–33.

Barjonet, P. E. (1980). 'L'influence sociale et des représentations des causes de l'accident de la route' . *Le Travail Humain*, **43**, 243–53.

Barker, (1965). 'Explorations in ecological psychology'. *American Psychologist*, **20**, 1–14.

Barney, W. D. (1973). 'TV viewing habits of 3-, 4- and 5-year old children'. *The New Zealand Psychologist*, **2**, 15–27.

Barocas, R. and Gorlow, L. (1967). 'Self-report personality measurement and conformity behaviour'. *Journal of Social Psychology*, **71**, 227–34.

Baron, R. A. (1977). *Human Aggression*. New York: Plenum.

Baron, R. A. (1979). 'Aggression, empathy, and race: effects of victim's pain cues, victim's race, and level of instigation on physical aggression'. *Journal of Applied Social Psychology*, **9**, 103–14.

Baron, R. A. (1989). 'Personality and organisational conflict: the Type A behaviour pattern and self-monitoring'. *Organisational Behaviour and Human Decision Processes*, **44**, 281–97.

Baron, R. A. and Bell, P. (1977). 'Sexual arousal and aggression by males: effects of types of erotic stimuli and prior provocation'. *Journal of Personality and Social Psychology*, **35**, 79–87.

Baron, R. A. and Byrne, D. (1987) *Social Psychology: Understanding Human Interaction* (5th edn). Boston: Allyn and Bacon.

Baron, R. A. and Byrne, D. (1991). *Social Psychology: Understanding Human Interaction* (6th edn). Boston: Allyn and Bacon.

Baron, R. A. and Ransberger, V. M. (1978). 'Ambient temperature and the occurrence of collective violence: the "long hot summer" revisited'. *Journal of Personality and Social Psychology*, **36**, 351–60.

Baron, R. A. and Richardson, D. R. (1991). *Human Aggression* (2nd edn). New York: Plenum.

Baron, R. M. and Rodin, J. (1978). 'Personal control as a mediator of crowding' in A. Baum, J. E. Singer and S. Valins (eds), *Advances in Environmental Psychology* (vol. 1). Hillsdale, NJ: Erlbaum.

Baron, R. S. (1986). 'Distraction–conflict theory: progress and problems' in L. Berkowitz (ed.), *Advances in Experimental Social Psychology* (vol. 20, pp. 1–40). New York: Academic Press.

Baron, R. S. and Roper, G. (1976). 'Reaffirmation of social comparison views of choice shifts: averaging and extremity effects in an autokinetic situation'. *Journal of Personality and Social Psychology*, **33**, 521–30.

Baron, R. S., Kerr, N. L. and Miller, N. (1992). *Group Process, Group Decision, Group Action.* Buckingham: Open University Press.

Barron, F. (1953). 'Some personality correlates of independence of judgement'. *Journal of Personality*, 21, 287–97.

Bar-Tal, D. (1976). *Prosocial Behaviour: Theory and Research.* Washington, DC: Hemisphere Press.

Bartlett, F. C. (1932). *Remembering.* Cambridge: Cambridge University Press.

Bartol, K. M. and Butterfield, D. A. (1976). 'Sex effects in evaluating leaders'. *Journal of Applied Psychology*, 61, 446–54.

Bates, A. (1964). 'Privacy – a useful concept?' *Social Forces*, 42, 432.

Batson, C. D. (1983). 'Sociobiology and the role of religion in promoting prosocial behaviour: an alternative view'. *Journal of Personality and Social Psychology*, 45, 1380–85.

Batson, C. D. and Coke, J. S. (1981). 'Empathy: a source of altruistic motivation for helping?' in J. P. Rushton and R. M. Sorrentino (eds), *Altruism and Helping Behaviour: Social, Personality, and Developmental Perspectives*, Hillsdale, NJ: Erlbaum.

Batson, C. D., Cochran, P. J., Biederman, M. F., Blosser, J. L., Ryan, M. J. & Vogt, B. (1978). 'Failure to help when in a hurry: Callousness or conflict?' *Journal of Personality and Social Psychology Bulletin*, 4, 97–101.

Batson, C. D., Duncan, B., Ackerman, P., Buckley, T. and Birch, K. (1981). 'Is empathic emotion a source of altruistic motivation?' *Journal of Personality and Social Psychology*, 40, 290–302.

Battisch, V. A., Assor, A., Messe, L. A. and Aronoff, J. (1985). 'Personality and person perception' in P. Shaver (ed.), *Review of Personality and Social Psychology* (vol. 6, pp. 185–208). Beverly Hills, CA: Sage.

Baum, A. and Davis, G. E. (1980). 'Reducing the stress of high-density living: an architectural intervention'. *Journal of Personality and Social Psychology*, 38, 471–81.

Baum, A. and Greenberg, C. I. (1975). 'Waiting for a crowd: the behavioral and perceptual effects of anticipated crowding'. *Journal of Personality and Social Psychology*, 32, 671–79.

Baum, A. and Valins, S. (1977). *Architecture and Social Behaviour: Psychological Studies of Social Density.* Hillsdale, NJ: Erlbaum.

Baum, A. and Valins, S. (1979). 'Architectural mediation of residential density and control: crowding and the regulation of social contact' in L. Berkowitz (ed.), *Advances in Experimental Social Psychology* (vol. 12, pp. 132–75). New York: Academic Press.

Baum, A., Singer, J. E. and Baum, C. S. (1981a). 'Stress and the environment'. *Journal of Social Issues*, 37, 4–35.

Baum, A., Fisher, J. D. and Solomon, S. K. (1981b). 'Type of information, familiarity, and the reduction of crowding stress'. *Journal of Personality and Social Psychology*, 40, 11–23.

Baumeister, R. F. and Covington, M. V. (1985). 'Self-esteem, persuasion, and retrospective distortion of initial attitudes'. *Electronic Social Psychology*, 1, 1–22.

Baumeister, R. F. and Darley, J. M. (1982). 'Reducing the biasing effect of perpetrator attractiveness in jury simulation'. *Personality and Social Psychology Bulletin*, 8, 286–92.

Baumeister, R. F., Chesner, S. P. Senders, P. S. and Tice, D. M. (1988). 'Who's in charge here? Group leaders do lend help in emergencies'. *Personality and Social Psychology Bulletin*, 14, 17–22.

Baumgarten-Tramer, F. (1948). 'German psychologists and recent events'. *Journal of Abnormal and Social Psychology*, 43, 452–65.

Baumrind, D. (1964). 'Some thoughts on ethics of research: after reading Milgram's "Behavioral study of obedience"'. *American Psychologist*, 19, 421–23.

Bavelas, A. (1968). 'Communications patterns in task-oriented groups' in D. Cartwright and A. Zander (eds), *Group Dynamics: Research and Theory* (3rd edn, pp. 503–11). London: Tavistock.

Baxter, J. C. (1970). 'Interpersonal spacing in natural settings'. *Sociometry*, 33, 444–56.

Baxter, T. L. and Goldberg, L. R. (1988). 'Perceived behavioral consistency underlying trait attributions to oneself and another: an extension of the actor–observer effect'. *Personality and Social Psychology Bulletin*, 13, 437–47.

Beattie, A. E. and Mitchell, A. A. (1985). 'The relationship between advertising recall and persuasion: an experimental investigation' in L. F. Alwitt and A. A. Mitchell (eds), *Psychological Processes and Advertising Effects: Theory, Research and applications*. Hillsdale, NJ: Erlbaum.

Beauvois, J. L. and Dubois, N. (1988). 'The norm of internality in the explanation of psychological events'. *European Journal of Social Psychology*, 18, 299–316.

Bechtel, R. (1977). *Enclosing Behaviour*. Stroudsbourg, PA: Dowden, Hutchinson & Ross.

Beck, L. and Ajzen, I. (1991). 'Predicting dishonest actions using the theory of planned behaviour'. *Journal of Research in Personality*, 25, 285–301.

Bell, L. G., Wicklund, R. A., Manko, G. and Larkin, C. (1976). 'When unexpected behaviour is attributed to the environment'. *Journal of Research in Personality*, 10, 316–27.

Bell, P. A. and Baron, R. A. (1974). 'Environmental influences on attraction: effects of heat, attitude similarity, and personal evaluations'. *Bulletin of the Psychonomic Society*, 4, 479–81.

Bem, D. J. (1967). 'Self perception: an alternative interpretation of cognitive dissonance'. *Psychological Review*, 74, 183–200.

Bem, D. J. (1972). 'Self-perception theory' in L. Berkowitz (ed.), *Advances in Experimental Social Psychology* (vol. 6, pp. 1–62). New York: Academic Press.

Bem, D. J. and Allen, A. A. (1974). 'On predicting some of the people some of the time: the search for cross-situational consistencies in behavior'. *Psychological Review*, 81, 506–20.

Bem, D. J. and McConnell, H. K. (1970). 'Testing the self-perception explanation of dissonance phenomena: on the salience of premanipulation attitudes'. *Journal of Personality and Social Psychology*, 14, 23–31.

Bem, S. L. (1981). 'Gender schema theory: a cognitive account of sex-typing'. *Psychological Review*, 88, 354–64.

Bennett, C. (1977). *Spaces for People: Human Factors in Design*. Englewood Cliffs, NJ: Prentice Hall.

Bennett, E. B. (1955). 'Discussion, decision, commitment and consensus in group decision'. *Human Relations*, 8, 25–73.

Benson, P. L., Karabenick, S. A. and Lerner, R. M. (1976). 'Pretty pleases: the effects of physical attractiveness, race, and sex on receiving help'. *Journal of Experimental Social Psychology*, 12, 409–15.

Benton, A. A. and Druckman, D. (1974). 'Constituent's bargaining orientation and intergroup negotiations'. *Journal of Applied Social Psychology*, 4, 141–50.

Beranek, L. L. (1966). 'Noise'. *Scientific American*, 215, 66–76.

Berger, J., Fisek, M. H., Norman, R. Z. and Zelditch, M., Jr (1977). *Status Characteristics and Social Interaction*. New York: Elsevier.

Berglas, S. (1987). 'The self-handicapping model of alcohol abuse' in H. T. Blane and K. E. Leonard (eds), *Psychological Theories of Drinking and Alcoholism* (pp. 305–45). New York: Guilford Press.

Berglas, S. and Jones, E. E. (1978). 'Drug choice as a self-handicapping strategy in response to noncontingent success'. *Journal of Personality and Social Psychology*, 36, 405–17.

Berkowitz, L. (1962). *Aggression: A Social Psychological Analysis*. New York: McGraw-Hill.

Berkowitz, L. (1970). 'The self, selfishness and altruism' in J. Macaulay and L. Berkowitz (eds), *Altruism and Helping Behaviour*. New York: Academic Press.

Berkowitz, L. (1972a). 'Frustrations, comparisons, and other sources of emotion arousal as contributors to social unrest'. *Journal of Social Issues*, 28, 77–91.

Berkowitz, L. (1972b). 'Social norms, feelings, and other factors affecting helping and altruism' in L. Berkowitz (ed.), *Advances in Experimental Social Psychology* (vol. 6, pp. 63–108). New York: Academic Press.

Berkowitz, L. (1974). 'Some determinants of impulsive aggression: role of mediated associations with reinforcements for aggression'. *Psychological Review*, 81, 165–76.

Berkowitz, L. (1978). 'Decreased helpfulness with increased group size through lessening the effects of the needy individual's dependency'. *Journal of Personality*, 46, 299–310.

Berkowitz, L. (1984). 'Some effects of thoughts on anti- and pro-social influences of media events: a cognitive-neoassociation analysis'. *Psychological Bulletin*, 95, 410–27.

Berry, J. W. (1967). 'Independence and conformity in subsistence level societies'. *Journal of Personality and Social Psychology*, 7, 415–18.

Berry, J. W. (1984). 'Cultural relations in plural societies: alternatives to segregation and their sociopsychological implications' in N. Miller and M. B. Brewer (eds), *Groups in Contact: The Psychology of Desegregation* (pp. 11–27). New York: Academic Press.

Berscheid, E. (1985). 'Interpersonal attraction' in G. Lindzey and E. Aronson (eds), *Handbook of Social Psychology* (3rd edn, vol. 2, pp. 413–84). New York: Random House.

Berscheid, E. and Walster, E. H. (1978). *Interpersonal Attraction* (2nd edn). Reading, MA: Addison-Wesley.

Berscheid, E., Graziano, W., Monson, T and Dermer, M. (1976). 'Outcome dependency: attention, attribution, and attraction'. *Journal of Personality and Social Psychology*, 34, 978–89.

Bexton, W. H., Heron, W. and Scott, T. H. (1954). 'Effects of decreased variation in the sensory environment'. *Canadian Journal of Psychology*, 8, 70–76.

Bickman, L. and Green, S. K. (1977). 'Situational cues and crime reporting: do signs make a difference?' *Journal of Applied Social Psychology*, 7, 1–8.

Bickman, L. and Rosenbaum, D. P. (1977). 'Crime reporting as a function of bystander encouragement, surveillance, and credibility'. *Journal of Personality and Social Psychology*, 35, 577–86.

Bierhoff, H. W. (1988). 'Affect, cognition, and prosocial behaviour' in K. Fiedler and J. Forgas (eds), *Affect, Cognition, and Social Behaviour* (pp. 167–82). Toronto: Hogrefe.

Billig, M. (1973). 'Normative communication in a minimal intergroup situation'. *European Journal of Social Psychology*, 3, 339–43.

Billig, M. (1976). *Social Psychology and Intergroup Relations*. London: Academic Press.

Billig, M. (1978). *Fascists: A Social Psychological View of the National Front*. London: Harcourt Brace Jovanovich.

Billig, M. (1987). *Arguing and Thinking: A Rhetorical Approach to Social Psychology*. Cambridge: Cambridge University Press.

Billig, M. (1991). *Ideology and Opinions: Studies in Rhetorical Psychology*. London: Sage.

Billig, M. and Cochrane, R. (1979). 'Values of political extremists and potential extremists: a discriminant analysis' *European Journal of Social Psychology*, 9, 205–22.

Billig, M. and Tajfel, H. (1973). 'Social categorisation and similarity in intergroup behaviour'. *European Journal of Social Psychology*, 3, 27–52.

Bilous, F. R; and Krauss, R. M. (1988). 'Dominance and accommodation in the conversational behaviours of same- and mixed-gender dyads'. *Language and Communication*, 8, 183–94.

Birdwhistell, R. (1970). *Kinesics and Context: Essays on Body Movement Communication*. Philadelphia, PA: University of Pennsylvania Press.

Blake, R. R. and Mouton, J. S. (1961). 'Reactions to intergroup competition under win/lose conditions'. *Management Science*, 7, 420–35.

Blake, R. R., Shepard, H. A. and Mouton, J. S. (1964). *Managing Intergroup Conflict in industry*. Texas: Gulf Publishing Co.

Bloom, L. (1970). *Language Development: Form and Function in Emerging Grammars*. Cambridge, MA: MIT Press.

Bochner, S. (1982). 'The social psychology of cross-cultural relations' in S. Bochner (ed,), *Cultures in Contact: Studies in Cross-Cultural Interaction*. Oxford: Pergamon.

Bochner, S. and Insko, C. A. (1966). 'Communicator discrepancy, source credibility, and opinion change'. *Journal of Personality and Social Psychology*, 4, 614–21.

Bodenhausen, G. V. and Lichtenstein, M. (1987). 'Social stereotypes and information-processing strategies: the impact of task complexity'. *Journal of Personality and Social Psychology*, 52, 871–80.

Bogardus, E. S. (1925). 'Measuring social distances'. *Journal of Applied Sociology*, 9, 299–308.

Boggs, S. D. H. and Simon, J. R. (1968). 'Differential effects of noise on tasks of varying complexity'. *Journal of Applied Psychology*, 52, 148–53.

Bohner, G., Bless, H., Schwarz N. and Strack, F. (1988). 'What triggers causal attributions? The impact of valence and subjective probability'. *European Journal of Social Psychology*, 18, 335–45.

Bond, C. F., Jr (1982). 'Social facilitation: a self-presentational view'. *Journal of Personality and Social Psychology*, 42, 1042–50.

Bond, C. F., Jr and Titus, L. J. (1983). 'Social facilitation: a meta-analysis of 241 studies'. *Psychological Bulletin*, 94, 265–92.

Bond, M. H. and King, A. Y. C. (1985). 'Coping with the threat of westernisation in Hong Kong' *International Journal of Intercultural Relations*, 9, 351–64.

Borden, R. J. (1980). 'Audience influence' in P. B. Paulus (ed.), *Psychology of Group Influence* (pp. 99–131). Hillsdale, NJ: Erlbaum.

Bornstein, G., Crum, L., Wittenbraker, J., Harring, K., Insko, C. A. and Thibaut, J. (1983). 'On the measurement of social orientations in the minimal group paradigm'. *European Journal of Social Psychology*, 13, 321–50.

Bossard, J. H. S. and Boll, E. S. (1950). *Ritual in Family Living*. Philadelphia: University of Pennsylvania Press.

Bothwell, R. K., Brigham, J. C. and Malpass, R. S. (1989). 'Cross-racial identification'. *Personality and Social Psychology Bulletin*, 15, 19–25.

Bourhis, R. Y. (1984). *Conflict and Language Planning in Quebec*. Clevedon: Multilingual Matters.

Bourhis, R. Y. and Giles, H. (1977.). 'The language of intergroup distinctiveness' in H. Giles (ed.), *Language, Ethnicity and Intergroup Relations* (pp. 119–35). London: Academic Press.

Bourhis, R. Y., Giles, H. and Lambert, W. E. (1975). 'Social consequences of accommodation one's style of speech: a cross-national investigation' *International Journal of the Sociology of Language*, 6, 55–72.

Bourhis, R. Y., Giles, H., Leyens, J-P. and Tajfel, H. (1979). 'Psycholinguistic distinctiveness: language divergence in Belgium' in H. Giles and R. St Clair (eds), *Language and Social Psychology* (pp. 158–85). Oxford: Blackwell.

Bourhis, R. Y., Giles, H. and Rosenthal, D. (1981). 'Notes on the construction of a 'Subjective Vitality Questionnaire' for ethnolinguistic groups'. *Journal of Multilingual and Multicultural Development*, 2, 144–55.

Bowlby, J. (1969). *Attachment and Loss. Volume 1: Attachment*. London: Hogarth.

Bowlby, J. (1988). *A Secure Base: Parent–Child Attachment and Healthy Human Development*. New York: Basic Books.

Bowman, C. H. and Fishbein, M. (1978). 'Understanding public reaction to energy proposals: an application of the Fishbein model'. *Journal of Applied Social Psychology*, 8, 319–40.

Bradbury, J. (1984). 'Violent offending and drinking patterns' *Institute of Criminology Monograph*. Victoria University of Wellington, Wellington.

Branthwaite, A., Doyle, S. and Lightbown, N. (1979). 'The balance between fairness and discrimination'. *European Journal of Social Psychology*, 2, 149–63.

Bray, R. M. and Noble, A. M. (1978). 'Authoritarianism and decisions of mock juries: evidence of jury bias and group polarisation'. *Journal of Personality and Social Psychology*, 36, 1424–30.

Breakwell, G. M. and Canter, D. V. (eds) (1993). *Empirical Approaches to Social Representations*. Oxford: Clarendon Press.

Breaugh, J. A. and Klimoski, R. J. (1981). 'Social forces in negotiation simulations'. *Personality and Social Psychology Bulletin*, 7, 290–95.

Breckler, S. J. (1984). 'Empirical validation of affect, behaviour, and cognition as distinct components of attitude'. *Journal of Personality and Social Psychology*, 47, 1191–1205.

Breckler, S. J. and Wiggins, E. C. (1989a). 'On defining attitude and attitude theory: once more with feeling' in A. R. Pratkanis, S. J. Breckler and A. G. Greenwald (eds). *Attitude Structure and Function* (pp. 407–27). Hillsdale, NJ: Erlbaum.

Breckler, S. J. and Wiggins, E. C. (1989b). 'Affect versus evaluation in the structure of attitudes'. *Journal of Experimental Social Psychology*, 25, 253–71.

Breckler, S. J., Pratkanis, A. R. and McCann, C. D. (1991). 'The representation of self in multidimensional cognitive space'. *British Journal of Social Psychology*, 30, 97–112.

Brehm, J. W. (1966). *A Theory of Psychological Reactance*. New York: Academic Press.

Brewer, M. B. (1968). 'Determinants of social distance among East African tribal groups'. *Journal of Personality and Social Psychology*, 10, 279–89.

Brewer, M. B. (1988). 'A dual process model of impression formation' in T. K. Srull and R. S. Wyer (eds), *Advances in Social Cognition: A Dual Process Model of Impression Formation* (vol. 1, pp. 1–36). Hillsdale, NJ: Erlbaum.

Brewer, M. B. (1991). 'The social-self: on being the same and different at the same time'. *Personality and Social Psychology Bulletin*, 17, 475–82.

Brewer, M. B. (1993). 'The role of distinctiveness in social identity and group behaviour' in M. A. Hogg and D. Abrams (eds), *Group Motivation: Social Psychological Perspectives* (pp. 1–16). London: Harvester Wheatsheaf.

Brewer, M. B. and Campbell, D. T. (1976). *Ethnocentrism and Intergroup Attitudes: East African Evidence*. New York: Sage.

Brewer, M. B. and Kramer, R. M. (1985). 'The psychology of intergroup attitudes and behavior'. *Annual Review of Psychology*, 36, 219–43.

Brewer, M. B. and Kramer, R. M. (1986). 'Choice behaviour in social dilemmas: effects of social identity, group size, and decision framing'. *Journal of Personality and Social Psychology*, 50, 543–49.

Brewer, M. B. and Lui, L. L. (1989). 'The primacy of age and sex in the structure of person categories'. *Social Cognition*, 7, 262–74.

Brewer, M. B. and Schneider, S. (1990). 'Social identity and social dilemmas: a double-edged sword' in D. Abrams and M. A. Hogg (eds), *Social Identity Theory: Constructive and Critical Advances* (pp. 169–84). London: Harvester Wheatsheaf.

Brewer, M. B., Dull, V. and Lui, L. (1981). 'Perceptions of the elderly: stereotypes as prototypes'. *Journal of Personality and Social Psychology*, 41, 656–70.

Brickner, M. A., Harkins, S. G. and Ostrom, T. M. (1986). 'Effects of personal involvement: thought-provoking implications of social loafing'. *Journal of Personality and Social Psychology*, 51, 763–70.

Bridgman, G. (1992). *Looking Back on a Decade of Television Violence: Media Watch 1992*. Auckland: Mental Health Foundation of New Zealand.

Brigham, J. C. (1971). 'Ethnic stereotypes'. *Psychological Bulletin*, 76, 15–38.

Brigham, J. C. (1991). *Social Psychology*. New York: Harper Collins.

Brigham, J. C. and Barkowitz, P. B. (1978). 'Do "they all look alike"?' The effect of race, sex, experience and attitudes on the ability to recognise face'. *Journal of Applied Social Psychology*, 8, 306–18.

Brigham, J. C. and Malpass, R. S. (1985). 'The role of experience and contact in the recognition of faces of own- and other-race persons'. *Journal of Social Issues*, 41, 139–56.

Brinthaupt, T. M., Moreland, R. L. and Levine, J. M. (1991). 'Sources of optimism among prospective group members'. *Personality and Social Psychology Bulletin*, 17, 36–43.

Britell, J. K. (1981). 'Ethics courses are making slow inroads'. *New York Times*, Education section, 26 April, p. 44.

Broadbent, D. E. (1979). 'Human performance and noise' in C. M. Harris (ed.), *Handbook of Noise Control*. New York: McGraw-Hill.

Broadbent, D. E. (1985). *Perception and Communication*. London: Pergamon.

Bronzaft, A. L. and McCarthy, D. P. (1975). 'The effects of elevated train noise on reading ability'. *Environment and Behaviour*, 7, 517–27.

Broome, B. J. (1983). 'The attraction paradigm revisited: response to dissimilar others'. *Human Communication Research*, 10, 137–51.

Broussard, I. G. (1979). Cited in D. E. Broadbent, 'Human performance and noise' in C. M. Harris (ed.), *Handbook of Noise Control*. New York: McGraw-Hill.

Broverman, I. L., Broverman, D. M., Clarkson, F. E., Rosencrantz, P. S. and Vogel, S. R. (1970). 'Sex-role stereotypes and clinical judgements of mental health'. *Journal of Consulting Psychology*, 34, 1–17.

Broverman, I. K., Vogel, S. R., Broverman, D. M., Clarkson, F. E. and Rosencrantz, P. S. (1972). 'Sex-role stereotypes: a current appraisal'. *Journal of Social Issues*, 28, 59–78.

Brown, G. W. and Harris, T. (1978). *Social Analysis of Depression*. London: Tavistock.

Brown, P. and Fraser, C. (1979). 'Speech as a marker of situation' in K. R. Scherer and H. Giles (eds), *Social Markers in Speech* (pp. 33–108). Cambridge: Cambridge University Press.

Brown, R. (1965). *Social Psychology*. New York: Free Press.

Brown, R. (1986). *Social Psychology* (2nd edn). New York: Free Press.

Brown, R. and Fish, D. (1983). 'The psychological causality implicit in language'. *Cognition*, 14, 237–73.

Brown, R. J. (1978). 'Divided we fall: an analysis of relations between sections of a factory workforce' in H. Tajfel (ed.), *Differentiation Between Social Groups: Studies in the Social Psychology of Intergroup Relations* (pp. 395–429). London: Academic Press.

Brown, R. J. (1988). *Group Processes: Dynamics Within and Between Groups*. Oxford: Blackwell.

Brown, R. J. and Abrams, D. (1986). 'The effects of intergroup similarity and goal interdependence on intergroup attitudes and task performance'. *Journal of Experimental Social Psychology*, 22, 78–92.

Brown, R. J., Condor, S., Matthews, A., Wade, G. and Williams, J. A. (1986). 'Explaining intergroup differentiation in an industrial organization'. *Journal of Occupational Psychology*, 59, 273–86.

Brown, R. J. and Turner, J. C. (1981). 'Interpersonal and intergroup behaviour' in J. C. Turner and H. Giles (eds), *Intergroup Behaviour* (pp. 33–65). Oxford: Blackwell.

Brown, R. J. and Wade, G. S. (1987). 'Superordinate goals and intergroup behaviour: the effects of role ambiguity and status on intergroup attitudes and task performance'. *European Journal of Social Psychology*, 17, 131–42.

Bruner, J. S. (1957). 'On perceptual readiness'. *Psychological Review*, 64, 123–52.

Bruner, J. S. (1958). 'Social psychology and perception' in E. E. Maccoby, T. M. Newcomb and E. L. Hartley (eds), *Readings in Social Psychology* (3rd edn, pp. 85–94). New York: Henry Holt.

Bruner, J. S. and Goodman, C. C. (1947). 'Value and need as organising factors in perception'. *Journal of Abnormal and Social Psychology*, 42, 33–44.

Bruner, J. S. and Tagiuri, R. (1954). 'The perception of people' in G. Lindzey (ed.), *Handbook of Social Psychology* (pp. 634–54). Reading, MA: Addison-Wesley.

Brunswik, E. (1956). *Perception and the Representative Design of Psychological Experiments* (2nd edn). Berkeley and Los Angeles, CA: University of California Press.

Bryan, J. H. and Test, M. A. (1967). 'Models and helping: naturalistic studies in aiding behavior'. *Journal of Personality and Social Psychology*, 6, 400–07.

Buchanan, P. J. (1987). 'AIDS and moral bankruptcy'. *New York Post*, 2 December, p. 23.

Buckner, H. T. (1965). 'A theory of rumour transmission'. *Public Opinion Quarterly*, 29, 54–70.

Budd, R. J., North, D. and Spencer, C. (1984). 'Understanding seat-belt use: a test of Bentler and Speckart's extension of the "theory of reasoned action"'. *European Journal of Social Psychology*, 14, 69–78.

Bugental, D. E., Love L. R. and Gianetto, R. M. (1971). 'Perfidious feminine faces'. *Journal of Personality and Social Psychology*, 17, 314–18.

Bulman, R. J. and Wortman, C. B. (1977). 'Attributions of blame and coping in the "real world": severe accident victims react to their lot'. *Journal of Personality and Social Psychology*, 35, 351–63.

Bunge, C. (1903). *Principes de Psychologie Individuelle et Sociale*. Paris: Alcan.

Burger, J. M. (1981). 'Motivational biases in the attribution of responsibility for an accident: a meta-analysis of the defensive attribution hypothesis'. *Psychological Bulletin*, 90, 496–513.

Burger, J. M. (1986). 'Increasing compliance by improving the deal: the that's-not-all technique'. *Journal of Personality and Social Psychology*, 51, 277–83.

Burgess, E. W. and Wallin, P. (1953). *Engagement and Marriage*. PA: Lipppencott.

Burgoon, J. K., Buller, D. B. and Woodall, W. G. (1989). *Nonverbal Communication: The Unspoken Dialogue*. New York: Harper & Row.

Burnham, W. H. (1910). 'The group as a stimulus to mental activity'. *Science*, 31, 761–67.

Burnstein, E. and McRae, A. (1962). 'Some effects of shared threat and prejudice in racially mixed groups'. *Journal of Abnormal and Social Psychology*, 64, 257–63.

Burnstein, E. and Vinokur, A. (1977). 'Persuasive argumentation and social comparison as determinants of attitude polarisation'. *Journal of Experimental Social Psychology*, 13, 315–32.

Bushman, B. J. (1984). 'Perceived symbols of authority and their influence on compliance'. *Journal of Applied Social Psychology*, 14, 501–08.

Bushman, B. J. (1988). 'The effects of apparel on compliance: a field experiment with a female authority figure'. *Personality and Social Psychology Bulletin*, 14, 459–67.

Buss, A. H. (1961). *The Psychology of Aggression*. New York: Wiley.

Byrd, R. E. (1938). *Alone*. New York: Putnam.

Byrne, D. (1971). *The Attraction Paradigm*. New York: Academic Press.

Byrne, D. and Clore, G. L. (1970). 'A reinforcement model of evaluative responses'. *Personality: An International Journal*, 1, 103–28

Byrne, D. and Kelley, K. (1981). *An Introduction to Personality* (3rd edn). Englewood Cliffs, NJ: Prentice Hall.

Byrne, D. and Wong, T. J. (1962). 'Racial prejudice, interpersonal attraction, and assumed dissimilarity of attitudes'. *Journal of Abnormal and Social Psychology*, 65, 246–52.

Cacioppo, J. T. and Petty, R. E. (1979). 'Attitudes and cognitive response: an electrophysiological approach'. *Journal of Personality and Social Psychology*, 37, 2181–99.

Cacioppo, J. T. and Petty, R. E. (1981). 'Electromyograms as measures of extent and affectivity of information processing'. *American Psychologist*, 36, 441–56.

Cacioppo, J. T. and Petty, R. E. (1982). 'The need for cognition'. *Journal of Personality and Social Psychology*, 42, 116–31.

Cacioppo, J. T. and Tassinary, L. G. (1990). 'Inferring psychological significance from physiological signals'. *American Psychologist*, 45, 16–28.

Calder, B. J. and Ross, M. (1973). *Attitudes and Behaviour*. Morristown, NJ: General Learning Press.

Calhoun, J. B. (1962). 'Population density and social pathology'. *Scientific American*, 206, 139–48.

Calhoun, J. B. (1971). 'Space and the strategy of life' in A. H. Esser (ed.), *Environment and Behaviour: The Use of Space by Animals and Men*. New York: Plenum.

Calkin, B. (1985). '"Joe Lunch Box": punishment and resistance in prisons'. *Race Gender Class*, 1, 5–16.

Callan, V. J., Gallois, C., Noller, P. and Kashima, Y. (1991). *Social Psychology* (rev. edn). Sydney: Harcourt Brace Jovanovich.

Callaway, M. R. and Esser, J. K. (1984). 'Groupthink: effects of cohesiveness and problem-solving procedures on group decision making'. *Social Behaviour and Personality*, 12, 157–64.

Callaway, M. R., Marriot, R. G. and Esser, J. K. (1985). 'Effects of dominance on group decision making: towards a stress-reduction explanation of groupthink'. *Journal of Personality and Social Psychology*, 49, 949–52.

Campbell, D. T. (1957). 'Factors relevant to the validity of experiments in social settings'. *Psychological Bulletin*, 54, 297–312.

Campbell, D. T. (1975). 'On the conflict between biological and social evolution and between psychology and moral tradition'. *American Psychologist*, 30, 1103–26.

Campbell, D. T. and Fairey, P. J. (1989). 'Informational and normative routes to conformity: the effect of faction size as a function of norm extremity and attention to the stimulus'. *Journal of Personality and Social Psychology*, 57, 457–68.

Campbell, J. D. and Fairey, P. J. (1985). 'Effects of self-esteem, hypothetical explanations, and verbalizations of expectancies on future performance'. *Journal of Personality and Social Psychology*, 48, 1097–111.

Cannavale, F. J. Scarr, H. A. and Pepitone, A. (1970). 'Deindividuation in the small group: further evidence'. *Journal of Personality and Social Psychology*, 16, 141–47.

Canter, D. (1969). 'An intergroup comparison of connotative dimensions in architecture'. *Environment and Behaviour*, 1, 37–48.

Cantor, N. and Kihlstrom, J. F. (1987). *Personality and Social Intelligence*. Englewood Cliffs, NJ: Prentice Hall.

Cantor, N. and Mischel, W. (1977). 'Traits as prototypes: effects on recognition memory'. *Journal of Personality and Social Psychology*, 35, 38–48.

Cantor, N. and Mischel, W. (1979). 'Prototypes in person perception' in L. Berkowitz (ed.), *Advances in Experimental Social Psychology* (vol. 12, pp. 3–52). New York: Academic Press.

Caplow, T. (1947). 'Rumors in war'. *Social Forces*, 25, 298–302.

Caporael, L. R., Lukaszewski, M. P. and Cuthbertson, G. H. (1983). 'Secondary baby talk: judgements by institutionalized elderly and their caregivers'. *Journal of Personality and Social Psychology*, 44, 746–54.

Caporael, L., Dawes, R., Orbell, J. and van de Kragt, A. (1989). 'Selfishness examined: cooperation in the absence of egoistic incentives'. *Behavioral and Brain Sciences*, 12, 683–99.

Carlsmith, J. M. and Anderson, C. A. (1979). 'Ambient temperature and the occurrence of collective violence: a new analysis'. *Journal of Personality and Social Psychology*, 37, 337–44.

Carlsmith, J. M. and Gross, A. E. (1969). 'Some effects of guilt on compliance'. *Journal of Personality and Social Psychology*, 11, 232–39.

Carlson, M., Marcus-Newhall, A. and Miller, N. (1989). 'Evidence for a general construct of aggression'. *Personality and Social Psychology Bulletin*, 15, 377–89.

Carlyle, T. (1841). *On Heroes, Hero-Worship, and the Heroic*. London: Fraser.

Carmichael, G. (1983). 'The transition to marriage: trends in age at first marriage and proportions marrying in Australia' cited in V. J. Callan, C. Gallois, P. Noller and Y. Kashima (1991), *Social Psychology* (2nd edn). Sydney: Harcourt Brace Jovanovich.

Carnevale, P. J. D., Pruitt, D. G. and Britton, S. D. (1979). 'Looking tough: the negotiator under constituent surveillance'. *Personality and Social Psychology Bulletin*, 5, 118–21.

Carrithers, M., Collins, S. and Lukes, S. (eds) (1986). *The Category of the Person*. Cambridge: Cambridge University Press.

Carter, L. F. and Nixon, M. (1949). 'An investigation of the relationship between four criteria of leadership ability for three different tasks'. *The Journal of Psychology*, 27, 245–61.

Cartwright, D. (1968). 'The nature of group cohesiveness' in D. Cartwright and A. Zander (eds), *Group Dynamics: Research and Theory* (3rd edn, pp. 91–109). London: Tavistock.

Cartwright, D. and Harary, F. (1956). 'Structural balance: a generalization of Heider's theory'. *Psychological Review*, 63, 277–93.

Carver, C. S. and Glass, D. C. (1978). 'Coronary-prone behaviour pattern and interpersonal aggression'. *Journal of Personality and Social Psychology*, 36, 361–66.

Carver, C. S. and Scheier, M. F. (1981). *Attention and Self-Regulation: A Control Theory Approach to Human Behaviour*. New York: Springer-Verlag.

Cary, M. S . (1978) . 'The role of gaze in the initiation of conversation'. *Social Psychology*, **41**, 269–71.

Cash, T. F., Kehr, J. A., Polyson, J. and Freeman, V. (1977). 'Role of physical attractiveness in peer attribution of psychological disturbance'. *Journal of Consulting and Clinical Psychology*, **45**, 987–93.

Cavan, S. (1963). 'Interaction in home territories'. *Berkeley Journal of Sociology*, **8**, 17–32.

Cavan, S. (1966). *Liquor License*. Chicago, IL: Aldine.

Chacko, T. I. (1982). 'Women and equal employment opportunity: some unintended effects'. *Journal of Applied Psychology*, **67**, 119–23.

Chaffee, S. H., Jackson-Beeck, M., Durall, J. and Wilson, D. (1977). 'Mass communication in political communication' in S. A. Renshon (ed.), *Handbook of Political Socialization: Theory and Research*. New York: Free Press.

Chaiken, S. (1979). 'Communicator physical attractiveness and persuasion'. *Journal of Personality and Social Psychology*, **37**, 1387–97.

Chaiken, S. (1980). 'Heuristic versus systematic information processing and the use of source versus message cues in persuasion'. *Journal of Personality and Social Psychology*, **39**, 752–66.

Chaiken, S. (1983). 'Physical appearance variables and social influence' in C. P. Herman, E. T. Higgins and M. P. Zanna (eds), *Physical Appearance, Stigma, and Social Behaviour: Third Ontario Symposium*. Hillsdale, NJ: Erlbaum.

Chaiken, S. (1987). 'The heuristic model of persuasion' in M. P. Zanna, J. M. Olsen and C. P. Herman (eds), *Social Influence: The Ontario Symposium* (vol. 5, pp. 3–39). Hillsdale, NJ: Erlbaum.

Chaiken, S. and Eagly, A. H. (1983). 'Communication modality as a determinant of persuasion: the role of communicator salience'. *Journal of Personality and Social Psychology*, **45**, 241–56.

Chaiken, S., Liberman, A. and Eagly, A. H., (1989). 'Heuristic and systematic information processing within and beyond the persuasion context' in J. S. Uleman and J. A. Bargh (eds). *Unintended Thought: Limits of Awareness, Intention, and Control*. New York: Guilford.

Chance, J. E. (1985). 'Faces, folklore, and research hypotheses'. Presidential address to the Midwestern Psychological Association convention.

Chandra, S. (1973). 'The effects of group pressure in perception: a cross-cultural conformity study'. *International Journal of Psychology*, **8**, 37–39.

Chaplin, W. F., John, O. P. and Goldberg, L. R. (1988). 'Conceptions of states and traits: dimensional attributes with ideals as prototypes'. *Journal of Personality and Social Psychology*, **54**, 541–57.

Chapman, L. J. (1967). 'Illusory correlation in observational report'. *Journal of Verbal Learning and Verbal Behaviour*, **6**, 151–55.

Chen, H., Yates, B. T. and McGinnies, E. (1988). 'Effects of involvement on observers' estimates of consensus, distinctiveness, and consistency'. *Personality and Social Psychology Bulletin*, **14**, 468–78.

Chesler, P. (1972). *Women and Madness*. Garden City, NY: Doubleday.

Chidester, T. R. (1986). 'Problems in the study of interracial interaction: pseudo-interracial dyad paradigm'. *Journal of Personality and Social Psychology*, **50**, 74–9.

Choi, S. C., Mirjafari, A. and Weaver, H. B. (1976). 'The concept of crowding: a critical review and proposal of an alternative approach'. *Environment and Behaviour*, **8**, 345–62.

Chomsky, N. (1957). *Syntactic Structures*. The Hague: Mouton.

Chomsky, N. (1959). 'Verbal behavior' review of Skinner's book. *Language*, **35**, 26–58.

Christensen, L. (1988). 'Deception in psychological research: when is its use justified?' *Personality and Social Psychology Bulletin*, **14**, 664–75.

Christian, J. J., Flyger, V. and Davis, D. E. (1960). 'Factors in the mass mortality of a herd of sika deer, *cervus nippon*'. *Chesapeake Science*, **1**, 79–95.

Christie, R. and Jahoda, M. (eds) (1954). *Studies in the Scope and Method of 'The Authoritarian Personality'*. New York: Free Press.

Cialdini, R. B. (1988). *Influence: Science and Practice* (2nd edn). Glenview, IL: Scott Foresman.

Cialdini, R. B. and Kenrick, D. T. (1976). 'Altruism as hedonism: a social development perspective on the relationship of negative mood state and helping'. *Journal of Personality and Social Psychology*, 34, 907–14.

Cialdini, R. B. and Petty, R. E. (1979). 'Anticipatory opinion effects' in R. Petty, T. Ostrom and T. Brock (eds)., *Cognitive Responses in Persuasion*. Hillsdale, NJ: Erlbaum.

Cialdini, R. B., Darby, B. L. and Vincent, J. E. (1973). 'Transgression and altruism: a case for hedonism'. *Journal of Personality and Social Psychology*, 9, 502–16.

Cialdini, R. B., Vincent, J. E., Lewis, S. K., Catalan, J., Wheeler, D. and Darby, B. L. (1975). 'Reciprocal concessions procedure for inducing compliance: the door-in-the-face technique'. *Journal of Personality and Social Psychology*, 31, 206–15.

Cialdini, R. B., Cacioppo, J. T., Bassett, R. and Miller, J. A. (1978). 'Low-balling procedure for producing compliance: commitment then cost'. *Journal of Personality and Social Psychology*, 36, 463–76.

Cialdini, R. B., Baumann, D. J. and Kenrick, D. T. (1981). 'Insights from sadness: a three-step model of the development of altruism as hedonism'. *Developmental Review*, 1, 207–23.

Clark, H. H. (1985). 'Language use and language users' in G. Lindzey and E. Aronson (eds), *Handbook of Social Psychology* (3rd edn, vol. 2, pp. 179–232). New York: Random House.

Clark, N. K. and Stephenson, G. M. (1989). 'Group remembering' in P. B. Paulus (ed.), *Psychology of Group Influence* (2nd edn, pp. 357–91). Hillsdale, NJ: Erlbaum.

Clark, N. K., Stephenson, G. M. and Rutter, D. R. (1986). 'Memory for a complex social discourse: the analysis and prediction of individual and group remembering'. *Journal of Memory and Language*, 25, 295–313.

Clark, R. D., III and Word, I. E. (1972) . 'Why don't bystanders help? Because of ambiguity?' *Journal of Personality and Social Psychology*, 24, 392–400.

Clark, R. D., III and Word, I. E. (1974). 'Where is the apathetic bystander? Situational characteristics of the emergency'. *Journal of Personality and Social Psychology*, 29, 279–87.

Clark, T. N. (1969). *Gabriel Tarde: On Communication and Social Influence*. Chicago, IL: University of Chicago Press.

Clarkson, J., Monaghan, S., Gilmore, R., Muir, R. and Crooks, T. (1985). 'Can child abuse be prevented?' *New Zealand Medical Journal*, 98, 1005–1006.

Clément, R. (1980). 'Ethnicity, contact and communication competence in a second language' in H. Giles, W. P. Robinson and P. M. Smith (eds), *Language: Social Psychological Perspectives* (pp. 147–54). Oxford: Pergamon.

Clore, G. L. (1976). 'Interpersonal attraction: an overview' in J. W. Thibaut, J. T. Spence and R. C. Carson, (eds). *Contemporary Topics in Social Psychology* (pp. 135–75). Morristown, NJ: General Learning Press.

Clore, G. L. and Byrne, D. (1974). 'A reinforcement–affect model of attraction' in T. L. Huston (ed.), *Foundations of Interpersonal Attraction* (pp. 143–65). New York: Academic Press.

Clyne, M. G. (1981). '"Second generation" foreigner talk in Australia'. *International Journal of the Sociology of Language*, 28, 69–80.

Clyne, M. G. (1985). *Multilingual Australia* (2nd edn). Melbourne: River Seine.

Coates, B., Pusser, H. E. and Goodman, I. (1976). 'The influence of *Sesame Street* and *Mister Rogers' Neighbourhood* on children's prosocial behaviour in preschool'. *Child Development*, 47, 138–44.

Coch, L. and French, J. R. P., Jr (1948). 'Overcoming resistance to change'. *Human Relations*, 1, 512–32.

Codol, J-P. (1975). 'On the so-called "superior conformity of the self" behaviour'. *European Journal of Social Psychology*, 5, 457–50.

Cohen, S. (1978). 'Environmental load and the allocation of attention' in A. Baum, J. E. Singer and S. Valins (eds), *Advances in Environmental Psychology* (vol. 1). Hillsdale, NJ: Erlbaum.

Cohen, C. (1987). 'Nuclear language'. *Bulletin of the Atomic Scientist*, June, 17–24.

Cohen, S., Glass, D. C. and Singer, J. E. (1973). 'Apartment noise, auditory discrimination and reading ability in children'. *Journal of Experimental Social Psychology*, 2, 407–22.

Cohen, S., Evans, G. W., Krantz, D. S. and Stokols, D. (1980). 'Physiological, motivational and cognitive effects of aircraft noise on children: moving from the laboratory to the field'. *American Psychologist*, 35, 231–43.

Cohn, N. (1966). *Warrant for Genocide. The Myth of the Jewish World Conspiracy and the Protocol of the Elders of Zion*. New York: Harper Row.

Cohn, N. (1975). *Europe's Inner Demons. An Enquiry Inspired by the Great Witch Hunt*. London: Chatto.

Collins, B. and Raven, B. H. (1969). 'Group structure: attraction, coalitions, communication, and power' in G. Lindzey and E Aronson (eds), *Handbook of Social Psychology* (vol. 4, pp. 102–204). Reading, MA: Addison-Wesley.

Collins, B. E. (1974). 'Four separate components of the Rotter I–E scale: belief in a difficult world, a just world, a predictable world, and a politically responsive world'. *Journal of Personality and Social Psychology*, 29, 381–91.

Condry, J. (1977). 'Enemies of exploration: self-initiated versus other-initiated learning'. *Journal of Personality and Social Psychology*, 35, 459–77.

Condry, J. C. and Ross, D. F. (1985). 'Sex and aggression: the influence of gender label'. *Child Development*, 56, 225–33.

Connell, R. W. (1972). 'Political socialization in the American family: the evidence reexamined'. *Public Opinion Quarterly*, 36, 323–33.

Cook, S. W. (1978). 'Interpersonal and attitudinal outcomes in cooperating interracial groups'. *Journal of Research and Development in Education*, 12, 97–113.

Cook, S. W. and Pelfrey, M. (1985). 'Reactions to being helped in cooperating interracial groups: a context effect'. *Journal of Personality and Social Psychology*, 49, 1231–45.

Cooper, H. M. (1979). 'Statistically combining independent studies: meta-analysis of sex differences in conformity'. *Journal of Personality and Social Psychology*, 37, 131–46.

Cooper, J. and Axom, D. (1982). 'Effort justification in psychotherapy' in G. Weary and H. Mirels (eds.), *Integrations of Clinical and Social Psychology*. London: Oxford University Press.

Cooper, J. and Croyle, R. T. (1984). 'Attitudes and attitude change'. *Annual Review of Psychology*, 35, 395–426.

Cooper, J. and Fazio, R. H. (1984). 'A new look at dissonance theory' in L. Berkowitz (ed.), *Advances in Experimental Social Psychology* (vol. 17, pp. 229–65). New York: Academic Press.

Costanzo, P. R. (1970). 'Conformity development as a function of self-blame'. *Journal of Personality and Social Psychology*, 14, 366–74.

Cottrell, N. B. (1972). 'Social facilitation' in C. McClintock (ed.), *Experimental Social Psychology* (pp. 185–236). New York: Holt, Rinehart and Winston.

Cottrell, N. B., Wack, D. L., Sekerak, G. J. and Rittle, R. H. (1968). 'Social facilitation of dominant responses by the presence of others'. *Journal of Personality and Social Psychology*, 9, 245–50.

Coupland, N., Coupland, J., Giles, H. and Henwood, K. (1988). 'Accommodating the elderly: invoking and extending a theory'. *Language in Society*, 17, 1–41.

Courtright, J. A. (1978). 'A laboratory investigation of groupthink'. *Communication Monographs*, 45, 229–46.

Cowen, W. L., Landes, J. and Schaet, D. E. (1958). 'The effects of mild frustration on the expression of prejudiced attitudes'. *Journal of Abnormal and Social Psychology*, 58, 33–38.

Cox, V. C., Paulus, P. B. and McCain, G. (1984). 'Prison crowding research: the relevance for prison housing standards and a general approach regarding crowding phenomena'. *American Psychologist*, 39, 1148–60.

Cozby, P. C. (1973). 'Self-disclosure: A literature review'. *Psychological Bulletin*, 79, 73–91.

Craddock, A. (1980). 'The impact of social change on Australian families'. *Australian Journal of Sex, Marriage and the Family*, 1, 4–14.

Cramer, R. E., McMaster, M. R., Bartell, P. A. and Dragna, M. (1988). 'Subject competence and minimization of the bystander effect'. *Journal of Applied Social Psychology*, 18, 1133–48.

Crocker, J. (1981). 'Judgement of covariation by social perceivers'. *Psychological Bulletin*, 90, 272–92.

Crocker, J., Fiske, S. T. and Taylor, S. E. (1984). 'Schematic bases of belief change' in J. R. Eiser (ed.), *Attitudinal Judgement* (pp. 197–226). New York: Springer-Verlag.

Crocker, J., Alloy, L. B. and Kayne, N. T. (1988). 'Attributional style, depression, and perceptions of consensus for events'. *Journal of Personality and Social Psychology*, 54, 840–46.

Crocker, J., Blaine, B. and Luhtanen, R. (1993). 'Prejudice, intergroup behaviour and self-esteem: enhancement and protection motives' in M. A. Hogg and D. Abrams (eds), *Group Motivation: Social Psychological Perspectives* (pp. 52–67). London: Harvester Wheatsheaf.

Crockett, W. H. (1965). 'Cognitive complexity and impression formation' in B. A. Maher (ed.), *Progress in Experimental Personality Research* (vol. 2, pp. 47–90). New York: Academic Press.

Crook, M. A. and Langdon, F. J. (1974). 'The effects of aircraft noise in schools around London Airport'. *Sound and Vibration*, 34, 221–32.

Crosby, F. (1982). *Relative Deprivation and Working Women*. New York: Oxford University Press.

Crosby, F., Bromley, S. and Saxe, L. (1980). 'Recent unobtrusive studies of black and white discrimination and prejudice: a literature review'. *Psychological Bulletin*, 87, 546–63.

Crosby, F., Pufall, A., Snyder, R. C., O'Connell, M. and Whalen, P. (1989). 'The denial of personal disadvantage among you, me, and all the other ostriches' in M. Crawford and M. Gentry (eds), *Gender and Thought* (pp. 79–99). New York: Springer-Verlag.

Crosby, F., Cordova, D. and Jaskar, K. (1993). 'On the failure to see oneself as disadvantaged: cognitive and emotional components' in M. A. Hogg and D. Abrams (eds), *Group Motivation: Social Psychological Perspectives* (pp. 87–104). London: Harvester Wheatsheaf.

Crusco, A. H. and Wetzel, C. G. (1984). 'The Midas touch: the effects of interpersonal touch on restaurant tipping'. *Personality and Social Psychology Bulletin*, 10, 512–17.

Crutchfield, R. A. (1955). 'Conformity and character'. *American Psychologist*, 10, 191–98.

Cunningham, M. R. (1979). 'Weather, mood, and helping behaviour: quasi experiments with the sunshine samaritan'. *Journal of Personality and Social Psychology*, 37, 1947–56.

Cunningham, M. R. (1986). 'Measuring the physical in physical attraction: quasi-experiments on the sociobiology of female beauty'. *Journal of Personality and Social Psychology*, 50, 925–35.

Currie, M. and Hogg, M. A. (1994). 'Subjective ethnolinguistic vitality and social adaptation among Vietnamese refugees in Australia'. *International Journal of the Sociology of Language*, 108, 97–115.

Cutrona, C. E., Russell, D. and Jones, R. D. (1985). 'Cross-situational consistency in causal attributions: does attributional style exist?' *Journal of Personality and Social Psychology*, 47, 1043–58.

Dabbs, J. M., Jr (1972). 'Sex, setting, and reaction to crowding on sidewalks'. *Proceedings of the 80th Annual Convention of the American Psychological Association*, 205–206.

Dakof, G. A. and Taylor, S. E. (1990). 'Victims' perceptions of social support: what is helpful from whom?' *Journal of Personality and Social Psychology*, 58, 80–89.

Darley, J. M. and Batson, C. D. (1973). 'From Jerusalem to Jericho: a study of situational and dispositional variables in helping behavior'. *Journal of Personality and Social Psychology*, 27, 100–108.

Darley, J. M. and Latane, B. (1968). 'Bystander intervention in emergencies: diffusion of responsibility'. *Journal of Personality and Social Psychology*, 8, 377–83.

Darlington, R. B. and Macker, D. F. (1966). 'Displacement of guilt-produced altruistic behaviour'. *Journal of Personality and Social Psychology*, 4, 442–43.

Darwin, C. (1872). *The Expression of Emotions in Man and Animals*. Chicago, IL: University of Chicago Press.

Davidowicz, L. C. (1975). *The War Against the Jews, 1933–1945*. New York: Holt, Rinehart & Winston.

Davidson, A. R. and Jacard, J. (1979). Variables that moderate the attitude–behaviour relation: results of a longtitudinal survey. *Journal of Personality and Social Psychology*, 37, 1364–76.

Davidson, L. R. and Duberman, L. (1982). 'Friendship: communication and interactional patterns in same-sex dyads'. *Sex Roles*, 8, 809–22.

Davies, J. C. (1962). 'Toward a theory of revolution'. *American Sociological Review*, 27, 5–19.

Davies, J. C. (1969). 'The J-curve of rising and declining satisfaction as a cause of some great revolutions and a contained rebellion' in H. D. Graham and T. R. Gurr (eds), *The History of Violence in America: Historical and Comparative Perspectives* (pp. 690–730). New York: Praeger.

Davis, J. A. (1959). 'A formal interpretation of the theory of relative deprivation.' *Sociometry*, 22, 280–96.

Davis, J. H. (1973). 'Group decision and social interaction: a theory of social decision schemes'. *Psychological Review*, 80, 97–125.

Davis, K. (1949). *Human Society*. New York: Macmillan.

Davis, M. H. (1980). 'Measuring individual differences in empathy'. *JSAS Catalogue of Selected Documents in Psychology*, 10, 85.

Dawes, R. M., Faust, D. and Meehl, P. E. (1989). 'Clinical versus actuarial judgement'. *Science*, 243, 1668–74.

Dean, L. M., Willis, F. N. and Hewitt, J. (1975). 'Initial interaction distance among individuals equal and unequal in military rank'. *Journal of Personality and Social Psychology*, 32, 294–99.

Deaux, K. (1976). *The Behaviour of Women and Men*. Monterey, CA: Brooks/Cole.

Deaux, K. (1984). 'From individual differences to social categories'. *American Psychologist*, 39, 105–16.

Deaux, K. (1985). 'Sex and gender'. *Annual Review of Psychology*, 36, 49–81.

Deaux, K. and Emswiller, T. (1974). 'Explanations of successful performance on sex-linked tasks: what is skill for the male is luck for the female'. *Journal of Personality and Social Psychology*, 29, 80–85.

Deaux, K. and Wrightsman, L. S. (1988). *Social Psychology* (5th edn). Belmont, CA: Brooks/Cole.

Deci, E. L. and Ryan, R. M. (1985). *Intrinsic Motivation and Self-determination in Human Behaviour*. New York: Plenum.

de Gilder, D. and Wilke, H .A. M. (in press). 'Social influence: investigating the boundaries of expectation states theory'. *European Review of Social Psychology*.

DeJong, W. (1979). 'An examination of self-perception mediation of the foot in the door effect'. *Journal of Personality and Social Psychology*, 37, 2171–80.

de Jong, P. F., Koomen, W. and Mellenbergh, G. J. (1988). 'Structure of causes for success and failure: a multidimensional scaling analysis of preference judgements'. *Journal of Personality and Social Psychology*, 55, 1024–37.

Dembroski, T. M. and MacDougall, J. M. (1978). 'Stress effects on affiliation preferences among subjects possessing the Type A coronary-prone behaviour pattern'. *Journal of Personality and Social Psychology*, 36, 23–33.

DePaulo, B. M. and Rosenthal, R. (1979). 'Telling lies'. *Journal of Personality and Social Psychology*, 37, 1713–22.

DePaulo, B. M., Lanier, K. and Davis, T. (1983). 'Detecting the deceit of the motivated liar'. *Journal of Personality and Social Psychology*, 45, 1096–103.

DePaulo, P. J. and DePaulo, B. M. (1989). 'Can deception by salespersons and customers be detected through nonverbal behavioral cues'. *Journal of Applied Social Psychology*, 19, 1552–77.

Deschamps, J-C. (1983). 'Social attribution' in J. Jaspars, F. D. Fincham and M. Hewstone (eds), *Attribution Theory and Research: Conceptual, Developmental and Social Dimensions* (pp. 223–40). London: Academic Press.

Deschamps, J-C. and Brown, R. J. (1983). 'Superordinate goals and intergroup conflict'. *British Journal of Social Psychology*, 22, 189–95.

Deutsch, M. (1975). 'Equity, equality and need: what determines which value will be used as a basis of distributive justice?' *Journal of Social Issues*, 31, 137–49.

Deutsch, M. and Gerard, H. B. (1955). 'A study of normative and informational social influences upon individual judgement'. *Journal of Abnormal and Social Psychology*, 51, 629–36.

Deutsch, M. and Krauss, R. M. (1960). 'The effect of threat upon interpersonal bargaining'. *Journal of Abnormal and Social Psychology*, 61, 181–89.

Devine, P. G. (1989). 'Stereotypes and prejudice: their automatic and controlled components'. *Journal of Personality and Social Psychology*, 56, 5–18.

Devine, P. G. and Malpass, R. S. (1985). 'Orienting strategies in differential face recognition'. *Personality and Social Psychology Bulletin*, 11, 33–40.

DeVos, G. A. and Hippler, A. E. (1969). 'Cultural psychology: comparative studies of human behavior' in G. Lindzey and E. Aronson (eds), *Handbook of Social Psychology* (2nd edn, vol. 4, pp. 322–417). Reading, MA: Addison-Wesley.

Diab, L. N. (1970). 'A study of intragroup and intergroup relations among experimentally produced small groups'. *Genetic Psychology Monographs*, 82, 49–82.

Dickens, C. (1854). *Hard Times*. Harmondsworth: Penguin.

Diehl, M. and Stroebe, W. (1987). 'Productivity loss in brainstorming groups: toward the solution of a riddle'. *Journal of Personality and Social Psychology*, 53, 497–509.

Diehl, M. and Stroebe, W. (1991). 'Productivity loss in idea-generating groups: tracking down the blocking effect'. *Journal of Personality and Social Psychology*, 61, 392–403.

Diener, E. (1976). 'Effects of prior destructive behaviour, anonymity, and group presence on deindividuation and aggression'. *Journal of Personality and Social Psychology*, 33, 497–507.

Diener, E. (1980). 'Deindividuation: the absence of self-awareness and self-regulation in group members' in P. B. Paulus (ed.), *Psychology of Group Influence* (pp. 209–42). Hillsdale, NJ: Erlbaum.

Diener, E., Fraser, S. C., Beaman, A. L. and Kelem, R. T. (1976). 'Effects of deindividuation variables on stealing by Halloween trick-or-treaters'. *Journal of Personality and Social Psychology*, 33, 178–83.

Dienstbier, R. A., Kahle, L. R., Willis, K. A. and Tunnell, G. B. (1980). 'The impact of moral theories on cheating: studies of emotion attribution and schema activation'. *Motivation and Emotion*, 4, 193–216.

Dion, K. L. (1972). 'Physical attractiveness and evaluation of children's transgressions'. *Journal of Personality and Social Psychology*, 24, 207–13.

Dion, K. L., Berscheid, E. and Walster, E. (1972). 'What is beautiful is good'. *Journal of Personality and Social Psychology*, 24, 285–90.

Dion, K. L. (1979). 'Intergroup conflict and intragroup cohesiveness' in W. G. Austin and S. Worchel (eds), *The Social Psychology of Intergroup Relations* (pp. 211–24). Monterey, CA: Brooks/Cole.

Dion, K. L. and Earn, B. M. (1975). 'The phenomenology of being a target of prejudice'. *Journal of Personality and Social Psychology*, 32, 944–50.

Dion, K. L., Earn, B. M. and Yee, P. H. N. (1978). 'The experience of being a victim of prejudice: an experimental approach'. *International Journal of Psychology*, 13, 197–214.

Dipboye, R. L. (1977). 'Alternative approaches to deindividuation'. *Psychological Bulletin*, 84, 1057–75

Dipboye, R. L., Arvey, R. D. and Terpstra, D. E. (1977). 'Sex and physical attractiveness of raters and applicants as determinants of resumé evaluations'. *Journal of Applied Psychology*, 61, 288–94.

Dittes, J. E. (1959). 'Attractiveness of group as function of self-esteem and acceptance by group'. *Journal of Abnormal and Social Psychology*, 59, 77–82.

Dittes, J. E. and Kelley, H. H. (1956). 'Effects of different conditions of acceptance upon conformity to group norms'. *Journal of Abnormal and Social Psychology*, 53, 100–07.

Doise, W. (1978). *Groups and Individuals: Explanations in Social Psychology*. Cambridge: Cambridge University Press.

Doise, W. (1982). 'Report on the European Association of Experimental Social Psychology'. *European Journal of Social Psychology*, 12, 105–11.

Doise, W. (1986). *Levels of Explanation in Social Psychology*. Cambridge: Cambridge University Press.

Doise, W., Clemence, A. and Lorenzi-Cioldi, F. (1993). *The Quantitative Analysis of Social Representations*. London: Harvester Wheatsheaf.

Dollard, J., Doob, L. W., Miller, N. E., Mowrer, O. H. and Sears, R. R. (1939). *Frustration and Aggression*. New Haven, CT: Yale University Press.

Doms, M. (1983). 'The minority influence effect: an alternative approach' in W. Doise and S. Moscovici (eds), *Current Issues in European Social Psychology*, (vol. 1, pp. 1–32). Cambridge: Cambridge University Press.

Doms, M. and van Avermaet, E. (1980). 'Majority influence, minority influence, and conversion behaviour: a replication'. *Journal of Experimental Social Psychology*, 16, 283–92.

Donnerstein, E. and Wilson, D. W. (1976). 'The effects of noise and perceived control upon ongoing and subsequent aggressive behavior'. *Journal of Personality and Social Psychology*, 34, 774–81.

Dovidio, J. F. (1984). 'Helping behaviour and altruism: an empirical and conceptual overview' in L. Berkowitz (ed.), *Advances in Experimental Social Psychology* (vol. 17, pp. 361–427). New York: Academic Press.

Dovidio, J. F. and Ellyson, S. L. (1985). 'Patterns of visual dominance behaviour in humans' in S. Ellyson and J. Dovidio (eds), *Power, Dominance, and Nonverbal Behaviour* (pp. 129–49). New York: Springer-Verlag.

Dovidio, J. F., Ellyson, S. L., Keating, C. J., Heltman, K. and Brown, C. E. (1988). 'The relationship of social power to visual displays of dominance between men and women'. *Journal of Personality and Social Psychology*, 54, 233–42.

Duck, S. (1977). *The Study of Acquaintance*. Farnborough: Saxon House.

Duck, S. (ed.) (1982). *Personal Relationships 4: Dissolving Personal Relationships*. London: Academic Press.

Duck, S. (1988). *Relating to Others*. Milton Keynes: Open University Press.

Duck, S. (1992). *Human Relationships* (2nd edn). London: Sage.

Duncan, S. (1969). 'Nonverbal communication'. *Psychological Bulletin*, 72, 118–37.

Duncan, S. L. (1976). 'Differential social perception and attribution of intergroup violence: testing the lower limits of stereotyping of blacks'. *Journal of Personality and Social Psychology*, 34, 590–98.

Dupuy, R. E. and Dupuy, T. N. (1977). *The Encyclopaedia of Military History*. London: Janes.

Dutton, D. G. and Lake, R. (1973). 'Threat of own prejudice and reverse discrimination in interracial situations'. *Journal of Personality and Social Psychology*, 28, 94–100.

Duval, S. and Wicklund, R. A. (1972). *A Theory of Objective Self-awareness*. New York: Academic Press.

Duveen, G. and Lloyd, B. B. (1993). 'An ethnographic approach to social representations' in G. M. Breakwell and D. V. Canter (eds), *Empirical Approaches to Social Representations*. Oxford: Clarendon Press, pp. 90–109.

Eagly, A. H. (1978). 'Sex differences in influenceability'. *Psychological Bulletin*, 85, 86–116.

Eagly, A. H. (1983). 'Gender and social influence: a social psychological analysis'. *American Psychologist*, 38, 971–81.

Eagly, A. H. (1987). *Sex Differences in Social Behaviour: A Social-role Analysis*. Hillsdale, NJ: Erlbaum.

Eagly, A. H. and Carli, L. (1981). 'Sex of researcher and sex-typed communications as determinants of sex differences in influenceability: a meta-analysis of social influence studies'. *Psychological Bulletin*, 90, 1–20.

Eagly, A. H. and Chaiken, S. (1984). 'Cognitive theories of persuasion' in L. Berkowitz (ed.), *Advances in Experimental Social Psychology* (vol. 17, pp. 268–359). New York: Academic Press.

Eagly, A. H. and Chaiken S. (1992). *The Psychology of Attitudes*. San Diego, CA: Harcourt Brace Jovanovich.

Eagly, A. H. and Crowley, M.(1986). 'Gender and helping behaviour: a meta-analytic review of the social psychological literature'. *Psychological Review*, 100, 283–308.

Eagly, A. H. and Chrvala, C. (1986). 'Sex differences in conformity: status and gender role interpretations'. *Psychology of Women Quarterly*, **10**, 203–20.

Eagly, A. H. and Steffen, V. J. (1984). 'Gender stereotypes stem from the distribution of women and men into social roles'. *Journal of Personality and Social Psychology*, **46**, 735–54.

Eagly, A. H. and Steffen, V. J. (1986). 'Gender and aggressive behaviour: a meta-analytic review of the social psychological literature'. *Psychological Bulletin*, **100**, 309–30.

Eagly, A. H., Wood, W. and Fishbaugh, L. (1981). 'Sex differences in conformity: surveillance by the group as a determinant of male nonconformity'. *Journal of Personality and Social Psychology*, **40**, 384–94.

Ebbinghaus, H. (1885). *Memory: A Contribution to Experimental Psychology*. (H. A. Ruger and C. E. Bussenius, trans. New York: Dover, 1964).

Edney, J. J. (1979). 'The nuts game: a concise commons dilemma analog'. *Environmental Psychology and Nonverbal Behaviour*, **3**, 252–54.

Edwards, A. L. (1957). *Techniques of Attitude Scale Construction*. New York: Appleton-Century-Crofts.

Edwards, J. and Chisholm, J. (1987). 'Language, multiculturalism and identity: a Canadian study'. *Journal of Multilingual and Multicultural Development*, **8**, 391–407.

Ehrlich, H. J. (1973). *The Social Psychology of Prejudice*. New York: Wiley.

Eibl-Eibesfeldt, I. (1972). 'Similarities and differences between cultures in expressive movements' in R. Hinde (ed.), *Non-verbal Communication* (pp. 297–314). Cambridge: Cambridge University Press.

Eichler, M. (1980). *The Double Standard: A Feminist Critique of Feminist Social Science*. London: Croom Helm.

Einhorn, H. J. and Hogarth, R. M. (1981). 'Behavioral decision theory: processes of judgement and choice'. *Annual Review of Psychology*, **32**, 53–88.

Eisen, S. V. (1979). 'Actor–observer differences in information inference and causal attribution'. *Journal of Personality and Social Psychology*, **37**, 261–72.

Eisenberg-Berg, N. (1979). 'Relationship of prosocial moral reasoning to altruism, political liberalism and intelligence'. *Developmental Psychology*, **15** 87–89.

Eisenberger, R. and Shank, D. M. (1985). 'Personal work ethic and effort training affect cheating'. *Journal of Personality and Social Psychology*, **49**, 520–28.

Eiser, J. R. (1986). *Social Psychology: Attitudes, Cognition and Social Behaviour*. Cambridge: Cambridge University Press.

Eiser, J. R. and Bhavnani, K. K. (1974). 'The effects of situational meaning on the behaviour of subjects in the prisoner's dilemma game'. *European Journal of Social Psychology*, **4**, 93–7.

Eiser, J. R. and Stroebe, W. (1972). *Categorization and Social Judgement*. London: Academic Press.

Ekman, P. (1971). 'Universals and cultural differences in facial expressions of emotion' in J. K. Cole (ed.), *Nebraska Symposium on Motivation* (vol. 19, pp. 207–84). Lincoln, NE: University of Nebraska Press.

Ekman, P. (1973). 'Cross-cultural studies of facial expression' in P. Ekman (ed.), *Darwin and Facial Expression* (pp. 169–222). New York: Academic Press.

Ekman, P. (1982). *Emotion in the Human Face*. New York: Cambridge University Press.

Ekman, P. and Friesen, W. V. (1971). 'Constants across cultures in the face and emotion'. *Journal of Personality and Social Psychology*, **17**, 124–29.

Ekman, P. and Friesen, W. V. (1972). 'Hand movements'. *Journal of Communication*, **22**, 353–74.

Ekman, P. and Friesen, W. V. (1974). 'Detecting deception from the body or face'. *Journal of Personality and Social Psychology*, **29**, 188–98.

Ekman, P. and Friesen, W. V. (1975). *Unmasking the Face*. Englewood Cliffs, NJ: Prentice Hall.

Ekman, P., Friesen, W. V. and Scherer, K. B. (1976). 'Body movement and voice pitch in deceptive interaction'. *Semiotica*, **16**, 23–27.

Ekman, P., Friesen, W. V., O'Sullivan, M., Chan, A., Diacoyanni-Tarlatzis, I., Heider, K., Krause, R., Lecompte, W. A., Pitcairn, T., Riccibitti, P. E., Scherer, K., Tomita, M. and Tzavaras, A. (1987). 'Universals and cultural differences in the judgements of facial expressions of emotion'. *Journal of Personality and Social Psychology*, 53, 712–17.

Elder, G. H., Jr (1969). 'Appearance and education in marriage mobility'. *American Sociological Review*, 34, 519–33.

Elkin, A. P. (1961). *The Aboriginal Australians*. London: Longman.

Ellemers, N., Wilke, H. and van Knippenberg, A. (1993). 'Effects of the legitimacy of low group or individual status on individual and collective identity enhancement strategies'. *Journal of Personality and Social Psychology*, 64, 766–78.

Elliot, A. J. (1981). *Child Language*. Cambridge: Cambridge University Press.

Ellis, R. J., Olson, J.. M. and Zanna, M. P. (1983). 'Stereotypic personality inferences following objective versus subjective judgements of beauty'. *Canadian Journal of Behavioral Science*, 15, 35–42.

Ellsworth, P. C., Carlsmith, J. M. and Henson, A. (1972). 'The stare as a stimulus to flight in human subjects: a series of field experiments'. *Journal of Personality and Social Psychology*, 21, 302–11.

Elms, A. C. (1975). 'The crisis of confidence in social psychology'. *American Psychologist*, 30, 967–76.

Elms, A. C. (1982). 'Keeping deception honest: justifying conditions for social scientific research strategies' in T. L. Beauchamp and R. Faden (eds), *Ethical Issues in Social Science Research*. Baltimore, MD: Johns Hopkins University Press.

Elms, A. C. and Milgram, S. (1966). 'Personality characteristics associated with obedience and defiance toward authoritative command'. *Journal of Experimental Research in Personality*, 1, 282–89.

Emler, N. and Hopkins, N. (1990). 'Reputon, social identity and the self' in D. Abrams and M. A. Hogg (eds), *Social Identity Theory: Constructive and Critical Advances* (pp. 113–130). London: Harvester Wheatsheaf.

Emler, N., Reicher, S. D. and Ross, A. (1987). 'The social context of delinquent conduct'. *Journal of Child Psychology and Psychiatry*, 28, 99–109.

Epstein, Y. M. (1981). 'Crowding stress and human behavior'. *Journal of Social Issues*, 37, 126–44.

Erber, R. (1991). 'Affective and semantic priming: effects of mood on category accessibility and inference'. *Journal of Experimental Social Psychology*, 27, 480–98.

Erber, R. and Fiske, S. T. (1984). 'Outcome dependency and attention to inconsistent information'. *Journal of Personality and Social Psychology*, 47, 709–26.

Eron, L. D. (1982). 'Parent–child interaction, television violence, and aggression of children'. *American Psychologist*, 37, 197–211.

Esser, J. K. and Komorita, S. S. (1975). 'Reciprocity and concession making in bargaining'. *Journal of Personality and Social Psychology*, 31, 864–72.

Evans, G. W. (1979). 'Behavioral and physiological consequences of crowding in humans'. *Journal of Applied Social Psychology*, 9, 27–46.

Evans, G. W. and Lovell, B. (1979). Design modifications in an open-plan school. *Journal of Educational Psychology*, 71, 41–49.

Evans, G. W., Jacobs, S. V. and Frager, N. B. (1982). 'Behavioral responses to air pollution' in A. Baum and J. E. Singer (eds), *Advances in Environmental Psychology* (vol. 4). Hillsdale, NJ: Erlbaum.

Evans, N. J. and Jarvis, P. A. (1980). 'Group cohesion: a review and re-evaluation'. *Small Group Behaviour*, 11, 359–70.

Evans-Pritchard, E. E. (1937). *Witchcraft, Oracles and Magic Among the Azande*. Oxford: Oxford University Press.

Exline, R. V. (1971). 'Visual interaction: the glances of power and preference' in J. K. Cole (ed.), *Nebraska Symposium on Motivation* (vol. 19, pp. 163–206). Lincoln, NE: University of Nebraska Press.

Exline, R. V., Ellyson, S. L. and Long, B. (1975). 'Visual behaviour as an aspect of power role relationships' in P. Pliner, L. Krames and T. Alloway (eds), *Nonverbal Communication of Aggression* (vol. 2, pp. 21–52). New York: Plenum.

Fajardo, D. M. (1985). 'Author race, essay quality, and reverse discrimination'. *Journal of Applied Social Psychology*, 15, 255–68.

Farr, R. M. and Moscovici, S. (eds) (1984). *Social Representations*. Cambridge: Cambridge University Press.

Farran, D. C. and Rarney, C. T. (1977). 'Infant day care and attachment behaviours toward mothers and teachers'. *Child Development*, 43, 1112–16.

Fazio, R. H. (1986). 'How do attitudes guide behaviour?' In R. M. Sorrentino and E. T. Higgins (eds), *Handbook of Motivation and Cognition*. New York: Guilford Press.

Fazio, R. H. (1989). 'On the power and functionality of attitudes: the role of attitude accessibility' in A. R. Pratkanis, S. J. Breckler and A. G. Greenwald (eds). *Attitude Structure and Function* (pp. 153–79). Hillsdale, NJ: Erlbaum.

Fazio, R. H. and Zanna, M. P. (1978). 'Attitudinal qualities relating to the strength of the attitude–behaviour relation'. *Journal of Experimental Social Psychology*, 14, 398–408.

Fazio, R. H. and Zanna, M. P. (1981). 'Direct experience and attitude–behaviour consistency' in L. Berkowitz (ed.), *Advances in Experimental Social Psychology* (vol. 14, pp. 161–202). New York: Academic Press.

Fazio, R. H., Zanna, M. P. and Cooper, J. (1977). 'Dissonance and self-perception: an integrative view of each theory's proper domain of application'. *Journal of Experimental Social Psychology*, 13, 464–79.

Fazio, R. H., Powell, M. C. and Herr, P. M. (1983). 'Toward a process model of the attitude–behaviour relation: accessing one's attitude upon mere observation of the attitude object'. *Journal of Personality and Social Psychology*, 44, 723–35.

Fazio, R. H., Sanbonmatsu, D. M., Powell, M. C. and Kardes, F. R. (1986). 'On the automatic activation of attitudes'. *Journal of Personality and Social Psychology*, 50, 229–38.

Feagin, J. (1972). 'Poverty: we still believe that God helps them who help themselves'. *Psychology Today*, 6, 101–29.

Feather, N. T. (1974). 'Explanations of poverty in Australian and American samples: the person, society and fate'. *Australian Journal of Psychology*, 26, 199–216.

Feather, N. T. (1985). 'Attitudes, values, and attributions: explanations of unemployment'. *Journal of Personality and Social Psychology*, 48, 876–89.

Feather, N. T. (1991). 'Human values, global self-esteem, and belief in a just world'. *Journal of Personality*, 59, 83–106.

Feather, N. T. (1993a). 'Attitudes towards the high achiever: value correlates and family resemblances'. Unpublished manuscript.

Feather, N. T. (1993b). 'Authoritarianism and attitudes towards high achievers'. *Journal of Personality and Social Psychology*, 65, 152–64.

Feather, N. T. (1994). 'Attitudes toward high achievers and reactions to their fall: theory and research toward tall poppies' in L. Berkowitz (ed.), *Advances in Experimental Social Psychology* (vol. 26, pp. 1–73). New York: Academic Press.

Feather, N. T. and Barber, J. G. (1983). 'Depressive reactions and unemployment'. *Journal of Abnormal Psychology*, 22, 185–95.

Feather, N. T. and Davenport, P. R. (1981). 'Unemployment and depressive affect: a motivational and attributional analysis'. *Journal of Personality and Social Psychology*, 41, 422–36.

Feather, N. T. and Simon, J. G. (1975). 'Reactions to male and female success and failure in sex-linked occupations: impressions of personality, causal attributions, and perceived likelihood of different consequences'. *Journal of Personality and Social Psychology*, 31, 20–31.

Feather, N. T. and Tiggerman, M. (1984). 'A balanced measure of attributional style'. *Australian Journal of Psychology*, 36, 267–83.

Feeney, J. A. and Noller, P. (1990). 'Attachment style as a predictor of adult romantic relationships'. *Journal of Personality and Social Psychology*, 58, 281–91.

Fehr, R. S. and Stern, J. A. (1970). 'Peripheral physiological variables and emotion: the James–Lange theory revisited'. *Psychological Bulletin*, 74, 411–24.

Felipe, N. and Sommer, R. (1966). 'Invasions of personal space'. *Social Problems*, 14, 206–14.

Ferguson, C. K. and Kelley, H. H. (1964). 'Significant factors in overevaluation of own group's product'. *Journal of Abnormal and Social Psychology*, 69, 223–28.

Fergusson, D. M., Horwood, L. J., Kershaw, K. L. and Shannon, F. T. (1986). 'Factors associated with reports of wife assault in New Zealand'. *Journal of Marriage and the Family*, 48, 407–12.

Festinger, L. (1950). 'Informal social communication'. *Psychological Review*, 57, 271–82.

Festinger, L. (1954). 'A theory of social comparison processes'. *Human Relations*, 7, 117–40.

Festinger, L. (1957). A *Theory of Cognitive Dissonance*. Stanford, CA: Stanford University Press.

Festinger, L. (1964). *Conflict, Decision and Dissonance*. Stanford, CA: Stanford University Press.

Festinger, L. (1980). *Retrospections on Social Psychology*. New York: Oxford University Press.

Festinger, L. and Carlsmith, J. M. (1959). 'Cognitive consequences of forced compliance'. *Journal of Abnormal and Social Psychology*, 58, 203–10.

Festinger, L., Schachter, S. and Back, K. (1950). *Social Pressures in Informal Groups: A Study of Human Factors in Housing*. New York: Harper.

Festinger, L., Pepitone, A. and Newcomb, T. M. (1952). 'Some consequences of deindividuation in a group'. *Journal of Personality and Social Psychology*, 47, 382–89.

Fidell, L. S. (1970). 'Empirical verification of sex discrimination in hiring practices in psychology'. *American Psychologist*, 25, 1094–98.

Fiedler, F. E. (1965). 'A contingency model of leadership effectiveness' in L. Berkowitz (ed.), *Advances in Experimental Social Psychology* (vol. 1, pp. 149–90). New York: Academic Press.

Fiedler, F. E. (1967). 'The effect of intergroup competition on group member adjustment'. *Personnel Psychology*, 20, 33–44.

Fiedler, F. E. (1971). *Leadership*. Morristown, NJ: General Learning Press.

Fiedler, F. E. (1981). 'Leadership effectiveness'. *American Behavioral Scientist*, 24, 619–32.

Fiedler, K. (1982). 'Causal schemata: review and criticism of research on a popular construct'. *Journal of Personality and Social Psychology*, 42, 1001–13.

Fincham, F. D. (1985). 'Attributions in close relationships' in J. H. Harvey and G. Weary (eds), *Attribution: Basic Issues and Applications*. Orlando, FL: Academic Press.

Fincham, F. D. and Bradbury, T. N, (1987). 'Cognitive processes and conflict in close relationships: an attribution–efficacy model'. *Journal of Personality and Social Psychology*, 53, 1106–18.

Fincham, F. D. and O'Leary, K. D. (1983). 'Causal inferences for spouse behaviour in maritally distressed and nondistressed couples'. *Journal of Social and Clinical Psychology*, 1, 42–57.

Fischer, C. S. (1982). *To Dwell Among Friends: Personal Networks in Town and City*. Chicago, IL: University of Chicago Press.

Fischer, W. F. (1963). 'Sharing in preschool children as a function of amount and type of reinforcement'. *Genetic Psychology Monographs*, 68, 215–45.

Fishbein, M. (1963). 'An investigation of the relationship between beliefs about an object and attitude toward that object'. *Human Relations*, 16, 233–39.

Fishbein, M. (1967a). 'A behaviour theory approach to the relation between beliefs about an object and the attitude toward the object' in M. Fishbein (ed.), *Readings in Attitude Theory and Measurement* (pp. 389–400). New York: Wiley.

Fishbein, M. (1967b). 'A consideration of beliefs and their role in attitude measurement' in M. Fishbein (ed.), *Readings in Attitude Theory and Measurement* (pp. 257–66). New York: Wiley.

Fishbein, M. (1971). 'Attitudes and the prediction of behaviour' in K. Thomas (ed.), *Attitudes and Behaviour* (pp. 52–83). London: Penguin.

Fishbein, M. and Ajzen, I. (1974). 'Attitudes toward objects as predictors of single and multiple behaviour criteria'. *Psychological Review*, 81, 59–74.

Fishbein, M. and Ajzen, I. (1975). *Belief, Attitude, Intention and Behaviour: An Introduction to Theory and Research*. Reading, MA: Addison-Wesley.

Fishbein, M. and Coombs, F. S. (1974). 'Basis for decision: an attitudinal analysis of voting behavior'. *Journal of Applied Social Psychology*, 4, 95–124.

Fishbein, M. and Feldman, S. (1963). 'Social psychological studies in voting behaviour. I: Theoretical and methodological considerations'. *American Psychologist*, 18, 388.

Fishbein, M., Ajzen, I. and Hinkle, R. (1980a). 'Predicting and understanding voting in American elections: effects of external variables' in I. Ajzen and M. Fishbein (eds), *Understanding Attitudes and Predicting Human Behaviour*. Englewood Cliffs, NJ: Prentice Hall.

Fishbein, M., Bowman, C. H., Thomas, K., Jacard, J. J. and Ajzen, I. (1980b). 'Predicting and understanding voting in British elections and American referenda: illustrations of the theory's generality' in I. Ajzen and M. Fishbein (eds). *Understanding Attitudes and Predicting Human Behaviour*. Englewood Cliffs, NJ: Prentice Hall.

Fisher, J. D., Rytting, M. and Heslin, R. (1976). 'Hands touching hands: affective and evaluative effects of an interpersonal touch'. *Sociometry*, 39, 416–21.

Fisher, J. D., Bell, P. A. and Baum, A. (1984). *Environmental Psychology* (2nd edn). New York: Holt, Rinehart and Winston.

Fisher, R. J. (1990). *The Social Psychology of Intergroup and International Conflict Resolution*. New York: Springer-Verlag.

Fisher, S. and Todd, A. D. (1983). *The Social Organization of Doctor–Patient Communication*. Washington, DC: Centre for Applied Linguistics.

Fishman, J. A. (1972). *Language and Nationalism*. Rowley, MA: Newbury House.

Fishman, J. A. (1989). *Language and Ethnicity in Minority Sociolinguistic Perspective*. Clevedon: Multilingual Matters.

Fiske, S. T. (1980). 'Attention and weight on person perception'. *Journal of Personality and Social Psychology*, 38, 889–906.

Fiske, S. T. (1993). 'Social cognition and social perception'. *Annual Review of Psychology*, 44, 155–94.

Fiske, S. T. and Neuberg, S. L. (1990). 'A continuum of impression formation, from category-based to individuating processes: influences of information and motivation on attention and interpretation' in L. Berkowitz (ed.), *Advances in Experimental Social Psychology* (vol. 23, pp. 1–74). New York: Academic Press.

Fiske, S. T. and Taylor, S. E. (1991). *Social Cognition* (2nd edn). New York: McGraw-Hill.

Fiske, S. T., Lau, R. R. and Smith, R. A. (1990). 'On the varieties and utilities of political expertise'. *Social Cognition*, 8, 31–48.

Flament, C. (1965). *Réseaux de communication et structures de groupe*. Paris: Dunod.

Fleishman, E. A. (1973). 'Twenty years of consideration and structure' in E. A. Fleishman and J. F. Hunt (eds), *Current Developments in the Study of Leadership*. Carbondale, IL: South Illinois University Press.

Fletcher, G. J. O. and Ward, C. (1988). 'Attribution theory and processes: a cross-cultural perspective' in M. H. Bond (ed.), *The Cross-cultural Challenge to Social Psychology* (pp. 230–44). Newbury Park, CA: Sage.

Fletcher, G. J. O., Danilovics, P., Fernandez, G., Peterson, D. and Reeder, G. D. (1986). 'Attributional complexity: an individual differences measure'. *Journal of Personality and Social Psychology*, 51, 875–84.

Fletcher, G. J. O., Fincham, F. D., Cramer, L. and Heron, N. (1987). 'The role of attributions in the development of dating relationships'. *Journal of Personality and Social Psychology*, 53, 481–89.

Flowers, M. L. (1977). 'A laboratory test of some implications of Janis's groupthink hypothesis'. *Journal of Personality and Social Psychology*, 35, 888–96.

Foa, E. B. and Foa, U. G. (1975). *Resource Theory of Social Exchange*. Morristown, NJ: General Learning Press.

Foa, E. B. and Foa, U. G. (1980). 'Resource theory: interpersonal behaviour as exchange' in K. J. Gergen, M. S. Greenberg and R. H. Willis (eds), *Social Exchange: Advances in Theory and Research*. New York: Plenum.

Fodor, E. M. and Smith, T. (1982). 'The power motive as an influence on group decision making'. *Journal of Personality and Social Psychology*, 42, 178–85.

Fogelson, R. M. (1970). 'Violence and grievances: reflections on the 1960's riot'. *Journal of Social Issues*, 26, 141–63.

Fong, G. T., Krantz, D. H. and Nisbett, R. E. (1986). 'The effects of statistical training on thinking about everyday problems'. *Cognitive Psychology*, 18, 253–92.

Forgas, J. P. (ed.) (1981). *Social Cognition: Perspectives on Everyday Understanding*. London: Academic Press.

Forgas, J. P. (1983). 'The effects of prototypicality and cultural salience on perceptions of people'. *Journal of Research in Personality*, 17, 153–73.

Forgas, J. P. (1985a). *Interpersonal Behaviour*. Sydney: Pergamon.

Forgas, J. P. (1985b). 'Person prototypes and cultural salience: the role of cognitive and cultural factors in impression formation'. *British Journal of Social Psychology*, 24, 3–17.

Forgas, J. P. and Dobosz, B. (1980). 'Dimensions of romantic involvement: towards a taxonomy of heterosexual relationships'. *Social Psychology Quarterly*, 43, 290–300.

Forgas, J. P., Morris, S. and Furnham, A. (1982). 'Lay explanations of wealth: attributions for economic success'. *Journal of Applied Social Psychology*, 12, 381–97.

Forgas, J. P., O'Connor, K. and Morris, S. (1983). 'Smile and punishment: the effects of facial expression on responsibility attributions by groups and individuals'. *Personality and Social Psychology Bulletin*, 2, 587–96.

Forsterling, F. and Rudolph, U. (1988). 'Situations, attributions and the evaluation of reactions'. *Journal of Personality and Social Psychology*, 54, 225–32.

Foss, R.D. and Dempsey, C.B. (1979). 'Blood donation and the foot-in-the-door technique'. *Journal of Personality and Social Psychology*, 37, 580–90.

Foucault, M. (1972). *The Archaeology of Knowledge*. London: Tavistock.

Fox, S. and Giles, H. (1993). 'Accommodating intergenerational contact: a critique and theoretical model'. *Journal of Ageing Studies*, 7, 423–51.

Franck, K. (1980). 'Friends and strangers: the social experience of living in urban and nonurban settings'. *Journal of Social Issues*, 52–71.

Frank, M. G. and Gilovich, T. (1989). 'Effect of memory perspective on retrospective causal attributions'. *Journal of Personality and Social Psychology*, 57, 399–403.

Fredericks, A.. J. and Dossett, D. L. (1983). 'Attitude–behaviour relations: a comparison of the Fishbein–Ajzen and the Bentler–Speckart models'. *Journal of Personality and Social Psychology*, 45, 501–12.

Freed, R. S. and Freed, S. A. (1989). 'Beliefs and practices resulting in female deaths and fewer females than males in India'. *Population and Environment*, 10, 144–61.

Freedman, J. (1975). *Crowding and Behaviour*. San Francisco, CA: Freeman.

Freedman, J. L. (1984). 'Effect of television violence on aggressiveness'. *Psychological Bulletin*. 92, 227–46.

Freedman, J., Heshka, S. and Levy, A. (1975) 'Population density and pathology: is there a relationship?' *Journal of Experimental Social Psychology*, 11, 539–52.

Freedman, J. L. and Fraser, S. C (1966): 'Compliance without pressure: the foot-in-the-door technique'. *Journal of Personality and Social Psychology*, 4, 195–202.

Freedman, J. L., Wallington, S. A. and Bless, E. (1967). 'Compliance without pressure: the effect of guilt'. *Journal of Personality and Social Psychology*, 7, 117–24.

Freeman, S., Walker, M. R., Bordon, R. and Latané, B. (1975). 'Diffusion of responsibility and restaurant tipping: cheaper by the bunch'. *Personality and Social Psychology Bulletin*, 1, 584–87.

Freides, D. (1974). 'Human information processing and sensory modality: cross-modal functions, information complexity, memory, and deficit'. *Psychological Bulletin*, 81, 284–310.

French, J. R. P. (1944). 'Organized and unorganized groups under fear and frustration'. *University of Iowa Studies of Child Welfare*, 20, 231–308.

French, J. R. P. and Raven, B. H. (1959). 'The bases of social power' in D. Cartwright (ed.), *Studies in Social Power* (pp. 118–49). Ann Arbor, MI: Institute for Social Research.

Freud, S. (1905). *Three Contributions to the Theory of Sex*. New York: Dutton.

Freud, S. (1921). *Group Psychology and the Analysis of the Ego*, in J. Strachey (ed.) (1953–64) *Standard Edition of the Complete Psychological Works* (vol. 18). London: Hogarth Press.

Freud, S. (1930). *Civilization and its Discontents*. London: Hogarth Press.

Frey, D. (1986). 'Recent research on selective exposure to information'. *Advances in Experimental Social Psychology*, 19, 41–80.

Frey, D. and Rosch, M. (1984). 'Information-seeking after decisions: the role of novelty of information and decision reversibility'. *Personality and Social Psychology Bulletin*, 10, 91–8.

Frick, R. W. (1985), 'Communication emotions: the role of prosodic features'. *Psychological Bulletin*, 97, 412–29.

Frieze, I. and Weiner, B. (1971). 'Cue utilization and attributional judgements for success and failure'. *Journal of Personality*, 39, 591–605.

Frohlich, N. and Oppenheimer, J. (1970). 'I get by with a little help from my friends'. *World Politics*, 23, 104–20.

Funder, D. C. (1982). 'On the accuracy of dispositional vs. situational attributions'. *Social Cognition*, 1, 205–22.

Funder, D. C. (1987). 'Errors and mistakes: evaluating the accuracy of social judgement'. *Psychological Bulletin*, 101, 75–90.

Furnham, A. (1982). 'Explanations for unemployment in Britain'. *European Journal of Social Psychology*, 12, 335–52.

Furnham, A. (1983). 'Attributions for affluence'. *Personality and Individual Differences*, 4, 31–40.

Furnham, A. (1986). 'Some explanations for immigration to, and emigration from, Britain'. *New Community*, 13, 65–78.

Furnham, A. and Bond, M. H. (1986). 'Hong Kong Chinese explanations for wealth'. *Journal of Economic Psychology*, 7, 447–60.

Gaertner, S. L. and Dovidio, J. F. (1977). 'The subtlety of white racism, arousal, and helping behavior'. *Journal of Personality and Social Psychology*, 35, 691–707.

Gaertner, S. L. and McLaughlin, J. P. (1983). 'Racial stereotypes: associations and ascriptions of positive and negative characteristics'. *Social Psychology Quarterly*, 46, 23–40.

Gaertner, S. L., Mann, J., Murrell, A. and Dovidio, J. F. (1989). 'Reducing intergroup bias: the benefits of recategorization'. *Journal of Personality and Social Psychology*, 57, 239–49.

Galizio, M. and Hendrick, C. (1972). 'Effect of musical accompaniment on attitude: the guitar as a prop for persuasion'. *Journal of Applied Social Psychology*, 2, 350–59.

Galle, O. R. and Gove, W. R. (1979). 'Crowding and behaviour in Chicago, 1949–1970' in J. R. Aiello and A Baum (eds), *Residential Crowding and Design*. New York: Plenum.

Galle, O. R., Gove, W. R. and McPherson, J. M. (1972). 'Population density and pathology: what are the relationships for man?' *Science*, 176, 23–30.

Gallois, C. (1993). 'The language and communication of emotion: interpersonal, intergroup, or universal'. *American Behavioral Scientist*, 36, 309–38.

Gallois, C. and Callan, V. J. (1986). 'Decoding emotional messages: influence of ethnicity, sex, message type, and channel'. *Journal of Personality and Social Psychology*, 51, 755–62.

Gallois, C., Callan, V. J. and Johnstone, M. (1984). 'Personality judgements of Australian Aborigine and white speakers: ethnicity, sex and context'. *Journal of Language and Social Psychology*, 3, 39–57.

Gallois, C., Barker, M., Jones, E. and Callan, V. J. (1992). 'Intercultural communication: evaluations of lecturers and Australian and Chinese students' in S. Iwawaki, Y. Kashima and K. Leung (eds), *Innovations in Cross-cultural Psychology* (pp. 86–102). Amsterdam: Swets and Zeitlinger.

Gallup, G. (1978). 'Gallup youth survey'. *Indianapolis Star*, 18 October.

Gardner, R. A. and Gardner, B. T. (1971). 'Teaching sign language to a chimpanzee'. *Science*, 165, 664–72.

Gardner, R. C. (1979). 'Social psychological aspects of second language acquisition' in H. Giles and R. St Clair (eds), *Language and Social Psychology* (pp. 193–220). Oxford: Blackwell.

Garfinkel, H. (1964). 'Studies of the routine grounds of everyday activities'. *Social Problems*, 11, 225–50.

Garfinkel, H. (1967). *Studies in Ethnomethodology*. Englewood Cliffs, NJ: Prentice Hall.

Garrett, P., Giles, H. and Coupland, N. (1989). 'The contexts of language learning: extending the intergroup model of second language acquisition' in S. Ting-Toomey and F. Korzenny (eds), *Language, Communication, and Culture* (pp. 201–21). Newbury Park, CA: Sage.

Gaskell, G. and Smith, P. (1985). 'An investigation of youths' attributions for unemployment and their political attitudes'. *Journal of Economic Psychology*, 6, 65–80.

Geen, R. G. (1968). 'Effects of frustration, attack, and prior training in aggressiveness upon aggressive behavior'. *Journal of Personality and Social Psychology*, 9, 316–21.

Geen, R. G. (1978). 'Some effects of observing violence on the behaviour of the observer' in B. A. Maher (ed.), *Process in Experimental Personality Research* (vol. 8). New York: Academic Press.

Geen, R. G. (1989). 'Alternative conceptions of social facilitation' in P. B. Paulus (ed.), *Psychology of Group Influence* (2nd edn, pp. 15–51). Hillsdale, NJ: Erlbaum.

Geen, R. G. (1991). 'Social motivation'. *Annual Review of Psychology*, 42, 377–99.

Geen, R. G. and Donnerstein, E. (eds) (1983). *Aggression: Theoretical and Empirical Reviews*. New York: Academic Press.

Geen, R. G. and Gange, J. J. (1977). 'Drive theory of social facilitation: twelve years of theory and research'. *Psychological Bulletin*, 84, 1267–88.

Geen, R. G. and O'Neal, E. C. (1969). 'Activation of cue-elicited aggression by general arousal'. *Journal of Personality and Social Psychology*, 11, 289–92.

Geen, R. G. and Quanty, M. (1977). 'The catharsis of aggression: an evaluation of a hypothesis' in L. Berkowitz (ed.). *Advances in Experimental Social Psychology*, (vol. 10, pp. 2–37). New York: Academic Press.

Geer, J. H. and Jarmecky, L. (1973). 'The effect of being responsible for reducing another's pain on subject's response and arousal'. *Journal of Personality and Social Psychology*, 26, 232–37.

Gelfand, D. M., Hartmann, D. P., Walder, P. and Page, B. (1973). 'Who reports shoplifters? A field-experimental study'. *Journal of Personality and Social Psychology*, 25, 276–85.

Gerard, H. B. and Hoyt, M. F. (1974). 'Distinctiveness of social categorization and attitude toward ingroup members'. *Journal of Personality and Social Psychology*, 29, 836–42.

Gerard, H. B. and Mathewson, G. C. (1966). 'The effects of severity of initiation on liking for a group: a replication'. *Journal of Experimental Social Psychology*, 2, 278–87.

Gergen, K. J. (1973). 'Social psychology as history'. *Journal of Personality and Social Psychology*, 26, 309–20.

Gergen, K. J., Gergen, M. M. and Meter, K. (1972). 'Individual orientations to prosocial behavior'. *Journal of Social Issues*, 28, 105–30.

Giles, H. (1978). 'Linguistic differentiation in ethnic groups' in H. Tajfel (ed.), *Differentiation between Social Groups: Studies in the Social Psychology of Intergroup Relations* (pp. 361–93). London: Academic Press.

Giles, H. (ed.) (1984). 'The dynamics of speech accommodation theory'. *International Journal of the Sociology of Language*, 46, whole issue.

Giles, H. and Byrne, J. L. (1982). 'The intergroup model of second language acquisition'. *Journal of Multilingual and Multicultural Development*, 3, 17–40.

Giles, H. and Coupland, N. (1991). *Language: Contexts and Consequences*, Milton Keynes: Open University Press.

Giles, H. and Johnson, P. (1981). 'The role of language in ethnic group relations' in J. C. Turner and H. Giles (eds), *Intergroup Behaviour* (pp. 199–43). Oxford: Blackwell.

Giles, H. and Johnson, P. (1987). 'Ethnolinguistic identity theory: a social psychological approach to language maintenance'. *International Journal of the Sociology of Language*, 68, 66–99.

Giles, H. and Powesland, P. F. (1975). *Speech Style and Social Evaluation*. London: Academic Press.

Giles, H. and Street, R. (1985). 'Communicator characteristics and behaviour' in M. L. Knapp and G. R. Miller (eds), *Handbook of Interpersonal Communication* (pp. 205–61). Beverly Hills, CA: Sage.

Giles, H., Taylor, D. M. and Bourhis, R. Y. (1973). 'Towards a theory of interpersonal accommodation through language: some Canadian data'. *Language in Society*, 2, 177–92.

Giles, H., Bourhis, R. Y. and Taylor, D. M. (1977). 'Towards a theory of language in ethnic group relations' in H. Giles (ed.), *Language, Ethnicity, and Intergroup Relations* (pp. 307–48). London: Academic Press.

Giles, H., Rosenthal, D. and Young, L. (1985). 'Perceived ethnolinguistic vitality: the Anglo- and Greek-Australian setting'. *Journal of Multilingual and Multicultural Development*, 6, 253–69.

Giles, H., Mulac, A., Bradac, J. J. and Johnson, P. (1987). 'Speech accommodation theory: the next decade and beyond', in *Communication Yearbook* (vol. 10, pp. 13–48). Newbury Park, CA: Sage.

Giles, H., Coupland, N., Henwood, K., Harriman, J. and Coupland, J. (1990). 'The social meaning of RP: an intergenerational perspective' in S. Ramsaran (ed.), *Studies in the Pronunciation of English: A Commemorative Volume in Honour of A. C. Gimson* (pp. 191–211). London: Routledge.

Glass, D. C. and Singer, J. E. (1972). *Urban Stress: Experiments on Noise and Social Stressors*. New York: Academic Press.

Glenn, N. and Hill, N. (1977). 'Rural–urban differences in attitudes and behavior in the United States'. *Annals of the American Academy of Political and Social Science*, 429, 36–50.

Goethals, G. R. and Darley, J. M. (1987). 'Social comparison theory: self-evaluation and group life' in B. Mullen and G. Goethals (eds), *Theories of Group Behaviour*. New York: Springer-Verlag.

Goethals, G. R. and Nelson, R. E. (1973). 'Similarity in the influence process: the belief–value distinction'. *Journal of Personality and Social Psychology*, 25, 117–22.

Goethals, G. R. and Zanna, M. P. (1979). 'The role of social comparison in choice shifts'. *Journal of Personality and Social Psychology*, 37, 1469–76.

Goffman, E. (1959). *The Presentation of Self in Everyday Life*. New York: Doubleday Anchor.

Goffman, E. (1961). *Asylums*. New York: Doubleday.

Goldberg, M. E. and Gorn, G. J. (1974). 'Children's reactions to television advertising: an experimental approach'. *Journal of Consumer Research*, 1, 69–75.

Goldberg, P. (1968). 'Are some women prejudiced against women?' *Trans-Action*, 5, 28–30.

Goldstein, A. P. (1987). 'Aggression' in R. J. Corsini (ed.), *Concise Encyclopedia of Psychology* (pp. 35–39). New York: Wiley.

Goldstein, J. H. (1980). *Social Psychology*. New York: Academic Press.

Goodman, M. (1964). *Race Awareness in Young Children* (2nd edn). New York: Cromwell-Collier.

Gorer, G. (1968). 'Man has no "killer" instinct' in M. F. A. Montagu (ed.), *Man and Aggression* (pp. 27–36). New York: Oxford University Press.

Gorsuch, R. L. and Ortbergh, J. (1983). 'Moral obligation and attitudes: their relation to behavioral intentions'. *Journal of Personality and Social Psychology*, 44, 1025–28.

Gosselin, C. and Wilson, G. (1980). *Sexual Variations*. New York: Simon and Schuster.

Gottlieb, J. and Carver, C. S. (1980). 'Anticipation of future interaction and the bystander effect'. *Journal of Experimental Social Psychology*, 16, 253–60.

Gouldner, A. W. (1960). 'The norm of reciprocity: a preliminary statement'. *American Sociological Review*, 25, 161–78.

Granberg, D. (1987). 'Candidate preference, membership group, and estimates of voting behavior'. *Social Cognition*, 5, 323–35.

Graumann, C. F. and Moscovici, S. (eds). (1986). *Changing Conceptions of Crowd Mind and Behaviour*. New York: Springer-Verlag.

Graumann, C. F. and Moscovici, S. (eds) (1987). *Changing Conceptions of Conspiracy*. New York: Springer-Verlag.

Greenberg, J. and Rosenfield, D. (1979). 'Whites' ethnocentrism and their attributions for the behaviour of blacks: a motivational bias'. *Journal of Personality*, 47, 643–57.

Greenberg, J., Williams, K. D. and O'Brien, M. K. (1986). 'Considering the harshest verdict first: biasing effects on mock juror verdict'. *Personality and Social Psychology Bulletin*, 12, 41–50.

Greene, K. B. (1979). 'The effects of community noise exposure on the reading and hearing ability of Brooklyn and Queens School Children'. Dissertation for the Program in Environmental Health Sciences, New York University.

Greenglass, E. R. (1982). *A World of Difference: Gender Roles in Perspective*. Toronto: Wiley.

Greenwald, A. G. and Pratkanis, A. R. (1984). 'The self' in R. S. Wyer, Jr and T. K. Srull (eds), *Handbook of Social Cognition* (vol. 3, pp. 129–78). Hillsdale, NJ: Erlbaum.

Greenwald, A. G. and Pratkanis, A. R. (1988). 'On the use of 'theory' and the usefulness of theory'. *Psychological Review*, 25, 575–79

Gregson, R. A. M. and Stacey, B. G. (1981). 'Attitudes and self-reported alcohol consumption in New Zealand'. *New Zealand Psychologist*, 10, 15–23.

Griffit, W. (1970). 'Environmental effects on interpersonal affective behaviour: ambient effective temperature and attraction'. *Journal of Personality and Social Psychology*, 15, 240–44.

Griffit, W. B. and Guay, P. (1969). '"Object" evaluation and conditioned affect'. *Journal of Experimental Research in Psychology*, 4, 1–8.

Griffit, W. B. and Veitch, R. (1971). 'Hot and crowded: influence of population density and temperature on interpersonal affective behavior'. *Journal of Personality and Social Psychology*, 17, 92–98.

Groff, B. D., Baron, R. S. and Moore, D. L. (1983). 'Distraction, attentional conflict, and drivelike behavior'. *Journal of Experimental Social Psychology*, 19, 359–80.

Gross, A. E. and Fleming, J. (1982). 'Twenty years of deception in social psychology'. *Personality and Social Psychology Bulletin*, 8, 402–08.

Gross, A. E., Wallston, B. S. and Piliavin, J. M. (1975). 'Beneficiary attractiveness and cost as determinants of responses to routine requests for help'. *Sociometry*, 38, 131–40.

Grusec, J. E. (1982). 'The socialization of altruism' in N. Eisenberg (ed.), *The Development of Prosocial Behaviour* (pp. 65–90). New York: Academic Press.

Grusec, J. E. and Redler, E. (1980). 'Attribution, reinforcement and altruism: a developmental analysis'. *Developmental Psychology*, 16, 525–34.

Grusec, J. E. and Skubiski, S. L. (1970). 'Model nurturance, demand characteristics of the modeling experiment, and altruism'. *Journal of Personality and Social Psychology*, 14, 352–59.

Grusec, J. E., Kuczynski, L., Rushton, J. P. and Simutis, Z. M. (1978). 'Modelling, direct instruction, and attributions: effects on altruism'. *Developmental Psychology*, 14, 51–57.

Guardo, C. J. and Meisels, M. (1971). 'Factor structure of children's personal space schemata'. *Child Development*, 42, 1307–1302.

Gubar, S. and Hoff, J. (eds). (1989). *For Adult Users Only: The Dilemma of Violent Pornography*. Bloomington, IN: Indiana University Press.

Guerin, B. (1986). 'Mere presence effects in humans: a review'. *Journal of Experimental Social Psychology*, 22, 38–77.

Guerin, B. (1989). 'Reducing evaluation effects in mere presence'. *Journal of Social Psychology*, **129**, 183–90.

Guerin, B. (1993). *Social Facilitation*. Cambridge: Cambridge University Press.

Guerin, B. and Innes, J. M. (1982). 'Social facilitation and social monitoring: a new look at Zajonc's mere presence hypothesis'. *British Journal of Social Psychology*, **21**, 7–18.

Guimond, S. and Dubé-Simard, L. (1983). 'Relative deprivation theory and the Québec Nationalist Movement: the cognitive–emotion distinction and the personal–group deprivation issue'. *Journal of Personality and Social Psychology*, **44**, 526–35.

Gurr, T. R. (1970). *Why Men Rebel*. Princeton, NJ: Princeton University Press.

Gutek, B. A. (1985). *Sex and the Workplace*. San Francisco, CA: Jossey-Bass.

Haas, A. (1979). 'Male and female spoken language differences: stereotypes and evidence'. *Psychological Bulletin*, **86**, 616–26.

Haines, H. (1980). 'The origins of modern social psychology'. PhD thesis, University of Auckland.

Haines, H. (1987). *Mental Health for Women*. Auckland: Reed Methuen.

Haines, H. and Vaughan, G. M. (1979). 'Was 1898 a great date in the history of social psychology?' *Journal for the History of the Behavioural Sciences*, **15**, 323–32.

Haire, M. and Grune, W. E. (1950). 'Perceptual defenses: processes protecting an organized perception of another personality'. *Human Relations*, **3**, 403–12.

Hall, B. J. and Gudykunst, W. B. (1986). 'The intergroup theory of second language ability'. *Journal of Language and Social Psychology*, **5**, 291–302.

Hall, E. T. (1966). *The Hidden Dimension*. New York: Doubleday.

Hall, E. T. (1979). 'Gender, gender roles, and nonverbal communication' in R. Rosenthal (ed.), *Skill in Nonverbal Communication* (pp. 32–67). Cambridge, MA: Oelgeschlager, Gunn and Hain.

Hall, E. T. and Braunwald, K. G. (1981). 'Gender cues in conversations'. *Journal of Personality and Social Psychology*, **40**, 99–110.

Hall, G. (1984). 'Women and violent crime: New Zealand 1950–1979'. *Papers of the Women's Studies Association Conference*, no. 6. Christchurch.

Hall, J. A. (1978). 'Gender effects in decoding nonverbal cues'. *Psychological Bulletin*, **85**, 845–57.

Hamilton, D. L. (1979). 'A cognitive attributional analysis of stereotyping' in L. Berkowitz (ed.), *Advances in Experimental Social Psychology* (vol. 12, pp. 53–84). New York: Academic Press.

Hamilton, D. L. and Gifford, R. K. (1976). 'Illusory correlation in interpersonal personal perception: a cognitive basis of stereotypic judgements'. *Journal of Experimental Social Psychology*, **12**, 392–407.

Hamilton, D. L. and Rose, T. L. (1980). 'Illusory correlation and the maintenance of stereotypic beliefs'. *Journal of Personality and Social Psychology*, **39**, 832–45.

Hamilton, D. L. and Zanna, M. P. (1972). 'Differential weighting of favorable and unfavorable attributes in impressions of personality'. *Journal of Experimental Research in Personality*, **6**, 204–12.

Hampson, S. E., John, O. P. and Goldberg, L. R. (1986). 'Category breadth and hierarchical structure in personality: studies in asymmetries in judgements of trait implications'. *Journal of Personality and Social Psychology*, **51**, 37–54.

Haney, C., Banks, C. and Zimbardo, P. (1973). 'Interpersonal dynamics in a simulated prison'. *International Journal of Criminology and Penology*, **1**, 69–97.

Hardin, G. (1968). 'The tragedy of the commons'. *Science*, **162**, 1243–48.

Harkins, S. G. (1987). 'Social loafing and social facilitation'. *Journal of Experimental Social Psychology*, **23**, 1–18.

Harkins, S. G. and Szymanski, K. (1987). 'Social loafing and social facilitation: new wine in old bottles' in C. Hendrick (ed.), *Review of Personality and Social Psychology: Group Processes and Intergroup Relations* (vol. 9, pp. 167–88). Newbury Park, CA: Sage.

Harkins, S. G. and Szymanski, K. (1989). 'Social loafing and group evaluation'. *Journal of Personality and Social Psychology*, 56, 934–41.

Harlow, H. F. (1958). 'The nature of love'. *American Psychologist*, 13, 673–85.

Harlow, H. F. and Harlow, M. K. (1965). 'The affectional systems' in A. M. Schrier, H. F. Harlow and F. Stollnitz (eds), *Behaviour of Non-human Primates* (vol. 2). New York: Academic Press.

Harlow, H. F. and Zimmermann, R. R. (1959). 'Affectional responses in the infant monkey'. *Science*, 130, 421.

Harries, K. D. and Stadler, S. J. (1983). 'Determinism revisited: assault and heat stress in Dallas, 1980'. *Environment and Behaviour*, 15, 235–56.

Harris, C. S. (1973). 'The effects of different types of acoustic stimulation on performance' in W. D. Ward (ed.), *Proceedings of the International Congress on Noise as a Public Health Problem*. Washington, DC: US Environmental Protection Agency.

Harris, E. E. (1970). *Hypothesis and Perception*. London: Allen and Unwin.

Harré, R. (1979). *Social Being: A Theory for Social Psychology*. Oxford: Blackwell.

Hart, P. T. (1990). *Groupthink in Government: A Study of Small Groups and Policy Failure*. Amsterdam: Swets & Zeitlinger.

Hartley, J. F. and Stephenson, G. M. (eds) (1992). *Employment Relations: The Psychology of Influence and Control at Work*. Oxford: Blackwell.

Hartman, T. and Mitchell, J. (1984). *A World Atlas of Military History 1945–1984*. London: Cooper/Secker and Warburg.

Hartmann, H., Kris, E. and Loewenstein, R. M. (1949). 'Notes on a theory of aggression'. *Psychoanalytic Study of the Child*, 3/4, 9–36.

Hartnett, J. J., Bailey, F. and Gibson, W. (1970). 'Personal space as influenced by sex and type of movement'. *Journal of Psychology*, 76, 139–44.

Harvey, J. H. (1987). 'Attributions in close relationships: research and theoretical developments'. *Journal of Social and Clinical Psychology*, 5, 420–34.

Harvey, J. H. and Weary, G. (1981). *Perspectives on Attributional Processes*. Dubuque, IA: W. C. Brown.

Haslam, S. A., Turner, J. C., Oakes, P. J., McGarty, C. and Hayes, B. K. (1992). 'Context-dependent variation in social stereotyping. 1: The effects of intergroup relations as mediated by social change and frame of reference'. *European Journal of Social Psychology*, 22, 3–20.

Hassett, J. (1981). 'But that would be wrong ...'. *Psychology Today*, November, 34–50.

Hastie, R. (1984). 'Causes and effects of causal attribution'. *Journal of Personality and Social Psychology*, 46, 44–56.

Hastie, R. (1988). 'A computer simulation model of person memory'. *Journal of Experimental Social Psychology*, 24, 423–47.

Hastie, R. (ed.) (1993). *Inside the Juror: The Psychology of Juror Decision Making*. Cambridge: Cambridge University Press.

Hastie, R. and Park, B. (1986). 'The relationship between memory and judgement depends on whether the judgement task is memory-based or on-line'. *Psychological Review*, 93, 258–68.

Hastie, R., Penrod, S. D. and Pennington, N. (1983). *Inside the Jury*. Cambridge, MA: Harvard University Press.

Hatfield, E. (1987). 'Love' in R. J. Corsini (ed.), *Concise Encyclopaedia of Psychology* (pp. 676–77). New York: Wiley.

Hatfield, E. and Walster, G. W. (1981). *A New Look at Love*. Reading, MA: Addison-Wesley.

Hawking, S. W. (1988). *A Brief History of Time: From the Big Bang to Black Holes*. London: Bantam.

Hayduk, L. A. (1983). 'Personal space: where we now stand'. *Psychological Bulletin*, 94, 293–335.

Heaven, P. C. L. (1990). 'Human values and suggestions for reducing unemployment'. *British Journal of Social Psychology*, 29, 257–64.

Hebb, D. O. and Thompson, W. R. (1968). 'The social significance of animal studies' in G. Lindzey and

E. Aronson (eds), *Handbook of Social Psychology* (2nd edn, vol. 2, pp. 729–74). Reading, MA: Addison-Wesley.

Hechinger, F. M. (1980). 'Studies examine the issue of ethics'. *New York Times*, 30 December, pp. C1, C3.

Heider, F. (1946). 'Attitudes and cognitive organization'. *Journal of Psychology*, 21, 107–12.

Heider, F. (1958). *The Psychology of Interpersonal Relations*. New York: Wiley.

Heider, F. and Simmel, M. (1944). 'An experimental study of apparent behavior'. *American Journal of Psychology*, 57, 243–59.

Heisler, G. (1974). 'Ways to deter law violators: effects of levels of threat and vicarious punishment on cheating'. *Journal of Consulting and Clinical Psychology*, 42, 577–82.

Heller, J., Groff, B. D. and Solomon, S. H. (1977). 'Toward an understanding of crowding: the role of physical interaction'. *Journal of Personality and Social Psychology*, 35, 183–90.

Henderson, J. and Taylor, J. (1985). 'Study finds bias in death sentences: killers of whites risk execution'. *Times Union*, 17 November, p. A–19.

Hendrick, C., Bixenstine, V. E. and Hawkins, G. (1971). 'Race vs. belief similarities as determinants of attraction: a search for a fair test'. *Journal of Personality and Social Psychology*, 17, 250–58.

Henley, N. M. (1973). 'The politics of touch' in P. Brown (ed.), *Radical Psychology* (pp. 421–33). New York: Harper and Row.

Henley, N. M. (1977). *Body Politics: Power, Sex, and Nonverbal Communication*. Englewood Cliffs, NJ: Prentice Hall.

Henley, N. M. and Harmon, S. (1985). 'The nonverbal semantics of power and gender: a perceptual study' in S. L. Ellyson and J. F. Dovidio (eds), *Power, Dominance, and Nonverbal Behaviour* (pp. 151–64). New York: Springer-Verlag.

Henriques, J., Holloway, W., Urwin, C., Venn, C. and Walkerdine, V. (1984). *Changing the Subject: Psychology, Social Regulation, and Subjectivity*. London: Methuen.

Hensley, T. R. and Griffin, G. W. (1986). 'Victims of groupthink: the Kent State University Board of Trustees and the 1977 gymnasium controversy'. *Journal of Conflict Resolution*, 30, 497–531.

Herek, G. M. and Glunt, E. K. (1988). 'An epidemic of stigma: public reaction to AIDS'. *American Psychologist*, 43, 886–91.

Herr, P. M., Sherman, S. J. and Fazio, R. H. (1983). 'On the consequences of priming: assimilation and contrast effects'. *Journal of Experimental Social Psychology*, 19, 323–40.

Hersh, S. (1970). *My Lai: A Report on the Massacre and Its Aftermath*. New York: Vintage Books.

Heslin, R. (1978). 'Responses to touching as an index of sex-role norms and attitudes'. Paper presented at the annual meeting of the American Psychological Association, Toronto.

Heslin, R. and Alper, T. (1983). 'Touch: a bonding gesture' in J. M. Wiemann and R. P. Harrison (eds), *Nonverbal Interaction* (pp. 47–75). Beverly Hills, CA: Sage.

Hess, E. H. (1965). 'The pupil responds to changes in attitude as well as to changes in illumination'. *Scientific American*, 212, 46–54.

Hewes, G. W. (1957). 'The anthropology of posture'. *Scientific American*, 196, 123–32.

Hewstone, M. R. C. (1986). *Understanding Attitudes to the European Community: A Social-psychological Study in Four Member States*. Cambridge: Cambridge University Press.

Hewstone, M. (1989). *Causal Attribution: From Cognitive Processes to Collective Beliefs*. Oxford: Blackwell.

Hewstone, M. and Antaki, C. (1988). 'Attribution theory and social explanations' in M. Hewstone, W. Stroebe, J-P. Codol and G. M. Stephenson (eds), *Introduction to Social Psychology: A European Perspective* (pp. 111–41). Oxford: Blackwell.

Hewstone, M. and Brown, R. J. (eds) (1986). *Contact and Conflict in Intergroup Encounters*. Oxford: Blackwell.

Hewstone, M. and Jaspars, J. M. F. (1982). 'Intergroup relations and attribution processes' in H. Tajfel (ed.), *Social Identity and Intergroup Relations* (pp. 99–133). Cambridge: Cambridge University Press.

Hewstone, M. and Jaspars, J. M. F. (1984). 'Social dimensions of attribution' in H. Tajfel (ed.), *The Social Dimension* (pp. 379–404). Cambridge: Cambridge University Press.

Hewstone, M. and Ward, C. (1985). 'Ethnocentrism and causal attribution in Southeast Asia'. *Journal of Personality and Social Psychology*, 48, 614–23.

Hewstone, M., Jaspars, J. M. F. and Lalljee, M. (1982). 'Social representations, social attribution and social identity: the intergroup images of "public" and "comprehensive" schoolboys'. *European Journal of Social Psychology*, 12, 241–69.

Hewstone, M., Stroebe, W., Codol, J-P. and Stephenson, G. M. (eds) (1988). *Introduction to Social Psychology*. Oxford: Blackwell.

Higgins, E. T. (1981). 'The "communication game": implications for social cognition' in E. T. Higgins, C. P. Herman and M. Zanna (eds), *Social Cognition: The Ontario Symposium* (vol. 1, pp. 343–92). Hillsdale, NJ: Erlbaum.

Higgins, E. T. (1987). 'Self-discrepancy: a theory relating self and affect'. *Psychological Review*, 94, 319–40.

Higgins, E. T. (1989). 'Self-discrepancy theory: what patterns of self-belief cause people to suffer?' in L. Berkowitz (ed.), *Advances in Experimental Social Psychology* (vol. 22, pp. 93–136). New York: Academic Press.

Higgins, E. T. and Bargh, J. A. (1987). 'Social cognition and social perception'. *Annual Review of Psychology*, 38, 369–425.

Higgins, E. T., Bargh, J. A. and Lombardi, W. (1985). 'The nature of priming effects on categorization'. *Journal of Experimental Psychology: Learning, Memory, and Cognition*, 11, 59–69.

Higgins, E. T., van Hook, E. and Dorfman, D. (1988). 'Do self-attributes form a cognitive structure?' *Social Cognition*, 6, 177–207.

Hilton, D. J. (1988). 'Logic and causal attribution' in D. J. Hilton (ed.), *Contemporary Science and Natural Explanation: Commonsense Conceptions of Causality*. Brighton: Harvester Press.

Hilton, D. J. (in press). 'A conversational model of causal explanation'. *Psychological Bulletin*.

Himmelfarb, S. and Eagly, A. H. (eds) (1974). *Readings in Attitude Change*. New York: Wiley.

Himmelweit, H. T., Humphreys, P. and Jaeger, M. (1985). *How Voters Decide: A Model of Vote Choice based on a Special Longitudinal Study Extending Over Fifteen Years and the British Election Surveys of 1970–1983*. Milton Keynes: Open University Press.

Hinde, R. A. (1982). *Ethology: Its Nature and Relations with Other Sciences*. London: Fontana.

Hockey, G. R. J. and Hamilton P. (1970). 'Arousal and information selection in short-term memory'. *Nature*, 226, 866–67.

Hoffman, C., Mischel, W. and Mazze, K. (1981). 'The role of purpose in the organization of information about behaviour: trait-based versus goal-based categories in person cognition'. *Journal of Personality and Social Psychology*, 40, 211–25.

Hoffman, C., Lau, I. and Johnson, D. R. (1986). 'The linguistic relativity of person cognition: an English–Chinese comparison'. *Journal of Personality and Social Psychology*, 51, 1097–105.

Hoffman, M. L. (1981). 'Is altruism part of human nature?' *Journal of Personality and Social Psychology*, 40, 121–37.

Hogg, M. A. (1985). 'Masculine and feminine speech in dyads and groups: a study of speech style and gender salience'. *Journal of Language and Social Psychology*, 4, 99–112.

Hogg, M. A. (1987). 'Social identity and group cohesiveness' in J. C. Turner, M. A. Hogg, P. J. Oakes, S. D. Reicher and M. S. Wetherell (eds), *Rediscovering the Social Group: A Self-categorization Theory* (pp. 89–116). Oxford: Blackwell.

Hogg, M. A. (1992). *The Social Psychology of Group Cohesiveness: From Attraction to Social Identity*. London: Harvester Wheatsheaf.

Hogg, M. A. (1993). 'Group cohesiveness: a critical review and some new directions'. *European Review of Social Psychology*, 4, 85–111.

Hogg, M. A. and Abrams, D. (1988). *Social Identifications: A Social Psychology of Intergroup Relations and Group Processes*. London: Routledge.

Hogg, M. A. and Abrams, D. (1990). 'Social motivation, self-esteem and social identity' in D. Abrams and M. A. Hogg (eds), *Social Identity Theory: Constructive and Critical Advances* (pp. 28–47). London: Harvester Wheatsheaf.

Hogg, M. A. and Abrams, D. (1993). 'Towards a single-process uncertainty-reduction model of social motivation in groups' in M. A. Hogg and D. Abrams (eds), *Group Motivation: Social Psychological Perspectives* (pp. 173–90). London: Harvester Wheatsheaf.

Hogg, M. A. and Hains, S. C. (1994). 'Intergroup relations and group solidarity: effects of group identification and social beliefs on depersonalized attraction'. Unpublished manuscript, University of Queensland.

Hogg, M. A. and Hardie, E. A. (1991). 'Social attraction, personal attraction, and self-categorization: a field study'. *Personality and Social Psychology Bulletin*, 17, 175–80.

Hogg, M. A. and McGarty, C. (1990). 'Self-categorization and social identity' in D. Abrams and M. A. Hogg (eds), *Social Identity Theory: Constructive and Critical Advances* (pp. 10–27). London: Harvester Wheatsheaf.

Hogg, M. A. and Sunderland, J. (1991). 'Self-esteem and intergroup discrimination in the minimal group paradigm'. *British Journal of Social Psychology*, 30, 51–62.

Hogg, M. A. and Turner, J. C. (1985). 'Interpersonal attraction, social identification and psychological group formation'. *European Journal of Social Psychology*, 15, 51–66.

Hogg, M. A. and Turner, J. C. (1987a). 'Social identity and conformity: a theory of referent informational influence' in W. Doise and S. Moscovici (eds), *Current Issues in European Social Psychology* (vol. 2, pp. 139–82). Cambridge: Cambridge University Press.

Hogg, M. A. and Turner, J. C. (1987b). 'Intergroup behaviour, self-stereotyping and the salience of social categories'. *British Journal of Social Psychology*, 26, 325–40.

Hogg, M. A., Joyce, N. and Abrams, D. (1984). 'Diglossia in Switzerland? A social identity analysis of speaker evaluations'. *Journal of Language and Social Psychology*, 3, 185–96.

Hogg, M. A., Turner, J. C., Nascimento-Schulze, C. and Spriggs, D. (1986). 'Social categorization, intergroup behaviour and self-esteem: two experiments'. *Revista de Psicología Social*, 1, 23–37.

Hogg, M. A., D'Agata, P. and Abrams, D. (1989). 'Ethnolinguistic betrayal and speaker evaluations among Italian Australians'. *Genetic, Social and General Psychology Monographs*, 115, 153–81.

Hogg, M. A., Turner, J. C. and Davidson, B. (1990). 'Polarized norms and social frames of reference: A test of the self-categorization theory of group polarization'. *Basic and Applied Social Psychology*, 11, 77–100.

Hogg, M. A., Cooper-Shaw, L. and Holzworth, D. W. (1993). 'Group prototypicality and depersonalized attraction in small interactive groups'. *Personality and Social Psychology Bulletin*, 19, 452–65.

Hogg, M. A., Hardie, E. A. and Reynolds, K. (1994). 'Prototypical similarity, self-categorization, and depersonalized attraction: a perspective on group cohesiveness'. *European Journal of Social Psychology*, 24.

Holahan, C. (1982). *Environmental Psychology*. New York: Random House.

Hollander, E. P. (1958). 'Conformity, status, and idiosyncrasy credit'. *Psychological Review*, 65, 117–27.

Hollander, E. P. (1967). *Principles and Methods of Social Psychology*. New York: Oxford University Press.

Hollander, E. P. (1985). 'Leadership and power' in G. Lindzey and E. Aronson (eds), *Handbook of Social Psychology* (3rd edn, vol. 2, pp. 485–537). New York: Random House.

Hollander, E. P. and Julian, J. W. (1970). 'Studies in leader legitimacy, influence, and innovation' in L. Berkowitz (ed.), *Advances in Experimental Social Psychology* (vol. 5, pp. 34–69). New York: Academic Press.

Holloway, S., Tucker, L. and Hornstein, H. A. (1977). 'The effects of social and nonsocial information on interpersonal behaviour of males: the news makes news'. *Journal of Personality and Social Psychology*, 35, 514–22.

Holtzworth-Munroe, A. and Jacobson, N. S. (1985). 'Causal attributions of married couples: when do they search for causes? What do they conclude when they do?' *Journal of Personality and Social Psychology*, 48, 1398–412.

Homans, G. C. (1961). *Social Behaviour: Its Elementary Forms*. New York: Harcourt, Brace & World.

Horai, J. (1977). 'Attributional conflict'. *Journal of Social Issues*, 33, 88–100.

Hornblow, A. R. (1980). 'The study of empathy'. *New Zealand Psychologist*, 2, 19–28.

Hornstein, G. A. (1985). 'Intimacy in conversational style as a function of the degree of closeness between members of a dyad'. *Journal of Personality and Social Psychology*, 42, 671–81.

Hornstein, H. A. (1970). 'The influence of social models on helping' in J. Macaulay and L. Berkowitz (eds), *Altruism and Helping Behaviour*. New York: Academic Press.

Horowitz, D. L. (1973). 'Direct, displaced and cumulative ethnic aggression'. *Comparative Politics*, 6, 1–16.

House, R. (1977). 'A 1976 theory of charismatic leadership' in J. G. Hunt and L. Larson (eds), *Leadership: The Cutting Edge* (pp. 189–207). Carbondale, IL: Southern Illinois University Press.

Hovland, C. I. and Sears, R. R. (1940). 'Minor studies in aggression. VI: Correlation of lynchings with economic indices'. *Journal of Psychology*, 2, 301–10.

Hovland, C. I. and Weiss, W. (1952). 'The influence of source credibility in communication effectiveness'. *Public Opinion Quarterly*, 15, 635–50.

Hovland, C. I., Lumsdaine, A. A. and Sheffield, F. D. (1949). *Experiments in Mass Communication*. Princeton, NJ: Princeton University Press.

Hovland, C. I., Janis, I. L. and Kelley, H. H. (1953). *Communication and Persuasion*. New Haven: Yale University Press.

Howard, J. A. (1985). 'Further appraisal of correspondent inference theory'. *Personality and Social Psychology Bulletin*, 11, 467–77.

Howard, J. W. and Rothbart, M. (1980). 'Social categorization and memory for ingroup and outgroup behavior'. *Journal of Personality and Social Psychology*, 38, 301–10.

Howell, D. C. (1987). *Statistical Methods for Psychology* (2nd edn). Boston, MA: PWS/Kent.

Howell, S., Epp, G., Reizenstein, J. E. and Alberight, C. (1976). *Shared Spaces in Housing for the Elderly*. Boston, MA: MIT Dept of Architecture.

Huesmann, L. R. (1988). 'An information processing model for the development of aggression'. *Aggressive Behaviour*, 14, 13–24.

Huesmann, L. R., Eron, L. D., Lefkowitz, M. M. and Walder, L. O. (1984). 'Stability of aggression over time and generations'. *Developmental Psychology*, 20, 1120–34.

Hughes, M. T. (1981). 'To cheat or not to cheat?' *Albany Times-Union*, 26 July, pp. B-1, B-3.

Hummert, M. L. (1990). 'Multiple stereotypes of elderly and young adults: a comparison of structure and evaluations'. *Psychology and Aging*, 5, 182–93.

Hunter, E. M. (1991). 'The intercultural and socio-historical context of Aboriginal personal violence in remote Australia'. *Australian Psychologist*, 26, 89–98.

Huston, T. L. and Korte, C. (1976). 'The responsive bystander: why he helps' in T. Lickona (ed.), *Morality: A Handbook of Moral Behaviour and Development*. (pp. 269–283). New York: Holt, Rinehart & Winston.

Ingham, A. G., Levinger, G., Graves, J. and Peckham, V. (1974). 'The Ringelmann effect: studies of group size and group performance'. *Journal of Experimental Social Psychology*, 10, 371–84.

Insel, P. M. and Lindgren, H. C. (1978). *Too Close for Comfort: The Psychology of Crowding*. Englewood Cliffs, NJ: Prentice Hall.

Insko, C. A. (1965). Verbal reinforcement of attitude. *Journal of Personality and Social Psychology*, 2, 621–23.

Insko, C. A. (1967). *Theories of Attitude Change*. New York: Appleton-Century-Crofts.

Insko, C. A., Nacoste, R. W. and Moe, J. L. (1983). 'Belief congruence and racial discrimination: review of the evidence and critical evaluation'. *European Journal of Social Psychology*, 13, 153–74.

Isen, A. M. (1970). 'Success, failure, attention, and reaction to others: the warm glow of success'. *Journal of Personality and Social Psychology*, 15, 294–301.

Isen, A. M. and Stalker, T. E. (1982). 'The effect of feeling state on evaluation of positive, neutral, and negative stimuli when you "accentuate the positive": do you "eliminate the negative"?' *Social Psychology Quarterly*, 45, 58–63.

Isen, A. M., Clark, M. and Schwartz, M. (1976). 'Duration of the effect of good mood on helping: "footprints on the sands of time"'. *Journal of Personality and Psychology*, 34, 385–93.

Isen, A. M., Horn, N. and Rosenhan, D. L. (1973). 'Effects of success and failure on children's generosity'. *Journal of Personality and Social Psychology*, 27, 239–47.

Isenberg, D. J. (1986). 'Group polarization: a critical review'. *Journal of Personality and Social Psychology*, 50, 1141–51.

Israel, J. and Tajfel, H. (eds) (1972). *The Context of Social Psychology: A Critical Assessment*. London: Academic Press.

Izraeli, D. N. and Izraeli, D. (1985). 'Sex effects in evaluating leaders: a replication study'. *Journal of Applied Psychology*, 70, 540–46.

Izraeli, D. N., Izraeli, D. and Eden, D. (1985). 'Giving credit where credit is due: a case of no sex bias in attribution'. *Journal of Applied Social Psychology*, 15, 516–30.

Jackson, J. and Harkins, S. G. (1985). 'Equity in effort: an explanation of the social loafing effect'. *Journal of Personality and Social Psychology*, 49, 1199–206.

Jacobs, R. and Campbell, D. T. (1961). 'The perpetuation of an arbitrary tradition through several generations of a laboratory microculture'. *Journal of Abnormal and Social Psychology*, 62, 649–58.

Jacoby, L. L., Kelly, C., Brown, J., and Jasechko, J. (1989). 'Becoming famous overnight: limits on the ability to avoid unconscious influences of the past'. *Journal of Personality and Social Psychology*, 56, 326–38.

Jahoda, G. (1979). 'A cross-cultural perspective on experimental social psychology'. *Personality and Social Psychology Bulletin*, 5, 142–48.

Jahoda, G. (1982). *Psychology and Anthropology: A Psychological Perspective*. London: Academic Press.

Jamieson, D. W. and Zanna, M. P. (1989). 'Need for structure in attitude formation and expression' in A. R. Pratkanis, S. J. Breckler and A. G. Greenwald (eds), *Attitude Structure and Function* (pp. 383–406). Hillsdale, NJ: Erlbaum.

Janis, I. L. (1954). 'Personality correlates of susceptibility to persuasion'. *Journal of Personality*, 22, 302–18.

Janis, I. L. (1967). 'Effects of fear arousal on attitude change: recent developments in theory and experimental research' in L. Berkowitz (ed.), *Advances in Experimental Social Psychology* (vol. 3, pp. 167–224). New York: Academic Press.

Janis, I. L. (1972). *Victims of Groupthink: A Psychological Study of Foreign Policy Decisions and Fiascoes*. Boston, MA: Houghton-Mifflin.

Janis, I. L. (1982). *Groupthink: Psychological Studies of Policy Decisions and Fiascoes* (2nd edn). Boston, MA: Houghton-Mifflin.

Janis, I. L. and Feshbach, S. (1953). 'Effects of fear-arousing communications'. *Journal of Abnormal and Social Psychology*, 48, 78–92.

Janis, I. L. and King, B. T. (1954). 'The influence of role-playing on opinion change'. *Journal of Abnormal and Social Psychology*, 49, 211–18.

Janis, I. L. and Mann, L. (1977). *Decision Making*. New York: Free Press.

Janis, I. L., Kaye, D. and Kirschner, P. (1965). 'Facilitating effects of "eating-while-reading" on responsiveness to persuasive communications'. *Journal of Personality and Social Psychology*, 1, 181–86.

Jaspars, J. M. F. (1980). 'The coming of age of social psychology in Europe'. *European Journal of Social Psychology*, **10**, 421–9.

Jaspars, J. M. F. (1986). 'Forum and focus: a personal view of European social psychology'. *European Journal of Social Psychology*, **16**, 3–15.

Jellison, J. and Arkin, R. (1977).' Social comparison of abilities: a self-presentation approach to decision making in groups' in J. M. Suls and R. L. Miller (eds), *Social Comparison Processes: Theoretical and Empirical Perspectives* (pp. 235–57). Washington, DC: Hemisphere.

Jellison, J. M. and Green, J. (1981). 'A self-presentation approach to the fundamental attribution error: the norm of internality'. *Journal of Personality and Social Psychology*, **40**, 643–49.

Jemmott, J. and Locke, S. (1984). 'Psychosocial factors, immunologic mediation, and human susceptibility to infectious diseases: how much do we know?' *Psychological Bulletin*, **95**, 78–108.

Jennings, H. H. (1943). *Leadership and Isolation*. New York: Longman, Green.

Jennings, M. K. and Niemi, R. G. (1968). 'The transmission of political values from parent to child'. *American Political Science Review*, **62**, 546–75.

Jodelet, D. (1991). *Madness and Social Representations*. London: Harvester Wheatsheaf.

Johnson, B. T. and Eagly, A. H. (1989). 'Effects of involvement on persuasion: a meta-analysis'. *Psychological Bulletin*, **106**, 290–314.

Johnson, D. W. and Johnson, F. P. (1987). *Joining Together: Group Theory and Group Skills* (3rd edn). Englewood Cliffs, NJ: Prentice Hall.

Johnson, R. D. and Downing, L. L. (1979). 'Deindividuation and valence of cues: effects on prosocial and antisocial behavior'. *Journal of Personality and Social Psychology*, **37**, 1532–38.

Johnston, L. and Hewstone, M. (1990). 'Intergroup contact: social identity and social cognition' in D. Abrams and M. A. Hogg (eds), *Social Identity Theory: Constructive and Critical Advances* (pp. 185–210). London: Harvester Wheatsheaf.

Jones, B., Gray, A., Kavanagh, D., Moran, M., Norton, P. and Seldon, A. (1994). *Politics UK* (2nd edn). Hemel Hempstead: Harvester Wheatsheaf.

Jones, E. E. (1979). 'The rocky road from acts to dispositions'. *American Psychologist*, **34**, 107–17.

Jones, E. E. and Davis, K. E. (1965). 'From acts to dispositions: the attribution process in person perception' in L. Berkowitz (ed.), *Advances in Experimental Social Psychology* (vol. 2, pp. 219–66). New York: Academic Press.

Jones, E. E. and Goethals, G. R. (1972). 'Order effects in impression formation: attribution context and the nature of the entity' in E. E. Jones, D. E. Kanouse, H. H. Kelley, R. E. Nisbett, S. Valins and B. Weiner (eds), *Attribution: Perceiving the Causes of Behaviour* (pp. 27–46). Morristown, NJ: General Learning Press.

Jones, E. E. and Harris, V. A. (1967). 'The attribution of attitudes'. *Journal of Experimental Social Psychology*, **3**, 1–24.

Jones, E. E. and McGillis, D. (1976). 'Correspondent inferences and the attribution cube: a comparative reappraisal' in J. H. Harvey, W. J. Ickes and R. F. Kidd (eds), *New Directions in Attribution Research* (vol. 1, pp. 389–420). Hillsdale, NJ: Erlbaum.

Jones, E. E. and Nisbett, R. E. (1972). 'The actor and the observer: divergent perceptions of the causes of behavior' in E. E. Jones, D. E. Kanouse, H. H. Kelley, R. E. Nisbett, S. Valins and B. Weiner (eds), *Attribution: Perceiving the Causes of Behaviour* (pp. 79–94). Morristown, NJ: General Learning Press.

Jones, E. E. and Sigall, H. (1971). 'The bogus pipeline: a new paradigm for measuring affect and attitude'. *Psychological Bulletin*, **76**, 349–64.

Jones, E. E., Davis, K. E. and Gergen, K. (1961). 'Role playing variations and their informational value for person perception'. *Journal of Abnormal and Social Psychology*, **63**, 302–10.

Jones, E. E., Wood, G. C. and Quattrone, G. A. (1981). 'Perceived variability of personal characteristics in ingroups and outgroups: the role of knowledge and evaluation'. *Personality and Social Psychology Bulletin*, **7**, 523–28.

Jones, S. E. and Yarbrough, A. E. (1985). 'A naturalistic study of the meanings of touch'. *Communication Monographs*, **52**, 19–56.

Jordan, N. (1953). 'Behavioral forces that are a function of attitudes and of behavioral organization'. *Human Relations*, **6**, 273–87.

Jorgensen, B. W. and Cervone, J. C. (1978). 'Affect enhancement in the pseudo recognition task'. *Personality and Social Psychology Bulletin*, **4**, 285–88.

Jourard, S. M. (1966). 'An exploratory study of body-accessibility'. *British Journal of Social and Clinical Psychology*, **5**, 221–31.

Jourard, S. M. (1971). *The Transparent Self*. New York: Van Nostrand.

Judd, C. M. and Park, B. (1988). 'Out-group homogeneity: judgements of variability at the individual and group levels'. *Journal of Personality and Social Psychology*, **54**, 778–88.

Jung, C. G. (1946). *Psychological Types or the Psychology of Individuation*. New York: Harcourt Brace. (First published 1922.)

Kahn, A. and Ryen, A. H. (1972). 'Factors influencing the bias towards one's own group'. *International Journal of Group Tensions*, **2**, 33–50.

Kahn, A., O'Leary, V. E., Krulewitz, J. E. and Lamm, H. (1980). 'Equity and equality: male and female means to a just end'. *Basic and Applied Social Psychology*, **1**, 173–197.

Kahneman, D. and Tversky, A. (1973). 'On the psychology of prediction'. *Psychological Review*, **80**, 237–51.

Kanazawa, H. and Loveday, L. (1988). 'The Japanese immigrant community in Brazil: language contact and shift'. *Journal of Multilingual and Multicultural Development*, **2**, 423–35.

Kanouse, D. E. and Hanson, L. R., Jr (1972). 'Negativity in evaluations' in E. E. Jones, D. E. Kanouse, H. H. Kelley, R. E. Nisbett, S. Valins and B. Weiner (eds), *Attribution: Perceiving the Causes of Behaviour* (pp. 47–62). Morristown, NJ: General Learning Press.

Kaplan, M. F. (1977). 'Discussion polarization effects in a modified jury decision paradigm: informational influence'. *Sociometry*, **40**, 262–71.

Kaplan, M. F. and Miller, L. E. (1978). 'Reducing the effects of juror bias'. *Journal of Personality and Social Psychology*, **36**, 1443–55.

Karlin, R. A., Epstein, Y. M. and Aiello, J. R. (1978). 'Strategies for the investigation of crowding' in A. Esser and B. Greenbie (eds), *Design for Community and Privacy*. New York: Plenum.

Karniol, R. (1982). 'Behavioral and cognitive correlates of various immanent justice responses in children: deterrent versus punitive moral systems'. *Journal of Personality and Social Psychology*, **43**, 881–820.

Kassin, S. M. (1979). 'Consensus information, prediction and causal attribution: a review of the literature and issues'. *Journal of Personality and Social Psychology*, **37**, 1966–81.

Kassin, S. M. and Pryor, J. B. (1985). 'The development of attribution processes' in J. Pryor and J. Day (eds), *The Development of Social Cognition* (pp. 3–34). New York: Springer-Verlag.

Kassin, S. M., Ellsworth, P. C. and Smith, V. L. (1989). 'The "general acceptance" of psychological research on eyewitness testimony'. *American Psychologist*, **44**, 1089–98.

Katsikitis, M., Pilowsky, I. and Innes, J. M. (1990). 'The quantification of smiling using a microcomputer-based approach'. *Journal of Nonverbal Behaviour*, **14**, 3–17.

Katz, D. (1960). 'The functional approach to the study of attitudes'. *Public Opinion Quarterly*, **24**, 163–204.

Katz, D. and Braly, K. (1933). 'Racial stereotypes of one hundred college students'. *Journal of Abnormal and Social Psychology*, **28**, 280–90.

Katz, I. and Haas, R. G. (1988). 'Racial ambivalence and American value conflict: correlational and priming studies of dual cognitive structures'. *Journal of Personality and Social Psychology*, **55**, 893–905.

Katz, I., Glass, D. C., Lucido, D. and Farber, J. (1979). 'Harm-doing and victim's racial or orthopaedic stigma as determinants of helping behaviour'. *Journal of Personality*, **47**, 340–64.

Katz, P. A. (1976). *Towards the Elimination of Racism*. New York: Pergamon.

Kazdin, A. E. and Bryan, J. H. (1971). 'Competence and volunteering'. *Journal of Experimental Social Psychology*, 7, 87–97.

Kelley, H. H. (1950). 'The warm–cold variable in first impressions of persons'. *Journal of Personality*, 18, 431–39.

Kelley, H. H. (1952). 'Two functions of reference groups' in G. E. Swanson, T. M. Newcomb and E. L. Hartley (eds), *Readings in Social Psychology* (2nd edn, pp. 410–14). New York: Holt, Rinehart & Winston.

Kelley, H. H. (1967). 'Attribution theory in social psychology' in D. Levine (ed.), *Nebraska Symposium on Motivation* (pp. 192–238). Lincoln, NE: University of Nebraska Press.

Kelley, H. H. (1972a). 'Causal schemata and the attribution process' in E. E. Jones, D. E. Kanouse, H. H. Kelley, R. E. Nisbett, S. Valins and B. Weiner (eds), *Attribution: Perceiving the Causes of Behaviour* (pp. 151–74). Morristown, NJ: General Learning Press.

Kelley, H. H. (1972b). 'Attribution in social interaction' in E. E. Jones, D. E. Kanouse, H. H. Kelley, R. E. Nisbett, S. Valins and B. Weiner (eds), *Attribution: Perceiving the Causes of Behaviour* (pp. 1–26). Morristown, NJ: General Learning Press.

Kelley, H. H. (1973). 'The process of causal attribution'. *American Psychologist*, 28, 107–28.

Kelley, H. H. (1979). *Personal Relationships: Their Structures and Processes*. Hillsdale, NJ: Erlbaum.

Kelley, H. H. and Michela, J. L. (1980). 'Attribution theory and research'. *Annual Review of Psychology*, 31, 457–501.

Kelley, H. H. and Thibaut, J. (1978). *Interpersonal Relations: A Theory of Interdependence*. New York: Wiley.

Kelley, K., Byrne, D., Przybyla, D. P. J., Eberly, C. C., Eberly, B. W., Greenlinger, V., Wan, C. K. and Grosky, J. (1985). 'Chronic self-destructiveness: conceptualization, measurement, and initial validation of the construct'. *Motivation and Emotion*, 9, 35–151.

Kelly, G. A. (1955). *The Psychology of Personal Constructs*. New York: Norton.

Kelman, H. C. (1967). 'Human use of human subjects: the problem of deception in social psychology'. *Psychological Bulletin*, 67, 1–11.

Kelvin, P. (1970). *The Bases of Social Behaviour: An Approach in Terms of Order and Value*. London: Holt, Rinehart & Winston.

Keneally, T. (1982). *Schindler's Ark*. Washington, DC: Hemisphere.

Kenrick, D. T. and MacFarlane, S. W. (1986). 'Ambient temperature and horn honking: a field study of the heat/aggression relationship'. *Environment and Behaviour*, 18, 179–191.

Kerckhoff, A. C. and Davis, K. E. (1962). 'Value consensus and need complementarity in mate selection'. *American Sociological Review*, 27, 295–303.

Kerr, N. L. (1978). 'Beautiful and blameless: effects of victim attractiveness and responsibility on mock jurors' verdicts'. *Journal of Personality and Social Psychology*, 4, 479–82.

Kerr, N. L. (1981). 'Social transition schemes: charting the group's road to agreement'. *Journal of Personality and Social Psychology*, 41, 684–702.

Kerr, N. L. (1983). 'Motivation losses in small groups: a social dilemma analysis'. *Journal of Personality and Social Psychology*, 45, 819–28.

Kerr, N. L. and Bray, R. M. (eds) (1982). *The Psychology of the Courtroom*. London: Academic Press.

Kerr, N. L. and Bruun, S. (1981). 'Ringelmann revisited: alternative explanations for the social loafing effect'. *Personality and Social Psychology Bulletin*, 7, 224–31.

Kerr, N. L. and MacCoun, R. J. (1985): 'The effects of jury size and polling method on the process and product of jury deliberation'. *Journal of Personality and Social Psychology*, 48, 349–63.

Kiesler, C. A. and Kiesler, S. B. (1969). *Conformity*. Reading, MA: Addison-Wesley.

Kilham, W. and Mann, L. (1974). 'Level of destructive obedience as a function of transmitter and executant roles in the Milgram obedience paradigm'. *Journal of Personality and Social Psychology*, 29, 696–702.

Kim, H. S. and Baron, R. S. (1988). 'Exercise and the illusory correlation: does arousal heighten stereotypic processing?' *Journal of Experimental Social Psychology*, 24, 366–80.

Kimble, G. A. (1961). *Hilgard and Marquis' Conditioning and Learning* (2nd edn). New York: Appleton-Century-Crofts.

Kinder, D. R. and Sears, D. O. (1981). 'Symbolic racism vs. threats to the good life'. *Journal of Personality and Social Psychology*, 40, 414–31.

King, G. A. and Sorrentino, R. M. (1988). 'Uncertainty orientation and the relationship between individual accessible constructs and person memory'. *Social Cognition*, 6, 128–49.

Kinloch, P. (1985). 'Alcohol, violence, and rape' in P. Kinloch (ed.), *Talking Health, Doing Sickness: Studies in Samoan Health*. Wellington: Victoria University Press.

Kinzel, A. S. (1970). 'Body buffer zone in violent prisoners'. *American Journal of Psychiatry*, 127, 59–64.

Kirkhart, R. O. (1963). 'Minority group identification and group leadership'. *Journal of Social Psychology*, 59, 111–17.

Kite, M. E. and Johnson, B. T. (1988). 'Attitudes toward older and younger adults: a meta-analysis'. *Psychology and Aging*, 3, 233–44.

Klapp, O. E. (1972). *Currents of Unrest*. New York: Holt, Rinehart and Winston.

Kleck, R. E., Buck, P. L., Goller, W. C., London, R. S., Pfieffer, J. R. and Vukcevic, D. P. (1968). 'Effect of stigmatizing conditions on the use of personal space'. *Psychological Reports*, 23, 111–18.

Kleinke, C. L. (1986). 'Gaze and eye contact: a research review'. *Psychological Bulletin*, 100, 78–100.

Kleinke, C. L., Bustos, A. A., Meeker, F. B. and Staneski, R. A. (1973). 'Effects of self-attributed and other-attributed gaze on interpersonal evaluations between males and females'. *Journal of Experimental Social Psychology*, 9, 154–63.

Klentz, B. and Beaman, A. L. (1981). 'The effects of type of information and method of dissemination on the reporting of a shoplifter'. *Journal of Applied Psychology*, 11, 64–82.

Klineberg, O. (1940). *Social Psychology*. New York: Holt.

Kineberg, O. and Hull, W. F. (1979). *At a Foreign University: An International Study of Adaptation and Coping*. New York: Praeger.

Knapp, M. L. (1978). *Nonverbal Communication in Human Interaction* (2nd edn). New York: Holt, Rinehart and Winston.

Knapp, M. L., Hart, R. P. and Dennis, H. S. (1974). 'An exploration of deception as a communication construct'. *Human Communication Research*, 1, 15–29.

Knottnerus, J. D. and Greenstein, T. N. (1981). 'Status and performance characteristics: a theory of status validation'. *Social Psychology Quarterly*, 44, 338–49.

Koffka, K. (1935). *Principles of Gestalt Psychology*. New York: Harcourt, Brace and World.

Kogan, N. and Wallach, M. A. (1964). *Risk Taking: A study in Cognition and Personality*. New York: Holt.

Kohen-Raz, R. (1968). 'Mental and motor development of kibbutz, institutionalized, and home-reared infants in Israel'. *Child Development*, 39, 489–504.

Kohn, I., Franck, K. and Fox, A. S. (1975). *Defensible Space Modifications in Row-house Communities*. National Science Foundation Report.

Komorita, S. S. and Esser, J. K. (1975). 'Frequency of reciprocated concessions in bargaining'. *Journal of Personality and Social Psychology*, 32, 699–705.

Konecni, V. J. (1979). 'The role of aversive events in the development of intergroup conflict' in W. G. Austin and S. Worchel (eds), *The Social Psychology of Intergroup Relations* (pp. 85–102). Monterey, CA: Brooks/Cole.

Konecni, V. J. and Ebbesen, E. (1976). 'Disinhibition versus the cathartic effect: artifact and substance'. *Journal of Personality and Social Psychology*, 34, 352–65.

Korte, C. (1971). 'Effects of individual responsibility and group communication on help-giving in an emergency'. *Human Relations*, 24, 149–59.

Kramer, R. M. and Brewer, M. B. (1984). 'Effects of identity on resource use in a simulated commons dilemma'. *Journal of Personality and Social Psychology*, 46, 1044–57.

Kramer, R. M. and Brewer, M. B. (1986). 'Social group identity and the emergence of cooperation in resource conservation dilemmas' in H. Wilke, D. Messick and C. Rutte (eds), *Psychology of Decisions and Conflict* (vol. 3). Frankfurt: Verlag Peter Lang.

Krauss, R. M., Curran, N. M. and Ferleger, N. (1983). 'Expressive conventions and the cross-cultural perception of emotion'. *Basic and Applied Social Psychology*, 4, 295–305.

Kraut, R. E. and Higgins, E. T. (1984). 'Communication and social cognition' in R. S. Wyer, Jr and T. K. Srull (eds), *Handbook of Social Cognition* (vol. 3, pp. 87–127). Hillsdale, NJ: Erlbaum.

Kraut, R. E. and Johnston, R. E. (1979). 'Social and emotional messages of smiling: an ethological approach'. *Journal of Personality and Social Psychology*, 37, 1539–53.

Kraut, R. E. and Poe, D. (1980). 'Behavioral roots of person perceptions: the deception judgements of the customs inspectors and laymen'. *Journal of Personality and Social Psychology*, 39, 784–98.

Kravitz, D. A. and Martin, B. (1986). 'Ringelmann rediscovered: the original article'. *Journal of Personality and Social Psychology*, 50, 936–41.

Krebs, D. L. (1975). 'Empathy and altruism'. *Journal of Personality and Social Psychology*, 32, 1134–46.

Krebs, D. L. and Miller, D. T. (1985). 'Altruism and aggression' in G. Lindzey and E. Aronson (eds), *Handbook of Social Psychology* (3rd edn, vol. 2, pp. 1–71). New York: Random House.

Krech, D. and Crutchfield, R. S. (1948). *Theory and Problems of Social Psychology*. New York: McGraw-Hill.

Krech, D., Crutchfield, R. and Ballachey, R. (1962). *Individual in Society*. New York: McGraw-Hill.

Krosnick, J. A. (1990). 'Expertise and political psychology'. *Social Cognition*, 8, 1–8.

Kruglanski, A. W. (1975). 'The endogenous–exogenous partition in attribution theory'. *Psychological Review*, 82, 387–406.

Krupat, E. and Guild, W. (1980). 'Defining the city: the use of objective and subjective measures of community description'. *Journal of Social Issues*, 36, 9–28.

Kubzansky, P. E. (1961). 'The effects of reduced environmental stimulation on human behaviour: a review' in A. D. Biderman and H. Zimmer (eds), *The Manipulation of Human Behaviour* (pp. 51–95). New York: Wiley.

Kuethe, J. L. and Weingartner, H. (1964). 'Male–female schemata of homosexual and non-homosexual penitentiary inmates'. *Journal of Personality*, 32, 23–31.

Kuhn, T. S. (1962). *The Structure of Scientific Revolutions*. Chicago, IL: University of Chicago Press.

Kulik, J. A. (1983). 'Confirmatory attribution and the perpetuation of social beliefs'. *Journal of Personality and Social Psychology*, 44, 1171–81.

Kulik, J. A. and Brown, R. (1979). 'Frustration, attribution of blame, and aggression'. *Journal of Experimental Social Psychology*, 15, 183–94.

Kun, A. and Weiner, B. (1973). 'Necessary versus sufficient causal schemata for success and failure'. *Journal of Research on Psychology*, 7, 197–207.

LaFrance, M. and Mayo, C. (1976). 'Racial differences in gaze behaviour during conversations: two systematic observational studies'. *Journal of Personality and Social Psychology*, 33, 547–52.

Lakoff, R. (1973). 'Language and women's place'. *Language in Society*, 2, 45–80.

Lakoff, R. (1975). *Language and Woman's Place*. New York: Harper and Row.

Lalljee, M. (1981). 'Attribution theory and the analysis of explanations' in C. Antaki (ed.), *The Psychology of Ordinary Explanations of Social Behaviour* (pp. 119–38). London: Academic Press.

Lambert, W. E., Hodgson, R. C., Gardner, R. C. and Fillenbaum, S. (1960). 'Evaluation reactions to spoken language'. *Journal of Abnormal and Social Psychology*, 60, 44–51.

Lambert, W. E., Mermigis, L. and Taylor, D. M. (1986). 'Greek Canadians' attitudes toward own group and other Canadian ethnic groups: a test of the multiculturalism hypothesis'. *Canadian Journal of Behavioural Sciences*, 18, 35–51.

Lamm, H. and Kayser, E. (1978). 'The allocation of monetary gain and loss following dyadic performance: the weight given effort and ability under conditions of low and high intradyadic attraction'. *European Journal of Social Psychology*, 8, 275–78.

Landman, J. and Manis, M. (1983). 'Social cognition: some historical and theoretical perspectives' in L. Berkowitz (ed.), *Advances in Experimental Social Psychology* (vol. 16, pp. 49–123). New York: Academic Press.

Landy, D. and Sigall, H. (1974). 'Beauty is talent: task evaluation as a function of the performer's physical attractiveness'. *Journal of Personality and Social Psychology*, 29, 299–304.

Lane, I. M. and Messé, L. A. (1971). 'Equity and the distribution of rewards'. *Journal of Personality and Social Psychology*, 20, 1–17.

Langer, E. J. (1975). 'The illusion of control'. *Journal of Personality and Social Psychology*, 32, 311 –28.

Langer, E. J. (1978). 'Rethinking the role of thought in social interaction' in J. H. Harvey, W. I. Ickes and R. F. Kidd (eds), *New Directions in Attribution Research* (vol. 2, pp. 35–58). Hillsdale, NJ: Erlbaum.

Langer, E. J., Blank, A. and Chanowitz, B. (1978). 'The mindlessness of ostensibly thoughtful action'. *Journal of Personality and Social Psychology*, 36, 635–42.

Langer, E. J., Bashner, R. S. and Chanowitz, B. (1985). 'Decreasing prejudice by increasing discrimination'. *Journal of Personality and Social Psychology*, 49, 113–20.

LaPiere, R. T. (1934). 'Attitudes vs. actions'. *Social Forces*, 13, 230–37.

LaPiere, R. T. and Farnsworth, P. R. (1936). *Social Psychology*. New York: McGraw-Hill.

Latané, B. (1981). 'The psychology of social impact'. *American Psychologist*, 36, 343–56.

Latané, B. and Dabbs, J. M., Jr (1975). 'Sex, group size and helping in three cities'. *Sociometry*, 38, 180–94.

Latané, B. and Darley, J. M. (1970). *The Unresponsive Bystander: Why Doesn't He Help?* New York: Appleton-Century-Crofts.

Latané, B. and Darley, J. M. (1976). 'Help in a crisis: bystander response to an emergency' in J. W. Thibaut and J. T. Spence (eds), *Contemporary Topics in Social Psychology* (pp. 309–332). Morristown, NJ: General Learning Press.

Latané, B. and Nida, S. (1980). 'Social impact theory and group influence: a social engineering perspective' in P. B. Paulus (ed.), *Psychology of Group Influence*. Hillsdale, NJ: Erlbaum.

Latané, B. and Rodin, J. (1969). 'A lady in distress: inhibiting effects of friends and strangers on bystander intervention'. *Journal of Experimental Social Psychology*, 5, 189–202.

Latané, B. and Wolf, S. (1981). 'The social impact of majorities and minorities'. *Psychological Review*, 88, 438–53.

Latané B., Williams, K. D. and Harkins, S. G. (1979). 'Many hands make light the work: the causes and consequences of social loafing.' *Journal of Personality and Social Psychology*, 37, 822–32.

Latin American Bureau (1982). *Falklands/Malvinas: Whose Crisis?* London: Latin American Bureau.

Laughlin, P. R. (1980). 'Social combination processes of cooperative problem solving groups on verbal intellective tasks' in M. Fishbein (ed.), *Progress in Social Psychology* (vol. 1, pp. 127–55). Hillsdale, NJ: Erlbaum.

Laughlin, P. R. and Ellis, A. L. (1986). 'Demonstrability and social combination processes on mathematical intellective tasks'. *Journal of Experimental Social Psychology*, 22, 177–89.

Leana, C. R. (1985). 'A partial test of Janis's groupthink model: effects of group cohesiveness and leader behaviour on defective decision making'. *Journal of Management*, 11, 5–17.

Leavitt, H. J. (1951). 'Some effects of certain communication patterns on group performance'. *Journal of Abnormal and Social Psychology*, 46, 38–50.

LeBon, G. (1908). *The Crowd: A Study of the Popular Mind*. London: Unwin. (Original work published 1896.)

Leibman, M. (1970). 'The effects of sex and race norms on personal space'. *Environment and Behaviour*, 2, 208–46.

Leiman, A. H. and Epstein, S. (1961). 'Thematic sexual responses as related to sexual drive and guilt'. *Journal of Abnormal and Social Psychology*, 63, 169–75.

Lemaine, G. (1966). 'Inégalité, comparison et incomparabilité: esquisse d'une théorie de l'originalité sociale'. *Bulletin de Psychologie*, 20, 24–32.

Lemaine, G. (1974). 'Social differentiation and social originality'. *European Journal of Social Psychology*, 4, 17–52.

Lepper, M. R., Greene, D. and Nisbett, R. E. (1973). 'Undermining children's intrinsic interest with extrinsic reward: a test of the overjustification hypothesis'. *Journal of Personality and Social Psychology*, 28, 129–37.

Lerner, M. J. (1977). 'The justice motive: some hypotheses as to its origins and forms'. *Journal of Personality*, 45, 1–52.

Lerner, M. J. and Miller, D. T. (1978). 'Just-world research and the attribution process: looking back and ahead'. *Psychological Bulletin*, 85, 1030–51.

Leventhal, H., Singler, R. and Jones, S. (1965). 'Effects of fear and specificity of recommendations upon attitudes and behaviour'. *Journal of Personality and Social Psychology*, 2, 20–29.

Leventhal, H., Watts, J. C., and Pagano, R. (1967). 'Effects of fear and instructions on how to cope with danger'. *Journal of Personality and Social Psychology*, 6, 313–21.

LeVine, R. A. and Campbell, D. T. (1972). *Ethnocentrism: Theories of Conflict, Ethnic Attitudes and Group Behaviour*. New York: Wiley.

Levine, J. M. and Moreland, R. L. (1990). 'Progress in small group research'. *Annual Review of Psychology*, 41, 585–634.

Levinger, G. (1964). 'Note on need complementarity in marriage'. *Psychological Bulletin*, 61, 153–57.

Levinger, G. (1980). 'Toward the analysis of close relationships'. *Journal of Experimental Social Psychology*, 16, 510–44.

Levinger, G., Senn, D. J. and Jorgensen, B. W. (1970). 'Progress toward permanence in courtship: a test of the Kerckhoff–Davis hypothesis'. *Sociometry*, 33, 427–43.

Levitt, E. and Klassen, A. (1974). 'Public attitudes towards homosexuality: part of the 1970 national survey by the Institute for Sex Research'. *Journal of Homosexuality*, 1, 29–43.

Lévy-Bruhl, L. (1925). *How Natives Think*. New York: Alfred A. Knopf.

Lewin, A. Y. and Duchan, L. (1971). 'Women in academia'. *Science*, 173, 892–95.

Lewin, K. (1943). 'Forces behind food habits and methods of change'. *Bulletin of National Research Council*, 108, 35–65.

Lewin, K. (1947). 'Frontiers in group dynamics'. *Human Relations*, 1, 5–42.

Lewin, K. (1951). *Field Theory in Social Science*. New York: Harper.

Lewin, K., Lippitt, R. and White, R. K. (1939). 'Patterns of aggressive behaviour in experimentally created "social climates"'. *Journal of Social Psychology*, 10, 271–99.

Lewis, A., Snell, M. and Furnham, A. (1987). 'Lay explanations for the causes of unemployment in Britain: economic, individualistic, societal or fatalistic?' *Political Psychology*, 8, 427–39.

Lewis, O. (1969). *A Death in the Sanchez Family*. New York: Secker and Warburg.

Leyens, J-P. (1983). *Sommes-nous tous des psychologues? Approche psychosociale de théories implicites de la personalité*. Brussels: Mardaga.

Leyens, J-P., Camino, L., Parke, R. D. and Berkowitz, L. (1975). 'Effects of movie violence on aggression in a field setting and as a function of group dominance and cohesion'. *Journal of Personality and Social Psychology*, 32, 346–60.

Leyens, J-P., Yzerbyt, V. Y. and Schadron, G. (1992). 'Stereotypes and social judgeability'. *European Review of Social Psychology*, 3, 91–120.

Liebrand, W., Messick, D. and Wilke, H. (eds) (1992). *Social Dilemmas: Theoretical Issues and Research Findings*. Oxford: Pergamon.

Liebrand, W. B. G. (1984). 'The effect of social motives, communication and group size in an *n*-person multi-stage mixed-motive game'. *European Journal of Social Psychology*, 14, 239–64.

Likert, R. (1932). 'A technique for the measurement of attitudes'. *Archives of Psychology*, 22, (140), 44–53.

Lilly, J. C. (1956). 'Mental effects of reduction of ordinary levels of physical stimuli on intact, healthy persons'. *Psychiatric Research Reports*, 5, 1–9.

Lim, R. G. and Carnevale, P. J. D. (1990). 'Contingencies in the mediation of disputes'. *Journal of Personality and Social Psychology*, 58, 259–72.

Limber, J. (1977). 'Language in child and chimp?' *American Psychologist*, 32, 280–95.

Lindzey, G. and Aronson E. (eds) (1985). *Handbook of Social Psychology* (3rd edn). New York: Random House.

Linskold, S. (1978). 'Trust development, the GRIT proposal, and the effects of conciliatory acts on conflict and cooperation'. *Psychological Bulletin*, 85, 772–93.

Linskold, S. and Han, G. (1988). 'GRIT as a foundation for integrative bargaining'. *Personality and Social Psychology Bulletin*, 14, 335–45.

Linssen, H. and Hagendoorn, L. (1994). 'Social and geographical factors in the explanation of European nationality stereotypes'. *British Journal of Social Psychology*, 23, 165–82.

Linville, P. W. (1982). 'Affective consequences of complexity regarding the self and others', in M. S. Clark and S. T. Fiske (eds), *Affect and Cognition: 17th Annual Carnegie Symposium on Cognition* (pp. 79–109). Hillsdale, NJ: Erlbaum.

Linville, P. W. (1987). 'Self-complexity as a cognitive buffer against stress-related depression and illness'. *Journal of Personality and Social Psychology*, 52, 663–76.

Linville, P. W., Fischer, G. W. and Salovey, P. (1989). 'Perceived distributions of the characteristics of in-group and out-group members: empirical evidence and a computer simulation'. *Journal of Personality and Social Psychology*, 57, 165–88.

Linz, D. G., Donnerstein, E. and Penrod, S. (1988). 'Effects of long-term exposure to violent and sexually degrading depictions of women'. *Journal of Personality and Social Psychology*, 55, 758–68.

Lipetz, M. E., Cohen, I. H., Dworin, J. and Rogers, L. (1970). 'Need complementarity, marital stability and marital satisfaction' in T. L. Huston (ed.), *Personality and Social Behaviour* (pp. 143–65). New York: Academic Press.

Lippa, R. A. (1990). *Introduction to Social Psychology*. Belmont, CA: Brooks/Cole.

Lippitt, R. and White, R. (1943). 'The 'social climate' of children's groups' in R. G. Barker, J. Kounin and H. Wright (eds), Child Behaviour and Development (pp. 5485–508). New York: McGraw-Hill.

Lippman, W. (1922). *Public Opinion*. New York: Harcourt and Brace.

Litton, I. and Potter, J. (1985). 'Social representations in the ordinary explanation of a "riot"'. *European Journal of Social Psychology*, 15, 371–88.

Liu, T. J. and Steele, C. M. (1986). 'Attributional analysis and self-affirmation'. *Journal of Personality and Social Psychology*, 51, 531–40.

Lloyd, B. B. and Duveen, G. (1992). *Gender Identities and Education: The Impact of Starting School*. Hemel Hempstead: Harvester Wheatsheaf.

Lock, A. (ed.) (1978). *Action, Gesture and Symbol: The Emergence of Language*, London: Academic Press.

Lock, A. (1980). *The Guided Reinvention of Language*. London: Academic Press.

Lockard, J. S., Kirkevold, B. C. and Kalk, D. F. (1980). 'Cost–benefit indexes of deception in nonviolent crime'. *Bulletin of the Psychonomic Society*, 16, 303–06.

Loftus, E. F. (1979). *Eyewitness Testimony*. Cambridge, MA: Harvard University Press.

Longley, J. and Pruitt, D. G. (1980). 'Groupthink: a critique of Janis's theory' in L. Wheeler (ed.), *Review of Personality and Social Psychology* (vol. 1, pp. 74–93). Beverly Hills, CA: Sage.

Lorenz, K. (1966). *On Aggression*. New York: Harcourt, Brace and World.

Lorenzi-Cioldi, F. and Doise, W. (1990). 'Levels of analysis and social identity' in D. Abrams and M. A. Hogg (eds), *Social Identity Theory: Constructive and Critical Advances* (pp. 71–88). London: Harvester Wheatsheaf.

Lorge, I. and Solomon, H. (1955). 'Two models of group behaviour in the solution of eureka-type problems'. *Psychometrika*, 20, 139–48.

Lott, A. J. and Lott, B. E. (1965). 'Group cohesiveness as interpersonal attraction'. *Psychological Bulletin*, 64, 259–309.

Lott, A. J. and Lott, B. E. (1972). 'The power of liking: consequences of interpersonal attitudes derived from a liberalized view of secondary reinforcement' in L. Berkowitz, (ed.), *Advances in Experimental Social Psychology* (vol. 6, pp. 109–148). New York: Academic Press.

Lott, A. J. and Lott, B. E. (1974). 'The role of reward in the formation of positive interpersonal attitudes' in T. L. Huston (ed.), *Foundations of Interpersonal Attraction* (pp. 171–89). New York: Academic Press.

Lott, A. J., Aponte, J. F., Lott, B. E. and McGinley, W. H. (1969). 'The effect of delayed reward on the development of positive attitudes towards persons'. *Journal of Experimental Social Psychology*, 5, 101–13.

Lott, B. E. (1961). 'Group cohesiveness: a learning phenomenon'. *Journal of Social Psychology*, 55, 275–86.

Lubek, I. (1979). 'A brief social psychological analysis of research on aggression in social psychology' in A. R. Buss (ed.), *Psychology in Social Context* (pp. 259–306). New York: Irvington.

Luce, R. D. and Raiffa, H. (1957). *Games and Decisions*. New York: Wiley.

Lueger, R. J. (1980). Person and situation factors influencing transgression in behaviour-problem adolescents. *Journal of Abnormal Psychology*, 89, 453–58.

Lumsdaine, A. A. and Janis, I. L. (1953). 'Resistance to "counterpropaganda" produced by one-sided and two-sided "propaganda" presentations'. *Public Opinion Quarterly*, 17, 311–18.

Lynch, K. (1960). *The Image of the City*. Cambridge, MA: MIT. Press.

Maass, A. and Clark, R. D., III (1983). 'Internalization versus compliance: differential processes underlying minority influence and conformity'. *European Journal of Social Psychology*, 13, 197–215.

Maass, A. and Clark, R. D., III (1984). 'Hidden impact of minorities: fifteen years of minority influence research'. *Psychological Bulletin*, 95, 428–50.

Maass, A. and Clark, R. D., III (1986). 'Conversion theory and simultaneous majority/minority influence: can reactance offer an alternative explanation?' *European Journal of Social Psychology*, 16, 305–09.

Maass, A., Clark, R. D., III and Haberkorn, G. (1982). 'The effects of differential ascribed category membership and norms on minority influence'. *European Journal of Social Psychology*, 12, 89–104.

Macaulay, J. R. and Berkowitz, L. (eds) (1970). *Altruism and Helping Behaviour: Social Psychological Studies of Some Antecedents and Consequences*. New York: Academic Press.

Mackie, D. M. (1986). 'Social identification effects in group polarization'. *Journal of Personality and Social Psychology*, 50, 720–28.

Mackie, D. M. and Cooper, J. (1984). 'Attitude polarization: the effects of group membership'. *Journal of Personality and Social Psychology*, 46, 575–85.

Mackie, D. M. and Worth, L. T. (1989). 'Processing deficits and the mediation of positive affect in persuasion'. *Journal of Personality and Social Psychology*, 57, 27–40.

MacKinnon, D. W. (1933). 'The violation of prohibitions in the solving of problems'. Doctoral dissertation, Harvard University, Cambridge.

MacNeil, M. and Sherif, M. (1976). 'Norm change over subject generations as a function of arbitrariness of prescribed norms'. *Journal of Personality and Social Psychology*, 34, 762–73.

Madden, T. J., Ellen, P. S. and Ajzen, I. (1992). 'A comparison of the theory of planned behaviour and reasoned action'. *Personality and Social Psychology Bulletin*, 18, 3–9.

Major, B. (1981). 'Gender patterns in touching behavior' in C. Mayo and N. M. Henley (eds). *Gender and Nonverbal Behaviour* (pp. 15–37). New York: Springer-Verlag

Major, B. and Adams, J. B. (1983). 'Role of gender, interpersonal orientation, and self-presentation in distributive justice behaviour'. *Journal of Personality and Social Psychology*, 45, 598–608.

Major, B. and Deaux, K. (1982). 'Individual differences in justice behavior' in J. Greenberg and R. L. Cohen (eds), *Equity and Justice in Social Behaviour* (pp. 43–76). New York: Academic Press.

Major, B. and Heslin, R. (1982). 'Perceptions of same-sex and cross-sex reciprocal touch: it's better to give than to receive'. *Journal of Nonverbal Behaviour*, 3, 148–63.

Major, B. and Konar, E. (1984). 'An investigation of sex differences in pay expectations and their possible causes'. *Academy of Management Journal*, 27, 777–92.

Malamuth, N. M. (1981). 'Rape proclivity among males'. *Journal of Social Issues*, 37, 138–57.

Malamuth, N. M. and Donnerstein, E. (1982). 'The effects of aggressive-pornographic mass media stimuli' in L. Berkowitz (ed.), *Advances in Experimental Social Psychology* (vol. 15, pp. 104–36). New York: Academic Press.

Malpass, R. S. and Kravitz, J. (1969). 'Recognition of faces of own and other race'. *Journal of Personality and Social Psychology*, 13, 330–34.

Manis, M. (1977). 'Cognitive social psychology'. *Personality and Social Psychology Bulletin*, 3, 550–66.

Mann, L. (1981). 'The baiting crowd in episodes of threatened suicide'. *Journal of Personality and Social Psychology*, 41, 703–09.

Mann, L., Newton, J. W. and Innes, J. M. (1982). 'A test between deindividuation and emergent norm theories of crowd aggression'. *Journal of Personality and Social Psychology*, 42, 260–72.

Mann, R. D. (1959). 'A review of the relationship between personality and performance in small groups'. *Psychological Bulletin*, 56, 241–70.

Mann, S. H. (1977). 'The use of social indicators in environmental planning' in I. Altman and J. F. Wohlwill (eds), *Human Behaviour and Environment* (vol. 2, pp. 307–30). New York: Plenum.

Manstead, A. S. R. and Semin, G. R. (1980). 'Social facilitation effects: mere enhancement of dominant responses?' *British Journal of Social and Clinical Psychology*, 19, 119–36.

Manstead, A. S. R., Proffitt, C. and Smart, J. L. (1983). 'Predicting and understanding mother's infant-feeding intentions and behaviour: testing the theory of reasoned action'. *Journal of Personality and Social Psychology*, 44, 657–71.

Mantell, D. M. (1971). 'The potential for violence in Germany'. *Journal of Social Issues*, 27, 101–12.

Marks, G. and Miller, N. (1985). 'The effect of certainty on consensus judgements'. *Personality and Social Psychology Bulletin*, 2, 165–77.

Marks, G. and Miller, N. (1987). 'Ten years of research on the false-consensus effect: an empirical and theoretical review'. *Psychological Bulletin*, 102, 72–90.

Markus, H. (1977). 'Self-schemata and processing information about the self'. *Journal of Personality and Social Psychology*, 35, 63–78.

Markus, H. (1978). 'The effect of mere presence on social facilitation: an unobtrusive test'. *Journal of Experimental Social Psychology*, 14, 389–97.

Markus, H. and Nurius, P. (1986). 'Possible selves'. *American Psychologist*, 41, 954–69.

Markus, H. and Sentis, K. P. (1982). 'The self in social information processing' in J. Suls (ed.), *Psychological Perspectives on the Self* (vol. 1, pp. 41–70). Hillsdale, NJ: Erlbaum.

Markus, H. and Zajonc, R. B. (1985). 'The cognitive perspective in social psychology' in G. Lindzey and E. Aronson (eds), *Handbook of Social Psychology* (3rd edn, vol. 1, pp. 137–230). New York: Random House.

Markus, H., Smith, J. and Moreland, R. L. (1985). 'Role of the self-concept in the social perception of others'. *Journal of Personality and Social Psychology*, 49, 1494–512.

Marques, J. M. (1990). 'The black-sheep effect: out-group homogeneity in social comparison settings' in D. Abrams and M. A. Hogg (eds), *Social Identity Theory: Constructive and Critical Advances* (pp. 131–51). London: Harvester Wheatsheaf.

Marques, J. M. and Yzerbyt, V. Y. (1988). 'The black sheep effect: judgemental extremity towards ingroup members in inter- and intra-group situations'. *European Journal of Social Psychology*, 18, 2872.

Marques, J. M., Yzerbyt, V. Y. and Leyens, J-P. (1988). 'The black sheep effect: judgmental extremity towards ingroup members as a function of group identification'. *European Journal of Social Psychology*, 18, 1–16.

Marrow, A. J. (1969). *The Practical Theorist: The Life and Work of Kurt Lewin*. New York: Basic Books.

Marsh, P., Rosser, E. and Harré, R. (1978). *The Rules of Disorder*. Milton Keynes: Open University Press.

Marshall, G. O. and Zimbardo, P. G. (1979). 'Affective consequences of inadequately explained physiological arousal'. *Journal of Personality and Social Psychology*, 37, 970–88.

Martens, R. (1969). 'Palmar sweating and the presence of an audience'. *Journal of Experimental Social Psychology*, 5, 371–74.

Martin, C. L. (1986). 'A ratio measure of sex stereotyping'. *Journal of Personality and Social Psychology*, 52, 489–99.

Martin, J. and Murray, A. (1983). 'Distributive injustice and unfair exchange' in K. S. Cook and D. M. Messick (eds), *Theories of Equity: Psychological and Sociological Perspectives*. New York: Praeger.

Martin, L. L. and Clark, L. F. (1990). 'Social cognition: exploring the mental processes involved in human social interaction' in M. W. Eysenck (ed.), *Cognitive Psychology: An International Review* (vol. 1, pp. 266–310). Sussex: Wiley.

Martin, R. (1987). 'Influence minorité et relations entre groupe' in S. Moscovici and G. Mugny (eds), *Psychologie de la Conversion*. Paris: Cossett de Val.

Martin, R. (1988). 'Ingroup and outgroup minorities: differential impact upon public and private response'. *European Journal of Social Psychology*, 18, 39–52.

Maser, A. L., Sorenson, P. H. and Kryter, K. D. (1978). 'Effects of intrusive sound on classroom behaviour: data from a successful lawsuit'. Paper presented at the Annual Meeting of the Western Psychological Association, San Francisco.

Maslach, C. (1979). 'Negative emotional biasing of unexplained arousal'. *Journal of Personality and Social Psychology*, 37, 953–69.

Mathews, K. E., Jr and Canon, L. K. (1975). 'Environmental noise level as a determinant of helping behavior'. *Journal of Personality and Social Psychology*, 32, 571–77.

Matthews, K. A. (1982). 'Psychological perspectives on the Type A behaviour pattern'. *Psychological Bulletin*, 91, 293–323.

Maxwell, G. M. and Coebergh, B.. (1986). 'Patterns of loneliness in a New Zealand population'. *Community Mental Health in New Zealand*, 2, 48–61.

McAndrew, F. (1993). *Environmental Psychology*. Monterey, CA: Brooks/Cole.

McArthur, L. A. (1972). 'The how and what of why: some determinants of consequences of causal attributions'. *Journal of Personality and Social Psychology*, 22, 171–93.

McArthur, L. Z. (1981). 'What grabs you? The role of attention in impression formation and causal attribution' in E. T. Higgins, C. P. Herman and M. P. Zanna (eds), *Social Cognition: The Ontario Symposium* (vol. 1, pp. 201–46). Hillsdale, NJ: Erlbaum.

McArthur, L. Z. and Baron, R. (1983). 'Toward an ecological theory of social perception'. *Psychological Review*, 90, 215–38.

McArthur, L. Z. and Friedman, S. A. (1980). 'Illusory correlation in impression formation: variations in the shared distinctiveness effect as a function of the distinctive person's age, race, and sex'. *Journal of Personality and Social Psychology*, 39, 615–24.

McArthur, L. Z. and Post, D. L. (1977). 'Figural emphasis and person perception'. *Journal of Experimental Social Psychology*, 13, 520–35.

McBride, G., King, M. G. and James, J. W. (1965). 'Social proximity effects on galvanic skin responses in adult humans'. *Journal of Psychology*, 61, 153–57.

McCain, G., Cox, V. C. and Paulus, P. B. (1976). 'The relationship between illness, complaints and degree to crowding in a prison environment'. *Environment and Behaviour*, 8, 283–90.

McCain, G., Cox, V. C., Paulus, P. B., Luke, A. and Abadzi, H. (1985). 'Some effects of reduction of extra-classroom crowding in a school environment'. *Journal of Applied Social Psychology*, 15, 503–15.

McCauley, C. (1989). 'The nature of social influence in groupthink: compliance and internalization'. *Journal of Personality and Social Psychology*, 57, 250–60.

McCauley, C., Coleman, G. and DeFusco, P. (1977). 'Commuters eye contact with strangers in city and suburban train stations: evidence of short-term adaptation to interpersonal overload in the city'. *Environmental Psychology and Nonverbal Behaviour*, 2, 215–225.

McClintock, C. G. and van Avermaet, E. F. (1982). 'Social values and rules of fairness' in V. J. Derlega and J. L. Grzelak (eds), *Cooperation and Helping Behaviour: Theory and Research* (pp. 43–71). New York: Academic Press.

McDougall, W. (1908). *An Introduction to Social Psychology*. London: Methuen.

McDougall, W. (1920). *The Group Mind*. London: Cambridge University Press.

McGarty, C. and Penny, R.E. C. (1988). 'Categorization, accentuation and social judgement'. *British Journal of Social Psychology*, 27, 147–57.

McGillicuddy, N. B., Welton, G. L. and Pruitt, G. D. (1987). 'Third-party intervention: a field experiment comparing three different models'. *Journal of Personality and Social Psychology*, 53, 104–12.

McGinnies, E. (1966). 'Studies in persuasion. III: Reactions of Japanese students to one-sided and two-sided communications'. *Journal of Social Psychology*, 70, 87–93.

McGovern, L. P. (1976). 'Dispositional social anxiety and helping behaviour under three conditions of threat'. *Journal of Personality*, 44, 84–97.

McGuire, W. J. (1964). 'Inducing resistance to persuasion' in L. Berkowitz (ed.), *Advances in Experimental Social Psychology* (vol. 1, pp. 191–229). New York: Academic Press.

McGuire, W. J. (1968). 'Personality and susceptibility to social influence' in E. F. Borgatta and W. W. Lambert (eds), *Handbook of Personality: Theory and Research* (pp. 1130–87). Chicago, IL: Rand-McNally.

McGuire, W. J. (1969). 'The nature of attitudes and attitude change' in G. Lindzey and E. Aronson (eds), *Handbook of Social Psychology* (2nd edn, vol. 3, pp. 136–314). Reading, MA: Addison-Wesley.

McGuire, W. J. (1986). 'The vicissitudes of attitudes and similar representational constructs in twentieth century psychology'. *European Journal of Social Psychology*, 16, 89–130.

McGuire, W. J. (1989). 'The structure of individual attitudes and attitude systems' in A. R. Pratkanis, S. J. Breckler and A. G. Greenwald, (eds) *Attitude Structure and Function* (pp. 37–69). Hillsdale, NJ: Erlbaum.

McGuire, W. J. and Papageorgis, D. (1961). 'The relative efficacy of various types of prior belief-defence in producing immunity against persuasion'. *Journal of Abnormal and Social Psychology*, 62, 327–37.

McKiethen, K. B., Reitman, J. S., Rueter, H. H. and Hirtle, S. C. (1981). 'Knowledge organization and skill differences in computer programmers'. *Cognitive Psychology*, 13, 307–25.

McMillen, D. L. (1971). Transgression, self-image, and compliant behaviour'. *Journal of Personality and Social Psychology*, 20, 176–79.

McNamara, T. F. (1987). 'Language and social identity: Israelis abroad'. *Journal of Language and Social Psychology*, 6, 215–28.

Mead, G. H. (1934). *Mind, Self and Society*, Chicago, IL: University of Chicago Press.

Meeus, W. and Raaijmakers, Q. (1986). 'Administrative obedience as a social phenomenon' in W. Doise and S. Moscovici (eds), *Current Issues in European Social Psychology* (vol. 2, pp. 183–230). Cambridge: Cambridge University Press.

Mehrabian, A. (1972). 'Nonverbal communication' in J. Cole (ed.), *Nebraska Symposium on Motivation* (vol. 19, pp. 107–62). Lincoln, NE: University of Nebraska Press.

Mehrabian, A. and Diamond, S. G. (1971). 'Effects of furniture arrangement, props, and personality on social interaction'. *Journal of Personality and Social Psychology*, **20**, 18–30.

Merei, F. (1949). 'Group leadership and institutionalization'. *Human Relations*, **2**, 23–39.

Mervis, C. B. and Rosch, E. (1981). 'Categorization of natural objects'. *Annual Review of Psychology*, **32**, 89–115.

Metalsky, G. I. and Abramson, L. Y. (1981). 'Attributional styles: toward a framework for conceptualization and assessment' in P. C. Kendall and S. D. Hollon (eds), *Cognitive–Behavioral Intentions: Assessment Methods*. New York: Academic Press.

Michelini, R. L. and Snodgrass, S. R. (1980). 'Defendant characteristics and juridic decisions'. *Journal of Research in Personality*, **14**, 340–50.

Middlebrook, P. N. (1980). *Social Psychology and Modern Life* (2nd edn). New York: Knopf.

Middlemist, R. D., Knowles, E. S. and Mutter, C. F. (1976). 'Personal space invasions in the lavatory: suggestive evidence for arousal'. *Journal of Personality and Social Psychology*, **33**, 541–46.

Midlarsky, E. and Bryan, J. H. (1972). 'Affect expressions and children's imitative altruism'. *Journal of Experimental Research in Personality*, **6**, 195–203.

Midlarsky, E. and Midlarsky, M. (1973). 'Some determinants of aiding under experimentally induced stress'. *Journal of Personality*, **1**, 305–27.

Midlarsky, M. and Midlarsky, E. (1976). 'Status inconsistency, aggressive attitude, and helping behavior'. *Journal of Personality*, **44**, 371–91.

Mikula, G. (1980). 'On the role of justice in allocation decisions' in G. Mikula (ed.), *Justice and Social Interaction*. New York: Springer-Verlag/Bern: Hans Huber.

Milardo, R. M., Johnson, M. P. and Huston, T. L. (1983). 'Developing close relationships: changing patterns of interaction between pair members and social networks'. *Journal of Personality and Social Psychology*, **44**, 964–76.

Milgram, S. (1963). 'Behaviour study of obedience'. *Journal of Abnormal and Social Psychology*, **67**, 371–378.

Milgram, S. (1974). *Obedience to Authority*. London: Tavistock.

Milgram, S. (1977a). 'A psychological map of New York City' in S. Milgram (ed.), *The Individual in a Social World* (pp. 54–67). Reading, MA: Addison-Wesley.

Milgram, S. (1977b). 'The experience of living in cities' in S. Milgram (ed.), *The Individual in a Social World* (pp. 24–41). Reading, MA: Addison-Wesley.

Milgram, S. (1992). *The Individual in a Social World: Essays and Experiments* (2nd edn). New York: McGraw-Hill.

Milgram, S. and Toch, H. (1969). 'Collective behaviour: crowds and social movements' in G. Lindzey and E. Aronson (eds), *Handbook of Social Psychology* (2nd edn, vol. 4, pp. 507–610). Reading, MA: Addison-Wesley.

Milham, J. (1974). 'Two components of need for approval score and their relationship to cheating following success and failure'. *Journal of Research in Personality*, **8**, 378–92.

Mill, J. S. (1869). *The Analysis of the Phenomenon of the Human Mind*. New York: Kelley.

Millar, M. G. and Tesser, A. (1986). 'Effects of affective and cognitive focus on the attitude–behaviour relation'. *Journal of Personality and Social Psychology*, **51**, 270–76.

Miller, C. E. (1989). 'The social psychological effects of group decision rules' in P. B. Paulus (ed.), *Psychology of Group Influence* (2nd edn, pp. 327–55). Hillsdale, NJ: Erlbaum.

Miller, D. T. (1977). 'Altruism and the threat to a belief in a just world'. *Journal of Experimental Social Psychology*, **13**, 113–24.

Miller, D. T. and Porter, C. A. (1980). 'Effects of temporal perspective on the attribution process'. *Journal of Personality and Social Psychology*, **39**, 532–41.

Miller, D. T. and Porter, C. A. (1983). 'Self-blame in victims of violence'. *Journal of Social Issues*, **39**, 139–52.

Miller, D. T and Ross, M. (1975). 'Self-serving biases in the attribution of causality: fact or fiction?' *Psychological Bulletin*, 82, 213–25.

Miller, J. G. (1984). 'Culture and the development of everyday social explanation'. *Journal of Personality and Social Psychology*, 46, 961–78.

Miller, N. and Brewer, M. B. (eds) (1984). *Groups in Contact: The Psychology of Desegregation*. New York: Academic Press.

Miller, N., Maruyama, G., Beaber, R. J. and Valone, K. (1976). 'Speed of speech and persuasion'. *Journal of Personality and Social Psychology*, 34, 615–25.

Miller, N., Brewer, M. B. and Edwards, K. (1985). 'Cooperative interaction in desegregated settings: a laboratory analogue'. *Journal of Social Issues*, 41, 63–79.

Miller, N. E. (1948). 'Theory and experiment relating psychoanalytic displacement to stimulus–response generalization'. *Journal of Abnormal and Social Psychology*, 43, 155–78.

Miller, N. E. and Bugelski, R. (1948). 'Minor studies in aggression: the influence of frustrations imposed by the ingroup on attitudes toward outgroups'. *Journal of Psychology*, 25, 437–42.

Minahan, N. M. (1971). 'Relationships among self-perceived physical attractiveness, body shape, and personality of teenage girls'. *Dissertation Abstracts International*, 32, 1249–50.

Minard, R. D. (1952). 'Race relations in the Pocahontas coal field'. *Journal of Social Issues*, 8, 29–44.

Mischel, W. (1968). *Personality and Assessment*. New York: Wiley.

Mita, T. H., Dermer, M. and Knight, J. (1977). 'Reversed facial images and the mere exposure hypothesis'. *Journal of Personality and Social Psychology*, 35, 597–601.

Mitchell, H. E. (1979). 'Informational and affective determinants of juror decision making'. PhD thesis, Purdue University.

Mitchell, R. (1971). 'Some social implications of higher density housing'. *American Sociological Review*, 36, 18–29.

Monson, T. C. and Hesley, J. W. (1982). 'Causal attributions for behaviour consistent or inconsistent with an actor's personality traits: differences between those offered by actors and observers'. *Journal of Experimental Social Psychology*, 18, 426–32.

Montagre, A. (1973). *Man and Aggression* (2nd edn). London: Oxford University Press.

Montepare, J. M. and Vega, C. (1988). 'Women's vocal reactions to intimate and casual male friends'. *Personality and Social Psychology Bulletin*, 14, 103–12.

Moore, B. S., Sherrod, D. R., Liu, T. J. and Underwood, B. (1979). 'The dispositional shift in attribution over time'. *Journal of Experimental Social Psychology*, 15, 553–69.

Moreland, R. L. (1985). 'Social categorization and the assimilation of "new" group members'. *Journal of Personality and Social Psychology*, 48, 1173–90.

Moreland, R. L. and Levine, J. M. (1982) 'Socialization in small groups: temporal changes in individual–group relations' in L. Berkowitz (ed.), *Advances in Experimental Social Psychology* (vol. 15, pp. 137–92). New York: Academic Press.

Moreland, R. L. and Levine, J. M. (1984). 'Role transitions in small groups' in V. Allen and E. van de Vliert (eds), *Role Transitions: Explorations and Explanations* (pp. 181–95). New York: Plenum.

Moreland, R. L. and Levine, J. M. (1989). 'Newcomers and oldtimers in small groups' in P. B. Paulus (ed.), *Psychology of Group Influence* (2nd edn, pp. 143–86). Hillsdale, NJ: Erlbaum.

Moreland, R. L. and Levine, J. M. (1994). *Understanding Small Groups*. Boston, MA: Allyn and Bacon.

Moreland, R. L., Levine, J. M. and Cini, M. (1993). 'Group socialization: the role of commitment' in M. A. Hogg and D. Abrams (eds), *Group Motivation: Social Psychological Perspectives* (pp. 105–29). London: Harvester Wheatsheaf.

Moreland, R. L., Hogg, M. A. and Hains, S. C. (1994). 'Back to the future: social psychological research on groups'. *Journal of Experimental Social Psychology*, 30, 505–33.

Moriarty, T. (1975). 'Crime, commitment and the responsive bystander: two field experiments'. *Journal of Personality and Social Psychology*, 31, 370–76.

Morley, I. E. and Stephenson, G. M. (1977). *The Social Psychology of Bargaining*. London: Allen and Unwin.

Morley, I. E., Webb, J. and Stephenson, G. M. (1977). 'Bargaining and arbitration in the resolution of conflict' in W. Stroebe, A. W. Kruglanski, D. Bar-Tal and M. Hewstone (eds), *The Social Psychology of Intergroup Conflict: Theory, Research and Applications* (pp. 117–34). Berlin: Springer-Verlag.

Morris, D. (1967). *The Naked Ape*. New York: McGraw-Hill.

Morris, W. N. and Miller, R. S. (1975). 'The effects of consensus-breaking and consensus preempting partners on reduction of conformity'. *Journal of Experimental Social Psychology*, **11**, 215–23.

Morton, T. L. (1978). 'Intimacy and reciprocity of exchange: a comparison of spouses and strangers'. *Journal of Personality and Social Psychology*, **36**, 72–81.

Moscovici, S. (1961). *La psychanalyse: son image et son public*. Paris: Presses Universitaires de France.

Moscovici, S. (1972). 'Society and theory in social psychology' in J. Israel and H. Tajfel (eds), *The Context of Social Psychology: A Critical Assessment* (pp. 17–68). New York: Academic Press.

Moscovici, S. (ed.) (1973). *Introduction à la psychologie sociale*. Paris: Larousse.

Moscovici, S. (1976). *Social Influence and Social Change*. London: Academic Press.

Moscovici, S. (1980). 'Toward a theory of conversion behaviour' in L. Berkowitz (ed.), *Advances in Experimental Social Psychology* (vol. 13, pp. 202–39). New York: Academic Press.

Moscovici, S. (1981). 'On social representation' in J. P. Forgas (ed.), *Social Cognition: Perspectives on Everyday Understanding* (pp. 181–209). London: Academic Press.

Moscovici, S. (1982). 'The coming era of representations' in J-P. Codol and J. P. Leyens (eds), *Cognitive Analysis of Social Behaviour* (pp. 115–50). The Hague: Martinus Nijhoff.

Moscovici, S. (1983). 'The phenomenon of social representations' in R. M. Farr and S. Moscovici (eds), *Social Representations* (pp. 3–69). Cambridge: Cambridge University Press.

Moscovici, S. (ed.) (1984). *Psychologie sociale*. Paris: Presses Universitaires de France.

Moscovici, S. (1985a). 'Social influence and conformity' in G. Lindzey and E. Aronson (eds), *Handbook of Social Psychology* (3rd edn, vol. 2, pp. 347–412). New York: Random House.

Moscovici, S. (1985b). *The Age of the Crowd*. Cambridge: Cambridge University Press.

Moscovici, S. (1988). 'Notes towards a description of social representations'. *European Journal of Social Psychology*, **18**, 211–50.

Moscovici, S. and Faucheux, C. (1972). 'Social influence, conforming bias, and the study of active minorities' in L. Berkowitz (ed.), *Advances in Experimental Social Psychology* (vol. 6, pp. 149–202). New York: Academic Press.

Moscovici, S. and Lage, E. (1976). 'Studies in social influence. III: Majority vs. minority influence in a group'. *European Journal of Social Psychology*, **6**, 149–74.

Moscovici, S. and Mugny, G. (1983). 'Minority influence' in P. B. Paulus (ed.), *Basic Group Processes* (pp. 41–64). New York: Springer-Verlag.

Moscovici, S. and Personnaz, B. (1980). 'Studies in social influence. V: Minority influence and conversion behaviour in a perceptual task'. *Journal of Experimental Social Psychology*, **16**, 270–82.

Moscovici, S. and Personnaz, B. (1986). 'Studies on latent influence by the spectrometer method. I: The impact of psychologization in the case of conversion by a minority or a majority'. *European Journal of Social Psychology*, **16**, 345–60.

Moscovici, S. and Zavalloni, M. (1969). 'The group as a polarizer of attitudes'. *Journal of Personality and Social Psychology*, **12**, 125–35.

Moscovici, S., Lage, E. and Naffrechoux, M. (1969). 'Influence of a consistent minority on the responses of a majority in a colour perception task'. *Sociometry*, **32**, 365–80.

Mudrack, P. E. (1989). 'Defining group cohesiveness: a legacy of confusion'. *Small Group Behaviour*, **20**, 37–49.

Mugny, G. (1982). *The Power of Minorities*. London: Academic Press.

Mugny, G. and Papastamou, S. (1982). 'Minority influence and psychosocial identity'. *European Journal of Social Psychology*, 12, 379–94.

Mugny, G. and Pérez, J. A. (1991). *The Social Psychology of Minority Influence*. Cambridge: Cambridge University Press.

Mulac, A., Studley, L. B., Wiemann, J. M. and Bradac, J. J. (1987). 'Male/female gaze in same-sex and mixed-sex dyads: gender-linked differences and mutual influence'. *Human Communication Research*, 13, 323–43.

Mulder, M. (1960). 'Communication structure, decision structure and group performance'. *Sociometry*, 23, 1–14.

Mullen, B. (1983). 'Operationalizing the effect of the group on the individual: a self-attention perspective'. *Journal of Experimental Social Psychology*, 19, 295–322.

Mullen, B. (1986). 'Atrocity as a function of lynch mob composition: a self-attention perspective'. *Personality and Social Psychology Bulletin*, 12, 187–97.

Mullen, B. and Hu, L. (1989). 'Perceptions of ingroup and outgroup variability: a meta-analytic integration'. *Basic and Applied Social Psychology*, 10, 233–52.

Mullen, B. and Johnson, C. (1990). 'Distinctiveness-based illusory correlations and stereotyping: a meta-analytic integration'. *British Journal of Social Psychology*, 29, 11–28.

Mullen, B. and Riordan, C. A. (1988).' Self-serving attributions for performance in naturalistic settings: a meta-analytic review'. *Journal of Applied Social Psychology*, 18, 3–22.

Mullen, B., Atkins, J. L., Champion, D. S., Edwards, C., Hardy, D., Story, J. E. and Vanderklok, M. (1985). 'The false consensus effect: a meta-analysis of 115 hypothesis tests'. *Journal of Experimental Social Psychology*, 21, 262–83.

Mullen, B., Salas, E. and Driskell, J. E. (1989). 'Salience, motivation, and artifact as contributions to the relation between participation rate and leadership'. *Journal of Experimental Social Psychology*, 25, 545–59.

Mullen, B., Johnson, C. and Salas, E. (1991). 'Productivity loss in brainstorming groups'. *Basic and Applied Social Psychology*, 12, 3–24.

Mullen, P. E. (1984). 'Mental disorder and dangerousness'. *Australian and New Zealand Journal of Psychiatry*, 18, 8–17.

Murchison, C. (ed.) (1935). *Handbook of Social Psychology*. Worcester, MA: Clark University Press.

Murphy, G. and Murphy, L. B. (1931). *Experimental Social Psychology*. New York Harper. (Rev. edn published with T. M. Newcomb in 1937).

Murphy, P., Williams, J. and Dunning, E. (1990). *Football on Trial: Spectator Violence and Development in the Football World*. London: Routledge.

Murstein, B. I. (1980). 'Love at first sight: a myth'. *Medical Aspects of Human Sexuality*. 14, 34, 39–41.

Myers, D. G. and Lamm, H. (1975). 'The polarizing effect of group discussion'. *American Scientist*, 63, 297–303.

Myers, D. G. and Lamm, H. (1976). 'The group polarization phenomenon'. *Psychological Bulletin*, 83, 602–27.

Nadler, A. (1986). 'Help seeking as a cultural phenomenon: differences between city and kibbutz dwellers'. *Journal of Personality and Social Psychology*, 51, 976–82.

Nahem, J. (1980). *Psychology and Psychiatry Today: A Marxist View*. New York: International Publishers.

Neisser, U. (1967). *Cognitive Psychology*. Englewood Cliffs, NJ: Prentice Hall.

Nemeth, C. (1970). 'Bargaining and reciprocity'. *Psychological Bulletin*, 74, 297–308.

Nemeth, C. (1981). 'Jury trials: psychology and law' in L. Berkowitz (ed.), *Advances in Experimental Social Psychology* (vol. 14, pp. 309–67). New York: Academic Press.

Nemeth, C. (1986). 'Differential contributions of majority and minority influence'. *Psychological Review*, 93, 23–32.

Nemeth, C. and Chiles, C. (1988). 'Modelling courage: the role of dissent in fostering independence'. *European Journal of Social Psychology*, **18**, 275–80.

Nemeth, C. and Wachtler, J. (1983). 'Creative problem solving as a result of majority vs. minority influence'. *European Journal of Social Psychology*, **13**, 45–55.

Nemeth, C., Swedlund, M. and Kanki, B. (1974). 'Patterning of the minority's response and their influence on the majority'. *European Journal of Social Psychology*, **4**, 53–64.

Nemeth, C., Wachtler, J. and Endicott, J. (1977). 'Increasing the size of the minority: some gains and some losses'. *European Journal of Social Psychology*, **7**, 15–27.

Neuberg, S. L. and Fiske, S. T. (1987). 'Motivational influences on impression formation: outcome dependency, accuracy-driven attention, and individuating processes'. *Journal of Personality and Social Psychology*, **53**, 431–44.

Newcomb, T. M. (1961). *The Acquaintance Process*. New York: Holt, Rinehart and Winston.

Newcomb, T. M. (1965). 'Attitude development as a function of reference groups: the Bennington study' in H. Proshansky and B. Seidenberg (eds), *Basic Studies in Social Psychology* (pp. 215–25). New York: Holt, Rinehart and Winston.

Newman, O. (1973). *Defensible Space*. New York: Macmillan.

Newman, O. (1975). *Design Guidelines for Creating Defensible Space*. Washington, DC: US Government Printing Office.

Ney, P. G. and Herron, J. L. (1985). 'Child abuse: mandatory reporting'. *New Zealand Medical Journal*, **98**, 703–05.

Ng, S. H. (1980). *The Social Psychology of Power*. London: Academic Press.

Ng, S. H. (1990). 'Androgenic coding of man and his memory by language users'. *Journal of Experimental Social Psychology*, **26**, 455–64.

Nieburg, H. (1969). *Political Violence: The Behavioural Process*. New York: St Martin's Press.

Nisbett, R. E., Zukier, H. and Lemley, R. E. (1981). 'The dilution effect: non-diagnostic information weakens the implications of diagnostic information'. *Cognitive Psychology*, **13**, 248–77.

Nisbett, R. E. and Ross, L. (1980). *Human Inference: Strategies and Shortcomings of Social Judgement*. Englewood Cliffs, NJ: Prentice Hall.

Nisbett, R. E., Krantz, D. H., Jepson, C. and Fong, G. T. (1982). 'Improving inductive inference' in D. Kahneman, P. Slovic and A. Tversky (eds), *Judgement Under Uncertainty: Heuristics and Biases* (pp. 445–62). New York: Cambridge University Press.

Noller, P. (1984). *Nonverbal Communication and Marital Interaction*. Oxford: Pergamon.

Noller, P. and Callan, V. J. (1990). *Adolescents in the Family*. London: Routledge and Kegan Paul.

Noller, P. and Ruzzene, M. (1991). 'Communication in marriage: the influence of affect and cognition' in G. J. O. Fletcher and F. D. Fincham (eds), *Cognition and Close Relationships* (pp. 203–33). Hillsdale, NJ: Erlbaum.

Nuttin, J. M. and Beckers, A. (1975). *The Illusion of Attitude Change: Towards a Response Contagion Theory of Persuasion*. London: Academic Press.

Oaker, G. and Brown, R. J. (1986). 'Intergroup relations in a hospital setting: a further test of social identity theory'. *Human Relations*, **39**, 767–78.

Oakes, P. J. (1987). 'The salience of social categories' in J. C. Turner, M. A. Hogg, P. J. Oakes, S. D. Reicher and M. S. Wetherell (eds), *Rediscovering the Social Group: A Self-categorization Theory* (pp. 117–41). Oxford: Blackwell.

Oakes, P. J. and Turner, J. C. (1990). 'Is limited information processing capacity the cause of social stereotyping?'. *European Review of Social Psychology*, **1**, 111–35.

Oakes, P. J., Haslam, S. A. and Turner, J. C. (1994). *Stereotyping and Social Reality*. Oxford: Blackwell.

Oliver, P. (1986). 'Rest home accommodation for the elderly: a civil rights perspective'. *Community Mental Health in New Zealand*, **3**, 74–91.

Olson, J. M. (1988). 'Misattribution, preparatory information, and speech anxiety'. *Journal of Personality and Social Psychology*, 54, 758–67.

Olson, J. M. and Zanna, M. P. (1993). 'Attitudes and attitude change'. *Annual Review of Psychology*, 44, 117–54.

Oppenheim, A. N. (1992). *Questionnaire Design. Interviewing and Attitude Measurement* (2nd edn). London: Pinter.

Orano, P. (1901). *Psicologia Sociale*. Bari: Lacerta.

Orne, M. T. (1962). 'On the social psychology of the psychology experiment: with particular reference to demand characteristics and their implications'. *American Psychologist*, 17, 776–83.

Ortony, A. and Turner, T. J. (1990). 'What's basic about basic emotions?' *Psychological Review*, 97, 315–31.

Orvis, B. R., Kelley, H. H. and Butler, D. (1976). 'Attributional conflicts in young couples' in J. H. Harvey, W. J. Ickes and R. F. Kidd (eds), *New Directions in Attribution Research* (vol. 1, pp. 353–86). Hillsdale, NJ: Erlbaum.

Orwell, G. (1962). *The Road to Wigan Pier*. Harmondsworth: Penguin.

Osborn, A. F. (1957). *Applied Imagination* (rev. edn). New York: Scribners.

Osgood, C. E. (1962). *An Alternative to War or Surrender*. Urbana, IL: University of Illinois Press.

Osgood, C. E., Suci, G. J. and Tannenbaum, P. H. (1957). *The Measurement of Meaning*. Urbana, IL: University of Illinois Press.

Oskamp, S. (1977). *Attitudes and Opinions*. Englewood Cliffs, NJ: Prentice Hall.

Oskamp, S. (1984). *Applied Social Psychology*. Englewood Cliffs, NJ: Prentice Hall.

Oskamp, S. (1991). *Attitudes and Opinions* (2nd edn). Sydney: Prentice Hall.

Osmond, H. (1957). 'Function as the basis of psychiatric ward design'. *Mental Hospitals*, 8, 23–30.

Ostrom, T. M. (1968). 'The relationship between the affective, behavioural, and cognitive components of attitude'. *Journal of Experimental Social Psychology*, 5, 12–30.

Ostrom, T. M. (1989a). 'Three catechisms for social memory' in P. R. Solomon, G. R. Goethals, C. M. Kelley and B. R. Stephens (eds), *Memory: Interdisciplinary Approaches* (pp. 201–20). New York: Springer-Verlag.

Ostrom, T. M. (1989b). 'Interdependence of attitude theory and measurement' in A. R. Pratkanis, S. J. Breckler and A. G. Greenwald, (eds). *Attitude Structure and Function* (pp. 11–36). Hillsdale, NJ: Erlbaum.

Page, R. R. (1978). 'Environmental influences on prosocial behaviour: the effect of temperature'. Paper presented at the Midwestern Psychological Association meeting, Chicago.

Pagel, M. D. and Davidson, A. R. (1984). 'A comparison of three social-psychological models of attitude and behavioral plan: prediction of contraceptive behavior'. *Journal of Personality and Social Psychology*, 47, 517–33.

Pandey, J. and Griffitt, W. (1974). 'Attraction and helping'. *Bulletin of Psychonomic Psychology*, 3, 123–24.

Pandey, J., Sinha, Y., Prakash, A. and Tripathi, R. C. (1982). 'Right–left political ideologies and attribution of the causes of poverty'. *European Journal of Social Psychology*, 12, 327–31.

Pantin, H. M. and Carver, C. S. (1982). 'Induced competence and the bystander effect'. *Journal of Applied Social Psychology*, 12, 100–11.

Parducci, A. (1968). 'The relativism of absolute judgements'. *Scientific American*, 219, 84–90.

Park, B. (1986). 'A method for studying the development of impressions of real people'. *Journal of Personality and Social Psychology*, 51, 907–17.

Park, B. and Hastie, R. (1987). 'Perception of variability in category development: instance- versus abstraction-based stereotypes'. *Journal of Personality and Social Psychology*, 53, 621–35.

Park, B. and Rothbart, M. (1982). 'Perception of outgroup homogeneity and levels of social categorization: memory for the subordinate attributes of ingroup and outgroup members'. *Journal of Personality and Social Psychology*, 42, 1051–68.

Parkinson, B. (1985). 'Emotional effects of false autonomic feedback'. *Psychological Bulletin*, **98**, 471–94.

Parsons, J. E., Adler, T. and Meece, J. L. (1984). 'Sex differences in achievement: a test of alternate theories'. *Journal of Personality and Social Psychology*, **46**, 26–43.

Patch, M. E. (1986). 'The role of source legitimacy in sequential request strategies of compliance'. *Personality and Social Psychology Bulletin*, **12**, 199–205.

Patterson, A. H. (1977). 'Methodological developments in environment–behaviour research' in D. Stokols (ed.) *Perspectives on Environment and Behaviour: Theory, Research, and Applications*, New York: Plenum Press.

Patterson, F. (1978). 'Conversations with a gorilla'. *National Geographic*, **154**, 438–65.

Patterson, M. L. (1983). *Nonverbal Behaviour: A Functional Perspective*. New York: Springer-Verlag.

Patterson, M. L., Mullens, S. and Romano, J. (1971). 'Compensatory reactions to spatial intrusion'. *Sociometry*, **34**, 114–21.

Paulus, P. B., Annis, A. B., Seta, J., Schkade, J. and Mathews, R. (1976). 'Density does affect task performance'. *Journal of Personality and Social Psychology*, **34**, 248–53.

Paulus, P. B., Dzindolet, M. T., Poletes, G. and Camacho, L. M. (1993). 'Perception of performance in group brainstorming: the illusion of group productivity'. *Personality and Social Psychology Bulletin*, **19**, 78–89.

Pavelchak, M. A., Moreland, R. L. and Levine, J. M. (1986). 'Effects of prior group memberships on subsequent reconnaissance activities'. *Journal of Personality and Social Psychology*, **50**, 56–66.

Pei, M. (1965). *The Story of Language* (2nd edn). Philadelphia, PA: Lippincott.

Penner, L. A. (1986). *Social Psychology: Concepts and Applications*. St Paul: West.

Penrod, S. (1983). *Social Psychology*. Englewood Cliffs, NJ: Prentice Hall.

Penrod, S. and Hastie, R. (1980). 'A computer simulation of jury decision making'. *Psychological Review*, **87**, 133–59.

Pepitone, A. (1981). 'Lessons from the history of social psychology'. *American Psychologist*, **36**, 972–85.

Peplau, L. A. and Perlman, D. (eds) (1982). *Loneliness: A Sourcebook of Current Theory, Research and Therapy*. New York: Wiley.

Perlman, D. and Oskamp, S. (1971). 'The effects of picture content and exposure frequency on evaluations of negroes and whites'. *Journal of Experimental Social Psychology*, **7**, 503–14.

Perry, D. G., Perry, L., Bussey, K., English, D. and Arnold, G. (1980). 'Processes of attribution and children's self-punishment following misbehaviour'. *Child Development*, **51**, 545–51.

Peters, L. H., O'Connor, E. J., Weekley, J., Pooyan, A., Frank, B. and Erenkrantz, B. (1984). 'Sex bias and managerial evaluation: a replication and extension'. *Journal of Applied Psychology*, **69**, 349–52.

Peters, L. H., Hartke, D. D. and Pohlmann, J. T. (1985). 'Fiedler's contingency theory of leadership: an application of the meta-analytic procedure of Schmidt and Hunter'. *Psychological Bulletin*, **97**, 274–85.

Peterson, C. (1980). 'Memory and the "dispositional shift"'. *Social Psychology Quarterly*, **43**, 372–80.

Peterson, C., Semmel, A., von Baeyer, C., Abramson, L. Y., Metalsky, G. I. and Seligman, M. E. P. (1982). 'The attributional style questionnaire'. *Cognitive Therapy and Research*, **6**, 287–300.

Pettigrew, T. F. (1958). 'Personality and sociocultural factors in intergroup attitudes: a cross-national comparison'. *Journal of Conflict Resolution*, **2**, 29–42.

Pettigrew, T. F. (1971). *Racially Separate or Together*. New York: McGraw-Hill.

Pettigrew, T. F. (1979). 'The ultimate attribution error: extending Allport's cognitive analysis of prejudice'. *Personality and Social Psychology Bulletin*, **5**, 461–76.

Pettigrew, T. F. (1981). 'Extending the stereotype concept' in D. L. Hamilton (ed.), *Cognitive Processes in Stereotyping and Intergroup Behaviour* (pp. 303–32). Hillsdale, NJ: Erlbaum.

Pettigrew, T. F. (1987). *Modern Racism: American Black-White Relations Since the 1960s*. Cambridge, MA: Harvard University Press.

Petty, R. E. and Cacioppo, J. T. (1979). 'Issue-involvement can increase or decrease persuasion by enhancing message-relevant cognitive responses'. *Journal of Personality and Social Psychology*, 37, 1915–26.

Petty, R. E. and Cacioppo, J. T. (1981). *Attitudes and Persuasion: Classic and Contemporary Approaches*. Dubuque, IA: Brown.

Petty, R. E. and Cacioppo, J. T. (1986). 'The elaboration likelihood model of persuasion' in L. Berkowitz (ed.), *Advances in Experimental Social Psychology* (vol. 19, pp. 123–205). New York: Academic Press.

Pevers, B. H. and Secord, P. F. (1973). 'Developmental changes in attribution of descriptive concepts to persons'. *Journal of Personality and Social Psychology*, 27, 120–8.

Pheterson, G. I., Keisler, S. B. and Goldberg, P. A. (1971). 'Evaluation of the performance of women as a function of their success, achievements, and personal history'. *Journal of Personality and Social Psychology*, 19, 114–18.

Phillips, D. P. (1986). 'Natural experiments on the effects of mass media violence on fatal aggression: strengths and weaknesses of a new approach' in L. Berkowitz (ed.), *Advances in Experimental Social Psychology* (vol. 19, pp. 207–50). New York: Academic Press.

Phillips, J. (1987). *A Man's Country? The Image of the Pakeha Male, a History*. Auckland: Penguin.

Piliavin, I. M., Piliavin, J. A. and Rodin, J. (1975). 'Costs, diffusion and the stigmatized victim'. *Journal of Personality and Social Psychology*, 32, 429–438.

Piliavin, J. A. and Charng, H-W. (1990). Altruism: a review of recent theory and research. *Annual Review of Sociology*, 16, 27–65.

Piliavin, J. A., Dovidio, J. F., Gaertner, S. L. and Clark, R. D., III (1981). *Emergency Intervention*. New York: Academic Press.

Platz, S. J. and Hosch, H. M. (1988). 'Cross-racial/ethnic eyewitness identification: a field study'. *Journal of Applied Social Psychology*, 18, 972–84.

Pomazal, R. J. and Clore, G. L. (1973). 'Helping on the highway: the effects of dependency and sex'. *Journal of Applied Social Psychology*, 3, 150–164.

Popper, K. (1969). *Conjectures and Refutations* (3rd edn). London: Routledge and Kegan Paul.

Potter, J. and Wetherell, M. S. (1987). *Discourse and Social Psychology: Beyond Attitudes and Behaviour*. London: Sage.

Potter, J., Stringer, P. and Wetherell, M. S. (1984). *Social Texts and Context: Literature and Social Psychology*. London: Routledge and Kegan Paul.

Potter, J., Wetherell, M. S., Gill, R. and Edwards, D. (1990). Discourse: noun, verb or social practice?' *Philosophical Psychology*, 3, 205–17.

Powell, M. C. and Fazio, R. M. (1984). 'Attitude accessibility as a function of repeated attitudinal expression'. *Personality and Social Psychology Bulletin*, 10, 139–48.

Pratkanis, A. R. and Greenwald, A. G. (1989). 'A sociocognitive model of attitude structure and function' in L. Berkowitz (ed.), *Advances in Experimental Social Psychology* (vol. 22, pp. 245–85). New York: Academic Press.

Prentice-Dunn, S. and Rogers, R. W. (1982). 'Effects of public and private self-awareness on deindividuation and aggression'. *Journal of Personality and Social Psychology*, 43, 503–13.

Pruitt, D. G. (1981). *Negotiation Behaviour*. New York: Academic Press.

Pruitt, D. G. (1986). 'Achieving integrative agreements in negotiation' in R. K. White (ed.), *Psychology and the Prevention of Nuclear War* (pp. 463–78). New York: New York University Press.

Pryor, J. B. and Ostrom, T. M. (1981). 'The cognitive organization of social information: a converging-operations approach'. *Journal of Personality and Social Psychology*, 41, 628–41.

Przybyla, D. P. J. (1985). 'The facilitating effects of exposure to erotica on male prosocial behaviour'. PhD thesis. State University of New York at Albany.

Pyszczynski, T. A. and Greenberg, J. (1981). 'Role of disconfirmed expectancies in the instigation of attributional processing'. *Journal of Personality and Social Psychology*, 40, 31–38.

Quattrone, G. A. (1986). 'On the perception of a group's variability' in S. Worchel and W. Austin (eds), *The Psychology of Intergroup Relations* (vol. 2, pp. 25–48). New York: Nelson-Hall.

Quattrone, G. A. and Jones, E. E. (1980). 'The perception of variability within ingroups and outgroups: implications for the law of small numbers'. *Journal of Personality and Social Psychology*, 38, 141–52.

Quigley-Fernandez, B. and Tedeschi, J. T. (1978). 'The bogus pipeline as lie detector: two validity studies'. *Journal of Personality and Social Psychology*, 36, 247–56.

Rabbie, J. M. and Bekkers, F. (1978). 'Threatened leadership and intergroup competition'. *European Journal of Social Psychology*, 8, 9–20.

Rabbie, J. M. and DeBrey, J. H. C. (1971). 'The anticipation of intergroup cooperation and competition under private and public conditions'. *International Journal of Group Tensions*, 1, 230–51.

Rabbie, J. M. and Horwitz, M. (1969). 'Arousal of ingroup–outgroup bias by a chance win or loss'. *Journal of Personality and Social Psychology*, 13, 269–77.

Rabbie, J. M. and Wilkens, G. (1971). 'Ingroup competition and its effect on intragroup relations'. *European Journal of Social Psychology*, 1, 215–34.

Rainwater, L. (1966). 'Fear and the house-as-haven in the lower class'. *Journal of the American Institute of Planners*, 32, 23–31.

Ramirez, J., Bryant, J. and Zillman, D. (1983). 'Effects of erotica on retaliatory behaviour as a function of level of prior provocation'. *Journal of Personality and Social Psychology*, 43, 971–78.

Rankin, R. E. and Campbell, D. T. (1955). 'Galvanic skin response to negro and white experimenters'. *Journal of Abnormal and Social Psychology*, 51, 30–33.

Raphael, B. (1985). *The Anatomy of Bereavement: A Handbook for the Caring Professions*. London: Hutchinson.

Rapoport, A. (1976). *Experimental Games and their Uses in Psychology*. Morristown, NJ: General Learning Press.

Raven, B. H. (1965). 'Social influence and power' in I. D. Steiner and M. Fishbein (eds), *Current Studies in Social Psychology* (pp. 371–82). New York: Holt, Rinehart and Winston.

Raven, B. H. and French, J. R. P. (1958). 'Legitimate power, coercive power and observability in social influence'. *Sociometry*, 21, 83–97.

Ray, M. L. (1988). *Short-term Evidence of Advertising's Long-term Effect*, Report no. 88–107. Cambridge, MA: Marketing Science Institute.

Reeder, G. D. and Brewer, M. B. (1979). 'A schematic model of dispositional attribution in interpersonal perception'. *Psychological Review*, 86, 61–79.

Regan, D. T. and Fazio, R. H. (1977). 'On the consistency of attitudes and behaviour: look to the method of attitude formation'. *Journal of Experimental Social Psychology*, 13, 38–45.

Regan, D. T., Williams, M. and Sparling, S. (1972). 'Voluntary expiation of guilt: a field experiment'. *Journal of Personality and Social Psychology*, 24, 42–45.

Regan, J. (1971). 'Guilt, perceived injustice, and altruistic behaviour'. *Journal of Personality and Social Psychology*, 18, 124–32.

Reicher, S. D. (1982). 'The determination of collective behaviour' in H. Tajfel (ed.), *Social Identity and Intergroup Relations* (pp. 41–83). Cambridge: Cambridge University Press.

Reicher, S. D. (1984). 'Social influence in the crowd: attitudinal and behavioural effects of deindividuation in conditions of high and low group salience'. *British Journal of Social Psychology*, 23, 341–50.

Reicher, S. D. (1987). 'Crowd behaviour as social action' in J. C. Turner, M. A. Hogg, P. J. Oakes, S. D. Reicher and M. S. Wetherell, *Rediscovering the Social Group: A Self-categorization Theory* (pp. 171–202). Oxford: Blackwell.

Reicher, S. D. and Emler, N. (1985). Delinquent behaviour and attitudes to formal authority. *British Journal of Social Psychology*, 24, 161–8.

Reicher, S. D. and Potter, J. (1985). 'Psychological theory as intergroup perspective: a comparative analysis of "scientific" and "lay" accounts of crowd events'. *Human Relations*, 38, 167–89.

Reisenzein, R. (1983). 'The Schachter theory of emotion: two decades later'. *Psychological Bulletin*, **94**, 239–64.

Reizenstein, J. E. (1982). 'Hospital design and human behaviour: a review of the recent literature' in A. Baum and J. E. Singer (eds), *Advances in Environmental Psychology: Environment and Health* (vol. 4, pp. 137–69). Hillsdale, NJ: Erlbaum.

Rhodes, N. and Wood, W. (1992). 'Self-esteem and intelligence affect influenceability: the mediating role of message reception'. *Psychological Bulletin*, **111**, 156–71.

Rhodewalt, F. and Strube, M. J. (1985). 'A self-attribution reactance model for health outcomes'. *Journal of Applied Social Psychology*, **15**, 330–44.

Rholes, W. S. and Pryor, J. B. (1982). 'Cognitive accessibility and causal attributions'. *Personality and Social Psychology Bulletin*, **8**, 719–27.

Rice, M. E. and Grusec, J. E. (1975). 'Saying and doing: effects on observer performance'. *Journal of Personality and Social Psychology*, **32**, 584–93.

Rice, R. W. (1978). 'Construct validity of the least preferred co-worker score'. *Psychological Bulletin*, **85**, 1199–237.

Rice, R. W., Instone, D. and Adams, J. (1984). 'Leader sex, leader success, and leadership process: two field studies'. *Journal of Applied Psychology*, **69**, 12–31.

Riess, M., Rosenfield, R., Melburg, V. and Tedeschi, J. T. (1981). 'Self-serving attributions: biased private perceptions and distorted public descriptions'. *Journal of Personality and Social Psychology*, **41**, 224–31.

Rimé, B. (1983). 'Nonverbal communication or nonverbal behaviour' in W. Doise and S. Moscovici (eds), *Current Issues in European Social Psychology* (vol. 1, pp. 85–141). Cambridge: Cambridge University Press.

Ringelmann, M. (1913). 'Recherches sur les moteurs animés: travail de l'homme'. *Annales de l'Institut National Agronomique*, **2**(12), 1–40.

Riopelle, A. J. (1987). 'Instinct' in R. J. Corsini (ed.), *Concise Encyclopaedia of Psychology* (pp. 599–600). New York: Wiley.

Rodin, J. (1976). 'Density, perceived choice and responses to controllable and uncontrollable outcomes'. *Journal of Experimental Social Psychology*, **12**, 546–78.

Rodin, J., Solomon, S. K. and Metcalf, J. (1979). 'Role of control in mediating perceptions of density'. *Journal of Personality and Social Psychology*, **36**, 988–99.

Roethlisberger, F. and Dickson, W. (1939). *Management and the Worker*. Cambridge, MA: Harvard University Press.

Rogers, R. W. and Prentice-Dunn, S. (1981). 'Deindividuation and anger-mediated interracial aggression: unmasking regressive racism'. *Journal of Personality and Social Psychology*, **41**, 63–73.

Rohner, R. P. (1974). 'Proxemics and stress: an empirical study of the relationship between living space and roommate turnover'. *Human Relations*, **27**, 697–702.

Rohner, R. P. (1976). 'A worldwide study of sex differences in aggression: a universalist perspective'. Paper presented at the meeting of the Eastern Psychological Association, New York.

Rokeach, M. (1948). 'Generalized mental rigidity as a factor in ethnocentrism'. *Journal of Abnormal and Social Psychology*, **43**, 259–78.

Rokeach, M. (ed.) (1960). *The Open and Closed Mind*. New York: Basic Books.

Rokeach, M. (1973). *The Nature of Human Values*. New York: Free Press.

Rokeach, M. and Mezei, L. (1966). 'Race and shared belief as factors in social choice'. *Science*, **151**, 167–72.

Rommetveit, R. (1974). *On Message Structure: A Framework for the Study of Language and Communication*. New York: Wiley.

Roper Report (1987). *Report of Ministerial Committee of Inquiry into Violence*. Wellington: Government Printer.

Rosch, E. (1978). 'Principles of categorization' in E. Rosch and B. B. Lloyd (eds), *Cognition and Categorization* (pp. 27–48). Hillsdale, NJ: Erlbaum.

Rosenberg, M. J. (1969). 'The conditions and consequences of evaluation apprehension' in R. Rosenthal and R. L. Rosnow (eds), *Artifact in Behavioral Research* (pp. 280–349). New York: Academic Press.

Rosenberg, M. J. and Hovland, C. I. (1960). 'Cognitive, affective, and behavioral components of attitude' in M. J. Rosenberg, C. I. Hovland, W. J. McGuire, R. P. Abelson & J. W. Brehm (eds), *Attitude Organization and Change: An Analysis of Consistency Among Attitude Components*. New Haven, CT: Yale University Press.

Rosenberg, S. and Sedlak, A. (1972). 'Structural representations of implicit personality theory' in L. Berkowitz (ed.), *Advances in Experimental Social Psychology* (vol. 6, pp. 235–97). New York: Academic Press.

Rosenberg, S., Nelson, C. and Vivekanathan, P. S. (1968). 'A multidimensional approach to the structure of personality impressions'. *Journal of Personality and Social Psychology*, **39**, 283–94.

Rosenberg, S. W. and Wolfsfeld, G. (1977). 'International conflict and the problem of attribution'. *Journal of Conflict Resolution*, **21**, 75–103.

Rosenfeld, H. M. (1965). 'Effect of approval-seeking induction on interpersonal proximity'. *Psychological Reports*, **17**, 120–22.

Rosenfield, D. & Stephan, W. G. (1977). 'When discounting fails: an unexpected finding'. *Memory and Cognition*, **5**, 97–102.

Rosenfield, D., Greenberg, J., Folger, R. and Borys, R. (1982). 'Effect of an encounter with a black panhandler on subsequent helping for blacks: tokenism or conforming to a negative stereotype?' *Personality and Social Psychology Bulletin*, **8**, 664–71.

Rosenthal, R. (1966). *Experimenter Effects in Behavioral Research*. New York: Appleton-Century-Crofts.

Rosenthal, R. and DePaulo, B. M. (1979). 'Sex differences in eavesdropping on nonverbal cues'. *Journal of Personality and Social Psychology*, **37**, 273–85.

Rosenthal, R. and Jacobson, L. F. (1968). *Pygmalion in the Classroom*. New York: Holt, Rinehart & Winston.

Rosnow, R. L. (1980). 'Psychology of rumor reconsidered'. *Psychological Bulletin*, **87**, 578–91.

Rosnow, R. L. (1981). *Paradigms in Transition: The Methodology of Social Enquiry*. Oxford: Oxford University Press.

Ross, E. A. (1908). *Social Psychology*. New York: Macmillan.

Ross, L. (1977). 'The intuitive psychologist and his shortcomings' in L. Berkowitz (ed.), *Advances in Experimental Social Psychology* (vol. 10, pp. 174–220). New York: Academic Press.

Ross, L. and Nisbett, R. E. (1991). *The Person and the Situation: Perspectives of Social Psychology*. New York: McGraw-Hill.

Ross, L., Lepper, M. R. and Hubbard, M. (1975). 'Perseverance in self-perception and social perception: biased attribution processes in the debriefing paradigm'. *Journal of Personality and Social Psychology*, **32**, 880–92.

Ross, L., Greene, D. and House, P. (1977). 'The "false consensus effect": an egocentric bias in social perception and attribution processes'. *Journal of Experimental Social Psychology*, **13**, 279–301.

Ross, M. and Fletcher, G. J. O. (1985). 'Attribution and social perception' in G. Lindzey and E. Aronson (eds), *Handbook of Social Psychology* (3rd edn, vol. 2, pp. 73–122). New York: Random House.

Rothbart, M. (1981). 'Memory processes and social beliefs' in D. L. Hamilton (ed.), *Cognitive Processes in Stereotyping and Intergroup Behaviour* (pp. 145–82). Hillsdale, NJ: Erlbaum.

Rothbart, M. and John, O. P. (1985). 'Social categorization and behavioral episodes: a cognitive analysis of intergroup contact'. *Journal of Social Issues*, **41**, 81–104.

Rothbart, M. and Park, B. (1986). 'On the confirmability and disconfirmability of trait concepts'. *Journal of Personality and Social Psychology*, **50**, 131–42.

Rotter, J. B. (1966). 'Generalized expectancies for internal versus external control of reinforcement'. *Psychological Monographs*, **80**, whole no. 609.

Rotter, J. B. (1980). 'Trust and gullibility'. *Psychology Today*, **14** (5), 35–38, 40, 42, 102.

Rowley, C. D. (1971). *Outcasts in White Australia*. Canberra: Australian National University Press.

Ruback, R. B. and Innes, C. A. (1988). 'The relevance and irrelevance of psychological research: the example of prison crowding'. *American Psychologist*, **43**, 683–93.

Rubin, A. M. (1978). 'Child and adolescent television use and political socialization'. *Journalism Quarterly*, **55**, 125–29.

Rubin, J. (1976). 'How to tell when someone is saying no'. *Topics in Culture Learning*, **4**, 61–65.

Rubin, J. (1980). 'Experimental research on third-party intervention in conflict: toward some generalizations'. *Psychological Bulletin*, **87**, 379–91.

Rubin, Z. (1973). *Liking and Loving: An Invitation to Social Psychology*. New York: Holt, Rinehart and Winston.

Ruckmick, C. A. (1912). 'The history and status of psychology in the United States'. *American Journal of Psychology*, **23**, 517–31.

Rumelhart, D. E. and Ortony, A. (1977). 'The representation of knowledge in memory' in C. R. Anderson, R. J. Spiro and W. E. Montague (eds), *Schooling and the Acquisition of Knowledge* (pp. 99–136). Hillsdale, NJ: Erlbaum.

Runciman, W. G. (1966). *Relative Deprivation and Social Justice*. London: Routledge and Kegan Paul.

Rusbult, C. E. and Zembrodt, I. M. (1983). 'Responses to dissatisfaction in romantic involvements: a multi-dimensional scaling analysis'. *Journal of Experimental Social Psychology*, **19**, 274–93.

Rushton, J. P. (1979). 'Effects of prosocial television and film material on the behaviour of viewers' in L. Berkowitz (ed.), *Advances in Experimental Social Psychology* (vol. 12, pp. 322–51). New York: Academic Press.

Rushton, J. P. (1980). *Altruism, Socialisation, and Society*. Englewood Cliffs, NJ: Prentice Hall.

Rushton, J. P. and Sorrentino, R. M. (1981). *Altruism and Helping Behaviour: Social, Personality, and Developmental Perspectives*. Hillsdale, NJ: Erlbaum.

Rushton, J. P. and Teachman, G. (1978). 'The effects of positive reinforcement, attributions, and punishment on model induced altruism in children'. *Personality, and Social Psychology Bulletin*, **4**, 322–25.

Russell, C. (1987). 'The brother and sister who fell in love'. *Woman's Day*, November (Australia).

Rutkowski, G. K., Gruder, C. L. and Romer, D. (1983). 'Group cohesiveness, social norms, and bystander intervention'. *Journal of Personality and Social Psychology*, **44**, 545–552.

Rutte, C. G. and Wilke, H. A. M. (1984). 'Social dilemmas and leadership'. *European Journal of Social Psychology*, **14**, 105–21.

Rutte, C. G. and Wilke, H. A. M. (1985). 'Preference for decision structure in a social dilemma situation'. *European Journal of Social Psychology*, **15**, 367–70.

Rutter, M. B., Yule, B., Quinton, O., Yule, W. and Berger, M. (1975). 'Attainment and adjustment in two geographic areas. III: Some factors accounting for area differences'. *British Journal of Psychiatry*, **126**, 520–33.

Ryan, E. B., Giles, H., Bartolucci, G. and Henwood, K. (1986). 'Psycholinguistic and social psychological components of communication by and with the elderly'. *Language and Communication*, **6**, 1–24.

Ryan, T. (1985). 'Human nature and the origins of war'. *Hurupaa* (3), 46–54.

Ryen, A. H. and Kahn, A. (1975). 'Effects of intergroup orientation on group attitudes and proxemic behavior'. *Journal of Personality and Social Psychology*, **31**, 302–10.

Sabini, J. and Silver, M. (1982). *The Moralities of Everyday Life*. New York: Oxford University Press.

Sachdev, I. and Bourhis, R. Y. (1990). 'Language and social identification' in D. Abrams and M. A. Hogg (eds), *Social Identity Theory: Constructive and Critical Advances* (pp. 211–29). London: Harvester Wheatsheaf.

Sagi, A. and Hoffman, M. (1976). 'Empathic distress in the newborn'. *Developmental Psychology*, **12**, 175–76.

Saint-Blancat, C. (1985). 'The effect of minority group vitality upon its sociopsychological behaviour and strategies'. *Journal of Multilingual and Multicultural Development*, 6, 31 –44.

Saks, M. J. (1978). 'Social psychological contributions to a legislative committee on organ and tissue transplants'. *American Psychologist*, 33, 680–90.

Sampson, E. E. (1977). 'Psychology and the American ideal'. *Journal of Personality and Social Psychology*, 35, 767–82.

San Antonio, P. M. (1987). 'Social mobility and language use in an American company in Japan'. *Journal of Language and Social Psychology*, 6, 191–200.

Sanders G. S. (1983). 'An attentional process model of social facilitation' in A. Hare, H. Blumberg, V. Kent and M. Davies (eds), *Small Groups*. London: Wiley.

Sanders, G. S. and Baron, R. S. (1977). 'Is social comparison relevant for producing choice shifts'. *Journal of Experimental Social Psychology*, 13, 303–14.

Sanders, G. S. and Mullen, B. (1983). 'Accuracy in perceptions of consensus: differential tendencies of people with majority and minority positions'. *European Journal of Social Psychology*, 13, 57–70.

Sanders, G. S., Baron, R. S. and Moore, D. L. (1978). 'Distraction and social comparison as mediators of social facilitation'. *Journal of Experimental Social Psychology*, 14, 291–303.

Sargant, W. (1957). *Battle for the Mind: A Physiology of Conversion and Brainwashing*. Garden City, NY: Doubleday.

Sato, K. (1987). 'Distribution of the cost of maintaining common resources'. *Journal of Experimental Social Psychology*, 23, 19–31.

Schachter, S. (1959). *The Psychology of Affiliation*. Stanford, CA: Stanford University Press.

Schachter, S. (1964). 'The interaction of cognitive and physiological determinants of emotional state' in L. Berkowitz (ed.), *Advances in Experimental Social Psychology* (vol. 1, pp. 49–80). New York: Academic Press.

Schachter, S. (1971). *Emotion, Obesity, and Crime*. New York: Academic Press.

Schachter, S. and Burdeck, H. (1955). 'A field experiment on rumor transmission and distortion'. *Journal of Abnormal and Social Psychology*, 50, 363–71.

Schachter, S. and Singer, J. E. (1962). 'Cognitive, social and physiological determinants of emotional state'. *Psychological Review*, 69, 379–99.

Schank, R. C. and Abelson, R. P. (1977). *Scripts, Plans, Goals, and Understanding: An Inquiry into Human Knowledge Structures*. Hillsdale, NJ: Erlbaum.

Scheier, M. F. and Carver, C. S. (1981). 'Private and public aspects of self' in L. Wheeler (ed.), *Review of Personality and Social Psychology* (vol. 2, pp. 189–216). London: Sage.

Scherer, K. R. (1974). 'Acoustic concomitants of emotional dimensions: judging affect from synthesised tone sequences' in S. Weitz (ed.), *Nonverbal Communication* (pp. 249–53). New York: Oxford University Press.

Scherer, K. R. (1978). 'Personality inference from voice quality: the loud voice of extroversion'. *European Journal of Social Psychology*, 8, 467–88.

Scherer, K. R. (1986). 'Vocal affect expression: a review and model for future research'. *Psychological Bulletin*, 22, 143–65.

Scherer, K. R. and Giles, H. (eds) (1979). *Social Markers in Speech*. Cambridge: Cambridge University Press.

Scherer, K. R., Abèles, R. P. and Fischer, C. S. (1975). *Human Aggression and Conflict*. Englewood Cliffs, NJ: Prentice Hall.

Schlenker, B. R., Nacci, P., Helm, B. and Tedeschi, J. T. (1976). 'Reactions to coercive and reward power: the effects of switching influence modes on target compliance'. *Sociometry*, 39, 316–23.

Schlenker, B. R., Weingold, M. F. and Hallam, J. R. (1990). 'Self-serving attributions in social context: effects of self-esteem and social pressure'. *Journal of Personality and Social Psychology*, 58, 855–63.

Schmidt, C. F. (1972). 'Multidimensional scaling of the printed media's explanations of the riot of the summer of 1967'. *Journal of Personality and Social Psychology*, 24, 59–67.

Schmitt, B. H., Gilovich, T., Goore, N. and Joseph, L. (1986). 'Mere presence and socio-facilitation: one more time'. *Journal of Experimental Social Psychology*, 22, 242–48.

Schneider, D. J., Hastorf, A. H. and Ellsworth, P. C. (1979). *Person Perception*. Reading, MA: Addison-Wesley.

Schofield, J. W. (1986). 'Black–white contact in desegregated schools' in M. Hewstone and R. J. Brown (eds), *Contact and Conflict in Intergroup Encounters* (pp. 79–92). Oxford: Blackwell.

Schopler, J. and Stockdale, J. (1977). 'An interference analysis of crowding'. *Environmental Psychology and Nonverbal Behaviour*, 1, 81–88.

Schul, Y. (1983). 'Integration and abstraction in impression formation'. *Journal of Personality and Social Psychology*, 44, 45–54.

Schul, Y. and Burnstein, E. (1985). 'The informational basis of social judgements: using past impression rather than the trait description in forming new impression'. *Journal of Experimental Social Psychology*, 21, 421–39.

Schullo, S. A. and Alperson, B. L. (1984). 'Interpersonal phenomenology as a function of sexual orientation, sex, sentiment, and trait categories in long-term dyadic relationships'. *Journal of Personality and Social Psychology*, 47, 983–1002.

Schwab, D. P. and Grams, R. (1985). 'Sex-related errors in job evaluation: a "real-world" test'. *Journal of Applied Psychology*, 70, 533–39.

Schwartz, B. (1968). 'The social psychology of privacy'. *American Journal of Sociology*, 73, 741–52.

Schwartz, S. H. (1975). 'The justice need and the activation of humanitarian norms'. *Journal of Social Issues*, 31, 111–36.

Schwartz, S. H. (1977). 'Normative influences on altruism' in L. Berkowitz (ed.), *Advances in Experimental Social Psychology* (vol. 10, pp. 222–79). New York: Academic Press.

Schwartz, S. H. and Clausen, G. T. (1970). 'Responsibility, norms and helping in an emergency'. *Journal of Personality and Social Psychology*, 16, 299–310.

Schwartz, S. H. and David, T. B.(1976). 'Responsibility and helping in an emergency: effects of blame, ability and denial of responsibility'. *Sociometry*, 39, 406–15.

Schwerin, H. S. and Newell, H. H. (1981). *Persuasion in Marketing*. New York: Wiley.

Scitovsky, T. (1980). 'Why do we seek more and more excitement?' *Stanford Observer*, October, p. 13.

Searle, J. (1979). *Expression and Meaning: Studies in the Theory of Speech Acts*. Cambridge: Cambridge University Press.

Sears, D. O. (1983). 'The person-positivity bias'. *Journal of Personality and Social Psychology*, 44, 233–50.

Sears, D. O. (1986). 'College sophomores in the laboratory: influences of a narrow data base on social psychology's view of human nature'. *Journal of Personality and Social Psychology*, 51, 515–30.

Sears, D. O. and Kinder, D. R. (1985). 'Whites' opposition to bussing: on conceptualizing and operationalizing group conflict'. *Journal of Personality and Social Psychology*, 48, 1141–47.

Sears, D. O., Peplau, L. A. and Taylor, S. E. (1991). *Social Psychology* (7th edn). Englewood Cliffs, NJ: Prentice Hall.

Sedikides, C. and Ostrom, T. M. (1988). 'Are person categories used when organizing information about unfamiliar sets of persons?' *Social Cognition*, 6, 252–67.

Seligman, M. E. P., Abramson, L. Y., Semmel, A. and von Baeyer, C. (1979). 'Depressive attributional style'. *Journal of Abnormal Psychology*, 88, 242–47.

Semin, G. R. (1980). 'A gloss on attribution theory'. *British Journal of Social and Clinical Psychology*, 19, 291–300.

Shaffer, D. R., Rogel, M. and Hendrick, C. (1975). 'Intervention in the library: the effect of increased responsibility on bystanders' willingness to prevent a theft'. *Journal of Applied Psychology*, 5, 303–19.

Shapiro, A. H. (1974). 'Effects of family density and mother's education on preschooler's motor skills'. *Perceptual and Motor Skills*, 38, 79–86.

Shapiro, P. N. and Penrod, S. (1986). 'Meta-analysis of facial identification studies'. *Psychological Bulletin*, 100, 139–56.

Sharma, N. (1981). 'Some aspects of attitude and behaviour of mothers' *Indian Psychological Review*, 20, 35–42.

Shaw, M. E. (1964). 'Communication networks' in L. Berkowitz (ed.), *Advances in Experimental Social Psychology* (vol. 1, pp. 111 –47). New York: Academic Press.

Shaw, M. E. (1966). 'Social psychology and group processes' in J. B. Sidowski (ed.), *Experimental Methods and Instrumentation in Psychology* (pp. 607–43). New York: McGraw-Hill.

Shaw, M. E. and Costanzo, P. R. (1982). *Theories of Social Psychology* (2nd edn). New York: McGraw-Hill.

Shaw, M. E., Rothschild, G. and Strickland, J. (1957). 'Decision process in communication networks'. *Journal of Abnormal and Social Psychology*, 54, 323–30.

Sheehan, P. W. (1983). 'Age trends and the correlates of children's television viewing'. *Australian Journal of Psychology*, 35, 417–31.

Sherif. M. (1935). 'A study of some social factors in perception'. *Archives of Psychology*, 27, 1–60.

Sherif, M. (1936). *The Psychology of Social Norms*. New York: Harper.

Sherif, M. (ed.) (1962). *Intergroup Relations and Leadership*. New York: Wiley.

Sherif, M. (1966). *In Common Predicament: Social Psychology of Intergroup Conflict and Cooperation*. Boston, MA: Houghton-Mifflin.

Sherif, M. and Sherif, C. W. (1953). *Groups in Harmony and Tension: An Integration of Studies in Intergroup Behaviour*. New York: Harper and Row.

Sherif, M. and Sherif, C. W. (1964). *Reference Groups*. New York: Harper and Row.

Sherif, M. and Sherif, C. W. (1967). 'Attitude as an individual's own categories: the social judgement–involvement approach to attitude and attitude change' in C. W. Sherif and M. Sherif (eds), *Attitude, Ego-involvement, and Change* (pp. 105–139). New York: Wiley.

Sherif, M., Harvey, O. J., White, B. J., Hood, W. and Sherif, C. (1961). *Intergroup Conflict and Cooperation: The Robbers Cave Experiment*. Norman, OK: University of Oklahoma Institute of Intergroup Relations.

Sherman, S. J., Presson, C. C. and Chassin, L. (1984). 'Mechanisms underlying the false consensus effect: the special role of threats to the self'. *Personality and Social Psychology Bulletin*, 10, 127–38.

Sherrod, D. R. (1974). 'Crowding, perceived control, and behavioral aftereffects'. *Journal of Applied Social Psychology*, 4, 171–86.

Shibutani, T. (1966). *Improvised News: A Sociological Study of Rumor*. Indianapolis, IA: Bobbs-Merrill.

Shotland, F. L. and Huston, T. L. (1979). 'Emergencies: what are they and do they influence bystanders to intervene?' *Journal of Personality and Social Psychology*, 37, 1822–34.

Shotland, R. L. and Heinold, W. D. (1985). 'Bystander response to arterial bleeding: helping skills, the decision-making process, and differentiating the helping response'. *Journal of Personality and Social Psychology*, 49, 347–56.

Shotter, J. (1984). *Social Accountability and Selfhood*. Oxford: Blackwell.

Showers, C. and Cantor, N. (1985). 'Social cognition: a look at motivated strategies'. *Annual Review of Psychology*, 36, 275–305.

Shure, G. H., Meeker, R. and Hansford, E. A. (1965). 'The effectiveness of pacifist strategies in bargaining games'. *Journal of Conflict Resolution*, 2, 106–17.

Shweder, R. A. and Bourne, E. J. (1982). 'Does the concept of the person vary cross-culturally?' in A. J. Marsella and G. M. White (eds), *Cultural Conceptions of Mental Health and Therapy* (pp. 97–137). Dordrecht, Holland: D. Reidel.

Siegel, A. E. and Siegel, S. (1957). 'Reference groups, membership groups, and attitude change'. *Journal of Abnormal and Social Psychology*, 55, 360–64.

Siegman, A. W. and Reynolds, M. A. (1983). 'Self-monitoring and speech in feigned and unfeigned lying'. *Journal of Personality and Social Psychology*, 45, 1325–33.

Sigall, H. and Ostrove, N., (1975). 'Beautiful but dangerous: effects of offender attractiveness and the nature of the crime on juristic judgement'. *Journal of Personality and Social Psychology*, 31, 410–14.

Sigelman, C. K., Berry, C. J. and Wiles, K. A. (1984). 'Violence in college students' dating relationships'. *Journal of Applied Social Psychology*, 5, 530–548.

Sillars (1981). 'Attributions and interpersonal conflict resolution' in J. H. Harvey, W. J. Ickes and R. F. Kidd (eds), *New Directions in Attribution Research* (vol. 3, pp. 281–305). Hillsdale, NJ: Erlbaum.

Silverman, I. (1971). 'Physical attractiveness and courtship'. *Sexual Behaviour*, September, pp. 22–25.

Simard, L., Taylor, D. M. and Giles, H. (1976). 'Attribution processes and interpersonal accommodation in a bilingual setting'. *Language and Speech*, 19, 374–87.

Simmel, E. C., Hahn, M. E. and Walters, J. K. (eds) (1983). *Aggressive Behaviour: Genetic and Neural Approaches*. Hillsdale, NJ: Erlbaum.

Simner, M. (1971). 'Newborn's response to the cry of another infant'. *Developmental Psychology*, 5, 136–150.

Simon, B. and Brown, R. J. (1987). 'Perceived intragroup homogeneity in minority–majority contexts'. *Journal of Personality and Social Psychology*, 53, 703–11.

Simonton, D. K. (1980). 'Land battles, generals and armies: individual and situational determinants of victory and casualties'. *Journal of Personality and Social Psychology*, 38, 110–19.

Simpson, J. A., Campbell, B. and Berscheid, E. (1986). 'The association between romantic love and marriage: Kephart (1967) twice revisited'. *Personality and Social Psychology Bulletin*, 12, 363–72.

Singer, J., Brush, C. and Lublin, S. (1965). 'Some aspects of deindividuation: identification and conformity'. *Journal of Experimental Social Psychology*, 1, 356–78.

Singer, J. D., and Small, M. (1972). *The Wages of War 1816–1965: A Statistical Handbook*. New York: Wiley.

Singh, R., Bohra, K. A. and Dalal, A. K. (1979). 'Favourableness of leadership situations studies with information integration theory'. *European Journal of Social Psychology*, 2, 253–64.

Sistrunk, F. and McDavid, J. W. (1971). 'Sex variable in conforming behavior'. *Journal of Personality and Social Psychology*, 2, 200–207.

Skevington, S. (1981). 'Intergroup relations and nursing'. *European Journal of Social Psychology*, 11, 43–59.

Skinner, B. F. (1963). 'Operant behavior'. *American Psychologist*, 18, 503–15.

Skowronski, J. J. and Carlston, D. E. (1989). 'Negativity and extremity biases in impression formation: a review of explanations'. *Psychological Bulletin*, 105, 131–42.

Slater, P. E. (1955). 'Role differentiation in small groups'. *American Sociological Review*, 20, 300–10.

Smedley, J. W. and Bayton, J. A. (1978). 'Evaluative race–class stereotypes by race and perceived class of subjects'. *Journal of Personality and Social Psychology*, 3, 530–35.

Smith, C. A., Smith, C. J., Kearns, R. A. and Abbott, M. W. (1993). Housing stressors, social support and psychological distress. *Social Science Medicine*, 37, 603–12.

Smith, C. P. (1983). 'Ethical issues: research on deception, informed consent, and debriefing' in L. Wheeler and P. Shaver (eds), *Review of Personality and Social Psychology* (vol. 4, pp. 297–328). Beverly Hills, CA: Sage.

Smith, D. L., Pruitt, D. G. and Carnevale, P. J. D. (1982). 'Matching and mismatching: the effect of own limit, other's toughness, and time pressure on concession rate in negotiation'. *Journal of Personality and Social Psychology*, 42, 876–83.

Smith, M. B., Bruner, J. S. and White, R. W. (1956). *Opinions and Personality*. New York: Wiley.

Smith, P. B. and Bond, M. H. (1993). *Social Psychology Across Cultures: Analysis and Perspectives*. London: Harvester Wheatsheaf.

Smith, P. M. (1985). *Language, the Sexes and Society*. Oxford: Blackwell.

Smolicz, J. J. (1983). 'Modification and maintenance: language among school children of Italian background in South Australia'. *Journal of Multilingual and Multicultural Development*, 4, 313–37.

Sniderman, P. M., Hagen, M. G., Tetlock, P. E. and Brady, H. E. (1986). 'Reasoning chains: causal models of policy reasoning in mass publics'. *British Journal of Political Science*, 16, 405–30.

Snyder, M. (1979). 'Self-monitoring processes' in L. Berkowitz (ed.), *Advances in Experimental Social Psychology* (vol. 12, pp. 88–131). New York: Academic Press.

Snyder, M. (1981). 'On the self-perpetuating nature of social stereotypes' in D. L. Hamilton (ed.), *Cognitive Processes in Stereotyping and Intergroup Behaviour* (pp. 183–212). Hillsdale, NJ: Erlbaum.

Snyder, M. (1984). 'When belief creates reality' in L. Berkowitz (ed.), *Advances in Experimental Social Psychology* (vol. 18, pp. 248–306). New York: Academic Press.

Snyder, M., Grether, J. and Keller, K. (1974). 'Staring and compliance: a field experiment on hitchhiking'. *Journal of Applied Social Psychology*, 4, 165–70.

Snyder, M. L., Stephan, W. G. and Rosenfield, D. (1978). 'Attributional egotism' in J. H. Harvey, W. Ickes and R. F. Kidd (eds), *New Directions in Attribution Research* (vol. 2, pp. 91–120). Hillsdale, NJ: Erlbaum.

Sommer, R. (1968). 'Intimacy ratings in five countries'. *International Journal of Psychology*, 3, 109–14.

Sommer, R. (1969). *Personal Space: The Behavioral Basis of Design*. Englewood Cliffs, NJ: Prentice Hall.

Sorrentino, R. M. and Field, N. (1986). 'Emergent leadership over time: the functional value of positive motivation'. *Journal of Personality and Social Psychology*, 50, 1091–99.

Sorrentino, R; M., King, G. and Lea, G. (1980). 'The influence of the minority on perception: a note on a possible alternative explanation'. *Journal of Experimental Social Psychology*, 16, 293–301.

Spence, J. T., Helmreich, R. L. and Stapp, J. (1974). 'The personal attributes questionnaire: a measure of sex role stereotypes and masculinity-femininity'. *JSAS Catalog of Selected Documents in Psychology*, 4, 127.

Spitz, R. A. (1945). 'Hospitalism: an inquiry into the genesis of psychiatric conditions in early childhood' in A. Freud, H. Hartman and E. Kris (eds), *The Psychoanalytic Study of the Child* (vol. 1, pp. 53–74). New York: International University Press.

Srull, T. K. (1983). 'Organizational and retrieval processes in person memory: an examination of processing objectives, presentation format, and the possible role of self-generated retrieval cues'. *Journal of Personality and Social Psychology*, 44, 1157–70.

Srull, T. K. and Wyer, R. S., Jr (1986). 'The role of chronic and temporary goals in social information processing' in R. M. Sorrentino and E. T. Higgins (eds), *Handbook of Motivation and Cognition: Foundations of Social Behaviour* (pp. 503–49). New York: Guilford Press.

Srull, T. K. and Wyer, R. S. (1989). 'Person memory and judgement'. *Psychological Review*, 96, 58–83.

Staats, C. K. and Staats, A. W. (1957). 'Meaning established by classical conditioning'. *Journal of Experimental Social Psychology*, 54, 74–80.

Stagner, R. and Congdon, C. S. (1955). 'Another failure to demonstrate displacement of aggression'. *Journal of Abnormal and Social Psychology*, 51, 695–96.

Stang, D. J. (1972). 'Conformity, ability, and self-esteem'. *Representative Research in Social Psychology*, 3, 97–103.

Stang, D. J. (1976). 'Group size effects on conformity'. *Journal of Social Psychology*, 98, 175–81.

Stangor, C. (1988). 'Stereotype accessibility and information processing'. *Personality and Social Psychology Bulletin*, 14, 694–708.

Stasser, G. and Davis, J. H. (1981). 'Group decision making and social influence: a social interaction sequence model'. *Psychological Review*, 88, 523–51.

Stasser, G., Kerr, N. L. and Davis, J. H. (1989). 'Influence processes and consensus models in decision-making groups' in P. B. Paulus (ed.), *Psychology of Group Influence* (2nd edn, pp. 279–326). Hillsdale, NJ: Erlbaum.

Staub, E. (1974). 'Helping a distressed person: social, personality and stimulus determinants' in

L. Berkowitz (ed.), *Advances in Experimental Social Psychology* (vol. 7, pp 294–341). New York: Academic Press.

Staub, E. (1977). *Positive Social Behaviour and Morality. I: Social and Personal Influences*. New York: Academic Press.

Staub, E. (1989). *The Roots of Evil: The Psychological and Cultural Origins of Genocide and Other Forms of Group Violence*. New York: Cambridge University Press.

St Claire, L. and Turner, J. C. (1982). 'The role of demand characteristics in the social categorization paradigm'. *European Journal of Social Psychology*, 12, 307–14.

Steinberg, R. and Shapiro, S. (1982). 'Sex differences in personality traits of female and male master of business administration students'. *Journal of Applied Psychology*, 67, 306–10.

Steiner, I. D. (1972). *Group Process and Productivity*. New York: Academic Press.

Steiner, I. D. (1976). 'Task-performing groups' in J. W. Thibaut and J. T. Spence (eds), *Contemporary Topics in Social Psychology* (pp. 393–422). Morristown, NJ: General Learning Press.

Steinmetz, S. K. and Straus, M. A. (1973). 'The family as cradle of violence'. *Society*, 10, 50–56.

Steir, C. (1978). *Blue Jolts: True Stories from the Cuckoo's Nest*. Washington, DC: New Republic Books.

Stephan, W. G. (1977). 'Cognitive differentiation in intergroup perception'. *Sociometry*, 40, 50–58.

Stephan, W. G. and Rosenfield, D. (1978). 'Effects of desegregation on racial attitudes'. *Journal of Personality and Social Psychology*, 36, 795–804.

Stephan, W. G. and Stephan, C. W. (1984). 'The role of ignorance in intergroup relations' in N. Miller and M. B. Brewer (eds), *Groups in Contact: The Psychology of Desegregation* (pp. 229–55). New York: Academic Press.

Stephan, W. G. and Stephan, C. W. (1985). 'Intergroup anxiety'. *Journal of Social Issues*, 41, 157–75.

Stephan, W. G., Berscheid, E. and Walster, E. (1971). 'Sexual arousal and heterosexual perception'. *Journal of Personality and Social Psychology*, 20, 93–101.

Stephenson, G. M., Abrams, D., Wagner, W. and Wade, G. (1986a). 'Partners in recall: collaborative order in the recall of a police interrogation'. *British Journal of Social Psychology*, 25, 341–43.

Stephenson, G. M., Clark, N. K. and Wade, G. (1986b). 'Meetings make evidence: an experimental study of collaborative and individual recall of a simulated police interrogation'. *Journal of Personality and Social Psychology*, 50, 1113–22.

Sternberg, R. J. (1988). *The Triangle of Love*. New York: Basic Books.

Stevens, S. S. (1972). 'Stability of human performance under intense noise'. *Journal of Sound and Vibration*, 21, 35–36.

Stewart, J. E. (1980). 'Defendant's attractiveness as a factor in the outcome of criminal trials: an observational study'. *Journal of Applied Social Psychology*, 10, 348–61.

Stogdill, R. (1974). *Handbook of Leadership*. New York: Free Press.

Stokols, D., Rall, M., Pinner, B. and Schopler, J. (1973). 'Physical, social and personal determinants of the perception of crowding'. *Environment and Behaviour*, 5, 87–115.

Stoner, J. A. F. (1961). 'A comparison of individual and group decisions including risk'. Masters thesis, Massachusetts Institute of Technology.

Storms, M. D. (1973). 'Videotape and the attribution process: reversing actor's and observer's points of view'. *Journal of Personality and Social Psychology*, 27, 165–75.

Storms, M. D. and Nisbett, R. E. (1970). 'Insomnia and the attribution process'. *Journal of Personality and Social Psychology*, 16, 319–28.

Stouffer, S. A., Suchman, E. A., DeVinney, L. C., Star, S. A. and Williams, R. M. Jr (1949). *The American Soldier. Volume 1: Adjustment During Army Life*. Princeton, NJ: Princeton University Press.

Straus, M. A., Gelles, R. J. and Steinmetz, S. K. (1980). *Behind Closed Doors: Violence in the American Family*. Garden City, NJ: Anchor Books.

Strickland, L. H., Aboud, F. E. and Gergen, K. J. (eds) (1976). *Social Psychology in Transition*. New York: Plenum Press.

Strodtbeck, F. L. and Lipinski, R. M. (1985). 'Becoming first among equals: moral considerations in jury foreman selection'. *Journal of Personality and Social Psychology*, 49, 927–36.

Strodtbeck, F. L., James, R. and Hawkins, C. (1957). 'Social status in jury deliberations'. *American Sociological Review*, 22, 713–18.

Stroebe, M. S. and Stroebe, W. (1983). 'Who suffers more? Sex differences in health risks of the bereaved'. *Psychological Bulletin*, 93, 279–301.

Stroebe, W. and Frey, B. S. (1982). 'Self-interest and collective action: the economics and psychology of public goods'. *British Journal of Social Psychology*, 21, 121–37.

Stroebe, W. and Stroebe, M. S. (1987). *Bereavement and Health*. New York: Cambridge University Press.

Stroebe, W., Stroebe, M. S., Gergen, K. J. and Gergen, M. (1982). 'The effects of bereavement on mortality: a social psychological analysis' in J. R. Eiser (ed.), *Social Psychology and Behavioural Medicine*. New York: Wiley.

Stroebe, W., Lenkert, A. and Jonas, K. (1988). 'Familiarity may breed contempt: the impact of student exchange on national stereotypes and attitudes' in W. Stroebe, A. Kruglanski, D. Bar-Tal and M. Hewstone (eds), *The Social Psychology of Intergroup Conflict: Theory, Research and Applications* (pp. 167–87). New York: Springer-Verlag.

Stroebe, W., Diehl, M. and Abakoumkin, G. (1992). 'The illusion of group effectivity'. *Personality and Social Psychology Bulletin*, 18, 643–650.

Strube, M. J. and Garcia, J. E. (1981). 'A meta-analytic investigation of Fiedler's contingency model of leadership effectiveness'. *Psychological Bulletin*, 90, 307–21.

Strube, M. J., Turner, C. W., Cerro, D., Stevens, J. and Hinchey, F. (1984). 'Interpersonal aggression and the Type A coronary-prone behaviour pattern: a theoretical distinction and practical implications'. *Journal of Personality and Social Psychology*, 47, 839–47.

Suls, J. M. and Miller, R. L. (eds) (1977). *Social Comparison Processes: Theoretical and Empirical Perspectives*. Washington, DC: Hemisphere.

Sumner, W. G. (1906). *Folkways*. Boston, MA: Ginn.

Sunafrank, M. J. and Miller, G. R. (1981). 'The role of initial conversations in determining attraction to similar and dissimilar strangers'. *Human Communication Research*, 8, 16–25.

Sundberg, N. D. (1977). *Assessment of Persons*. Englewood Cliffs, NJ: Prentice Hall.

Swann, W. B., Jr (1984). 'Quest for accuracy in person perception: a matter of pragmatics'. *Psychological Review*, 91, 457–77

Sweeney, P. D., Anderson, K. and Bailey, S. (1986). 'Attribution style in depression: a meta-analytic review'. *Journal of Personality and Social Psychology*, 50, 974–91.

Swim, J., Borgida, E. and Maruyama, G. (1989). 'Joan McKay versus John McKay: do gender stereotypes bias evaluation?' *Psychological Bulletin*, 105, 409–29.

Szasz, T. (1970). *The Manufacture of Madness*. New York: Delta.

Szymanski, K. and Harkins, S. G. (1987). 'Social loafing and self-evaluation with a social standard'. *Journal of Personality and Social Psychology*, 53, 891–97.

Taft, R. (1973). 'Migration: problems of adjustment and assimilation in immigrants' in P. Watson (ed.), *Psychology and Race* (pp. 224–39). Harmondsworth: Penguin.

Tajfel, H. (1957). 'Value and the perceptual judgement of magnitude'. *Psychological Review*, 64, 192–204.

Tajfel, H. (1959). 'Quantitative judgement in social perception'. *British Journal of Psychology*, 50, 16–29.

Tajfel, H. (1969). 'Social and cultural factors in perception' in G. Lindzey and E. Aronson (eds), *Handbook of Social Psychology* (vol. 3, pp. 315–94). Reading, MA: Addison-Wesley.

Tajfel, H. (1970). 'Experiments in intergroup discrimination'. *Scientific American*, 223, 96–102.

Tajfel, H. (1972a). 'Experiments in a vacuum' in J. Israel and H. Tajfel (eds), *The Context of Social Psychology: A Critical Assessment*. London: Academic Press.

Tajfel, H. (1972b). 'La catégorisation sociale' in S. Moscovici (ed.), *Introduction à la psychologie sociale* (vol. 1, pp. 272–302). Paris: Larousse.

Tajfel, H. (1974). 'Social identity and intergroup behaviour'. *Social Science Information*, 13, 65–93.

Tajfel, H. (1978). 'Intergroup behaviour. II: Group perspectives' in H. Tajfel and C. Fraser (eds), *Introducing Social Psychology* (pp. 423–45). Harmondsworth: Penguin.

Tajfel, H. (1981a). 'Social stereotypes and social groups' in J. C. Turner and H. Giles (eds), *Intergroup Behaviour* (pp. 144–67). Oxford: Blackwell.

Tajfel, H. (1981b). *Human Groups and Social Categories: Studies in Social Psychology*. Cambridge: Cambridge University Press.

Tajfel, H. (1982). 'Social psychology of intergroup relations'. *Annual Review of Social Psychology*, 33, 1–39.

Tajfel, H. (ed.) (1984). *The Social Dimension: European Developments in Social Psychology*. Cambridge: Cambridge University Press.

Tajfel, H. and Billig, M. (1974). 'Familiarity and categorization in intergroup behaviour'. *Journal of Experimental Social Psychology*, 10, 159–70.

Tajfel, H. and Fraser, C. (eds) (1978). *Introducing Social Psychology*. Harmondsworth: Penguin.

Tajfel, H. and Turner, J. C. (1979). 'An integrative theory of intergroup conflict' in W. G. Austin and S. Worchel (eds), *The Social Psychology of Intergroup Relations* (pp. 33–47). Monterey, CA: Brooks/Cole.

Tajfel, H. and Wilkes, A. L. (1963). 'Classification and quantitative judgement'. *British Journal of Psychology*, 54, 101–14.

Tajfel, H., Billig, M., Bundy R. P. and Flament, C. (1971). 'Social categorization and intergroup behaviour'. *European Journal of Social Psychology*, 1, 149–77.

Tanford, S. and Penrod, S. (1984). 'Social influence model: a formal integration of research on majority and minority influence processes'. *Psychological Bulletin*, 95, 189–225.

Tanter, R. (1966). 'Dimension of conflict behaviour within and between nations, 1958–1960'. *Journal of Conflict Resolution*, 10, 41–64.

Tanter, R. (1969). 'International war and domestic turmoil: some contemporary evidence' in H. D. Graham and T. R. Gurr (eds), *Violence in America* (pp. 550–69). New York: Bantam Books.

Tarde, G. (1890). *Les lois de l'imitation*. Paris: Alcan.

Tarde, G. (1898). *Etudes de psychologie sociale*. Paris: V. Giard and E. Briére.

Taylor, A. J. W. (1987). *Antarctic Psychology*. Wellington: Science Information Publishing Centre.

Taylor, D. M. and Brown, R. J. (1979). 'Towards a more social social psychology'. *British Journal of Social and Clinical Psychology*, 18, 173–79.

Taylor, D. M. and Jaggi, V. (1974). 'Ethnocentrism and causal attribution in a S. Indian context'. *Journal of Cross-cultural Psychology*, 5, 162–71.

Taylor, D. M. and McKirnan, D. J. (1984). 'A five-stage model of intergroup relations'. *British Journal of Social Psychology*, 23, 291–300.

Taylor, S. E. (1981). 'The interface of cognitive and social psychology' in J. Harvey (ed.), *Cognition, Social Behaviour, and the Environment* (pp. 189–211). Hillsdale, NJ: Erlbaum.

Taylor, S. E. (1982). 'Social cognition and health'. *Personality and Social Psychology Bulletin*, 8, 549–62.

Taylor, S. E. and Fiske, S. T. (1975). 'Point-of-view and perceptions of causality'. *Journal of Personality and Social Psychology*, 32, 439–45.

Taylor, S. E. and Fiske, S. T. (1978). 'Salience, attention, and attribution: top of the head phenomena' in L. Berkowitz (ed.), *Advances in Experimental Social Psychology* (vol. 11, pp. 249–88). New York: Academic Press.

Taylor, S. E. and Koivumaki, J. H. (1976). 'The perception of self and others: acquaintanceship, affect, and actor–observer differences'. *Journal of Personality and Social Psychology*, 33, 403–408.

Taylor, S. E. and Thompson, S. C. (1982). 'Stalking the elusive "vividness" effect'. *Psychological Review*, 89, 155–81.

Taylor, S. E., Fiske, S. T., Etcoff, N. L. and Ruderman, A. J. (1978). 'Categorical and contextual bases of person memory and stereotyping'. *Journal of Personality and Social Psychology*, 36, 778–93.

Taylor, S. P. and Sears, J. D. (1988). 'The effects of alcohol and persuasive social pressure on human physical aggression'. *Aggressive Behaviour*, 14, 237–43.

Taynor, J. and Deaux, K. (1973). 'Equity and perceived sex differences: role behaviour as defined by the task, the mode, and the actor'. *Journal of Personality and Social Psychology*, 32, 381–90.

Teger, A. (1970). 'Defining the socially responsible response'. Paper presented at the 78th annual meeting of the American Psychological Association.

Teger, A. I. and Pruitt, D. G. (1967). 'Components of group risk taking'. *Journal of Experimental Social Psychology*, 3, 189–205.

Tellis, G. J. (1987). *Advertising Exposure, Loyalty, and Brand Purchase: A Two-stage Model of Choice*. Report no. 87–105. Cambridge, MA: Marketing Science Institute.

Terry, D. J. and Hogg, M. A. (in press). 'Group norms and the attitude-behavior relationship: a role for group identification'. *Personality and Social Psychology Bulletin*.

Terry, D., Gallois, C. and McCamish, M. (1993). 'The theory of reasoned action and health care behaviour' in D. Terry, C. Gallois and M. McCamish (eds), *The Theory of Reasoned Action: Its Application to Aids-preventive Behaviour* (pp. 1–27). Oxford: Pergamon.

Tesser, A. and Paulhus, D. L. (1976). 'Toward a casual model of love'. *Journal of Personality and Social Psychology*, 34, 1095–105.

Tesser, A. and Shaffer, D. R. (1990). 'Attitudes and attitude change'. *Annual Review of Psychology*, 41, 479–523.

Tesser, A., Gatewood, R. and Driver, M. (1968). 'Some determinants of gratitude'. *Journal of Personality and Social Psychology*, 9, 233–36.

Tetlock, P. E. (1979). 'Identifying victims of groupthink from public statements of decision makers'. *Journal of Personality and Social Psychology*, 37, 1314–24.

Tetlock, P. E. (1983). 'Policymakers' images of international conflict'. *Journal of Social Issues*, 39, 67–86.

Tetlock, P. E. (1984). 'Cognitive style and political belief systems in the British House of Commons'. *Journal of Personality and Social Psychology*, 46, 365–75.

Tetlock, P. E. (1988). 'Monitoring the integrative complexity of American and Soviet policy rhetoric: what can be learned?' *Journal of Social Issues*, 44, 101–31.

Tetlock, P. E. (1989). 'The structural bases of consistency among political attitudes: effects of political expertise and attitude importance. Structure and function in political belief systems' in A. R. Pratkanis, S. J. Breckler and A. G. Greenwald (eds), *Attitude Structure and Function* (pp. 129–51). Hillsdale, NJ: Erlbaum.

Tetlock, P. E. and Boettger, R. (1989). 'Accountability: a social magnifier of the dilution effect'. *Journal of Personality and Social Psychology*, 57, 388–98.

Tetlock, P. E. and Kim, J. I. (1987). 'Accountability and judgement processes in a personality prediction task'. *Journal of Personality and Social Psychology*, 52, 700–09.

Tetlock, P. E. and Levi, A. (1982). 'Attribution bias: on the inconclusiveness of the cognition–motivation debate'. *Journal of Experimental Social Psychology*, 18, 68–88.

Tetlock, P. E., Peterson, R. S., McGuire, C., Chang, S. and Feld, P. (1992). 'Assessing political group dynamics: a test of the groupthink model'. *Journal of Personality and Social Psychology*, 63, 403–25.

Thakerar, J. N., Giles, H. and Cheshire, J. (1982). 'Psychological and linguistic parameters of speech accommodation theory' in C. Fraser and K. R. Scherer (eds), *Advances in the Social Psychology of Language* (pp. 205–55). Cambridge: Cambridge University Press.

Thibaut, J. W. and Kelley, H. H. (1959). *The Social Psychology of Groups*. New York: Wiley.

Thomas, W. I. and Znaniecki, F. (1918). *The Polish Peasant in Europe and America* (vol. 1). Boston, MA: Badger.

Thoreau, H. D. (1854). *Walden*. New York: Signet.

Thorndike, E. L. (1940). *Human Nature and the Social Order*. New York: Macmillan.

Thurstone, L. L. (1928). 'Attitudes can be measured'. *American Journal of Sociology*, 33, 529–54.

Thurstone, L. L. (1931). 'The measurement of social attitudes'. *Journal of Abnormal and Social Psychology*, 26, 249–69.

Tilker, H. (1970). 'Socially responsible behaviour as a function of observer responsibility and victim feedback'. *Journal of Personality and Social Psychology*, 14, 95–100.

Titus, H. E. and Hollander, E. P. (1957). 'The California F scale in psychological research (1950–1955)'. *Psychological Bulletin*, 54, 47–74.

Toch, H. (1969). *Violent Men*. Chicago: Aldine.

Toi, M. and Batson, C. D. (1982). 'More evidence that empathy is a source of altruistic motivation'. *Journal of Personality and Social Psychology*, 43, 281–92.

Tolstoy, L. (1869). *War and Peace*. Harmondsworth: Penguin.

Trager, G. L. (1958). 'Paralanguage: a first approximation'. *Studies in Linguistics*, 13, 1–12.

Triandis, H. C. (1971). *Attitude and Attitude Change*. New York: Wiley.

Triandis, H. C. (ed.) (1976). *Variations in Black and White Perceptions of the Social Environment*. Champaign, IL: University of Illinois Press.

Triandis, H. C. (1977). *Interpersonal Behaviour*. Monterey, CA: Brooks/Cole.

Triandis, H. C. (1980) 'Values, attitudes and interpersonal behavior' in H. H. Howe and M. M. Page (eds), *Nebraska Symposium on Motivation* (vol. 27). Lincoln, NE: University of Nebraska Press.

Triandis, H. C. and Davis, E. G. (1965). 'Race and belief as shared determinants of behaviour intentions'. *Journal of Personality and Social Psychology*, 2, 715–25.

Triandis, H. C., Vassiliou, V., Vassiliou, G., Tanaka, Y. and Shanmugam, A. (eds) (1972). *The Analysis of Subjective Culture*. New York: Wiley.

Tripathi, R. C. and Srivasta, R. (1981). 'Relative deprivation and intergroup attitudes'. *European Journal of Social Psychology*, 11, 313–18.

Triplett, N. (1898). 'The dynamogenic factors in pacemaking and competition'. *American Journal of Psychology*, 2, 507–33

Turner, J. C. (1978). 'Social categorization and social discrimination in the minimal group paradigm' in H. Tajfel (ed.), *Differentiation Between Social Groups* (pp. 101–40). London: Academic Press.

Turner, J. C. (1980). 'Fairness or discrimination in intergroup behaviour? A reply to Branthwaite, Doyle and Lightbown'. *European Journal of Social Psychology*, 10, 131–47.

Turner, J. C. (1981a). 'Some considerations in generalizing experimental social psychology' in G. M. Stephenson and J. M. Davis (eds), *Progress in Applied Social Psychology* (vol. 1, pp 3–34). Chichester: Wiley.

Turner, J. C. (1981b). 'The experimental social psychology of intergroup behaviour' in J. C. Turner and H. Giles (eds), *Intergroup Behaviour* (pp. 66–101). Oxford: Blackwell.

Turner, J. C. (1982). 'Towards a cognitive redefinition of the social group' in H. Tajfel (ed.), *Social Identity and Intergroup Relations* (pp. 15–40). Cambridge: Cambridge University Press.

Turner, J. C. (1983). 'Some comments on "the measurement of social orientations in the minimal group paradigm"'. *European Journal of Social Psychology*, 13, 351–68.

Turner, J. C. (1984). 'Social identification and psychological group formation' in H. Tajfel (ed.), *The Social Dimension: European Developments in Social Psychology* (vol. 2, pp. 518–38). Cambridge: Cambridge University Press.

Turner, J. C. (1985). 'Social categorization and the self-concept: a social cognitive theory of group behaviour' in E. J. Lawler (ed.), *Advances in Group Processes: Theory and Research* (vol. 2, pp. 77–122). Greenwich, CT: JAI Press.

Turner, J. C. (1991). *Social Influence*. Buckingham: Open University Press.

Turner, J. C. and Oakes, P. J. (1986). 'The significance of the social identity concept for social psychology with reference to individualism, interactionism and social influence'. *British Journal of Social Psychology*, 25, 237–52.

Turner, J. C. and Oakes, P. J. (1989). 'Self-categorization and social influence' in P. B. Paulus (ed.), *The Psychology of Group Influence* (2nd edn, pp. 233–75). Hillsdale, NJ: Erlbaum.

Turner, J. C., Hogg, M . A., Oakes, P. J., Reicher, S. D. and Wetherell, M. S. (1987). *Rediscovering the Social Group: A Self-categorization Theory*. Oxford: Blackwell.

Turner, J. C., Wetherell, M. S. and Hogg, M . A. (1989). 'Referent informational influence and group polarization'. *British Journal of Social Psychology*, 28, 135–47.

Turner, M. E., Pratkanis, A. R., Probasco, P. and Leve, C. (1992). 'Threat, cohesion, and group effectiveness: testing a social identity maintenance perspective on groupthink'. *Journal of Personality and Social Psychology*, 63, 781–96.

Turner, R. H. (1974). 'Collective behavior' in R. E. L. Faris (ed.), *Handbook of Modern Sociology* (pp. 382–425). Chicago, IL: Rand-McNally.

Turner, R. H. and Killian (1957). *Collective Behaviour*. Englewood Cliffs, NJ: Prentice Hall.

Tversky, A. and Kahneman, D. (1974). 'Judgement under uncertainty: heuristics and biases'. *Science*, 185, 1124–31.

Tyerman, A. and Spencer, C. (1983). 'A critical test of the Sherifs' robbers cave experiments: intergroup competition and cooperation between groups of well acquainted individuals'. *Small Group Behaviour*, 14, 515–31.

Tyler, T. and Sears, D. O. (1977). 'Coming to like obnoxious people when we have to live with them'. *Journal of Personality and Social Psychology*, 35, 200–11.

Ulman, R. B. and Abse, D. W. (1983). 'The group psychology of mass madness: Jonestown'. *Political Psychology*, 4, 637–61.

Ussher, J. (1991). *Women's Madness: Misogyny or Mental Illness?* London: Harvester Wheatsheaf.

Valenstein, E. S. (1975). 'Brain stimulation and behaviour control'. *Nebraska Symposium on Motivation*, 22, 251–92.

Valins, S. (1966). 'Cognitive effects of false heart-rate feedback'. *Journal of Personality and Social Psychology*, 4, 400–408.

Valins, S. and Nisbett, R. E. (1972). 'Attribution processes in the development and treatment of emotional disorders' in E. E. Jones, D. E. Kanouse, H. H. Kelley, R. E. Nisbett, S. Valins and B. Weiner (eds), *Attribution: Perceiving the Causes of Behaviour* (pp. 137–50). Morristown, NJ: General Learning Press.

van der Pligt, J. (1984). 'Attributional false consensus, and valence: two field studies'. *Journal of Personality and Social Psychology*, 46, 57–68.

van Dijk, T. A. and Wodak, R. (eds) (1988). *Discourse, Racism and Ideology* (special issues of *Text*, 8, nos 1 and 2). Amsterdam: Mouton de Gruyter.

van Dijk, T . A. (1987). *Communicating Racism: Ethnic Prejudice in Thought and Talk*. Newburg Park, CA: Sage.

van Knippenberg, A. and Ellemers, N. (1993). 'Strategies in intergroup relations' in M. A. Hogg and D. Abrams (eds), *Group Motivation: Social Psychological Perspectives* (pp. 17–32). London: Harvester Wheatsheaf.

van Knippenberg, A. and van Oers, H. (1984). 'Social identity and equity concerns in intergroup perceptions'. *British Journal of Social Psychology*, 23, 351–61.

Vanneman, R. D. and Pettigrew, T. F. (1972). 'Race and relative deprivation in the urban United States'. *Race*, 13, 461–86.

Vaughan, G. M. (1964). 'The trans-situational aspects of conforming behaviour'. *Journal of Personality*, 32, 335–540.

Vaughan, G. M. (ed.) (1972). *Racial Issues in New Zealand: Issues and Insights*. Auckland: Akarana Press.

Vaughan, G. M. (1978a). 'Social change and intergroup preferences in New Zealand'. *European Journal of Social Psychology*, 8, 297–314.

Vaughan, G. M. (1978b). 'Social categorization and intergroup behaviour in children' in H. Tajfel (ed.), *Differentiation Between Social Groups: Studies in the Social Psychology of Intergroup Relations* (pp. 339–60). London: Academic Press.

Vaughan, G. M. (1988). 'The psychology of intergroup discrimination'. *New Zealand Journal of Psychology*, 17, 1–14.

Vaughan, G. M. and Guerin, B. (1994). 'Norman Triplett: social psychologist or sport psychologist?' Unpublished paper, University of Auckland.

Vine, I. (1983). 'Sociobiology and social psychology: rivalry or symbiosis? The explanation of altruism'. *British Journal of Social Psychology*, 22, 1–11.

Vinokur, A. and Burnstein, E. (1974). 'The effects of partially shared persuasive arguments on group-induced shifts: a problem-solving approach'. *Journal of Personality and Social Psychology*, 29, 305–15.

Vinokur-Kaplan, D. (1978). 'To have or not-to-have another child: family planning attitudes, intentions, and behavior'. *Journal of Applied Social Psychology*, 8, 29–46.

Von Neumann, J. and Morgenstern, O. (1944). *Theory of Games and Economic Behaviour*. Princeton, NJ: Princeton University Press.

Vygotsky, L. S. (1962). *Thought and Language*. New York: Wiley.

Walker, I. and Mann, L. (1987). 'Unemployment, relative deprivation, and social protest'. *Personality and Social Psychology Bulletin*, 13, 275–83.

Walker, I. and Pettigrew, T. F. (1984). 'Relative deprivation theory: an overview and conceptual critique'. *British Journal of Social Psychology*, 23, 301–10.

Walkley, F. H. (1984). 'The relationship between interpersonal distance and violence in imprisoned offenders'. *Criminal Justice and Behaviour*, 11, 331–40.

Walster, E. (1966). 'Assignment of responsibility for an accident'. *Journal of Personality and Social Psychology*, 3, 73–79.

Walster, E. and Festinger, L. (1962). 'The effectiveness of "overheard" persuasive communications'. *Journal of Abnormal and Social Psychology*, 65, 395–402.

Walster, E., Walster, G. W., Piliavin, J. and Schmidt, L. (1973). 'Playing hard-to-get: understanding an elusive phenomenon'. *Journal of Personality and Social Psychology*, 26, 113–21.

Walster, E., Walster, G. W. and Berscheid, E. (1978). *Equity Theory and Research*. Boston, MA: Allyn and Bacon.

Warren, P. E. and Walker, I. (1991). 'Empathy, effectiveness and donations to charity: social psychology's contribution'. *British Journal of Social Psychology*, 30, 325–37.

Watson, D. (1982). 'The actor and the observer: how are the perceptions of causality divergent?' *Psychological Bulletin*, 92, 682–700.

Watson, J. B. (1913). 'Psychology as a behaviourist views it'. *Psychological Review*, 20, 158–77.

Watson, J. B. (1930). *Behaviourism*. New York: W. W. Norton.

Watson, O. M. and Graves, T. D. (1966). 'Quantitative research in proxemic behaviour'. *American Anthropoloyist*, 68, 971–85.

Waxman, C. (1977). *The Stigma of Poverty*. New York: Pergamon.

Webb, E. J., Campbell, D. T., Schwartz, R. D. and Sechrest, L. (1969). *Unobtrusive Measures: Nonreactive Research in the Social Sciences*. Chicago: Rand-McNally.

Weber, R. and Crocker, J. (1983). 'Cognitive processes in the revision of stereotypic beliefs'. *Journal of Personality and Social Psychology*, 45, 961–77.

Wegner, D. M. (1986). 'Transactive memory: a contemporary analysis of the group mind' in B. Mullen and G. R. Goethals (eds), *Theories of Group Behaviour* (pp. 185–208). New York: Springer-Verlag.

Wegner, D. M., Erber, R. and Raymond, P. (1991). 'Transactive memory in close relationships'. *Journal of Personality and Social Psychology*, 61, 923–29.

Weiner, B. (1979). 'A theory of motivation for some classroom experiences'. *Journal of Educational Psychology*, **71**, 3–25.

Weiner, B. (1985). '"Spontaneous" causal thinking'. *Psychological Bulletin*, **97**, 74–84.

Weiner, B. (1986). *An Attributional Theory of Motivation and Emotion*. New York: Springer-Verlag.

Weinstein, N. (1980). 'Unrealistic optimism about future life events'. *Journal of Personality and Social Psychology*, **5**, 806–20.

Weinstein, N. (1989). 'Why it won't happen to me: perceptions of risk factors and illness susceptibility'. *Science*, **246**, 1232–33.

Weiten, W. (1980). 'The attraction–leniency effect in jury research: an examination of external validity'. *Journal of Applied Social Psychology*, **10**, 340–47.

Wells, G. L. and Turtle, J. W. (1988). 'What is the best way to encode faces?' in M. Gruneberg, P. E. Morris and R. N. Sykes (eds), *Practical Aspects of Memory: Current Research and Issues* (vol. 1, pp. 163–68). Chichester: Wiley.

West, C. (1984). *Routine Complications*. Bloomington, IA: Indiana University Press.

West, S. G. and Brown, T. J. (1975). 'Physical attractiveness, the severity of the emergency, and helping: a field experiment and interpersonal simulation'. *Journal of Experimental Social Psychology*, **11**, 531–38.

West, S. G., Whitney, G. and Sehnedler, R. (1975). 'Helping a motorist in distress: the effects of sex, race and neighbourhood'. *Journal of Personality and Social Psychology*, **31**, 691–98.

Westie, F. R. and DeFleur, M. L. (1959). 'Automatic responses and their relationship to race attitudes'. *Journal of Abnormal and Social Psychology*, **58**, 340–47.

Wetherell, M. S. (1986). 'Linguistic repertoires and literary criticism: new directions for a social psychology of gender' in S. Wilkinson (ed.), *Feminist Social Psychology* (pp. 77–95). Milton Keynes: Open University Press.

Wetherell, M. S. (1987). 'Social identity and group polarization' in J. C. Turner, M. A. Hogg, P. J. Oakes, S. D. Reicher and M. S. Wetherell, *Rediscovering the Social Group: A Self-categorization Theory* (pp. 142–70). Oxford: Blackwell.

Wetherell, M. S. and Potter, J. (1992). *Mapping the Language of Racism*. London: Harvester Wheatsheaf.

Wetzel, C. G. and Walton, M. D. (1985). 'Developing biased social judgements: the false consensus effect'. *Journal of Personality and Social Psychology*, **49**, 1352–59.

Weyant, J. (1978). 'The effect of mood states, costs and benefits on helping'. *Journal of Personality and Social Psychology*, **36**, 1169–76.

Whitcher, S. J. and Fisher, J. D. (1979). 'Multidimensional reaction to therapeutic touch in a hospital setting'. *Journal of Personality and Social Psychology*, **37**, 87–96.

White, P. A. (1988). 'Causal processing: origins and development'. *Psychological Bulletin*, **104**, 36–52.

White, P. A. and Younger, D. P. (1988). 'Differences in the ascription of transient internal states to self and other'. *Journal of Experimental Social Psychology*, **24**, 292–309.

Whorf, B. L. (1956). *Language, Thought and Reality*. Cambridge, MA: MIT Press.

Whyte, W. F. (1943). *Street Corner Society* (2nd edn). Chicago, IL: University of Chicago.

Wicker, A. W. (1969). 'Attitudes versus actions: the relationship of verbal and overt behavioral responses to attitude objects'. *Journal of Social Issues*, **25**, 41–78.

Wicker, A. W. (1979). *An Introduction to Ecological Psychology*. Monterey, CA: Brooks/Cole.

Wicklund, R. A. (1975). 'Objective self-awareness' in L. Berkowitz (ed.), *Advances in Experimental Social Psychology* (vol. 8, pp. 233–75). New York: Academic Press.

Widdicombe, S. and Wooffitt, R. (1994). *The Language of Youth Subcultures*. London: Harvester Wheatsheaf.

Widmeyer, W. N., Brawley, L. R. and Carron, A. V. (1985). *The Measurement of Cohesion in Sports Teams: The Group Environment Questionnaire*. London, Ontario: Sports Dynamics.

Wiemann, J. M. and Giles H. (1988). 'Interpersonal communications' in M. Hewstone, W. Stroebe, J-P.

Codol and G. M. Stephenson (eds), *Introduction to Social Psychology* (pp. 199–221). Oxford: Blackwell.

Wilder, D. A. (1977). 'Perceptions of groups, size of opposition and social influence'. *Journal of Experimental Social Psychology*, 13, 253–68.

Wilder, D. A. (1984). 'Predictions of belief homogeneity and similarity following social categorization'. *British Journal of Social Psychology*, 23, 323–33.

Wilder, D. A. (1986). 'Social categorization: implications for creation and reduction of intergroup bias' in L. Berkowitz (ed.), *Advances in Experimental Social Psychology* (vol. 19, pp. 291–355). New York: Academic Press.

Wilder, D. A. and Shapiro, P. N. (1984). 'Role of out-group cues in determining social identity'. *Journal of Personality and Social Psychology*, 47, 342–48.

Wilder, D. A. and Shapiro, P. N. (1989). 'Role of competition-induced anxiety in limiting the beneficial impact of positive behaviour by an outgroup member'. *Journal of Personality and Social Psychology*, 56, 60–69.

Wilke, H. and Lanzetta, J. T. (1970). 'The obligation to help: the effects of amount of prior help on subsequent helping behavior'. *Journal of Experimental Social Psychology*, 6, 488–93.

Williams, J. A. (1984). 'Gender and intergroup behaviour: towards and integration'. *British Journal of Social Psychology*, 23, 311–16.

Williams, J. E. and Best, D. L. (1982). *Measuring Sex Stereotypes: A Thirty Nation Study*. Beverly Hills, CA: Sage.

Williams, J. G. and Solano, C. H. (1983). 'The social reality of feeling lonely: friendship and reciprocation'. *Personality and Social Psychology Bulletin*, 2, 237–42.

Williams, K. D. and Karau, S. J. (1991). 'Social loafing and social compensation: the effects of expectations of co-worker performance'. *Journal of Personality and Social Psychology*, 61, 570–81.

Williams, K. D., Harkins, S. G. and Latane, B. (1981). 'Identifiability as a deterrent to social loafing: two cheering experiments'. *Journal of Personality and Social Psychology*, 40, 303–11.

Williams, K. D., Karau, S. J. and Bourgeois, M. (1993). 'Working on collective tasks: social loafing and social compensation' in M. A. Hogg and D. Abrams (eds), *Group Motivation: Social Psychological Perspectives* (pp. 130–48). London: Harvester Wheatsheaf.

Williamson, G. M. and Clark, M. S. (1989). 'Providing help and relationship type as determinants of changes in moods and self-evaluations'. *Journal of Personality and Social Psychology*, 56, 722–34.

Wilson, E. O. (1975). *Sociobiology: The New Synthesis*. Cambridge, MA: Harvard University Press.

Wilson, E. O. (1978). *On Human Nature*. Cambridge, MA: Harvard University Press.

Winch, R. (1958). *Mate Selection: A Study of Complementary Needs*. New York: Harper & Row.

Wineman, J. D. (1980). 'The design of office environments'. Paper presented at the Environmental Design Research Association Conference, Charleston.

Winsborough, H. (1965). 'The social consequences of high population density'. *Law and Contemporary Problems*, 30, 120–26.

Wishner, J. (1960). 'Reanalysis of "impressions of personality"'. *Psychological Review*, 67, 96–112.

Wispe, L. G. (1972). 'Positive forms of social behaviour: an overview'. *Journal of Social Issues*, 28, 1–19.

Witkin, H. A., Mednick, S. A., Schulsinger, F., Bakkestrom, E., Christiansen, K. D., Goodenough, D. R., Philip, J., Rubin, D. B. and Stocking, M. (1976). 'Criminality in XYY and XXY men'. *Science*, 198, 547–55.

Wittgenstein, L. (1953). *Philosophical Investigations*. Oxford: Blackwell.

Wolfgang, A. and Wolfgang, J. (1968). 'Personal space: an unobtrusive measure of attitudes toward the physically handicapped'. *Proceedings of the 76th Annual Convention of the American Psychological Association*, pp. 653–54.

Wood, G. S. (1982). 'Conspiracy and the paranoid style: causality and deceit in the eighteenth century'. *William and Mary Quarterly*, 39, 401–41.

Wools, R. and Canter, D. (1970). 'The effect of the meaning of buildings on behavior'. *Applied Ergonomics*, 1, 144–50.

Worchel, S. (1979). 'Cooperation and the reduction of intergroup conflict: some determining factors' in W. Austin and S. Worchel (eds), *The Social Psychology of Intergroup Relations* (pp. 262–73). Monterey, CA: Brooks/Cole.

Worchel, S. and Novell, N. (1980). 'Effect of perceived environmental conditions during cooperation on intergroup attraction'. *Journal of Personality and Social Psychology*, 38, 764–72.

Worchel, S., Andreoli, V. A. and Folger, R. (1977). 'Intergroup cooperation and intergroup attraction: the effect of previous interaction and outcome of combined effort'. *Journal of Experimental Social Psychology*, 13, 131–40.

Worchel, S., Cooper, J. and Goethals, G. R. (1988). *Understanding Social Psychology* (4th edn). Chicago: Dorsey Press.

Wrightsman, L. S. (1964). 'Measurement of philosophies of human nature'. *Psychological Reports*, 14, 743–51.

Wundt, W. (1897). *Outlines of Psychology*. New York: Stechert.

Wyer, R. S., Jr (1976). 'An investigation of relations among probability estimates'. *Organizational Behaviour and Human Performance*, 15, 1–18.

Wyer, R. S., Jr and Gordon, S. E. (1982). 'The recall of information about persons and groups'. *Journal of Experimental Social Psychology*, 18, 128–64.

Wyer, R. S., Jr and Gordon, S. E. (1984). 'The cognitive representation of social information' in R. S. Wyer, Jr and T. K. Srull (eds), *Handbook of Social Cognition* (vol. 2, pp. 73–150). Hillsdale, NJ: Erlbaum.

Wyer, R. S., Jr and Martin, L. L. (1986). 'Person memory: the role of traits, group stereotypes, and specific behaviours in the cognitive representation of persons'. *Journal of Personality and Social Psychology*, 50, 661–75.

Wyer, R. S., Jr and Srull, T. K. (1981). 'Category accessibility: some theoretical and empirical issues concerning the processing of social stimulus information' in E. T. Higgins, C. P. Herrnan and M. P. Zanna (eds), *Social Cognition: The Ontario Symposium* (vol. 1, pp. 161–98). Hillsdale, NJ: Erlbaum.

Wyer, R. S. and Srull, T. K. (1984). *Social Cognition*. Hillsdale, NJ: Erlbaum.

Wyer, R. S., Jr and Srull, T. K. (1986). 'Human cognition in its social context'. *Psychological Review*, 93, 322–59.

Yancey, W. L., (1971). 'Architecture and social interaction: the case of a large-scale public housing project'. *Environment and Behaviour*, 3, 3–21.

Yarwood, A. T. and Knowling, M. (1982). *Race Relations in Australia: A History*. Sydney: Methuen.

Yates, B. T. and Mischel, W. (1979). 'Young children's preferred attentional strategies for delaying gratification'. *Journal of Personality and Social Psychology*, 37, 286–300.

Younger, J. C., Walker, L. and Arrowood, A. J. (1977). 'Post-decision dissonance at the fair'. *Personality and Social Psychology Bulletin*, 3, 247–87.

Youngson, R. M. (1989). *Grief: Rebuilding Your Life after Bereavement*. London: David & Charles.

Yukl, G. (1981). *Leadership in Organizations*. Englewood Cliffs, NJ: Prentice Hall.

Yzerbyt, V. Y., Schadron, G., Leyens, J-P. and Rocher, S. (1994). 'Social judgeability: the impact of meta-informational cues on the use of stereotypes'. *Journal of Personality and Social Psychology*, 66, 48–55.

Zaccaro, S. J. (1984). 'Social loafing: the role of task attractiveness'. *Personality and Social Psychology Bulletin*, 10, 99–106.

Zahn-Waxler, C., Radke-Yarrow, M. and King, R. A. (1979). 'Child-rearing and children's prosocial initiations toward victims of distress'. *Child Development*, 50, 319–30.

Zajonc, R. B. (1965). 'Social facilitation'. *Science*, 1429, 269–74.

Zajonc, R. B. (1968). 'Attitudinal effects of mere exposure'. *Journal of Personality and Social Psychology*, 9, 1–27.

Zajonc, R. B. (1980). 'Cognition and social cognition: a historical perspective' in L. Festinger (ed.), *Retrospections on Social Psychology* (pp. 180–204). New York: Oxford University Press.

Zajonc, R. B. (1989). 'Styles of explanation in social psychology'. *European Journal of Social Psychology*, 19, 345–68.

Zanna, M. P. and Hamilton, D. L. (1972). 'Attribute dimensions and patterns of trait inferences'. *Psychonomic Science*, 27, 353–54.

Zanna, M. P. and Rempel, J. K. (1988). 'Attitudes: a new look at an old concept' in D. Bar-Tal and A. W. Kruglanski, (eds), *The Social Psychology of Knowledge* (pp. 315–34). Cambridge: Cambridge University Press.

Zanna, M. P., Kiesler, C. A. and Pilkonis, D. A. (1970). 'Positive and negative affect established by classical conditioning'. *Journal of Personality and Social Psychology*, 14, 321–28.

Zillman, D. (1979). *Hostility and Aggression*. Hillsdale, NJ: Erlbaum.

Zillman, D. (1984). *Connections Between Sex and Aggression*. Hillsdale, NJ: Erlbaum.

Zillman, D. (1988). 'Cognition–excitation interdependencies in aggressive behaviour'. *Aggressive Behaviour*, 14, 51–64.

Zillmann, D. and Bryant, J. (1984). 'Effects of massive exposure to pornography' in N. M. Malamuth and E. Donnerstein (eds), *Pornography and Sexual Aggression* (pp. 115–138). New York: Academic Press.

Zimbardo, P. G. (1970). 'The human choice: individuation, reason, and order versus deindividuation, impulse, and chaos' in W. J. Arnold and D. Levine (eds), *Nebraska Symposium on Motivation 1969* (vol. 17, pp. 237–307). Lincoln, NE: University of Nebraska Press.

Zimbardo, P. G. (1971). 'The Stanford Prison experiment'. Script of the slide show.

Zimbardo, P. G. and Leippe, M. R. (1991). *The Psychology of Attitude Change and Social Influence*, New York: McGraw-Hill.

Zimbardo, P. G., Weisenberg, M., Firestone, I. and Levy B. (1965). 'Communication effectiveness in producing public conformity and private attitude change'. *Journal of Personality*, 33, 233–56.

Zimbardo, P. G., Haney, C., Banks, W. C. and Jaffe, D. (1982). 'The psychology of imprisonment' in J. C. Brigham and L. Wrightsman (eds), *Contemporary Issues in Social Psychology* (4th edn, pp. 230–35). Monterey, CA: Brooks/Cole.

Zlutnick, S. and Altman, I. (1972). 'Crowding and human behaviour' in J. Wohlwill and D. Carson (eds), *Environment and the Social Sciences* (pp. 44–60). Washington, DC: American Psychological Association.

Zuckerman, M., Lazzaro, M. M. and Waldgeir, D. (1979). 'Undermining effects of the foot-in-the-door technique with extrinsic rewards'. *Journal of Applied Social Psychology*, 9, 292–96.

Zuckerman, M., DePaulo, B. M. and Rosenthal, R. (1981). 'Verbal and non-verbal communication of deception' in L. Berkowitz (ed.), *Advances in Experimental Social Psychology* (vol. 14, pp. 1–59). New York: Academic Press.

Zuckerman, M., Miserandino, M. and Bernieri, F. (1983). 'Civil inattention exists – in elevators'. *Personality and Social Psychology Bulletin*, 9, 578–86.

Zukier, H. (1986). 'The paradigmatic and narrative modes in goal-guided inference' in R. M. Sorrentino and E. T. Higgins (eds), *Handbook of Motivation and Cognition: Foundations of Social Behaviour* (pp. 465–502). New York: Guilford Press.

Author index

······················

Subject index